Band 158: G. Cyranek, A. Kachru, H. Kaiser (Hrsg.), Informatik und „Dritte Welt". X, 302 Seiten. 1988.

Band 159: Th. Christaller, H.-W. Hein, M. M. Richter (Hrsg.), Künstliche Intelligenz. Frühjahrsschulen, Dassel, 1985 und 1986. VII, 342 Seiten. 1988.

Band 160: H. Mäncher, Fehlertolerante dezentrale Prozeßautomatisierung. XVI, 243 Seiten. 1987.

Band 161: P. Peinl, Synchronisation in zentralisierten Datenbanksystemen. XII, 227 Seiten. 1987.

Band 162: H. Stoyan (Hrsg.), Begründungsverwaltung. Proceedings, 1986. VII, 153 Seiten. 1988.

Band 163: H. Müller, Realistische Computergraphik. VII, 146 Seiten. 1988.

Band 164: M. Eulenstein, Generierung portabler Compiler. X, 235 Seiten. 1988.

Band 165: H.-U. Heiß, Überlast in Rechensystemen. IX, 176 Seiten. 1988.

Band 166: K. Hörmann, Kollisionsfreie Bahnen für Industrieroboter. XII, 157 Seiten. 1988.

Band 167: R. Lauber (Hrsg.), Prozeßrechensysteme '88. Stuttgart, März 1988. Proceedings. XIV, 799 Seiten. 1988.

Band 168: U. Kastens, F. J. Rammig (Hrsg.), Architektur und Betrieb von Rechensystemen. 10. GI/ITG-Fachtagung, Paderborn, März 1988. Proceedings. IX, 405 Seiten. 1988.

Band 169: G. Heyer, J. Krems, G. Görz (Hrsg.), Wissensarten und ihre Darstellung. VIII, 292 Seiten. 1988.

Band 170: A. Jaeschke, B. Page (Hrsg.), Informatikanwendungen im Umweltbereich. 2. Symposium, Karlsruhe, 1987. Proceedings. X, 201 Seiten. 1988.

Band 171: H. Lutterbach (Hrsg.), Non-Standard Datenbanken für Anwendungen der Graphischen Datenverarbeitung. GI-Fachgespräch, Dortmund, März 1988, Proceedings. VII, 183 Seiten. 1988.

Band 172: G. Rahmstorf (Hrsg.), Wissensrepräsentation in Expertensystemen. Workshop, Herrenberg, März 1987. Proceedings. VII, 189 Seiten. 1988.

Band 173: M. H. Schulz, Testmustergenerierung und Fehlersimulation in digitalen Schaltungen mit hoher Komplexität. IX, 165 Seiten. 1988.

Band 174: A. Endrös, Rechtsprechung und Computer in den neunziger Jahren. XIX, 129 Seiten. 1988.

Band 175: J. Hülsemann, Funktioneller Test der Auflösung von Zugriffskonflikten in Mehrrechnersystemen. X, 179 Seiten. 1988.

Band 176: H. Trost (Hrsg.), 4. Österreichische Artificial-Intelligence-Tagung. Wien, August 1988. Proceedings. VIII, 207 Seiten. 1988.

Band 177: L. Voelkel, J. Pliquett, Signaturanalyse. 224 Seiten. 1988.

Band 178: H. Göttler, Graphgrammatiken in der Softwaretechnik. VIII, 244 Seiten. 1988.

Band 179: W. Ameling (Hrsg.), Simulationstechnik. 5. Symposium. Aachen, September 1988. Proceedings. XIV, 538 Seiten. 1988.

Band 180: H. Bunke, O. Kübler, P. Stucki (Hrsg.), Mustererkennung 1988. 10. DAGM-Symposium, Zürich, September 1988. Proceedings. XV, 361 Seiten. 1988.

Band 181: W. Hoeppner (Hrsg.), Künstliche Intelligenz. GWAI-88, 12. Jahrestagung. Eringerfeld, September 1988. Proceedings. XII, 333 Seiten. 1988.

Band 182: W. Barth (Hrsg.), Visualisierungstechniken und Algorithmen. Fachgespräch, Wien, September 1988. Proceedings. VIII, 247 Seiten. 1988.

Band 183: A. Clauer, W. Purgathofer (Hrsg.), AUSTROGRAPHICS '88. Fachtagung, Wien, September 1988. Proceedings. VIII, 267 Seiten. 1988.

Band 184: B. Gollan, W. Paul, A. Schmitt (Hrsg.), Innovative Informations-Infrastrukturen. I. I. I. – Forum, Saarbrücken, Oktober 1988. Proceedings. VIII, 291 Seiten. 1988.

Band 185: B. Mitschang, Ein Molekül-Atom-Datenmodell für Non-Standard-Anwendungen. XI, 230 Seiten. 1988.

Band 186: E. Rahm, Synchronisation in Mehrrechner-Datenbanksystemen. IX, 272 Seiten. 1988.

Band 187: R. Valk (Hrsg.), GI – 18. Jahrestagung I. Vernetzte und komplexe Informatik-Systeme. Hamburg, Oktober 1988. Proceedings. XVI, 776 Seiten.

Band 188: R. Valk (Hrsg.), GI – 18. Jahrestagung II. Vernetzte und komplexe Informatik-Systeme. Hamburg, Oktober 1988. Proceedings. XVI, 704 Seiten.

Band 189: B. Wolfinger (Hrsg.), Vernetzte und komplexe Informatik-Systeme. Industrieprogramm zur 18. Jahrestagung der GI, Hamburg, Oktober 1988. Proceedings. X, 229 Seiten. 1988.

Band 190: D. Maurer, Relevanzanalyse. VIII, 239 Seiten. 1988.

Band 191: P. Levi, Planen für autonome Montageroboter. XIII, 259 Seiten. 1988.

Band 192: K. Kansy, P. Wißkirchen (Hrsg.), Graphik im Bürobereich. Proceedings, 1988. VIII, 187 Seiten. 1988.

Band 193: W. Gotthard, Datenbanksysteme für Software-Produktionsumgebungen. X, 193 Seiten. 1988.

Band 194: C. Lewerentz, Interaktives Entwerfen großer Programmsysteme. VII, 179 Seiten. 1988.

Band 195: I. S. Bátori, U. Hahn, M. Pinkal, W. Wahlster (Hrsg.), Computerlinguistik und ihre theoretischen Grundlagen. Proceedings. IX, 218 Seiten. 1988.

Band 197: M. Leszak, H. Eggert, Petri-Netz-Methoden und -Werkzeuge. XII, 254 Seiten. 1989.

Band 198: U. Reimer, FRM: Ein Frame-Repräsentationsmodell und seine formale Semantik. VIII, 161 Seiten. 1988.

Band 199: C. Beckstein, Zur Logik der Logik-Programmierung. IX, 246 Seiten. 1988.

Band 200: A. Reinefeld, Spielbaum-Suchverfahren. IX, 191 Seiten. 1989.

Band 201: A. M. Kotz, Triggermechanismen in Datenbanksystemen. VIII, 187 Seiten. 1989.

Band 202: Th. Christaller (Hrsg.), Künstliche Intelligenz. 5. Frühjahrsschule, KIFS-87, Günne, März/April 1987. Proceedings. VII, 403 Seiten. 1989.

Band 203: K. v. Luck (Hrsg.), Künstliche Intelligenz. 7. Frühjahrsschule, KIFS-89, Günne, März 1989. Proceedings. VII, 302 Seiten. 1989.

Band 204: T. Härder (Hrsg.), Datenbanksysteme in Büro, Technik und Wissenschaft. GI/SI-Fachtagung, Zürich, März 1989. Proceedings. XII, 427 Seiten. 1989.

Band 205: P. J. Kühn (Hrsg.), Kommunikation in verteilten Systemen. ITG/GI-Fachtagung, Stuttgart, Februar 1989. Proceedings. XII, 907 Seiten. 1989.

Band 206: P. Horster, H. Isselhorst, Approximative Public-Key-Kryptosysteme. VII, 174 Seiten. 1989.

Informatik-Fachberichte 204

Herausgeber: W. Brauer
im Auftrag der Gesellschaft für Informatik (GI)

T. Härder (Hrsg.)

Datenbanksysteme in Büro, Technik und Wissenschaft

GI/SI-Fachtagung
Zürich, 1.-3. März 1989
Proceedings

Springer-Verlag
Berlin Heidelberg New York
London Paris Tokyo

Herausgeber
Theo Härder
Universität Kaiserslautern, Fachbereich Informatik
Erwin-Schrödinger-Straße, D–6750 Kaiserslautern

CR Subject Classification (1987): D.2.6, H.2-3, H.4.1, I.2.1,
I.2.3-4, I.3.5, J.6

ISBN-13: 978-3-540-50894-6   e-ISBN-13: 978-3-642-74571-3
DOI: 10.1007/978-3-642-74571-3

CIP-Titelaufnahme der Deutschen Bibliothek.
Datenbanksysteme in Büro, Technik und Wissenschaft: GI/SI-Fachtagung; proceedings. – Berlin;
Heidelberg; New York; London; Paris; Tokyo: Springer.
NE: Gesellschaft für Informatik
1989. Zürich, 1.-3. März 1989. – 1989
   (Informatik-Fachberichte; 204)

NE: GT

2145/3140 – 543210 – Gedruckt auf säurefreiem Papier

Vorwort

Im Bereich der Datenbankverwaltung haben neue Anwendungen und Einsatzbereiche zahlreiche neuartige Forschungsvorhaben und herausfordernde Entwicklungsaufgaben hervorgebracht. Sie bilden seit Jahren weltweit einen Schwerpunkt der Datenbankforschung, wobei man sich weniger auf theoretische Fragestellungen als vielmehr auf aktuelle Themen der Praxis konzentriert. Als wichtige Gebiete, die auch dieser Tagung ihren Namen gegeben haben, lassen sich hier Anwendungen in den weiten Bereichen der Büroinformationssysteme, der Technik sowie der Wissenschaft nennen. Heute werden bereits aussichtsreiche Lösungsvorschläge in vielen Forschungsprojekten untersucht und durch Prototyp-Implementierungen getestet, so daß jetzt auch erste Aussagen über das Leistungsverhalten solcher DB-gestützter Anwendungen erwartet werden können.

Die Fachtagung "Datenbanksysteme in Büro, Technik und Wissenschaft" (BTW) versteht sich als wissenschaftliches Forum für die oben genannte Thematik im deutschsprachigen Raum. Nach erfolgreichen Fachtagungen in Karlsruhe 1985 und in Darmstadt 1987 findet die dritte BTW-Tagung vom 1.-3. März 1989 an der Eidgenössischen Technischen Hochschule Zürich statt. Sie wird zum ersten Mal als gemeinsame Fachtagung der Gesellschaft für Informatik (GI) und der Schweizer Informatiker Gesellschaft (SI), vertreten durch den Fachausschuß 2.5 "Rechnergestützte Informationssysteme" der GI und der Fachgruppe DBTA (Data Bases - Theory and Application) der SI, veranstaltet.

Gemessen an der Zahl und Qualität der eingereichten Beiträge war die Resonanz auf den "Call for Papers" für die Tagung sehr gut. Erfreulicherweise kam auch eine große Anzahl der Beiträge von Entwicklern und Anwendern aus der Praxis. Das Programmkomitee erhielt insgesamt etwa 50 Langbeiträge und 30 Kurzbeiträge, aus denen es das Programm für diese Tagung zusammenstellen konnte. Die hohe Zahl der Beiträge zeigt, daß sich die "BTW" inzwischen als Tagungsreihe sowie als "Diskussionsforum für die Praxis" fest etabliert hat.

An dieser Stelle möchte ich allen Autoren ausdrücklich für ihre Mühe und ihre Arbeit danken, auch wenn sie nicht mit ihrem Beitrag in diesem Tagungsband vertreten sind. Das Programmkomitee hat sich seine Auswahlentscheidung nicht leicht gemacht. Alle Lang- und Kurzbeiträge wurden von mindestens drei Gutachtern bewertet; bei recht hohem wissenschaftlichem Niveau der Beiträge mußten wegen der begrenzten Vortragszeit oft zusätzliche Kriterien wie thematische Orientierung bei der Auswahlentscheidung berücksichtigt werden. Es wurde darauf geachtet, daß die in den Langbeiträgen dargestellten Ergebnisse als wissenschaftlich gesichert gelten können, während bei den Kurzbeiträgen auch Projektberichte, Anwendererfahrungen oder interessante Forschungsideen und -ansätze mit vorläufigem Charakter akzeptiert wurden. Daraus entstand eine Mischung aus 15 Langbeiträgen und 20 Kurzbeiträgen, die hoffentlich die wesentlichen aktuellen Entwicklungen des breiten BTW-Forschungsspektrums widerspiegeln. Das Tagungsprogramm wird zusätzlich gestützt durch zwei eingeladene Beiträge, welche die Themen "Anfragesprachen für objektorientierte Datenbanksysteme" und "Analyse des Verhältnisses von Anwendungs- und Datenbanksystemen" behandeln, die die Datenbankforschung wohl noch für geraume Zeit beschäftigen werden.

Die Durchführung einer Tagung ist nur mit vielfältiger Unterstützung möglich, die mir bereitwillig und in erheblichem Umfang gewährt wurde. Dafür möchte ich mich bedanken: bei den Autoren der eingereichten Beiträge, bei den Mitgliedern des Programmkomitees, bei den Gutachtern der Beiträge, bei der Tagungsleitung (siehe nächste Seite), bei den unterstützenden Institutionen, beim Springer-Verlag für die schnelle Erstellung der Proceedings.

Ganz besonders bedanken möchte ich mich bei den Mitgliedern des Organisationskomitees unter Leitung von Dr. R. Marti. Ebenso gilt mein Dank den vielen "anonymen" Helfern; stellvertretend für sie darf ich hier meine Mitarbeiter M. Gaß, Dr. B. Mitschang, H. Neu und A. Sikeler nennen.

Kaiserslautern, im Dezember 1988   Theo Härder

Tagungsleitung

Prof. Dr. C.A. Zehnder, ETH Zürich (Vorsitz)
Prof. Dr. H.P. Frei, ETH Zürich
Prof. Dr. K. Bauknecht, Uni Zürich

Programmkomitee

Prof. Dr. T. Härder, Uni Kaiserslautern (Vorsitz)
Prof. Dr. H.-J. Appelrath, Uni Oldenburg
Prof. Dr. K. Bauknecht, Uni Zürich
Dr. M. Bärtschi, BBC Brown Boveri AG
Dr. H. Biller, Siemens AG
Dr. R. Brägger, CAP GEMINI (Schweiz) AG
Dr. P. Dadam, IBM Deutschland GmbH
Dr. K. Dittrich, FZI Karlsruhe
Prof. Dr. H.-D. Ehrich, TU Braunschweig
Prof. Dr. H.P. Frei, ETH Zürich
Prof. Dr. G. Lausen, Uni Mannheim
Dr. H.C. Mayr, KMK Kreutz & Mayr Ges. f. Datent. mbH
Dr. A. Meier, Schweizerischer Bankverein
Prof. Dr. A. Reuter, Uni Stuttgart
Prof. Dr. H.-J. Schek, TH Darmstadt
Prof. Dr. G. Schlageter, FernUni Hagen
Prof. Dr. Stucky, Uni Karlsruhe (TH)
Dipl.-Inform. H. Thoma, Ciba-Geigy AG
Prof. Dr. A.M. Tjoa, Uni Wien
Prof. Dr. H. Wedekind, Uni Erlangen-Nürnberg

Organisationskomitee

Dr. R. Marti, Vorsitz
Dr. A. Dudler, P. Janes, F. Oertly,
W. Rüttener, Frau G. Unseld, Dr. P. Ursprung
ETH Zürich

Als weitere Gutachter standen dem Programmkomitee zur Verfügung

K. Abramowicz

J. Böhme

H. Eirund

G. Engels

R. Erbe

W. Gotthard

M. Härtig

U. Herrmann

Ch. Hübel

K. Hülsmann

H. Jasper

Bin Jiang

U. Kessler

P. Klarhold

H. Knolle

A. Kotz

R. Kramer

K. Küspert

V. Linnemann

F. Lohmann

M. Marmann

R. Marti

R. Meyer

K. Neumann

M. Nussbaum

V. Obermeit

A. Oberweis

H.-P. Paul

P. Pistor

M. Ranft

Th. Raupp

S. Rehm

B. Schiefer

M. Scholl

D. Stieger

N. Südkamp

R. Unland

W. Waterfeld

Ch. Wieland

W. Wilkes

A. Wolf

B. Wüthrich

M. Wyle

P. Zabback

Inhaltsverzeichnis

Integrität

Wissensbasierte DB-Ansätze

Implementierungsaspekte

Rekursion

Query Languages for Object-Oriented Database Systems:
Analysis and a Proposal

François Bancilhon
Altaïr*
BP 105, 78153 Le Chesnay Cédex
France

Abstract

This paper discusses the problem of query languages for object-oriented database systems. We first discuss the general problem of designing such a language. Then we restrict ourselves to the specific context of the O_2 system. After presenting the main features of the system, we use its specificity to propose a query language. The query language is defined formally and through examples.

1   Introduction

Object-oriented database systems (OODBS) have recently received a lot of attention from the research community. Products and prototypes have been developed at a past pace over the last few years [Banerjee et al 87], [Bancilhon et al 88], [Fishman et al. 87], [Maier *et al* 84]. However, OODBS's have to compete against relational systems whose main strength is their query language. Therefore, one of the major problems which must be solved for such systems is that of the query language.

In this paper, I address the general problem of designing a query language for object-oriented database systems. I discuss the main issues to be investigated and I propose one solution for a specific object-oriented system O_2, currently being implemented in the Altaïr group. The rest of the paper is organized as follows: Section 2 defines what I mean by an object-oriented database system. Section 3 presents the various uses of a query language

---

*Altaïr is a consortium funded by IN2 (the computer subsidiary of the Intertechnique Group), INRIA (Institut National de Recherche en Informatique et Automatique and LRI (the research lab of the University of Paris XI, Orsay). It was created for five years and started operating in September of 1986

and defines the notion of query facility. Section 4 presents and discusses the issues in designing a query language for an object-oriented database system. Section 5 presents the O_2 data model. Section 6 presents the formal syntax and semantics of the language and gives example queries.

2   Definition of an object-oriented database system

It is not the purpose of this paper to give a definition of an object-oriented database system. The topic is subject to considerable debate and it will probably take some time before the community agrees on a common definition. My objective in this section is simply to set up the framework in which the query language should be discussed. I believe that an object-oriented DBMS should satisfy two criteria: it should be a DBMS, and it should be an object-oriented system. The first criterion translates into five features: persistence, secondary storage management, concurrency, recovery and an *ad hoc* query facility. The second one translates into seven features: complex objects, object identity, encapsulation, types or classes, inheritance, overriding and late binding, extensibility and computational completeness. Let me now briefly comment each point.

Complex objects are built from simple ones by applying to them object constructors. The three minimal constructors that the system should have are sets, lists and tuples.

In a model with *object identity*, an object has an existence which is independent of its value. Thus two objects can either be identical (they are the same object) or they can be equal (they have the same value). This has two implications: object sharing (two distinct objects can share a common sub-component) and object updates (we can modify an object without changing its identity).

The idea of *encapsulation* comes from abstract data types. In this approach, an object has an interface part and an implementation part. The interface part is the specification of the set of operations (the methods) that can be performed on the object. It is the only visible part of the object. The implementation part has a data part and a procedure part. The data part is the representation or state of the object and the procedure part describes, in some programming language, the implementation of each operation.

Whether a system supports *types or classes* is a touchy issue. A *type*, in an object-oriented system, summarizes the common structure of a set of objects with the same characteristics. It corresponds to the notion of an abstract data type. The notion of *class* is different. Its specification is the same as that of a type, but it is more of a run time notion. It contains two aspects: an object factory (to generate new objects) and an object warehouse (to store all the objects of a class).

Classes and types are organized into *inheritance* hierarchies. Each class or type can be specialized into a more specific class or type which inherits all its methods and structure and contains some extra ones.

Methods can be redefined for more specific types. This yields *overloading*, i.e., the fact that a given method name means different things depending on the object to which it is applied. Overloading implies that the binding of the method name to the actual piece of code which executes it must be done at run time, this is *late binding*.

From a programming language point of view *computational completeness* is obvious: it simply means that one can program any computable function, using the system. It is however new from a database system point of view.

Extensibility means that the system comes with a set of predefined types or classes which can be extended. This set is extensible in the following sense: there is a means to define new types or and there is no distinction between system defined and user defined types.

I now turn to the database system characteristics: *persistence* is the ability of data to survive the execution of a process, and to be eventually reusable in another process.

Disk management includes the classical features one finds in a DBMS: index management, data clustering and data buffering.

Concurrency means that the system should insure harmonious cooperation between users working simultaneously on the database. The system should therefore support the standard notion of atomicity of a sequence of operations and of controlled sharing.

Recovery means that, in case of hardware or software failure, the system should recover, i.e., be brought back to some coherent point.

A query facility consists in providing the functionality of an *ad hoc* query language. It does not have to be done under the form of a query language but the service has to be provided, for instance a graphical browser could very well be sufficient to fulfill this functionality. The service consists in allowing the user to ask reasonable queries to the database without too much difficulty. This paper discusses the issue of providing this facility with a query language.

3 Usage of the query language

David Maier [Maier 88] defines an *ad hoc* query facility by the three following characteristics: it should be

- *high level:* this implies declarativity and associative access. It also means that reasonable queries should be easily and concisely expressed.

- *optimizable:* this means that the system can take the user query and find a good strategy to optimize them, using the physical access paths such as indices.

- *application independent*, which means that a specific user interface, targeted to a given application is not an *ad hoc* query facility.

The first question worth asking concerns the objectives of such a query language. I think it can be used in three ways, which are the ways query languages such as SQL are currently used, and that in the specific case of an object-oriented query language, it might be used in a fourth way. Two modes of usage are what the languages were meant for: *ad hoc* querying or data manipulation in an application program. As it is often the case, the tool has also been used differently, mainly to write simple programs.

3.1   As an *ad hoc* query facility

This applies to all query languages and is the mode privileged by relational systems. This is the primary use of a query language: people who have simple data to extract from an information system should be given a simple means to formulate their question. Ease of expression, declarativity and efficiency are the three main criteria that such a language should satisfy. This mode will apply to every possible system, thus it makes sense for object-oriented database system: the user, instead of accessing the database through the programming language will access it for simple tasks through the query language.

3.2   As an access language to the database

This essentially applies to relational systems which were meant to be used only through their query language. SQL was also designed as a means of accessing data in a relational database from an application program (written in C, PL1 or Cobol). It is a mixed success in that sense, because of the impedance mismatch [Bancilhon et Maier 87]. Normally, in an object-oriented database system, there is no need for this functionality because the programming language allows for direct data manipulation: the data manipulation language and the programming language are supposed to be integrated.

3.3   To write simple programs

Once one gives a tool to people, they tend very often to use it for different purposes, simply because they like it or because they find it easy to use for this new purpose. Thus SQL has generated the so-called SQL programmer, who writes entire applications in SQL directly without resorting to any other language. Only simple applications can be written this way (due to the limited power of the language), but there are many such applications. It is unclear whether, given a query language, users of object-oriented database systems will tend to use it this way; after all, they are supposed to be given a good application programming language.

3.4   To take shortcuts in the programming language

This only applies to object-oriented systems. Assume we have a simple and easy to use query language to express even complex queries, this language is going to be simpler and more readable than the actual programming language of the system and the programmer will be tempted to call it from its program to solve some data manipulation problems.

4   Issues in the design of a query language

I list here the critical problems one must solve and the crucial questions one must answer when designing an object-oriented query language.

1. Can the query language violate encapsulation?

2. What do we query? data or methods, or both?

3. What should be the style of the query language?

4. Should the query language be integrated in the programming language?

5. What should the relationship with the type system be?

I now comment on each one of these issues in detail.

4.1   Relationship with encapsulation

In an object-oriented system, each object has associated with it a set of methods (operations) by which one can operate on the object. The idea of encapsulation is that these methods are the *only* way to operate on objects. If the query language cannot violate encapsulation, then basically the only access to objects is through methods and data is invisible. Conversely, if we want to see data, we must be able to violate encapsulation.

Encapsulation is a mechanism to enforce a good structuration of the code and a good programming discipline. Because the query language is only used to query the data and in an interactive mode, there is less reason to enforce this encapsulation. This statement should be moderated in the case of updates in the query (of the style "replace"). It should also be moderated in the case where the query language is embedded in the programming language. So we are back to an authorization problem: the query language should have a different behavior when it is used as an *ad hoc* query facility, as an embedded data manipulation language, or as a programming language.

I claim that in the first case it should be allowed to violate encapsulation, and that in the two other cases it should strictly respect it. Here is an example showing that in the query mode, one wants a different behavior. Take the classical example of a stack: it is represented as an object with two operations, *pop* and *push*. When manipulating that stack in a program, we do not want the client programmers to see the stack implementation or content. However, when querying the system through a browser (assume a graphical interface), we do not want to see an icon which we can pop and push, but we want to see a complete picture of a stack with its entire content. On the contrary, if we allow the query language to violate encapsulation in the embedded or in the programming language mode, we are giving the user a means of violating encapsulation and loosing all the benefit of the approach.

Thus, *the query language should be able to violate encapsulation in the* ad hoc *query mode and should not when used for programming purposes.*

4.2   Data vs. methods

Because methods will be used by database designers to glorify data (i.e. to generate virtual attributes), it is necessary to be able to query them. Here is an example demonstrating this need: consider the *person* object with the instance variable *birth_date*. A good way of improving this object is by introducing a "computed field" *age*, which computes the age from the birth date and the current date. This computed field is usually represented by a method of the person object. Thus, if we disallow the user to query on methods, he will be forced to recompute the age in the query whenever he needs to query on that field.

Because sometimes methods will only be used to store entire application programs, it is necessary to be able to query data directly. Here is an example showing that we should be allowed to query data and not only methods: consider the *employee* object and assume the designer has encapsulated everything and uses only two methods *fire* and *hire*. Then there are no ways to browse through the database.

Thus, *the query language should be able to see data and apply methods to objects.*

4.3 Style

There are basically four choices in the style of the query language. It can be *ad hoc*; it can be SQL-like; it can be functional; or finally it can be logic-based. Notice that I do not count SQL as logic like language, mainly because the reason why one would stick to an SQL like syntax is not that it is logic based, but that it is a standard (i.e. the important thing is not relational calculus, but the *select-from-where* clause).

I have absolutely no religious belief concerning logic or functional approaches to the problem. I believe the first problem is SQL vs. the other languages. The main advantages of SQL are market driven: the language is a standard, people understand its concepts, the name is catchy, even for people who don't understand anything to it. The main drawbacks are that the language is ugly and clumsy.

Logic based language have the advantage of being considered declarative by most people.

Both logic and functional languages have the advantage of relying on good technologies. They also both have the drawback of scaring people away, for no specific reason (maybe they just look too "theoretical").

Let me add one more thing at this stage: *syntax is important.* Many programming language designers and query language designers have made the mistake of believing syntax is unimportant and their languages, even though they had interesting features or intrinsic qualities, failed because, due to an ugly syntax, the resulting queries and programs were unreadable or too hard to understand.

Thus, *the style of the query language is a matter of taste.*

4.4 Integration in the programming language

The query language could be a subset of the programming language or it could be a distinct language. In the later case, the programming language could call the query language, and/or the query language could call the programming language.

Three situations can occur in order of increasing interest: (i) the query language is distinct from the programming language and there is an impedance mismatch between the two languages, such as the one between SQL and C, due to the difference in style of the language, (ii) the query language is distinct but it mixes well with the programming language and calling it from a program is rather natural and (iii) the query language is a subset of the programming language. In the first situation, we have failed in fulfilling one of the major objectives of object-oriented database systems: solving the impedance mismatch of relational systems. In the second case, we have improved the situation but the programmer still has to learn two different languages. The last case is a sure winner: there is no impedance mismatch, the user only learns one language and he still has the benefit of a user-friendly query language.

Thus, if possible, *the query language should be a subset of the programming language.*

4.5 Relationship with the type or class system

Many query languages refer to types in their query formulation. They can refer to types for various reasons: for correctness purposes or simply to extract information. I think the issue is a little bit confused by the definition of what is a type in a database system, so let me try to clarify that first.

Consider the following statements:

```
(1)      type t is tuple(a: int, b: string);
(2)      x of type t;
(3)      x of type tuple(a: int, b: string);
```

The first statement is purely a type statement, it creates a type with name t. It gives no information about the database content. The second statement is purely a data statement: it states that the database contains an object of name x and of type t, it tells us something about the content of the database but nothing about the type system. The third statement is a mixture of the two situations, it gives information about the type *and* about the data.

Depending on the system, commands of each category are allowed. Usually, programming languages have a tendency to do things more cleanly and use statements of type 1 and 2 only. Relational systems only accept commands of the third type, thus the schema contains type information and data information. This approach has also been used in many other database systems and gave the impression that types were used in queries while only data was: in a system with mixed mode, the only way to access data is through its type. Thus the QUEL statement "range of x is R" which can be understood as a type declaration for the variable x is in fact a statement that x must run over the set *value* R.

In fact the only information needed is that concerning the data and not the types. Programming languages need type information to increase their correctness. But in the case of *ad hoc* query languages, we are in an interpreted mode and we are not so concerned with correctness.

Concerning the form of type checking, whether we use compile-time or run-time type checking is more of a performance argument: *ad hoc* queries could be type checked at run-time and canned queries could be checked at compile-time.

One last important point: type information is currently used in database systems, not for correctness purposes but for performance purposes. Knowing the exact type of the data allows to compile operation down into machine code thus increasing performance. This is an argument for compile time type-checking. Note that no type information is needed in the query for that: the system can derive the type information from the schema. The query only reference the data and the schema tells the system the type of the referenced data.

Thus, *no type information is needed in the query formulation; type information can be derived by the system and used for checking purposes and optimization purposes at compile time*

5   A quick tour of the O_2 model

This section describes and presents the specificity of the O_2 data model, [Lécluse et al 88], [Bancilhon et al 88]. It just describes the features which are necessary to explain the query language. It also simplifies some of the features of the model for the sake of clarity.

The O_2 data model relies on two kinds of concepts: values on which we can perform a predefined set of primitives and objects which have identity and encapsulate values and user defined methods. Values have types which specify their structure and objects have classes.

We are given a set of *atoms* (integers, floats, booleans and strings), and an alphabet A of attributes names.

An *object* is a triple *(oid, value, methods)* consisting of an object identifier, a value and a set of methods. The *object identifier* uniquely identifies the object throughout the system. Classes identify the common structure of a set of objects. A class consists of a name, a type t and a set of methods M. Every object in the class will have a value of type t and will have the same set of methods M.

A *value* is defined recursively as follows:

- An atom is value of type atom.

- If $v_1, v_2, ..., v_n$ are values of type t, then $\text{set}(v_1, v_2, ..., v_n)$ is a value of type set(t). Two set values with the same elements in a different order, or with different number of occurrences of the same elements are equal.

- If $v_1, v_2, ..., v_n$ are objects of class c, then $\text{set}(v_1, v_2, ..., v_n)$ is a value of type set(c). Two set values with the same elements in a different order, or with different number of occurrences are equal.

- If $v_1, v_2, ..., v_n$ are values or objects of type or classes respectively $t_1, t_2, ..., t_n$, then $\text{tuple}(a_1: v_1, a_2: v_2, ..., a_n: v_n)$ is a value of type $\text{tuple}(a_1: t_1, a_2: t_2, ..., a_n: t_n)$. One does not change a tuple value by changing the order of its attributes.

- If $v_1, v_2, ..., v_n$ are values of type t, then $\text{list}(v_1, v_2, ..., v_n)$ is a value of type list(t).

- If $v_1, v_2, ..., v_n$ are objects of class c, then $\text{list}(v_1, v_2, ..., v_n)$ is a value of type list(c).

Note that, because objects have identifiers, several objects can share a common component and objects can be cyclic.

A *named* object or value is an object or a value with a name.

Persistence is defined in the model as follows: every named object or value is persistent. Every component of a persistent object or value is persistent. Nothing else is persistent. The query language should be able to reach all persistent data and only persistent data.

The set of objects of a given class is the *extension* of that class. Upon user request, the system offers automatic extension maintenance as follows: given a class c, it creates a named value of type set(c) with name c and automatically inserts every newly created object of class c into it.

The *schema* consists of classes, types and named values or objects.

The O_2 programming interface consists of two languages: the *schema command* language and the *programming* language for methods. The former allows the user to create classes and types. The later is used to write the body of the methods.

Methods are procedures taking as inputs objects and values and returning a value or an object. For the purpose of this discussion, methods will be assumed purely applicative, i.e. they create or return objects or values without updating any of the existing ones.

Methods in the model are written using a programming language. That programming language is the extension of an existing programming language to which several extensions are added. In the current implementation of the system, methods can be written in C and Basic. The extensions we make to the existing programming languages are (i) primitives to declare object classes and value types, (ii) primitives to pass messages to objects and (iii) primitives to manipulate structured values. I do not present the type and class declaration primitives since they would not add anything to this discussion. The two other types of primitives will be presented later on, because they in fact make the query language.

This short presentation ignores many of the important features of the O_2 data model. For instance, inheritance, exceptional attributes and exceptional methods were not presented because they do not impact the query language design.

I now present an example database. It is described by the sequence of commands which create it.

```
add class Place_to_go
        type tuple( name: string,
                    address:  tuple(country: string,
                                    city: string,
                                    street: string)
                    description: string,
                    phone: integer,
                    things_to_do: set(Thing_to_do))
        with extension
```

This creates a class of objects having a tuple structure. The tuple has five fields. Field *address* is itself a tuple value. Fields *name, description* and *phone* are atomic values and the field *things_to_do* is a set of objects of class Thing_to_do. The extension clause means that there is a set value named Place_to_go which contains all the instances of that class. The next command creates the class Thing_to_do.

```
add class Thing_to_do
        type tuple( name: string,
                    description: string,
                    location: Place_to_go,
                    closing day: string,
                    fee: integer)
        with extension
```

The next command creates the Tour class. The schedule field is a list of tuples. Notice that this class is created without extension.

```
add class Tour
        type tuple(name: string,
                   maximum_number: int,
                   schedule: list(tuple(what: Thing_to_do,
                                        when: Date)))
```

The last class is the Date class. This class has four methods day, day_in_week, month and year which returns respectively an integer, a string, a string and an integer.

```
add class Date
        type integer
        method day: integer,
        method day_in_week: string,
        method month: string,
        method year: integer,
```

The actual code of the methods is not shown in this example.

```
add object the_Eiffel_tower: Place_to_see
```

This declares a named object of class Place_to_see with name "the_Eiffel_tower".

```
add value packages: set(Tour)
```

This declares a named value of type set(Tour) with name "packages".

```
add object today: Date
```

This declares a named object of type Date with name "today". The actual initialization and maintenance of these objects is not shown in this example.

6   The query language

6.1   Design choices

According to our previous discussion, the following design decision for the language were made.

1. The query language violates encapsulation in its *ad hoc* mode. It does not in its programming or embedded mode.

2. The query language sees data and can apply methods to objects.

3. The query language is functional in nature. Its syntax follows the syntax of the CO_2 language and is set oriented.

4. The query language is a subset of the programming language.

5. The query language ignores types and the type hierarchy. Type checking is performed at run time in the query mode and at compile time in the programming mode.

We already discussed points (1), (2), and (5). All is left to show is how to obtain the inclusion of the query language in the programming language and why we chose this style of query language.

Here is how we obtain the inclusion of the query language in the programming language: because of the specificity of the data model, values and objects are distinguished and there are some special primitives to manipulate the structured values. Because the programming language is the extension of a existing programming language, this set of primitives is clearly identified. Thus we have simply chosen to take this set of primitives to be our query language. Note that this came free with the data model.

Here is my main motivation for choosing a functional approach. The model should be clean and have a well defined semantics. This leaves us with the choice between functional and logic. Logic is not the best approach to deal with complex object models having a set constructor because it introduces its own set constructor the meta-level. In a logic based system, we deal only with predicates and predicates are defined as "sets of things". Thus, there is meta constructor set in the model since an answer to a query is a set of things. This is fine, as long as there are no other set constructors in the model, which is the case of Prolog for instance. If one tries to introduce a set constructor in the data model, there is a difficulty in dealing with two set constructors one at the data level and the other one at the metadata level. I believe this is the source of the difficulty of people trying to introduce sets in logic programming, [Tsur and Zaniolo 86], [Kuper]. In the functional approach there is no meta constructor and queries only return objects, thus sets can be introduced naturally in the model without disturbing anything.

6.2   General form of queries

Loosely speaking, a query is an expression of the form $e(x_1, x_2, ...,x_n)$ where the x_i's are free variables. For any database, it defines a partial mapping which associates with each collection of n objects or values of the database, an object or a value of the database. Thus, queries are parameterized and, to be evaluated, they have to be assigned parameters (objects or values). Therefore, only closed queries (those without any free variables) can be actually evaluated. Open queries (those with free variables) are only used to build and define other queries.

The semantics of a query $f(x_1, x_2, ..., x_n)$ is defined as follows: for every database D, f defines a partial mapping $(O \cup V)^n \to O \cup V$, where O an V are the sets of persistent objects and values of the database.

6.3   Query syntax and semantics

We are given: the set of atoms (integers, booleans, strings and reals), the alphabet of attribute names A, the alphabet of the persistent names of the database and the alphabet of method names.

Queries are defined as follows:

6.3.1   Entering the database

- If n is the name of a named object or value of the database, then n is a closed query. It returns the object or the value associated with this name.

6.3.2   Dealing with atoms

- a, where a is an atom, is a closed query returning this atom.

- x + y, x - y, x * y are queries with free variables x and y. They associate to every couple of integers or reals their sum, difference and product.

- x and y, x or y are queries with free variables x and y. They associate to the two booleans x and y their product and their sum.

- not(x) is a query with free variable x. It associates with the boolean value x its negation.

6.3.3   Base queries for tuples

- x.a, where a is an attribute name, is a query with free variable x. It associates with every tuple value having an attribute a, its a-component.

6.3.4   Base queries for lists

- x[i] is a query with free variables and i. It associates with each list value x (of length at least equal to i) and every integer value i, the i-th element of x.

- sublist(x, i, j) is a query with free variables x, i and j. It associates with each list value x, each integer i and each integer j, the sublist starting with the i-th element and ending with the j-th. If i is greater than j then the list is empty. If i is less than 0 then the sublist start at the 0-th element, if j is greater than the length of x then the sublist ends with the last element of x.

- count(x) is a query with free variable x. It associates, with every list value, x its length.

- concat(x, y) is a query with free variable x and y. It associates with every couple of list values x and y their concatenation.

- flatten(x) is a query with free variable x. It associates with each list of lists x the concatenation of its members.

6.3.5 Base queries for sets

- element(x) is a query with free variable x. It associates with every singleton set value x, the element of the singleton.

- x union y is a query with free variables x and y. It associates to every couple of set values x and y their union.

- x minus y is a query with free variables x and y. It associates to every couple of set values x and y their set difference.

- x inter y is a query with free variables x and y. It associates to every couple of set values x and y their set intersection.

- flatten(x) is a query with free variable x. It associated with each set of sets x the union of its elements.

- count(x) is a query with free variable x. It associates with each set x its cardinality.

6.3.6 Base queries for constructing objects

- set() is a closed query, it returns the empty set value.

- tuple() is a closed query, it returns the empty tuple value.

- list() is a closed query, it returns the empty list value.

- $set(x_1, x_2, ..., x_n)$ is a query with free variables $x_1, x_2, ..., x_n$. It associates with every n objects $x_1, x_2, ..., x_n$ or with every n values $x_1, x_2, ..., x_n$ the set value containing them. Note that one cannot mix objects and values in the same set.

- $tuple(a_1: x_1, a_2: x_2, ... , a_n: x_n)$ where the a_i's are distinct attribute names is a query with free variables $x_1, x_2, ..., x_n$. It associates to the n objects or values $x_1, x_2, ..., x_n$ the tuple having its attribute a_i equal to x_i. Note that in this case the input variables can be assigned a mix of objects and values.

- $list(x_1, x_2, ..., x_n)$ is a query with free variables $x_1, x_2, ..., x_n$. It associates with every n objects $x_1, x_2, ..., x_n$ or with every n values $x_1, x_2, ..., x_n$ the list value containing them. Note that one cannot mix objects and values in the same list.

6.3.7 Message passing

- x m$(x_1, x_2, ..., x_n)$, where m is an n-ary method name, is a query with free variables $x_1, x_2, ..., x_n$. It associates with every object x having method m and every objects or values $x_1, x_2, ..., x_n$, the result of the application of m$(x_1, x_2, ..., x_n)$ on x.

6.3.8 Base predicate queries

- (x = y), is a query with free variable x and y. It returns the value true if the two values x and y are equal or if the two objects x and y are identical. It returns the value false if the two values x and y are not equal or if the two objects x and y are not identical.

- (x in y) is a query with free variables x and y. It returns true if the value or object x belongs to the set value y. It returns false if the value or object x does not belong to the set value y.

- (x included in y) is a query with free variables x and y. It returns true if the set value x belongs is included in the set value y. It returns false if the set value x is not included in the set value y.

6.3.9 Constructing queries from queries

- if $f(x_1, x_2, ..., x_n)$ is a query with free variables $x_1, x_2, ..., x_n$,

  if $f_1(x_{11}, x_{12}, ..., x_{1n_1})$ are queries with free variables $x_{11}, x_{12}, ..., x_{1n_1}$,

  if $f_2(x_{21}, x_{22}, ..., x_{2n_2})$ is a query with free variables $x_{21}, x_{22}, ..., x_{2n_2}$,

  ...

  if $f_n(x_{n_1}, x_{n_2}, ..., x_{nn_n})$ is a query with free variables $x_{n_1}, x_{n_2}, ..., x_{nn_n}$,

  then $f(f_1(x_{11}, x_{12}, ..., x_{1n_1}), f_2(x_{21}, x_{22}, ..., x_{2n_2}), ... f_n(x_{n_1}, x_{n_2}, ..., x_{nn_n}))$ is a query with free variables $x_{11}, x_{12}, ..., x_{1n_1}, x_{21}, x_{22}, ..., x_{2n_2}, ..., x_{n_1}, x_{n_2}, ..., x_{nn_n}$. Notice that some of the x_{ij}'s might be the same. The query is defined as the composition of f with the f_i's modulo variable repetition.

- if q$(x, x_1, x_2, ..., x_n)$ is a query, if p$(x, y_1, y_2, ..., y_p)$ is a query, then

  set(q$(x, x_1, x_2, ..., x_n)$: x in z and p$(x, y_1, y_2, ..., y_p)$)

  is a query with free variables $x_1, x_2, ..., x_n, z, y_1, y_2, ..., y_p$. If z is a set, it defines a new query which builds a set consisting of the image by q of the subset of z satisfying p. In other words:

  set(q$(x, a_1, a_2, ..., a_n)$: x in c and p$(x, b_1, b_2, ..., b_p)$) =

  {q$(x, a_1, a_2, ..., a_n)$ such that x in c and p$(x, b_1, b_2, ..., b_p)$}

- if q$(x, x_1, x_2, ..., x_n)$ is a query, if p$(x, y_1, y_2, ..., y_p)$ is a query, then

  list(q$(x, x_1, x_2, ..., x_n)$: x in z and p$(x, y_1, y_2, ..., y_p)$)

is a query with free variables $x_1, x_2, ..., x_n, z\ y_1, y_2, ..., y_p$. If z is a list, it defines a new query which builds a list consisting of the image by q of the sublist of z satisfying p.

- if $p(x, x_1, x_2, ..., x_n)$ is a query with free variables $x, x_1, x_2, ..., x_n$ then

  for all x in y : $p(x, x_1, x_2, ..., x_n)$

  is a query with free variable $x_1, x_2, ..., x_n, y$. It defines a predicate taking the value true if all the elements of the set or list value y satisfy $p(x, x_1, x_2, ..., x_n)$.

- if $p(x, x_1, x_2, ..., x_n)$ is a query with free variables $x, x_1, x_2, ..., x_n$ then

  there exists x in y : $p(x, x_1, x_2, ..., x_n)$

  is a query with free variable $x_1, x_2, ..., x_n, y$. It defines a predicate taking the value true if one of the elements of the set or list value y satisfies $p(x, x_1, x_2, ..., x_n)$.

6.3.10   Defining and re-using queries

Given an expression $e(x_1, x_2, ..., x_n)$ defining a query, we attach a name to that query to re-use it in other query expressions with the following statement:

define query $f(x_1, x_2, ..., x_n)$: $e(x_1, x_2, ..., x_n)$
Then we can use $f(x_1, x_2, ..., x_n)$ in place of $e(x_1, x_2, ..., x_n)$

6.4   Example queries

This section presents a number of example queries based on the database described in Section 5.

Where is the Eiffel Tower?

```
the_Eiffel_tower.address
```

What is 2 and 2?

```
2 + 2
```

What is the description of the things I can do at the Eiffel tower?

```
set(x.description : x in the_Eiffel_tower.things_to_do)
```

What is the price of a visit to the Eiffel tower increased by 10%?

```
element(set(x.fee : x in the_Eiffel_tower.things_to_do and
            x.name = ''visit'')) * 1.1
```

What are the activities in Paris for less than 10 francs?

```
set(x.name : x in Thing_to_do and
            (x.location.address.city = ''Paris'' and x.fee <= 10))
```

Is there a tour which takes me to the Eiffel Tower and the Arc de Triomphe ?

```
define goes-to(x, y) :
     there exists z in  x.schedule : x.what.location.name = y

there exists x in packages :
            (goes-to(x, ''Eiffel Tower'') and
             goes_to(x, ''Lido''))
```

What is open today?

```
set(x.name : x in Thing_to_do and
            not(x.closing_day = today day))
```

What is the first stop of each tour which can take 50 persons?

```
set(x.schedule[1] : x in packages and
                    x.maximum_number >= 50)
```

What is the last stop of tours starting today?

```
define last(x) : x[count(x)]
set(last(x.schedule) : x in packages and
                    x.schedule[1].when = today)
```

Print the names and the number of stops of the tours passing through Paris.

```
set(tuple(x.name, number: count(x.schedule)) :
   x in Packages and
   (there exists y in x.schedule
                such that y.what.location.address.city = ''Paris'' ))
```

For each place to go, list the name, the street and the description.

```
set(tuple(name: x.name,
        street: x.address.street,
        description: x.description) :
   x in Place_to_go)
```

7   Conclusion

In this paper, I have described a query language for an object oriented database system. The query language uses the specificity of the O_2 database system, namely the distinction between objects and values and the existence, in the data manipulation language, of primitives to manipulate structured values. The result is a query language which is fully embedded in the data manipulation language thus solving the impedance mismatch. We are currently implementing a first version of the interpreter of this query language. This is one of the three experiments we are conducting on query languages in O_2. The other ones are Lifoo (a functional language) and Reloop (an SQL like language).

8 Acknowledgements

I wish to thank Christophe Lécluse and Michel Scholl for their comments on an earlier version of this paper, and Sophie Cluet for highly stimulating discussions on the topic. This also benefited from conversations with Claude Delobel. The reader will have noticed strong similarities between this query language and the FAD database programming language (this is probably due to my lack of imagination), so I am in debt to Setrag Khoshafian, Ted Briggs and Patrick Valduriez. There also a complete (and intentional) match between the query language and a subset of CO_2 and I thank its designers Christophe Lécluse and Philippe Richard.

References

[Atwood 85] T. Atwood, "An object-oriented DBMS for design support applications", *Ontologic Inc. Report.*

[Bancilhon 88] F. Bancilhon, "Object-oriented database systems", *Proceedings of the ACM SIGACT-SIGMOD-SIGART Conference on the Principles of Database Systems*, Austin, Texas, May 1988.

[Bancilhon et Maier 87] F. Bancilhon et D. Maier, "Multilanguage object-oriented database systems: new answer to old database problems?", *Proceedings of the second INRIA-ICOT Workshop on Computer Science and Artificial Intelligence*, Cannes, October 87.

[Bancilhon et al 88] F. Bancilhon, G. Barbedette, V. Benzaken, C. Delobel, S. Gamerman, C. Lécluse, P. Pfeffer, P. Richard et F. Velez, "The design and implementation of O_2, an object-oriented database system", *Proceedings of the ooDBS II Workshop*, Bad Munster, RFA, September 1988.

[Banerjee et al 87] J. Banerjee, H.T. Chou, J. Garza, W. Kim, D. Woelk, N. Ballou and H.J. Kim, "Data model issues for object-oriented applications", ACM TOIS, January 1987.

[Dadam et al 86] P. Dadam et al, "A DBMS prototype to support extended NF2 relations: an integrated view on flat tables and hierarchies", *Proceedings ACM Sigmod*, Washington 1986.

[Fishman et al. 87] D. Fishman et al, "Iris: an object-oriented database management system", *ACM TOIS 5:1, January 86, pp 48-69.*

[Kuper] G. Kuper, "Logic programming with sets", *Proceedings 6th PODS*, San Diego, March 1987.

[Lécluse et al 88] C. Lécluse, P. Richard and F. Velez, "O_2, an Object-Oriented Data Model", *Proceedings of the ACM-SIGMOD Conference*, Chicago, June 1988.

[Maier *et al* 84] D. Maier, J. Stein, A. Otis, A. Purdy, "Development of an object-oriented DBMS" *Report CS/E-86-005*, Oregon Graduate Center, April 86

[Maier 88] D. Maier, *Private conversation.*

[Tsur and Zaniolo 86] S. Tsur and C. Zaniolo, "LDL: a logic-based data-language", *Proceeding of the 85 Conference on VLDB*, September 1985

[Zaniolo 86] C. Zaniolo, "Object-oriented programming in Prolog ", *Proceedings of the first workshop on Expert Database Systems*, 1985.

EINE LOGISCHE ANALYSE DES VERHÄLTNISSES VON ANWENDUNGS- UND DATENBANKSYSTEMEN

H. Wedekind
Lehrstuhl Informatik VI
Universität Erlangen-Nürnberg

Zusammenfassung:

Der Transaktionsbegriff wird mit Hilfe der klassischen Logik analysiert. Der Begriff ist auf die Betriebsmittelverwaltung beschränkt. Eine Erweiterung zu Problemlösungszyklen auf der Grundlage der konstruktiven Logik ohne tertium-non-datur wird untersucht. Eine Klassifikation von Externoperationen wird vorgetragen,mit denen Realaktionen eingrenzbar sind. Konzeptionelle Schemata werden auf die Art/Gattungs-Relation und die Teil/Ganze-Relation zurückgeführt, um Objekte mit Vererbung und Komplexobjekte unterscheiden zu können.

Summary:

The transaction concept of database systems is analyzed from the point of view of classical logic. Transactions of this type are confined to resource management. An extension to problem solving cycles is outlined using constructive logic without the famous tertium-non-datur. A taxonomy of operations affecting states outside a transaction system is investigated and predicates of real actions are considered. Objects of a conceptional schema are studied from the species-genus and part-whole relationship point of view, in order to distinguish objects with inheritance from complex objects.

0.   VORBEMERKUNGEN

Der Terminus "logische Analyse" wurde von den Logikern des Wiener Kreises um Rudolf Carnap in den 20-er Jahren dieses Jahrhunderts eingeführt. Gegenstand der logischen Analyse ist das Bemühen, die in den Gebrauchs- und Wissenschaftssprachen verdeckten logischen Formen und Konzepte aufzuzeigen, um damit Grundlagen für mögliche Weiterentwicklungen aufzuzeigen. Das Fachgebiet "Datenbanksysteme" steht mit seinen erfolgreichen konventionellen Anwendungen an einem Abschluß und Anfang zugleich. Mit den Ausdrücken "Database Extensions", "Non-Standard-Datenbanksysteme", "Future DB-Systems", etc. werden neue Anwendungsfelder genannt, die mit den Datenbanksystemen zusammen auf ihre logischen Strukturen und Annahmen untersucht werden müssen. Logische Analysen wollen zeigen, was möglich ist. "Die Erforschung der Logik bedeutet die Erforschung aller Gesetzmäßigkeit. Und außerhalb der Logik ist alles Zufall" (Wittgenstein, Tractatus 6.2)

1.   TRANSAKTION UND PROBLEMLÖSUNGSZYKLUS ALS LOGISCHE KONZEPTE

1.1 Die Transaktion auf der Grundlage der klassischen Logik

Der Transaktionsbegriff gehört neben der Einführung eines global geltenden Konzeptionellen Schemas zu den wesentlichen Komponenten konventioneller Datenbanksysteme. Während das Konzeptionelle Schema von den Ausdrucksmitteln des verwendeten Datenmodells abhängig ist und somit von einer Sprach- und Modellierungsvielfalt determiniert wird, ist das Transaktionskonzept in den letzten fünfzehn Jahren mit einer hohen Präzision und Eindeutigkeit herausgearbeitet worden. Das Akronym ACID wurde gebildet, um die Hauptmerkmale einer Transaktion, nämlich die Atomarität, die C(K)onsistenzerhaltung, die Isolation und die Dauerhaftigkeit hervorzuheben. Die Eigenschaften ACID machen die Transaktion zu einem operativen Konzept, das wegen der erforderlichen leistungsfähigen Protokoll-, Sperr- und Recoverykomponenten einen hohen Implementierungsaufwand verlangt. Atomarität bedeutet, daß eine Transaktion von außen gesehen nur ganz oder gar nicht abläuft. Es gibt nur definite Zustände, von denen Consistenz verlangt wird. Isolation bedeutet, daß eine Transaktion in einem Mehrtransaktionsbetrieb so ablaufen soll, als handele es sich um einen seriell arbeitenden Eintransaktionsbetrieb. Dauerhaftigkeit nun ist die Garantie, daß das Ergebnis der Transaktion nicht rückgängig gemacht werden kann. Eine Veränderung der Ergebnisse kann nur durch eine andere Transaktion erfolgen. Üblicherweise wird eine Transaktion als Klammerung dargestellt, wobei die öffnende Klammer BOT (Begin of Transaction) und die schließende Klammer EOT (End of Transaction) genannt wird. Die entsprechenden Aussagen, die für Dritte sichtbare, konsistente Sachverhalte (Zustände) darstellen, sollen mit A bzw. B bezeichnet werden:

$$\begin{array}{cc} A & B \\ (\text{----------------->}) \\ \text{BOT} & \text{EOT} \end{array}$$

Eine strenge, mengentheoretische Definition des Transaktionsbegriffs wird von Bernstein e.a. [5, S. 27] vorgetragen, wobei auf die Leseoperationen $r_i(x)$ und Schreiboperationen $w_i(x)$ einer Transaktion i mit Bezug auf ein Datenobjekt x eingegangen wird. Die mengentheoretische Definition Bernsteins ist vorteilhaft, wenn die Planung der Konflikte von Lese- und Schreiboperationen der Transaktion i, $r_i(x)$ bzw. $w_i(x)$, mit $r_j(x)$ bzw. $w_j(x)$, also den Lese- und Schreiboperationen einer Transaktion j bzgl. des gleichen Objektes x, untersucht werden soll. Will man den logischen Kern des Transaktionsbegriffs bloßlegen, so genügt eine deskriptive mengentheoretische Definition nicht, da Mengenlehre bereits auf logischen Konstruktionen aufbaut. Wir tragen hier eine operative, kalkülorientierte Definition des Transaktionsbegriffs vor. Ein Kalkül ist dabéi nichts anderes als die Herstellung irgendwelcher Figuren nach Regeln. Was ein Kalkül ist, versteht jeder, der Steinchen, die calculi, im Spiel auf einem Brett nach Regeln hin- und herschieben kann. Voraussetzungsfreie Kalküle als Basis der Aussagen- und Prädikatenlogik zu nehmen, geht auf Leibniz und noch ausgeprägter auf Frege zurück. Damit wird der Zirkel aufgelöst, der in einer axiomatischen Theorie der Logik steckt und der darin besteht, daß jede axiomatische Theorie (so auch die Mengenlehre) schon Logik voraussetzt.
Ein Kalkül mit Aussagen über Sachverhalte (nicht mit "Steinchen") zum Vollzug einer Transaktion sieht wie folgt aus:

o Notation:

    oo   => ist der Regelpfeil.

        Die allgemeine Form einer Regel ist $a_{i1}, a_{i2},\ldots,a_{in} => b_i$. Die a's und b's sind logisch nicht weiter zerlegbare Elementaraussagen, die Sachverhalte (Zustände) darstellen. Mit $i=1,\ldots,n$ liegt ein Regelsystem vor, das durch A=>B abgekürzt wird.

    oo   Konjunktion ($\wedge$) und Adjunktion ($\vee$) werden über die Regeln

        $a,b => a \wedge b$; $a => a \vee b$; $b => a \vee b$

        eingeführt.

    oo $\top$ bzw. $\bot$ sind die Zeichen für beliebig wahre bzw. beliebige falsche Aussagen.

o   Transaktionskalkül:

1) $a => \top$ <u>Ex-quodlibet-verum:</u> Aus einer beliebigen Aussage kann eine wahre abgeleitet werden.

2) $A => B$ Transaktionsregelsystem: Es werden die zulässigen Übergänge operativ bestimmt.

3) $b \wedge \neg b => \bot$ Prinzip vom ausgeschlossenen Widerspruch oder <u>principium contradictionis:</u> Niemand kann beides tun, b ableiten und somit garantieren und b nicht ableiten. D.h., wenn eine Transaktion freigegeben und ein b verkündet

wurde, kann sie nicht mehr zurückgesetzt werden ($\neg$ b). Die <u>redo-Operation</u> muß die Aussage b auf jeden Fall erhalten. Regel 3) darf nicht in Transaktionskalkülen angewendet werden, weil mit b gegenüber der Transaktionsumgebung eine Verpflichtung besteht und $\neg$ b nicht behauptet werden darf.

4) $\top \Rightarrow$ b $\vee \neg$ b

Prinzip vom ausgeschlossenen Dritten oder das <u>tertium-non-datur:</u> Das gültige Ende einer Transaktion wird erreicht oder nicht erreicht, ein Drittes gibt es nicht. Man formuliert an dieser Stelle auch häufig wie folgt: Das Prädikat EOT kommt einer Transaktion zu oder nicht zu.

5) $\bot \Rightarrow$ c

und specialiter

$\neg$ b $\Rightarrow$ a

<u>Ex-falso-quodlibet:</u> Aus einer falschen Aussage (Fehler) darf zu einer beliebigen Aussage c, d.h. aber auch über $\neg$ b $\Rightarrow$ a zu einer Anfangsaussage a übergegangen werden. In reinen Logikkalkülen kann diese Regel in keiner Ableitung angewendet werden. Im Spezialfall des Transaktionskalküls darf diese Regel, d.h. das Zurücksetzen auf den Anfang (<u>undo-Operation</u>) nur herangezogen werden, wenn man zu $\bot$ nicht über 3) kommt. Aufgabe der Implementierung des Transaktionskalküls ist es, durch geeignete Maßnahmen dafür zu sorgen, daß 3) niemals anwendbar wird.

Die durch die berühmten lateinischen Namen gekennzeichneten Regeltypen 1), 3), 4) und 5) sind Forderungen der klassischen Logik. Die Besonderheit des der klassischen Logik zugrunde liegenden Kalküls liegt darin, daß mit Ausnahme von 5) (ex-falso-quodlibet) Elementaraussagen und ihre Negation paarweise auftreten, d.h. mit b stets $\neg$ b. Man nennt deshalb die Aussagen eines solchen Paares primitiv-komplementär [16, S. 87]. Diese Bezeichnung bezieht sich nur auf die logische Erscheinungsform. Die Implementierung eines Transaktionskalküls mit seiner Fiktion, daß nur Anfangs- und Endzustände sichtbar sein sollen, ist hingegen sehr komplex. So muß, um die Regel 5), die undo-Operation, als Spezialfall realisieren zu können, das System ein "Erinnerungsvermögen" haben, um im Fehlerfall invers auf den Ausgangspunkt zurückzugelangen. Technisch gilt gleiches vom Widerspruchsprinzip 3). Geht ein b verloren, so muß es wiederhergestellt werden (redo-Operation). Regel 3) darf somit niemals angewendet werden, weil das "quid iuris" (was gilt), die Frage der Transaktionsumgebung, ein für allemal verläßlich (committed) beantwortet sein muß, um Fehlerfortpflanzungen zu vermeiden.

Wir halten fest: Der klassische Logikkalkül unterscheidet sich vom Transaktionskalkül nur durch die unterschiedliche Interpretation (Verbot, Erlaubnis) des ex falso quodlibet 5) und des principium contradictionis 3). Das ex-falso- quodlibet 5) ist im Logikkalkül <u>nicht</u> anzuwenden und das principium contradictionis 3) ist im Transaktionskalkül <u>nicht</u> zu benutzen (Verbot). Regel 3) kann im Logikkalkül zwecks Beweisführung und Regel 5) kann im Transaktionskalkül zwecks Recovery herangezogen werden (Erlaubnis). Im Mittelpunkt des Transaktionskalküls steht die Konsistenzerhaltung, im Logikkalkül dagegen geht es um den Beweis der Ableitbarkeit steht die Konsistenzerhaltung, im Logikkalkül dagegen geht es um den Beweis der Ableitbarkeit oder Nicht-Ableitbarkeit.

Die Nichtanwendbarkeit des ex-falso-quodlibet hat in der Geschichte der Logik dazu geführt, die Regel ganz wegzulassen. Man nennt, wenn das tertium-non-datur auch noch entfällt, den Kalkül dann Minimalkalkül [Johansson 1937]. Der Minimalkalkül hat den Nachteil, daß dann die Schlußweise der Kontraposition nicht mehr gilt. Da ex-falso-quodlibet ohne technische Hilfen gar nicht anwendbar ist, das Verbot somit praktisch nicht übertretbar ist, kann man es auch gelten lassen.

1.2   Problemlösungszyklen auf der Grundlage der konstruktiven Logik

Es ist eine bedeutende Erkenntnis Anfang dieses Jahrhunderts gewesen [Brouwer 1907], herausgefunden zu haben, daß alle Regeln rein formal, ohne irgendwelche Bezüge zu Inhalten von Aussagen, gelten, bis auf das tertium-non-datur 4). Die logisch nicht zu begründenden Transaktionsregeln 2) des Anwenders sind selbstverständlich ebenfalls nur inhaltlich zu begründen. Ob in A=>B logische Schlüsse möglich sind oder nicht, ist eine Frage der konkreten Anwendung. Ein logischer Schluß ist jedenfalls ein Übergang von gewissen Aussagen (den Prämissen) zu einer weiteren Aussage (der Konklusion). Es bleibt zu fragen, welche dieser Übergänge "logisch" heißen sollen [Lorenzen]. Der Programmierstil, in dem A=>B dargestellt wird, ist auf jeden Fall belanglos.

Das tertium-non-datur gilt nur bei der inhaltlichen Festlegung auf wahrheitsdefinite (wertedefinite) Aussagen, das sind Aussagen, von denen man weiß, daß sie entweder wahr oder falsch sind.   Nicht-wahr impliziert falsch und nicht-falsch impliziert wahr. Gibt man das tertium-non-datur auf, so kann man die nicht-formale Frage nach Wahrheit oder Falschheit offen halten, um die relevanten Sachverhalte noch zu klären. Die Wahrheitsdefinitheit des tertium-non-datur ist eine Fiktion. Die Frage ist nur, ob man diese Fiktion rechtfertigen kann. Gelingt dies nicht, so muß man die klassische Logik bzw. das klassische Transaktionskonzept verlassen. Man gelangt zur konstruktiven Logik, die man früher in psychologisierender Manier auch intuitionistische Logik nannte. Offene Wahrheitswerte stellen ein Problem dar, für das, wenn es überhaupt behandelt werden soll, ein Konstruktionsverfahren vorliegen oder, im schlimmeren Fall, sogar entwickelt werden muß. Statt Wahrheitsdefinitheit wird jetzt Bestimmbarkeit durch ein Verfahren gefordert (Verfahrensdefinitheit). Konstruktiv hilft bei offenen Aussagen auch die z.B. von Codd [7] für Nullwerte eingeführte mehrwertige Logik nicht weiter, da kein Lösungsverfahren für das Problem der offenen Aussagen angeboten wird. Darüber hinaus gibt es eine Fülle dreiwertiger Logiken [z.B. Lukasiewicz 1930, Heyting 1930, Kleene 1938, Blau 1938]. Der Coddsche Vorschlag entspricht dem von Kleene, wobei der Ansatz in summa unbegründet bleibt.   Man kann verfahrensmäßig bei dreiwertigen Logiken nur so vorgehen, indem die offenen Aussagen den falschen zuzuschlagen sind, womit die Zweiwertigkeit wieder-hergestellt wird. Im Reich der Informatik ist mit Drei- und Mehrwertigkeiten logisch wenig anzufangen.

Jede Logik anerkennt den Satz vom Widerspruch. Eine Aussage, in der der Satz vom Widerspruch akzeptiert wird, ist absurd[1]). Eine wahrheitserhaltende Transaktion kann deshalb die Regel 3) als Verbotsregel nicht aufgeben und muß nach Beendigung und Freigabe von b diese Aussage auf jeden Fall wiederholen können (redo). In der Arbeit von Stonebraker und Neuhold über "Future Directions im DBMS Research" [21], die viel Aufsehen verursacht hat, wird die Aufgabe dieses Prinzips nahegelegt ("transactions which can be undone after committing", S. 30). Im Kern bedeutet diese Forderung den Ausmarsch aus der Logik, was hoffentlich nicht beabsichtigt ist. Eine Logik ohne komplementäres Widerspruchsprinzip ist nicht denkbar. In der konstruktiven Logik und damit in einem neu einzuführenden konstruk-tiven Begriff "Problemlösungszyklus" wird statt des komplementären Negationsbegriff des tertium-non-datur die konstruktive (intuitionistische) Negation (auch schwache Negation genannt) eingeführt:

6) $a_{i1}, a_{i2}, \ldots, a_{in} \Rightarrow \perp$

Die Idee der konstruktiven Negation stammt von Heyting (1930). Die Aufgabe des tertium-non-datur und die Akzeptanz der schwachen Negation ist für einen neuen, konstruktiven Begriff eines Transaktions- oder Problemlösungszyklus von entscheidender Bedeutung. Mit der Einführung von Regel 6) im Kalkül und der expliziten Einführung des Negationszeichens-durch die Definition $\neg a =_{Def} a \Rightarrow \perp$ geht es nicht einfach um das unmittelbare Zusprechen oder Absprechen eines Prädikates, es steht somit nicht die Frage zur Debatte, ob eine Aussage als wahr oder falsch, als kalkülmäßig ableitbar oder nicht ableitbar behauptet werden darf, sondern es geht um Verfahren, um Beweise, um Widerlegungen, die aufgezeigt werden müssen, um Regel 6) zu realisieren. Die konstruktive Negation ist somit keine Verbotsregel wie die Widerspruchsregel, sondern eine Handlungsaufforderung. Der konstruktive Problemlösungszyklus fordert wie der klassische Logikkalkül eine Nachweispflicht, aber ohne tertium-non-datur. Darüber hinaus soll der konstruktive Problemlösungszyklus wie der klassische Transaktionskal-kül konsistenzerhaltend sein.

Die konstruktive Negation wird von Gabbay [10] treffend als "negation as inconsistency" (NAI) bezeichnet, um sie vom klassischen, komplementären "negation as failure" (NAF) abzugrenzen. Es geht beim NAI nicht um das Hamletsche "to be or not to be". Das ist eben hier nicht die Frage. Konstruktiv handelt es sich um den Nachweis des Unerwünschten, des NOGOOD, wie es

---

[1]) Hierzu gehört der Satz "Ich irre mich jetzt." Der Satz vom Wider-spruch wird praktisch akzeptiert.

Frage. Konstruktiv handelt es sich um den Nachweis des Unerwünschten, des NOGOOD, wie es bei deKleer [8] in seinem "Assumption-Based-Truth-Maintenance-System (ATMS)" heißt. Die konstruktive Logik und ihr Konzept des Problemlösungszyklus ist verfahrensorientiert und verfahrensinteressiert und nicht bloß fehlerorientiert im komplementären Sinne. Statt Wahrheitsdefinitheit von Aussagen wird die allgemeine Verfahrensdefinitheit eingeführt, und damit liegt eine echte Erweiterung der klassischen Logik mit ihrer Fiktion wahrheitsdefiniter Aussagen vor. Es gelten alle konstruktiven Schlüsse auch klassisch. Allgemein gilt die Umkehrung nicht (z.B. gilt die deMorgansche Äquivalenz konstruktiv nur in einer Richtung). Konstruktive Logik ist keine neue Logik, sondern eine umfassendere. Sie entspricht genau den Forderungen nach aktiven Datenbanken, wie sie im Aufsatz von Neuhold und Stonebraker über den Laguna Beach Workshop vorgetragen werden [21, S. 28]. Der Irrtum der "Laguna Beach Participants", von Wiederhold liebevoll "die Beach Boys" genannt (so Schlageter [25]), liegt in dem Glauben, man könne eine Datenbank-Erweiterung ohne Logikerweiterung schaffen. Bloße Erweiterungen um Mechanismen wie Regel-, Alerter- oder Trigger-Manager sind nur Dienste, die ohne Logik-Konzepte passiv im Raume stehen bleiben. Würden Informatiker sich mit der Geschichte ihres Grundlagenfaches "Logik" befassen, dann wüßten sie, daß die Konzepte einer präskriptiven, Aktivitäten fordernden Logik längst ausgearbeitet vorliegen. In der Lehre obsiegt leider nur die bloß deskriptive, klassische Logik mit dem tertium-non-datur; ihre konstruktive, auch informatik-spezifische Erweiterung wird, wenn überhaupt, als heterodoxe Variante unter "ferner liefen" neben anderen Formalkalkülen behandelt. Daß das tertium-non-datur mit seiner Wahrheitsdefinitheit gravierende inhaltliche Voraussetzungen macht, deren Zutreffen erst einmal nachzuweisen ist, wird übersehen. Nur die konstruktive Logik ist rein formal, inhaltsfrei und deshalb für ein allgemeineres Konzept der Problemlösungszyklen geeignet. Das Grundlagenwerk von Beckstein [4] zeigt hier neue Wege auf, wie insbesondere die konstruktive Negation technisch zu behandeln ist. Formal wird in der konstruktiven (dialogischen) Logik ein Problemlösungszyklus beendet, wenn der modus ponens abgearbeitet wurde, also aus einem a;a => b auf ein wahrheitsdefinites b übergegangen werden kann [12, S. 78 ff].

Wer einen Fehler konstruktiv nachweisen kann, der muß auch Antwort auf die Frage geben, warum diese Inkonsistenz entstanden ist. Regel 6) ist somit gleichsam auch eine Einladung zum Forward-Recovery (Randell), d.h. die ex-falso-quodlibet-Regel 5) sollte nicht bloß als eine undo-Operation, als eine Backward-Recovery-Maßnahme aufgefaßt werden. Backward-Recovery-Maßnahmen können durch bloßes Datenprotokollieren des Anfangszustandes (BOT) oder benutzerdefinierter Zwischenzustände (Sicherungspunkte) durchgeführt werden. In vielen Fällen, insbesondere dann, wenn der Transaktionsprozeß so weit fortgeschritten ist, daß ein Zurück nicht mehr möglich oder zu kostspielig ist, wird ein Forward-Recovery ($\perp$=>c) als Fehlerkompensation unumgänglich. Eine Logik kann dazu in concreto nichts sagen, bis auf die Forderung, daß c ein quodlibet, etwas Beliebiges ist, also auch einen fehlerbereinigten Zustand in der Zukunft darstellt. Beckstein [4] führt zur Registrierung des Ableitungsschemas A=>B ein Assumption-Based-Truth-Maintenance-System (ATMS) ein, das viel mehr ist als ein bloßes

Protokollieren von Anfangs- und Zwischenzuständen. Eine Fehlerentstehung kann in einem Netz zurückverfolgt und u.U. während des Transaktionsablaufes beseitigt werden.

1.3 Geltungsbereich des klassischen Transaktions- und des konstruktiven Problemlösungszyklus

Der Geltungsbereich des klassischen Transaktionskonzepts mit der scharfen Komplementärregel des tertium-non-datur als Fiktion oder - wie man in der Informatik sagt - als virtuelle Eigenschaft läßt sich sehr genau umreißen. Das Konzept findet vornehmlich Anwendung in der Betriebsmittelverwaltung, im Ressourcenmanagement. In diesem Bereich können definite Zustände angenommen werden. Sie stimmen mit den Aussagen ihrer Spezifikation überein oder sie tun dies nicht. Das ist das typische komplementäre "negation as failure". Es ist nun fast schon tragisch zu nennen, daß das im Gebiet "Datenbanksysteme" entwickelte klassische Transaktionskonzept im Bereich der Betriebssysteme bisher kaum Anklang gefunden hat. Gerade hier aber hat das Konzept sein Hauptanwendungsgebiet. Es ist kaum auszumachen, weshalb Entwerfer von Betriebssystemen vor der Implementierung des Transaktionskonzeptes zurück- schrecken. Erstaunlich bleibt ebenfalls, daß der Remote Procedure Call (RPC), Kanalprogramme, Interprozeß-Kommunikationen etc. nicht nach dem Transaktionskonzept abgewickelt werden. Im Bereich der Datenverwaltung, wo Daten als Betriebsmittel zur Debatte stehen, ist das Transaktionskonzept stark verbreitet. Das Buch von Bernstein e.a. [5] ist eine umfassende Darstellung der klassischen Transaktionstheorie als Theorie des Ressourcenmanagements. Es fehlt in diesem Buch die Behandlung der geschachtelten Transaktionen, also das Zulassen von Subtransaktionen, die in eine übergeordnete Transaktion eingebettet sind. Mengentheoretisch bereitet das Durcharbeiten verschachtelter Transaktionen noch große Schwierigkeiten (laut mündlicher Mitteilung von P.A. Bernstein). Als Kalküle sind tiefere Klammerstrukturen hingegen problemlos.

Ein zweites Anwendungsfeld des klassischen Transaktionsbegriffs sind wahrheitsdefinit gemachte Benutzeroperatoren. Der Benutzer kann in einem Menü von Operatoren eine Auswahl treffen. Vom Transaktionssystem wird ihm die sog. Ausführsemantik "exactly once" garantiert, oder es wird ihm mitgeteilt, daß aus systematischen Gründen die aufgerufene Operation nicht ablaufen kann. Auf jeden Fall verbleibt der Benutzer nicht im Unsicheren.

Das Anwendungsfeld des konstruktiven Konzepts der Problemlösungszyklen ist das "problem solving". Beim Problemlösen sind Aussagen und ihre Zusammensetzungen per se nicht wahr- heitsdefinit. Ein Verfahren muß her, um die Aussagen Schritt für Schritt in die Wahrheitsde- finitheit zu überführen. Fehler im Sinne des negation as failure (NAF) treten jetzt noch gar nicht auf. Inkonsistenzen im Sinne des negation as inconsistency (NAI) sind es, die uner- wünscht sind und beseitigt werden müssen. Das kann zeitlich gesehen ein langer Prozeß sein. Wenn man in der gängigen Praxis der Non-Standard-Datenbanken von Langzeittransaktionen spricht, dann handelt es sich um eine sehr unpräzise Wiedergabe des konstruktiven Zykluskon- zepts, das zeitraubende Problemlösungsoperationen verlangen kann. Zeit spielt originär in der klassischen und konstruktiven Logik keine Rolle, sie wird explizit operativ nicht eingeführt. Es handelt sich eben um extensionale Logiken, d.h. also um extensionale Sprachen, deren Umfang von Ausdrücken eindeutig durch den Umfang der Teilausdrücke bestimmt wird. Für Verbindungsoperationen (Junktoren) von Teilausdrücken ist eindeutig eine Wahrheitsfunktion (klassisch) oder ein Regelwerk (konstruktiv) definiert. Bei intensionalen Logiken, zu denen die Modallogiken, insbesondere auch die temporale Logik, gehören, ist dies nicht der Fall. Zwei Aussagen **A** und **B** mögen wahr sein. Wenn **A** notwendig und **B** bloß möglich ist, ist ihre konjunktive Zusammensetzung noch lange nicht wahr.

1.4 Wie kann eine Verbindung zwischen betriebsmittelverwaltenden Transaktionen und Problemlösungszyklen hergestellt werden?

Es dürfte in den Darlegungen des vorangegangenen Abschnitts deutlich geworden sein, daß Transaktionen und Problemlösungszyklen mit ihrem klassich-logischen bzw. konstruktiv-logischen Unterbau in ihrer Bedeutung gleichberechtigt nebeneinander stehen und daß es um Argumente geht, wenn die Geltung des einen oder des anderen Konzepts zu begründen ist. Das tertium-non-datur wird als das entscheidende Kriterium angesehen, das Datenbanksysteme und ihre möglichen Erweiterungen unterscheidet. So wie dieses Prinzip das Grundlagenfach "Logik" durchschneidet, so setzt es eine operative Grenzlinie zwischen konventionellen Transaktionen und Problemlösungszyklen. Beide unterscheiden sich durch abgeschlossene, komplementäre Möglichkeiten [sic, non] auf der einen und offene Möglichkeiten[2] [sic, non, non-liquet (es ist noch nicht entschieden)] auf der anderen Seite. Ist ein unbekanntes Land sofort als "falsch" zu bewerten, weil man es nicht kennt, oder ist erst ein Abwarten und Untersuchen vonnöten, bevor man sich entscheidet?
Daß man sich entscheiden muß, steht hier außer Frage. Es geht somit um den Kenntnisstand, und der ist bei einer geregelten, bloß fehlererkennenden Betriebsmittel- und Datenvergabe im allgemeinen hoch, jedoch bei einer fehlerklassifizierenden und fehlerbeseitigenden Tätigkeit äußerst eingeschränkt. Die in [14] dargestellten vier Fehlerbehandlungphasen: "<u>Erkennung</u>, <u>Eindämmung</u>, <u>Klassifizierung</u>, <u>Beseitigung</u>", haben für Transaktionen nur in den ersten beiden, "problemlosen" Phasen Geltung. Klassifizierende Untersuchungen sind für Transaktionssysteme, die bloß auf definite Zustände bedacht sind, von untergeordneter Bedeutung, und Fehlerbeseitigungen finden nur einseitig im "Zurückgehen" auf schon als korrekt erkannte Zustände statt (backward recovery in der Form von Undo- und Redo-Operationen). Wenn konstruktiv zu behandelnde Fehlerbeseitigungsprobleme auftreten, ziehen "Transaktionssysteme" sich vornehm, d.h. klassisch logisch, zurück und deklarieren einfach ihre Unzuständigkeit. <u>Passives</u> Garantieren von korrekten Zuständen ist die Hauptsache, ein Einbeziehen von Verfahren zur <u>aktiven</u>

---

[2]   Nach Kripke ist in der Regel die Metapher "Welt" in angemessener Weise durch "Möglichkeiten" zu ersetzen (siehe Kripke, S: Naming and Necessity, Harvard University Press, 2. Aufl., 1980, S. 15)

Fehlerbeseitigung steht außerhalb.

Eine Verbindung zwischen betriebsmittelverwaltenden Transaktionen und Problemlösungszyklen kann hergestellt werden, wenn nicht nur die gewöhnlichen Speichermedien wie Halbleiterspeicher und Platten, sondern der gesamte Eingabe-Ausgabe-Verkehr mit Sichtgeräten in eine transaktionale Kontrolle einbezogen werden. Zu diesem Thema ist von Pausch [22] eine bedeutende Dissertation veröffentlicht worden. Pausch kann zeigen, daß "transaktional" arbeitende Terminaltreiber mit einigem Aufwand implementiert werden können. Der Benutzer am Bildschirm kann Teilergebnisse seiner Transaktion sehen, ein Problem lösen und dann ein "Abort" bzw. ein "Commit" geben. Es dürfte klar sein, daß mit dieser Art von "conversational transactions" das Postulat wertedefiniter Aussagen mit seiner rigorosen Recoverybehandlung aufgegeben wurde. Streng genommen handelt es sich nicht mehr um eine Transaktion, weil der Mensch einbezogen wird, und der ist nun mal kein Betriebsmittel. Es kommen intensionale, inhaltliche Aspekte hoch, während klassische Transaktionen ihre Betriebsmittel bloß extensional, umfänglich disponieren. "Conversational transactions" sind auch nicht mehr serialisierbar, d.h. nicht jede serielle Permutation wird als potentionell mögliche Ablauffolge anerkannt. Wenn Inhalte dazukommen, ändert sich vieles. Die klassische wie auch die konstruktive Logik sind extensionale Logiken. Da aber die konstruktive Logik bloß Verfahrens- bzw. Dialogdefinitheit voraussetzt, kann sie "gerettet" werden, die klassische Logik mit ihrem tertium-non-datur geht bei einem dialogischen bzw. konversationellen Öffnen unter, und mit ihr das Transaktionskonzept in strengem Sinne.

Im folgenden betrachten wir Ausgabeoperationen, das sind Operationen, die im Auftrage einer Transaktion ablaufen und Zustände beeinflußen, die außerhalb des wiederherstellbaren Speichers liegen, der vom Transaktionssystem verwaltet wird. Ausgabeoperationen dienen nicht nur der Ergebnisdarstellung, sondern können auch Anfragen nach Eingaben, z.B. auch nach noch nicht wertedefiniten Aussagen zum Gegenstand haben. In Anlehnung an Pausch [22] wird in Bild 1 eine Klassifikation dieser Ausgabeoperationen vorgetragen.

Alle nicht transaktionsgesteuerten Operationen gelten als ungeschützt (<u>Bereich A</u>). Hat die (Ausgabe-)Operation Wirkung im Hinblick auf wiederherstellbare (recoverable) Speicher, so liegt ein klassisches Transaktionssystem vor (<u>Bereich B</u>). Ausgaben über Sichtgeräte gelten konventionell als nicht wiederherstellbar. Es war die Aufgabe von Pausch, zu zeigen, daß der <u>Bereich C</u> durch "transactionale" Terminaltreiber in den <u>Bereich B</u> im Hinblick auf Wiederherstellbarkeit überführt werden kann. Was die Logik anbetrifft, so bleibt weiterhin ein eigenständiger Bereich bestehen. Keine Wertedefinitheit, keine Serialisierbarkeit, dafür inhaltsbezogene Probleme als nichttriviale Fragestellungen.

Man nimmt in einfachen Datenbanksystemen im allgemeinen an, daß Ausgabeoperationen bis nach dem EOT hinausgezögert werden können, d.h. andere, insbesondere Eingabeoperationen sind nicht abhängig von der Ausgabe. Bei Realaktionen als Ausgabe (z.B. Bewegung eines Roboterarms, Bohren eines Lochs ...) ist ein Hinauszögern in der Regel nicht möglich. Einige

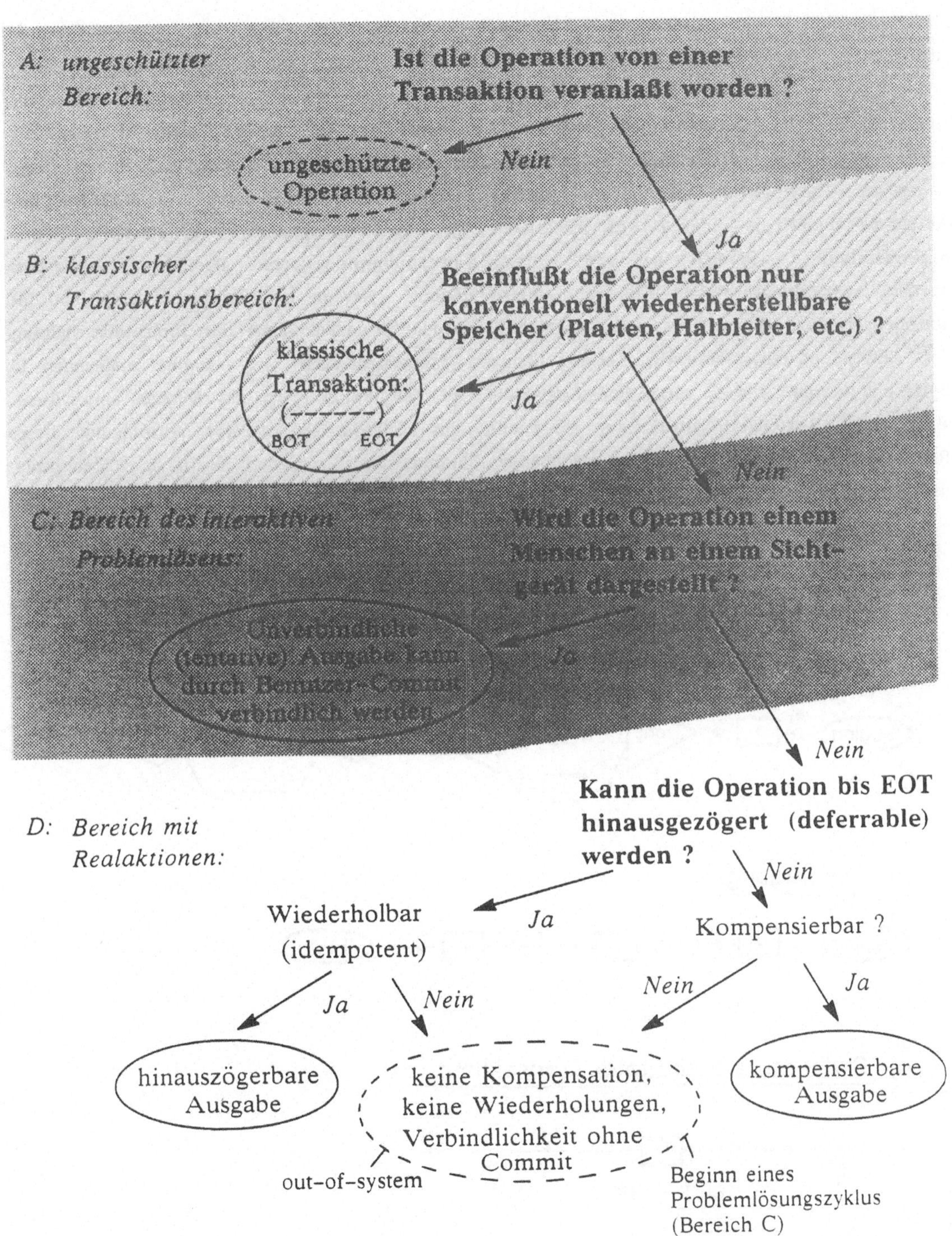

Bild 1: Klassifikation von Ausgabeoperationen

30

dieser die äußere Welt tatsächlich verändernden Operationen sind auch nicht <u>wiederholbar</u> und auch häufig nicht <u>kompensierbar</u>. Wir bezeichnen den <u>Bereich D</u> als den Bereich der Realaktionen, weil die Verzögerbarkeit, die Wiederholbarkeit (ohne Nebenwirkung) und die Kompensierbarkeit Realoperationen treffender eingrenzen als die häufig zitierte Zeiteinhaltung ($\Delta t < \Delta t_{max}$). Die Ausführungen in der Literatur über Real<u>zeit</u>transaktionen sind in der Regel wegen der Konzentration auf die bloß relativ geltenden Zeitbeschränkungen sehr ungenau. Eine Ausnahme bildet die Analyse von Zörntlein [34]. Hier wird gezeigt, wie klassische Datenbanktransaktionen (Bereich B) von realen Anwendungsprozessoren (Bereich D) gesteuert werden. Anwendungsprozesse, die Transaktionen steuern, werden in Anlehnung an [2] und [6] Skripte genannt. Sie verfügen über Zustände, die den aktuellen Stand der Problembearbeitung der Anwendung repräsentieren. Skripte können Transaktionsinput und -output zueinander in Beziehung setzen. Bild 2 zeigt eine Realaktion. Im Teilbild 2a wird das Schema einer Realaktion mit allen Kontrollstrukturen dargestellt. Aus Teilbild 2b ist eine Ausprägung dieser Realaktion zu ersehen. Teilbild 2c macht den Zusammenhang zwischen Skript und Transaktion deutlich.

a) <u>Schema:</u>

b) <u>Ausprägung:</u>

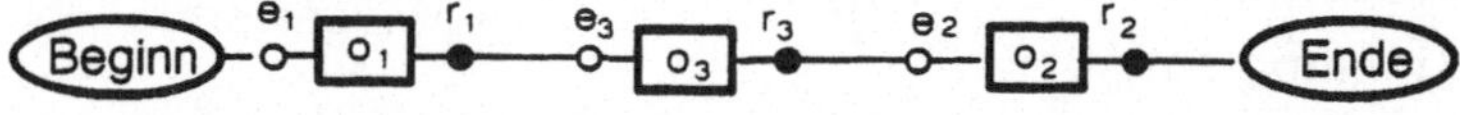

c) <u>Skript mit eingebetteter Transaktion:</u>

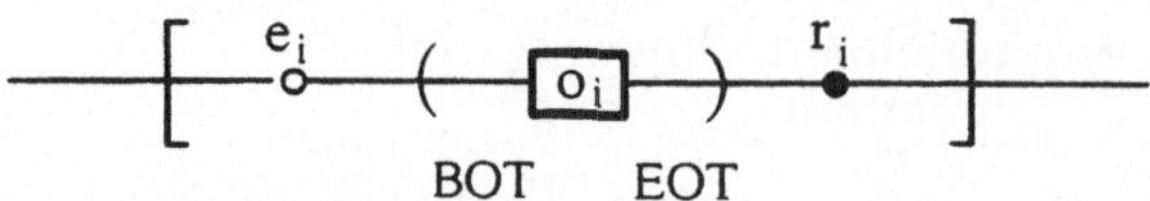

<u>Bild 2:</u> Typischer Ablauf einer Realaktion

Im Falle der mechanischen Fertigung etwa stellen **Beginn** und **Ende** überprüfbare, d.h. meßbare Zustände eines Teils dar. Zwischen **Beginn** und **Ende** liegen meßtechnisch nicht verifizierbare Werkstücke vor. Die e_i und r_i sind Eingangs-und Ausgangsmeldungen über Realtzeitaktionen im technischen System. Ohne besondere Vorkehrungen sind e_i und r_i unwiderruflich, ohne "commit", d.h. die Meldungen sind das Resultat von Operationen, die in der Klassifikation von Bild 1 mit "out-of-system" gekennzeichnet sind. BOT und EOT im Teilbild 2c) stellen Sicherungspunkte auf einem wiederherstellbaren Speicher dar. Jede Datenbankoperation wird als Subtransaktion aufgefaßt, für die das ACID-Prinzip gilt. Durch das Mittel der transaktionalen Einkapselung einer Operation o_i kann es gelingen, die durch r_i initialisierte Ausgabeoperation in die EOT-Behandlung einzubeziehen, um somit die höhere Qualität "hinauszögerbar" (Bild 1) zu erlangen. Jedoch können Wiederholbarkeit bzw. Kompensierbarkeit von r_i-Folgen externe, technische Probleme sein, die in Problösungszyklen (Bereich B) gehandhabt werden müssen.

Zum Abschluß dieses Abschnittes soll noch eine Bemerkung zur Kompensation angefügt werden. Bild 1 könnte den falschen Eindruck erwecken, als sei Kompensation in klassischen Transaktionen (Bereich B) oder Problemlösungszyklen (Bereich C) nicht erlaubt. Das Gegenteil ist der Fall. Zu bedenken ist, daß Bild 1 Ausgabeoperationen klassifiziert, die außerhalb des Transaktionssystems Wirkung haben. Bleiben wir innerhalb des Transaktionssystems, so ist es nützlich, die Klassifikation von Operationen nach Reuter [24, S. 41] heranzuziehen. Reuter teilt Operationen ganz allgemein wie folgt ein:

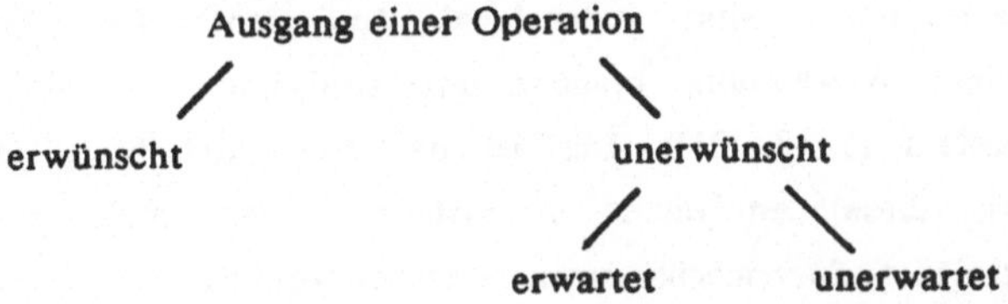

Der Fall "unerwünscht-erwartet" kann von internen Kompensationen in den Bereichen B und C abgedeckt werden. In der Arbeit von Leikauf [15] in diesem Tagungsband wird präzise dargetan, wie ein klassisches Transaktionssystem um eine Kompensationskomponente erweitert werden kann. Unerwartete Operationen, die indefinite Ausgänge einbeziehen sollen, können hingegen nur in Problemlösungszyklen behandelt werden.

1.5 Extension und Intension

Klassische und konstruktive Logik sind rein formal, d.h., die Geltung von Aussagen kommt zustande allein auf Grund der Form ihrer Zusammensetzung mit logischen Partikeln. Mit Bezug auf die Gegenstände, die sie beschreiben, sind beide extensional oder umfänglich. Ein einstelliges Prädikat beschreibt eine Klasse, ein mehrstelliges eine Relation. Wenn man aus dem Bereich B der klassischen Betriebsmitteltransaktionen in den Bereich der Problemlösungszyklen gelangen will, dann genügt der Übergang zu einer "anderen" extensionalen Logik durch Aufgabe des tertium-non-datur allein nicht. Die konstruktive Logik ist jedoch eine Grundvoraussetzung für ein nicht-betriebsmittelorientiertes Problemlösen. In Problemlösungszyklen sind intensionale, inhaltliche Logiken als Erweiterung der konstruktiven Logik von Bedeutung. Zu den intensionalen Logiken gehören insbesondere alle Modallogiken, die temporale Logik, die epistemische Logik und viele mehr. Die Intension, der Inhalt orientiert sich am <u>Begriff</u> eines Gegenstandes, nicht am <u>Umfang</u>. Ob man vom Begriff "Mensch" oder von der Menge "Mensch" spricht, muß ja wohl unterschieden werden können. Wer intensional redet, der ist an Umfängen, an Tupeln als Elemente einer Menge nicht interessiert. Die Menge kann für "Intensionalisten" im Grenzfall auch unendlich sein. Der "Extensionalist" hingegen verlangt Endlichkeit, denn er will ja die Äquivalenz zweier Prädikate, sagen wir P und Q, feststellen. Das kann er nur, wenn endlich viele Gegenstände in Betracht kommen, um die extensionale Äquivalenz von P und Q behaupten zu können. Wiederkäuer und Paarzeher sind bekanntlich extensional äquivalent, da bisher noch jeder Wiederkäuer auch ein Paarzeher ist und umgekehrt. Intensional sind beide Prädikate verschieden. Das eine Prädikat ist ein Terminus mit Bezug auf den Verdauungsapparat, das andere ein Wort der Tierorthopädie. Der Bereich B in Bild 1 ist rein extensional ohne Inhalte zu denken. Zwei Transaktionen R und S heißen extensional äquivalent, wenn aus "die Aussagen, die R produziert, sind wahr" der Satz "die Aussagen, die S produziert, sind wahr" folgt und umgekehrt. Alle erfolgreichen Transaktionen sind extensional äquivalent, ebenso alle gescheiterten. Die extensionale Äquivalenz von Transaktionen führt bei den Ablaufschemata von Transaktionen zu dem wichtigen Erfordernis des seriellen Ablaufs. Alle Permutationen von seriellen, erfolgreichen Transaktionen sind extensional äquivalent. Der konkrete Ablauf ('history' nach Bernstein) einer Anwendung braucht nur äquivalent zu sein mit einer der seriellen Permutationen (Bernstein [5, S. 31]). Das ist der Kern der Serialisierbarkeitstheorie. Technisch schwierig ist es, diese Äquivalenz herzustellen. Man muß einen azyklischen Serialisierungsgraphen durch geeignete Sperrmechanismen herstellen können.

Wir gehen zur Intensionalität über und können bei dem glänzend geschriebenen Werk von Bernstein e.a. [5] bleiben. Zwei Transaktionen sind intensional äquivalent (Bernstein spricht von "view equivalent" und gibt dem Terminus eine extensionale Deutung [5, S.39]), wenn sie die gleiche Wirkung haben, besser: wenn ihre Ergebnisse verwendungsgleich sind. Wer an Ergebnissen als Problemlösung interessiert ist, dem genügen bloß "extensionale Wahrheiten" eines Kalküls nicht. Umgekehrt ist das extensionale, betriebsmittelorientierte Transaktionsdenkens so erfolgreich geworden, weil es invariant gegenüber dem Problem der Anwendungen ist. Was ist zu tun? Im Kern stehen Umsetzungsregelwerke zur Debatte, um intensional gedachte Abläufe (Transaktionen, Problemlösungszyklen) in extensionale, betriebsmittelorientierte Abläufe umzusetzen. Geht das? Die Antwort Bernsteins [5, S. 41] lautet: "From the theoretical standpoint, it is hopeless to expect efficient schedulers to be based on view serializability. Technically, it can be shown that an efficient scheduler that produces exactly the set of all view serializable histories can only exist if the famous P=NP? problem has an affirmative answer. This is considered very unlikely, as it would imply that a wide variety of notoriously difficult problems would be solvable by efficient algorithms."

Die Bernsteinsche Formulierung zeigt ein Fundamentalproblem der Informatik auf. Man kann die Bernsteinsche Aussage auch im Sinne der logischen Analyse anders formulieren: "Die Extensionalitätsthese, wonach alle Rede über Intensionen sich auf die Rede über Extension zurückführen läßt, gilt nicht" [19, S. 627]. Wir wollen es bei diesen theoretischen Andeutungen belassen. Ein Weg aus dieser Extension/Intension-Problematik scheint uns die noch nicht richtig verstandene Arbeit von Eswaran e.a. [9] über logische Sperren, auch Prädikatensperren genannt, zu sein. Vielleicht liegt dieses Mißverständnis an der zweifelhaften, unpräzisen Bezeichnung "logisch". Im Sinne der logischen Analyse heißen logische Sperren intensionale Sperren und physische Sperren werden extensionale Sperren genannt. Wer intensional sperrt, der sperrt keine Einzelobjekte, die umfänglich unter ein Prädikat fallen. Alle möglichen, im Extremfall auch unendlich viele Objekte unterliegen einer intensionalen Sperre. Auf diese Weise wird erreicht, daß gemeinsame Betriebsmittel des extensionalen Bereichs B in Bild 1 (shared devices) wie exklusiv-verfügbare Betriebsmittel (non-shared devices) angesehen werden können. Wenn Problemlösungszyklen des Bereichs C in Bild 1 zur Debatte stehen, dann sollten alle Benutzer eines tatsächlichen oder möglichen Betriebsmittels eine gemeinsame, intensionale Basis haben. Denn es kann nicht sein, daß zwei Problemlöser (Entwerfer) unter ein und demselben Begriff verschiedene Extensionen (von Tupeln) ausgeliefert bekommen. Diese unter dem Begriff "Phantomproblem" behandelte Inkonsistenz ist logisch unhaltbar. Eine intensionale Behandlung des Phantom-Problems ist in [26] zu finden. Gleiche Intensionen (Inhalte), denen mehrere Extensionen (Umfänge) zukommen sollen, sind logische Verstöße. "Wenn 'Schlot' und 'Schornstein' wirklich gleichbedeutend sind, muß jeder Schornstein auch Schlot genannt werden dürfen und umgekehrt. Kann man das nicht (etwa, weil man Schornsteine von weniger als 30 m Höhe nicht Schlot nennen darf), so liegt eben keine intensionale Bedeutungsgleichheit vor" [27, S. 46]. Das zentrale Problem der Entwurfstransaktionen, besser Problemlösungszyklen, ist nicht, möglichst raffinierte Checkout/Checkin-Mechanismen [18, 13] zu konzipieren, sondern effiziente Umsetzungen von (einfachen) intensionalen Sperren in extensionale Sperren zu schaffen. Ob eine Sperre lang oder kurz gesetzt wird, ist beim Problemlösen ohne Bedeutung. Es geht um das Problem, nicht um die Datenbank. Der Änderungsdienst von entwurfsrelevanten Daten, also das Verbindlichmachen von Problemlösungen für alle, ist in technischen Organisationen sowieso einer zentralen Stelle (Normenbüro) überantwortet, die genau bestimmt, "was" von welchem Zeitpunkt an gilt. Problemlöser sind Leser und keine "Verkünder", keine Schreiber. Das Schreiben obliegt einen "Gesetzgeber", der dann und wann wie ein Parlament auch mal in Aktion tritt. "Datenbänkler" tun so, als bestünde die Möglichkeit, daß jeder x-beliebe zu jeder Zeit verbindliche Gesetze für alle erlassen kann.

Pausch [22, S. 79] schlägt vor, den Gedanken der intensionalen Sperren auch auf physikalische Bewegungen, z.B. eines Roboterarms oder eines Förderbandes, auszudehnen. Die Idee ist, sich den dreidimensionalen Raum vor der Nutzung reservieren zu lassen. Wenn r_l die Zielkoordinaten eines Roboterarms sind, die von der Datenbankoperation o_i, ermittelt wurden, dann bedeutet eine intensionale Sperre die Reservierung eines wie immer gearteten Bahnkontinuums als Betriebsmittel, das a priori zur Verfügung zu stellen ist. Eine fehlerhafte Ausführung jedenfalls ist bei intensionalen Betriebsmitteln problemlos isolierbar, womit eine Kompensierbarkeit und Wiederholbarkeit erleichtert wird. Der zweite Teil, die physikalische Anschlußbewegung (Abschluß der Roboterarmbewegung, dann Schließen einer Spannvorrichtung und ihre Hardwareverzögerungen), ist ein Protokollproblem, also die Regelung der Interaktion zweier Partner. Die temporale Logik als intensionale Logik mit ihren Grundrelationen "früher/später" tritt dann an die Stelle einer intensionalen Sperrlogik. Allgemein kann man den Begriff der "Intensionalen Synchronisation" einführen (vgl. auch [34, S. 86] zum Thema "Sperren und Protokolle").

2. INTENSIONALITÄT UND EXTENSIONALITÄT BEIM SCHEMAENTWURF

2.1 Objekte in einer Art/Gattungs-Relation (is-a relation)

Die intensionalen und extensionalen Sichtweisen sind wesentliche Kriterien der logischen Analyse von Datenbank- und Anwendungssystemen. Da Datenbanksysteme beide Aspekte zu überdecken versuchen, ist häufig auch nicht klar, in welchem Sinne argumentiert wird. Datenbanksysteme als Betriebsmittelverwalter sind extensional gedacht. Als Verwalter von Begriffssystemen sind sie intensional aufzufassen. Die Schwierigkeit in Diskussionen mag durch eine kleine Anekdote verdeutlicht werden. Im vergangenen Herbst auf einer Wanderung mit Andreas Reuter durch die Fränkische Schweiz sahen wir die Abdrücke von Paarzehern im Schlamm des Weges. Es entspann sich eine Diskussion, wie wohl die extensional äquivalenten, mengengleichen Termini "Paarzeher" und "Wiederkäuer", die, wie wir bereits wissen, intensional nicht äquivalent, d.h. nicht synonym sind, für die somit nicht dieselben Verwendungsnormen gelten, in einem Konzeptionellen Datenbankschema zu fassen sind. Obwohl die uns begleitenden Ehefrauen verständlicherweise unruhig wurden, war die Diskussion u.a. auch erhellend, weil zwei Standpunkte in klassischer Weise aufeinander trafen, der des "Extensionalisten" (Reuter) und der des "Intensionalisten" (Autor). Da wir beide keine Ideologen sind, konnte der Disput transsubjektiv, einvernehmlich geklärt werden. Andreas Reuter schlug vor, eine wie immer auch zu benennende Relation X mit allen Paarzeher- und Wiederkäuerattributen einzuführen, um dann die Sichten PAARZEHER und WIEDERKÄUER durch Projektion intensional "draufzusetzen". Mein Ansatz als Intensionalist war, PAARZEHER und WIEDERKÄUER direkt als Basisrelationen zu formulieren und das für mich lästige Problem der extensionalen Äquivalenz per Integritätsbedingung zu lösen, d.h. extensional zu fordern, daß ein Tupel mit seinem Primärschlüssel in PAARZEHER auch mit seinem Primärschlüssel in WIEDERKÄUER zu erscheinen hat. Dem Relationenmodell folgend, kommt es bekanntlich nur auf die Primärschlüssel an; der Rest kann, wenn noch keine wahrheitsdefiniten Aussagen möglich sind, durch Nullwerte aufgefüllt werden. Andreas Reuter vertrat nachdrücklich die berühmte Extensionalitätsthese, die bei Mittelstraß [19] breit erläutert wird. Die Extensionalitätsthese im Sinne einer Reduktionsthese besagt, daß sich die Rede über Intension auf die Rede über Extension zurückführen läßt, daß also zur logischen Analyse von Aussagen der Begriff der Extension hinreichend ist. In der Sprache der Datenbanksysteme heißt dies, daß es im System immer Mechanismen (z.B. den View-Mechanismus) geben muß, um die intensionalen Aussagen auf ihre Extensionen, d.h. ihre Tupelmengen zurückzuführen. Daß die Extensionalitätsthese nicht immer gilt, der breite Bereich der intensionalen Logiken wird durchweg nicht erfaßt, steht heute außer Frage. Da Datenbanksysteme die Extensionalitätsthese in axiomatischer Grundsätzlichkeit fordern, sind ihre Beschränkungen evident.

Was ist extensional zu tun, wenn PAARZEHER und WIEDERKÄUER extensional nicht zusammenfallen, was ja bloß ein empirischer Tatbestand ist, der nicht notwendig sein muß? Trivialerweise müssen dann auch zwei getrennte Relationen angelegt werden. Was muß getan werden, wenn nicht nur über die Arten PAARZEHER und WIEDERKÄUER, sondern auch über die Gattung RINDER geredet werden soll? Seit dem bedeutenden Aufsatz von Smith/Smith [28] gibt es hierfür eine extensionale Lösung im Relationenmodell, obwohl die Abstraktion von der Art (species) zur Gattung (genus) eine intensionale Äquivalenz (Abstraktion) voraussetzt. Unter dem Aspekt RINDER sind PAARZEHER und WIEDERKÄUER intensional gleich (es gelten gleiche Verwendungsregeln, -normen, -operatoren), d.h., es kommt bei der Gattung gar nicht auf die spezifischen Eigenschaften der Arten an. Seit Smith/Smith [27] wird in der Literatur (auch in der "Objekt-Orientierten"[3]) [1]) FAHRZEUG als Gattung mit seinen diversen Arten (LUFT, WASSER,-LAND-Fahrzeuge etc.) als Beispiel genommen. Vielfach wird auch das Beispiel mit KONTO als Gattung und mit SPARKONTO und GIROKONTO als Arten zur Demonstration angeführt.

Das Problem all dieser Beispiele ist, daß das Wichtigste, nämlich die Verwendungsregeln-, norm, -operatoren, nicht explizit angegeben werden. Je alltäglicher die Begriffe, umso schwieriger das Herausstellen ihrer Verwendungen, bezüglich derer sie invariant sind. Wir konzentrieren uns auf das Beipiel KONTO und erklären in Bezug auf die Operation "gutschreiben" (und in gleicher Weise "belasten") SPARKONTO und GIROKONTO verwendungsgleich, d.h. synonym. Die Äquivalenzrelation: gutschreiben (SPARKONTO) <-> gutschreiben (GIROKONTO) bedeutet nichts anderes als: reden (Samstag) <-> reden (Sonnabend), d.h. reden unter Verwendung von Samstag besagt nichts anderes als reden unter Verwendung von Sonnabend. Also kann man unter diesem

---

[3]) Stoyan [29] unterscheidet zwischen Verarbeitungsmodell, Programmiersprachen und Programmierstilen. Programmiersprachen basieren konstitutiv auf einem Verarbeitungsmodell. Stoyan spricht z.B. von anweisungs-basierten (PASCAL) und objektbasierten (SmallTalk) Sprachen. Der Programmierstil, dem ein Programmierer folgt, ist bloß ein regulatives Kriterium und wird durch das Beiwort "-orientiert" wiedergegeben. Z.B. kann ein Programmierer mit einer anweisungs-basierten Sprache objekt-orientiert oder funktions-orientiert programmieren. Programmierstile sind wie Baustile anscheinend "Geschmacksache". Aus diesem Aspekt ist der "dunkle" Begriff "Objekt-Orientierte Datenbanksysteme" zu kritisieren.

Aspekt sagen: Samstag = Sonnabend, obwohl Samstag im Süddeutschen und Sonnabend im Norddeutschen gängige Sub-Verwendungsnormen sind, von denen per Äquivalenz abgesehen (abstrahiert) wird.

Man erkennt sofort: Intensionalität stellt sich, wenn man spezifisch werden muß, in den Operatoren dar. "gutschreiben" bzw. "belasten" machen SPARKONTO = GIROKONTO, obwohl beide banktechnisch eine völlig unterschiedliche Funktion haben, von der abgesehen (abstrahiert) wird.

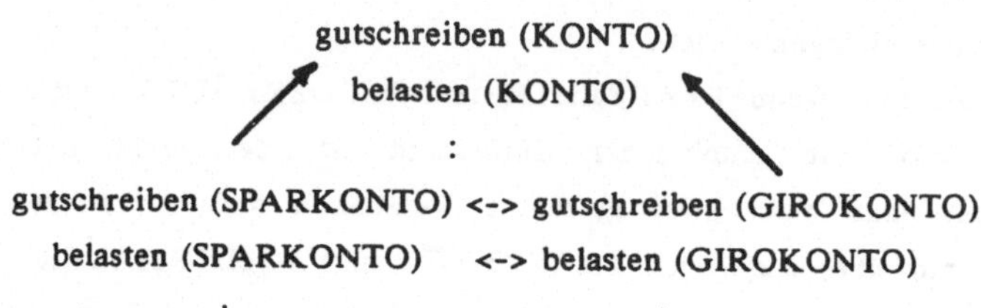

Äquivalenz heißt: gegenseitige Ersetzbarkeit. SPARKONTO und GIROKONTO sind in Bezug auf "gutschreiben" und "belasten" gegenseitig ersetzbar[4]). Das Austauschen (gegenseitiges Ersetzen) kann man redeökonomisch auch lassen und einfach KONTO sagen, womit die Abstraktion unter operativen Aspekten auch durch den (Gattungs-) Namen kenntlich gemacht wird.

Es ist wert, hervorgehoben zu werden, daß bei der Entwicklung eines Konzeptionellen Schema ein neues "Objekt" (wie man heute sagt), z.B. KONTO, intensional eingeführt wird, die Absicherung des "Neuen" aber extensional erfolgt, so als ob man dem Neuen noch nicht richtig traut. Das scheinbar wohl bestellte Feld der Extensionalität gilt offensichtlich als sicherer Boden. Die Absicherung des Mastes "KONTO" durch Trossen, durch extensionale Integritätsbedingungen geschieht, indem gefordert wird, daß die mengentheoretische Vereinigung von SPARKONTEN-Tupeln und GIROKONTEN-Tupeln eine Untermenge von KONTEN-Tupeln zu sein hat.

Aus dem Aspekt der logischen Analyse ist der mit dem Begriff der Objekthierarchisierung verbundene Terminus "Vererbung" (inheritence) relativ uninteressant. Vererbung ist eine biologische Metapher. "To inherit" ist intensional äquivalent (synonym) mit dem logisch aufzufassenden Terminus "to share", der eine konjunktive Verknüpfung beinhaltet. Daß Attribute von KONTO auch in den "Objekten" SPARKONTO und GIROKONTO verfügbar sein sollten, gilt alleine schon aufgrund der Äquivalenzrelation, die das Oberobjekt KONTO

---

[4]) Formal kann die gegenseitige Ersetzbarkeit (Äquivalenz) wie folgt formuliert werden: $[N_1=N_2] \rightarrow [A(N_1) \leftrightarrow A(N_2)]$. Oder: [SPARKONTO = GIROKONTO] $\rightarrow$ [gutschreiben (SPARKONTO) <-> gutschreiben (GIROKONTO)]. In den Aussagen $A(N_1)$ bzw. $A(N_2)$ darf nichts über die Eigennamen N_1 und N_2 ausgesagt werden, z.B., daß beide glücklicherweise aus extensionaler Sicht keine nicht druckbaren "four-letter-words", sondern "nine-letter-words" sind.

sollten, gilt alleine schon aufgrund der Äquivalenzrelation, die das Oberobjekt KONTO konstituiert.

2.2 Objekte in einer Teil/Ganze-Relation (part-of relation)

In der Debatte um Extensionalität und Intensionalität im Konzeptionellen Schema stehen nicht nur homogene Objekte einer Art-Gattungsrelation zur Diskussion. Eine heterogene Objektbildung, wie sie am Beispiel einer Stückliste häufig vorgeführt wird und allgemein von Smith/Smith [28] mit dem Terminus "Aggregation" belegt wurde, basiert auf dem anderen, großen Relationstypus, der Teil/Ganze-Beziehung. Daß die Aggregation auch eine Gleichheit voraussetzt, diese Erkenntnisleistung kann man vielleicht auch auf den Umstand zurückführen, daß Frau Diane Smith bei Paul Lorenzen in Erlangen Logik studiert hat. In der Theorie der Gleichheit wird die Äquivalenz $N_1 = N_2 \to A(N_1) \leftrightarrow A(N_1)$, die schließlich zu einem Gattungsbegriff führt, abstrakte Gleichheit genannt. Ihr steht die konkrete Gleichheit (auch Identität genannt) gegenüber, die in Kennzeichnungen benötigt wird. Nehmen wir an, in einer Stückliste von Maschinenteilen sei festgelegt, daß das Zusammenbauteil, das wir zunächst mit dem Variablennamen x benennen wollen, aus n Teilen von T_1 und m Teilen von T_2 montiert werden kann.

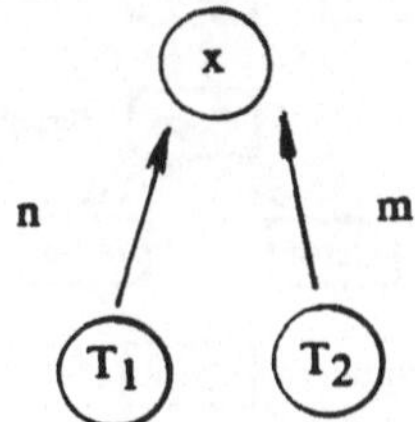

Der Satz "Das Teil x, das aus n-mal T_1 und m-mal T_2 zusammengesetzt ist" wird Kennzeichnung (definite description) genannt. Kennzeichnungen sind einstellige Aussageformen A(x), die nur von genau einem Gegenstand erfüllt werden. Durch Davorsetzen des Kennzeichnungsoperators ι wird diese Einzigkeitsbedingung hervorgehoben. Der Operator ι bindet zugleich die Variable x, so daß für $\iota_x(A(x))$ auch ein eindeutiger Eigenname eingeführt werden kann, z.B. $T_3 =$ Def $\iota_x(A(x))$, mit A(x) als formalisierte Darstellung des obigen Satzes. Bekannte Kennzeichnungen in der Literatur sind: Venus $=$Def ι_x der Stern x, der Abendstern oder Morgenstern ist (Frege), und Mond $=$Def ι_x der Himmelskörper x, der ein natürlicher Satellit der Erde ist. Mit der Theorie der Kennzeichnung führte Frege das Begriffspaar Sinn und Bedeutung eines Namens ein. Im Anschluß hieran hat Carnap zwischen Intension (Sinn) und Extension (Bedeutung) unterschieden. "Von der Bedeutung (Extension) eines Namens als dem benannten Gegenstand ist sein Sinn als die Weise seines Gegebenseins zu unterscheiden. [19, S. 259]. In dieser Lesart ist der Eigenname, z.B. T_3, extensional als Teil vieler Teile, der Kennzeichnungsterm ι_x A(x) jedoch intensional zu verstehen. Die Eindeutigkeitsbedingung einer Kennzeichnung verlangt nun eine Identitätsforderung als konkrete Äquivalenzrelation.

Wenn x in $\iota_x\,A(x)$ durch y ersetzt werden kann, dann muß y=x, sein, d.h. y ist mit x identisch[5]).

Es ist bekannt, daß mathematische Funktionen (n:1-Abbildungen) als Kennzeichnungen dargestellt werden können[6]). Damit ist die gesamte Theorie der funktionalen Abhängigkeit auf die Kennzeichnungstheorie reduzierbar, was in der Datenbankwelt unbeachtet blieb. Funktionale

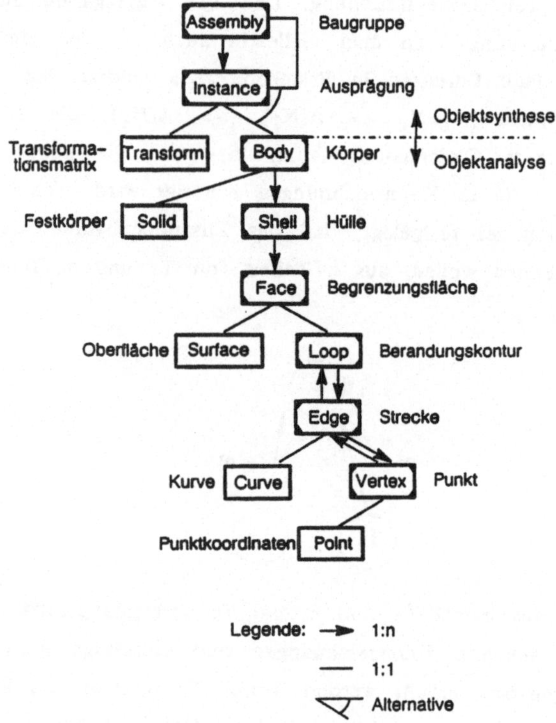

Bild 3: Schema eines komplexen Raumobjektes

---

5)   Man notiert die Eindeutigkeit einer Kennzeichnung formal wie folgt:
$\forall_{xy}[A(x)\wedge(A(y)] \to (x=y).$

6)   z.B. $z = x^2 + 1$, mit $y = x^2$: $x+y = \iota_z A(x,y,z)$
     $x \cdot y = \iota_z M(x,y,z)$ $x^2+1 = \iota_z A(\iota_y M(x,x,y),1,z)$

Abhängigkeiten fallen hier bekanntlich vom Himmel und werden nicht durch eine logische Normierung rekonstruiert. Die Theorie der komplexen Objekte, die mit dem CODASYL-SET oder einer funktionalen Beziehung zwischen MEMBER- und OWNER-RECORD begann, ist in gleicher Weise durch die Kennzeichnungstheorie bestimmt. Betrachten wir in Bild 3 das Konzeptionelle Schema eines komplexen Raumobjektes, wie es von Wilson [33] entwickelt und u.a. in Wedekind [32] detaillierter beschrieben wird.

Die Begriffe der Topologie (Nachbarschaftstopologie) sind von den Begriffen der Geometrie streng getrennt. Die "tief-liegenden" Subobjekte des komplexen Gesamtobjektes "Assembly" stehen in einem n:m Verhältnis, was durch Doppelpfeile mit gegenseitigen Richtungen angegeben wird. Da jeder Pfeil als Kennzeichnung aufzufassen ist, gilt in diesen Fällen die Doppelkennzeichnung, ein komplizierter Zusammenhang, der im Molekülmodell von Härder [12] unterstützt wird. In Darstellungen ist es häufig üblich, n:m-Beziehungen durch Einführung eines künstlichen Objektes in zwei Funktionalbeziehungen bzw. Kennzeichnungen aufzulösen.

Komplexe Objekte, bzw. Komplexobjekte, wie man heute schon kontrahierend sagt, sind typische "Ausleseobjekte". Es ist eine schwierige implementierungstechnische Aufgabe, z.B. T_3 als "Assembly" bis zu seiner Punktgeometrie (point) hinunter effizient wiederaufzufinden. Dieser Prozeß geht entlang von Kennzeichnungen $T =_{Def} \iota_x A(x)$, die Eindeutigkeitsforderungen voraussetzen. Eine Eindeutigkeitsforderung ist so streng und einschneidend, daß praktisch ohne Anwendungswissen nur identische Objekte als gleich angesehen werden können (konkrete Gleichheit). Die "lockere" Verwendungsgleichheit der Art-Gattung-Beziehungen, die im Falle des Bebuchens von Konten dargestellt wurde und die zu objekt-orientierten Programmierstilen bzw. zu objekt-basierten Programmiersprachen führt, ist wegen ihrer "abstrakten" Gleichheit wesentlich "liberaler". In einem Komplexobjekt vom Typ Raumobjekt kann man so ohne weiteres nichts ändern, da über Integritätsbedingungen bis auf die wenig einschränkende, toplogische, extensional aufzufassende Eulersche Gleichung nichts bekannt ist. Wer wagt es schon, z.B. den Durchmesser eines Kreises, topologisch als "Face" gedacht, zu ändern? Er muß damit rechnen, daß Kreise mit kleinem Durchmesser geometrisch ganz anders als "Surface" erzeugt und technisch hergestellt werden als Kreise mit großem Durchmesser. An die Geometrie in Bild 3 schließen sich die technischen Herstellverfahren, sprich die NC-Programme an. Wer wagt es schon, z.B. eine konvexe Oberfläche in eine topologisch gleiche, konkave Oberfläche umzuformen und die Änderung automatisch in den NC-Programmen zu berücksichtigen? Die entscheidenden Integritätsbedingungen in Komplexobjekten sind eben intensionaler Art, und hier liegen die Grenzen. Es macht keinen Sinn, Komplexobjekte einzuführen, deren Integrität nicht beherrscht wird. Ein Komplexobjekt "Unternehmung" bzw. "Fabrik" gehört in die Kategorie des groben Unfuges. Das Komplexobjekt "Assembly" und sein Änderungsdienst kann im Rahmen eines "alles-oder-nichts"-Transaktionskonzeptes nicht verteidigt werden. Denn es geht hier nicht um Betriebsmittelverwaltung, sondern um Problemlösungen. Damit schließt sich der Kreis "Komplexobjekt" und "Aktive Datenbanken", von Datenschema und Operationsschema.

3.   SCHLUSSBEMERKUNGEN

Das Anliegen dieses Aufsatzes ist es, deutlich zu machen, mit welchen logischen Mitteln der klassische Datenbankansatz und sein Transaktions- und Schemakonzept erweitert werden können. Klassischen Transaktionen stehen Problemlösungszyklen als Erweiterung gegenüber, und Extensionalität muß durch Intensionalität ergänzt werden, wobei die Extensionalitätsthese eine bloß eingeschränkte Bedeutung hat. Es ist nicht einzusehen, weshalb Datenbanksysteme und ihre Anwendungsfelder auf den Fall der mechanistischen Umsetzung von Intension in Extension beschränkt bleiben sollen. Interaktive Lösungen müssen angestrebt werden, wenn insbesondere auch Komplexobjekte zur Verarbeitung anstehen. In Problemlösungszyklen auf der Grundlage von betriebsmittelverwaltenden Transaktionen zu arbeiten, wobei der Bereich der Realaktionen nicht ausgespart werden kann, ist als ein Fernziel moderner Datenbankanwendungen anzusehen.

41

Literatur

[1] Bancilhon, F., e.a.: The design and implementation of O_2, an object-oriented system, in: Dittrich, K.R. (Hrsg.): Proc. Advanced Object-Oriented Database Systems, Bad Münster am Stein-Ebernburg, Sept. 1988, Springer Verlag, S. 1-22

[2] Barron, J.: Dialogue and Process Design for Interactive Information Systems Using Taxis, in: Proc. ACM SIGOA Conf. on Office Information Systems, Philadelphia, 1982, S. 12-20

[4] Beckstein, C.: Zur Logik der Logik-Programmierung - Ein konstruktiver Ansatz, Springer Verlag, 1988

[5] Bernstein, P.A., Hadzilacos, V. und Goodman, N.: "Concurrency Control and Recovery in Database Systems". Addison-Wesley Publishing Company, 1987

[6] Borgida, A.: Mylopoulos, J.L., Wong, H.K.T.: Generalization as a Basis for Software Specification. In: On Conceptual Modelling: Perspectives from Artificial Intelligence, Databases and Programming Languages (eds. Brodie, M.L.: Mylopoulos, J.L., Schmidt, J.W.), Springer-Verlag, Berlin, Heidelberg, New York, 1984

[7] Codd, E.F.: More Commentary on Missing Information in Relational Databases, in: ACM SIGMOD RECORD, Vol. 16 (1987), S. 42-50

[8] deKleer, J.: An Assumption-Based Truth Maintenance System, in: AI-Journal Vol. 28 (1986), S. 127-162

[9] Eswaran, K.P., Gray, J., Lorie, R., Traiger, I.: The notion of consistency and predicate locks in a database system, in: Comm. ACM, Vol. 19 (1976), No. 11, S. 624-633.

[10] Gabbay, D.M. und Seryot, M.J.: Negation as Inconsistency, in: Journal of Logic Programming, Vol. 1 (1986), S. 1-35

[11] Halbert, D., O'Brien, P.D.: Using Types and Inheritance in object-oriented Programming, in: IEEE Software, September 1987, S. 7179

[12] Härder, Th., et al.: PRIMA - A DBMS Prototype Supporting Engineering Applications, Sonderforschungsbereich 124, Report 22/87, Univ. Kaiserslautern, 1987

[13] Haskin, R., Lorie, R.: On extending the functions of a relational database system, Research Report, RJ 3182, IBM Res. Lab., San Jose, Cal., 1981

[14] Jablonski, S., Wedekind, H., Zörntlein, G.: Fehlerbehandlung in Flexiblen Fertigungssystemen, in: Informatik Forschung und Entwicklung, Band 3 (1988), Heft 2, S. 53-63

[15] Leikauf, P.: Konsistenzsicherung durch Verwaltung von Konsistenzverletzungen, in diesem Tagungsband

[16] Lorenzen, P.: Formale Logik, Sammlung Göschen, Band 1176/1176a, de Gruyter Verlag, Berlin, 1970

[17] Lorenzen, P.: Lehrbuch der Konstruktiven Wissenschaftstheorie, BI-Verlag, Mannheim, 1987

[18] Lorie, R., Plouffe, W.: Complex Objects and their Use in Design Transactions, in: Proc. Engineering Design Applications, Database Week 1983, S. 115-121

[19] Mittelstraß (Hrsg.): Enzyklopädie Philosophie und Wissenschaftstheorie, Band 1, BI Verlag, Mannheim, 1980

[20] Nau, H.-W. und Wedekind, H.: Die Spezifikation von Nullwerten als Problem einer wissensbasierten Büroautomatisierung, in diesem Tagungsband

[21] Neuhold, E. und Stonebraker, M. (Hrsg.): Future Directions in DBMS Research, Technical Report 88/001 University of California in Berkeley/International Computer Science Institute (ICSI). Abgedruckt im Datenbank-Rundbrief, Ausgabe 2, Nov. 88, S. 22-31

[22] Pausch, R.: Adding Input and Output to the Transactional Model, Dissertation, Carnegie Mellon University, CMU-CS-88-171, August 1988

[23] Rehm, S., e.a.: Support for design processes in a structurally object-oriented database system, in: Proc. Advances in Object-Oriented Database System, Sept. 27-30, 1988, Springer Verlag, S. 80-97

[24] Reuter, A.: Fehlerbehandlung in Datenbanksystemen - Datenbank-Recovery, Carl Hanser Verlag, München, 1981

[25] Schlageter, G.: Der Report "Future Directions in DBMS Research" auf der VLDB 88, in: Datenbank-Rundbrief, Ausgabe 2, Nov. 88, S. 32-33

[26] Schreier, U., Wedekind, H.: Supporting Concurrent Access to Facts in Logic Programs, in: C. Beeri, J.W. Schmidt, U. Dayal (Hrsg.): Proc. of the 3rd Intern. Conf. on Data and Knowledge Bases, Jerusalem, June 28-30, 1988, S. 102-108

[27] Seiffert, H.: Einführung in die Wissenschaftstheorie, Band 1, C.H. Beck Verlag, München, 1975

[28] Smith, J.M. und Smith D.C.P.: Database Abstraction: Aggregation and Generalization, in: ACM TODS, Vol.2 (1977), No.2, S. 105-133

[29] Stoyan, H.: Programmiermethoden der Künstlichen Intelligenz, Band 1, Springer Verlag, 1988

[30] Wedekind, H.: Datenbanksysteme I, Bibliographisches Institut, 2. Aufl., Mannheim, 1981

[31] Wedekind, H.: Die Komposition beim Datenbank-Schemaentwurf als Kennzeichnung, in: Angewandte Informatik, 1985, Heft 10, S. 420-423

[32] Wedekind, H.: Die Problematik des Computer Integrated Manufacturing (CIM) - Zu den Grundlagen eines strapazierten Begriffes, in: Informatik-Spektrum, Band 11 (1988), S. 29-39

[33] Wilson, P.R. et al.: Interfaces for data transfer between solid modelling systems, in: IEEE Comp. Graph. Appl., January 1985, S. 41-51

[34] Zörntlein, G.: Flexible Fertigungssysteme, - Belegung, Steuerung, Datenorganisation -, Carl Hanser Verlag, München, 1988

Entwurf eines Datenbank-Prototyps
für geowissenschaftliche Anwendungen

Friedrich Lohmann, Karl Neumann, Hans-Dieter Ehrich

Informatik, Abt. Datenbanken
Technische Universität Braunschweig
Postfach 3329, D-3300 Braunschweig

Kurzfassung: In dieser Arbeit wird die Konzeption eines Nichtstandard-Datenbanksystems für
geowissenschaftliche Anwendungen vorgestellt. Das System bietet eine objektorientierte Datenbanksprache mit einer erweiterbaren Menge von geometrischen Datentypen; in Anwendungsprogrammen ist die Datenbanksprache als eingebettete Datenteilsprache verfügbar, wobei von der
Datenbank gelesene Objektmengen nach einem Abstrakten-Datentyp-Ansatz manipuliert werden
können. Ein spezieller NF2-Datenbankkern ist als Grundlage für eine effiziente Implementierung
vorgesehen.

Abstract: This paper presents the design of a non-standard database system for geoscientific
applications. The system offers an object-oriented database language with an extensible set of
geometric data types; in application programs, the database language is available as an embedded
data sublanguage, and sets of objects read from the database can be manipulated by operations
offered in abstract data type modules. A special NF2 database kernel is to provide the basis for
an efficient implementation.

1. Einleitung

Gegenwärtig existieren im Bereich der Nichtstandard-Datenbanksysteme zahlreiche Forschungs-
projekte, deren Aktivitäten zwei Schwerpunkten zugeordnet werden können. Diese Schwerpunkte
sind zum einen die Entwicklung neuer, an die jeweilige Anwendung angepaßter Daten- oder Ob-
jektmodelle [NR86, ScS86, HNSE87] mit zugehörigen Sprachen und deren theoretischer Fundierung
[BK86, PA86, SSE87, HG88] und zum anderen die Bereitstellung von neuartigen Datenbankarchi-
tekturen, die diese Anwendungen effizient unterstützen [CDWF86, Me87, Sc87, ALPS88]. Auf der
Ebene der Datenbanksprachen setzen sich dabei Konzepte wie *Objektorientiertheit* und *Erweiterbarkeit* durch [BM86, DD86, LKDP87, WSSH88]. Bei den Implementierungsaspekten rückt das
NF2-Relationenmodell [SP82, ScS83] als Implementierungs-Datenmodell immer mehr in den Vordergrund [KTW85, DDKL87, KW87].

Zum Entwurf eines geowissenschaftlichen Datenbanksystems als zentrale Komponente innerhalb
des DFG-Schwerpunktprogrammes „Digitale geowissenschaftliche Kartenwerke" [Vi85, Vi88] greifen wir diese aktuellen Forschungsergebnisse auf. Es geht dabei zunächst um die Bereitstellung
einer Benutzerschnittstelle, die es ermöglicht, die sehr verschiedenen Daten der ca. 25 am Schwerpunktprogramm beteiligten Gruppen zu vereinheitlichen und so untereinander austauschbar zu
machen. Des weiteren soll das Datenbanksystem auch Sprachmittel bieten, die kartographische
Anwendungen unterstützen.

Diese Arbeit wurde von der Deutschen Forschungsgemeinschaft (DFG) gefördert unter Az. Eh 75/3-4.

Aus diesen Anforderungen wurde eine geowissenschaftliche *Datenbanksprache* abgeleitet, die im nächsten Abschnitt vorgestellt wird. Sie zeichnet sich aus durch eine Zweiteilung des Datenbankschemas in fest vorgegebene und frei definierbare Objekttypen mit Generalisierungshierarchien und Beziehungsklassen sowie durch ihre semantische Fundierung, die sich auf das Konzept der Trennung zwischen Objekt- und Datenschicht [Eh85] stützt. In Abschnitt 3 beschreiben wir die *Anwendungsprogrammschnittstelle* unseres Datenbanksystems. Es wurde eine Einbettungsstrategie mit Vorübersetzung gewählt, wobei Mengen von komplexen geowissenschaftlichen Objekten im Anwendungsprogramm mittels automatisch generierter Operationen bequem manipuliert werden können. Zur Vorbereitung von Implementierungsaspekten charakterisieren wir in Abschnitt 4 zunächst die unterste Systemschicht, den sogenannten *Geo-Kern*, den wir von einer anderen Forschungsgruppe übernehmen [SW86, Sc87, HSWW88]. Darauf aufbauend wird in Abschnitt 5 die schrittweise *Übersetzung von Anfragen* unserer deskriptiven Datenbanksprache auf die prozedurale Schnittstelle dieses Kerns diskutiert. Abschnitt 6 schließlich stellt die geplante Gesamtkonzeption unseres Datenbanksystems dar. Des weiteren findet sich hier eine Zusammenfassung der Erfahrungen, die wir mit einem ersten Prototyp bereits sammeln konnten.

2. Datenbanksprache

In diesem Abschnitt sollen die geowissenschaftliche Datenbanksprache und das zugrundeliegende Objektmodell soweit beschrieben werden, wie es für das Verständnis dieser Arbeit erforderlich ist. Die Darstellung ist bewußt sehr knapp und überblicksartig gehalten, da Sprache und Objektmodell bereits an anderer Stelle ausführlich vorgestellt wurden. Für eine detailliertere Beschreibung muß auf [LN87, ELNR88, Ne88] verwiesen werden.

Der geowissenschaftlichen Datenbanksprache liegt ein spezielles *Geo-Objektmodell* zugrunde, das durch Erweiterung des bekannten ER-Modells [Ch76] entwickelt wurde. Als Modellierungskonzepte bietet das Geo-Objektmodell – ähnlich wie das ER-Modell – Objektklassen und Beziehungsklassen. Jedes Objekt wird in der Datenbank repräsentiert durch seine Attributwerte. Dabei sind nicht nur atomare Objektklassen zugelassen, sondern auch komplexe Objektklassen, d. h. ein Objekt kann zusammengesetzt sein aus einer Menge oder Liste von Unterobjekten gleichen Typs oder aus einzelnen Unterobjekten verschiedenen Typs (Aggregation). Darüber hinaus ist es möglich, unterschiedliche Objektklassen zu allgemeineren Klassen zu generalisieren.

Das Geo-Objektmodell unterstützt eine grundsätzliche konzeptionelle Trennung zwischen den Informationen über geowissenschaftliche Gegebenheiten *(Geoobjekte)* und deren grafischen Darstellungen in Landkarten *(Kartenobjekte)*. Dabei können Geoobjektklassen, entsprechend den Erfordernissen des jeweiligen Anwendungsfalles, vom Benutzer frei definiert werden, während das Attributschema der Karten und Kartenobjekte fest vordefiniert ist. Spezielle Konstrukte der Datenbanksprache ermöglichen es, aus Geoobjekten, die in einer Landkarte grafisch dargestellt werden sollen, entsprechende Kartenobjekte abzuleiten.

Eine charakteristische Eigenschaft geowissenschaftlicher Objekte liegt darin, daß sie in der Regel eine räumliche Ausdehnung besitzen. Zur Unterstützung dieser wichtigen Eigenschaft bietet das Geo-Objektmodell zusätzlich zu den herkömmlichen Datentypen spezielle *geometrische Datentypen*: Die Typen POINTS (Mengen von Punkten in der Ebene), LINES (Mengen von Linienzügen in der Ebene) und POLYGONS (Mengen von Polygonflächen in der Ebene) sind bereits im Datenbanksystem vordefiniert, zusammen mit einer Vielzahl von Operationen, z. B. für die Berechnung von Schnitt-Geometrien, zur Längen- und Flächenberechnung usw. Diese drei geometrischen Datentypen sind für viele Anwendungsfälle bereits ausreichend. Darüber hinaus besteht jedoch für den Benutzer die Möglichkeit, weitere geometrische Datentypen zu definieren, die er für seinen speziellen Anwendungsfall zusätzlich benötigt, etwa zweidimensionale Spline-Kurven, wie in [Sc86] erwähnt, ferner Raster, Raumpunktmengen usw. Nachdem solche benutzerdefinierten Typen dem

Datenbanksystem bekanntgemacht worden sind, können sie wie alle anderen Datentypen in Datenbankanweisungen benutzt werden.

Die geowissenschaftliche Datenbanksprache bietet die erforderlichen Anweisungen zur Handhabung der Konzepte des Geo-Objektmodells: In ihrem Datendefinitionsteil können Anweisungen zur Definition und zum Löschen von atomaren und komplexen Geoobjektklassen, von Beziehungsklassen und Generalisierungen formuliert werden, und in ihrem Datenmanipulationsteil bietet sie Anweisungen zum Erzeugen, Wiederfinden, Ändern und Löschen von Geoobjekten, Beziehungen, Karten und Kartenobjekten sowie zur alphanumerischen und grafischen Ausgabe.

Die Sprache weist einige Ähnlichkeiten zur relationalen Datenbanksprache QUEL [SWKH76] auf: Wie in QUEL, so dienen auch in der Geo-Datenbanksprache sog. Range-Variablen dazu, sich auf in der Datenbank gespeicherte Objekte zu beziehen; ferner sind im Qualifikationsteil der Datenbankanweisungen nur Prädikate ohne explizite Quantoren vorgesehen. Die Bedeutung der Sprache läßt sich durch einen zugrundeliegenden Objektkalkül mit geschachtelten Mengenausdrücken präzise festlegen [Ne88].

Anhand einfacher Beispiele, auf die in den folgenden Abschnitten Bezug genommen wird, sollen nun die Anweisungen zur Definition und zum Wiederfinden von Geoobjektklassen vorgestellt werden. Das Geoobjektschema für eine Datenbank, in der Ausgangsdaten für die Berechnung der Bodenerosion in einem Untersuchungsgebiet [BH88] gespeichert werden sollen, könnte wie folgt definiert werden:

```
DEFINE_GEOOBJ Bodenareal
    (Bezeichnung     KEY STRING (5),
     Geometrie       POLYGONS,
     Bodenart        STRING (20));

DEFINE_GEOOBJ Parzelle
    (Bezeichnung     KEY STRING (5),
     Geometrie       POLYGONS,
     Anbaufrüchte            LIST_OF GEOOBJ Anbaujahr
        (Jahr               INTEGER,
         Fruchtart          STRING (20)));
```

Die Objekte der atomaren Klasse „Bodenareal" sind jeweils charakterisiert durch ihre Bezeichnung, ihre Geometrie (Polygonflächen) und die Bodenart (z. B. Lehm, lehmiger Sand, toniger Lehm, Ton); die Objekte der komplexen Klasse „Parzelle" werden beschrieben durch ihre Bezeichnung, ihre Geometrie (ebenfalls Polygonflächen) sowie durch die Liste der in verschiedenen Jahren jeweils angebauten Feldfrüchte (z. B. Getreide, Zuckerrüben, Raps).

Nach dem Einfügen der Daten in diese Klassen können mittels RETRIEVE-Anweisungen Auswertungen durchgeführt werden. Dabei erzeugt jede RETRIEVE-Anweisung eine temporäre Objektklasse, die für die Dauer einer „Sitzung" in der Datenbank gespeichert wird. Das jeweilige Objektschema ergibt sich aus der angegebenen Zielliste; diese ist bei komplexen Objektklassen geschachtelt.

Für jede Objektklasse, auf die in einer RETRIEVE-Anweisung Bezug genommen werden soll, muß zunächst eine Range-Variable deklariert werden, z. B.

```
RANGE_OF b IS Bodenareal IN_WINDOW (4404000,5768000,4406000,5770000);
RANGE_OF p IS Parzelle   IN_WINDOW (4404000,5768000,4406000,5770000);
RANGE_OF a IS p.Anbaujahr;
```

Die IN_WINDOW-Angabe schränkt den Gültigkeitsbereich der Variablen b und p auf das angegebene geometrische Fenster ein, das hier gerade dem gewünschten Untersuchungsgebiet entspricht.

Die folgende RETRIEVE-Anweisung erzeugt nun eine komplexe temporäre Objektklasse mit dem Namen „Schnittfläche":

```
RETRIEVE_GEOOBJ_INTO Schnittfläche
   (Bezeichnung     = p.Bezeichnung CAT b.Bezeichnung,
    Geometrie       = INTERSECTION (p.Geometrie, b.Geometrie),
    Bodenart        = b.Bodenart,
    Anbau           = SET_OF GEOOBJ Anbaujahr
       (Jahr           = a.Jahr,
        Fruchtart      = a.Fruchtart))
WHERE CUT (p.Geometrie, b.Geometrie)
  AND a.Jahr >= 1986;
```

Jedes Objekt dieser Klasse repräsentiert eine Fläche mit einheitlicher Bodenart und einheitlichem Anbau von Feldfrüchten. Die Geometrie ergibt sich jeweils aus einer Parzelle und einem Bodenareal durch Flächenverschneidung mit Hilfe des geometrischen Operators INTERSECTION; die Bezeichnung wird durch Konkatenation der Bezeichnungen von Parzelle und Bodenareal gebildet. Vom Bodenareal wird die in der Fläche vorgefundene Bodenart übernommen, von der Parzelle ein Teil der Informationen über die angebauten Feldfrüchte (als Menge von Unterobjekten).

In dem durch WHERE eingeleiteten Qualifikationsteil der Anfrage bestimmt die CUT-Operation, daß nur nichtleere Schnittflächen gespeichert werden sollen und daß nur die Anbaujahre ab 1986 von Interesse sind. Anders als in vergleichbaren Sprachen, etwa den in [HMMS87] oder [RKB87] vorgeschlagenen, bleibt der Qualifikationsteil auch bei komplexen Objektklassen einfach und nicht geschachtelt.

Die so konstruierte temporäre Klasse „Schnittfläche" kann mit Hilfe einer PRINT_GEOOBJ-Anweisung in alphanumerischer Form ausgegeben werden:

```
RANGE_OF s IS Schnittfläche;
PRINT_GEOOBJ s ON TERMINAL;
```

Wir wollen nun diese sehr kurze Einführung in die Datenbanksprache abschließen und uns im nächsten Abschnitt den Fragen der Anwendungsprogramm-Schnittstelle zuwenden.

3. Anwendungsprogrammierung

Um einen möglichst großen Bereich von Anwendungen zu unterstützen, sollten Datenbanksysteme außer einer interaktiven Schnittstelle auch die Möglichkeit bieten, von Anwendungsprogrammen aus direkt auf die Datenbank zuzugreifen. Eine solche Anwendungsprogramm-Schnittstelle erlaubt es, komplexere Auswertungen auf in der Datenbank gespeicherten Daten durchzuführen (z. B. Erosions- und Akkumulations-Berechnungen auf der Grundlage von statistischen Modellen [BH88]); ferner erlaubt sie die Entwicklung von einfach zu benutzenden Dialog-Schnittstellen für spezielle, immer wiederkehrende Datenbankoperationen.

Für die Anwendungsprogramm-Schnittstelle des Geo-Datenbanksystems wurde eine *Einbettungs-Strategie* gewählt, d. h. Anwendungsprogramme bestehen aus einer Mischung von Datenbankanweisungen und Anweisungen der Programmiersprache. Gegenüber anderen Ansätzen (prozedurale Schnittstellen, integrierte Datenbank-Programmiersprachen, vgl. z. B. [LP83, ESW88]) bietet die Einbettung zwei wichtige Vorteile: Zum einen kann in Anwendungsprogrammen dieselbe Datenbanksprache verwendet werden wie an der interaktiven Schnittstelle, und zum anderen ist keine Änderung der Programmiersprache und damit des Programmiersprachen-Übersetzers erforderlich, denn die Datenbankanweisungen können von einem Vorübersetzer (im folgenden *Datenbanksprach-Übersetzer* genannt) in Aufrufe entsprechender Module des Datenbankverwaltungssystems übersetzt werden. In Anwendungsprogrammen dürfen die Datenbankanweisungen parametrisiert werden, d. h. anstelle von Datenwerten können Programmvariable entsprechenden Typs angegeben werden.

Die in Abschnitt 2 als Beispiel angegebene RETRIEVE-Anweisung könnte – zusammen mit den zugrundeliegenden Range-Deklarationen – also auch in einem Anwendungsprogramm stehen. Anstelle der konstanten Bedingung „a.Jahr >= 1986" im Qualifikationsteil könnte flexibler „a.Jahr >= :jahr" geschrieben werden; dabei ist „jahr" eine Programmvariable, an die vorher die jeweils gewünschte Jahreszahl zugewiesen wurde.

Da das Geo-Datenbanksystem die Handhabung beliebig geschachtelter komplexer Objekte ermöglicht, ist auch für Anwendungsprogramme ein objektorientierter Zugriff auf die Datenbank wünschenswert. Während [ESW88] eine solche Objektorientierung durch Definition entsprechend geschachtelter Record- und Arraytypen in Pascal erreicht, verfolgen wir beim Geo-Datenbanksystem einen auf den Ideen der Datenabstraktion [LG86] beruhenden Ansatz: Alle erforderlichen Objekttypen, Objektmengentypen, Objektlistentypen und geometrischen Datentypen werden dem Anwendungsprogramm als Abstrakte-Datentyp-Module (ADT-Module) mit den benötigten Operationen zur Verfügung gestellt. Als Programmiersprache wurde aufgrund dieses Ansatzes Modula-2 [Wi85] gewählt, da diese Sprache die Datenabstraktion durch ihr Konzept der Definitions- und Implementationsmodule gut unterstützt.

Als Beispiel wollen wir annehmen, daß die in Abschnitt 2 berechnete temporäre Objektklasse „Schnittfläche" in einem Anwendungsprogramm gelesen und weiterverarbeitet werden soll. Zu diesem Zweck müssen zunächst ADT-Module für den Objekttyp „Schnittfläche" und den Objektmengentyp „SET_OF_Schnittfläche", ferner für den Unterobjekttyp „Anbaujahr" und den entsprechenden Mengentyp „SET_OF_Anbaujahr" generiert werden. Diese Generierung erfolgt weitgehend automatisch mit Hilfe von zwei Werkzeugen, dem *Objekttyp-Generator* und dem *Objekttyp-Übersetzer*. Der Objekttyp-Generator erhält als Eingabe die RETRIEVE-Anweisung aus Abschnitt 2 zusammen mit den zugrundeliegenden Range-Deklarationen. Unter Zuhilfenahme des Datenbankkatalogs, in dem die Objektschemata der referenzierten Klassen „Bodenareal" und „Parzelle" beschrieben sind, erzeugt er hieraus ebenenweise die folgende Pseudocode-Spezifikation der beteiligten Objekt- und Objektmengentypen:

```
OBJECTTYPES

    SET_OF_Schnittfläche = SET_OF (Schnittfläche);

    Schnittfläche =
    OBJECT
        Bezeichnung      STRING (10),
        Geometrie        POLYGONS,
        Bodenart         STRING (20),
        Anbau            SET_OF_Anbaujahr
    END;

    SET_OF_Anbaujahr = SET_OF (Anbaujahr);
```

```
Anbaujahr =
OBJECT
    Jahr            INTEGER,
    Fruchtart       STRING (20)
END

  END_OBJECTTYPES
```

Aus dieser Pseudocode-Spezifikation – die der Benutzer auch „von Hand" hätte schreiben können – erzeugt der Objekttyp-Übersetzer Definitions- und Implementationsmodule für die vier spezifizierten Typen. Die ADT-Module für die Objekttypen „Schnittfläche" und „Anbaujahr" enthalten dabei u. a. Operationen zum Erzeugen von Objekten sowie zum Lesen und zum Ändern einzelner Attributwerte; die ADT-Module für die Objektmengentypen „SET_OF_Schnittfläche" und „SET_OF_Anbaujahr" beinhalten Operationen zum Erzeugen einer leeren Menge, zum Einfügen und Entfernen von Objekten, zur Prüfung, ob ein Objekt in der Menge vorkommt, zur Berechnung der Anzahl der aktuell enthaltenen Elemente usw.

Auf ähnliche Weise erzeugt eine weitere Komponente des Systems, der *Datentyp-Übersetzer*, die ADT-Module für vom Benutzer spezifizierte geometrische Datentypen. Der Typ POLYGONS beispielsweise könnte wie folgt spezifiziert werden:

```
DATATYPES
    DB_TYPE POLYGONS            REPR SET (SINGLE_POLYGON);
    NON_DB_TYPE SINGLE_POLYGON  REPR LIST (SINGLE_POINT) (MIN = 3);
    NON_DB_TYPE SINGLE_POINT    REPR TUPLE (X: CARDINAL, Y: CARDINAL);
END_DATATYPES
```

POLYGONS wird in dieser Spezifikation in mehreren Stufen auf den Grunddatentyp CARDINAL zurückgeführt: Polygonmengen werden als Mengen von Einzelpolygonen erklärt, Einzelpolygone als Listen ihrer Stützpunkte (Einzelpunkte, mind. 3) und Einzelpunkte wiederum als Paare kartesischer Koordinaten (CARDINAL-Werte).

Die vom Datentyp-Übersetzer erzeugten ADT-Module für die Typen POLYGONS, SINGLE_POLYGON und SINGLE_POINT enthalten alle Operationen, die für das Zerlegen und Aufbauen von Werten dieser Typen erforderlich sind. Weitere geometrische Operationen, wie etwa Flächenverschneidungen, Flächeninhaltsberechnungen etc., müssen vom Benutzer selbst programmiert und als Modul dem Datentyp-Übersetzer zur Verfügung gestellt werden.

Der Datentyp-Übersetzer macht die mit DB_TYPE gekennzeichneten Typen sowie die zugehörigen vom Benutzer geschriebenen geometrischen Operationen auch dem Datenbanksprach-Übersetzer bekannt, so daß diese auch in Datenbankanweisungen verwendet werden können. Die mit NON_DB_TYPE gekennzeichneten Typen (im Beispiel SINGLE_POLYGON und SINGLE_POINT) dienen hingegen lediglich als „Hilfstypen", um die Bearbeitung komplexerer Geometrien (im Beispiel von POLYGONS-Werten, also Polygonmengen) in Anwendungsprogrammen zu ermöglichen; sie können in Datenbankanweisungen nicht verwendet werden.

Durch die Integration aller benötigten Typen als ADT-Module wird für den Anwendungsprogrammierer das Lesen und Verarbeiten von Daten aus der Datenbank sehr einfach. Als Beispiel wollen wir das folgende Programmstück betrachten, das auf den Beispielen aus Abschnitt 2 beruht; es wird berechnet, in wieviel Prozent der Gesamtfläche des Untersuchungsgebietes Lehmboden vorliegt:

```
/* Deklaration von Programmvariablen */

VAR schnitt_menge: SET_OF_Schnittfläche;
    einzel_fläche, gesamt_fläche, lehm_fläche, lehm_prozente: REAL;

/* Berechnung der temporären Objektklasse "Schnittfläche"
   (Datenbank-Anweisungen) */

... wie in Abschnitt 2 ...

/* Kopieren der temporären Objektklasse in die
   Programmvariable "schnitt_menge" (Datenbank-Anweisungen) */

RANGE_OF s IS Schnittfläche;
WRITE_GEOOBJ s INTO :schnitt_menge;

/* Berechnung der Gesamtfläche des Untersuchungsgebietes sowie
   der Summe aller Lehmflächen im Untersuchungsgebiet */

gesamt_fläche := 0.0;
lehm_fläche   := 0.0;

FOR schnitt: Schnittfläche IN  schnitt_menge  DO
    /* Bearbeitung der einzelnen Objekte */
    einzel_fläche := AREA (Schnittfläche.VALUE_Geometrie (schnitt));
    gesamt_fläche := gesamt_fläche + einzel_fläche;
    IF Schnittfläche.VALUE_Bodenart (schnitt) = "Lehm"
    THEN lehm_fläche := lehm_fläche + einzel_fläche
    END
END;

/* Berechnung des Prozentsatzes Lehmfläche zu Gesamtfläche */

lehm_prozente := lehm_fläche * 100 / gesamt_fläche;
...
```

Mittels der WRITE-Anweisung wird die Geoobjektklasse „Schnittfläche", die mit der RETRIEVE-Anweisung aus Abschnitt 2 berechnet wurde, in die Programmvariable „schnitt_menge" gelesen, die gerade vom entsprechenden Typ SET_OF_Schnittfläche ist. Das FOR-Konstrukt erlaubt es, in einer vom System bestimmten Reihenfolge alle Elemente der Objektmenge zu bearbeiten; die Einzelobjekte werden nacheinander an die Laufvariable „schnitt" zugewiesen. Es handelt sich hierbei um ein Sprachkonstrukt, das die Ausdrucksfähigkeit von Modula-2 erweitert; es wird daher vor der Bearbeitung des Programms durch den Datenbanksprach-Übersetzer von einem weiteren Vorübersetzer, dem *Sprachkonstrukt-Übersetzer*, durch den Aufruf entsprechender Prozeduren ersetzt, die in den ADT-Modulen für Objektmengentypen enthalten sind. Die Operationen „Schnittfläche.VALUE_Geometrie" und „Schnittfläche.VALUE_Bodenart" sind enthalten in dem vom Objekttyp-Übersetzer erzeugten ADT-Modul für den Objekttyp „Schnittfläche"; der Aufruf dieser Operationen liefert den Geometrie- bzw. Bodenartwert des jeweils durch die Variable „jahr" bezeichneten Objektes.

Wir wollen uns mit dieser kurzen Übersicht über die Konzeption der Anwendungsprogramm-Schnittstelle begnügen; eine genauere Beschreibung findet sich in [Lo88]. Gleichzeitig beenden wir hiermit die Beschreibung der Anwendersicht auf das System und diskutieren im folgenden die Grundlagen der Implementierung.

4. Benutzerschnittstelle des Geo-Kerns

Der für die Verwaltung der Datenbasis gewählte Geo-Kern realisiert das *NF2-Relationenmodell* mit zusätzlichen *geometrischen Datentypen* und deren Unterstützung durch *räumliche Indexe* [SW86, Sc87, WHSW88]. Als Benutzerschnittstelle wird eine Sammlung von Prozeduren angeboten, die jeweils entsprechende Funktionen realisieren. So gibt es beispielsweise Prozeduren zum Definieren und Löschen von Relationenschemata; andere Prozeduren ermöglichen die Zusammenstellung von Qualifikationsformeln und Projektionslisten. Zur Bildung der Qualifikationsformeln sind Teilformeln der Art „Attribut Vergleichsoperator Konstante" möglich. Bei geometrischen Attributen werden die Vergleiche IN_WINDOW und INTERSECTS_WINDOW direkt vom Kern ausgewertet [HSWW88].

Zur Erhöhung der Effizienz wurde auf allen Implementierungsschichten des Geo-Kerns eine mengenorientierte Behandlung der NF2-Tupel realisiert. An der Benutzerschnittstelle spiegelt sich diese Mengenorientierung in dem Konzept der Übergabebereiche wider, die als Zwischenbehälter für Mengen von NF2-Tupeln fungieren. Eine Anfrage wird gestellt, indem man dem Geo-Kern eine Projektionsliste übergibt, eventuell mit zugehörigen Filterprädikaten. Das System stellt daraufhin die Antwortmenge zusammen, die immer aus einer Teilstruktur einer gespeicherten NF2-Relation besteht, und füllt einen Ergebnisübergabebereich mit dieser Tupelmenge. Bei der Eröffnung eines Übergabebereiches wird vom System automatisch ein zugehöriger (impliziter) Zeiger generiert, mit dessen Hilfe Attribute von Tupeln oder Subtupeln gelesen werden können; dabei wird der Zeiger mittels der Navigationskommandos UP, DOWN, NEXT, FIRST, PRIOR auf die entsprechenden Attribute positioniert.

Das folgende Programmstück illustriert die Anwendung dieser Prozeduren des Geo-Kerns. Zunächst wird die Struktur einer NF2-Relation „Parzelle" angegeben, auf die sich die folgende Anfrage bezieht: Es sollen alle Namen von Parzellen, die in einem bestimmten Weltausschnitt liegen, zusammen mit ihren Anbaufrüchten von 1986 an am Bildschirm angezeigt werden.

```
RELATION Parzelle (Name        STRING,
                   Geometrie   POLYGON_GEO,
                   SUBRELATION Anbaufrüchte
                               (Jahr       INTEGER,
                                Fruchtart  STRING));

VAR Parzellen_Name, Fruchtart_Bezeichnung: STRING;

RETRIEVE (RELATION:   Parzelle,
          ATTRIBUTES: Parzelle(Name,Anbaufrüchte(Fruchtart)),
          PREDICATES: Parzelle(Geometrie IN_WINDOW (...) AND
                               Anbaufrüchte(Jahr GE 1986)),
          RETURN:     Result_Buffer);

OPEN (Result_Buffer, RETURN: No_of_Tuples);
```

```
FOR i = 1 TO No_of_Tuples DO
BEGIN
    NEXT (Result_Buffer);
    READ (Result_Buffer, Parzellen_Name);
    DISPLAY (Parzellen_Name);
    DOWN (Result_Buffer, RETURN: No_of_Subtuples);
    FOR j = 1 TO No_of_Subtuples DO
    BEGIN
        NEXT (Result_Buffer);
        READ (Result_Buffer, Fruchtart_Bezeichnung);
        DISPLAY (Fruchtart_Bezeichnung)
    END;
    UP (Result_Buffer)
END;
```

Zunächst wird mit der Kern-Prozedur RETRIEVE der Suchvorgang angestoßen. Man erkennt die Projektionsliste (ATTRIBUTES: ...) und das Qualifikationsprädikat (PREDICATES: ...), das hier auch den geometrischen Vergleichsoperator IN_WINDOW enthält. Im Übergabebereich „Result_Buffer" werden die Ergebnistupel abgelegt. Danach erfolgt das Durchmustern des Übergabebereiches mittels der erwähnten Positionier-Prozeduren NEXT, DOWN, UP. Als weitere Kern-Prozeduren treten noch die Routinen OPEN zum Eröffnen von Übergabebereichen und READ zum Transferieren von Attributinhalten aus dem Übergabebereich in Variable der Wirtssprache auf.

Neben den in diesem Beispiel aufgeführten gibt es noch eine Reihe weiterer Prozeduren, etwa zum Einfügen und Löschen von Tupeln in Übergabebereiche, zum Anlegen von (räumlichen) Indexen, zum Transferieren von Tupelmengen aus Übergabebereichen in NF2-Relationen etc. Zur Erläuterung dieser Funktionen sei auf [SW86, HSWW88, WHSW88] verwiesen.

Geoobjektklassen können direkt durch Kernrelationen implementiert werden, da lediglich Hierarchien auf Hierarchien abgebildet werden müssen. Außerdem stellt der Geo-Kern Mengen- sowie Tupelkonstrukte bereit, so daß auf der Ebene der *Datendefinition* nur wenig Arbeit zu leisten ist. Die Transformation von *Anfragen* der Geo-Datenbanksprache auf die Kernschnittstelle gestaltet sich komplexer. Dies wird anhand eines Beispiels im nächsten Abschnitt dargestellt.

5. Übersetzung von Anfragen

Bei der Übersetzung von Anfragen unserer Datenbanksprache gehen wir in zwei Stufen vor: Im ersten Schritt werden die Datenbankanweisungen syntaktisch/semantisch analysiert und dann auf Mengenausdrücke abgebildet, die denen aus den bekannten Tupel- oder Bereichskalkülen [Ul82, Ma83] ähnlich sind; im zweiten Schritt werden die Mengenausdrücke in Programmstücke mit eingebetteten Aufrufen des Geo-Kerns übersetzt. Das Ausführen dieser Programme schließlich bewirkt die Interpretation der Mengenausdrücke über dem aktuellen Datenbankzustand.

Diese Vorgehensweise wollen wir an der in Abschnitt 2 diskutierten Anfrage illustrieren, bei der die komplexe Objektklasse „Schnittfläche" aus Exemplaren von „Bodenarealen" und „Parzellen" berechnet wird.

```
RANGE_OF b IS Bodenareal IN_WINDOW(4404000,5768000,4406000,5770000);
RANGE_OF p IS Parzelle IN_WINDOW(4404000,5768000,4406000,5770000);
RANGE_OF a IS p.Anbaujahr;
RETRIEVE_GEOOBJ_INTO Schnittfläche
   (Bezeichnung = p.Bezeichnung CAT b.Bezeichnung,
    Geometrie   = INTERSECTION (p.Geometrie, b.Geometrie),
    Bodenart    = b.Bodenart,
    Anbau       = SET_OF GEOOBJ Anbaujahr
                    (Jahr     = a.Jahr,
                     Fruchtart = a.Fruchtart))
WHERE CUT (p.Geometrie, b.Geometrie)
   AND a.Jahr >= 1986;
```

Der zu dieser Anfrage äquivalente Mengenausdruck enthält neben den wie üblich gebildeten Termen und Formeln als wesentliche Neuerung ein *Mengengleichheits-Prädikat*. Dieses drückt die Mengenbildung von Subobjekten aus.

```
{ s' | ∃ p ∈ Parzelle ∃ b ∈ Bodenareal
   (cut (Geometrie(p),Geometrie(b)) ∧
    within (Geometrie(p),(4404000,5768000,4406000,5770000)) ∧
    within (Geometrie(b),(4404000,5768000,4406000,5770000)) ∧
    Bezeichnung(s') = cat (Bezeichnung(p),Bezeichnung(b)) ∧
    Geometrie(s') = intersection (Geometrie(p),Geometrie(b)) ∧
    Bodenart(s') = Bodenart(b) ∧
    Anbau(s') = { a' | ∃ a ∈ Anbaujahr(p)
                       (Jahr(a) ≥ 1986 ∧
                        Jahr(a') = Jahr(a) ∧
                        Fruchtart(a') = Fruchtart(a) )} )}
```

Zur Umsetzung solcher geschachtelter Mengenausdrücke auf die Schnittstelle des Geo-Kerns werden zunächst alle mit logischem Und verknüpften Teilformeln, die vom Kern direkt ausgewertet werden können, aus den Qualifikationsprädikaten entfernt und als Filterprädikate für die Kernprozedur RETRIEVE vorgemerkt. Dann ist für jede Objektvariable o, die im Kontext „∃ o ∈ *Geoobjektklasse*" vorkommt, ein Aufruf der RETRIEVE-Prozedur zu generieren. Dabei muß die jeweilige Projektionsliste alle Attribute enthalten, die im zu übersetzenden Mengenausdruck vorkommen. In unserem Beispiel sind deshalb die folgenden beiden RETRIEVE-Aufrufe zu generieren:

```
RETRIEVE (RELATION:   Parzelle,
          ATTRIBUTES: Parzelle(Bezeichnung, Geometrie,
                               Anbaufrüchte(Jahr, Fruchtart)),
          PREDICATES: Parzelle(Geometrie IN_WINDOW
                               (4404000,5768000,4406000,5770000)
                               AND
                               Anbaufrüchte(Geometrie IN_WINDOW
                                   (4404000,5768000,4406000,5770000)
                                   AND Jahr GE 1986)),
          RETURN:     Parzelle_Buffer);

RETRIEVE (RELATION:   Bodenareal,
          ATTRIBUTES: Bodenareal(Bezeichnung, Geometrie, Bodenart),
          PREDICATES: -
          RETURN:     Bodenareal_Buffer);
```

Die Auswertung der verbleibenden Prädikate des WHERE-Teils und der Wertzuweisungen aus der ursprünglichen Zielliste wird von geschachtelten DO-Schleifen durchgeführt, deren Schachtelungsstruktur durch die Reihenfolge der Existenzquantoren im zu übersetzenden Mengenausdruck gegeben ist. Neben diesen Schleifen werden als weitere Konstrukte der Wirtssprache noch Variablen passenden Typs benötigt, die als Parameter der Übergabebereichsfunktionen READ und WRITE zum Transfer von Attributwerten dienen. In unserem Beispiel werden zu diesem Zweck folgende Variablen deklariert:

```
VAR  b_Bezeichnung : STRING,    p_Bezeichnung : STRING,
     b_Bodenart    : STRING,    a_Fruchtart   : STRING,
     a_Jahr        : INTEGER,
     b_Geometrie   : POLYGONS,  p_Geometrie   : POLYGONS;
```

Weitere Aktionen bestehen im Einrichten einer NF2-Relation mit passendem Schema, die die Ergebnismenge der zu übersetzenden Anfrage aufnehmen kann, sowie eines entsprechenden Übergabebereichs. Wir gehen davon aus, daß die Relation „Schnittfläche" und der Übergabebereich „Schnittfläche_Buffer" bereits eingerichtet sind. Damit ergibt sich folgendes Programmstück, das zusammen mit den oben angegebenen RETRIEVE-Aufrufen den übersetzten Mengenausdruck darstellt:

```
 1  OPEN (Parzelle_Buffer, RETURN: No_of_Parzelle_Tuples);
 2  FOR p=1 TO No_of_Parzelle_Tuples DO
 3  BEGIN
 4    NEXT (Parzelle_Buffer);
 5    READ (Parzelle_Buffer, p_Bezeichnung);
 6    READ (Parzelle_Buffer, p_Geometrie);
 7    OPEN (Bodenareal_Buffer, RETURN: No_of_Bodenareal_Tuples);
 8    FOR b=1 TO No_of_Bodenareal_Tuples DO
 9    BEGIN
10      NEXT (Bodenareal_Buffer);
11      READ (Bodenareal_Buffer, b_Bezeichnung);
12      READ (Bodenareal_Buffer, b_Geometrie);
13      READ (Bodenareal_Buffer, b_Bodenart);
14      IF cut(p_Geometrie, b_Geometrie)
15      THEN NEXT (Schnittfläche_Buffer);
16           WRITE (Schnittfläche_Buffer,
17                   cat(p_Bezeichnung, b_Bezeichnung);
18           WRITE (Schnittfläche_Buffer,
19                   intersection(p_Geometrie, b_Geometrie);
20           WRITE (Schnittfläche_Buffer, b_Bodenart);
21           DOWN (Schnittfläche_Buffer);
22           DOWN (Parzelle_Buffer, RETURN: No_of_Anbaujahr_Subtuples);
23           FOR a=1 TO No_of_Anbaujahr_Subtuples DO
24           BEGIN
25             NEXT (Parzelle_Buffer);
26             READ (Parzelle_Buffer, a_Jahr);
27             READ (Parzelle_Buffer, a_Fruchtart);
28             NEXT (Schnittfläche_Buffer);
29             WRITE (Schnittfläche_Buffer, a_Jahr);
30             WRITE (Schnittfläche_Buffer, a_Fruchtart);
31           END; /* Anbaujahr_Subtuples */
32           UP (Parzelle_Buffer);
33           UP (Schnittfläche_Buffer)
34      FI /* cut (p_Geometrie, b_Geometrie) */
35    END; /* Bodenareal_Tuples */
36    CLOSE (Bodenareal_Buffer)
37  END; /* Parzelle_Tuples */
38  CLOSE (Parzelle_Buffer);
39  INSERT (RELATION: Schnittfläche, BUFFER: Schnittfläche_Buffer);
```

Man erkennt die systematische Umsetzung des Mengenausdrucks; so entsprechen beispielsweise die Zeilen 1–4 dem Konstrukt „∃ p ∈ Parzelle", die Zeilen 7–10 entsprechen „∃ b ∈ Bodenareal". Da die beiden IN_WINDOW-Prädikate bereits vom Kern überprüft worden sind, braucht in Zeile 14 nur noch die Bedingung „cut(Geometrie(p),Geometrie(b))" ausgewertet werden, bevor in den Zeilen 16–20 die Wertzuweisungen an die Attribute der Ergebnisrelation durchgeführt werden. Die Zeilen 23–31 beinhalten die Berechnung der Werte der Subtupel-Attribute. Außerdem treten noch zahlreiche Aufrufe der in Abschnitt 4 beschriebenen Positionierprozeduren auf, z. B. in den Zeilen 21, 22, 32, 33. Nachdem im Ergebnisübergabebereich alle Tupel mit ihren Subtupeln aufgebaut worden sind, werden sie als letzte Aktion, Zeile 39, in die Resultatsrelation „Schnittfläche" geschrieben.

Aus diesem Programmstück und den weiter oben angegebenen RETRIEVE-Aufrufen sowie den Variablen-Deklarationen wird ein Modul gebildet, das zur Laufzeit des Anwendungsprogramms, in das die Anfrage eingebettet ist, aufgerufen wird. Die ursprüngliche Datenbankanfrage wird dabei im Anwendungsprogramm durch den Aufruf dieses Moduls ersetzt.

Die Übersetzung anderer Datenbankanweisungen, etwa DELETE oder UPDATE, ähnelt zwar dem Vorgehen bei Anfragen, setzt sich jedoch aus mehreren Teilschritten zusammen. Zur Erläuterung dieser Sachverhalte verweisen wir aus Platzgründen auf [Ne88]. Dort wird auch die Umsetzung der Karten- und Kartenobjekt-Konstrukte diskutiert.

6. Gesamtkonzeption und Ausblick

Verglichen mit der inzwischen klassischen Vorgehensweise bei der Implementierung von relationalen Datenbanksystemen [Hä87] weist unser System zwei wesentliche Unterschiede auf: zum einen die Werkzeuge, die die Einbettung in die Programmiersprache und die Erweiterbarkeit der Datenbanksprache um neue Datentypen realisieren (siehe Abschnitt 3), zum anderen die Tatsache, daß als Impementierungsschicht der in Abschnitt 4 vorgestellte Geo-Kern benutzt wird. Die tieferen Systemschichten, wie Speicherungs- und Zugriffssysteme, wurden deshalb von uns hier nicht betrachtet.

Die daraus resultierende Gesamtkonzeption des Datenbanksystems stellt sich wie folgt dar: Aus den für die jeweilige Anwendung relevanten Datenbankanweisungen erzeugen der *Objekttyp-Generator* und der *Objekttyp-Übersetzer* die ADT-Module, die benötigt werden, um die von der Datenbank gelesenen Objektmengen im Anwendungsprogramm handhaben zu können. Analog generiert der *Datentyp-Übersetzer* aus Datentyp-Spezifikationen die ADT-Module für die Handhabung benutzerdefinierter Geometrietypen; darüber hinaus macht er die neu definierten Datentypen den übrigen Systemkomponenten bekannt, so daß diese Typen auch in den Datendefinitions- und Datenmanipulations-Anweisungen der Datenbanksprache verwendet werden können. Das eigentliche Anwendungsprogramm wird nacheinander von zwei Vorübersetzern bearbeitet: Zunächst ersetzt der *Sprachkonstrukt-Übersetzer* jedes Auftreten des neu eingeführten Sprachkonstruktes für die Iteration über Objektmengen durch entsprechende Prozeduraufrufe. Hierauf folgt die Bearbeitung durch den *Datenbanksprach-Übersetzer*: Dieser ersetzt die in das Anwendungsprogramm eingestreuten Datenbankanweisungen, wie in Abschnitt 5 ausgeführt, in mehreren Schritten durch entsprechende Module. Zum Schluß können das Anwendungsprogramm und alle neu generierten Module durch einen Programmiersprachen-Übersetzer in ausführbaren Objektcode umgesetzt werden.

Eine Untermenge der in Abschnitt 2 kurz vorgestellten Datenbanksprache wurde inzwischen durch einen ersten experimentellen Prototyp implementiert [JN88]. Dieser stützt sich auf eine relationale Datenbankmaschine (IDM 500 [Br84]) und bietet zunächst nur atomare Geoobjektklassen, aber bereits die wichtigsten geometrischen Datentypen mit zugehörigen Operationen. Des weiteren wurden die Konzepte der Karten und Kartenobjekte vollständig implementiert. Bei ersten realistischen Anwendungen, die im Rahmen des erwähnten Schwerpunktprogrammes durchgeführt wurden [Os87, He88, Ti88], zeigte sich neben der Adäquatheit der entworfenen Datenbanksprache auch die Problematik der langen Antwortzeiten eines Nichtstandard-Datenbanksystems, das auf der Basis eines konventionellen Datenbanksystems implementiert ist. Ähnliche Erfahrungen sind bereits aus anderen Projekten bekannt (etwa [HHLM87] und [AL88]). Durch den im zweiten Prototyp zur Implementierung vorgesehenen Geo-Kern hoffen wir jedoch, die Antwortzeiten erheblich reduzieren zu können.

Literatur

[AL88]   Appelrath, H.J.; Lorek, H.: Der Einsatz von Prolog-Werkzeugen für Geo-Datenbanken. Proc. Non-Standard-Datenbanken für Anwendungen der Graphischen Datenverarbeitung, Lutterbach, H. (Hrsg.), Dortmund 1988, 147–165.

[ALPS88]   Andersen, F.; Linnemann, V.; Pistor, P.; Südkamp, N.: AIM-P, User Manual for the Online Interface of the Heidelberg Data Base Language (HDBL) Prototype Implementation. TN 86.01, Heidelberg 1988.

[BH88]   Bork, H.-R.; Hensel, H.: Computer-Aided Construction of Erosion Maps. In [NLfB88].

[BK86]   Bancilhon, F.; Khoshafian, S.: A Calculus for Complex Objects. Proc. 5th Symp. on Principles of Database Systems, 1986, 53–59.

[BM86]   Batory, D.S.; Mannino, M.: Panel on Extensible Database Systems. Proc. SIGMOD'86, Zaniolo, C. (Hrsg.), 1986, 187–190.

[Br84]   Britton Lee Inc.: IDM Software Reference Manual, Version 1.7. Los Gatos (CA), 1984.

[CDWF86]   Carey, M.J.; DeWitt, D.J.; Frank, D.; Graefe, G.; Muralikrishna, M.; Richardson, J.E.; Shekita, E.J.: The Architecture of the EXODUS Extensible DBMS. In [DD86], 52–65.

[Ch76]   Chen, P.P.: The Entity-Relationship Model – Toward a Unified View of Data. ACM Transactions on Database Systems, Vol. 1, No. 1, 1976, 9–36.

[DD86]   Dittrich, K.; Dayal, U. (Hrsg.): Proc. Int. Workshop on Object-Oriented Database Systems. Pacific Grove 1986.

[DDKL87]   Dadam, P.; Dillmann, R.; Kemper, A.; Lockemann, P.C.: Objektorientierte Datenhaltung für die Roboterprogrammierung. Informatik Forschung und Entwicklung, Band 2, Nr. 2, 1987, 151–170.

[Eh85]   Ehrich, H.-D.: Spezifikation konzeptioneller Schemata mit abstrakten Datentypen und Versionen. Proc. GI-Fachgespräch „Entwurf von Informationssystemen – Methoden und Modelle". Mayr, H.C.; Meyer, B.E. (Hrsg.). Tutzing 1985, 1–19.

[ELNR88]   Ehrich, H.-D.; Lohmann, F.; Neumann, K.; Ramm, I.: A Database Language for Scientific Map Data. In [NLfB88].

[ESW88]   Erbe, R.; Südkamp, N.; Walch, G.: An Application Program Interface for a Complex Object Database. Proc. 3rd Int. Conf. on Data and Knowledge Bases, Jerusalem 1988.

[Hä87]   Härder, T.: Realisierung von operationalen Schnittstellen. In: Datenbank-Handbuch. Lockemann, P.C.; Schmidt, J.W. (Hrsg.). Springer: Heidelberg 1987, 163–335.

[He88]   Heitland, M.: Der Einsatz eines Geo-Datenbanksystems auf dem Gebiet der Bodenerosion. Studienarbeit, TU Braunschweig 1988.

[HG88]   Hohenstein, U; Gogolla, M.: A Calculus for an Extended Entity-Relationship Model Incorporating Arbitrary Data Operations and Aggregate Functions. Proc. 7th Int. Conf. on Entity-Relationship Approach, Batini, C. (Hrsg.), North Holland, Amsterdam, erscheint 1988.

[HHLM87] Härder, T.; Hübel, C.; Langenfeld, S.; Mitschang, B.: KUNICAD – ein datenbankgestütztes geometrisches Modellierungssystem für Werkstücke. Informatik Forschung und Entwicklung, Band 2, Nr. 1, 1987, 1–18.

[HMMS87] Härder, T.; Meyer-Wegener, K.; Mitschang, B.; Sikeler, A.: PRIMA - a DBMS Prototype Supporting Engineering Applications. In [SKH87], 433–442.

[HNSE87] Hohenstein, U.; Neugebauer, L.; Saake, G.; Ehrich, H.-D.: Three-Level-Specification of Databases Using an Extended Entity-Relationship Model. Proc. Informationsbedarfsermittlung und -analyse für den Entwurf von Informationssystemen, Linz 1987, 58–88.

[HS86] Hommel, G.; Schindler, S. (Hrsg.): GI – 16. Jahrestagung, Proceedings I. Berlin 1986.

[HSWW88] Horn, D.; Schek, H.-J.; Waterfeld, W.; Wolf, A.: Spatial Access Paths and Physical Clustering in a Low-Level Geo-Database System. In [NLfB88].

[JN88] Jungclaus, R.; Neumann, K.: Benutzerhandbuch zum ersten Prototypen des Braunschweiger Geo-Datenbanksystems. Informatik-Bericht Nr. 88-01, TU Braunschweig 1988.

[KTW85] Kappel, G.; Tjoa, A.M.; Wagner, R.R.: Form Flow Systems Based on NF2-Relations. Proc. Datenbanksysteme für Büro, Technik und Wissenschaft. Blaser, A.; Pistor, P. (Hrsg.). Karlsruhe 1985, 234–252.

[KW87] Kemper, A.; Wallrath, M.: Konzepte zur Integration abstrakter Datentypen in R2D2. Proc. Datenbanksysteme für Büro, Technik und Wissenschaft. Schek, H.J.; Schlageter, G. (Hrsg.). Darmstadt 1987, 344–359.

[LG86] Liskov, G.; Guttag, J.: Abstraction and Specification in Program Development. McGraw-Hill: 1986.

[LKDP87] Linnemann, V.; Küspert, K.; Dadam, P.; Erbe, R.; Kemper, A.; Südkamp, N.; Walch, G.; Wallrath, M.: Design and Implementation of an Extensible Database Management System Supporting User Defined Types and Functions. TR 87.12.011, Heidelberg 1987.

[LN87] Lipeck, U.W.; Neumann, K.: Modelling and Manipulating Objects in Geoscientific Databases. In: Entity-Relationship Approach: Ten Years of Experience in Information Modelling (Proc. Int. Conf.), Spaccapietra, S. (Hrsg.). North-Holland, Amsterdam 1987, 67–86.

[Lo88] Lonmann, F.: Processing Non-Standard Database Objects in a Higher Level Programming Language - An Abstract Data Type Approach. Proc. Int. Workshop on Software Engineering and its Applications, Toulouse, erscheint 1988.

[LP83] Lacroix, M.; Pirotte, A.: Comparison of Database Interfaces for Application Programming. Information Systems, Vol. 8, No. 3, 1983, 217–229.

[Ma83] Maier, D.: The Theory of Relational Databases. Pitman, 1983.

[Me87] Meier, A.: Erweiterung relationaler Datenbanksysteme für technische Anwendungen. Springer: Heidelberg 1987.

[Ne88] Neumann, K.: Eine geowissenschaftliche Datenbanksprache mit benutzerdefinierbaren geometrischen Datentypen. Dissertation, TU Braunschweig 1988.

[NR86] Noltemeier, H.; Ruland, D.: Datenmodellierung in Geo-Datenbanken. In [HS86], 470–482.

[NLfB88] Niedersächsisches Landesamt für Bodenforschung (Hrsg.): Construction and Display of Geoscientific Maps Derived from Databases (Proc. Int. Coll.). Geologisches Jahrbuch, Sonderband, Hannover, erscheint 1988.

[Os87] Osterhold, A.: Der Einsatz eines geowissenschaftlichen Datenbanksystems im Bereich der Ökologie. Studienarbeit, TU Braunschweig 1987.

[PA86] Pistor, P.; Andersen, F.: Designing a Generalized NF2 Data Model with an SQL-Type Language Interface. Proc. 12th VLDB 1986, Kambayashi, Y. (Hrsg.), 1986, 278–288.

[RKB87] Roth, A. M.; Korth, H. F.; Batory, D. S.: SQL/NF: A Query Language for ¬1NF Relational Databases. Information Systems 12 (1987), 99–144.

[Sc86]   Schek, H.-J.: Datenbanksysteme für die Verwaltung geometrischer Objekte. In [HS86], 483–497.

[Sc87]   Schek, H.-J.: Ein Datenbank-Kernsystem für anwendungsspezifische Schichten – Architektur der DASDBS-Familie. Informationstechnik 3 (1987), 153–164.

[ScS83]   Schek, H.-J.; Scholl, M.H.: Die NF2-Relationenalgebra zur einheitlichen Manipulation externer, konzeptueller und interner Datenstrukturen. Proc. Sprachen für Datenbanken, 1983, 113–133.

[ScS86]   Schek, H.-J.; Scholl, M.H.: The Relational Model with Relational-Valued Attributes. Information Systems 11 (1986), 137–147.

[SKH87]   Stocker, P. M.; Kent, W.; Hammersley, P. (Hrsg.): Proc. of the 13th Int. Conf. on Very Large Data Bases. Brighton 1987.

[SP82]   Schek, H.-J.; Pistor, P.: Data Structures for an Integrated Data Base Management and Information Retrieval System. Proc. 8th VLDB, 1982, 197–207.

[SSE87]   Sernadas, A.; Sernadas, C.; Ehrich, H.-D.: Object-Oriented Specification of Databases: An Algebraic Approach. In [SKH87], 107–116.

[SW86]   Schek, H.-J.; Waterfeld, W.: A Database Kernel System for Geoscientific Applications. Proc. 2nd Int. Symposium on Spatial Data Handling, Seattle 1986, 273–288.

[SWKH76]   Stonebraker, M.; Wong, E.; Kreps, P.; Held, G.: The Design and Implementation of INGRES. ACM Transactions on Database Systems, Vol. 1, No. 3, 1976, 189–222.

[Ti88]   Tietjen, S.: Einrichtung von virtuellen Basiskarten auf einem geowissenschaftlichen Datenbanksystem am Beispiel von Island. Studienarbeit, TU Braunschweig 1988.

[Ul82]   Ullman, J.D.: Principles of Database Systems. 2nd ed., Computer Science Press, Rockville (Md.) 1982.

[Vi85]   Vinken, R.: Digitale geowissenschaftliche Kartenwerke – ein neues Schwerpunktprogramm der Deutschen Forschungsgemeinschaft. Nachrichten aus dem Karten- und Vermessungswesen, Reihe I, Heft 95 (1985), 163–173.

[Vi88]   Vinken, R.: Digital geoscientific Maps: A Dream or a Chance? In [NLfB88].

[WHSW88]   Waterfeld, W.; Horn, D.; Schek, H.-J.; Wolf, A.: How to Make Spatial Access Methods Extensible? Proc. 3rd Int. Symp. on Spatial Data Handling, Sydney 1988.

[Wi85]   Wirth, N.: Programming in Modula 2, Third corrected Edition. Springer: Berlin, Heidelberg, New York, Tokyo 1985.

[WSSH88]   Wilms, P.F.; Schwarz, P.M.; Schek, H.-J.; Haas, L.M.: Incorporating Data Types in an Extensible Database Architecture. Proc. 3rd Int. Conf. on Data and Knowledge Bases, Jerusalem 1988.

CADBASE - ein Datenhaltungssystem für Objekt- und Versions-Management in rechnerunterstützten Engineering-Anwendungen

Jutta Loers, Franz Josef Schmid, Wolfgang Wenderoth
Siemens AG, München

Abstract

Zur Lösung der Datenhaltungsproblematik in rechnerunterstützten Engineering Systemen sind besonders objektorientierte Ansätze geeignet. Es wird ein Objektmodell vorgestellt, das sowohl Objektbeschreibungen in anwendungsspezifischen Repräsentationen ermöglicht als auch die Betrachtung von Objekten in alternativen und versionierten Zuständen unterstützt. Die semantische Datenkonsistenz läßt sich durch ein Beziehungskonzept sichern. Anwendungstools greifen über eine funktionale, objektorientierte Schnittstelle zu. Zur Erzeugung anwendungsspezifischer Ausprägungen der Schnittstelle wird ein Generierungskonzept vorgestellt. Auf Basis der vorgestellten Konzepte wurde eine erste Ausbaustufe des objektorientierten Datenhaltungssystems CADBASE realisiert.

Zielsetzung:

Ausgangspunkt zur Konzeption einer Datenhaltung für rechnerunterstützte Engineering-Anwendungen sind Überlegungen zur Behandlung von Objekten. Objekte sind Verarbeitungseinheiten wie z.B. elektronische Komponenten, mechanische Bauteile oder Software-Komponenten, auf welche Engineering Tools angewendet werden. Objekte sind charakterisiert durch komplexe Strukturen und große Datenmengen und werden von einer Vielzahl von Tools in unterschiedlichen Darstellungen wie z.B. logische und physikalische Beschreibung, funktionale Spezifikation oder Programm-Quellen bearbeitet. Objekte besitzen Beziehungen zwischen ihren darstellungsspezifischen Ausprägungen und müssen in zeitabhängigen Zuständen (Versionen) abrufbar sein. Zur Versorgung von Tools mit Objekten ist eine performante Programmschnittstelle erforderlich. Da die Ablaufumgebung von Engineering Systemen typischerweise aus vernetzten grafikfähigen Arbeitsplatzrechnern besteht, ist ein Verteilkonzept in der Datenhaltung erforderlich.

Diese Anforderungen sind durch klassische kommerzielle Datenbank-Management-Systeme unabhängig von ihrem Typ (Netzwerk, hierarchisch, relational) nicht adäquat zu erfüllen /WEN87/, /DIT87/. Ihre Stärken wie leistungsfähige satzorientierte Verarbeitung in dialoggeführten Anwendungen können in rechnerunterstützten Engineering-Anwendungen nur begrenzt genutzt werden. Insbesondere ist auf Anwendungs-Ebene keine Objekt-Verarbeitung möglich. Versions-Management auf Anwendungsebene wird ebenfalls nicht unterstützt.

Zur adäquaten Lösung dieses Datenhaltungs-Problems wird ein objektorientiertes Datenhaltungssystem für Nicht-Standard Anwendungen benötigt. Über die klassischen Anforderungen wie Mehrbenutzer-Fähigkeit, Unterstützung der Datenverteilung, Datensicherheit und Datenschutz sind folgende Zielsetzungen zu erfüllen:

- Definition eines Objekt-Modells, das einen performanten Objektzugriff durch eine Vielzahl von Tools in unterschiedlichen Darstellungen unterstützt.

- Objektorientierte Daten-Definitionssprache zur Definition von Objekttypen und Beziehungstypen zwischen Objekten zur Sicherung der semantischen Datenkonsistenz. Insbesondere sollen damit die Bildung von Objekt-Hierarchien oder -Netzen, die Bildung von Objektkonfigurationen und die Formulierung von Objekt-Äquivalenzen ermöglicht werden.

- Objektorientierte Daten-Manipulationssprache.

- Unterstützung des Versionsgeschehens.

CADBASE - ein objektorientiertes Datenhaltungssystem zur Verwaltung komplexer Engineering-Objekte und deren Beziehungen zueinander - trägt den aufgezeigten Anforderungen und Zielsetzungen Rechnung.

Objektmodell und Versionenkonzept

Zur Unterstützung einer performanten Objektverwaltung sowie Objektbearbeitung liegt CADBASE die folgende Objektmodellierung zugrunde, die auf Konzepten von /MIT85/, /HÄR85/ und /DIT87/ basiert.

Ein komplexes Objekt beschreibt eine Einheit, die im Anwendungsprozeß individuell festgelegt wird (z.B.: Software-Entwicklung: Software-Modul, CAD/CAM: Baugruppe). Es wird mit einem Objektnamen eindeutig bezeichnet und durch die Hierarchiestufen Repräsentation, Alternative und Version baumartig strukturiert. Die Bedeutung der einzelnen Hierarchiestufen läßt sich dabei wie folgt interpretieren:

- Als *Repräsentation* wird eine Objektdarstellung verstanden, die das Objekt in einer bestimmten Form beschreibt und von verschiedenen Funktionen bearbeitet wird (z.B.: Software-Modul: Spezifikation, Implementierung, Dokumentation, Baugruppe: Layout).

- *Alternativen* beschreiben in einer Repräsentation gleichberechtigte Varianten, die parallel zueinander während des gesamten Anwendungsprozesses bestehen können.

- Die zeitliche Entwicklung des Datenbestandes einer Alternative wird in *Versionen* modelliert.

Dieses Objektmodell bildet für unterschiedliche Anwendungen einen geeigneten Rahmen, um komplexe Objekte eindeutig zu klassifizieren und Zusammenhänge zwischen Objekten schon durch das Modell auszudrücken.

Über die Konkatenation von Objektname mit den Bezeichnungen für Repräsentation, Alternative und Version wird ein Objekt an der Datenhaltungsschnittstelle eindeutig identifiziert (vgl. Bild 1).

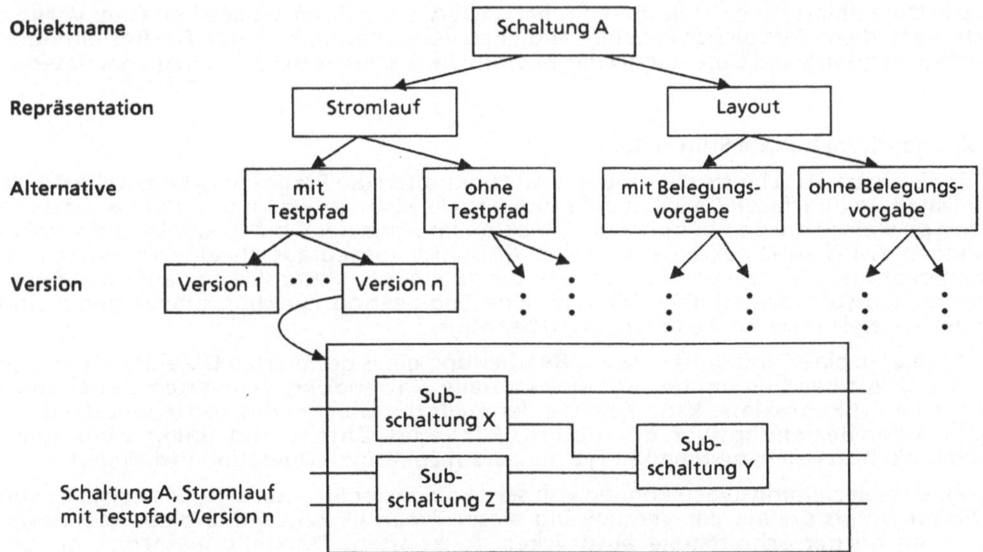

Bild 1: Beispiel der Objektmodellierung im Anwendungsbereich CAD-Elektronik

Objekte sind in CADBASE bestimmten definierten Objekttypen eindeutig zugeordnet. Dabei unterscheidet man zwischen unstrukturierten und strukturierten Typen:

60

- Der Typ *unstrukturiertes Objekt* beschreibt ein Objekt aus Sicht der Datenhaltung als unstrukturierte komplexe Einheit. Die innere Objektstrukturierung (Datenstrukturen, Formate) ist ausschließlich der Anwendung bekannt.

- Strukturierte Objekttypen dienen der Ausprägung spezieller anwendungsspezifischer Objektstrukturen, die an der Datenhaltungsschnittstelle den Anwendungen zur Verfügung stehen. Diese Ausprägungen stellen eine verarbeitungsorientierte Betrachtungsweise von Objekten dar. Eine objektorientierte Datendefinitionssprache dient als Instrument zur Beschreibung von strukturierten Objekttypen.

Zwischen Objekten lassen sich Beziehungen herstellen, welche wiederum definierten Beziehungstypen zugeordnet werden. Ein Beziehungstyp wird definiert durch die Angabe der Typen von Objekten, zwischen welchen Beziehungen hergestellt werden sollen und durch die Definition von Attributtypen, mit welchen sich die Beziehungen beschreiben lassen.

Standardmäßig enthält CADBASE die Beziehungstypen „Objektliste", „Objektäquivalenz", „Objekthierarchie", „Objektverwendung" und „Objektkonfiguration"

Im Rahmen der Objektbearbeitung unterscheidet CADBASE Versionen und Arbeitsstände. Versionen stellen explizit vom Anwender festgeschriebene unveränderbare Datenbestände dar. Die schreibende Bearbeitung eines Objektes ist ausschließlich im Zustand Arbeitsstand möglich.

Die Erzeugung eines Arbeitsstandes findet auf Basis einer Version wahlweise innerhalb derselben Alternative oder einer neuen Alternative der betrachteten Repräsentation statt.

Eine Version wird stets durch ein Freigabeverfahren aus einem bestehenden Arbeitsstand gebildet. Das Versionshandling unterliegt dabei strengen Integritätskontrollen, die auf Basis der Inhalte der Standardbeziehungen von CADBASE durchgeführt werden. Beispielsweise wird eine Versionsfreigabe zurückgewiesen, wenn in ihrer Objekthierarchie veränderbare Subobjekte (Arbeitsstände) vorliegen. CADBASE entnimmt diese Information der Beziehung Objekthierarchie. Desweiteren führt CADBASE nur dann das Löschen einer Version durch, wenn diese Version sich in keiner aktuellen Verwendung befindet. Die Beziehungen Objektverwendung und Objektäquivalenz liefern die hierfür notwendigen Analysedaten.

Objektorientierte höhere Schnittstelle

CADBASE besitzt als Schnittstelle zu den CAE-Funktionen die Programmschnittstelle CADIF (CAE-Database-Interface). CADIF ist eine funktionale Schnittstelle im Sinne des abstrakten Datentyps, welche die Bearbeitung von Objekten im Sinne des Objektmodells und von Beziehungen zwischen Objekten ermöglicht. CADIF ist ausgeprägt als eine in Funktionsklassen geordnete Menge von Funktionen. Die zu einer Funktionsklasse gehörigen Funktionen bilden softwaretechnisch Module. Eine Engineering Funktion bindet genau die Module ein, welche sie für die Anwendung benötigt.

CADIF bietet je eine Funktionsklasse zur Bearbeitung eines definierten Objekttyps sowie je eine Klasse zur Bearbeitung der für eine spezielle Anwendung definierten Beziehungstypen. Eine Funktionsklasse kann keine anderen als die Objekte des korrespondierenden Objekt- oder Beziehungstyps bearbeiten. Für jedes Objekt sind damit über seine Zugehörigkeit zu einem bestimmten Typ die darauf zulässigen Operationen definiert.

Objekt- oder Beziehungstypen können von sehr komplexer Struktur sein. Die Leistung von CADIF zur Unterstützung der Verabeitung dieser Typen besteht darin, diese komplexen Strukturen an der Schnittstelle ausdrücken zu können. Darstellungsformat an der Datenhaltungsschnittstelle ist also nicht ein Satz oder eine Folge von Sätzen. Darstellungsformat ist vielmehr ein Baum, ein Netz oder eine Liste. Somit ist CADIF wegen dieser Eigenschaft eine höhere Datenhaltungsschnittstelle.

Eine CADIF-Funktionsklasse kann jeweils nur auf Objekten genau eines Typs operieren. Umgekehrt kann es für einen Objekttyp aber mehrere Funktionsklassen geben. Für diesen Sachverhalt verwendet CADBASE den Begriff „Sicht": Auf Objekte eines bestimmten Typs kann man in verschiedenen Sichten zugreifen. Einer Sicht ist ein bestimmtes Darstellungsformat von Daten an der Schnittstelle zugeordnet. In Abweichung von der üblichen Verwendung des Begriffs ist eine Sicht eindeutig einem Objekt- oder Beziehungstyp zugeordnet.

Die Bearbeitung von Objekten mit CADIF findet immer innerhalb einer Sicht statt. Pro Sicht gibt es je eine Funktion zum Öffnen sowie zum Schließen der Sicht. Beim Öffnen einer Sicht ist der Name des Objekts, welches bearbeitet werden soll an CADBASE zu übergeben. Es muß natürlich ein Element aus der Menge der Objekte des sichtspezifischen Typs sein. Innerhalb einer geöffneten Sicht stehen Funktionen zur Datenbearbeitung wie GET, PUT, COMMIT, UNDO, ... sowie spezielle Kommandos zur Unterstützung eines komplexen Selektionsmechanismus zur Verfügung.

Im folgenden sei ein Beispiel einer CADIF-Funktionsreihenfolge gegeben, wie sie in einem Engineering Tool zu programmieren wäre:

db : = IDENTIFY (<Name der Datenbasis>, ...);

    (* Eröffnet die Sitzung mit einer bestimmten Datenbasis und stellt die Variable *db* zur weiteren Verwendung bereit   *)

set : = <*SICHTNAME*>-VIEW (*db*, <Objektname>, ...);

    (* Eröffnet die Sicht zur Bearbeitung der mit <Objektname> bezeichneten Objekts und stellt es in der Variablen *set* bereit   *)

while not ENDOFDATA (*set*, ...) do

   elem : = GET (*set*, ...);

    (* Liest Eintrag für Eintrag aus dem bezeichneten Objekt (der Variablen *set*) und liefert das Ergebnis in der Variablen *elem*. Der Typ von *elem* ist sichtspezifisch.*)

oder:

   set : = PUT (*set*, *elem*, ...);

    (* Trägt ein Element *elem* in das Objekt (die Variable *set*) ein   *)

oder:

   <Aufbau eines Selektionskiteriums in einer Variablen *selkrit* mit CADIF-Mitteln>

   set : = SELECT (*set*, *selkrit*, ...);

    (* Liefert in der Variablen *set* alle Elemente des Objekts, welche nach dem Selektionskriterium *selkrit* Treffer darstellen. Anschließend kann wie oben aufgezeigt mit GET Treffer für Treffer gelesen werden.*)

db : = RELEASE (*set*, ...);

    (* Schließt die Bearbeitung der Sicht *)

Das Beispiel soll auch einen Eindruck vermitteln, wie die Theorie des abstrakten Datentyps in der Realisierung der Schnittstelle CADIF verwendet wurde.

Generierungsaspekte

Ein Vorteil von CADIF liegt darin, komplexe Strukturen zu verarbeiten. Diese Strukturen sind applikationsspezifisch und werden erst über die Definition von Objekt- und Beziehungstypen bei der Installation von CADBASE für eine bestimmte Anwendung festgelegt. Unter Beibehaltung der Philosophie der sichtspezifischen Funktionen sind aus diesem Grund höhere als herkömmliche Implementierungstechniken einzusetzen, um einer speziellen Anwendung einen für ihre Umgebung kompletten Satz von Schnittstellenfunktionen bieten zu können.

Zur Lösung dieses Problems bietet sich die Verwendung von Generierungstechniken an. Voraussetzung für eine Generierung von sichtspezifischen Kommandos ist die Existenz einer Data Definition Language (DDL) und eines Data Dictionary (DD). Über die DDL sind beim Einrichten einer Datenbasis die für die spezielle Anwendung benötigten Beziehungstypen zu beschreiben und die Information im DD abzulegen. Über den DDL - Compiler werden gemäß der Beschreibung die Datenbasisstrukturen angelegt. Aufgabe eines

Schnittstellengenerators ist es dann, den für einen speziellen Beziehungstyp notwendigen Satz der sichtspezifischen Kommandos zu erzeugen. Dafür benötigt er neben der Beschreibung der Ablagestrukturen als weitere Eingabe die Beschreibung des Zugriffsformats an der CADIF-Schnittstelle. Diese Struktur ist immer eine Teilmenge des zugeordneten Beziehungstyps. Ihre Beschreibung erfolgt ebenfalls mit der DDL und ist im DD abgelegt.

Der generierte Code für die Datenzugriffskommandos enthält neben den notwendigen Typ- und Variablenvereinbarungen, welche aus der DD - Information abgeleitet werden, eine Anwendung der Kernsystemschnittstelle auf eine vorher erzeugte Datenbasis sowie eine Umsetzung der so erhaltenen Daten auf die an der CADIF-Schnittstelle abzubildende Struktur (bzw. in umgekehrter Richtung). Die vom Generator abgelieferten Sourcen sind zu übersetzen und in die anwendenden Programme einzubinden.

Realisierungsstand und Ausblick

CADBASE liegt qualitätsgesichert in einer ersten Ausbaustufe vor. Der Leistungsumfang umfaßt Ablage und Verwaltung von Objekten vom Typ *unstrukturiertes Objekt* sowie die Unterstützung der standardmäßig enthaltenen Beziehungstypen „Objektliste", „Objektäquivalenz", „Objekthierarchie", „Objektverwendung" und „Objektkonfiguration". Die dafür notwendigen CADIF-Funktionsklassen sind im CADBASE-Kern realisiert.

CADBASE ist in ringartig vernetzten Sicomp WS30-Workstations (Token-Ring) voll mehrbenutzerfähig und enthält für produktive Anwendungen notwendige Logging- und Recovery-Mechanismen.

Für die physikalische Ablage von Objekten greift CADBASE auf UNIX-FMS zurück. Die Ablage von Beziehungen erfolgt über eine Abbildung auf SQL in das als Kern verwendete relationale Datenbanksystem Informix.

Mit dieser Ausbaustufe sollen in der praktischen Anwendung Erfahrungen gesammelt werden, z. B. durch Einsatz für das Konfigurationsmanagement des CADBASE-Systems selbst. Sie ist zugleich Basis für weitere Forschungs- und Entwicklungsschritte.

Ziel ist die Verwirklichung eines objektorientierten Datenbankkernsystems zur Ablösung des relationalen DBS. Die Konzepte dafür orientieren sich an den Eigenschaften objektorientierter Programmiersprachen. Auf Anwendungsebene sind weitergehende Arbeiten notwendig zur Realisierung von Werkzeugen zur freien Definierbarkeit beliebiger Objekt- und Beziehungstypen. Dies beinhaltet auch die Realisierung eines Schnittstellengenerators zur automatischen Erweiterung der Schnittstelle CADIF.

Literatur

/DIT87/ Dittrich, Kotz, Mülle: Database Support for VLSI Design: The DAMASCUS-System, in CAD-Schnittstellen und Datentransferformate im Elektronikbereich, Springer Verlag 1987

/HÄR85/ Härder T., Keller W., Mitschang B., Siepmann E., Zimmermann G.: Datenstrukturen und Datenmodelle für den VLSI-Entwurf, SFB 124, Report Nr. 26/85, Universität Kaiserslautern, Fachbereich Informatik

/MIT85/ Mitschang G.: Charakteristiken des Komplex-Objekt-Begriffs und Ansätze für dessen Realisierung, Informatik Fachberichte Nr. 94, Springer-Verlag 1985

/WEN87/ Wenderoth W., Leßenich H. R.: Trends und Konzepte für ein Datenhaltungssystem im Bereich CAD-Elektronik, Tagungsband CAT' 1987

/LES87/ Leßenich, Munford, Dentler: Realisierung der Datenhaltungsschnittstellen eines CAE-Systems mittels Programmgeneratoren, Informatik-Fachberichte 136, Springer-Verlag 1987

ENTWURF UND REALISIERUNG EINES DATENBANK-SYSTEMS FÜR DAS GEOMETRIESYSTEM VEGAS

A. Wälchli, Dipl. Informatik-Ing. ETH
Institut für Informationssysteme, ETH Zürich
ETH-Zentrum, CH-8092 Zürich

ZUSAMMENFASSUNG:

Bei vielen rechnergestützten Anwendungen in Technik und Wissenschaft fallen Daten mit komplizierter Struktur an, welche längerfristig gespeichert werden müssen. Anhand eines Beispiels werden drei verschiedene Ansätze gezeigt, wie sich die Strukturen dreidimensionaler geometrischer Objekte auf relationale Datenmodelle abbilden lassen. Der für das neue Geometriesystem VEGAS (ein für den praktischen Einsatz ab 1989 an schweizerischen Gymnasien vorgesehenes Konstruktions-system) gewählte Ansatz arbeitet mit abstrakten Datentypen. Ein auf dieser Basis entwickeltes Datenbanksystem konnte in kurzer Zeit realisiert werden und zeichnet sich durch gutes Laufzeitverhalten auch auf Kleinrechnern aus. Die wichtigsten Eigenschaften und verwendeten Techniken sowie erste Erfahrungen werden vorgestellt, die sich im praktischen Einsatz ergaben.

ABSTRACT

In many technical and scientific application fields data with highly sophisticated structures have to be managed by a database system. For that reason, three different ways to store geometric objets in a relational database system will be discussed and what kind of support such a system is able to offer. It is shown, how abstract data types in an extended relational database system can be used very successfully in terms of efficiency and implementation time. The practical application area of the implemented system VEGAS is 3D-geometry in schools.

INHALTSANGABE:

Das Relationenmodell ist seit Beginn der siebziger Jahren in unzähligen theoretischen Arbeiten studiert worden und hat seine praktische Verwendbarkeit in verschiedenen Implementierungen unter Beweis gestellt. Bei der Verwaltung komplexer Objekte zeigen jedoch relationale Datenbank-Verwaltungssysteme, vordergründig gesehen, ein schlechtes Effizienzverhalten. Der Grund liegt in der Zerlegung strukturierter Information und deren Organisation in Tabellen als (ungeordnete) Menge von Datensätzen.

Diese Schwäche lässt sich am Beispiel dreidimensionaler geometrischer Objekte gut darstellen. Die erste Normalform des *klassischen Relationenmodells* verlangt, dass die einzelnen Datenwerte atomar und somit ohne eigene Struktur sein müssen. Bei geometrischen Anwendungen muss die Information auf mehrere Relationen und die Daten auf eine Vielzahl verschiedener Speicherplätze verteilt werden. Abfragen und Manipulationsoperationen werden dadurch für den Anwender untragbar langsam.

Das *erweiterte relationale Datenbanksystem XRS* [Meier et al. 87] wurde eigens für die Verwaltung strukturierter Objekte entworfen mit dem Ziel, logisch (z.B. geometrisch) zusammengehörende Tupel in unterschiedlichen Relationen dem System übergeben zu können. XRS benützt hierzu das Surrogatkonzept zur Definition von Beziehungen, sowie spezielle Relationentypen für die Modellierung komplexer Objekte. Mehrdimensionale Dateien unterstützen den Zugriff auf Datensätze mit mehreren gleichwertigen Schlüsselwerten, womit Anfragen vom Typ Punkt-, Teilpunkt-, Teilbereich- und Nachbarschaftsfragen möglich sind.

Die Verwaltung hierarchisch strukturierter Objekte unter Beibehaltung des relationalen Zugriffs ist damit in XRS effizient möglich, doch sind noch nicht alle Probleme für einen raschen Zugriff gelöst. Zwischen Teilobjekten besteht oft eine Ordnung, die durch den mengenorientierten Ansatz des Relationenmodells verloren geht. Zeitaufwendige Konvertierungsroutinen und die Verwaltung künstlich erzeugter Daten sind zur Wiederherstellung der Ordnung nötig. Bei der Entwicklung effizienter Datenbanksysteme für strukturierte Objekte ist deshalb eine bessere Berücksichtigung der inneren Struktur des Objekts nötig. Bekannte Studien gehen in die Richtung, bessere Speichermethoden zu finden. Das eigentliche Problem liegt jedoch bei den heute noch völlig unzureichenden Möglichkeiten zur Modellierung und einfachen Handhabung strukturierter Objekte.

Für Systeme der Grössenordnung des Geometriesystems VEGAS [Loacker/Wälchli/Zehnder 88] (ca. 5 MByte Programmtext) ist es absolute Notwendigkeit, dass jede Systemkomponente zur Begrenzung der Komplexität des Gesamtsystems möglichst viel beiträgt. Ein wesentliches Element ist dabei die konsequente Anwendung des Prinzips des 'Information Hiding', dass heisst der Realisierung abstrakter Maschinen für die nächsthöhere Verarbeitungsschicht. Eine datenbankmässige Unterstützung hat in Anwendung dieses Prinzips logisch zusammengehörende Objektteile als Dateneinheit für Modellierung und Bearbeitung anzubieten und die dahinter stehende Struktur zu verbergen. Dazu eignen sich insbesondere abstrakte Datentypen zur Definition der Wertebereiche von Attributen [Stonebraker 84].

Es existieren bereits einige objektorientierte Erweiterungen relationaler Datenbanksysteme, z.B. das NF^2-Modell [Schek/Pistor 82], bei welchem Attribute relationenwertige Ausdrücke aufweisen dürfen, oder rekursive Datenmodelle [Lamersdorf/Schmidt 83], wo das Beschreiben strukturierter Datenobjekte durch rekursiv definierte Datentypen erlaubt ist. Beide Ansätze erfordern einen hohen Implementationsaufwand und bilden für sich äusserst komplexe Systeme, was Probleme beim Laufzeitverhalten ergibt und deren Anwendbarkeit einschränkt. Wie Kemper und Wallrath in ihrer Ist-Zustands-Analyse über die Verwendbarkeit von Datenbanksystemen für das geometrische Modellieren richtig festhalten [Kemper/Wallrath 87], ist zur Zeit ADT-INGRES [Stonebraker et al. 83] das einzige (auf Grossrechnersystemen) einsatzfähige Datenbanksystem, welches eine teilweise objektorientierte Schnittstelle sowie Möglichkeiten zur Modellierung strukturierter Objekte anbietet.

Das *erweiterte relationale Datenbanksystem VEGADB* wurde in der kurzen Entwicklungszeit von nur $1^{1}/_{2}$ Jahren realisiert und bildet ein kompaktes, überschaubares System für den Einsatz auf Kleinrechnern. Für VEGADB ist erstmals ein Datenbank*kern* konzipiert worden, welcher abstrakte Datentypen direkt unterstützt und über eine erweiterbare Schnittstelle anbietet. Es können beliebig komplexe Strukturen verwaltet werden, was neue Möglichkeiten zur Modellierung strukturierter Objekte schafft, da logisch zusammengehörende Daten nicht mehr auf mehrere Relationen aufgeteilt werden müssen. Die Integration spezieller Prozeduren zur Verwaltung abstrakter Datentypen erlaubt eine optimale Unterstützung des Benutzers und die Einfachheit relationaler Datenbankschnittstellen bleibt voll erhalten. Die Anzahl abstrakter Datentypen ist in VEGADB jederzeit erweiterbar und verleiht dem System eine grosse Flexibilität, wie sie in bisherigen Systemen nicht zu finden ist.

Voraussetzung für die einfache Handhabung der Datensätze im Relationenmodell ist die Einschränkung der Wahl der Wertebereiche von Attributen auf Basistypen, auf die sich das Daten banksystem mit Standardoperationen beziehen kann. Um die daraus erzielbare Vereinfachung für Benutzer und Datenbanksystem bei Einbezug abstrakter Datentypen nicht zu verlieren, wurde für VEGADB folgendes Konzept entwickelt und realisiert (Figur 1): die Definition abstrakter Datentypen (ADT = Abstract Data Type) umfasst einen festen Satz von Operationen (ADP = Abstract Datatype Procedure) und zugehörigen Anwendungsregeln. Diese werden vom Datenbanksystem bei der Verwaltung von Ausprägungen eines abstrakten Datentyps miteinbezogen, analog zu den Standardoperationen bei Basistypen. Die Operationen werden in einem erweiterten Metadatenbankschema im Quelltext gespeichert, um die korrekte Interpretation des Datenbestands auch für künftige Anwendungen zu sichern. Aus den Quellprogrammen werden nach abgeschlossener Definition die für das Datenbanksystem benötigten Manipulationsprozeduren generiert. Die Verwaltung der Daten abstrakter Datentypen ist während des Betriebs gleich wie bei einfachen Daten.

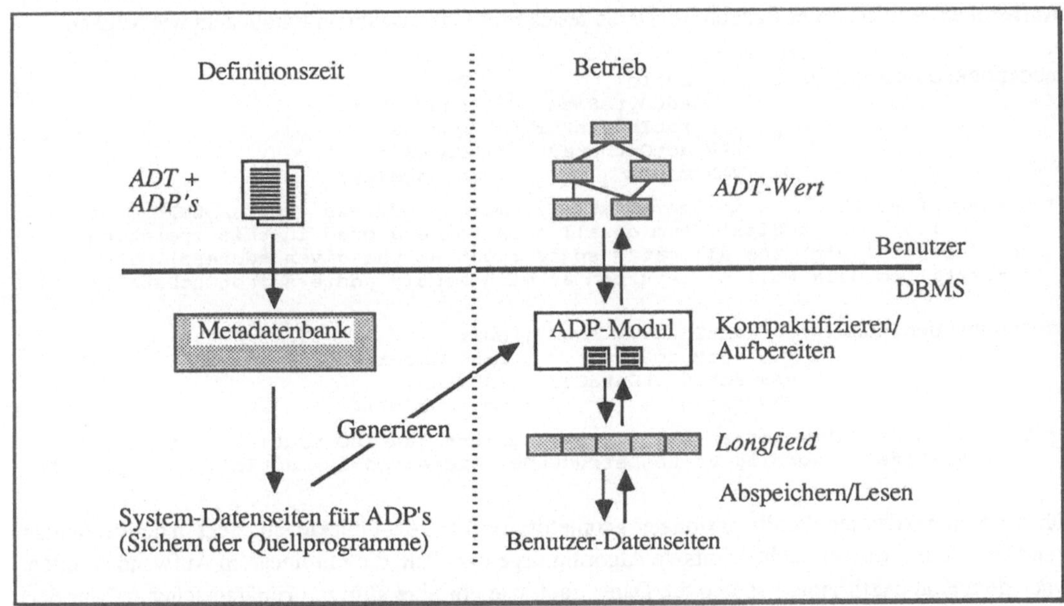

Figur 1:   Abbildungsmechanismus von ADT-Werten in VEGADB

Als wichtigstes technisches Problem stellt sich die Abbildung von Werten abstrakter Datentypen vom Primär- auf den Sekundärspeicher und umgekehrt. Die Voraussetzung ist ein Datenbanksystem, welches variabel lange Datenfelder zulässt. Wichtig ist ein sauber durchdachtes Konzepts, um die häufig sehr umfangreichen Daten zwischen Datenbankschnittstelle zum Anwender und dem Seitenpuffer nur genau einmal zu kopieren (aus Sicherheitsgründen ist ein einmaliges Kopieren nötig). Für die Abbildung der im Primärspeicher i.a. in komplexen Zeigerstrukturen abgelegten Werte abstrakter Datentypen auf einen linearen, zusammenhängenden Speicherbereich werden die ADP's "Kompaktifizieren" und "Aufbereiten" verwendet. Diese besitzen wie alle anderen ADP's ein fest vorgegebenes Ein- und Ausgabeprotokoll. Die Abbildung verläuft folgendermassen (vgl. Figur 1): Strukturinhärente Algorithmen bilden die Daten vorerst im Primärspeicher auf einen zusammenhängenden Block ab (Kompaktifizieren), worauf diese als unformatierte Daten abgepeichert werden können (normale DB-Operation). Das Lesen der Daten erfolgt umgekehrt ebenfalls in zwei Schritten:

nach dem Kopieren der Daten vom Sekundärspeicher auf einen zusammenhängenden Primär-speicherblock (DB-Operation) werden durch einen einfachen Algorithmus die i.a. ungültigen Adressen aktualisiert (Aufbereiten). Der gesamte Abbildungsmechanismus ist entlastet von der Verwaltung künstlich erzeugter Information und der zeitraubenden Wiederherstellung der Ordnung unter logisch zusammengehörender Daten. Die durch die Kompaktifizierung vorgenommene Clusterung legt die Verwaltung der Daten abstrakter Datentypen auf eigenen Seiten nahe, was die Anzahl der Sekundärspeicherzugriffe auf ein Minimum beschränkt.

In VEGADB sind zur vollständigen Spezifikation eines ADT's vom Datenbankadministrator insgesamt sechs verschiedene ADP's anzugeben, die alle dazu dienen, eine einheitliche Datenbank-schnittstelle anzubieten. Zu den beiden ADP's "Kompaktifizieren" und "Aufbereiten" kommen die ADP's "Vergleichen" (definiert eine Ordnung auf einem abstrakten Datentyp), "Wertebereich-Überprüfen", "Konsistenz-Überprüfen" sowie "Grösse-Berechnen" hinzu. Für die Verwaltung der Daten abstrakter Datentypen sind jedoch die ersten beiden ADP's "Kompaktifizieren" und "Aufbereiten" von zentraler Bedeutung. Deren festes Ein-und Ausgabeprotokoll sieht wie folgt aus:

```
PROCEDURE CompactifyADT (     adtId           : ADT;
                              adtByteSize     : LongNumber;
                              adtInDataPtr    : ADDRESS;
                          VAR adtOutDataPtr   : ADDRESS;
                          VAR msgId           : MessageId);
(* Compactifies the data delivered at main memory address 'adtInDataPtr' of
   total size 'adtByteSize' (sum of all data to be stored in this operation,
   not identical with the allocated space right at the given address). The
   compactified data will be returned at main memory address 'adtOutDataPtr'.*)


PROCEDURE UpdateADT (     adtId           : ADT;
                          adtByteSize     : LongNumber;
                      VAR adtInOutDataPtr : ADDRESS;
                      VAR msgId           : MessageId);
(* Updates data delivered at main memory address 'adtInOutDataPtr' of size
   'adtByteSize' according to the structure referenced by 'adtId'.          *)
```

Für das Kompaktizieren dreidimensionaler geometrischer VEGAS-Objekte, abgelegt in der bekannten Randdarstellung, wurden nicht-rekursive Algorithmus entwickelt, die mit linearem Aufwand arbeiten. Nach dem Kompaktifizieren stellen die Daten nach wie vor eine gültige Primärspeicherstruktur dar, wodurch das Aufbereiten sehr einfach wird. Die einzige durchzuführende Aufbereitungsoperation ist daie Addition eines festen Offsets zu allen Primärspeicheradressen. Beide Algorithmen benutzen systemnahe Operationen, sind jedoch in den Datenbankkern eingebettet, wodurch eine korrekte Verwendung sichergestellt ist.

Zur verbesserten datenbankmässigen Unterstützung gehört auch die Entlastung des Anwenders bei der Vergabe von Identifikationsschlüsselwerten. Hierzu wird in VEGADB das Surrogatkonzept (s. z.B. [Meier 1987]) verwendet: ein spezielles Attribut 'Surrogat' in jeder Relation enthält die vom System erzeugten invarianten Merkmalswerte individueller Tupel einer Datenbank und kann damit als Identifikationsschlüssel dienen. Die Surrogatwerte können wie in XRS vom System zur Definition von Beziehungen benutzt werden oder, wie in VEGADB dank der Verwendung eines virtuellen Speicherkonzepts, zur Einbindung von zugriffsbeschleunigender Information.

Die kurze Entwicklungszeit und das gute Laufzeitverhalten haben den Entscheid für die Neuentwicklung des Datenbanksystems VEGADB bestätigt, zumal wertvolle Erfahrungen bei der Einbettung abstrakter Datentypen in einen erweiterbaren Datenbankkern gewonnen werden konnten. Die Architektur unterscheidet sich von herkömmlichen Vorschlägen durch das Vorhandensein eines durch das Datenbanksystem generierten Moduls, welches die zu den ADT's zugehörigen ADP's enthält. Dieses ADP-Modul ist auf technischer Seite für die Erweiterbarkeit des Datenbankkerns verantwortlich. Abstrakte Datentypen werden auch systemintern zur Verwaltung der Zugriffshilfen und eines einfachen Datenkatalogs verwendet. Die in VEGADB realisierte Lösung ist auf Anwendungsbereiche beschränkt, wo die *Verwaltung* strukturierter Objekte im Vordergrund steht, und die eigentliche Datenverarbeitung im Primärspeicher erfolgt.

LITERATURHINWEISE:

[Kemper/Wallrath 87]

Kemper A., Wallrath M.: An Analysis of Geometric Modeling in Database Systems. In: ACM Computing Surveys, Vol. 19, No. 1, New York 1987.

[Lamersdorf/Schmidt 83]

Lamersdorf W., Schmidt J.W.: Rekursive Datenmodelle. Informatik-Fachberichte Nr. 83, Springer-Verlag, Berlin 1983, S. 148-168.

[Loacker/Wälchli/Zehnder 88]

Loacker H.-B., Wälchli A., Zehnder C.A.: VEGAS - Ein rechnergestütztes Unterrichtssystem für Raumgeometrie und Konstruktion. Institut für Informationssysteme, ETH Zürich, Herbst 1988.

[Meier 87]

Meier A.: Erweiterung relationaler Datenbanksysteme für technische Anwendungen. Informatik-Fachberichte Nr. 135, Springer-Verlag, Berlin 1987.

[Meier et al. 87]

Meier A., Durrer K., Heiser G., Petry E., Wälchli A., Zehnder C.A.: XRS: Ein erweitertes relationales Datenbanksystem zur Verwaltung von technischen Objekten und Versionen. Bericht Nr. 76 Instituts für Informatik der ETH Zürich, Zürich 1987.

[Schek/Pistor 82]

Schek H.-J., Pistor P.: Data structures for an integrated data base management and retrieval system. In: Proc. of the 8th International Conference on Very Large Databases. VLDB Endowment, Saratoga (CA), 1982.

[Stonebraker et al. 83]

Stonebraker M., Rubenstein B., Guttman A.: Application of abstract data types and abstract indices to CAD databases. In: Proc. of ACM SIGMOD Conference on Engineering Design Applications. ACM, New York 1983.

[Stonebraker 84]

Stonebraker M.: Adding Semantic Knowledge to a Relational Database System. In: Brodie M., Mylopoulos J., Schmidt J.W. (Hrsg.): On Conceptual Modelling. Springer-Verlag, New York 1984, S. 333-353.

Die Datenhaltung der CADLAB–Workstation: Konzept und Realisierung

Gerd Kachel, Thomas Kathöfer, Bernd Nelke
CADLAB
Kooperation Uni-GH Paderborn/Nixdorf Computer AG

1   Einleitung

Der Benutzer heutiger CAD-Systeme zur Unterstützung des Entwurfs integrierter Systeme wird vor eine Reihe von Problemen gestellt. Er muß mit verschiedenen komplexen Software-Werkzeugen, die sich dem Anwender gegenüber unterschiedlich verhalten und die untereinander nur schwer Daten und Ergebnisse austauschen können, arbeiten. Deshalb wird gewünscht, integrierte CAD-Systeme zu schaffen. Ziel der Integration ist es, ein System zu bieten, das eine gemeinsame Datenbasis und eine einheitliche, allgemeine Benutzeroberfläche für verschiedene Software-Werkzeuge bereitstellt.

Zusätzliche Ziele sind die dynamische Erweiterbarkeit und Konfigurierbarkeit eines solchen Systems und die Offenheit der Architektur, so daß Programme, die nicht als Quellen vorliegen oder systemfremd sind, leicht in das System eingebracht werden können.

CADLAB, eine Kooperation der Nixdorf Computer AG und der Universität Gesamthochschule Paderborn, hat sich zum Ziel gesetzt, ein solches System zu entwickeln und darin Werkzeuge zum Schaltkreisentwurf einzubringen. Dieses System wird als CADLAB–Workstation [6] bezeichnet.

Eine Basiskomponente der CADLAB–Workstation ist das Datenhaltungssystem, daß im folgenden beschrieben wird. Um seine Einordnung zu zeigen, wird zunächst die Architektur der CADLAB–Workstation vorgestellt. Im Abschnitt 3 wird der Aufbau der Datenhaltung beschrieben. In Abschnitt 4 folgt eine Erläuterung des internen Datenmodells der Datenhaltung und schließlich im Abschnitt 5 ein Ausblick auf weitere Arbeiten im CADLAB auf dem Gebiet der Datenhaltung für CAD im Schaltkreis- und Systementwurf.

2   Die CADLAB–Workstation

Den Integrationsrahmen der CADLAB–Workstation (Bild 1) bildet zum einen ein User Interface Management System, mit dem Benutzeroberflächen als Anwenderschnittstellen von Programmen generiert werden können [5,6], zum anderen das Datenhaltungssystem. In diesen Rahmen werden die Software-Werkzeuge eingefügt. Die CADLAB–Workstation ist primär für den Schaltkreisentwurf konzipiert, ist aber so flexibel, daß sie auch für andere komplexe Anwendungen wie z.B. die Software-Produktion eingesetzt werden kann. Die Entwicklung basiert auf Standards wie X-Window für die Graphik, C als Programmiersprache und Unix[1] als Betriebssystem.

---

[1]UNIX ist ein eingetragenes Warenzeichen von AT&T

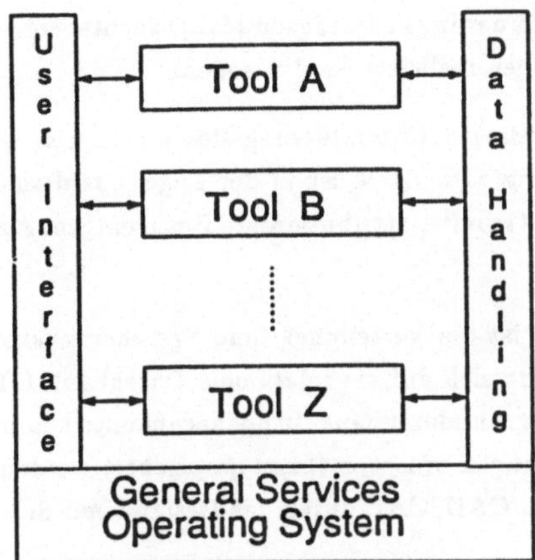

Bild 1 : Die CADLAB–Workstation Software Architektur

3   Die Datenhaltung der CADLAB–Workstation

[6,12] nennen als Anforderungen an ein Datenbank-Managementsystem (DBMS) im Bereich von CAD/CAE-Anwendungen hohen Durchsatz, leichte Konfigurierbarkeit, große Allgemeinheit, Erweiterbarkeit, einfache Schnittstellen zum Anwendungsprogrammierer, ein Datenmodell zur Verwaltung vielfältiger Datenbeziehungen, Wahl zwischen verschiedenen Graden der Integration von Software, Mehrbenutzerfähigkeit und Netzwerkfähigkeit.

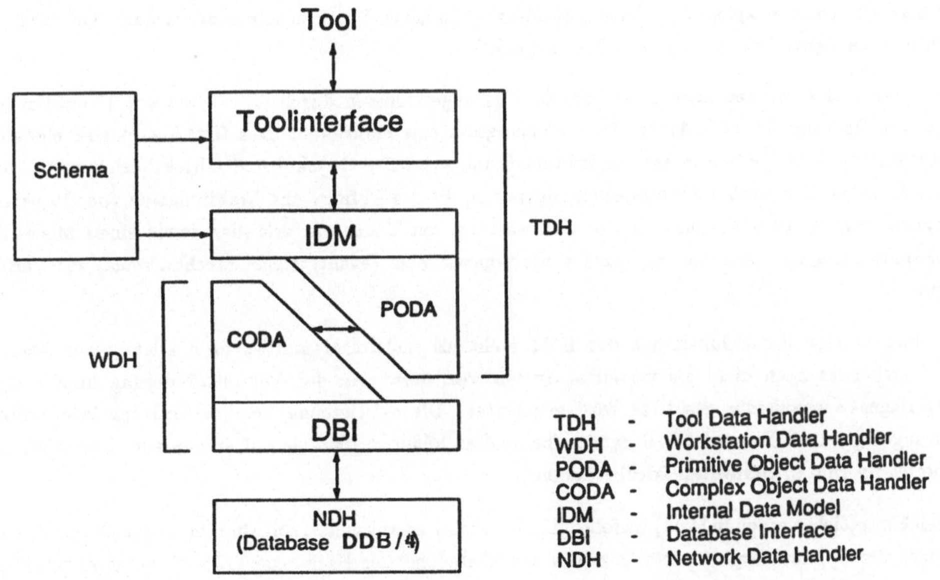

Bild 2 : Architektur des Datenhaltungssystems

Ausgehend von den genannten Anforderungen wurde ein Mehrschichtenkonzept entworfen (Bild 2), mit dem Schritt für Schritt diese Vorstellungen realisiert werden sollen.

Das Konzept gewährleistet eine direkte Unterstützung des strukturell objektorientierten Datenmodells (IDM) der CADLAB-Datenhaltung. Das IDM ist in der Lage, aus dem Entity-Relationship -Modell [2] abgeleitete Konstrukte (Entities, Attribute, attributierbare Beziehungen, Aggregate und Gruppierungen) zu unterstützen.

Unterste Ebene der Datenhaltung ist die Verteilungs- und Speicherungskomponente. Die aktuelle Implementierung der Datenhaltung stützt sich auf die relationale Datenbank **DDB/4** (Nixdorf Computer AG) ab[2]. DDB/4 ist die verteilte Hintergrunddatenbank, in der sogenannte komplexe Objekte als in dieser Ebene unteilbare Einheit und die Beziehungen zwischen ihnen gespeichert werden. Ein komplexes Objekt in der Datenhaltung kann z.B. im Bereich CAD/CAE durch das Design einer Schaltung gebildet werden.

Mit Hilfe einer prozeduralen Schnittstelle (**DBI**) wird die relationale Sichtweise von DDB/4 von der graphenorientierte Sicht der Beziehungen zwischen komplexen Objekten in der Datenhaltung entkoppelt. Hier liegt der Übergang von einer netzwerkweiten Speicherung von komplexen Objekten hin zur rechnerlokalen Verwaltung (**CODA**) von komplexen Objekten. DBI und CODA bilden einen Prozeß, den **WDH**.

Die Verwaltung komplexer Objekte umfaßt die Zuteilung der komplexen Objekte an Anwendungsprozesse (Werkzeuge), die Verwaltung der Konfigurationsinformationen und die Interpretation der Informationen, die sich in einem komplexen Objekt befinden, für die Anwendungen.

Innerhalb eines komplexen Objekts befinden sich primitive Objekte oder Verweise auf komplexe Objekte, die sich, wie die komplexen Objekte, zu einem Graph von Objekten zusammenfügen. Mit primitiven Objekten können z.B. im Schaltkreisentwurf einzelne Bauelemente repräsentiert werden. Ein komplexes Objekt kann somit als eine eigene, graphenorientierte Datenbank primitiver Objekte aufgefaßt werden. Auf diese Daten wird über eine eigene Verwaltung (**PODA**) zugegriffen.

PODA und CODA werden nach oben hin (Bild 2) abgeschlossen durch einen Satz von Operationen, die das interne Datenmodell (**IDM**) des Datenhaltungssystems realisieren. Das IDM bietet eine einheitliche, applikationsunabhängige Sichtweise auf komplexe und primitive Objekte und Objektbeziehungen. An der Schnittstelle des IDM werden Operationen angeboten, die die Abfrage und Manipulation von Objekten, die Konfigurierung der Datenhaltung und die Verwaltung von Benutzern erlauben sowie einen Mechanismus zur ereignisabhängigen Ausführung von Benutzeroperationen (event/trigger-Mechanismus) zur Verfügung stellen.

Eine erste Version der Schnittstelle des IDM steht als multi-user/multi-prozeß Lösung zur Verfügung. Diese Version ist noch nicht als verteiltes System realisiert. An der Vervollständigung hinsichtlich des event/trigger-Mechanismus des IDM wird gearbeitet. Die existierende Version wird zur Integration von Werkzeugen genutzt. Es wird z.Z. darauf aufbauend an höherwertigen Schnittstellen zur Anwenderseite hin gearbeitet (in Bild 2: **Schema, Toolinterface**).

Vergleichbare Ziele werden in [4,11] verfolgt. Unser Ansatz ist spezieller, soll aber im Vergleich zu allgemeinen Ansätzen durch benutzergesteuerte Lokalität von Daten mittels komplexer Objekte einen entsprechenden Effizienzgewinn ermöglichen. In [8,9,13] wird ein Satz von aufeinander aufbauenden Werkzeugen entwickelt, die speziell für CAD/CAE geeignet sind. Für die weitere Entwicklung der Datenhaltung im CADLAB sind

---

[2]Eine relationale Datenbank ist nicht notwendige Basis. Realisierungen auf anderen Grundlagen sind ebenfalls möglich.

Ergänzungen in Richtung des Design Management wie in [1,8,14], der Versionsunterstützung wie in [7], und der Konsistenzsicherung wie in [10] geplant.

4 Das interne Datenmodell – IDM

Das IDM ist die Basis der weiteren Entwicklung der Datenhaltung und erste Grundlage der Integration von Werkzeugen in die Datenhaltung der CADLAB–Workstation. Die Funktionalität des IDM wird im folgenden kurz beschrieben.

Das IDM erlaubt die Abbildung der realen Welt, z.B Entwurfsanwendungen, auf Objekte und Objektbeziehungen in Form von Objektgraphen (anders als z.B. das relationale Modell [3]). Objekte können im IDM komplexe Objekte oder primitive Objekte sein. Komplexe Objekte sind untereinander durch gerichtete n:m-Beziehungen verbunden. Damit entsteht ein gerichteter Graph mit den komplexen Objekten als Knoten und den Beziehungen zwischen ihnen als Kanten. Ein komplexes Objekt enthält eine Menge von primitiven Objekten oder von Verweisen auf andere komplexe Objekte, die ebenfalls einen gerichteten Graphen bilden. Primitive Objekte tragen die Nutzinformationen in komplexen Objekten, komplexe Objekte sind nichtüberlappende Zugriffseinheiten aus der Hintergrunddatenbank und können selbst eigenständige Attribute zu ihrer Beschreibung besitzen.

An der Schnittstelle zum IDM werden Gruppen von Operationen, die es erlauben, eine Datenbank gemäß des IDM aufzubauen, bereitgestellt. Durch Manipulationsoperationen können Objekte geschaffen und beschrieben werden und Beziehungen zwischen Objekten aufgebaut werden. Allgemeine oder selektierende Suche nach Objekten erfolgt durch Navigation im Objektgraphen. Dabei werden Objekte, spezifiziert nach Typ, Name, Identifikation und Art der Beziehung relativ zu einem Ausgangsobjekt bestimmt. Um nicht integrierte Werkzeuge zu unterstützen, gibt es die Möglichkeit, Daten in der Datenhaltung als strukturlose Zeichenfolge ähnlich wie Betriebssystemdateien zu behandeln.

Das IDM unterstützt Datenkonsistenz durch implizite Transaktionen. Jede Operation am IDM bildet eine Transaktion mitsamt Wiederaufsetzen beim Scheitern dieser Operation. Zusätzlich bilden Operationen zum Öffnen und Schließen von komplexen Objekten Transaktionsklammern, die durch zwischenzeitliche Operationen zum Sichern oder Abbrechen der Bearbeitung modifiziert werden können.

Neben dieser Funktionalität, die die Verarbeitung der Daten der Applikation erlaubt, werden Operationen für die weiteren Aufgaben eines Datenhaltungssystems vom IDM angeboten (wie z.B zur Verwaltung von Benutzern und Benutzergruppen).

Besonders wichtig für technische Anwendungen auf Datenbanken ist ein flexibler und mächtiger Mechanismus der Konsistenzsicherung. Hier bietet die Datenhaltung an der IDM-Schnittstelle den objektorientierten, prozeßübergreifenden event/trigger-Mechanismus. Der Anwender spezifiziert Ereignisse (über Angabe bestimmter Objekte oder Operationen), auf die er mit von ihm definierten Aktionen (die dann z.B. die Konsistenz herstellen können) reagieren möchte. Tritt nun eines dieser Ereignisse ein, so wird automatisch die zugehörige Aktion ausgeführt.

5 Aktuelle und zukünftige Arbeiten in der Datenhaltung

Das Datenhaltungssystem wird z.Z. bezüglich Laufzeiteffizienz und Platzbedarf untersucht und optimiert. Das existierende System wird so modifiziert, daß es von der unterliegenden relationalen Datenbank unabhängig wird. Es werden Lösungen erstellt, so daß die Datenhaltung auf allgemeinen Plattformen zur Verfügung steht. Parallel dazu wird die Realisierung eines sicheren und schnellen verteilten Systems in einer heterogenen Rechnerumgebung angegangen.

Gleichzeitig wird das System an seinen oberen Schnittstellen zu den Anwendungen hin ausgebaut. Ziel ist eine anwenderfreundliche Datenhaltungsschnittstelle auf hohem Abstraktionsniveau. Hier sind Sprachen (DDL) und zugehörige Werkzeuge zur deskriptiven Beschreibung von konzeptionellen und applikativen Schemata basierend auf dem erweiterten Entity-Relationship -Modell in der Entwicklung. Weiterhin wird es eine DML geben, die Anfragen auf dem Niveau der DDL erlaubt. In Zukunft folgen anwenderunterstützende Werkzeuge wie Reportprogramme, Objekt-Browser und Hilfen für den Systemverwalter.

6 Literaturverzeichnis

1. G.P. Barabino, G. Bisio, M. Marchesi; "A Modular System for Data Management in VLSI Design";
   IEEE, International Conference on Computer Design 1984,
   VLSI in Computers, pp 796-801, 1984

2. P.P. Chen; "The entity-relationship model: towards a unified view of data";
   ACM Transactions on Database Systems, 1, 11, pp 77-84, 1976

3. C.J. Date; "An Introduction to Data Base Systems, Volume II";
   Addison Wesley, 1984

4. K. Dittrich, A. Kotz, J. Mülle; "Database Support for VLSI Design: The DAMASCUS System";
   in: M.H. Ungerer (Hrsg):
   "CAD-Schnittstellen und Datentransferformate im Elektronikbereich";
   Springer Verlag, pp 62-81, 1986

5. K.Gottheil, G. Kachel, Th. Kathöfer, B. Kleinjohann, E.Kupitz, B. Nelke;
   "The Integrated CADLAB Workstation CWS";
   CADLAB Report 1/87, Januar 1987

6. K. Gottheil, G. Kachel, Th. Kathöfer, H.J.Kaufmann, B. Kleinjohann,
   E. Kupitz, J. Miller, B. Nelke, F.J. Rammig, B. Steinmüller, C. White;
   "The CADLAB Workstation CWS - An Open, Generic System for Tool Integration";
   Proc. of the IFIP WG 10.2, Paderborn, 1987;
   Tool Integration and Design Environments, north-holland, pp 167-184, 1988

7. R.H. Katz, M. Anwarrudin, E. Chang; "A Version Server for Computer-Aided Design Data";
   23th Design Automation Conference 1986, pp 27-33, Proceedings

8. R.H. Katz; "A Database Approach for Managing VLSI Design Data";
   19th Design Automation Conference 1982, pp 274-282, Proceedings

9. K.H. Keller; "An Electronic Circuit CAD-Framework";
   University of California Berkeley, Report, 1984

10. A.M. Kotz, K.R. Dittrich, J.M. Mülle; "Supporting Semantic Rules by a Generalized Event/Trigger Mechanism";
    J.W. Schmidt, S.Ceri, M. Missikoff (editors):
    Advances in Database Technology, EDBT'88,
    Springer Verlag, pp 76-91, 1988

11. V. Linnemann, K. Küspert, P.Dadam, P. Pistor, R. Erbe, A. Kemper, N. Südkamp, G. Walch, M. Wallrath;
    "Design and Implementation of an Extensible Database Management System";
    25th VLDB Conference 1988, pp 294-305, Proceedings

12. P. Lockemann, K. Dittrich, M. Adams, M. Bever, B. Ferkinghoff,
    W. Gotthard, A. Kotz, R.-P. Liedtke, B. Lüke, J. Mülle;
    "Database Requirements of Engineering Applications – An Analysis";
    Forschungszentrum für Informatik, Universität Karlsruhe,
    Interner Bericht Nr.12/85

13. A.R. Newton; "The General Structure of OCT";
    University of California Berkeley, Report, 1986

14. P. van der Wolf, T.G.R van Leuken; "Object Type Oriented Data Modeling for VLSI Data Management";
    25th Design Automation Conference 1988, pp 351-356, Proceedings

PANDA: An Extensible DBMS
Supporting Object-Oriented Software Techniques*

Max J. Egenhofer
Andrew U. Frank
National Center for Geographic Information and Analysis
and
Department of Surveying Engineering
University of Maine
Orono, ME 04469, USA
MAX@MECAN1.bitnet
FRANK@MECAN1.bitnet

Abstract

The PANDA databases management system was designed for non-standard applications which deal with spatial data. It supports an object-oriented program design with modularization, encapsulation, and reusability, and can be easily embedded into complex applications, such as spatial information systems or cartographic expert systems. It is presented how complex objects and their operations are defined. A layered structure on top of the programmer's interface provides object operations which include potentially complex consistency constraints.

1   Introduction

The interface of a non-standard DBMS must fit well into the methods used for the implementation of the applications; therefore, it is important that database methods and techniques fit well within a software engineering environment. Software engineering techniques, such as the concept of abstract data types [Guttag 1977] [Parnas 1978] [Zilles 1984] and abstract object types [Sernades 1987], in which each module encapsulates an object type with all its pertinent operations, are commonly used for applications; however, database management systems do not sufficiently support them. Their interfaces to programming languages, like Embedded SQL, have demonstrated to be incompatible with sophisticated software engineering concepts and cumbersome [Christensen 1987].

This short version of a longer report [Egenhofer 1988b] describes the software engineering techniques used in PANDA [Frank 1982], an object-oriented database tailored for applications with spatial data. PANDA is an acronym for <u>Pa</u>scal <u>N</u>etwork <u>Da</u>tabase Management System. The system was originally designed as a network DBMS with object-oriented concepts and enhancements for storage and access of spatial data and evolved over the years to an object-oriented design. PANDA consists of about 40,000 lines of program code and has been running for several years, primarily used for research and teaching in undergraduate and graduate courses. Its development started at the Swiss Federal Institute for Technology, Zurich, and has been continued at the University of Maine. Code was transferred

---

*This work was partially funded by a grant from NSF under No. IST-8609123 and equipment grants from Digital Equipment Corporation.

between such vastly different hardware and operating systems as DEC-10 (under TOPS-10), IBM 370 (under VM/CMS), and VAX/MicroVAX (under VMS).

PANDA's data model is based upon the basic concepts of abstraction: classification, generalization, and aggregation [Brodie 1984]. The term *object* is used for a single occurrence (instantiation) of data; *type*, *class*, or *abstract data type*, refer to sorts of objects; *superclass* describes the grouping of several classes in an is_a relation (generalization) [Dahl 1966]; and *subclass* is the specialization of a superclass. *Inheritance* defines a superclass in terms of one or more other classes, propagating the properties of the superclass to all subclasses transitively.

PANDA's DB kernel manages storage and retrieval of data from persistent storage devices, buffers pages and records to improve performance, provides facilities for transaction management, incorporates structures for logical access (hashing, B*-trees, Field Tree for spatial access [Frank 1983]), and provides generic structures for aggregation and generalization. The kernel is built in a layered and modular structure so that it can be easily extended by additional parts, e.g., a multi-user facility. The extensible part of PANDA is the definition of the application-specific classes based on the definition of value types which can be arbitrarily complex acyclic abstract data types.

The paper starts with a brief discussion of PANDA's software environment. Section 3 focuses on PANDA's object model. The four phases during the definition of complex classes are presented. In section 4 the implementation of object operations in a layered structure on top of the generic programmer's interface is presented. The paper concludes that better object-oriented programming languages can help to implement object-oriented databases closer to the designed models.

2   Software Engineering Aspects

An abstract data type (ADT) is a mathematical structure which fully defines the behavior (semantics and operations) of objects. Abstract data types are specified as an algebra describing what sorts of objects (types) are dealt with, and what kinds of operations they are subject to. A set of axioms determines the effects of the operations. Abstract data types can be combined in layers, where higher-level abstract data types are first described independently (specifications), and it is then shown how this behavior can be achieved using other, hierarchically lower abstract data types (abstract implementation [Olthoff 1985] [Frank 1986]).

The software engineering environment of PANDA supports *modularization, encapsulation, reusability*, and *transportability*. Programmers are motivated to write object-oriented code as the implementation of ADTs in a standardized way such that other programmers can easily read and correct it. Modularization is achieved by using a Pascal precompiler [Egenhofer 1988a], which provides types and routines from one module to another, with type checking across modules. The implementation of operations is encapsulated into the module. A highly modular programming style requires that the modules are managed in a controlled library system providing the user information about existing ADTs, their operations, and their specifications. The precompiler is embedded into a library management system with hierarchical directory structure where several versions of modules can be kept in parallel. Transportability of code among different Pascal compilers and various hardware is guaranteed by the precompiler, because only the precompiler itself, not the particular code, must be adapted to fit specific compiler features.

3   Object Definition

An object-oriented data model gives rise to the formation of arbitrarily complex classes, the majority of which is composed of a (limited) number of lower structured parts, here called *components*. The same components occur repeatedly as part of various classes, and it is more economical to define and reuse components, instead of defining redundantly a multitude of very similar classes. Though this may resemble a traditional entity-attribute type of concept, it is only the object-oriented implementation of several classes with the same components which are defined only once and reused in every class they are part of. The decomposition of objects into components releases the application designer from redundant definitions of specific object operations for the structures. Considerable overhead is removed by defining the operations for the value types and applying them for classes. Users are not aware of this decomposition because they see only objects and operations upon them.

PANDA's object definition consisting of *value types*, *classes*, and a generalized *objectType* adopts the modular concept and fits well into the layered architecture. An application model is defined in standardized operations that are easily integrated into the kernel. The operations are implemented as short Pascal routines which are executed during PANDA's startup. This approach releases the database administrator from recompiling the entire DBMS code; instead, only the initialization modules for each class and an interface module must be compiled, and (shareable) images linked. A systematic implementation with strict naming conventions allows the generation of code for these modules. Currently, code is generated partially from definitions in a text file; a more user friendly generation immediately from a graphical schema design is being investigated. The four phases of the object definition are distinguished.

3.1 Phase 1: Declaration of User Terms

The kernel was originally initiated with templates for the names of the classes, components, links, and paths. These templates must be replaced with the particular names used in the schema design of the application.

3.2 Phase 2: Definition of Value Types

A value type is the Pascal implementation of an abstract data type in a single programming unit, consisting of a type definition and a set of pertinent operations, and serves as class component. The type definition can be any simple data type, such as integer, string, real, etc., or any structured type, such as array or record, except types for dynamically allocated variables, such as pointers[1]. Value types can be built upon other value types by using their definitions and methods. Due to restrictions of current compilers, only acyclic combinations of value types are permitted.

Each value type must provide a set of fundamental operations necessary for indexing and hashing structures of objects. For example, hashing requires a function that calculates a hash value, and an operation that compares two values for equality. The implementation of these operations depends upon the structure and the semantics of the class. Unlike traditional databases that support only a limited, hardcoded set of types, PANDA is extensible. This implies that the operations for the supporting structures are not predefined and must be provided by the application designer.

3.3 Phase 3: Composition of Classes

The properties of a class are determined by its own components and the components transitively inherited from its superclasses. Details about the implementation of a class are hidden, such that modules outside of the class definition are not aware of the decomposition into object components. Class components are implemented as Pascal records. Inheritance is simulated with the help of variant records, which is necessary due to the lacking support of inheritance in Pascal.

These type definitions are not yet sufficient for the object definition. Programming languages of the FORTRAN/Algol type separate compilation and execution of code into two phases which provide different levels of information. During compilation, variables and types are named, and types may be composed from other types. During executing, the names and the relation between a variable and its

---

[1]This limitation is with respect to the intended persistency of objects.

type is not accessible by the user code. Likewise, it is not possible to find out whether a type is part of another structured type.

In order to provide the compile time knowledge also during execution, the relations between each class and its components, its immediate superclass, possible aggregations, and logical access paths must be defined explicitly as programming code. PANDA has the database administrator write these standardized routines which will be executed by the kernel during startup, initializing the user's model. For each class, the composition of the type and the corresponding ini-routine are combined in a separate module.

3.4   Phase 4: Definition of Database Objects

All classes are specializations of the most general superclass *objectType* from which all pertinent DB-operations are inherited. The objectType is implemented as a Pascal record with varying parts for each specific class. It combines all specific classes into a single, compatible type to which common (system) components, such as tuple identifiers and aggregate pointers, are added.

4   A Layered Structure of Object Operations

The object-oriented approach requires the definition of complex objects *and* their pertinent operations. While the knowledge about the composition of complex classes is essential to the database kernel, the object operations are the application programmer's tools to manipulate objects. The programmer's interface of the DBMS kernel is a collection of object-oriented manipulation and retrieval operations which can be called from the application programs. These operations are defined for the generalized objectType, and are compatible with any class. Conceptually, all database operations, such as *store*, *delete*, and *update*, are inherited to each class of the schema. Their implementation on top of the programmers's interface is a layered structure of model-specific object operations. This is the location to implement consistency checks. A layered structure of object operations has been developed which is generally applicable for any object-oriented application. Based upon the fundamental object operations, more complex operations can be defined. By restricting the operations to a single task, the code for the routines stays small and correctness can be verified more easily.

The structure of these operations is the same for every application: First, the operations are defined to make a specific object, and to assign values to and access them from an object. Then, unary object operations for storing, modifying, deleting, and accessing individual objects are defined based upon the generic DB-operations offered in the programmer's interface. Another layer treats all binary operations manipulating aggregates. These operations are exploited in the next layer to form complex object operations, including complex consistency constraints.

4.1   Level 1: Make, Get, and Put Operations

The first layer is a collection of modules with the basic operations to manipulate the individual description of a single object: creating an instance (*make*), assigning values to (*put*), and extracting values from an instance (*get*). These operations hide the implementation of the classes from the user, preventing uncontrolled access. Since the properties of a superclass are propagated to all subclasses, *get* and *put* operations are compatible with objects of the subclasses as well.

For each class a separate module contains these operations. Their implementation is trivial, and the code can be generated with the knowledge of the object description. Simple consistency constraints, such as checking whether a value lies within a range, can be added to the put operations.

4.2 Level 2: Unary Object Operations

The second layer covers all database operations to store, update, delete, and access a single object which are inherited from the common superclass *objectType*. The implementation of these operations is straightforward because the generic object operations are part of the programmer's interface and can be immediately applied to each object class. Depending on the definition of the class, different access methods are supported, such as access with a key value and spatial access. For each class, a separate module with the specific object operations is implemented.

4.3 Level 3: Binary Object Operations

The third layer comprises aggregate operations that always envolve two objects. Standard operations are the addition of a part to an aggregate, the removal of a part from an aggregate, cancellation of an entire aggregate, and the access of parts of an aggregate. The operations which establish links among objects require that the corresponding objects have been loaded into the database before. Reversely, remove and cancel dissolve the links without deleting the previously linked objects from the database. For each aggregation, a separate module with the aggregate operations is implemented.

Three types of access operations for aggregates are distinguished: (1) iterating over all aggregate components, similar to a FOR EACH loop in CLU [Liskov 1981], (2) getting a specific aggregate component with a certain value, and (3) getting the composite object part of an aggregate. The second access method is only efficiently supported if a sorted access path was defined.

4.4 Level 4$^+$: Complex Object Operations

The fourth and later layers combine operations of the lower levels to form more complex operations.

The level structure is open and can be extended according to the complexity of the application. Entire applications have been written in this highly structured form. The advantage of the object layers is that very complex operations can be implemented by combining other object operations. Following the rule that no object operation may use other operations of a higher level, a well-structured application package can be designed.

5 Conclusion

The close relation between the implementation of object-oriented databases and object-oriented software techniques has been explained. For an object-oriented database it is of vital interest to tie into the software environment of the application. PANDA's object-oriented programmer's interface facilitates applications on top which conform with an object-oriented design.

With the growing complexity of the application the layered structure of complex object operations can be extended beyond the four basic layers introduced. The embedding of consistency constraints into these object operations is a natural and object-oriented way, starting with very general operations, and constraining them more and more.

Conventional programming languages do not easily support the implementation of object-oriented databases and often, methods must be simulated to match the model. Using a language that supports multiple inheritance, clearer designs and more condensed implementations become possible.

References

[Brodie 1984] M.L. Brodie. On the Development of Data Models. In: M.L. Brodie et al., editors, On Conceptual Modelling, Springer Verlag, New York (NY), 1984.

[Christensen 1987] A. Christensen and T.U. Zahle. A Comparison of Self-Contained and Embedded Database Languages. In: P. Stocker and W. Kent, editors, Proceedings 13th VLDB Conference, Brighton, England, September 1987.

[Dahl 1966] O.-J. Dahl and K. Nygaard. SIMULA—An Algol-based Simulation Language. Communications of the ACM, 9(9), September 1966.

[Egenhofer 1988a] M. Egenhofer and A. Frank. A Precompiler For Modular, Transportable Pascal. SIGPLAN Notices, 23(3), March 1988.

[Egenhofer 1988b] M. Egenhofer and Andrew Frank. Object-Oriented Software Techniques in PANDA. Technical Report 96, Surveying Engineering Program, University of Maine, Orono (ME), December 1988.

[Frank 1982] A. Frank. PANDA—A Pascal Network Database System. In: G.W. Gorsline, editor, Proceedings of the Fifth Symposium on Small Systems, Colorado Springs (CO), 1982.

[Frank 1983] A. Frank. Problems of Realizing LIS: Storage Methods for Space Related Data: The Field Tree. Technical Report 71, Institut for Geodesy and Photogrammetry, Swiss Federal Institute of Technology (ETH), Zurich, Switzerland, 1983.

[Frank 1986] A. Frank and W. Kuhn. Cell Graph: A Provable Correct Method for the Storage of Geometry. In: D. Marble, editor, Second International Symposium on Spatial Data Handling, Seattle (WA), 1986.

[Guttag 1977] J. Guttag. Abstract Data Types And The Development Of Data Structures. Communications of the ACM, June 1977.

[Liskov 1981] B. Liskov et al. CLU Reference. Lecture Notes in Computer Science, Springer Verlag, New York (NY), 1981.

[Olthoff 1985] W. Olthoff. An Overview on ModPascal. SIGPLAN Notices, 20(10), October 1985.

[Parnas 1978] D.L. Parnas and J.E. Share. Language Facilities for Supporting the Use of Data Abstraction in the Development of Software Systems. Technical Report, Naval Research Laboratory, Washington (DC), 1978.

[Sernades 1987] A. Sernades et al. Object-Oriented Specification of Databases: An Algebraic Approach. In: P. Stocker and W. Kent, editors, Proceedings 13th VLDB Conference, Brighton, England, September 1987.

[Zilles 1984] S.N. Zilles. Types, Algebras, and Modelling. In: M.L. Brodie et al., editors, On Conceptual Modelling, Springer Verlag, New York (NY), 1984.

Eine Testumgebung zur Untersuchung paralleler Verarbeitungsstrategien in komplexen Transaktionen

G. Schiele

Universität Stuttgart - Institut für Informatik
Azenbergstr. 12, D-7000 Stuttgart 1

Kurzfassung: Dieser Artikel beschreibt einen Mechanismus zur einfachen Implementierung und Evaluierung unterschiedlicher paralleler Ausführungsschemata für jegliche Art komplexer Transaktionen. Der Artikel basiert auf der Idee, die algorithmischen Aspekte der Berechnung von der Beschreibung des parallelen Ausführungsplans zu trennen. Die Eignung dieses Ansatzes wird durch Präsentation eines parallelen Ausführungsschemas für eine massiv parallele Anwendung belegt - der Berechnung transitiver Hüllen auf einer SQL-Datenbank. Anhand der Resultate dieses Experimentes wurde eine Anzahl notwendiger Erweiterungen der gegenwärtigen Implementierung abgeleitet. Einige Argumente belegen die Sichtweise, daß dieser Ansatz in allen Gebieten des Umganges mit nicht klassischen, "strukturierten" Transaktionen hilfreich ist.

Abstract: This paper describes a mechanism for easily implementing and evaluating different parallel execution schemes for any given complex transaction. It rests on the idea to seperate the algorithmic aspects of the computation from the description of the parallel execution plan. We show the use of this approach by demonstrating a parallel execution scheme for a massively parallel application - the transitive closure processing on a SQL database. From the results of this experiments, we will derive a number of necessary extensions to our current implementation. Some arguments are given to support the view of this approach being useful in all areas of handling non-classical, 'structured' transactions.

1. Einleitung

In Datenbanksystemen hat die Parallelverarbeitung eine sehr lange Tradition, indem der parallele Zugriff mehrerer Transaktionen auf dieselbe Datenbank unterstützt wird. Dies ist allerdings eine sehr spezielle Art der Parallelität, da nur wirklich unabhängige Transaktionen parallel verarbeitet werden. Transaktionen, die auf denselben Datenbestand zugreifen, werden durch geeignete Synchronisationsmechanismen serialisiert. Tatsächlich erfolgt daher eine geschachtelte Verarbeitung einfacher sequentieller Programme auf disjunkten Datenbeständen. Nur der Benutzer sieht Parallelität, wobei es dessen Aufgabe ist, den Grad der Parallelität durch die Programmierung der Transaktionen zu spezifizieren (Transaktionsgröße, Sperrmodi, usw.).

Dieses Modell ist für klassische Transaktionssysteme geeignet, wo viele kurze Transaktionen auf jeweils sehr kleinen Datenbeständen operieren [1]. Neue Typen von Datenbankapplikationen erfordern neue Systemarchitekturen, welche echte Parallelität auch innerhalb von Transaktionen unterstützen. Diese Anforderungen wurden zwar weitgehend erkannt [2],[3],[4],[21], aber abgesehen von den Datenbankmaschinen wurden nur sehr geringe

Fortschritte auf diesem Gebiet gemacht. Datenbankmaschinen sind allerdings kein typisches Beispiel, da sie eine Art hartverdrahteter Parallelität benutzen. Deshalb ist abhängig von den verwendeten Transaktionstypen auch nur sehr bedingt eine Leistungssteigerung zu erwarten.

Die allgemeinere Frage beschäftigt sich mit der automatischen Erkennung inhärenter Parallelität in komplexen Transaktionen auf jedem Niveau.

In diesem Artikel wird die Idee eines Entwicklungssystems zur Ausführung komplexer Transaktionen in parallelen Aktionen, basierend auf einem Standard-SQL-Datenbanksystem, präsentiert. Die Eignung dieses Ansatzes als Test- und Entwicklungsumgebung zur schnellen Implementierung komplexer Transaktionen wird anhand einer Anwendung, der Berechnung der transitiven Hülle eines Graphen, demonstriert.

Diese Arbeit ist Teil des PROSPECT-Projektes (**PR**ocessor *Organizations Supporting Parallel Execution in Complex Transactions*; [5],[18],[19],[20]).

2. Parallelität in komplexen Transaktionen

Spricht man über Parallelverarbeitung, wird darunter gewöhnlich die Vektorisierung numerischer Berechnungen oder massive Parallelität in den Connection Machine Architekturen [6] verstanden. Es gibt ein gemeinsames Merkmal numerischer Probleme und solcher die in kleinere Subprobleme zerlegt werden können und auf eine hohe Anzahl von Prozessoren abgebildet werden: das Problem hat eine invariante homogene Struktur hinsichtlich der iterativen Zerlegung der Gesamtaufgabe in kleinere Einheiten derselben Art. Beispiele hierfür sind einerseits einfache Datenstrukturen wie Vektoren und Matrizen und andererseits reguläre Problemstrukturen

wie lineare Gleichungssysteme, Differentialgleichungssysteme, usw.

Die Analyse komplexer Transaktionen in Nichtstandard Datenbanksystemen [7], wie beispielsweise CAD- oder Expertensysteme, zeigt, daß keine dieser Eigenschaften hier zutrifft. Datenbankschemata zur Repräsentation komplexer CAD-Objekte sind von ihrer Struktur weit komplexer als Matrizen, sodaß keine offensichtliche Zerlegung erkennbar ist. Auch Inferenzprozesse weisen in ihrer algorithmischen Struktur sehr viel weniger Regelmäßigkeit auf, als etwa lineare Gleichungssysteme.

Als Konsequenz ergibt sich die Notwendigkeit für einen allgemeineren und dynamischeren Ansatz zur Erkennung und Auswertung von Parallelität in datenbankorientierten Anwendungen. Der Ansatz sollte nicht an Hardware-Strukturen gebunden sein, wie dies bei den Datenbankmaschinen der Fall ist. Ferner sollte idealerweise eine Anwendung in eng gekoppelten homogenen Systemen, wie auch in lokalen oder dezentralen Netzen inhomogener Systeme möglich sein. Nicht zuletzt muß die Architektur heutiger Großrechner - Mehrprozessorsysteme, Anzahl und Mächtigkeit von Kanälen und Kontrolleinheiten, usw. - berücksichtigt werden.

2.1 Arten der Parallelverarbeitung

Die Behauptung, daß klassische Datenbanksysteme Transaktionen nur strikt sequentiell verarbeiten ist nicht ganz korrekt. Einige Systeme nutzen Parallelität im Zusammenhang mit ihrer internen Verwaltung wie das Ausschreiben modifizierter Seiten, Schreiben der Protokolldatei oder der asynchronen Kommunikation mit anderen Knoten. Diese Art der Parallelität auf niederer Ebene ist vollkommen unabhängig vom Inhalt einer Transaktion. Beispiele für echte Parallelität bei der Bearbeitung von Datenbankanfragen finden sich in sehr wenigen Systemen. System R^* [8] verwendet Parallelität bei der Verbundberechnung über zwei unterschiedliche Knoten und während der Commit-Bearbeitung. Die Gamma Datenbankmaschine [9] wurde für alle Arten der Parallelität entworfen, aber bis jetzt beschränkten sich Experimente auf parallele Verbundberechnung, Selektionen, etc. Diesbezügliche Publikationen erlauben keine Voraussage, wie eine Erweiterung erfolgen kann. Die Beschreibung des PRIMA Storage Servers [10] enthält einige Hinweise zur Verwendung von Parallelität, allerdings scheint dieses System noch nicht einsetzbar zu sein.

Die einzige kommerziell verfügbare Maschine welche transaktionsinterne Parallelität verwendet, ist Teradata's DBC 1012 [11]. Durch Speicherungsstrukturen, basierend auf Hash-Techniken, können Daten einer Anfrage parallel von den Platten gelesen werden. Dies ist allerdings auch in klassischen Datenbanksystemen möglich, wie z.B. DB2. Eine Änderung der Prozessor- oder E/A-Architektur wäre nicht erforderlich. Auch dies ist daher eine sehr eingeschränkte Art der Parallelität, welche nur sehr spezielle Anfragen unterstützt.

Schlüsselprobleme sind die unterschiedlichen Kriterien zur Dekomposition einer komplexen Anfrage in kleinere Subaufträge und die Forderung, daß ein System zur Bearbeitung komplexer Transaktionen in der Lage sein sollte, jedes dieser Kriterien anzuwenden, abhängig sowohl von der Problemstruktur, wie auch von globalen Systemparametern. Grundsätzlich können komplexe Anfragen in kleinere Aufträge zerlegt werden, indem eine Zerteilung hinsichtlich folgender Merkmale erfolgt:

Datenabhängig: Operationen auf großen Datenmengen können als parallele Operationen auf disjunkten Teilmengen ausgeführt werden. Diesen Ansatz verwenden Teradata und - bis zu einem gewissen Grad - System R^*.

Funktionsabhängig: Eine komplexe Operation wird gewöhnlich durch Ausführung einfacherer Operationen realisiert, welche iterativ weiter zerlegt werden können. Für einige dieser Funktionen stehen eventuell spezialisierte Prozessoren zur Verfügung, beispielsweise für das Sortieren, das Suchen auf Platten oder Spezialberechnungen. Diese Zerteilung kann entweder statisch oder aber dynamisch erfolgen. Die prominentesten Vertreter dieses Ansatzes sind die Datenbankmaschinen.

Lastabhängig: In Mehrprozessorumgebungen kann die Entscheidung, was parallel auf welchem Prozessor verarbeitet werden soll lastabhängig erfolgen. Da die theoretischen Grundlagen der dynamischen Lastverteilung weitgehend fehlen, existieren diesbezüglich nur sehr wenige Ansätze.

Abhängig von der Ebene der Implementierung: Die Ausführung einer DML-Anweisung erfolgt durch eine dynamische Abstraktion, welche die Wartung redundanter Daten wie Zugriffspfade, Protokollsätze, Kataloginformationen, etc. umfaßt. Setzt man eine geeignete Systemarchitektur voraus, kann dies bis zu einem gewissen Grad parallel, in einer der Pipeline-Technik vergleichbaren Weise, erfolgen. Dies ist die einzige Art von Parallelität, die - wenn überhaupt - in heutigen Systemen gefunden werden kann.

Offensichtlich können diese Kriterien nahezu willkürlich kombiniert werden, um die Struktur eines gegebenen Problems zu analysieren. Das Datenbanksystem selbst mag in der Lage sein, einzelne Schritte während der Bearbeitung einer DML-Anweisung parallel auszuführen. Einige dieser Schritte können hinsichtlich der Datenpartitionen parallelisiert werden. Und andererseits mag all dies Gegenstand der Anforderungen an die Lastbalancierung sein. Es

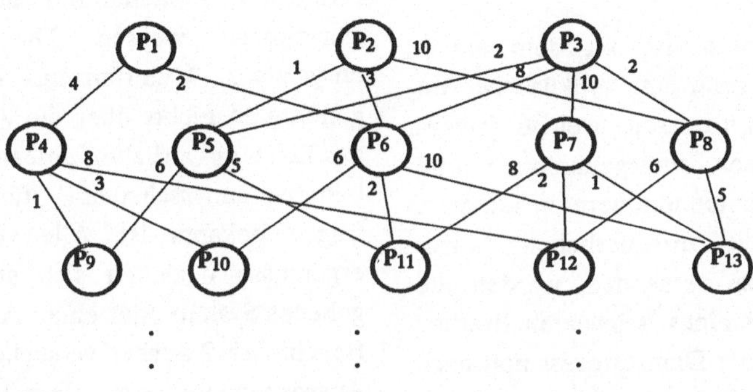

Bild 2.1: Datenstruktur der Stücklistenverarbeitung

stellt sich daher die Frage, wann welche komplexe Anfrage mittels welchen Kriteriums zerteilt werden soll.

2.2 Bestimmung probleminhärenter Parallelität

Eine generelle Antwort auf diese Frage zu geben, übersteigt sicher den Anspruch dieses Artikels. Stattdessen soll anhand eines einfachen Beispiels ein Eindruck von dem Problem und der Notwendigkeit einer Testumgebung für Parallelverarbeitung vermittelt werden.

Als Beispiel diene die klassische Stücklistenverarbeitung, welche zwar theoretisch aufgearbeitet wurde, aber von gängigen Datenbanksystemen kaum unterstützt wird. Bild 2.1 zeigt einen Auszug eines typischen Stücklistengraphen zusammen mit dem relationalen Schema. Die Bestimmung aller elementaren, d.h. nicht weiter zerlegbaren Komponenten eines gegebenen Teiles ist im Vergleich mit einer gewöhnlich Datenbankanfrage komplex. Sie erfordert den rekursiven Abstieg im Kompositionsgraph, was ein Spezialfall der transitiven Hülle ist [12]. Unter Vernachlässigung der Details rekursiver Anfragen auf Relationen, genüge eine intuitive Erläuterung, wie Parallelität bezüglich dieses Problems eingesetzt werden kann. Es existieren eine ganze Reihe möglicher Ansätze:

- Beginnend mit einem gegebenen Teil, bestimmt man dessen unmittelbare Komponenten und erzeugt parallele Aufträge zur weiteren Zerlegung derselben. Jede Komponente wird auf dieselbe Art behandelt. Dies ist ein Beispiel der Pipeline-Technik.

- Angenommen, es existieren Dienstprozesse für zusammenhängende nicht überlappende

Teilenummern, so gibt man die Eingabeteilenummer dem zuständigen Prozess. Als Ausgabe erhält man die Menge der Komponentennummern, welche wiederum an die zuständigen Prozesse gesendet werden. Der Grad der Parallelität hängt von der Verteilung der auftretenden Teilenummern ab. Dies ist ein Beispiel für datenabhängige Parallelität.

- Der nächste Ansatz ist mit dem ersten vergleichbar. Es gebe eine willkürliche Anzahl von Dienstprozessen, welche jeweils eine Teilenummer entgegennehmen und dessen Komponentennummern bestimmen. Aber anstatt die erforderlichen Folgeaufträge selbst zu versenden, werden die Nummern mittels eines "schwarzen Brettes" veröffentlicht. Jeder Dienstprozess holt nach vollendeter Bearbeitung eines Auftrags einen neuen Auftrag vom schwarzen Brett. Diese Technik ist eine Kombination von funktions- und lastabhängiger Parallelität.

Darüber hinaus gibt es noch viele weitere Möglichkeiten der parallelen Stücklistenverarbeitung. Neben den erwähnten Breadth-First-Algorithmen lassen sich auch Depth-First-Strategien einsetzen. Aber dies ist hier nicht von Bedeutung; die interessantere Frage angesichts der vielfältigen Möglichkeiten zur parallelen Berechnung einer vergleichsweise einfachen rekursiven Anfrage ist vielmehr: Wie erstellt man tatsächlich ein paralleles Programm zur Berechnung komplexer Anfragetypen und welchen Ausführungsplan wählt man basierend auf welchen Informationen? Dies beschreibt präzise, was mittels der Testumgebung für Parallelverarbeitung untersucht werden soll.

2.3 Randbedingungen einer Implementierung

Um zu bestimmen, welche Art der Parallelität hinsichtlich einer gegebenen Problemstruktur, einer Prozessorarchitektur, eines Datenbanksystems, etc., welches Maß an Leistungssteigerung ergibt, müssen alle relevanten Strategien implementiert und meßtechnisch ausgewertet werden. Dies ist ein sehr ehrgeiziges Unterfangen, da im Grunde genommen nichts über die Auswirkungen auf das Leistungsverhalten unterschiedlicher Parallelberechnungsschemata für Datenbankanfragen bekannt ist. Alle verfügbaren Meßergebnisse beziehen sich stets auf **ein** gegebenes System oder einen Anfragetyp [13] für Benchmark-Zwecke, versuchen aber nie, die Auswirkungen von Parallelität auf das Leistungsverhalten zu bestimmen.

Das Schreiben und Testen paralleler Programme ist bekanntermaßen sehr schwierig, umsomehr, wenn der parallele Algorithmus komplexe Anfragen mit irregulären Datenstrukturen beinhaltet. Eine erschöpfende Untersuchung aller unterschiedlichen paralleler Verarbeitungsschemata in unterschiedlichen Teilen des Systems erscheint daher als ein prohibitiv schwieriges Unterfangen.

Aus diesem Grunde wurde die Testumgebung für Parallelverarbeitung - im folgenden mit dem nicht sehr phantasievollen Begriff **Scheduler** bezeichnet - entworfen. Die zugrundeliegende Idee ist eine Trennung des algorithmischen Teils der Verarbeitung, d.h. der komplexen Anfrage, von der Beschreibung des parallelen Ausführungsschemas (Skript). Betrachtet man das Beispiel aus Bild 2.1, stellt man fest, daß die Einheiten der Parallelverarbeitung, unabhängig von der konkreten Strategie, stets dieselben sind: Ein gegebenes Teil wird mittels einer einfachen Datenbankoperation in seine Komponenten zerlegt. Der

Scheduler erlaubt nun die Kodierung des algorithmischen Teils des Problems als simples sequentielles Programm. Eine zusätzliche Komponente zur Beschreibung und Kontrolle des parallelen Ausführungsplans, welcher daten-, funktions- oder lastabhängig sein kann, garantiert die Flexibilität. Im nächsten Kapitel erfolgt eine kurze Beschreibung, wie diese Separierung erreicht werden kann.

3. Skripte zur Parallelverarbeitung

Es ist sehr einfach, das grundlegende Konzept der Testumgebung mittels der Analogie der Petri-Netze [14] zu verstehen. Diese sind ein formales Mittel zur Beschreibung der Dynamik asynchroner Prozeßsysteme. Es gibt aber keinen Grund, Petri-Netz-Konstrukte aus der umgekehrten Sichtweise als reale Kontrollinstanz zu verwenden. Setzt man eine Menge einfacher Dienstleistungsprozesse voraus, welche gerade die Teiloperationen der zerlegten komplexen Anfrage umfassen, so beschreibt und steuert ein Skript mit Petri-Netz-Konstrukten, wie die parallelen Prozesse die Gesamtverarbeitung leisten. Zusätzlich benötigt man daher einen Interpreter, eben gerade den Scheduler, welcher die Ausführungseinheiten tatsächlich entsprechend den Spezifikationen des Skripts startet und stoppt.

3.1 Der Scheduler - Basiskonzepte

Betrachten wir das Beispiel aus Bild 2.1 und den ersten Typ der parallelen Verarbeitung näher. Will man die ursprüngliche Anfrage zur Bestimmung der elementaren Komponenten und deren Quantitäten berechnen, so ersetzt man die Anfrage durch Subaufträge derselben Struktur für jede unmittelbare Komponente des ursprünglichen Teils. Die Subaufträge werden wiederum nach dem gleichen Prinzip ersetzt, usw. Das Programm (Dienst) welches eine dieser parallelen Berechnungen im-

plementiert, arbeitet grundsätzlich wie folgt (vgl. Bild 3.1):

- Lese die Eingabeteilenummer und stelle die Datenbankanfrage zur Bestimmung der Komponentennummern.

- Starte unmittelbar parallele Berechnungen desselben Typs für jede Komponente.

- Warte auf die rückzumeldenden Quantitäten, um das Gesamtergebnis zu bestimmen.

Es sind daher zwei Arten von Terminierungszuständen hinsichtlich dieses Programmes zu unterscheiden: Der erste Zustand drückt aus, daß ein Auftrag **berechnet** wurde, dieser aber vor seiner tatsächlichen Beendigung noch auf die Beendigung anderer Aufträge wartet. Der zweite Zustand drückt aus, daß ein Auftrag aus der Sicht abhängiger (wartender) Aufträge **beendet** ist. Die Unterscheidung dieser zwei Zustände ist im wesentlichen das, was die parallele Programmierung so schwierig gestaltet. Der Scheduler verbirgt diese Komplexität vor dem Programmierer der partiellen Berechnung und ersetzt diese durch die einheitliche und sehr einfache Notation der **Ereignisse**, deren Funktionsweise im folgenden erläutert wird.

Auftrag T führt die Datenbankanfrage aus, erhält alle Komponentennummern und erzeugt neue Aufträge mit willkürlichen Namen T_1, T_2, um dieselbe Tätigkeit auf der nächsttieferen Ebene auszuführen. Anschließend erzeugt T das bedingte Ereignis *"Ich bin berechnet, wenn T_1 und T_2 beendet sind"*. Anstatt diese Bedingungen selbst zu testen, wird die Ereignisbeschreibung an den Scheduler übergeben und die Bearbeitung des Auftrages T abgeschlossen, d.h. der entsprechende Prozeß kann einen neuen Auftrag entgegennehmen (vgl.Bild 3.2).

Der Scheduler verwaltet und überwacht alle Ereignisse. Im wesentlichen müssen beim Eintreten eines Ereignisses alle von diesem Ereig-

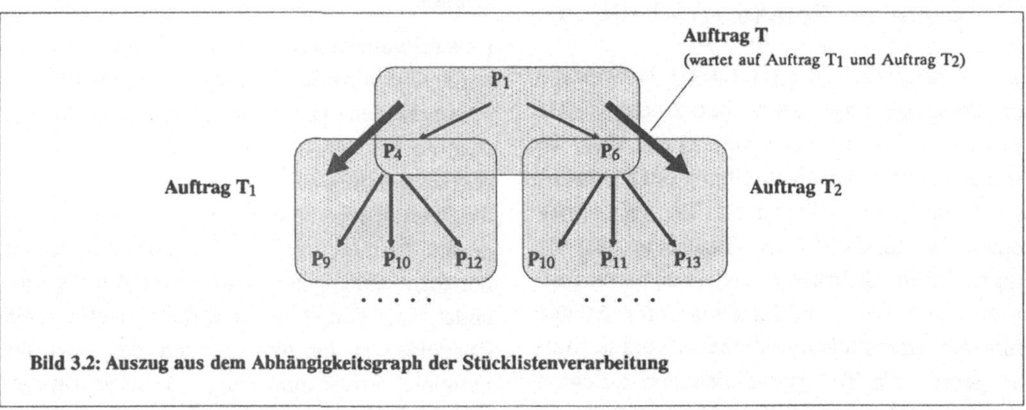

Anfrage: Bestimme alle Komponenten des Teiles P_1

<u>Auftragsstruktur:</u>
Nehme einen Auftrag entgegen;
Bestimme die Komponenten des Teils;
Erzeuge für jede Komponente einen neuen Auftrag;
Warte auf die Ergebnisse der Subaufträge;

<u>Beispiel:</u>
Auftrag T: Teil P_1
Komponente von P_1: P_4, P_6
Auftrag T_1: Teil P_4, Auftrag T_2: Teil P_6
Warte auf die Ergebnisse von Auftrag T_1 und Auftrag T_2

Bild 3.1: Auftragsstruktur der Stücklistenverarbeitung

Bild 3.2: Auszug aus dem Abhängigkeitsgraph der Stücklistenverarbeitung

nis abhängigen Aufträge gestartet bzw. logisch beendet werden. Andererseits kann ein eintretendes Ereignis andere Ereignisse eintreten lassen und damit weitere Aufträge starten. Die Basisfunktionen des Schedulers sind im einzelnen:

Define-an-Event: Hiermit erzeugt ein Auftrag (task) ein Ereignis, d.h. einen Eintrag im Scheduler, welcher einen Namen und eine Eintrittsbedingung bestehend aus Verküpfungen anderer Ereignisse besitzt. Standardereignisse wie Start- und Terminierungsereignisse werden besonders unterstützt (das Startereignis TRUE drückt beispielsweise die sofortige Ausführung eines Auftrags aus) und von beliebigen benutzerdefinierten Ereignissen unterschieden.

Define-a-Task: Hiermit kann ein Auftrag Subaufträge definieren, welche implizit an ihre Standard Start- und Terminierungsereignisse gebunden sind.

Receive-a-Task: Mittels dieser Funktion drückt ein Dienstleistungsprozess seine Bereitschaft aus, einen neuen Auftrag zu akzeptieren. Implizit ergibt sich aus einem Aufruf dieser Funktion gleichzeitig das Bearbeitungsende des vorherigen Auftrages, d.h. dieser gilt dann als beendet.

Wait-on-Event: Diese Funktion erlaubt die Suspendierung eines Programmes bis zum Eintritt eines beliebigen Ereignisses und wird von einem übergelagerten Kontrollprogramm zur Erkennung der Terminierung der Gesamtberechnung verwendet.

Modify-an-Event: Mittels dieser Funktion kann dynamisch die Eintrittsbedingung eines definierten Ereignisses geändert werden.

<table>
<tr><td>Eintrittsbedingung:</td><td>"E1 wenn E2 oder E3"</td></tr>
<tr><td>Skript:</td><td>Define-an-Event (E1, initial ^ count: 1)
Define-an-Event (E2, initial ^ count: x)
Define-an-Event (E3, initial ^ count: y)
Modify-an-Event (modified ^ event: E1, triggering ^ event: E2, count: 1)
Modify-an-Event (modified ^ event: E1, triggering ^ event: E3, count: 1)</td></tr>
<tr><td>Erläuterung:</td><td>Ereignis E1 wird mit dem Initialwert 1 des Zählers definiert, die Ereignisse E2 und E3 mit beliebigen Werten. Mittels der Funktion Modify-an-Event wird der Wert des Ereignisses E1 um den Betrag 1 dekrementiert, wenn eines der Ereignisse E2 oder E3 eintritt. E1 tritt dann ebenfalls ein, da dessen Zähler den Wert Null erreicht.</td></tr>
</table>

Bild 3.3: Skript einer disjunktiven Ereignisdefinition

Der reale Scheduler enthält eine ganze Reihe zusätzlicher Funktionen, die obigen sollten aber genügen, einen Eindruck von der Funktionsweise zu vermitteln.

3.2 Implementierungsaspekte - Die Tandem Umgebung

Die Idee der Trennung des algorithmischen Teils und des Skripts zur Steuerung des Ausführungsszenàrios, ist ein sehr allgemeines Konzept, welches im Rahmen dieses Artikels nicht diskutiert werden kann. Auch die gegenwärtige Implementierung beschränkt sich auf einen Scheduler mit einfacher Struktur, die aber mächtig genug ist, die interessantesten Fälle paralleler Ausführungsschemata zu realisieren. Die wichtigsten Vereinfachungen sind:

- Die Bedingungen für das Eintreten eines Ereignisses werden mittels Zählern ausgedrückt. Bei der Definition eines Ereignisses erhält dieser Zähler einen beliebigen positiven Wert. Bei jeder Beendigung eines Auftrages wird der Zähler des assoziierten Terminierungsereignisses implizit um den Betrag 1 dekrementiert. Explizit können die Zähler durch Aufrufe der Basisfunktion Modify-an-Event um einen bestimmten Betrag sowohl dekrementiert als auch inkre-

mentiert werden. Ist der Wert eines Zählers kleiner oder gleich Null, tritt das zugehörige Ereignis ein. Trotz dieser Einschränkung ist die Verwendung disjunktiver und konjunktiver Eintrittsbedingungen durch Ereignishierarchien möglich (siehe Bild 3.3).

- Alle Ereignisse sind permanent, d.h. ist ein Ereignis eingetreten, so wird diese Tatsache nie vergessen. Dies erscheint sehr natürlich, in einem späteren Kapitel werden aber Situationen beschrieben, in denen vergängliche oder wiederholbare Ereignisse geeigneter wären.

Da die gesamte Testumgebung als Teil des Projektes PROSPECT implementiert wurde, nutzt sie die Eigenschaften des Betriebssystems GUARDIAN [15]. Das verwendete Datenbanksystem ist NonStop SQL [16].

Die ursprüngliche Idee - welche im Kontext sehr komplexer Transaktionen noch nützlich sein könnte - sah eine Speicherung der Skripte zur Parallelverarbeitung in der Datenbank vor. Aus Effizienzgründen wurde aber entschieden, die Skripte in einer spezialisierten Speicherungsstruktur im Adressraum des Schedulers zu halten. Der Scheduler ist daher ein Prozess, wobei alle Aufrufe von Basisfunktionen der auftragsverarbeitenden Dienstleistungsprozesse mittels Nachrichten realisiert wurden - GUARDIAN ist ein nachrichtenbasiertes verteiltes Betriebssystem, welches insbesondere sehr schnelle Kontextwechsel erlaubt (ein Prozeßwechsel ist unter 500 Maschineninstruktionen möglich).

Es sei noch ein relevanter Aspekt dieses, wie auch aller konventioneller Betriebssysteme erwähnt: Da die maximal erlaubte Anzahl der Prozesse je Prozessor meist noch recht niedrig ist, ist die Notation der Terminierung einer Auftragsbearbeitung sehr hilfreich. Sobald ein Auftrag im "terminiert"-Status ist, d.h. der algorithmische Teil der Auftragsverarbeitung abgeschlossen ist und die erforderliche Ereignisverwaltung an den Scheduler übermittelt wurde, kann der Prozess für die Verarbeitung eines anderen Teiles des parallelen Ausführungsskriptes genutzt werden.

Nach der Erläuterung der Ausführungszyklen wird anhand einer massiv parallelen Anwendung die Leistungsfähigkeit des Schedulers, basierend auf konkreten Meßergebnissen belegt, und das eventuelle Argument eines nicht vertretbaren Overheads, welcher den Scheduler zum Flaschenhals werden läßt, entkräftet.

3.3 Unterstützung massiv paralleler Anwendungen

Massiv parallele Anwendungen werden durch eine sehr hohe Anzahl potentiell parallel ausführbarer Aufträge von äußerst geringem Umfang charakterisiert. Typischerweise wird ein Auftrag bei dieser Verarbeitungsform nur aus dem Lesen oder Schreiben weniger Datensätze und der Definition neuer Aufträge bestehen. Da schon erste praktische Erfahrungen mit Parallelisierungsstrategien komplexer Transaktionen zeigten, daß massiv parallele Skripte mit einfachsten Formen der Aufträge sehr häufig eindeutig zu favorisieren sind, wurde auf deren effiziente Bearbeitung durch den Scheduler bei dessen Implementierung in

besonderem Maße Wert gelegt. Die Zielsetzung war zu zeigen, daß der Scheduler auch in diesem Fall in der Lage ist, die Verarbeitung effizient zu steuern. Dies drückt sich in einer linearen Durchsatzsteigerung mit zunehmender Anzahl zur Verfügung stehender Prozessoren aus.

Es sei allerdings ausdrücklich festgehalten, daß gerade bei massiv parallelen Verarbeitungsschemata nicht der gesamte Einsatz des Schedulers als Overhead bezeichnet werden darf. Aufgrund der radikalen Reduzierung der Komplexität des gestellten Problems durch eine funktionale Zerlegung in Aufträge von einfachster Struktur, erfolgt logischerweise eine Verlagerung der probleminhärenten Komplexität in die die Ausführung kontrollierende Instanz, den Scheduler. Dieser leistet daher in hohem Maße problemspezifische Arbeit als Verwalter der gesamten dynamischen Kontrollinformation. Die Reduzierung der algorithmischen Komplexität erfolgt somit auf Kosten einer Erhöhung der Komplexität der Kontrollschemata. Als Overhead darf streng genommen nur der Anteil der Interprozeßkommunikation gelten.

Massiv parallele Anwendungen zeichnen sich gewöhnlich durch eine im voraus unvorhersehbare, aber sehr hohe Anzahl auszuführender Auftäge, ein hohes Maß **redundanter** Aufträge und ungewöhnliche Synchronisationsanforderungen aus. Neue Aufträge sind stets sofort ausführbar, d.h. nicht an Startaufträge gebunden, und unabhängig von anderen Aufträgen, insbesondere von den durch sie selbst definierten Folgeaufträgen (es existieren keine Wartebedingungen). Ein Beispiel hierfür ist die in Kapitel 4 diskutierte massiv parallele Berechnung der transitiven Hülle. Das Ende der Gesamtverarbeitung kann einerseits durch die erfolgte Verarbeitung jedes entstandenen Auftrages oder aber durch das Eintreten eines bestimmten Ereignisses (beispielsweise das Finden einer speziellen Lösung durch einen beliebig Auftrag) definiert sein. Beide Fälle werden durch entsprechende Konzepte durch den Scheduler unterstützt:

- **Wächter** ermöglichen eine Überwachung bestimmter Dienstklassen (eine Menge von Prozessen welche alle denselben Dienst zur Verfügung stellen). Ein Wächter benachrichtigt ein Programm mittels eines Ereignisses, sobald die assoziierte Klasse alle vorhandenen Aufträge bearbeitet hat (da Aufträge Folgeaufträge stets vor ihrer logischen Beendigung definieren, entstehen keine zeitlichen Abhängigkeitsprobleme, das Ende der Gesamtverarbeitung der Klasse durch einen Wächter zu erkennen).

- **Ausführungszyklen**, welche am Rande bemerkt auch die Transaktionsverwaltung umfassen und daher jede Form der Verarbeitung ähnlich der Transaktionsklammerung umschließen, dienen zur Spezifikation eines Synchronisationspunktes zu einer beliebigen Zeit während der Gesamtverarbeitung. Wird der Synchronisationspunkt, ausgelöst durch ein wohldefiniertes Ereignis, durch einen beliebigen Auftrag gefordert, so wird die Gesamtverarbeitung auf kontrollierte Weise unterbrochen. Alle bisher unsynchronisiert ablaufenden Aktivitäten werden gemäß unterschiedlicher Modi zu einer globalen Synchronisation gezwungen. Jeder Modus spezifiziert dabei, wie weitere Aufrufe von Basisfunktionen während dieser globalen Synchronisationsphase behandelt werden sollen: Werden diese akzeptiert oder ignoriert? Ist die Definition neuer Aufträge erlaubt? ... Ferner wird festgelegt, was mit bereits definierten aber noch nicht verarbeiteten Aufträgen bzw. mit Aufträgen, deren Startereignisse während der Synchronisationsphase eintreten, geschehen soll. Insgesamt steht ein Spektrum von dem "sanften Auslaufen" der Verarbeitung (nur

die Neudefinition von Aufträgen wird verhindert), bis hin zur "radikalen Unterbrechung" (die Basisfunktionen werden blockiert und nicht bearbeitete Aufträge gelöscht) zur Verfügung, was alle praktisch auftretenden Fälle abdeckt.

3.4 Nachrichtenpuffer

Zur Reduzierung des Aufwandes für die Interprozesskommunikation, wurde die Möglichkeit zur **transparenten** Verwendung von Nachrichtenpuffern realisiert. Nachrichtenpuffer beziehen sich im wesentlichen auf das Versenden von Aufträgen. Einerseits werden dabei neue Folgeaufträge gepuffert an den Scheduler übermittelt, d.h. nicht als Einzelnachrichten sondern als Paket mit einer größeren Anzahl von Aufträgen. Andererseits werden auszuführende Aufträge ebenfalls in Paketen an die Dienstleistungsprozesse übermittelt. Die optimale Paketgröße wird dynamisch mittels einfacher Heuristiken durch den Scheduler ermittelt.

Nachrichtenpuffer wurden weniger aus Effizienzgründen realisiert, vielmehr erfolgte dies, um störende Einflüsse der Interprozesskommunikation auf laufende Messungen weitestgehend zu eliminieren.

3.5 Lastbalancierung

Aus Komplexitätsgründen ist bisher nur eine sehr rudimentäre Lastbalancierungsstrategie implementiert, welche bei homogenen Aufträgen allerdings vollkommen ausreichend ist.

- Es ist garantiert, daß alle Dienstleistungsprozesse einer Klasse jeweils dieselbe Anzahl auszuführender Aufträge erhalten. Dies garantiert eine gleichmäßige Systemauslastung.

- Dienstleistungsprozesse werden nicht überlastet. Obwohl seitens des Betriebssystems die Möglichkeit besteht, mehrere Aufträge gleichzeitig asynchron an einen Prozess zu senden, welcher diese sequentiell als Einzelnachrichten in der korrekten Reihenfolge empfängt, erhält jeder Dienstprozess zu einem Zeitpunkt nur eine fest vorgebene Anzahl auszuführender Aufträge. Falls erforderlich, werden auszuführende Aufträge durch den Scheduler gepuffert. Dieser Mechanismus ermöglicht schnelle globale Synchronisationsphasen, da sich jeweils nur eine beschränkte Menge auszuführender Aufträge tatsächlich bei den Dienstprozessen befindet. Der Scheduler ist in der Lage, eine prinzipiell unbegrenzte Anzahl von Aufträgen zwischenzuspeichern. Dies erlaubt die Realisierung von Anwendungen mit explosionsartig anwachsenden Mengen ausführbarer Aufträgen.

4. Massiv parallele Berechnung der transitiven Hülle

Eine massiv parallele Berechnung der transitiven Hülle eines Graphen ist durch eine Zerlegung des Problems in Aufträge einfachster Struktur sehr leicht möglich. Vergleicht man die massiv parallele Strategie mit anderen Algorithmen, beispielsweise der sequentiellen, mengenorientierten Delta-Iteration [18], stellt man eine verblüffende Einfachheit fest.

Eine Basisrelation $GRAPH(Anfangsknoten, Endknoten)$ beschreibe alle Kanten des Graphen. Eine zweite Relation $HÜLLE(Von, Nach)$ diene zur Speicherung der zu berechnenden transitiven Hülle. Zur Erläuterung der zugrundeliegenden Idee sei die Struktur der Einzelaufträge vorab definiert:

Jeder Auftrag besteht aus einem Startknoten K_s und einem aktuellen Knoten K_a. Das Paar (K_s, K_a) drückt aus, daß die Knoten K_s und K_a durch einen transitiven Kantenzug verbunden sind. Gegenstand der Auftragsverarbeitung ist nun die Bestimmung aller direkten Nachfolger K_i des Knotens K_a durch einen einfachen Zugriff auf die Relation $GRAPH$. Für jeden Nachfolger wird ein Tupel der Form (K_s, K_i) in die Relation $HÜLLE$ geschrieben, da K_s mit K_i verbunden ist. Scheitert dieser Versuch, d.h. existiert bereits ein Tupel (K_s, K_i) wird der Knoten K_i aus der Menge der gefundenen Nachfolger gestrichen. Für alle erfolgreich eingetragenen Nachfolger K_i wird abschließend ein neuer Auftrag zur weiteren Evaluierung definiert. Damit ist die Bearbeitung des Auftrages vollständig abgeschlossen. Es bestehen im Sinne des definierten Terminierungsbegriffs keinerlei Abhängigkeiten zu den Folgeaufträgen. Jeder Auftrag wird *isoliert* bearbeitet.

Die Gesamtverarbeitung wird durch die Definition eines Auftrages der Form (K_s, K_s) für jeden Knoten K_s des Graphen gestartet und endet mit der Verarbeitung des letzten definierten Folgeauftrages (das Ende wird mit einem Wächter erkannt). Da der Graph endlich ist, d.h. nur aus einer endlichen Menge von Ausgangsknoten und Kanten besteht, endet die Verarbeitung. Daß die vollständige transitive Hülle berechnet wird, ist aufgrund des Algorithmus' unmittelbar einleuchtend.

Je nach Größe des Graphen entsteht schon beim Start der Berechnung eine relativ große Anzahl auszuführender Aufträge und je nach Vernetzungsgrad sehr schnell sehr viele Folgeaufträge. Das Maß der Redundanz ist beträchtlich.

4.1 Leistungsmessungen

Grundlage der Leistungsbewertung des Schedulers bildete die massiv parallele Berechnung der transitiven Hülle. Dieses extreme Beispiel eignet sich aufgrund folgender Eigenschaften besonders, die an den Scheduler gestellten Anforderungen zu überprüfen.

Antwortzeit [sec]	Berechnungsart
1385	<u>Delta-Iteration</u> sequentiell
1260	<u>Massiv parallel</u> zentrale Datenbank 1 Prozessor 1 Dienstprozess "sequentielle" Variante
455	<u>Massiv parallel</u> partitionierte Datenbank 2 Prozessoren 8 Dienstprozesse

Tabelle 4.1: Meßergebnisse

Einerseits handelt es sich bei der Hüllenberechnung um eine komplexe Datenbankanwendung, d.h. es wird das Zusammenspiel mit dem Datenbanksystem mitberücksichtigt. Andererseits werden durch die sehr hohe Anzahl auszuführender Aufträge die Kontrollmechanismen des Schedulers heftig beansprucht. Damit ist eine fundierte Leistungsbewertung möglich.

Die Messungen wurden zum Teil im *High Performance Research Center* von Tandem Computers in Frankfurt ausgeführt.

Tabelle 4.1 vermittelt einen ersten Eindruck von der Leistungsfähigkeit des Konzeptes. Diese Meßserie wird durch folgende Parameter beschrieben:

– **Mengengerüst:** Die Basisrelation *GRAPH* beinhaltete 303 Datensätze (Kanten). Dies entsprach 101 unterschiedlichen Knoten mit durchschnittlich 3 Nachfolgern. Die Hülle dieses Graphen besteht aus 13736 Datensätzen (Pfaden). Es wurde bewußt eine relativ kleine Datenmenge gewählt, einerseits um Einflüsse physikalischer E/A vor-

erst noch auszuschließen - diese würden eine erste Interpretation der Ergebnisse unnötig erschweren - und andererseits um die Laufzeiten der Einzelberechnungen zu begrenzen, da der Gesamtumfang der Meßserien beträchtlich war.

– **Konfiguration 1:** Es wurden zwei Prozessoren mit jeweils 4 Dienstprozessen (diese Anzahl erwies sich als optimal) verwendet. Eine Besonderheit des Betriebssystems GUARDIAN ist die feste Zuordnung jeder Platte zu einem *Plattenprozess* und damit zu einem Prozessor. Um jeden Prozessor mit gleichen E/A-Anteilen zu belasten, wurde die Datenbank partitioniert, d.h. je eine Partition der Relationen *GRAPH* und *HÜLLE* je einem Prozessor zugeordnet.

– **Vergleichskriterien:** Als Vergleichsgrundlage wurden zwei weitere Berechnungsvarianten ausgewählt. Zum einen ist dies eine sequentielle Berechnung der transitiven Hülle mittels der Delta-Iteration (**Variante 1**). Im Gegensatz zu der massiv parallelen Berechnung, verwendet die Delta-Iteration eine mengenorientierte Strategie und belastet damit die Datenbank stärker. Zum anderen wurde die massiv parallele Variante durch die Verwendung einer zentralen, d.h. nicht partitionierten Datenbank, eines einzigen Dienstprozesses zur Verarbeitung der Aufträge und nur eines Prozessors "sequentialisiert" (**Variante 2**).

– **Ergebnisse:** Die parallele Berechnung weist eine Leistungssteigerung um den Faktor 3.0 gegenüber Variante 1 (Delta-Iteration) und Faktor 2.8 gegenüber Variante 2 (sequentialisierte Berechnung) auf. Ferner konnte eine nahezu 100%ige Auslastung beider Prozessoren bei der parallelen Berechnung verifiziert werden. Ein interessanter Aspekt ist der Anteil der redundanten Aufträge bei der parallelen Version: ca 70% aller

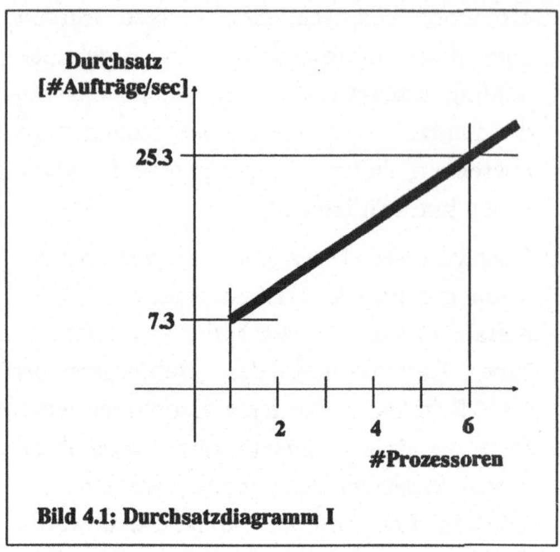

Bild 4.1: Durchsatzdiagramm I

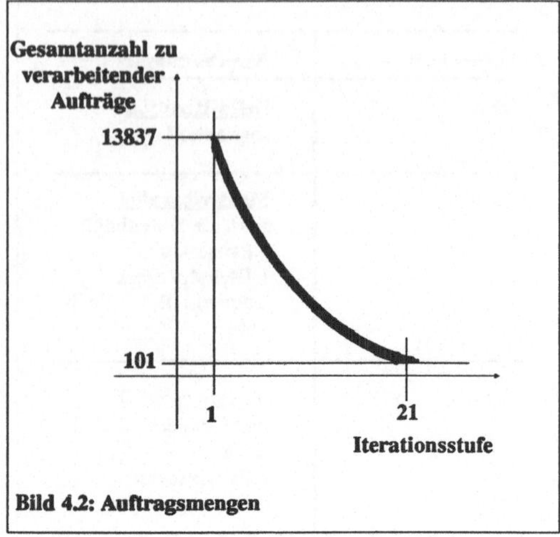

Bild 4.2: Auftragsmengen

Aufträge sind redundant und damit nutzlos! Versuche, diesen Anteil durch geeignete Mechanismen bei der Auftragsverarbeitung zu reduzieren, ergaben schlechtere Antwortzeiten. Die Duplikateliminierung über das Datenbanksystem erwies sich stets als effizienter.

Nachdem die grundsätzliche Funktionsfähigkeit des Schedulers nachgewiesen war, blieb noch, dessen Verhalten bei einer höheren Anzahl zur Verfügung stehender Prozessoren zu beobachten.

– **Konfiguration 2:** Bei dieser Meßreihe wurde für den Scheduler ein privater Prozessor reserviert. Abgesehen von dieser Änderung wurde wie bei Konfiguration 1 jedem Prozessor je eine Partition der Datenbank und 4 Dienstprozesse zugeordnet.

Bild 4.1 zeigt das Resultat: Die Durchsatzsteigerung, definiert in berechneten Aufträgen pro Sekunde, ist linear mit steigender Anzahl verwendeter Prozessoren. Auch in diesem Fall konnte eine nahezu 100%ige Prozessorauslastung beobachtet werden.

Damit ist bestätigt, daß der Scheduler selbst bei massiv parallelen Datenbankanwendungen nicht zum Flaschenhals wird und daher in der Lage ist alle Arten paralleler Skripte effizient zu realisieren.

4.2 Spezielle Meßreihen

Eine weitere Meßreihe untersuchte den Einfluß der Nachrichtenpuffer. Um die Anzahl der auszuführenden Aufträge, und damit auch die Gesamtanzahl an Nachrichten, leicht variieren zu können, wurde der Berechnungsalgorithmus geringfügig erweitert: Jeder Auftrag bestimmt nun nicht mehr nur die direkten Nachfolger eines Knotens, sondern alle Nachfolger bis zu einem spezifizierten Wert, der **Iteratiosstufe**. Algorithmisch ändert sich durch diesen "Trick" nichts, d.h. insbesondere die Anzahl der Zugriffe auf die Datenbank bleibt unverändert. Bild 4.2 zeigt die Abhängigkeit der Anzahl zu verarbeitender Aufträge von der verwendeten Iterationsstufe. Dabei ist ab Iterationsstufe 21 die Gesamtanzahl der Aufträge gleich der Anzahl der Knoten des Graphen (101). Diese Meßreihe wurde in Konfiguration 1 durchgeführt. Bild 4.3 zeigt das Resultat: Bei sehr niederer Iterationsstufe ist die Nachrichtenpufferung notwendig, um störende Einflüsse des Schedulers zu vermeiden.

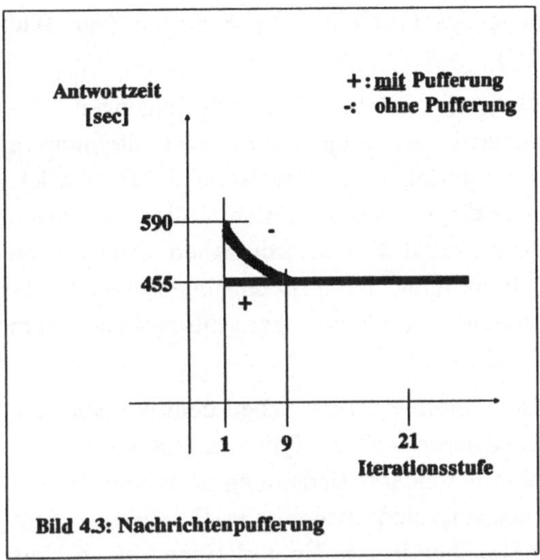

Bild 4.3: Nachrichtenpufferung

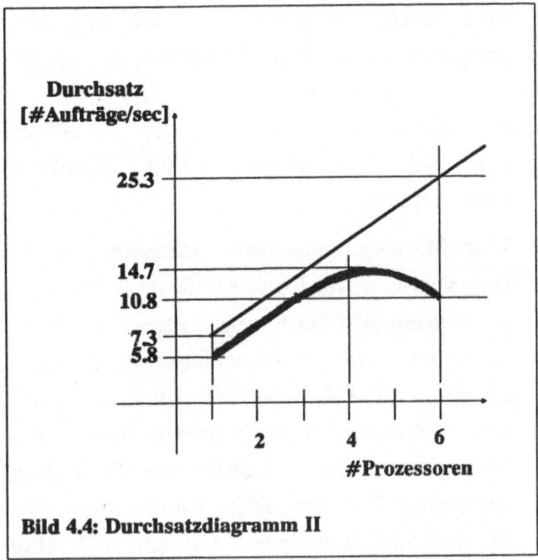

Bild 4.4: Durchsatzdiagramm II

Bei einer letzten Meßreihe wurde bewußt ein Flaschenhals eingebaut: die parallele Berechnung geschah auf einer zentralen Datenbank. Alle Datenzugriffe werden nun über einen Prozessor abgewickelt. Abgesehen von dieser Änderung wurde Konfiguration 2 verwendet. Bild 4.4 zeigt das erwartete Verhalten: Mit zunehmender Anzahl verwendeter Prozessoren flacht die Durchsatzsteigerung zuerst ab und fällt schließlich unter den erzielten Maximalwert. Dies ist die Folge eines sich vor dem zentralen Plattenprozeß bildenden Konvois, bestehend aus sequentiell zu bearbeiteten E/A-Operationen. Übersteigt die Auftragsrate die maximale Durchsatzrate des Plattenprozesses, entsteht der Konvoi.

4.3 Weitere Einsatzgebiete des Schedulers

Die in diesem Kapitel untersuchte Anwendung der massiv parallelen Hüllenberechnung, diente im wesentlichen nur zu einer Leistungsbewertung des Schedulers. Denkbar ist eine Anwendung als spezieller Rekursionsoperator auf Relationen, da klassische relationale Datenbanksysteme keine Mittel zur Formulierung rekursiver Anfragen besitzen.

Allgemein dient der Scheduler als Testumgebung zur flexiblen Implementierung beliebiger komplexer Transaktionen. Im wesentlichen sollen dabei unterschiedliche Parallelisierungsstrategien bezüglich ihrer Effizienz beurteilt werden. Momentan werden im Rahmen des Projektes PROSPECT folgende Gebiete bearbeitet:

- **Parallelisierungsstrategien in SQL:** Untersucht werden u.a. parallele Selektionen und Projektionen, parallele Zugriffe auf Datenpartitionen und parallelisierte Strategien der Verbundberechnung (Hash-Joins, horizontale und vertikale Partitionierung von Mehrfachverbunden).

- **Deduktive Datenbanksysteme:** Ziel ist die Implementierung einer Deduktionskomponente auf einem SQL-Datenbanksystem. Die Regeln der zugrundeliegenden Logiksprache, werden in einer Zwischendarstellung auf Rule/Goal-Graphen [23] abgebildet. Der Deduktionsmechanismus basiert auf einer dynamischen Zerlegung des Graphen in Teilbäume und deren Abbildung auf SQL-Anweisungen. Jede Anfrage wird durch eine parallele Ausführung der entsprechenden SQL-Anweisungen gelöst. Untersucht werden die Einflüsse unterschiedlicher Abbildungsstrategien (Umfang der SQL-Anweisungen) und Parallelisierungsschemata.

- **Modellierung komplexer Beziehungen in Datenbanken:** Im Rahmen diese Teilprojektes werden Abbildungsmethoden komplexer Strukturen, wie sie in technischen Anwendungen, im CAD-Bereich und in regelbasierten Systemen vorkommen, auf Datenbanken untersucht. Neben der Definition geeigneter Datenmodelle, welche eine Abbildung der komplexen Objekte auf eine relationale Datenbank erlauben, wird eine Anfragesprache zur Modifikation der Objekte entwickelt. Die effiziente Realisierung der Modifikationsoperatoren basiert im wesentlichen auf vielfältigen Parallelisierungsstrategien.

5. Ausblick

Obwohl die Basismechanismen des Schedulers eine große Vielfalt möglicher Kontrollflüsse bieten, liegen einige Ideen zur Erweiterung und Verbesserung der Flexibilität des Modells vor.

5.1 Flexiblere Ereignisdefinitionen

Die Beschränkung der Eintrittsbedingungen von Ereignissen auf Zähler ist an vielen Stellen recht hinderlich. Folgendes Beispiel soll dies verdeutlichen.

Bild 5.1 zeigt einen einfachen Abhängigkeitsgraphen. Die Erstellung eines entsprechenden Skripts unter Wahrung des maximalen Parallelitätsgrades (T3, T4 und T5 parallel) ist recht mühselig (vgl. Bild 5.2). Wären konjunktive Eintrittsbedingungen erlaubt, wäre eine Lö-

sung des Problems weit einfacher (vgl. Bild 5.3).

Generell wären Eintrittsbedingungen bestehend aus konjunktiven oder disjunktiven Normalformen von Einzelereignissen nützlich. Allerdings wird durch die steigende Komplexität der erforderlichen dynamischen Überprüfung dieser Bedingungen eine Realisierung aus Leistungsgesichtspunkten kaum möglich sein.

Des weiteren sollten neben dem permanenten Ereignistyp weitere Typen angeboten werden. Von besonderer Bedeutung in diesem Zusammenhang sind **dynamische** Ereignisse. Diese treten bei jedem Überschreiten des Zählers des Wertes Null ein und lösen alle abhängigen Aktivitäten wiederholt aus. Damit wird eine einfache Beschreibung von Standardaktivitäten ohne jeweils erforderliche Neudefinition der beteiligten Ereignisse und Aufträge möglich. **Vergängliche** Ereignisse lösen bei ihrem Eintreten einmalig alle abhängigen Aktionen aus, ihre Defintion erlischt aber mit dem Eintreten.

5.2 Rücksetzbare Ereignisse

In der gegenwärtigen Implementierung wird ausschließlich das konventionelle Transaktionsparadigma unterstützt. D.h. es stehen nur flache Transaktionen zur Sicherung komplexer zeitraubender Berechnungen zur Verfügung. Als Konsequenz kann im Fehlerfall nur die Gesamttransaktion zurückgesetzt werden, was in vielen Situationen nicht toleriert werden kann. Stattdessen sollte das Rücksetzen kleinerer Einheiten möglich sein, da oft die Möglichkeit zur Beendigung der Transaktion auf einem anderen Weg besteht. Benötigt wird daher ein Konzept zur Realisierung geschachtelter Transaktionen [17] angewandt auf die Ereignis- und Auftragskonzepte des Schedulers. Es sollte die Möglichkeit bestehen,

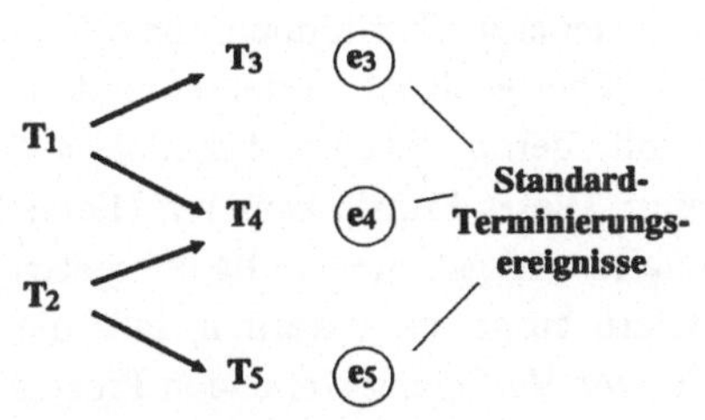

Bild 5.1: Abhängigkeitsgraph

Define-an-event (e_{34}, init ^ cnt: 2)
Define-an-event (e_{45}, init ^ cnt: 2)
Modify-an-event (mod ^ ev: e_{34}, cnt: 1, trigg ^ ev: e_3)
Modify-an-event (mod ^ ev: e_{34}, cnt: 1, trigg ^ ev: e_4)
Modify-an-event (mod ^ ev: e_{45}, cnt: 1, trigg ^ ev: e_4)
Modify-an-event (mod ^ ev: e_{45}, cnt: 1, trigg ^ ev: e_5)
Define-a-task (T_1, trigg-ev: e_{34})
Define-a-task (T_2, trigg-ev: e_{45})
Define-a-task (T_3, trigg-ev: true, term ^ ev: e_3)
Define-a-task (T_4, trigg-ev: true, term ^ ev: e_4)
Define-a-task (T_5, trigg-ev: true, term ^ ev: e_5)

Erläuterung:
init ^ cnt ... initial count
mod ^ ev ... modified event
trigg ^ ev ... triggering event
term ^ ev ... termination event

Bild 5.2: Zugehöriges Skript

Define-a-task (T_1, trigg-ev: e_3 and e_4)
Define-a-task (T_2, trigg-ev: e_4 and e_5)
Define-a-task (T_3, trigg-ev: true)
Define-a-task (T_4, trigg-ev: true)
Define-a-task (T_5, trigg-ev: true)

Bild 5.3: Erweitertes Skript

gezielt alle durch ein bestimmtes Ereignis ausgelösten Aufträge rückzusetzen. Diese Aufträge könnten allerdings zwischenzeitlich weitere Ereignisse ausgelöst haben, welche nun ebenfalls zurückgesetzt werden müssen. Praktisch erfordert die Rücksetzung eines Ereignisses daher die Kompensierung ganzer Serien von Aufträgen in der korrekten Reihenfolge und die Wiederherstellung aller beteiligten Ereignisse.

5.3 Automatische Generierung der Skripte

Wie das Beispiel aus den Bildern 5.1 bis 5.3 zeigt, kann die Erstellung eines Skriptes sehr schnell unübersichtlich und fehleranfällig werden. Es ist daher geplant einen Übersetzer zu entwickeln, welcher zumindest eine halbautomatische Generierung von Skripten, basierend auf geeignet erweiterten Abhängigkeitsgraphen leistet.

Parallel dazu werden Werkzeuge entwickelt, welche eine Analyse der durch den Scheduler erzeugbaren Protokolldatei ermöglichen. Die Protokolldatei enthält Protokollsätze für jede Aktivität des Schedulers. Mittels der Analyse sollten Standardfehler in Skripten, wie beispielsweise die Erzeugung von Deadlocks oder zu einem falschen Zeitpunkt ausgelöste Aktivitäten, leicht bestimmbar sein [22].

5.4 Inhaltsbezogene Lastbalancierung und Auftragsverteilung

Die rein auf der Anzahl auszuführender Aufträge basierende rudimentäre Lastbalancierung sollte inhaltsbezogen erweitert werden. Der Scheduler wählt, basierend auf einer geeigneten Beschreibung eines Auftrages hinsichtlich dessen Ressourcenbedarfs, einen geeigneten Dienstleistungsprozeß der angegebenen Klasse aus. Diese Auswahl muß vorausschauend unter zusätzlicher Berücksichtigung globaler Systemparameter und aktueller Lastmessungen geschehen, vorausgesetzt sie soll wirksam sein.

Zur effizienten Realisierung weiterer Kooperationsstrukturen, muß die inhaltsabhängige Auftragsvergabe auch durch den Anwender selbst möglich sein, d.h. durch den Programmierer der partiellen Funktionen. Das Klassenprinzip der Dienstprozesse, jeder Prozess einer Klasse ist gleichwertig, ist oft nicht ausreichend. Die kontextfreie Programmierung der Dienstprozesse kann zu einschränkend sein, da eine gezielte Vergabe eines Auftrages an einen ganz bestimmten Prozess, der beispielsweise gewisse Vorarbeiten nicht mehr leisten müßte, nicht möglich ist.

5.5 Verteilte Version

Die in Kapitel 4 belegte Leistungsfähigkeit des Schedulers für Systeme mit mehreren Prozessoren und einer Vielzahl von Prozessen gilt natürlicherweise nur bis zu einer bestimmten Grenze. Die lineare Durchsatzsteigerung, welche in einem vollständig ausgebauten System von Tandem mit 16 Prozessoren noch möglich ist, wird bei einer noch höheren Anzahl sehr schnell ein Ende finden. Eine verteilte Version des Schedulers soll diese Problematik, ebenso wie eine Verteilung auf ein heterogenes Rechnernetz lösen.

Entwickelt wird ein Konzept **hierarchischer Scheduler**. Die Menge der zu Verfügung stehenden Prozessoren wird partitioniert, wobei Systemgrenzen möglichst nicht überschritten werden sollten und die Partitionsgröße auf das Leistungsverhalten eines Schedulerprozesses abgestimmt ist. Jeder Partition wird ein lokaler Scheduler zugeordnet, dessen Funktionsweise dem bisherigen Konzept entspricht. Jeder lokale Scheduler kann Dienste anderer Partitionen beanspruchen, indem er über geeignet zu definierende Protokolle mit deren lokalen Schedulern kommuniziert. Dieses Prinzip kann auf Hierarchien von lokalen und ggf. mehrstufig übergelagerten Schedulern ausgeweitet werden, falls die Anzahl der zur Verfügung stehenden Prozessoren sehr groß ist. In diesem Zusammenhang wird hauptsächlich die Problematik einer globalen Lastverteilung von entscheidender Bedeutung sein.

6. Schlußbemerkungen

Im Rahmen dieses Artikels wurde versucht, die grundlegenden Ideen einer Testumgebung zur flexiblen Beschreibung und Ausführung paralleler Verarbeitungsschemata in komplexen Datenbanktransaktionen zu vermitteln. Die Eignung der Umgebung für unterschiedlichste parallele Strategien wird durch eine Trennung des algorithmischen Teils der zu realisierenden Funktion von dem Skript, welches die Art der Parallelität beschreibt, erreicht. Ein großer Vorteil des Ansatzes ist das Verbergen von Parallelität, Asynchronität, etc. vor dem Programmierer, der die Komponenten einer komplexen Transaktion implementiert.

Dieser Ansatz kann in einem weiten Gebiet paralleler und verteilter Systeme hilfreich sein. Die Leistungsfähigkeit wurde an dem extremen Beispiel der massiv parallelen Berechnung transitiver Hüllen, d.h. spezieller Rekursionsoperatoren auf Datenbankrelationen, nachgewiesen. Des weiteren liegen positive Erfahrungen bei der halbautomatischen Erstellung von parallelen Ausführungsplänen in deduktiven Datenbanksysemen, der Stücklistenverarbeitung und der internen Parallelisierung von SQL vor.

Es wurde eine Anzahl notwendiger Erweiterungen der derzeitigen Version erläutert, welche in absehbarer Zukunft die Möglichkeit zur Realisierung und Bewertung geschachtelter Transaktionen oder anderer verallgemeinerter Transaktionsmodelle mit den Mittel der parallelen Testumgebung ermöglichen.

7. Literatur

[1]   Gray, Jim; The Transaction Concept: Virtues and Limitations, VLDB 81, Cannes, 1981

[2]   IEEE Transactions On Computers, special issue on database machines, Vol. C-28, No. 6, 1979

[3]   Proc. of the Kiawah Workshop on Expert Database Systems, South Carolina, 1984

[4]   Proc. of the Asilomar Workshop on High Performance Transaction Systems, Asilomar, 1985

[5]   Reuter, A.; Duppel, N.; Peinl, P.; Schiele, G.; Zeller, H.; An Outlook on PROSPECT, University of Stuttgart, 1986

[6]   Hillis, D.; The Connection Machine, MIT Press, 1985

[7]   Härder, T.; Reuter, A.; Concepts for Implementing a Centralized Database Management System, Proc. ICS Nuernberg, Teubner Verlag, pp28-59, 1983

[8]   Williams, R.; R*: An Overview of the Architecture, Proc. Int. Conference on Database Systems, Jerusalem, 1982

[9]   Gerber, R.; DeWitt, D.; The Impact of Hardware and Software Alternatives on the Performance of the Gamma Database Machine, University of Wisconsin-Madison, Computer Sciences Department Technical Report #708, 1987

[10] Kuespert, K.; Dadam, P.; Guenauer, J.; Cooperative Object Buffer Management in the Advanced Information Management Prototype, Proc. Of VLDB 1987, Brighton, 1987

[11] Neches, P.; The Anatomy of a Database Computer System, spring COMPCON, San Francisco, 1985

[12] Dayal, U.; Smith, J.; PROBE: A Knowledge-Oriented DBMS, Proc. Islamorada Workshop on Large Scale Knowledge Base and Reasoning Systems, 1985

[13] DeWitt, D.; Smith, M.; Boral H.; A Single-User Performance Evaluation of the Teradata Database Machine, Proc. 2nd International Workshop on High Performance Transaction Systems, Asilomar, Oct. 1987

[14] Genrich, H.; Lautenbach, K.; System Modelling with High-Level Petri Nets, Theoretical Computer Science, Vol. 13, 1981

[15] System Description Manual, Tandem Computers Inc., Cupertino, CA, 1985

[16] Introduction to NonStop SQL, Tandem Computers Inc., Cupertino, CA, 1987

[17] Haerder, T.; Rothermel, K.; Concepts for Transaction Recovery in Nested Transactions, SIGMOD 87, San Francisco, pp239-248, 1987

[18] Duppel, N., Peinl, P., Schiele, G., Zeller, H.; Progress Report #1 of PROSPECT, University of Stuttgart, 1987

[19] Duppel, N., Peinl, P., Schiele, G., Zeller, H.; Progress Report #2 of PROSPECT, University of Stuttgart, 1987

[20] Duppel, N., Schiele, G., Zeller, H.; Progress Report #3 of PROSPECT, University of Stuttgart, 1988

[21] Härder, T.; Reuter, A.; Database Systems for Non-Standard-Applications, Proc. ICS 1983, pp. 452-466

[22] Zuse, K.; Petri-Netze, Braunschweig, Vieweg, 1980

[23] Ullman, J.; Implementation of Logical Query Languages for Databases, ACM Transactions on Database Systems, Vol. 10, No. 3, pp289-321, 1985

Sperren disjunkter, nicht-rekursiver komplexer Objekte mittels objekt- und anfragespezifischer Sperrgraphen

U. Herrmann[1,2], P. Dadam[1], K. Küspert[1], G. Schlageter[2]

[1] Wissenschaftliches Zentrum Heidelberg der IBM,
Tiergartenstr. 15, 6900 Heidelberg

[2] FernUniversität Hagen, Praktische Informatik I,
Postfach 940, 5800 Hagen

Überblick

Die Benutzung von Datenbanksystemen im Bereich der sogenannten Nicht-Standard-Anwendungen wie etwa CAD/CAM, Robotik und Künstliche Intelligenz führt zu zahlreichen neuen Anforderungen. Dazu zählen vor allem die Verwaltung komplexer Objekte und die Unterstützung von Workstation-Server-Umgebungen mit den dort vorherrschenden langen Transaktionen. Traditionelle Synchronisationsverfahren für den Mehrbenutzerbetrieb weisen im Hinblick auf diese Anforderungen gravierende Nachteile auf: Entweder werden Transaktionen, die eigentlich parallel ablaufen könnten, unnötigerweise serialisiert, oder aber der systeminterne Aufwand für die Mehrbenutzerkontrolle steigt drastisch an, was sich auf das gesamte Systemverhalten einer Anwendung stark leistungsmindernd auswirken kann.

In der vorliegenden Arbeit wird ein neuartiges, aus dem bekannten DAG-Sperrverfahren von System R abgeleitetes Synchronisationsverfahren vorgeschlagen, das diese Nachteile traditioneller Techniken vermeidet. Das vorgestellte Verfahren erlaubt bei akzeptablem Aufwand einen hohen Grad an Parallelität auf disjunkten, nicht-rekursiven komplexen Objekten. Dies wird durch die Verwendung von angepaßten Sperrgranulaten innerhalb der Struktur von komplexen Objekten und durch die Vorwegnahme von Sperreskalationen erreicht. Sperrgranulate innerhalb der Struktur komplexer Objekte spiegeln sich in objektspezifischen Sperrgraphen wider; die Vorwegnahme von Sperreskalationen zeigt sich im sogenannten anfragespezifischen Sperrgraphen. Die Größe der zu sperrenden Granulate und die entsprechenden Sperrmodi werden mit Hilfe von Informationen über die Struktur der berührten komplexen Objekte automatisch so aus einer Anfrage abgeleitet, daß der Durchsatz des Datenbanksystems möglichst hoch zu werden verspricht. Der Nutzen dieses Verfahrens wird zunächst qualitativ bewertet und anschließend anhand eines konkreten Zahlenbeispiels genauer quantifiziert.

Abstract

The use of database systems in the fields of so-called non-standard applications like CAD/CAM, robotics, and artificial intelligence leads to many new requirements. Some of the most important ones are the support of complex objects and of workstation-server environments with long transactions. With regard to these requirements traditional techniques for concurrency control reveal some severe drawbacks: Either transactions are serialized unnecessarily or the overhead for concurrency control grows drastically which reduces the performance of the whole system.

In this paper a new technique for concurrency control is proposed which is derived from the well-known DAG-locking mechanism of System R. The proposed technique avoids the disadvantages of traditional methods. With acceptable overhead a high degree of parallelism is achieved on disjoint, non-recursive complex objects. This is attained by the use of appropriate locking granules within the structure of complex objects and by the anticipation of lock escalations. Lock granules within the structure of complex objects are represented in the object-specific lock graphs; the query-specific lock graphs show the anticipation of lock escalations. The size of the lock granules and the corresponding lock modes are derived automatically from a query by using information about the structure of the complex objects. This is done in a way that the throughput of the whole system is expected to be as high as possible. The benefits of the proposed technique are first evaluated qualitatively and then demonstrated by using a concrete numerical example.

1 Einleitung

Herkömmliche Datenbanksysteme sind in erster Linie für den Einsatz im administrativ-betriebswirtschaftlichen Bereich ausgelegt. Die Entwicklung im Datenbankbereich geht jedoch in den letzten Jahren immer mehr dahin, daß ein Datenbanksystem auch sogenannte Nicht-Standard-Anwendungen wie CAD/CAM, Robotik, Künstliche Intelligenz usw. unterstützen soll [BlPi85, ScSc87, Ditt88, Lutt88]. Die Benutzung von Datenbanken im Bereich der Nicht-Standard-Anwendungen führt zu zahlreichen neuen Anforderungen. Zu den wichtigsten zählen die Verwaltung von *komplexen Objekten* und die Unterstützung von *Workstation-Server-Umgebungen* mit *langen Transaktionen* [HaLo82, LoPl83, BaBu84, Lori85, KDG87, HHMM88].

Das Konzept der *komplexen Objekte* erlaubt es Benutzern einer Datenbank, viele "flache", d.h. einfach strukturierte Objekte (meist als 'Tupel' bezeichnet) als eine Einheit mit einer bestimmten Struktur zu betrachten und als Ganzes zu bearbeiten (strukturelle, operationale und verhaltensmäßige Objektorientierung im Sinne von [Ditt86, KWD88]). In der vorliegenden Arbeit wird ein Datenmodell zugrunde gelegt, das disjunkte, nicht-rekursive komplexe Objekte (d.h. hierarchisch strukturierte komplexe Objekte) unterstützt. Ein Beispiel für ein solches Datenmodell ist das NF^2-Datenmodell [JaSc82, ScSc86]. Durch das Konzept der komplexen Objekte und deren Realisierung im Datenbanksystem wird die Verarbeitung der für Nicht-Standard-Anwendungen typischen Objekte (komplex strukturierte Konstruktionsdaten usw.) aus Benutzersicht wesentlich vereinfacht und auch systemseitig beschleunigt, da sich dem Datenbanksystem interne Optimierungsmöglichkeiten verschiedenster Art eröffnen [Härd88].

Eine *Transaktion* stellt in der vorliegenden Arbeit - wie im Datenbankbereich üblich - die Einheit für die Konsistenzerhaltung der Daten dar. Diese Arbeit geht davon aus, daß ein Datenbanksystem dafür zu sorgen hat, daß mehrfaches Lesen derselben Daten innerhalb einer Transaktion zu demselben Ergebnis führt (Konsistenzebene 3) [GLPT76]. Transaktionen im administrativ-betriebswirtschaftlichen Bereich sind i.d.R. *kurz*, d.h. ihre Dauer liegt im Bereich von Sekunden oder maximal Minuten. In Nicht-Standard-Anwendungen, z.B. beim Design-Prozeß eines Chips, können Transaktionen dagegen u.U. Tage oder Wochen dauern. Solche *langen Transaktionen* [KLMP84, KSUW85] müssen beispielsweise auch Systemzusammenbrüche aller Art und Systemabschaltungen überleben. In diesen Umgebungen stößt das klassische Transaktionskonzept an seine Grenzen. Der Begriff des *Benutzers* oder der *conversational transaction* [LoPl83] ist besser geeignet als der der klassischen Transaktion. In der vorliegenden Arbeit wird von *kurzen Transaktionen* gesprochen, wenn es sich um klassische Transaktionen auf der zentralen Datenbank handelt, und von *langen Transaktionen*, wenn Benutzer auf Workstations gemeint sind. Neben den vorherrschenden langen Transaktionen gibt es aber im Bereich der Nicht-Standard-Anwendungen nach wie vor auch kurze Transaktionen (etwa zum Ad-hoc-Zugriff auf einzelne Daten oder für statistische Auswertungen), die ebenfalls vom System in geeigneter Weise unterstützt werden müssen. Ein Datenbanksystem, das den Anspruch erhebt, für Nicht-Standard-Anwendungen geeignet zu sein, muß somit sowohl komplexe Objekte als auch lange (und kurze) Transaktionen unterstützen.

In Nicht-Standard-Anwendungen ist es zudem oft wünschenswert, daß verschiedene Benutzer oder Benutzergruppen die Möglichkeit haben, komplexe Objekte aus der zentralen Datenbank auf *Arbeitsplatzrechner*, d.h. *Workstations*, auszulagern ("Check-Out"). Bei diesen Arbeitsplatzrechnern kann es sich z.B. um Graphik-Workstations im Konstruktionsbereich o.ä. handeln. Die ausgelagerten Daten stellen - zumindest vorübergehend - private, lokale Datenbanken dar. Auf Workstations geänderte Daten können nach Abschluß der Änderungen wieder in die zentrale Datenbank eingebracht werden ("Check-In"). Heutzutage arbeiten oft verschiedene Arbeitsgruppen unabhängig voneinander mit ihren privaten Datenbanken. Geeignete Maßnahmen müssen sicherstellen, daß sich die privaten Datenbanken untereinander und im Vergleich zur zentralen Datenbank immer in einem konsistenten oder zumindest wohldefinierten Zustand befinden. Speziell unter dem Gesichtspunkt der Synchronisation langer Transaktionen auf komplexen Objekten weisen jedoch traditionelle Techniken der Mehrbenutzerkontrolle einige gravierende Nachteile auf.

Die *optimistischen Synchronisationsverfahren* [KuRo81] scheiden von vorn herein für die Verwendung in Workstation-Server-Umgebungen mit langen Transaktionen aus, da bei diesen Verfahren Zugriffskonflikte erst am Transaktionsende erkannt werden und es sich von selbst verbietet, im Falle eines Zugriffskonflikts die Arbeit von vielleicht einigen Wochen durch Rücksetzen der Transaktion zunichte zu machen. Bei *Sperrverfahren* [GLPT76] wird bei einem Zugriff auf Daten sofort geprüft, ob der entsprechende Zugriff erlaubt ist oder nicht. Die Erkennung von Konflikten erfolgt somit erheblich früher (u.U. schon bei Transaktionsbeginn) als bei optimistischen Verfahren. Aus diesem Grund werden in der vorliegenden Arbeit ausschließlich Synchronisationsverfahren untersucht, die auf der Verwendung von Sperren basieren. In dieser Arbeit sind mit "Sperren" immer *transaktionsorientierte Sperren* gemeint; aktionsorientierte Sperren, z.B. auf Indexen [BaSc77], werden nicht betrachtet.

Ein Datenbanksystem, das komplexe Objekte unterstützt, sollte - z.B. bei der Bearbeitung von komplexen Konstruktionsdaten - auch die Synchronisation von Zugriffen auf *Teile* von komplexen Objekten zulassen. Die Synchronisation solcher Zugriffe führt bei Anwendung der *klassischen Sperrtechniken* jedoch zu unbefriedigenden Ergebnissen. Wenn komplexe Objekte nur als Ganzes als Sperrgranulat verwendet werden können, reduziert dies die Parallelität unnötig stark, da möglicherweise sehr viele Daten ohne Grund lange Zeit blockiert werden. Auf der anderen Seite führen einzelne Tupel, also die Basiselemente von komplexen Objekten, als Sperrgranulat zu einem großen Aufwand im Hinblick auf die Verwaltung der Sperren und die Konflikttests. Die genannten Nachteile fallen bei langen

Transaktionen mit ihren langen Sperren besonders stark ins Gewicht. Neben der Größe der Sperrgranulate haben die entsprechenden Sperrmodi einen großen Einfluß auf den möglichen Parallelitätsgrad. Je restriktiver die Sperrmodi sind, desto geringer ist die Parallelität. Insbesondere im Hinblick auf lange Transaktionen ist es somit sehr wichtig, die benötigten Daten so wenig restriktiv wie nötig zu sperren.

Ein *Synchronisationsverfahren für komplexe Objekte* sollte also bestimmte Sperrgranulate *innerhalb* komplexer Objekte unterstützen und über einen Mechanismus zur "optimalen" Bestimmung der zu sperrenden Granulate und zur Auswahl der entsprechenden Sperrmodi verfügen.

In *dieser Arbeit* wird ein neuartiges Synchronisationsverfahren vorgestellt, das auf die speziellen Anforderungen disjunkter, nicht-rekursiver komplexer Objekte zugeschnitten ist. Das Verfahren basiert auf der Verwendung von Sperrgranulaten verschiedener Größe innerhalb komplexer Objekte. Die Sperrgranulate innerhalb komplexer Objekte sind in den entsprechenden objektspezifischen Sperrgraphen enthalten. Durch die Vorwegnahme von Sperreskalationen läßt das Verfahren einen hohen Parallelitätsgrad bei akzeptablem Verwaltungsaufwand zu. Aus einer Anfrage[1] werden unter Benutzung von Informationen über die Struktur der berührten Objekte die Granulate und Sperrmodi abgeleitet, die den größtmöglichen Durchsatz des Datenbanksystems erwarten lassen. Mit Hilfe dieser "optimalen" Granulate und Sperrmodi baut das Synchronisationsverfahren während der Analyse der Anfrage den entsprechenden anfragespezifischen Sperrgraphen auf. Aus dem anfragespezifischen Sperrgraphen werden zur Laufzeit der Anfrage die benötigten Sperranforderungen abgeleitet.

In *Kapitel 2* wird zunächst eine mögliche Klassifizierung und Repräsentationsform komplexer Objekte vorgestellt. Eine Diskussion existierender Sperrverfahren und deren Verwendung in Nicht-Standard-Anwendungen folgt in *Kapitel 3*. *Kapitel 4* und *Kapitel 5* stellen den zentralen Teil der vorliegenden Arbeit dar. In *Kapitel 4* wird aufgezeigt, welche Anforderungen an ein Sperrverfahren für Nicht-Standard-Anwendungen gestellt werden müssen, um bei akzeptablem Aufwand Parallelität innerhalb komplexer Objekte zu ermöglichen. *Kapitel 5* enthält einen Vorschlag für spezielle Sperrtechniken auf disjunkten, nicht-rekursiven komplexen Objekten unter Verwendung von Sperrgranulaten innerhalb der Struktur komplexer Objekte. Schlußfolgerungen in *Kapitel 6* runden die vorliegende Arbeit ab.

2 Klassifizierung und Darstellung komplexer Objekte

In [BaBu84] wird eine Klassifizierung komplexer Objekte in disjunkte bzw. nicht-disjunkte und rekursive bzw. nicht-rekursive komplexe Objekte vorgenommen. *Disjunkte* komplexe Objekte besitzen im Gegensatz zu *nicht-disjunkten* komplexen Objekten keinerlei gemeinsame Daten. Komplexe Objekte werden als *rekursiv* bezeichnet, wenn sie andere komplexe Objekte desselben Typs enthalten. Ist dies nicht der Fall, spricht man von *nicht-rekursiven* komplexen Objekten.

Disjunkte, nicht-rekursive komplexe Objekte sind die am besten untersuchte Art von komplexen Objekten. Sie besitzen eine hierarchische Struktur. Ein Ansatz, solche Strukturen zu beschreiben, ist das NF^2-Datenmodell bzw. dessen Erweiterungen [PiAn86, ScSc86]. Dieser Ansatz läßt in der Verallgemeinerung zu, daß ein Attribut in einer Relation wiederum relationenwertig, d.h. eine Menge oder eine Liste, oder aber auch ein (komplexes) Tupel sein darf. In Abbildung 1 ist die Struktur der Relation "zellen" als ein Beispiel für disjunkte, nicht-rekursive komplexe Objekte zu finden. M, L bzw. T bedeutet Menge, Liste bzw. (komplexes) Tupel. Die Blätter des Objektschema-Baumes bestehen aus "atomaren" Datentypen ohne innere Struktur, z.B. aus einer Zeichenkette (str) oder einer Integer-Zahl (int). Zu den einzelnen Knoten des Objektschema-Baumes sind die entsprechenden Attributnamen hinzugefügt. Das Suffix "_id" an einem Attributnamen bedeutet, daß es sich bei dem entsprechenden Attribut um einen Schlüssel handelt. Auf dieses Beispiel wird in den folgenden Kapiteln des öfteren Bezug genommen. Die Relation "zellen" modelliert eine Fertigungszelle, in der sich verschiedene Zellen-Objekte befinden, die von diversen Robotern bearbeitet werden. Ein Roboter kann mit verschiedenen Effektoren (Werkzeugen) ausgerüstet sein. Eine solche Relation könnte etwa im Bereich der Verwaltung von Fertigungszellen eines Automobil- oder Flugzeugherstellers Anwendung finden [GFR87]. Abbildung 2 enthält eine mögliche Ausprägung, das komplexe Objekt Zelle "ze1".

Gerade im Bereich der Nicht-Standard-Anwendungen gibt es auch ein breites Anwendungsspektrum für *nicht-disjunkte, nicht-rekursive* komplexe Objekte [Mits86]. Beispiele für Fälle, in denen es sinnvoll ist, daß verschiedene komplexe Objekte gemeinsame Daten haben, sind etwa Bauteil-Bibliotheken und Normteil-Kataloge. *Rekursive*

---

[1] Der Begriff *Anfrage* wird in dieser Arbeit als Oberbegriff für Lese-(SELECT), Änderungs-(ASSIGN/UPDATE), Einfüge-(INSERT) und Lösch-(DELETE)-Anweisungen verwendet.

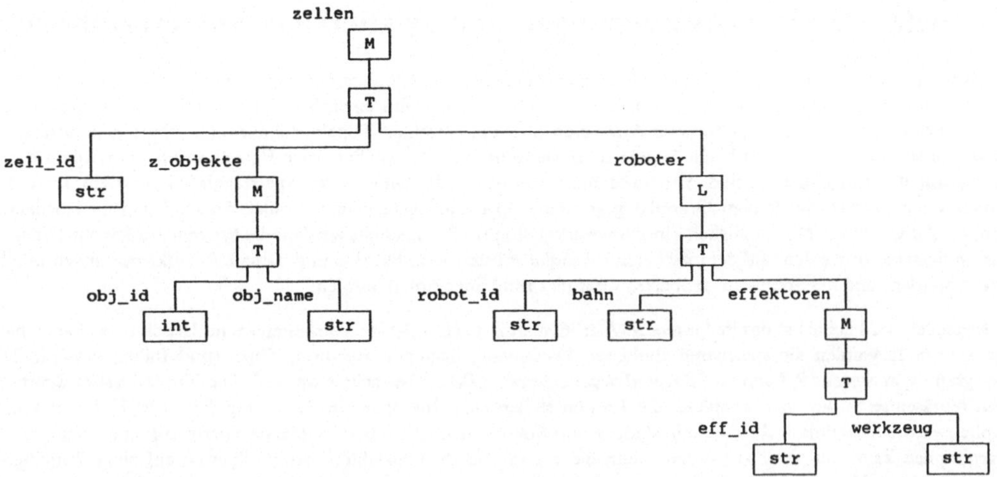

Abbildung 1. Disjunkte, nicht-rekursive komplexe Relation "zellen": Objektschema

komplexe Objekte, die sowohl *disjunkt* als auch *nicht-disjunkt* sein können, eignen sich u.a. sehr gut zur Modellierung von Stücklistenproblemen. - In dem vorliegenden Papier werden aus Platzgründen ausschließlich disjunkte, nicht rekursive komplexe Objekte näher betrachtet. Die Untersuchung der übrigen oben vorgestellten Arten komplexer Objekte ist Gegenstand zukünftiger Arbeiten.

Noch ein paar Worte zur Terminologie: Im folgenden wird davon ausgegangen, daß die Attributwerte eines komplexen Objekts entweder nicht weiter strukturiert sind, aus Daten gleichen Typs bestehen oder aber aus Daten verschiedenen Typs zusammengesetzt sein dürfen. Bei nicht weiter strukturierten (atomaren) Attributwerten handelt es sich beispielsweise um Daten des Typs integer oder real. Attributwerte wie etwa eine Menge oder eine Liste, die aus Daten gleichen Typs bestehen, werden in dieser Arbeit als *homogen* strukturiert bezeichnet. Von *heterogen* strukturierten Attributwerten wird gesprochen, wenn ein Attributwert aus Daten verschiedenen Typs zusammengesetzt sein darf. Dieser Fall liegt etwa vor, wenn es sich bei einem Attributwert um ein (komplexes) Tupel handelt, das Attribute verschiedenen Typs enthält.

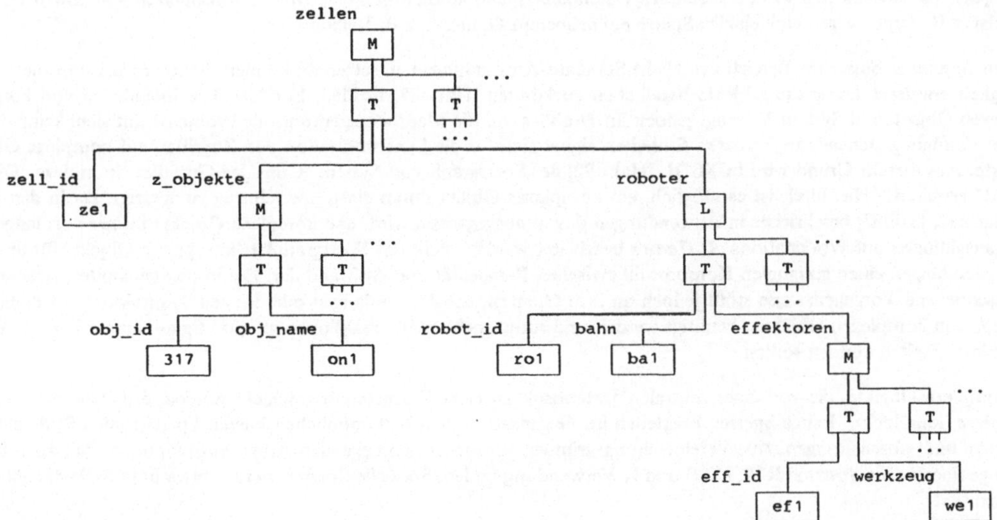

Abbildung 2. Disjunkte, nicht-rekursive komplexe Relation "zellen": Komplexes Objekt Zelle "zel"

3 Nicht-Standard-Anwendungen und existierende Sperrverfahren

Die Synchronisationskomponente eines Datenbanksystems für Nicht-Standard-Anwendungen muß - wie in der Einleitung erläutert - so fein und so wenig restriktiv wie nötig sperren, um einen hinreichenden Parallelitätsgrad zu erhalten. Feine Sperren, z.B. auf atomaren Attributen oder auf einzelnen Tupeln, führen u.U. schon in traditionellen Anwendungen und erst recht in Nicht-Standard-Anwendungen zu übermäßig vielen Einzelsperren. Zur Reduzierung der Anzahl der Einzelsperren sind *Sperreskalationen* erforderlich. Unter einer Sperreskalation versteht man den Tausch vieler Sperren auf feinem Granulat gegen eine Sperre auf gröberem Granulat. Sperreskalationen bedeuten ebenfalls Aufwand: die Notwendigkeit einer Sperreskalation muß festgestellt werden, die Sperren auf feinem Granulat müssen freigegeben werden, auf dem gröberen Granulat müssen Konflikttests und Tests auf Verklemmungen durchgeführt werden, und die Sperre auf gröberem Granulat muß angefordert werden.

Im folgenden wird zunächst das in *System R* [Astr76] realisierte (DAG-)Sperrverfahren exemplarisch näher betrachtet. Für System R wurden die sperrbaren Einheiten Datenbank, Segment, Relation, Tupel (und Index) gewählt. Der Sperrgraph von System R kann als *"directed acyclic graph" (DAG)* betrachtet werden. Die Knoten dieses Sperrgraphen repräsentieren die Sperrgranulate; die Kanten stellen eine Enthaltensein-Beziehung dar. Mit Hilfe des Sperrgraphen wird ein Protokoll für die Anforderung von Sperren definiert [GLPT76]. Eine Sperre auf einen Knoten des Sperrgraphen kann nur gewährt werden, wenn die entsprechende Transaktion bereits Sperren auf allen Vorgängern des betrachteten Knotens hält. Die Sperren auf Vorgängerknoten müssen dabei das Recht einschließen, den gerade betrachteten Knoten in dem angeforderten Modus sperren zu dürfen. Eine Warnsperre im Modus IS (Intention Shared) bzw. IX (Intention eXclusive) gewährt beispielsweise das Recht, einen Nachfolgerknoten im Modus S (Shared) bzw. X (eXclusive) zu sperren. Sperren werden immer ausgehend von der Wurzel des Sperrgraphen (Datenbank) angefordert und zur Wurzel hin freigegeben. Ein Knoten ist *explizit* im Modus S gesperrt, wenn wenigstens für einen Pfad von der Wurzel zum betrachteten Knoten entsprechende Sperren gehalten werden. Für eine explizite X-Sperre müssen alle Pfade zwischen der Wurzel und dem betrachtetem Knoten geeignet gesperrt sein. Wenn wenigstens ein Vorgängerknoten eines Knotens im Modus S gesperrt ist, bedeutet dies, daß auf dem entsprechenden Knoten eine *implizite* S-Sperre liegt. Eine X-Sperre auf jedem Vorgängerknoten bewirkt eine implizite X-Sperre für den betrachteten Knoten.

Der Durchsatz eines Datenbanksystems hängt in hohem Maße von der Größe der gesperrten Granulate ab [RiSt77]. Je größer die gesperrten Granulate sind, desto geringer ist der Aufwand für die Verwaltung der Sperren, aber desto geringer ist auch der mögliche Parallelitätsgrad. Um die widersprüchlichen Ziele eines geringen Verwaltungsaufwands und eines hohen Parallelitätsgrads einander näherzubringen, wurden sowohl System R [Date85] als auch DB2 [CLSW84] und der OS/2 EE Database Manager [ChMy88] mit einem Mechanismus zur *automatischen Sperreskalation* ausgestattet. Sobald ein bestimmter Grenzwert für die Anzahl der gewährten Sperren auf den Ausprägungen eines Objekttyps überschritten wird, wandelt das Datenbanksystem automatisch eine Menge von Sperren auf feinem Granulat, z.B. Tupel, gegen eine einzige Sperre auf gröberem Granulat, z.B. Relation, um.

Um *System R* besser im Bereich der Nicht-Standard-Anwendungen einsetzen zu können, wurde es u.a. um die Fähigkeit *erweitert*, komplexe Objekte handhaben zu können [HaLo82, LoPl83, Lori85]. Die Integration von komplexen Objekten in System R bringt jedoch im Hinblick auf die Mehrbenutzerkontrolle Probleme mit sich: keine der zur Verfügung stehenden sperrbaren Einheiten eignet sich für die Synchronisation von Zugriffen auf komplexe Objekte. Aus diesem Grund wird in XSQL [HaLo82] der Sperrgraph von System R um das Granulat "komplexes Objekt" erweitert. Hierdurch ist es möglich, ein komplexes Objekt durch *einen* Sperreintrag zu sperren. Da in den in [HaLo82, LoPl83] beschriebenen Anwendungen davon ausgegangen wird, daß komplexe Objekte immer von langen Transaktionen auf Workstations *als Ganzes* bearbeitet werden, stellt das Sperrgranulat "komplexes Objekt" für diese Anwendungen einen geeigneten Kompromiß zwischen Parallelität und Aufwand dar. Die in den genannten Arbeiten beschriebene Vorgehensweise stößt jedoch an ihre Grenzen, sobald von langen oder kurzen Transaktionen lediglich *Teile* von komplexen Objekten benötigt werden und somit mehrere Transaktionen gleichzeitig auf einem komplexen Objekt arbeiten können sollten.

Komplexe Objekte, die von einer zentralen Datenbank zu einer Workstation geschickt werden, erhalten eine *lange Sperre* (long lock). Lange Sperren überleben im Gegensatz zu den herkömmlichen kurzen Sperren auch Systemabstürze und -abschaltungen. Aus Vereinfachungsgründen wird in der vorliegenden Arbeit angenommen, daß auch für lange Sperren die Sperrmodi IS, IX, S und X Verwendung finden. Spezielle Sperren werden etwa in [KSUW85] näher diskutiert.

```
A1:   SELECT o                              A2:   SELECT r
      FROM z IN zellen, o IN z.z_objekte          FROM z IN zellen, r IN z.roboter
      WHERE z.zell_id = 'ze1'                      WHERE z.zell_id = 'ze1' AND
                                                         r.bahn INTERSECTS 'punkt (x,y)'
                                                   FOR UPDATE

A3:   SELECT o                              A4:   SELECT z.zell_id, z.z_objekte, z.roboter
      FROM z IN zellen, o IN z.z_objekte          FROM z IN zellen
      WHERE z.zell_id = 'ze1' AND                 WHERE z.zell_id = 'ze1'
            o.obj_id = '317'
      FOR UPDATE

A5:   SELECT z.zell_id, z.z_objekte,        A6:   SELECT z
             r.robot_id, r.effektoren, r.bahn     FROM z IN zellen
      FROM z IN zellen, r IN z.roboter            WHERE z.zell_id = 'ze1'
      WHERE z.zell_id = 'ze1'
```

Abbildung 3. Beispiele: Anfragen[2] A1, A2, A3, A4, A5 und A6

4 Anforderungen an ein Sperrverfahren für Nicht-Standard-Anwendungen

Da sowohl zu grobe (komplexes Objekt, Relation) als auch zu feine (Tupel) Sperrgranulate möglichst vermieden werden sollten, stellt die Verfügbarkeit von *abgestuften Sperrgranulaten* innerhalb komplexer Objekte eine Grundvoraussetzung für ein effizientes Sperrverfahren auf solchen Objekten dar.

Ein Beispiel dazu ist in Abbildung 3 zu finden. Anfrage A1 ist die Anforderung einer Workstation, alle Z_Objekte der Zelle "ze1" auszulagern, um sie zu lesen. Mit Anfrage A2 verlangt eine andere Workstation bestimmte Roboter, um sie zu ändern. Beide Anfragen sind exemplarisch in einer Anfragesprache verfaßt, die eine Erweiterung von SQL darstellt[3]. Die Anfragen A1 und A2 greifen auf verschiedene Teile des komplexen Objekts Zelle "ze1" zu und könnten daher an sich parallel ausgeführt werden. Ein Zugriffskonflikt auf logischer Ebene liegt nicht vor. Bei der Verwendung von je einer Sperre auf ganzen komplexen Objekten vom Typ "zellen" werden A1 und A2 jedoch unnötigerweise serialisiert. Auf der anderen Seite führt das Sperren der kleinstmöglichen Einheiten, nämlich der Ausprägungen von Datentypen ohne innere Struktur (den atomaren Attributen), insbesondere bei Anfrage A1 zu einer nicht mehr tolerierbaren Anzahl von Sperren, da innerhalb einer Zelle u.U. Hunderte von Z_Objekten vorhanden sein können.

Letztlich bestimmt werden Parallelität und Aufwand von der Tatsache, welche Granulate in welchem Modus gesperrt sind. Das Ziel der Synchronisationskomponente eines Datenbanksystems muß also sein, so zu sperren, daß der Durchsatz - unter Wahrung der Konsistenz der Daten - optimal zu werden verspricht. Dies bedeutet, daß die gesperrten Granulate so klein wie möglich, aber auch nur so klein wie nötig sein sollen. Wie im folgenden gezeigt wird, kann dieses Ziel durch eine *geeignete Vorwegnahme von Sperreskalationen* erreicht werden.

Das Setzen "optimaler" Sperren könnte im Prinzip *manuell* durch die Benutzer erfolgen. Dieser Ansatz hat jedoch einige entscheidende Nachteile: zum einen ist das geeignete Setzen von Sperren ein sehr komplexes Problem, das sowohl gute Kenntnisse der Synchronisationsproblematik als auch der Implementierung eines komplexen Objekts (interne Datenstrukturen) erfordert; zum anderen ist es sowohl im Hinblick auf mögliche Konsistenzverletzungen als auch im Hinblick auf die Wahl geeigneter Sperrgranulate nicht sinnvoll, dies dem Benutzer zu überlassen. Erschwerend kommt hinzu, daß die zugrundeliegenden Strukturen, d.h. die sperrbaren Einheiten, i.d.R. von Relation zu Relation verschieden sind. Es bietet sich somit an, die Bestimmung "optimaler" Sperren *automatisch* durch das Datenbanksystem durchführen zu lassen. Ein entsprechender Mechanismus muß in der Lage sein, aus einer *Anfrage* unter Berücksichtigung von *strukturellen* und ggf. *statistischen Informationen* die zu sperrenden Granulate und die dazugehörenden Sperrmodi in einer Weise abzuleiten, die einen "optimalen" Durchsatz erwarten läßt. Darauf wird im folgenden Kapitel näher eingegangen.

---

[2] Die Beispiel-Anfragen sind möglichst einfach gehalten, um eine tiefergehende und hier überflüssige Sprachdiskussion zu vermeiden. Insbesondere in Fällen, in denen das Anfrage-Ergebnis eine bestimmte, nicht-flache Struktur haben soll, werden die entsprechenden Anfragen erheblich komplizierter. Das im folgenden vorgestellte Verfahren ist jedoch ohne Probleme auch bei beliebig komplexen Anfragen anwendbar.

[3] Es handelt sich im wesentlichen um die Heidelberg Database Language (HDBL). HDBL ist die Anfragesprache des Advanced Information Management Prototype (AIM-P), der zur Zeit am Wissenschaftlichen Zentrum Heidelberg der IBM entwickelt und bereits prototypisch in Anwendungen eingesetzt wird [Dada86, Dada88].

5 Spezielle Sperrtechniken für komplexe Objekte

In den nächsten Abschnitten werden zuerst ein allgemeiner Sperrgraph für disjunkte, nicht-rekursive komplexe Objekte und objektspezifische Sperrgraphen eingeführt. Danach folgt die Vorstellung eines Verfahrens zur Bestimmung "optimaler" Sperranforderungen. Bei diesem Verfahren werden zuerst die für die Synchronisation wichtigen Informationen aus einer Anfrage extrahiert. Im nächsten Schritt erfolgt unter Verwendung gewisser, im folgenden beschriebener Regeln die eigentliche Bestimmung "optimaler" Sperranforderungen. Auf diese Weise sollen Sperreskalationen so weit wie möglich vorweggenommen werden. Die "optimalen" Sperranforderungen führen zu den anfragespezifischen Sperrgraphen. Während der Ausführung einer Anfrage wird jeweils *vor* dem Zugriff auf Daten eines bestimmten Granulats die Information aus dem anfragespezifischen Sperrgraphen geholt, in welchem Modus die Daten dieses Granulats zu sperren sind. Mit dieser Information erfolgt ein Aufruf an den Sperrverwalter. Wenn der Sperrverwalter die Sperre gewährt, dann hat die entsprechende Transaktion das Recht, die gewünschten Daten zu bearbeiten. Eine Bewertung des vorgestellten Verfahrens rundet das Kapitel 5 ab.

5.1 *Allgemeiner Sperrgraph für disjunkte komplexe Objekte*

Um Parallelität innerhalb komplexer Objekte zu ermöglichen, wird der in Kapitel 3 bereits erwähnte Sperrgraph (DAG) in zweierlei Hinsicht erweitert. Zum einen werden Sperrgranulate benötigt, die bzgl. ihrer Größe zwischen Tupel und Relation liegen. Darüber hinaus muß ein Sperrgraph für komplexe Objekte beliebige Strukturen unterstützen, da die Struktur und "Tiefe" komplexer Objekte von Relation zu Relation unterschiedlich sein kann. In Abbildung 4 ist ein *allgemeiner Sperrgraph für disjunkte komplexe Objekte* dargestellt, der die beiden genannten Forderungen erfüllt. Die Knoten im Sperrgraph stellen die sperrbaren Einheiten, d.h. die Sperrgranulate, dar. Die *basic lockable units (BLU)* sind die kleinsten sperrbaren Einheiten[4]. Beispiele für basic lockable units könnten Attributwerte des Typs integer oder real sein. *Homogeneous lockable units (HoLU)* bestehen aus Daten desselben Datentyps, etwa einer Menge (Relation) oder einer Liste von Teilobjekten gleichen Typs (vgl. "homogen strukturierte Attributwerte" in Kap. 2). *Heterogeneous lockable units (HeLU)* dürfen aus Teilobjekten verschiedenen Typs bestehen (vgl. "heterogen strukturierte Attributwerte" in Kap. 2). Ein Beispiel hierfür ist etwa ein einzelnes Tupel, das i.d.R. Attribute verschiedenen Typs enthält.

Die Unterscheidung zwischen HoLUs und HeLUs ist nötig, um sowohl homogene als auch heterogene Sperreskalationen sauber mit dem vorgestellten Sperrgraphen erfassen und unterscheiden zu können. Wenn Sperren auf Objekten *gleichen Typs* zu einer Sperre auf einer HoLU zusammengefaßt werden, wollen wir von *homogener Sperreskalation* sprechen. Analog dazu kann es sinnvoll sein, Sperren auf Daten *verschiedenen Typs* zu einer Sperre auf einer HeLU zusammenzufassen. In diesem Fall handelt es sich um *heterogene Sperreskalation*. Die Pfeile in Abbildung 4 deuten an, daß ein Sperrgranulat u.U. aus anderen Sperrgranulaten zusammengesetzt sein kann. Der allgemeine Sperrgraph unterstützt somit beliebige Strukturen. Beispielsweise ist eine Menge von Listen von Integer-Zahlen für die Sperrkomponente eine HoLU, die aus HoLUs besteht, die wiederum aus BLUs zusammengesetzt sind. Sperrbare Einheiten wären in diesem Fall die gesamte Menge, genau eine Liste oder - im Extremfall - genau eine Integer-Zahl. Der traditionelle Sperrgraph von System R ist ein Spezialfall des allgemeinen Sperrgraphen: "Datenbank" kann als eine HeLU aufgefaßt werden, "Segment" ebenfalls, "Relation" ist eine HoLU, und die einzelnen "Tupel" stellen die kleinsten sperrbaren Einheiten, die BLUs, dar[5].

---

[4] Die Anzahl der BLUs einer Relation - speziell einer komplexen Relation - ist i.d.R. recht groß. Wenn man zuläßt, daß jede einzelne BLU separat gesperrt werden kann, führt dies zu einem sehr hohen Aufwand (vgl. Attributsperren), ohne daß der Gewinn an Parallelität in einem entsprechenden Verhältnis steht. Aus diesem Grund ist es günstiger, die BLUs einer Hierarchiestufe eines Teilobjekts eines komplexen Objekts zu einer *basic lockable unit** zusammenzufassen. Auf diese Weise wird der Sperraufwand stark reduziert, ohne die mögliche Parallelität wesentlich einzuschränken. In der komplexen Relation "zellen" könnten beispielsweise die BLUs "obj_id" und "obj_name" zu einer einzigen BLU* zusammengefaßt werden. Sobald eines der beiden Attribute von einer Transaktion berührt wird, wird die BLU* mit beiden Attributen zusammen gesperrt.

[5] Indexe werden in dieser Arbeit nicht betrachtet.

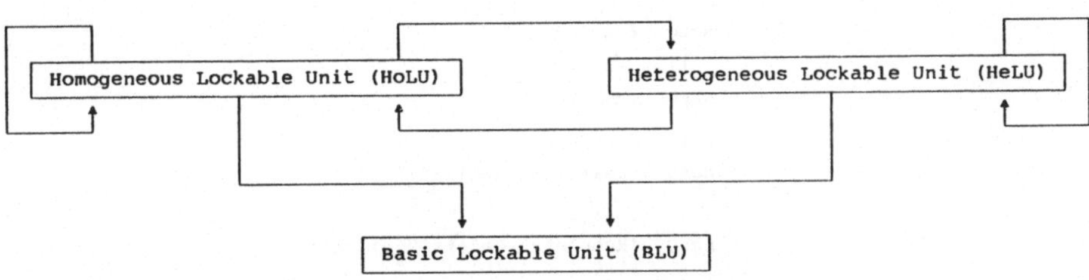

Abbildung 4. Sperrgraph: Allgemeiner Sperrgraph für disjunkte komplexe Objekte

5.2 Objektspezifischer Sperrgraph

Unter Benutzung des allgemeinen Sperrgraphen und bestimmter einfacher Ableitungsregeln kann für jede Relation aus den Kataloginformationen sehr einfach ein *objektspezifischer Sperrgraph* konstruiert werden, der die atomar sperrbaren Einheiten der entsprechenden Relation enthält. Die Ableitungsregeln geben an, welcher Attributtyp zu welcher Art sperrbarer Einheit umgeformt werden muß. Im folgenden sind exemplarisch einige Ableitungsregeln angegeben:

1. Ein Attribut des Typs "Liste" wird zu einer HoLU.
2. Ein Attribut des Typs "Menge" wird zu einer HoLU.
3. Ein Attribut des Typs "Komplexes Objekt" wird zu einer HeLU.
4. Ein Attribut des Typs "Integer" wird zu einer BLU.
5. usw.

Haben verschiedene komplexe Relationen verschiedene Strukturen, so unterscheiden sich auch die dazugehörenden objektspezifischen Sperrgraphen strukturell. Auf diese Weise wird der Tatsache Rechnung getragen, daß jede komplexe Relation eine eigene Struktur und Tiefe haben kann. Der objektspezifische Sperrgraph von disjunkten, nichtrekursiven komplexen Relationen hat stets eine hierarchische Struktur. In Abbildung 5 ist der objektspezifische Sperrgraph der komplexen Relation "zellen" zu finden. Die Zuordnung zwischen den Knoten dieses Graphen und den Attributen des zugehörigen Objektschemas (Abbildung 1) dürfte weitgehend selbsterklärend sein.

5.3 Bestimmung einer "optimalen" Sperranforderung

Die *einfachste Möglichkeit* zur automatischen Bestimmung der zu sperrenden Granulate besteht darin, die in einer Anfrage spezifizierten Attribute ohne weitere Optimierung als Sperrgranulat zu übernehmen. Wenn wie etwa in Anfrage A1 oder A3 (siehe Abbildung 3) in der SELECT-Klausel einer Anfrage eine Ausprägung eines komplexen Attributs spezifiziert ist, dann wird die zugehörige HeLU gesperrt. Andernfalls - z.B. in Anfrage A4 - bilden die zu den in der SELECT-Klausel angegebenen Attributen gehörenden Granulate - in A4 sind dies eine BLU und zwei HoLUs - die zu sperrenden Einheiten (vgl. ein ähnliches Verfahren in [DüKc88]). Dieser Ansatz führt jedoch in einigen Fällen zu unbefriedigenden Ergebnissen: Wird etwa wie in Anfrage A1 auf ein komplexes Attribut ("z_objekte") ohne einschränkende WHERE-Bedingung zugegriffen, bewirkt die genannte Vorgehensweise, daß während der Ausführung der Anfrage mit hohem Aufwand jedes komplexe Objekt (HeLU "z_objekte") des entsprechenden komplexen Attributs *einzeln* gesperrt werden muß und erst nach dem Überschreiten des entsprechenden Grenzwerts eine ebenfalls teure (homogene) Sperreskalation durchgeführt wird. Durch das sofortige Sperren des komplexen Attributs (HoLU "z_objekte") könnte man den Sperraufwand erheblich reduzieren. Neben der Einsparung von Sperraufwand würde ein geeignetes *Preclaiming* auf gröberen Granulaten die Wahrscheinlichkeit für Verklemmungen im Vergleich zu Sperreskalationen während der Laufzeit drastisch reduzieren [Weik88]. Auf der anderen Seite werden bei der Anwendung von Preclaiming oftmals Daten unnötigerweise bzw. unnötig lange gesperrt. **Es wird somit ein Mechanismus benötigt, der für eine Anfrage durch eine semantische Analyse dieser Anfrage unter Verwendung von strukturellen und statistischen Informationen entscheidet, ob die Vorwegnahme von (homogenen) Sperreskalationen sinnvoll ist oder nicht.** Der Fall liegt ähnlich, wenn etwa wie in Anfrage A4 *alle* Attribute eines komplexen Objekts spezifiziert sind. Es bereitet weniger Aufwand, nicht erst nacheinander die zu den einzelnen Attributen gehörenden Granulate zu sperren, sondern sofort das ganze komplexe Objekt (heterogene Sperreskalation). Es ist möglich, daß die beiden o.g. Fälle in einer Anfrage auf verschiedenen Hierarchiestufen eines Teilobjekts und in verschiedenen Attributen beliebig häufig auftreten (Anfrage A5). Gerade dann kann durch die Vorwegnahme von sowohl homogenen als auch hete-

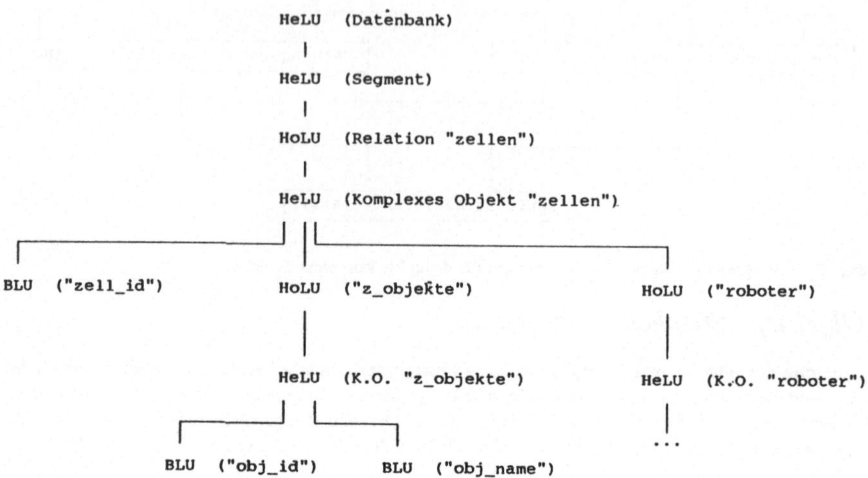

Abbildung 5. Objektspezifischer Sperrgraph: Komplexe Relation ʼzellenʼ

rogenen Sperreskalationen der Sperraufwand u.U. drastisch reduziert werden. (Die gleiche Aussage gilt insbesondere auch für die in dieser Arbeit aus Platzgründen nicht näher betrachteten komplizierteren Anfragen, bei denen z.B. das Anfrage-Ergebnis eine bestimmte, nicht-flache Struktur haben soll.)

Im folgenden werden unter *"optimalen" Granulaten* genau die Granulate verstanden, die am Ende gesperrt wären, wenn eine Anfrage unter Verwendung von Sperreskalationen zur Laufzeit abgearbeitet würde.

Es gibt Fälle, in denen aus einer Anfrage (zufällig) die ʼoptimalenʼ Sperrgranulate direkt abgeleitet (übernommen) werden können. Eine anschließende Optimierung stellt dann lediglich überflüssigen Aufwand dar und führt zu keiner Verbesserung mehr. Die Synchronisationskomponente eines Datenbanksystems für Nicht-Standard-Anwendungen sollte jedoch in jedem Fall über einen Mechanismus zur Optimierung der Granulate und Modi verfügen, da es viele Fälle gibt, in denen eine Anfrage nicht die ʼoptimalenʼ Granulate - spezifiziert über Attribute - enthält bzw. enthalten kann. Ein Benutzer, der aufgrund einer Sicht (View) nur einen Teil eines komplexen Objekts sieht, oder der nicht über alle strukturellen Informationen (auch im Hinblick auf gemeinsame Daten!) verfügt, oder der sich einfach nicht um Fragen der Synchronisation kümmern möchte, kann bzw. will nicht dafür sorgen, daß jede Anfrage direkt das ʼoptimaleʼ Sperrgranulat enthält. Wenn beispielsweise Joins zwischen flachen Tabellen vom Datenbanksystem mit Hilfe komplexer Objekte materialisiert sind, oder wenn existierende Anwendungsprogramme, die auf flachen Objekten arbeiten, auf ein Nicht-Standard-Datenbanksystem mit komplexen Objekten aufgesetzt werden sollen, muß das Ergebnis eine flache Struktur haben. Die Struktur der berührten komplexen Objekte entspricht somit nicht der bei der Ausgabe gewünschten und in der Anfrage spezifizierten Struktur, so daß nicht von vorn herein z.B. ein komplexes Attribut in der Anfrage spezifiziert werden kann. Eine automatische Optimierung sorgt dafür, daß unabhängig von den spezifizierten Attributen stets in einer Weise gesperrt wird, die den größten Durchsatz erwarten läßt.

Der *Mechanismus* zur Bestimmung der ʼoptimalenʼ Granulate (und Modi) besteht aus zwei Schritten. Im *ersten Schritt* werden unter Benutzung der objektspezifischen Sperrgraphen der berührten komplexen Relationen die in einer Anfrage spezifizierten Attribute aus der Anfrage extrahiert. Darüber hinaus wird aus einer Anfrage abgeleitet, auf welches Attribut in welcher Weise, d.h. lesend, ändernd, einfügend oder löschend, zugegriffen wird und für welche Attribute in einer ggf. vorhandenen WHERE-Bedingung welche Arten von Bedingungen, z.B. Test auf Gleichheit mit einer Konstanten, angegeben sind. Danach erfolgt im *zweiten Schritt* eine Optimierung der im ersten Schritt gewonnenen Informationen. **Durch die Optimierung soll erreicht werden, daß zur Laufzeit so wenig homogene bzw. heterogene Sperreskalationen wie möglich anfallen**[6]. Gleichzeitig sollen die gesperrten Granulate so klein wie möglich sein, um einen hohen Grad an Parallelität zu gewährleisten. Die Vorwegnahme von Sperreskalationen wird mit Hilfe folgender *Regeln* erreicht:

---

[6] *Hot-Spot-Daten* [Reut82, Weik88], d.h. Daten, auf die sehr häufig zugegriffen wird, werden hier nicht näher betrachtet. Bei dieser Art von Daten kann es u.U. günstiger sein, auf die Vorwegnahme von Sperreskalationen zu verzichten, da Sperren auf gröberen Granulaten die Anzahl der Pseudokonflikte ansteigen lassen.

(1) Werden voraussichtlich mindestens G_1 Ausprägungen einer HoLU gelesen bzw. geändert, wird statt der Ausprägungen sofort die HoLU selbst entsprechend gesperrt (Vorwegnahme homogener Sperreskalation).
(2) Liest bzw. ändert eine Anfrage mindestens G_2 Komponenten einer HeLU, wird statt der Komponenten sofort die HeLU selbst entsprechend gesperrt (Vorwegnahme heterogener Sperreskalation).

Das *Kernproblem* bei der Anwendung beider Regeln ist die Entscheidung, ob beim Zugriff auf Daten während der Abarbeitung einer Anfrage direkt eine Sperre auf gröberem Granulat angefordert werden soll oder ob es günstiger ist, doch feinere Granulate zu sperren. Die Entscheidung des vorgeschlagenen Mechanismus, welche Granulate zur Laufzeit gesperrt werden, hängt in erster Linie von einer geeigneten Abschätzung für die Anzahl der Ausprägungen bzw. Komponenten, die eine Anfrage innerhalb eines komplexen Objekts voraussichtlich bearbeiten wird, und darüber hinaus noch von den Grenzwerten G_1 und G_2 in den o.g. Regeln ab.

Bei der *Anwendung von Regel 1* kommt es entscheidend darauf an, aus einer Anfrage möglichst exakt abzuleiten, auf wieviele Ausprägungen in den berührten Attributen bzw. Relationen während der Abarbeitung der Anfrage voraussichtlich zugegriffen wird. Diese Information steht in engem Zusammenhang mit der WHERE-Bedingung einer Anfrage. Ist **keine WHERE-Bedingung bzgl. eines bestimmten Attributs** spezifiziert, werden *alle* Ausprägungen bearbeitet, und es ist dann stets sinnvoll, für das entsprechende Attribut die homogene Sperreskalation vorwegzunehmen (vgl. Anfrage A1, Attribut "z_objekte"; A5, "roboter"). Ist **eine WHERE-Bedingung bzgl. eines bestimmten Attributs** spezifiziert, bestimmt die Selektivität der WHERE-Bedingung die Anzahl der voraussichtlich berührten Ausprägungen. Die Selektivität einer WHERE-Bedingung ist u.a. abhängig vom Definitionsbereich eines Attributs und der Verteilung der aktuellen Daten. Eine exakte Bestimmung der Selektivität einer WHERE-Bedingung ist viel zu aufwendig, da eine genaue Inspektion der betroffenen Daten durchzuführen wäre, also eine Art "Vorausführung" der Anfrage. Es lassen sich jedoch auch ohne eine derartige exakte Analyse Aussagen über die Selektivität einer WHERE-Bedingung machen. Wenn etwa eine WHERE-Bedingung einen Ausdruck des Typs "Schlüsselattribut = Konstante" (vgl. z.B. Anfrage A6) enthält, dann wird mit Sicherheit nur eine Ausprägung bearbeitet und ein Sperren des gröberen Granulats verbietet sich von selbst. Im Falle des Vorliegens einer unscharfen WHERE-Bedingung werden dagegen voraussichtlich "viele" Ausprägungen bearbeitet (vgl. Anfrage A2). Somit ist es günstig, sofort die ganze HoLU zu sperren. Mit Hilfe der genannten und weiterer, ähnlicher Annahmen[7] sind die meisten der für die Praxis relevanten Fälle erfaßt. Damit existiert eine (hinreichend) genaue Entscheidungsgrundlage für die Vorwegnahme homogener Sperreskalationen.

Die Informationen, die zur *Anwendung von Regel 2* benötigt werden, können direkt aus einer Anfrage und den entsprechenden Strukturdaten im Systemkatalog extrahiert werden.

Die Wahl der *Grenzwerte G_1 und G_2* ermöglicht eine Reduzierung des Sperraufwands auf Kosten der Parallelität bzw. eine Erhöhung der Parallelität auf Kosten des Sperraufwands. Die Festlegung beider Grenzwerte muß so erfolgen, daß für die Gesamtheit aller Zugriffe auf eine bestimmte komplexe Relation ein "optimaler" Kompromiß zwischen Parallelität und Sperraufwand gefunden wird. Bei der Definition einer komplexen Relation werden für die Grenzwerte, die innerhalb dieser Relation gelten sollen, entweder vom Datenbanksystem bestimmte, global voreingestellte Werte angenommen, oder es werden vom Datenbankverwalter entsprechende Angaben erwartet. Falls nötig erfolgt später von Zeit zu Zeit eine Anpassung dieser Werte an die aktuellen Erfordernisse. Die Grenzwerte G_1 und G_2 können prozentual, z.B. 10 % aller Ausprägungen, oder auch absolut, z.B. 500 Ausprägungen, angegeben werden.

Die Regeln (1) und (2) werden so lange in objektspezifischen Sperrgraphen "bottom-up" angewendet, bis keine Granulate mehr zusammengefaßt werden können. Auf diese Weise erfolgt einmalig *vor der Ausführung* einer Anfrage die Bestimmung der "optimalen" Sperranforderungen. Erst *während der Laufzeit* der entsprechenden Anfrage werden die "optimalen" Sperranforderungen dazu verwendet, vom Sperrverwalter Sperren auf die benötigten Daten zu erwerben (siehe Beispiel weiter unten).

Das folgende *Beispiel* möge die gewählte Vorgehensweise nochmals verdeutlichen: Bei der Anwendung des vorgestellten Mechanismus auf Anfrage A5 liefert **Schritt 1**, daß während der Ausführung von A5 auf die BLUs "zell_id", "robot_id" und "bahn" sowie auf die HoLUs "z_objekte" und "effektoren" lesend zugegriffen wird. Darüber hinaus existiert in A5 eine WHERE-Bedingung, die fordert, daß das Schlüsselattribut "zell_id" gleich einer Konstanten sein muß. In **Schritt 2** folgert der beschriebene Mechanismus (bei entsprechenden Grenzwerten G_1 und G_2) zuerst unter Verwendung von Regel 2, daß es günstig ist, die BLUs "robot_id" und "bahn" und die HoLU "effektoren" zusammenzufassen und zur Laufzeit sofort die HeLU "roboter" zu sperren (Vorwegnahme heterogener Sperreskalation).

---

[7] Bei der Zugriffspfadauswahl wurden ähnliche Probleme der Selektivitätsberechnung von Prädikaten - u.a. mit Hilfe von Statistiken - weitgehend gelöst [Seli79].

Da in A5 keine WHERE-Bedingung bzgl. des komplexen Attributs "roboter" spezifiziert ist, erkennt der beschriebene Mechanismus dann aufgrund von Regel 1, daß durch eine Sperre auf der HoLU "roboter" eine homogene Sperreskalation vorweggenommen werden kann. Danach faßt der Mechanismus die BLU "zell_id" und die HoLUs "z_objekte" und "roboter" zusammen und schreibt vor, daß zur Laufzeit sofort eine komplette HeLU "zellen" zu sperren ist (Vorwegnahme heterogener Sperreskalation). Da bzgl. des Schlüsselattributs "zell_id" der HoLU "zellen" eine WHERE-Bedingung der Art "Schlüsselattribut = Konstante" angegeben ist, umfaßt das Anfrage-Ergebnis genau eine Zelle. Es verbietet sich also von selbst, zur Laufzeit im voraus die ganze Relation "zellen", d.h. die entsprechende HoLU, zu sperren. Das hier vorgestellte Verfahren liefert also als Ergebnis, daß es bei Anfrage A5 am günstigsten ist, zur Laufzeit beim Zugriff auf Zelle "ze1" sofort diese Zelle (HeLU) als Ganzes zu sperren.

Es handelt sich bei der beschriebenen Vorgehensweise zwar um *eine Art von Preclaiming innerhalb der Struktur komplexer Objekte*, aber *nicht* um *Preclaiming im traditionellen Sinn*: Erst dann, wenn *zur Laufzeit* einer Anfrage tatsächlich auf bestimmte Ausprägungen zugegriffen wird, erfolgt - falls der beschriebene Mechanismus so entschieden hat - nach den Prinzipien vorweggenommener Sperreskalation das Sperren grober, "optimaler" Granulate. Bei dem Zugriff auf Daten (komplexe Objekte) während der Abarbeitung einer Anfrage ist genau bekannt, um welche Attributausprägungen es sich jeweils handelt. Somit können exakt die Granulate (Attributausprägungen) innerhalb komplexer Objekte gesperrt werden, in denen tatsächlich Daten bearbeitet werden. Eine gewisse Unschärfe, d.h. zuviel gesperrte Daten, wird bei der beschriebenen Vorgehensweise - ebenso wie bei der Sperreskalation zur Laufzeit - bewußt in Kauf genommen, um den Sperraufwand zu reduzieren. Durch die Auswertung der WHERE-Bedingung einer Anfrage und die Grenzwerte G_1 und G_2 in den o.g. Regeln wird die mögliche Unschärfe bei der Vorwegnahme von Sperreskalationen jedoch so stark eingeschränkt, daß der eingesparte Sperr- und Eskalationsaufwand im Durchschnitt die unnötigerweise reduzierte Parallelität zu rechtfertigen verspricht. Bei *Preclaiming im traditionellen Sinn* müssen dagegen bereits bei Transaktions- oder Anfragebeginn sehr grobe Granulate, z.B. ganze Relationen, gesperrt werden, da zu diesem Zeitpunkt noch nicht bekannt ist, welche Ausprägungen während der Abarbeitung der Anfrage tatsächlich bearbeitet werden, d.h. eine eventuell vorhandene WHERE-Bedingung erfüllen. Diese Vorgehensweise führt - im Gegensatz zu dem in dieser Arbeit vorgestellten Verfahren - i.d.R. zu einer nicht mehr tolerierbaren Zahl unnötigerweise gesperrter Daten.

Auch bei Anwendung des vorgeschlagenen Verfahrens der vorweggenommenen Sperreskalationen können nach wie vor noch *Sperreskalationen zur Laufzeit* auftreten. Dies ist beispielsweise der Fall, wenn die Analyse einer WHERE-Bedingung nicht zur Vorwegnahme einer Sperreskalation geführt hat, sich aber während der Ausführung einer Anfrage herausstellt, daß doch "viele" Daten vorhanden sind, die die WHERE-Bedingung erfüllen. Bei hinreichender Genauigkeit der Analyse einer WHERE-Bedingung sollte dieser Fall jedoch nur selten vorkommen.

Zur Auswertung einer WHERE-Bedingung - sei es über einen Index oder durch sequentielle Suche - benötigt man ebenfalls Sperren. Der in dieser Arbeit beschriebene Mechanismus sorgt ausschließlich dafür, daß die Daten eines komplexen Objekts, die bearbeitet (d.h. zur Workstation übertragen) werden, falls eine eventuell vorhandene WHERE-Bedingung erfüllt ist, in einer "optimalen" Art und Weise gesperrt werden. Um dieses Ziel zu erreichen, analysiert der vorgeschlagene Mechanismus wie beschrieben die in einer Anfrage enthaltene WHERE-Bedingung selbst und schätzt deren voraussichtliche Selektivität ab. Die zur Auswertung einer WHERE-Bedingung notwendigen Sperren und die damit verbundenen Probleme, z.B. das Phantom-Problem, stellen dagegen einen eigenen Problemkreis dar.

Die Vorwegnahme von Sperreskalationen birgt aber auch eine gewisse *Gefahr* in sich. Wenn etwa alle Roboter einer Zelle von einer Transaktion gelesen werden sollen, führt die Vorwegnahme von Sperreskalationen dazu, daß sofort beim Zugriff auf diese Zelle alle zugehörigen Roboter zusammen gesperrt werden (vorweggenommene homogene Sperreskalation). Eine zweite Transaktion, die nur auf Robotern arbeitet, die erst ganz am Ende der ersten Transaktion von dieser tatsächlich benötigt werden, wird u.U. unnötigerweise blockiert. Gerade im Hinblick auf lange Transaktionen auf Workstations ist jedoch zu erwarten, daß die Verringerung des Aufwandes die unnötige Reduzierung der Parallelität aufwiegt. Wenn nämlich eine lange Transaktion Daten aus der zentralen Datenbank benötigt, fordert sie in vielen Fällen alle Daten "relativ früh" an, d.h. einer kurzen Check-Out-Phase steht eine sich anschließende lange Verarbeitungsphase gegenüber. Entweder werden alle angeforderten Daten gesperrt und der entsprechenden Transaktion zur Verfügung gestellt, oder keine. Der Zeitraum, in dem parallel andere Transaktionen auf noch nicht berührten Robotern arbeiten könnten, ist nur kurz. Falls sich herausstellen sollte, daß der Preis, der an Parallelität bezahlt werden muß, um den Aufwand zu reduzieren, doch zu hoch ist, kann man die Vorwegnahme von Sperreskalationen z.B. von weiteren statistischen Daten abhängig machen und Regel 1 bzw. 2 entsprechend erweitern: nur wenn weniger als eine bestimmte Anzahl Ausprägungen existieren, wird von vorn herein die entsprechende HoLU bzw. HeLU als Ganzes gesperrt.

```
HeLU   (Datenbank)   (IS)

 |

HeLU   (Segment)     (IS)

 |

HoLU   (Relation "zellen")    (IS)

 |

HeLU   (Komplexes Objekt "zellen")    (S)
```

Abbildung 6. Anfragespezifischer Sperrgraph: Granulate und Modi bei Anfrage A5

5.4 Anfragespezifischer Sperrgraph

Mit der "optimalen" Zuordnung zwischen Sperrgranulat und Sperrmodus wird der *anfragespezifische Sperrgraph* erzeugt. In Abbildung 6 ist beispielsweise der zu Anfrage A5 (Abbildung 3) gehörende anfragespezifische Sperrgraph zu finden[8]. Aufgrund der einfachen Struktur dieser Anfrage ergibt sich hier auch ein sehr einfach strukturierter anfragespezifischer Sperrgraph. Der anfragespezifische Sperrgraph enthält die Information, in welchem Modus die zu den verschiedenen Granulaten gehörenden Ausprägungen gesperrt werden müssen, bevor auf die entsprechenden Daten zugegriffen werden darf. Wenn etwa während der Ausführung einer Anfrage die Relation "zellen" benötigt wird, extrahiert die Synchronisationskomponente aus dem dazugehörenden anfragespezifischen Sperrgraphen, in welchem Modus eine Sperre auf die Relation "zellen" zu erwerben ist, und generiert einen entsprechenden Aufruf an den Sperrverwalter. Erst der Sperrverwalter entscheidet mit Hilfe der Sperrtabelle nach Konflikttests, ob die angeforderte Sperre gewährt werden kann oder nicht.

5.5 Qualitative und quantitative Bewertung

Vorteile des vorgestellten Sperrverfahrens sind

1. die Bereitstellung von angepaßten Sperrgranulaten innerhalb der Hierarchie komplexer Objekte,
2. die automatische Bestimmung "optimaler" Sperranforderungen durch die Vorwegnahme homogener und heterogener Sperreskalationen,
3. die Schaffung der Voraussetzungen für eine effiziente Behandlung von nicht-disjunkten, (nicht-)rekursiven komplexen Objekten und
4. die Erleichterung des Austauschs der Sperrtechnik im Hinblick auf die Erweiterbarkeit des Datenbanksystems durch die strikte Trennung der einzelnen Phasen
   a. Anfrage-Analyse
      1) Erzeugung des objektspezifischen Sperrgraphen,
      2) Bestimmung der "optimalen" Sperranforderungen,
      3) Erzeugung des anfragespezifischen Sperrgraphen und
   b. Anfrage-Ausführung
      Anforderung der Sperren aufgrund der Informationen im anfragespezifischen Sperrgraphen.

Nachteile des vorgestellten Sperrverfahrens sind

1. ein etwas erhöhter Aufwand zur einmaligen Erzeugung der objekt- und anfragespezifischen Sperrgraphen *vor* der eigentlichen Ausführung der Anfrage im Zuge der Anfrageanalyse und
2. eine gewisse Abhängigkeit von einer "gefühlvollen" Bestimmung der in den angegebenen Regeln enthaltenen Grenzwerte G_1 und G_2, da es in Extremfällen zum Setzen zu grober bzw. zu feiner Sperren kommen kann.

Folgendes *Zahlenbeispiel* (Abbildung 7) soll mit Hilfe der Anfragen A1, A2, A4 und A5 (siehe Abbildung 3) auf den Ausprägungen des Objektschemas der Abbildung 1 die in den vorangegangenen Abschnitten gemachten Aussagen untermauern: Es wird angenommen, daß in der Relation "zellen" 100 Zellen vorhanden sind, 1 Zelle durchschnittlich 500 Z_Objekte und 20 Roboter enthält und 1 Roboter im Mittel 50 Effektoren verwendet. Wenn man davon ausgeht, daß alle atomaren Daten einer Hierarchiestufe eines Teilobjekts jeweils in einem Datentupel gespeichert und somit auch als Einheit gesperrt werden (BLU[*]), sind 1 + 500 + 20 + 20 * 50 = 1.521 Datentupel durchschnittlich zur

---

[8] Die zur Auswertung der WHERE-Bedingung benötigten Sperren werden hier nicht näher betrachtet.

Abspeicherung einer Zelle notwendig. Die Speichereinheiten (Tupel), die die Informationen zur Abbildung der Hierarchie enthalten, werden in diesem Beispiel vernachlässigt. Ihre Anzahl variiert je nach Art der Implementierung [DGW85, Dada86]. Diese Tatsache ist im hier betrachteten Zusammenhang jedoch nur von sekundärer Bedeutung; es kommt hier in erster Linie auf die Größenordnungen an. Die in der Tabelle angegebenen Werte für die Anzahl der Sperren und Sperreskalationen bezeichnen die Größenordnung, in denen sich diese Zahlen bewegen. Die genauen Werte hängen u.a. von dem Punkt ab, bei dem Sperreskalationen durchgeführt werden. Die zur Auswertung einer WHERE-Bedingung benötigten Sperren werden im folgenden nicht näher betrachtet, da hierzu diverse Annahmen über die Existenz und Struktur von Zugriffspfaden erforderlich wären. Darüber hinaus enthalten die angegebenen Anzahlen von Sperren nicht die Anzahl der ggf. anfallenden Warnsperren (IS, IX), da diese hier nicht ins Gewicht fällt. Es wird angenommen, daß die WHERE-Bedingung in Anfrage A2 60 % der entsprechenden vorhandenen Ausprägungen qualifiziert. Weiterhin wird angenommen, daß eine homogene Sperreskalation durchgeführt wird, sobald 10 % der Granulate einer Hierarchiestufe in einem Teilbaum gesperrt sind.

Das *Sperren von einzelnen Datentupeln* (1) erlaubt zwar den maximal möglichen Parallelitätsgrad, verbietet sich aber auf Grund des immensen Sperraufwands von selbst.

Bei Verwendung der *Sperrgranulate des erweiterten System R* (2) wird generell ein ganzes komplexes Objekt gesperrt. Sobald eine Anfrage lediglich einen Teil eines komplexen Objekts benötigt, führt diese Vorgehensweise dazu, daß u.U. sehr viele Daten unnötigerweise blockiert werden.

Die Alternativen (1) und (2) sind also - wie schon in Kapitel 3 gezeigt - für Nicht-Standard-Anwendungen nur sehr bedingt geeignet. Sie wurden lediglich aus Vergleichsgründen in die Betrachtungen mit einbezogen.

Die Verwendung der *Sperrgranulate des objektspezifischen Sperrgraphen bei gleichzeitiger Bestimmung der zu sperrenden Granulate ohne weitere Optimierung direkt aus einer Anfrage* (3) führt im Vergleich zu den Alternativen (1) und (2) zu genaueren Sperren bei weniger Aufwand. Es werden die zu den in einer Anfrage spezifizierten Attributen gehörenden HoLUs, HeLUs bzw. BLU's gesperrt. Dies führt zu der in der Tabelle angegebenen Anzahl von Sperren und bringt u.U. auch ein gewisse Anzahl von Sperreskalationen zur Laufzeit mit sich.

In Alternative (4) werden sowohl die *Sperrgranulate des objektspezifischen Sperrgraphen* als auch die *Vorwegnahme von Sperreskalationen* mit Hilfe des in der vorliegenden Arbeit beschriebenen Verfahrens zugrunde gelegt. Man sieht deutlich, daß diese Alternative im Vergleich zur Alternative (3) einen erheblich geringeren Sperraufwand verursacht. Dabei werden nur genauso viele Daten wie bei Alternative (3) unnötigerweise blockiert, d.h. bei beiden Alternativen ist ein gleich hoher Parallelitätsgrad möglich. Darüber hinaus ist bei der Vorwegnahme von Sperreskalationen (4) die Wahrscheinlichkeit für Verklemmungen und die damit verbundenen teuren Rücksetzungen geringer als bei Sperreskalationen zur Laufzeit (3).

	(1)	(2)	(3)	(4)
A1	500 Sperren u = 0	1 Sp. (k.O. "zellen") u = 1.021	51 Sp. (HeLU "z_objekte"), 1 ho. Sperresk. u = 0	1 Sp. (HoLU "z_objekte") u = 0
A2	612 Sp. u = 0	1 Sp. (k.O. "zellen") u = 909	3 Sp. (HeLU "roboter"), 1 ho. Sperresk. u = 408	1 Sp. (HoLU "roboter") u = 408
A4	1.521 Sp. u = 0	1 Sp. (k.O. "zellen") u = 0	4 Sp. (BLU* "zell_id"", HoLU "z_objekte", HoLU "roboter"), 1 he. Sperresk. u = 0	1 Sp. (HeLU "zellen") u = 0
A5	1.521 Sp. u = 0	1 Sp. (k.O. "zellen") u = 0	10 Sp. (BLU* "zell_id", HoLU "z_objekte", BLU* "robot_id, bahn"), HoLU "effektoren"), 1 ho. Sperresk., 3 he. Sperresk. u = 0	1 Sp. (HeLU "zellen") u = .0

(u = unnötigerweise gesperrte Datentupel)

Abbildung 7. Tabelle: Zahlenbeispiel

6 Schlußfolgerungen und Ausblick

In der vorliegenden Arbeit wurde ein *Synchronisationsverfahren* vorgestellt, das besonders für Nicht-Standard-Anwendungen geeignet ist. Es ist zu erwarten, daß das vorgeschlagene Sperrverfahren vor allem im Hinblick auf komplexe Objekte und lange Transaktionen eine hohe Parallelität bei vertretbarem Aufwand zuläßt. Dieses Ziel wird durch die Verwendung von Sperrgranulaten innerhalb der Struktur von komplexen Objekten und durch die Vorwegnahme von Sperreskalationen erreicht. Die zu sperrenden Granulate und die entsprechenden Sperrmodi werden mit Hilfe von Informationen über die Struktur der berührten Objekte automatisch so aus einer Anfrage abgeleitet, daß der zu erwartende Durchsatz so hoch wie möglich ist. Je tiefer komplexe Objekte strukturiert sind, je länger Transaktionen dauern und je restriktiver die benötigten Sperrmodi sind, desto höher verspricht die Steigerung des Durchsatzes durch das vorgestellte Verfahren zu sein.

Ein wichtiges Thema für die zukünftige Arbeit ist es zu untersuchen, wie durch eine geschickte Ausnutzung der *Nicht-Disjunktheit* von komplexen Objekten eine weitere Steigerung des Durchsatzes erreicht werden kann. Die grundlegende Voraussetzung, die Nicht-Disjunktheit komplexer Objekte ausnutzen zu können, ist die Verfügbarkeit geeigneter Sperrgranulate. Der in der vorliegenden Arbeit eingeführte Sperrgraph für disjunkte komplexe Objekte kann so erweitert werden, daß er den Anforderungen nicht-disjunkter komplexer Objekte genügt. Neben geeigneten Sperrgranulaten benötigt man zur Synchronisation von Transaktionen auf nicht-disjunkten komplexen Objekten entsprechende Regeln zur effizienten Anforderung von Sperren. Darüber hinaus kann insbesondere im Hinblick auf lange Transaktionen eine enge Zusammenarbeit der Synchronisationskomponente und des Zugriffsrechte-Verwalters (Autorisierungs-Komponente) eines Nicht-Standard-Datenbanksystems zu einer erheblichen Steigerung des Parallelitätsgrades führen [WKS88]. Beispielsweise ist es möglich, daß im gegebenen Anwendungsfall alle Effektoren in einer gemeinsamen Bibliothek, die nur von bestimmten Transaktionen geändert werden darf, zusammengefaßt sind. Die Relation "zellen" enthält in diesem Fall lediglich logische Verweise in die Effektor-Bibliothek. Wenn eine Transaktion, die nicht das Recht hat, die Effektor-Bibliothek zu ändern, eine exklusive Sperre auf eine Zelle hält, ist es überflüssig, auch die Effektoren, die zu der bearbeiteten Zelle gehören, exklusiv zu sperren. Eine S-Sperre auf die entsprechenden Effektoren reicht hier völlig aus.

Weitere Themen für die zukünftige Arbeit sind die Durchführung von *Simulationen* im Hinblick auf die Leistungsfähigkeit des vorgestellten Verfahrens, die Integration von *Indexen* in das vorgestellte Verfahren, der Aspekt der *Erweiterbarkeit* [Linn88], die Behandlung des *Phantom-Problems* insbesondere für lange Transaktionen, ein geschicktes *Freigeben von Sperren* ("De-Eskalation") und die Einführung spezieller *Sperrmodi* für Workstation-Server-Umgebungen [LoPl83, KSUW85].

Danksagung

Die Autoren möchten sich bedanken bei den Mitarbeitern des AIM-Teams - insbesondere bei R. Gimnich, P. Pistor, E. Roman und N. Südkamp - für ihre ständige Diskussionsbereitschaft und ihre konstruktiven Kommentare, die dieses Papier verbessert haben.

Literaturverzeichnis

Astr76   M. M. Astrahan, M. W. Blasgen, D. D. Chamberlin, K. P. Eswaran, J. N. Gray, P. P. Griffiths, W. F. King, R. A. Lorie, P. R. McJones, J. W. Mehl, G. R. Putzolu, I. L. Traiger, B. W. Wade, V. Watson, *System R: Relational Approach to Database Management*, ACM Transactions on Database Systems, Vol. 1, No. 2 (June 1976), pp. 97 - 137.

BaBu84   D. S. Batory, A. P. Buchmann, *Molecular Objects, Abstract Data Types, and Data Models: A Framework*, Proceedings 10th International Conference on Very Large Data Bases (Singapore; August 27 - 31, 1984), pp. 172 - 184.

BaSc77   R. Bayer, M. Schkolnick, *Concurrency of Operations on B-Trees*, Acta Informatica 9 (1977), pp. 1 - 21.

BlPi85   A. Blaser, P. Pistor, *Tagungsband der GI-Fachtagung "Datenbanksysteme für Büro, Technik und Wissenschaft"*, Informatik-Fachberichte 94, Springer-Verlag, ISBN 3-540-15196-6 (Karlsruhe, März 1985).

ChMy88   P. Y. Chang, W. W. Myre, *OS/2 EE Database Manager overview and technical highlights*, IBM Systems Journal, Vol. 27, No. 2 (1988), pp. 105 - 118.

CLSW84 J. M. Cheng, C. R. Loosley, A. Shibamiya, P. S. Worthington, *IBM Database 2 performance: Design, implementation, and tuning,* IBM Systems Journal, Vol. 23, No. 2 (1984), pp. 189 - 210.

Dada86 P. Dadam, K. Küspert, F. Andersen, H. Blanken, R. Erbe, J. Günauer, V. Lum, P. Pistor, G. Walch, *A DBMS Prototype to Support Extended NF^2-Relations: An Integrated View on Flat Tables and Hierarchies,* Proc. ACM SIGMOD (Washington; May 28 - 30, 1986), pp. 356 - 367.

Dada88 P. Dadam, K. Küspert, N. Südkamp, R. Erbe, V. Linnemann, P. Pistor, G. Walch, *Managing Complex Objects in R^2D^2,* HECTOR, Volume II: Basic Projects; G. Krüger, G. Müller (eds.); Springer-Verlag, ISBN 3-540-19137-2; pp. 304 - 331.

Date85 C. J. Date, *An Introduction to Database Systems, Volume II, Third Edition,* Addison-Wesley Publishing Company, Inc.; ISBN 0-201-14474-3 (July 1985).

DGW85 U. Deppisch, J. Günauer, G. Walch, *Speicherungsstrukturen und Adressierungstechniken für komplexe Objekte des NF^2-Relationenmodells,* Tagungsband der GI-Fachtagung "Datenbanksysteme in Büro, Technik und Wissenschaft"; Informatik-Fachberichte 94, Springer-Verlag (Karlsruhe, März 1985), pp. 441 - 459.

Ditt86 K. R. Dittrich, *Object-oriented Database Systems: The Notion and the Issues,* Proceedings International Workshop on Object-Oriented Database Systems (Pacific Grove; September 23 - 26, 1986), pp. 2 - 4.

Ditt88 K. R. Dittrich, *Advances in Object-Oriented Database Systems, Proc. 2nd International Workshop on Object-Oriented Database Systems; Bad Münster am Stein-Ebernburg (FRG), September 27 - 30, 1988;* Lecture Notes in Computer Science 334; K. R. Dittrich (Ed.); Springer-Verlag, ISBN 0-387-50345-5.

DüKe88 M. Dürr, A. Kemper, *Transaction Control Mechanism for the Object Cache Interface of R^2D^2,* Proc. of the Third International Conference on Data and Knowledge Bases (Jerusalem; June 28 - 30, 1988); C. Beeri, J.W. Schmidt, U. Dayal (eds.), pp. 81 - 89.

GFR87 E. Grill, J. Flittner, W. Rauch, *Integration of CAx via Relational Databases,* Information Management 1/87, pp. 54 - 64.

GLPT76 J. N. Gray, R. A. Lorie, G. R. Putzolu, I. L. Traiger, *Granularity of Locks and Degrees of Consistency in a Shared Data Base,* in: "Modelling in Database Management Systems", G. M. Nijssen (ed.), North Holland Publishing Company (1976), pp. 365 - 394.

HaLo82 R. L. Haskin, R. A. Lorie, *On Extending the Functions of a Relational Database System,* Proceedings ACM SIGMOD (Orlando; June 2-4, 1982), pp. 207 - 212.

Härd88 T. Härder, *The PRIMA Project - Design and Implementation of a Non-Standard Database System,* University Kaiserslautern, SFB 124, Report No. 26/88 (March 1988).

HHMM88 T. Härder, C. Hübel, K. Meyer-Wegener, B. Mitschang, *Processing and transaction concepts for cooperation of engineering workstations and a database server,* Data & Knowledge Engineering, Vol. 3, No. 2; Special Issue: First International Conference on Data and Knowledge Systems for Manufacturing and Engineering (September 1988), pp. 87 - 107.

JaSc82 G. Jaeschke, H.-J. Schek, *Remarks on the Algebra of Non First Normal Form Relations,* Proceedings of the Fourth ACM SIGACT-SIGMOD Symposium on Principles of Database Systems (Los Angeles; March 29 - 31, 1982), pp. 124 - 138.

KDG87 K. Küspert, P. Dadam, J. Günauer, *Cooperative Object Buffer Management in the Advanced Information Management Prototype,* Proceedings 13th International Conference on Very Large Data Bases (Brighton; September 01 - 04, 1987), pp. 483 - 492; also available as: Technical Report TR 87.02.002, IBM Scientific Center Heidelberg (Heidelberg, February 1987).

KLMP84 W. Kim, R. Lorie, D. McNabb, W. Plouffe, *A Transaction Mechanism for Engineering Design Databases,* Proceedings 10th International Conference on Very Large Data Bases (Singapore; August 27 - 31, 1984), pp. 355 - 362.

KSUW85 P. Klahold, G. Schlageter, R. Unland, W. Wilkes, *A Transaction Model Supporting Complex Applications in Integrated Information Systems,* Proc. ACM SIGMOD (Austin; May 28 - 31, 1985), pp. 388 - 401.

KuRo81 H. T. Kung, J. T. Robinson, *On Optimistic Methods for Concurrency Control,* ACM Transactions on Database Systems, Vol. 6, No. 2 (June 1981), pp. 213 - 226.

KWD88 A. Kemper, M. Wallrath, M. Dürr, *Object Orientation in R^2D^2,* HECTOR, Volume II: Basic Projects; G. Krüger, G. Müller (eds.); Springer-Verlag, ISBN 3-540-19137-2; pp. 332 - 354.

Linn88 V. Linnemann, K. Küspert, P. Dadam, P. Pistor, R. Erbe, N. Südkamp, G. Walch, A. Kemper, M. Wallrath, *Design and Implementation of an Extensible Database Management System Supporting User Defined Data Types and Functions,* Proceedings 14th International Conference on Very Large Data Bases (Los Angeles; August 29 - September 01, 1988), pp. 294 - 305.

LoPl83 R. Lorie, W. Plouffe, *Complex Objects and Their Use in Design Transactions,* Proc. ACM SIGMOD, Database Week, Engineering Design Applications (San Jose; May 23 - 26, 1983), pp. 115 - 121.

Lori85 R. Lorie, W. Kim, D. McNabb, W. Plouffe, A. Meier, *Supporting Complex Objects in a Relational System for Engineering Databases,* in "Query Processing in Database Systems"; W. Kim, D. S. Reiner, Don S. Batory (eds.); Springer-Verlag, ISBN 0-387-13831-5, pp. 145 - 155.

Lutt88 H. Lutterbach, *Tagungsband der Fachtagung "Non-Standard Datenbanken für Anwendungen der Graphischen Datenverarbeitung"; Dortmund; 21. - 22. März, 1988;* Informatik-Fachberichte 171, Springer-Verlag, ISBN 3-540-19175-5.

Mits86 B. Mitschang, *MAD - ein Datenmodell zur Verwaltung von komplexen Objekten,* Universität Kaiserslautern, Fachbereich Informatik, SFB 124, Report Nr. 20/85 (Sommer 1986).

PiAn86 P. Pistor, F. Andersen, *Designing a Generalized NF^2 Model with an SQL-Type Language Interface,* Proceedings 12th International Conference on Very Large Data Bases (Kyoto; August 25 - 28, 1986), pp. 278 - 288.

Reut82   A. Reuter, *Concurrency on High-Traffic Data Elements,* Proceedings of the First ACM SIGACT-SIG-MOD Symposium on Principles of Database Systems (Los Angeles; March 29 - 31, 1982), pp. 83 - 92.

RiSt77   D. R. Ries, M. Stonebraker, *Effects of Locking Granularity in a Database Management System,* ACM Transactions on Database Systems, Vol. 2, No. 3 (September 1977), pp. 233 - 246.

ScSc86   H.-J. Schek, M. H. Scholl, *The Relational Model with Relation-Valued Attributes,* Information Systems, Vol. 11, No. 2 (1986), pp. 137 - 147.

ScSc87   H.-J. Schek, G. Schlageter, *Tagungsband der GI-Fachtagung "Datenbanksysteme in Büro, Technik und Wissenschaft"; Darmstadt; 01. - 03. April, 1987;* Informatik-Fachberichte 136, Springer-Verlag, ISBN 3-540-17736-1.

Seli79   P. G. Selinger, M. M. Astrahan, D. D. Chamberlin, R. A. Lorie, T. G. Price, *Access Path Selection in a Relational Database Management System,* Proceedings ACM SIGMOD (Boston; May 31 - June 01, 1979), pp. 23 - 34.

Weik88   G. Weikum, *Transaktionen in Datenbanksystemen,* Internationale Computer-Bibliothek, H. Zima (Hrsg.); Addison-Wesley Verlag (Deutschland) GmbH, Bonn; ISBN 3-925118-91-8 (1988).

WKS88   W. Wilkes, P. Klahold, G. Schlageter, *Complex and Composite Objects in CAD/CAM Databases,* University of Hagen, Informatik Berichte Nr. 80 (Hagen; April 1988).

Ein allgemeines Modell für Sperren in Nicht-Konventionellen Datenbanken[*]

Rainer Unland, Gunter Schlageter

FernUniversität Hagen
Lehrstuhl Praktische Informatik I
Feithstr. 140
D-5800 Hagen 1

1. Einleitung

Die Entwicklung und Implementierung sogenannter nicht-konventioneller Datenbanksysteme genießt gegenwärtig eine sehr hohe Priorität in der Datenbankwelt. Vorschläge reichen von der Verbesserung bzw. Aufwertung herkömmlicher Datenbanksysteme (z. B. AIM-P /LDEG85/) bis hin zur vollständigen Neukonzeption (z. B. ORION /WoKi87/). Ein sehr erfolgsversprechender Ansatz scheint dabei die Idee des Datenbankkernsystems (/HäRe85/) zu sein, wie sie z. B. in DASDBS (/PSSW87/), OMS (/FrBo89/) oder PRIMA (/Härd88/) verwirklicht wurde. Hierbei wird angenommen, daß **ein** Datenbanksystem bzw. dessen Datenmodell alleine nicht in der Lage sein wird, für alle denkbaren Anwendungen eine geeignete und effiziente Unterstützung zu bieten. Vielmehr ist davon auszugehen, daß eine Reihe von Anwendungen derart komplex sind, daß sie nur durch spezielle, anwendungsspezifische Datenmodelle ausreichend unterstützt werden können. Das Datenbankkernsystem realisiert dabei die (gemeinsamen) unteren Schichten und stellt dadurch die Basis zur Verfügung, auf die anwendungsspezifische Datenmodelle abgebildet werden können. Die Architektur von Datenbankkernsystemen entspricht damit einer Schichtenarchitektur (/HäRe85/).

Bisher wurde bereits sehr viel Arbeit in die Entwicklung eines geeigneten Speichersystems und der dazugehörigen Zugriffspfade investiert. Weniger Aufmerksamkeit fand dagegen die Konzeption eines adequaten Transaktionsmanagers. Aber gerade das Transaktionsmanagement in nicht-konventionellen Anwendungen stellt sehr vielschichtige und komplexe Anforderungen (siehe z. B.: /DKML84/, /KSUW85/, /LoPl83/). Da sich neuere Anwendungen zum Teil ganz erheblich in ihrer Handhabung von und in ihren Ansprüchen an Daten bzw. Objekte(n) unterscheiden, muß der Transaktionsmanager sehr flexibel und anpassungsfähig ausgelegt sein. Unglücklicherweise können die Ansprüche unterschiedlicher Anwendungsumgebungen aber nicht nur anders geartet sein, sondern sie können sich sogar widersprechen. Als Konsequenz aus dieser Erkenntnis ergibt sich, daß **ein** fest vorgegebener Transaktionsmanager nur ein mehr oder weniger zufriedenstellender Kompromiß sein kann. Aus diesem Grunde sind wir der Meinung, daß es notwendig ist, eine Art flexiblen und erweiterbaren Baukasten für das Transaktionsmanagement bereitzustellen. Ein solcher Baukasten soll dabei nicht das Instrumentarium sein, mit dem der Endbenutzer operiert. Vielmehr soll er die Grundlage für das vom Datenbank-Spezialisten zu entwickelnde Anwender-Modell sein, d.h. der Baukasten muß die Basisoperationen zur Verfügung stellen, die für die Entwicklung des Anwendermodells (in Bezug auf die Synchronisationsaspekte) notwendig sind. Der Baukasten ist damit der gleichen Schicht zuzuordnen, die auch das Datenmodell des Datenbankkernsystems realisiert.

In diesem Papier werden wir uns auf die Konzepte beschränken, die notwendig sind, um einen Baukasten für die Synchronisation zur Verfügung stellen zu können. Andere Aspekte, wie z. B. lange und geschachtelte Transaktionen, Recovery oder die Unterstützung von kooperativer Arbeitsweise (z. B. durch Kommunikationsmechanismen) werden nicht behandelt.

Der Baukasten für die Synchronisation muß zunächst einmal eine geeignete und ausreichende Menge von Basis-Sperrmodi zur Verfügung stellen. Weiterhin sollte nicht nur die Möglichkeit bestehen, Sperren an Transaktionen zu binden (wie im klas-

---

[*] Diese Arbeit entstand im Rahmen des von der DFG geförderten Schwerpunktprogramms 'Objektbanken für Experten'

sischen Falle), sondern Sperren sollten auch an Objekte gebunden werden können (die Notwendigkeit dieser Forderung wird im weiteren noch klar werden). Der Baukasten sollte natürlich in der Lage sein, Anforderungen wie z. B. die Serialisierbarkeit ebenso wie die anwendungs- bzw. benutzerabhängige Konsistenz zu unterstützen. Auch sollte die Arbeit z. B. auf unterschiedlichen Versionsmodellen (Zeitversionen, Versionsgraphen, usw.) ebenso gefördert werden, wie der Umgang mit Bibliotheks- oder Standardobjekten (Objekte, die nicht mehr geändert werden können).

Diese Arbeit entstand im Rahmen des von der DFG geförderten Schwerpunktprogramms *'Objektbanken für Experten'*. Der hier vorgestellte Baukasten soll innerhalb dieses Schwerpunktprogramms zunächst in DASDBS und OMS eingebaut werden. Innerhalb dieser Kooperationen ist dann auch abzuklären, in welcher Form die hier vorgestellten Konzepte auf die tieferen Schichten des Datenbankkernsystems abgebildet werden können.

Auf den folgenden Seiten können aus Platzgründen nur recht abstrakt die groben Ideen zum Baukasten vorgestellt werden. Der interessierte Leser sei auf die Papiere /Unla88/ und /UnSc88/ verwiesen.

2. Der Baukasten-Ansatz zur Synchronisation

2.1 Sperrmodi

Konventionelle Datenbanksysteme arbeiten lediglich mit einem exklusiven (X-) und einem gemeinsamen (S-) Sperrmodus (hierarchische Sperren werden hier nicht betrachtet). Da Transaktionen in diesen Umgebungen in der Regel nur von kurzer Dauer sind, sind diese beiden Sperrmodi i. d. R. auch ausreichend. Nichtkonventionelle Anwendungen verhalten sich jedoch völlig anders. Transaktionen sind üblicherweise interaktiv, häufig geschachtelt und von langer Dauer. Aus diesem Grunde werden Objekte bzw. Daten auch für eine erheblich längere Zeit blockiert. In solchen Umgebungen macht es daher durchaus Sinn, die bisherigen Sperrmodi zu überdenken, mit dem Ziel, eine Anzahl von Sperrmodi zu entwickeln, die exakt zu den Operationen passen, die auf dem Objekt ausgeführt werden sollen.
Uns erscheinen dabei mindestens die Sperren laut Figur 2.1 notwendig zu sein.

Exklusive Sperre (X-Sperre): erlaubt das Lesen, Ändern und Löschen eines Objektes.
Update-Sperre (U-Sperre): erlaubt das Lesen und Ändern eines Objektes, nicht aber das Löschen.
Ableitungs-Sperre (A-Sperre): erlaubt das Lesen einer Objektversion und das Ableiten einer neuen Objekversion aus der alten.
Gemeinsame Sperre (S-Sperre): erlaubt nur das Lesen eines Objektes.
Browse-Sperre (B-Sperre): erlaubt jederzeit das (schmutzige) Lesen eines Objektes.

Figur 2.1: Sperrmodi

Die Ableitungssperre ist eine Sperre, die im Zusammenhang mit Versionen von Interesse ist. Sie erlaubt das Erzeugen einer neuen Objektversion aus einer alten, wobei die alte Version erhalten bleibt. Die neue Version wird Nachfolger der alten.

2.2 Die Semantik von Sperren

Sperrverfahren regeln den Zugang zu den Daten in einer relativ restriktiven Art und Weise: Grundsätzlich besitzt eine Transaktion zunächst einmal überhaupt keine Rechte, auf den Daten der Datenbank zu arbeiten. Erst über die (konkurrierende) Bewerbung um und den Erhalt von Sperren werden notwendige Rechte erworben. Im weiteren wird zwischen **Sperrbesitzer** und **Sperrbewerber** unterschieden. Ein Sperrbesitzer besitzt bereits eine Sperre auf einem Objekt, während ein Sperrbewerber eine solche noch erwerben möchte.
Untersucht man den Sperrvorgang genauer, so stellt man fest, daß eine Sperre zwei Formen von Konsequenzen mit sich bringt:

1. Der Sperrbesitzer darf bestimmte Operationen auf dem gesperrten Objekt durchführen und
2. alle anderen, parallelen Transaktionen können - abhängig von der Art der Sperre - in ihren Möglichkeiten eingeschränkt werden, ebenfalls auf dem Objekt zu arbeiten.

Diese Zerlegung der Auswirkungen einer Sperre erlaubt es, eine Unterscheidung vorzunehmen zwischen den Operationen bzw. Rechten, die dem Sperrbesitzer zugestanden werden (1.) und den Einschränkungen, die Sperrbewerbern auferlegt werden (2.). Auswirkung 1 wird im folgenden **Innenwirkung** einer Sperre genannt werden, Auswirkung 2 **Außenwirkung**.

Betrachtet man noch einmal Figur 2.1, so wird deutlich, daß hier die Innenwirkungen der einzelnen Sperrmodi aufgeführt sind.

Die Betrachtung der Außenwirkungen läßt einigen Interpretationsspielraum offen. Während in konventionellen Systemen die operationale Integrität durch das System garantiert werden soll, möchte man diese strenge Sicht in nicht-konventionellen Anwendungen gelegentlich etwas abmildern, indem dem Benutzer eine gewisse Verantwortlichkeit für den korrekten Ablauf von Operationen auf Objekten überlassen werden soll. Daher muß bei den Außenwirkungen zwischen Konflikten unterschieden werden, bei denen Konsistenzverletzungen unvermeidlich sein können, und solchen, die dann zu keinen Konsistenzverletzungen führen, wenn der Benutzer geeignet (d. h. konsistenzwahrend) auf den Objekten arbeitet. Zwei parallele Update-Operationen auf einem Objekt vertragen sich in diesem Sinne auf keinen Fall (zumindest dann nicht, wenn ein Objekt vom System als eine nicht zerlegbare (atomare) Einheit aufgefaßt wird, so daß die Update-Operationen nicht als auf unterschiedlichen Subkomponenten ausgeführt betrachtet werden können). Dagegen können sich eine Update- und eine Lese-Operation auf demselben Objekt dann vertragen, wenn eine mögliche Änderung des Objektes durch den Updater für den Leser keine negativen Konsequenzen mit sich bringt. Legt man diese Semantik zugrunde, so ergeben sich die folgenden minimalen Außenwirkungen (in Klammern die erlaubten Operationen und die, deren Ausführung erlaubt werden könnte (möglich)):

  X-Sperre: Lesen, Ableiten, Ändern und Löschen verboten
  U-Sperre: Ableiten, Ändern und Löschen verboten, (Lesen möglich)
  A-Sperre: Ändern und Löschen verboten, (Lesen erlaubt, Ableiten möglich)
  S-Sperre: Löschen verboten, (Lesen erlaubt, Ableiten oder/und Ändern möglich)
  B-Sperre: (alles erlaubt)

2.3 Kompatibilität von Sperren

Um nun ein generelles Verfahren zur Definition von Sperrmodi zu ermöglichen, sollte es erlaubt sein, die Innen- und Außenwirkung einer Sperre im Rahmen der vorgegebenen Möglichkeiten jeweils individuell festzulegen. Eine Sperranforderung besteht demnach aus der Festlegung der Innenwirkung und der Wahl der dazu gewünschten Außenwirkung. Die zu einer vorgegebenen Innenwirkung möglichen Außenwirkungen können der Kompatibilitäts-Matrix (Tabelle 2.1) entnommen werden.

In der Kompatibilitätsmatrix sind die mit + und - belegten Operationen festgelegt und nicht veränderbar. Bei einem + ist demnach die dazugehörige Operation (Spalte) immer erlaubt, bei einem - immer verboten. Ein * in einer Zeile gibt an, daß die entsprechende Innenwirkung mit der entsprechenden Außenwirkung kombiniert werden darf aber nicht muß.

Um im folgenden eine Sperre präzise beschreiben zu können, muß neben der Innenwirkung ihre Außenwirkung angegeben werden. **X/Y** soll daher eine Sperre bezeichnen, die die Innenwirkung X mit der Außenwirkung Y kombiniert. Aus der obigen Kompatibilitätsmatrix läßt sich nun entnehmen, daß gewisse Operationen grundsätzlich erlaubt (+) oder verboten (-) sind, so daß Kombinationen wie B/A oder X/S nicht vorkommen können. Da die Zeilen für X und B kein * enthalten, gibt es für diese beiden Sperrtypen generell nur die Sperrkombination X/B und B/X. Ersetzt man nun in den übrigen Zeilen * durch + oder -, so lassen sich insgesamt neun verschiedene Möglichkeiten ableiten, Sperrkombinationen zu definieren: B/X, S/U, S/A, S/S, A/A, A/S, U/S, U/B, und X/B.

Auch in anderen Arbeiten zum Thema Synchronisation in nicht-konventionellen Datenbanken ist festgestellt worden, daß die bekannten Sperrmodi in vielen neueren Anwendungsumgebungen (vor allem in CAD/CAM-Umgebungen) nicht ausreichen. Alle uns bekannten Vorschläge für neue Sperrmodi (z. B. /KSUW85/, /LoPl83/) lassen sich durch unseren Baukasten nachbilden. Insbesondere läßt sich auch der mittlerweile allgemein als wesentlich akzeptierte CHECKOUT / CHECKIN-Mechanismus durch die U/S Sperre modellieren.

Außenwirkung

Innenwirkung		B	S	A	U	X
	B	+	+	+	+	+
	S	+	+	*	*	−
	A	+	+	*	−	−
	U	+	*	−	−	−
	X	+	−	−	−	−

Transaktionspererre

Objektsperre		B	S	A	U	X
	PX	+	+	+	+	+
	PU	+	+	+	+	−
	PSA	+	+	$+^1$	−	−
	PXA	+	+	$+^2$	−	−
	PS	+	+	−	−	−

+ = erlaubt, - = nicht erlaubt, * = möglich
1 beliebig häufiges Ableiten erlaubt
2 nur einmaliges Ableiten erlaubt

Tabelle 2.1: Kompatibilitätsmatrix Innen-/Außenwirkung

Tabelle 2.2: Kompatibilitätsmatrix Transaktions-/Objektsperre

2.4 Die Objektsperre

Bisher wurde immer (implizit) vorausgesetzt, daß Sperren an Transaktionen gebunden sind. Eine solch enge Auslegung ist in nicht-konventionellen Anwendungen unter Umständen zu einschränkend. Ähnlich dem Lebensverlauf eines Menschen, der ledig geboren wird und irgendwann den Zustand verheiratet erreichen kann (der keinen Rücksprung mehr zum Zustand ledig erlaubt), kann es auch bei Objekten solche Lebensabschnitte geben. Betrachtet man z. B. den Versionsgraphen eines Objektes, so wird häufig der Standpunkt vertreten, daß innere Knoten nicht mehr änderbar sein sollen, da eine solche Änderung i. d. R. auch Konsequenzen für die von dieser Version abgeleiteten Versionen oder Varianten nach sich zieht. Ein möglicher Weg zur Realisierung von solchen Einschränkungen ist die Bindung von Sperren an Objekte. Solche Arten von Sperren, im weiteren **Objektsperren** genannt, wirken wie Transaktionssperren, die nur eine Innenwirkung besitzen, d. h. wird eine Objektsperre gesetzt, so kann als Erwerber der Sperre die Gemeinschaft aller (potentiellen) Transaktionen angesehen werden. Die Operationen der Innenwirkung sind weiterhin erlaubt; alle Operationen, die nicht zur Innenwirkung gehören, sind verboten. Eine weitere, ganz wesentliche Eigenschaft von Objektsperren ist, daß sie dauerhaft (persistent) sind. Daher soll die Objektsperre von der Transaktionssperre durch Voranstellen eines P unterschieden werden. Eine einmal festgelegte Objektsperre darf weder aufgehoben noch abgeschwächt werden. Sie kann nur noch verschärft werden.

Die folgenden Objektsperren lassen sich direkt ableiten:
PU-Sperre: Sie verbietet generell das Löschen eines Objektes, während alle anderen Operationen erlaubt sind.
PA-Sperre: Sie verbietet generell das Ändern und Löschen eines Objektes. Ableiten und Lesen sind weiterhin erlaubt.
PS-Sperre: Sie verbietet auf Dauer das Ableiten, Ändern und Löschen eines Objektes. Damit ist nur noch das Lesen möglich.

Von den angegebenen Objektsperren lohnt es sich insbesondere, die PA-Sperre noch eingehender zu untersuchen. Sie erlaubt zunächst einmal das Ableiten einer neuen Objektversion, macht aber keine Aussage darüber, ob dieses Ableiten ein einmaliger

Vorgang sein soll oder beliebig häufig wiederholt werden darf. Eine solche Differenzierung kann aber durchaus nützlich sein. Erlaubt man nur ein einmaliges Ableiten, so würde das dazu führen, daß nur (lineare) Versionslisten erzeugt werden können (z.B. Zeitversionen). Der andere Fall ist allgemeiner, da er das Erzeugen von Versionsgraphen erlaubt. Wegen der großen Bedeutung von Zeitversionen erscheint die obige Differenzierung der PA-Sperre durchaus geboten zu sein, so daß zwischen einer **PXA-Sperre** (einmaliges Ableiten) und einer **PSA-Sperre** (beliebig häufiges Ableiten) unterschieden werden kann.

Führt man jetzt noch die **PX-Sperre** als die Sperre ein, mit der jedes Objekt 'geboren' wird, so besitzt jedes Objekt genau eine Objektsperre, die dann im Laufe seines Lebens verschärft werden kann. Mit seiner Geburt wird die PX-Sperre gesetzt. Diese führt zu keinerlei Einschränkungen und muß auch nicht vom Sperrprotokoll beachtet werden (da sie, ähnlich wie die B-Sperre, keinerlei Konsequenzen nach sich zieht).

Wie sich Objekt- und Transaktionssperren vertragen, ist in Tabelle 2.2 dargestellt.

Die durch Objektsperren realisierten Zugriffseinschränkungen ließen sich prinzipiell auch über andere Mechanismen erreichen (z. B. Integritätsbedingungen oder Zugriffsrechte). Der hier eingeschlagene Weg besitzt jedoch den erheblichen Vorteil, daß das zusätzliche Wissen ausgenutzt werden kann, um den Sperraufwand erheblich zu verringern:
Beispielsweise bewirkt die PS-Sperre, daß das gesperrte Objekt nicht mehr vom Sperrprotokoll berücksichtigt zu werden brauchen, da generell nur noch Lesen erlaubt ist und Konflikte damit ausgeschlossen sind. Eine PS-Sperre eignet sich damit hervorragend, um z. B. Bibliotheksobjekte zu modellieren. Solche Objekte dürfen nicht geändert werden. Angenommen ein Bibliotheksobjekt *BO* ist Subkomponente in mehreren komplexen Objekten. Falls eines dieser komplexen Objekte jetzt exklusiv gesperrt würde, so könnte ein anderer Sperrbewerber normalerweise auf keines der verbleibenden komplexen Objekte zugreifen (da *BO* exklusiv gesperrt ist). Mit Hilfe der PS-Sperre ist ein solcher Zugriff aber erlaubt, da das Sperrprotokoll *BO* nicht beachten muß. Solche Situationen sind gerade in Entwicklungs-Umgebungen sehr häufig.

Literatur

/DKML84/ Dittrich, K.R.; Kotz, A. M.; Mülle, J. A.; Lockemann, P.C.: *Datenbankkonzepte für Ingenieuranwendungen: Eine Übersicht über den Stand der Entwicklung.* Proc. 14.te GI Jahrestagung, Braunschweig, 1984.

/FrBo88/ Freitag, J.; Bode, T.: *Ein allgemeiner Speicherobjektmanager als Implementierungsbasis für komplexe Objekte in einem Objektmanagementsystem,* Proc. BTW, Zürich, Schweiz, 1989

/Härd88/ Härder, T. (Editor): *The PRIMA Project: Design and Implementation of a Non-Standard Database System,* Forschungsbericht SFB 124, Universität Kaiserslautern, 1988

/HäRe85/ Härder, T.; Reuter, A.: *Architektur von Datenbanksystemen für Non-Standard-Anwendungen.* PROC. BTW, Karlsruhe, 1985

/KSUW85/ Klahold, P.; Schlageter, G.; Wilkes, W.; Unland, R.; *A Transaction Model Supporting Complex Applications in Integrated Information Systems,* Proc. ACM-Sigmod, Austin, Texas, 1985

/LDEG85/ Lum, V.; Dadam; P.; Erbe, R.; Guenauer,. J.; Pistor, P.; Walch, G.; Warner, H.; Woodfill, J.: *Design of an Integrated DBMS to Support Advanced Applications,* Proc. BTW, Karlsruhe, 1985

/LoPl83/ Lorie, R.; Plouffe, W.: *Complex Objects and Their Use in Design Transactions,* Proc. Databases for Engineering Applications, ACM-Database Week, 1983

/PSSW87/ Paul, H.B.; Schek, H.J.; Scholl, M.H., Weikum, G.; Deppisch, U.: *Architecture and Implementation of the DARMSTADT Database Kernel System,* Proc. ACM-SIGMOD, San Francisco, Kalifornien, 1987

/Unla88/ Unland, R.: *A Flexible and Adaptable Tool-Kit Approach for Concurrency Control in Non-Standard Database Systems,* Forschungsbericht, FernUniversität Hagen, (zur Veröffentlichung eingereicht), 1988

/UnSc88/ Unland, R.; Schlageter, G.: *Ein allgemeines Modell für Sperren in Nicht-Konventionellen Datenbanken,* Forschungsbericht, FernUniversität Hagen, 1988

/WoKi87/ Woelk, D.; Kim, W.: *Multimedia Information Management in an Object-Oriented Database System,* Proc. VLDB, Brighton, England, 1987

Autorisierung und Zugriffsüberwachung in strukturell objekt-orientierten Datenbanksystemen

Heribert Pfefferle

Software AG, Darmstadt

Martin Härtig, Klaus Dittrich

Forschungszentrum Informatik an der Universität Karlsruhe
Haid-und-Neu-Straße 10-14, D-7500 Karlsruhe 1

Kurzfassung

Autorisierung und Zugriffskontrolle wurden für Betriebssysteme und konventionelle (z.B. relationale) Datenbanksysteme intensiv untersucht. Objekt-orientierte Datenbanksysteme stellen jedoch neue Anforderungen und bieten neue Möglichkeiten, die es erforderlich machen, die Probleme und Lösungen auf diesem Gebiet wiederaufzugreifen. Strukturell objekt-orientierte Datenbanksysteme bilden eine größere Teilklasse und zeichnen sich dadurch aus, daß sie komplexe Objektstrukturen speichern und bearbeiten können. Das vorliegende Papier stellt die wichtigsten Konzepte eines Vertreters dieser Klasse vor. Anschließend werden die Anforderungen, die strukturell objekt-orientierte Datenbanksysteme an Autorisierung und Zugriffskontrolle stellen, abgeleitet und es wird ein Schutzkonzept präsentiert, das diesen Anforderungen gerecht wird. Abschließend werden einige Implementierungsaspekte diskutiert.

Abstract

Discretionary access control has been extensively studied for advanced operating systems and for traditional (e.g. relational) database systems (DBS). With the recent advent of object-oriented database systems, however, problems and solutions in this area have to be reconsidered as new requirements arise and new opportunities become available. Structurally object-oriented database systems are a major subclass that specifically provides features to deal with complexly structured objects in their entirety. This paper reviews the salient concepts of a typical representative of that class. It then summarizes the requirements of discretionary access control in this context and introduces a comprehensive concept fulfilling them. Finally, some aspects of its implementation are discussed.

1. Strukturell objekt-orientierte Datenbanksysteme

In den letzten Jahren wurden große Anstrengungen unternommen, die Vorteile der Datenbanktechnologie auch ingenieurwissenschaftlichen Anwendungen zugänglich zu machen. Es stellte sich dabei sehr bald heraus, daß hierfür die verfügbaren Datenbanksysteme, die für den Einsatz im betriebswirtschaftlich-administrativen Bereich konzipiert waren, wenig geeignet sind [Sidl80]. Diese Systeme bieten meist eines der "klassischen" Datenmodelle an (relational, hierarchisch, Netzwerk; [Date83]) und können als *satz-orientiert* charakterisiert werden: Daten werden in Form von einfachen, flachen Sätzen (Tupel) oder homogenen Mengen solcher Sätze modelliert. Beziehungen zwischen Sätzen sind relativ einfach. Die operationale Schnittstelle stellt generische Operatoren für den Zugriff und die Manipulation einzelner Sätze und ihrer Attribute bzw. homogener Mengen solcher Sätze zur Verfügung.

"Non-Standard-" Anwendungen wie CAD/CAM, CASE, Wissensrepräsentation etc. stellen neuartige Anforderungen an die Datenhaltung [Lock85]. Die zu modellierenden Objekte weisen eine komplexe interne Struktur auf und setzen sich typischerweise aus anderen, heterogenen Objekten zusammen. Objekte können zur Dokumentation verschiedener Entwicklungsstufen in mehreren Versionen vorliegen und sind meist durch eine Vielfalt weiterer Beziehungen miteinander verbunden. Operationen sind oftmals typspezifisch und nicht mehr atomar, sondern bearbeiten komplex strukturierte Einheiten in ihrer Gesámtheit.

Die Ausdrucksmöglichkeiten satz-orientierter Datenmodelle sind nicht mächtig genug, um diese Art von Anwendungen in befriedigender Weise zu unterstützen. Dagegen haben sich objektorientierte Datenmodelle [DiDa86, Ditt87, Banc88] als sehr geeignet erwiesen, den Anforderungen von "Non-Standard-" Anwendungen gerecht zu werden. Sie zeichnen sich in erster Linie durch die Fähigkeit aus, beliebige Objektstrukturen — unabhängig von ihrer internen Struktur, Größe und/oder ihrem Verhalten — durch genau ein Datenbank-Objekt repräsentieren zu können. Nach [DiKL89, DiDa86] lassen sich drei Klassen von objekt-orientierten Datenbanksystemen unterscheiden:

— *strukturell objekt-orientierte* Datenbanksysteme stellen Mechanismen (sowohl Strukturen als auch generische Operatoren) zur Verfügung, welche die Darstellung und Bearbeitung von strukturierten (aus anderen Objekten aufgebauten) Objekten erlauben.

— *verhaltensmäßig objektorientierte* Datenbanksysteme erlauben dem Benutzer die Definition von Objekttypen zusammen mit typspezifischen Operatoren (z.B. im Sinne abstrakter Datentypen).

— *voll objekt-orientierte* Datenbanksysteme vereinen die Eigenschaften von strukturell und verhaltensmäßig objekt-orientierten Datenbanksystemen.

Wir konzentrieren uns in diesem Papier auf strukturell objekt-orientierte Datenbanksysteme und stellen zunächst einen Vertreter aus dieser Klasse von Systemen vor, der uns als Anschauungsobjekt zur Erläuterung unserer Schutzkonzepte dient.

Das EODM von DAMOKLES

Im Rahmen des DAMOKLES-Projekts [DiGL87] wird ein Datenbanksystem entwickelt und prototypisch implementiert, dessen Konzepte speziell für den Einsatz in Software-Produktionsumgebungen (CASE) und verwandten Anwendungsgebieten zugeschnitten sind. Das *Entwurfsobjekt-Datenmodell* (EODM; [DAMO88, Abra87]) von DAMOKLES kann als eine (allerdings mächtige) Erweiterung des Entity-Relationship Ansatzes charakterisiert werden. Die wichtigsten Konzepte des EODM werden im folgenden kurz beschrieben; Abbildung 1 illustriert sie an einem Beispiel.

Ein *Objekt* ist eine selbständig existierende Einheit eines bestimmten Typs, beschrieben durch deskriptive und strukturelle Eigenschaften. Die *deskriptiven* Eigenschaften werden durch Attribute spezifiziert, die Objekten Elemente einfacher oder zusammengesetzter Wertemengen zuordnen. Ein Objekt kann *strukturiert* sein und aus Unterobjekten und Unterbeziehungen bestehen. Ein strukturiertes Objekt kann selbst wieder Unterobjekt in einem anderen strukturierten Objekt werden, so daß sich eine Objekthierarchie ergibt. Es kann auch Überlappungen geben, wenn ein Objekt gleichzeitig Komponente in verschiedenen strukturierten Objekten ist. Mit "Anker" bezeichnen wir ein Objekt ohne seine Komponenten.

Ein weiteres Konzept zum Umgang mit Objekten sind *Versionen*. Versionen beziehen sich immer auf ein zugrundeliegendes generisches Objekt, wobei jede Version die Eigenschaften seines generischen Objekts *ererbt*. Versionen werden genauso wie Objekte behandelt: sie können deskriptive und strukturelle Eigenschaften haben, können wiederum versionsbehaftet sein und in Beziehungen eingebracht werden. Die Menge der Versionen eines generischen Objekts ist geordnet und kann linear, baumartig oder azyklisch verwaltet werden.

Ferner werden in DAMOKLES *Beziehungen* als n-stellige Assoziationen von Objekten angeboten. Beziehungen werden zu Beziehungstypen zusammengefaßt und können wie Objekttypen mit Attributen versehen werden. Beziehungsexemplare können wie Objekte als Unterbeziehungen in strukturierte Objekte eingefügt werden.

Objekte und Beziehungen erhalten beim Einfügen in eine Datenbasis einen systemvergebenen, eindeutigen *Datenbankschlüssel* (Surrogat). Der Datenbankschlüssel bleibt während der Lebenszeit eines Exemplars unverändert und wird nach dem Löschen des Exemplars kein zweites Mal vergeben. Einige Operatoren liefern als Ergebnis zunächst nur den betreffenden Datenbankschlüssel. Mit Hilfe des Datenbankschlüssels kann der Anwender mit den Objekten arbeiten, bevor er sie endgültig in seinen Arbeitsbereich einliest.

Die Menge der Objekte und Beziehungen kann logisch auf mehrere *Datenbasen* verteilt werden. Eine Datenbasis kann als Behälter interpretiert werden, in den eine beliebige Anzahl von Objekten und Beziehungen eingebracht werden kann. Während (strukturierte) Objekte vollständig in einer Datenbasis enthalten sein müssen, können Beziehungen Objekte aus verschiedenen Datenbasen verbinden. Datenbasen dienen in DAMOKLES ferner als Einheit der Verteilung in einer Server-Workstation Architektur.

Objekte können in beliebiger Weise zwischen Datenbasen kopiert und transferiert werden. Darüberhinaus bietet DAMOKLES mit seinen "Design Transactions" (Entwurfstransaktionen) [Rehm88] ein Konzept zur Unterstützung von parallelen Entwurfsprozessen und der kontrollierten Zusammenarbeit mehrerer Entwickler. Während einer Entwurfstransaktion kann ein Entwerfer mittels eines Checkout/Checkin Mechanismus Objekte zeitweilig aus "öffentlichen" Datenbasen in seine "private" Datenbasis ausleihen und dort bearbeiten.

Für jedes der beschriebenen Konzepte bietet die Datenmanipulationssprache des EODM geeignete Operatoren an. Beispiele für solche Operatoren sind:

— Generieren/Löschen von Datenbasen/Objekten/Versionen/Beziehungen,
— Ein-/Ausfügen von Komponenten in/aus komplexen Objekten,
— Navigieren innerhalb komplexer Objekte, in Versionsgraphen und entlang von Beziehungen,
— Kopieren oder Transferieren eines komplexen Objekts zwischen Datenbasen,
— Aus-/Einlagern eines komplexen Objekts aus einer Datenbasis in eine andere (Checkout/-in).

2. Schutz in strukturell objekt-orientierten Datenbanksystemen

In einem Datenbanksystem ist Zugriffsschutz vor allem deshalb wichtig, weil der Integrationsgrad der Daten besonders hoch ist — Datenintegration ist bekanntlich ein wesentliches Ziel des Datenbankeinsatzes — und verschiedene Benutzer unter verschiedenen Gesichtspunkten auf dieselben physisch vorhandenen Daten zugreifen. Mit einem Schutzkonzept soll verhindert werden, daß nichtlegitimierte Benutzer in ein System eindringen und/oder daß ein an sich legitimer Benutzer in einem System Operationen ausführt, für die er keine Erlaubnis hat.

Einem Schutzsystem obliegt es, zum einen Zugriffsrechte zu definieren, die festlegen, welche Benutzer wie auf welche Daten zugreifen dürfen und zum anderen diese Beschränkungen mit Hilfe eines Überwachungssystems durchzusetzen. Nach [Denn82], [Ditt83], [HsKM79] und [Schi81] kann

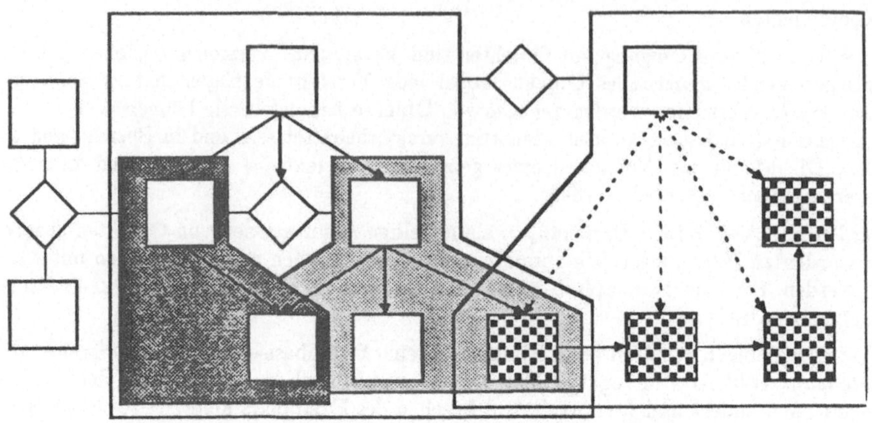

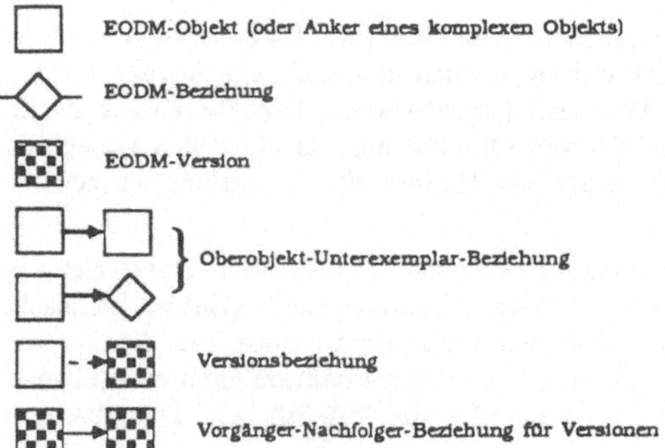

Abb. 1: Beispiel für eine DAMOKLES-Datenbasis (Exemplarebene)

ein Schutzsystem durch folgende Merkmale charakterisiert werden:

(a) Mit den *Subjekten* wird spezifiziert, welche Instanzen im System Zugriffsrechte erhalten sollen. Subjekte sind aktive Systembestandteile wie Benutzer, Benutzergruppen, Programme oder auch Kombinationen aus Benutzer und Programm.

(b) *Schutzobjekte* sind die Bestandteile des Systems, die vor unberechtigtem Zugriff geschützt werden sollen, auf die sich also die Zugriffsrechte beziehen. Schutzobjekte können beispielsweise Dateien, Datenbankrelationen oder ausführbare Programme sein.

(c) Mit *Operationen* bezeichnet man die von den Subjekten ausgelösten Aktionen auf Objekte, die vom Schutzsystem unterschieden werden können. Beispiele für Operationen sind: Schreiben in eine Datei, Suchen in einem Directory oder Ausführen eines Programms. Auch die Vergabe von Rechten kann als eine Operation aufgefaßt werden, denn damit ist eine Änderung in den Schutzinformationen verbunden.

(d) Durch die Vergabe von *Rechten* werden Subjekte zu Operationen an Objekten berechtigt. Ein wichtiges Merkmal bei diesem Vorgang ist die *Detaillierung* des vergebenen Rechts, d.h. in welchen Portionen Zugriffsrechte vergeben werden können.

(e) Die *Autorisierung* legt fest, wie Rechte an Subjekte vergeben bzw. von ihnen zurückgerufen werden.

(f) Die *Zugriffsüberwachung* ist dafür verantwortlich, nicht erlaubte Aktionen im System zu erkennen und zu verhindern.

Beim Entwurf eines Schutzsystems für ein Datenbanksystem müssen diese Merkmale unter Berücksichtigung des Datenmodells und des intendierten Anwendungsgebietes geeignet gewählt werden. Dabei werden insbesondere die Eigenschaften (b), (c) und (d) durch das zugrundeliegende Datenmodell beeinflußt. Ihnen gilt deshalb unser Hauptinteresse.

Die neuen Konzepte, die objekt-orientierte gegenüber satz-orientierten Datenbanksystemen auszeichnen, stellen zusätzliche Anforderungen an ein Schutzsystem:

— Der Informationsgehalt eines Objekts ist nicht allein durch seine Attribute, sondern durch weitere Eigenschaften (strukturelle Eigenschaften, Versionen) gegeben, die individuell schützbar sein sollten.

— Bei der Festlegung der Schutzobjekte müssen nicht nur atomare Objekte, sondern insbesondere strukturierte Objekte berücksichtigt werden.

— Infolgedessen muß der Zusammenhang zwischen Rechten auf strukturierten Objekten und deren Komponenten in sinnvoller Weise definiert werden.

— Änderungen in der Struktur von zusammengesetzten Objekten müssen der Zugriffskontrolle unterworfen werden.

— Mit den komplexen Objektstrukturen taucht in verstärktem Maße ein Problem auf, das auch bei Systemen nach dem Netzwerk- oder hierarchischen Modell in der Literatur unter dem Namen *Pass-Through-Problem* beschrieben wurde [HsKM79]: zum Zugriff auf ein bestimmtes Objekt muß ein anderes Objekt *überquert* werden, auf das man eigentlich keinen Zugriff hätte.

Weitere Anforderungen resultieren aus dem Anwendungsgebiet, das unseren Forschungsarbeiten zugrundeliegt: Im Entwurfsbereich müssen "private" Arbeitsbereiche unterstützt und Konzepte wie Entwurfstransaktionen und Checkout/Checkin-Mechanismen beim Entwurf eines Schutzsystems berücksichtigt werden. Schließlich darf das Leistungsverhalten des Datenbanksystems durch die Integration von Schutzmechanismen nicht über Gebühr beeinträchtigt werden.

3. Konzeptentwurf

Wir wollen nun das für DAMOKLES entworfene Schutzkonzept vorstellen. Dazu orientieren wir uns an den im letzten Abschnitt beschriebenen Merkmalen eines Schutzsystems und beschreiben, wie diese in unserem Falle definiert sind. Einige Beispiele am Ende des Kapitels illustrieren die entwickelten Konzepte.

Wir haben uns für ein *positives* Schutzkonzept entschieden: jede Aktion im System muß explizit autorisiert werden, das Fehlen eines Rechts wird als "Aktion nicht erlaubt" interpretiert. Um eine im EODM von DAMOKLES angebotene Operation durchführen zu können, ist i.a. mehr als ein Recht notwendig. Dies liegt zum einen daran, daß unser Schutzsystem zweistufig konzipiert ist und Schutz sowohl auf Exemplar-, als auch auf Datenbasisebene vorsieht. Zum anderen erstreckt sich eine EODM-Operation meist auf mehrere Schutzobjekte, für die entsprechende Rechte vorhanden sein müssen.

3.1 Subjekte

Unser Schutzkonzept sieht als eigenständige Einheiten Benutzer vor, die man zu Benutzergruppen zusammenfassen darf. Eine Benutzergruppe darf selbst wieder Mitglied in anderen Benutzergruppen werden, womit eine Benutzergruppenhierarchie aufgebaut werden kann. Die gleichzeitige Mitgliedschaft in mehreren Gruppen ist erlaubt. Jeder Benutzer kann Gruppen bilden und wird dadurch deren *Verwalter* mit dem Recht, neue Benutzer in die Gruppe aufzunehmen und Mitglieder aus der Gruppe zu entfernen; der Gruppenverwalter kann seine Rolle an andere Mitglieder übertragen. Als weitere eigenständige Einheiten werden Programme berücksichtigt, die analog zu Benutzern eine hierarchische und überlappende Programmgruppenstruktur bilden können.

Als Subjekte wählen wir dann Paare (B,P), wobei B ein Benutzer oder eine Benutzergruppe und P ein Programm oder eine Programmgruppe ist. Dies gestattet es, bei der Autorisierung zu berücksichtigen, mit welchem Programm P ein Benutzer B auf bestimmte Objekte zugreifen darf. Für P (B) können auch die Gruppen "all_progs" ("all_users") gewählt werden, so daß ein Benutzer mit jedem beliebigen Programm auf die Daten zugreifen oder ein Programm von jedem Benutzer auf den Daten ausgeführt werden darf. Die Gruppenhierarchien für Benutzer und Programme dienen dazu, mittels einer Autorisierung gleich mehreren "zusammengehörenden" Benutzern (z.B. einer Projektgruppe) bzw. Programmen Rechte erteilen zu können: Die Mitglieder einer Benutzer- oder Programmgruppe erben diejenigen Zugriffsrechte, die für die Gruppe ausgesprochen wurden.

Das Schutzsystem sieht auch einen Datenbankadministrator vor, der bestimmte Verwaltungsaufgaben übernimmt, wie zum Beispiel neue Benutzer einzufügen oder vorhandene Benutzer zu entfernen. Er besitzt jedoch nur die zur Bewältigung dieser Verwaltungsaufgaben notwendigen Privilegien. Für weitergehende Aktionen muß er wie jeder andere Benutzer mit Zugriffsrechten ausgestattet werden.

3.2 Schutzobjekte

Die Wahl der Schutzobjekte wird in erheblichem Maße von dem zugrundeliegenden Datenmodell bestimmt. Wie bereits bei den Anforderungen im letzten Kapitel erläutert, muß berücksichtigt werden, daß EODM- Objekte und Beziehungen verschiedene -"Arten" von Information tragen, die differenzierten Schutz erfordern. Es ist daher sinnvoll, Objekte und Beziehungen für Schutzzwecke zunächst in feinere Einheiten aufzuspalten, die dann die "kleinsten zu schützenden" Granulate, die *atomaren* Schutzobjekte bilden (siehe Abbildung 2):

- ein Objekt wird aufgeteilt in
  - einen deskriptiven Teil D (Attribute des Objekts)
  - einen strukturellen Teil S (Unterexemplare des Objekts)
  - und einen versionstragenden Teil V (Versionen des Objekts)
- eine Beziehung wird aufgeteilt in
  - einen deskriptiven Teil A (Attribute der Beziehung)
  - und einen relationstragenden Teil R (Rollen der Beziehung)

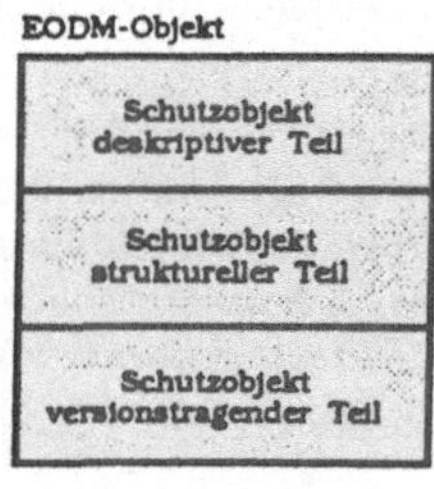

Abb. 2: atomare Schutzobjekte in DAMOKLES

Ein strukturell objekt-orientiertes Datenbanksystem macht es natürlich erforderlich, auch strukturierte Objekte als Einheiten der Autorisierung und Zugriffskontrolle vorzusehen. Strukturierte Objekte führen zu *molekularen* Schutzobjekten; sie umfassen alle von dem Anker des Objekts aus über die Oberobjekt-Unterexemplar-Beziehung erreichbaren Komponenten des Objekts. Für ein generisches Objekt nehmen wir ferner alle zugehörigen Versionen in das molekulare Schutzobjekt mit auf. Auf die Wechselwirkung zwischen molekularen und atomaren Schutzobjekten kommen wir bei der Erläuterung der Autorisierung zurück.

Die bisher definierten Schutzobjekte entsprechen der Exemplarebene. Als weitere Schutzobjekte wählen wir ganze Datenbasen. Auch hier wird das Zusammenwirken zwischen dem Schutzobjekt Datenbasis und den darin enthaltenen atomaren und molekularen Schutzobjekten zu klären sein.

3.3 Operationen

Aufgrund der großen Zahl von Operatoren, die in der Datenmanipulationssprache (DML) des EODM angeboten werden, ist es nicht sinnvoll, jede DML-Operation auch als Operation im Sinne des Schutzsystems aufzufassen. Insbesondere die Autorisierung würde dadurch zu unübersichtlich. Wir zerlegen daher die DML-Operatoren und fassen die resultierenden "Elementaroperationen" in *Operationsklassen* zusammen. Die Semantik einer Operationsklasse hängt davon ab, auf welches Schutzobjekt eine Operation ausgeführt wird. Wir unterscheiden die folgenden vier Klassen:

- Operationsklasse *Exist*
  - Objekte: den Datenbankschlüssel lesen
  - Beziehungen: den Datenbankschlüssel lesen
- Operationsklasse *Read*
  - Datenbasen: Objekte und Beziehungen lesen
  - Objekte: die Attribute lesen
                   die Datenbankschlüssel der Unterexemplare lesen
                   die Datenbankschlüssel der Versionen lesen
  - Beziehungen: die Attribute lesen
                   die Datenbankschlüssel in den Rollen lesen
- Operationsklasse *Write*
  - Datenbasen: Objekte und Beziehungen ändern/löschen
  - Objekte: die Attribute ändern
                   Unterexemplare einfügen oder ausfügen
                   Versionen einfügen oder löschen
  - Beziehungen: die Attribute ändern
                   die Datenbankschlüssel in den Rollen ändern
- Operationsklasse *Delete*
  - Datenbasen: Datenbasis löschen
  - Objekte: Objekt löschen
  - Beziehungen: Beziehung löschen

Offensichtlich macht die im letzten Abschnitt erläuterte Zerlegung der EODM-Objekte und Beziehungen in feinere Schutzobjekte nur für die Operationsklassen *Read* und *Write* Sinn.

Auf den Operationsklassen definieren wir eine Ordnung mit der Bedeutung, daß ein Recht für eine Klasse die Rechte für alle vorausgehenden Operationsklassen implizit einschließt. Die Ordnung ist wie folgt definiert:

$$Exist < Read < Write < Delete$$

3.4 Rechte, Autorisierung und Zugriffskontrolle

Der Begriff "Recht" führt die in den vorigen Abschnitten für das Schutzsystem definierten Merkmale Subjekt, Schutzobjekt und Operation zusammen: Mit dem Recht R=(O,K) erhält ein Subjekt die Erlaubnis, Operationen aus der Klasse K auf dem Schutzobjekt O auszuführen.

Das Erteilen (und Zurückrufen) von Rechten, die *Autorisierung*, wird dynamisch (d.h. während des laufenden Systembetriebs) und *dezentral* durchgeführt. Dazu ist den EODM-Objekten und Beziehungen, sowie den Datenbasen jeweils genau ein *Besitzer* zugeordnet (eine Zerlegung der Exemplare in feinere Einheiten ist bzgl. der Besitzeigenschaft nicht sinnvoll). Nur der Besitzer eines Schutzobjekts kann Rechte für dieses Schutzobjekt an Subjekte vergeben (und auch wieder zurückrufen). Zunächst ist der Benutzer, der ein Exemplar erzeugt, auch dessen Besitzer; er kann jedoch die Besitzeigenschaft an andere Benutzer oder Benutzergruppen übergeben; im letzteren Fall übernimmt der Gruppenverwalter die Autorisierung.

Die Strukturierungsmöglichkeiten des EODM hatten bei der Festlegung der Schutzobjekte die Einführung von atomaren und molekularen Schutzobjekten erforderlich gemacht. Diese Unterscheidung spiegelt sich auch bei den Rechten wider. *Einfache* Rechte beziehen sich auf atomare Schutzobjekte und ermöglichen es, bei der Autorisierung zwischen den D-, S- und V-Teilen von Objekten bzw. den D- und R-Teilen von Beziehungen zu differenzieren. Um dem Benutzer möglichst hohen Komfort zu bieten, zwingen wir ihn jedoch nicht, jedes atomare Schutzobjekt einzeln zu autorisieren, sondern erlauben ihm, mit einer Autorisierungsoperation Rechte für alle Teile eines Objekts oder einer Beziehung zu vergeben.

Die molekularen Schutzobjekte führen zu *komplexen* Rechten. Diese erlauben es, Rechte für ein strukturiertes Objekt einschließlich aller direkten und indirekten Komponenten, sowie — im Falle von generischen Objekten — aller Versionen zu vergeben. Dabei sind die folgenden Regeln zu beachten:

— Komplexe Rechte erstrecken sich nur auf die Komponenten (Versionen), die denselben Besitzer haben. Haben die Komponenten eines strukturierten Objekts verschiedene Besitzer, muß ein Subjekt von *allen* autorisiert werden, um mit dem gesamten Objekt arbeiten zu können.

— Komplexe Rechte beziehen sich auf aktuelle *und* zukünftige Komponenten/Versionen ("intensionales" Recht).

— Wurde das komplexe Recht nur für den D-, S-, V- oder R- Teil eines Objektes oder einer Beziehung vergeben, bezieht es sich auch nur auf den entsprechenden Teil der Komponenten/Versionen.

Wir haben uns bisher mit der Autorisierung beschäftigt und wenden uns nun der Frage zu, welche Rechte zur Ausführung von Operationen notwendig sind. Wie bereits in der Einleitung zu diesem Kapitel angedeutet, wird zwischen Schutz auf Datenbasis- und Exemplarebene unterschieden: Mit Ausnahme von Operationen wie "create_object", die nur Datenbasen betreffen, sind grundsätzlich sowohl geeignete *Exemplarrechte* auf den betroffenen Exemplaren als auch geeignete *Datenbasisrechte* auf den betroffenen Datenbasen notwendig. Dadurch wird es möglich (im Zusammenspiel mit datenbasisübergreifenden Operatoren wie "checkout"), die *tatsächlich* auf einem Schutzobjekt erlaubten Operationen von der Datenbasis abhängig zu machen, in der sich das Schutzobjekt befindet: Beispielsweise kann man einem Benutzer die Bearbeitung eines Objekts in dessen "privater" Datenbasis erlauben, während ihm dies (für dasselbe Objekt!) in der "öffentlichen" Datenbasis der Projektgruppe nicht gestattet ist. Ein weiterer Vorteil der Unterscheidung zweier Schutzebenen liegt darin, daß man in vielen Fällen frühzeitig und mit minimalem Aufwand bereits auf Datenbasisebene feststellen kann, daß für eine gewünschte Operation keine Autorisierung vorliegt (da entsprechende Datenbasisrechte fehlen).

Zum Lesen der Attribute eines Objektes reicht (auf Exemplarebene) das entsprechende einfache Recht für das atomare Schutzobjekt (D-Teil) aus. Die meisten Operatoren des EODM erstrecken sich jedoch auf mehrere Exemplare und folglich auch auf mehrere Schutzobjekte, für die geeignete (Exemplar-)Rechte vorhanden sein müssen. Navigationsoperatoren beispielsweise betreffen sowohl das Ausgangsexemplar als auch das Ziel der Suche. Ein Subjekt, das von einem Oberobjekt zu dessen Komponenten navigieren möchte, braucht deshalb das *Read*-Recht auf dem strukturellen (S-) Teil des Oberobjektes *und* das *Exist*-Recht auf den Komponenten. An dieser Stelle wird auch deutlich, wie das Pass-Through-Problem gelöst ist: Zur Navigation über die Objektstruktur oder entlang von Beziehungen genügen Rechte auf dem strukturellen (S-) Teil von Objekten bzw. dem relationstragenden (R-) Teil von Beziehungen, sowie das *Exist*-Recht auf dem Ziel der Navigation; Rechte auf dem deskriptiven Teil (Attribute) der überquerten Exemplare sind nicht erforderlich.

Zur Ausführung von Operatoren, die strukturierte Objekte als Ganzes bearbeiten (z.B. die Attribute des Objektes und aller seiner Komponenten lesen), sind entsprechende Rechte auf allen betroffenen Schutzobjekten notwendig. Geeignete Besitzverhältnisse vorausgesetzt, können diese aber bekanntlich mittels der komplexen Rechte durch *eine* Autorisierungsoperation erteilt werden.

Besonderes Interesse gilt den datenbasisübergreifenden Operatoren, die es gestatten, Objekte zwischen Datenbasen auszutauschen. Soll ein Objekt kopiert werden, benötigt man *Read*-Rechte auf der Quelldatenbasis und dem betreffenden Objekt, sowie *Write*-Recht auf der Zieldatenbasis. Um ein Objekt in eine andere Datenbasis transferieren zu können, ist das *Write*-Recht auf der Quelldatenbasis, das *Delete*-Recht für das Objekt und schließlich das *Write*-Recht auf der Zieldatenbasis notwendig. Checkout-Operationen können in zwei Modi aufgerufen werden: Im Schreibmodus kann das ausgelagerte Objekt in der Zieldatenbasis geändert, im Lesemodus darf es dort nur gelesen werden. Lesendes Auslagern verhält sich bzgl. der Rechte ähnlich wie Kopieren. Für schreibendes Auslagern ist das *Delete*-Recht auf dem Objekt notwendig, da beispielsweise auch Komponenten des Objekts gelöscht werden dürfen. Auf Datenbasisebene ist das *Read*-Recht für die Ausleihdatenbasis ausreichend. Dies mag zunächst überraschen, hat seinen Grund aber im vorgesehenen Anwendungsbereich von DAMOKLES: Benutzer können auf diese Weise dazu gebracht werden, für ihre Arbeit benötigte Objekte in ihre "privaten" Arbeitsbereiche auszulagern (indem man ihnen keine *Write*-Rechte auf "öffentlichen" Datenbasen, sondern nur für bestimmte darin enthaltene Objekte erteilt).

Wir wollen nun noch auf eine weitere Eigenschaft des Schutzkonzeptes eingehen, die ebenfalls im Hinblick auf das Anwendungsszenarium von DAMOKLES von besonderer Bedeutung ist. Bei der für den Entwurfsbereich charakteristischen arbeitsteiligen Entwicklung eines Systems bearbeiten die einzelnen Mitglieder einer Projektgruppe über längere Zeiträume genau abgegrenzte Teilaufgaben. Hierfür notwendige "private" Arbeitsbereiche können leicht über "private" Datenbasen realisiert werden, für die ein Entwickler nur sich selbst Datenbasisrechte gibt, sodaß niemand sonst Zugriff hat. Darüberhinaus besteht die Möglichkeit, Datenbasen im Modus "no_instance_access_control" anzulegen: Für den Zugriff auf solche Datenbasen werden nur geeignete Datenbasisrechte benötigt und geprüft, Exemplarrechte sind nicht erforderlich. Dadurch werden die Kosten für den Zugriffsschutz auf ein Minimum reduziert! Ein Entwickler wird deshalb diesen Mechanismus z.B. für seine privaten Datenbasen nutzen, auf denen er seine eigentliche Entwicklungsarbeit verrichtet. Für den Austausch von Objekten (z.B. Arbeitsergebnissen) zwischen seinen privaten Datenbasen und "Gruppendatenbasen" stehen ihm die beschriebenen datenbasisübergreifenden Operatoren zur Verfügung. Ist für die Gruppendatenbasis (die beispielsweise der Integration des Gesamtsystems dient) auch auf Exemplarebene Zugriffsschutz gefordert, garantiert die Zugriffskontrolle bei den datenbasisübergreifenden Operatoren, daß keine Schutzverletzungen auftreten. Beim Auslagern z.B. (entsprechendes gilt für das Einlagern) werden wie oben beschrieben in der Gruppendatenbasis Exemplarrechte überprüft. Der erläuterte Mechanismus unterstreicht einmal mehr die Nützlichkeit des Datenbasiskonzeptes in DAMOKLES.

3.5 Beispiele

Dieser Abschnitt erläutert die vorgestellten Konzepte anhand einiger Beispiele. Dabei gehen wir von der in Abbildung 3 dargestellten Benutzer- und Programmhierarchie aus. Abbildung 4 zeigt die Beispieldatenbasis *modules*, die dem Benutzer *Ziegler* gehört. Sie enthält nur einfache und strukturierte Objekte, die Objektbesitzer sind bei den Exemplaren vermerkt.

In Abbildung 5 sind die vergebenen Zugriffsrechte dargestellt. Bei allen Beispielen wird vorausgesetzt, daß der Benutzer *König* mit dem Programm *Editor schreibend* auf die *Datenbasis modules* zugreifen darf (*right_0*). Sonst sind zu diesem Zeitpunkt keine weiteren Datenbasisrechte erteilt. Da nur die Objektbesitzer Zugriffsrechte für ihre Objekte vergeben dürfen, hat der Benutzer *Ziegler* das Datenbasisrecht *right_0* und die Exemplarrechte *right_1*, *right_2*, *right_3* und *right_4* und der Benutzer *Keller* die Exemplarrechte *right_5* und *right_6* vergeben.

Das Zugriffsrecht *right_1* ist ein einfaches Recht und ermächtigt den Benutzer *König*, mit dem Programm *Editor* die Attribute des Objekts *system* (nur das Ankerobjekt) zu *ändern*. Der Benutzer *König* darf auch tatsächlich schreibend auf dieses Objekt zugreifen, weil er auch das entsprechende Datenbasisrecht besitzt.

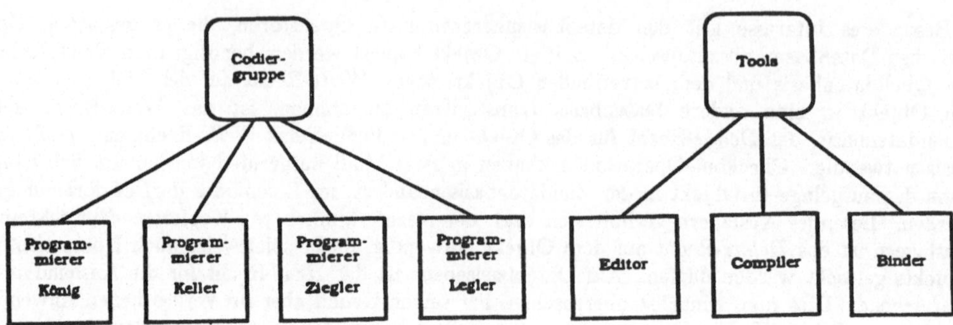

Abb. 3: Benutzer- und Programmhierarchie für die Beispiele

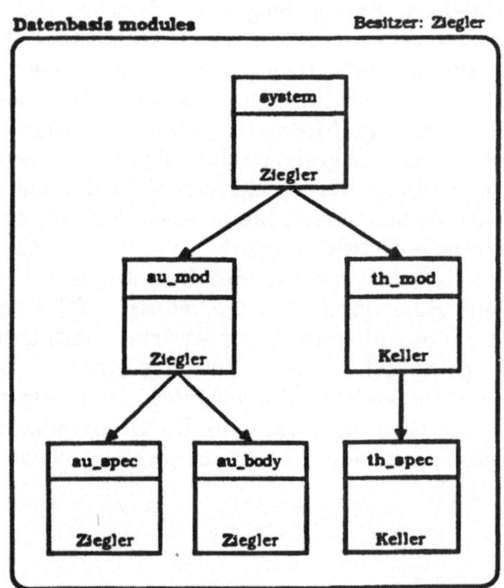

Abb. 4: Datenbasis für die Beispiele

Das Recht *right_2* ist komplex, es gilt also nicht nur für *system*, sondern auch für alle direkten und indirekten Komponenten von *system*, die dem Autorisierer gehören. Der Benutzer *König* darf also mit dem Programm *Editor* die Datenbankschlüssel der Objekte *system*, *au_mod*, *au_spec* und *au_body* lesen. Die Objekte *th_mod* und *th_spec* werden nicht tangiert, weil sie dem Benutzer *Keller* gehören.

Mit dem Recht *right_3* wird der Benutzer *König* ermächtigt, mit dem Programm *Editor* die Datenbankschlüssel der Unterexemplare des Objekts *au_mod* zu lesen. Er darf die Datenbankschlüssel tatsächlich lesen, weil er mit dem Programm *Editor* in der *Datenbasis modules* schreiben und damit lesen darf, und weil er für alle Unterobjekte die entsprechenden *Exist*-Rechte besitzt.

```
--> (König, Editor):          right_0: (modules, Write)
--> (König, Editor):          right_1: (system.D, Write, Simple)
--> (König, Editor):          right_2: (system, Exist, Complex)
--> (König, Editor):          right_3: (au_mod.S, Read, Simple)
--> (Codiergruppe, Tools):    right_4: (system.D, Read, Simple)
--> (König, Editor):          right_5: (th_mod.S, Read, Simple)
--> (König, Editor):          right_6: (th_spec, Delete, Simple)
```

Abb. 5: Rechte für die Beispiele

Der Benutzer *Ziegler* ermächtigt mit dem Zugriffsrecht *right_4* alle Benutzer der Benutzergruppe *Codiergruppe* dazu, mit allen Programmen der Programmgruppe *Tools* die Attribute seines Objekts *system* zu lesen. Für das Subjekt sind alle Kombinationen aus der Benutzerliste {*König, Keller, Ziegler, Legler*} und der Programmliste {*Editor, Compiler, Binder*} möglich. Jedoch kann nur der Benutzer *König* mit dem Programm *Editor* dieses Exemplarrecht nutzen, weil er auch das benötigte Datenbasisrecht besitzt.

Mit dem Recht *right_5* wird dem Benutzer *König* erlaubt, mit dem Programm *Editor* die Datenbankschlüssel der Unterobjekte von *th_mod* zu lesen. Das nützt ihm allerdings nicht viel, da er für keines der Unterobjekte das entsprechende *Exist*-Recht besitzt.

Ähnlich sind die Verhältnisse, wenn zusätzlich noch das Zugriffsrecht *right_6* ausgesprochen wird. Der Benutzer *König* wird mit diesem Recht ermächtigt, mit dem Programm *Editor* das Objekt *th_spec* zu löschen. Er darf das Objekt jedoch nicht löschen, weil er mit dem Datenbasisrecht zwar schreibend auf die *Datenbasis modules* zugreifen darf, jedoch kein Schreibrecht für den strukturellen Teil des Objekts *th_mod*

Angenommen, der Benutzer *Keller* möchte die Attribute des komplexen Objekts *au_mod* lesen. Dann benötigt er zunächst die *Read*-Rechte auf den deskriptiven Teil der Objekte *au_mod, au_spec* und *au_body*. Darüber hinaus benötigt er das *Read*-Recht auf den strukturellen Teil des Objekts *au_mod* und die *Exist*-Rechte auf die Objekte *au_spec* und *au_body* (die implizit über die *Read*-Rechte auf den deskriptiven Teil der Objekte vergeben wurden). Außerdem wird noch das *Read*-Recht auf die Datenbasis *modules* benötigt.

4. Implementierungsentwurf

Unerlaubte Aktionen werden im Datenbanksystem dadurch verhindert, daß die Überwachungskomponente vor der Ausführung einer Operation entscheidet, ob die Operation erlaubt ist oder zurückgewiesen werden muß. Dazu muß sie auf die gespeicherten Schutzinformationen (Rechte, Benutzer- und Programmhierarchie) zurückgreifen. Beim Entwurf der Schutzinformation stellt sich die Frage, ob man komplexe Rechte

— zum *Autorisierungszeitpunkt* entsprechend der Objekthierarchie und unter Berücksichtigung der "Besitzverhältnisse" zu einfachen Rechten *expandiert*

— so speichert, "wie sie vergeben wurden" und die Verfügbarkeit eines einfachen Rechts *zum Überprüfungszeitpunkt berechnet*

Subjekte entsprechend der Benutzer-/Programmhierarchie zum Autorisierungszeitpunkt zu expandieren, ist nicht ratsam: kleine Änderungen in der Gruppenzusammensetzung könnten zu immensen Änderungen in der Schutzinformation führen (man beachte, daß i.a auch Datenbasen auf anderen Rechnern betroffen wären).

Ähnliche Argumente gelten bzgl. der Expandierung komplexer Rechte. Wir entscheiden uns daher (und aus Gründen der einfacheren Implementierbarkeit) für die Berechnung geeigneter Rechte zum Überprüfungszeitpunkt. Neben der Objektstruktur wird hierfür auch die Benutzer- und Programmgruppenstruktur benötigt. Um eine möglichst hohe Effizienz zu erreichen, werden letztere während der Laufzeit in entsprechen aufbereiteter Form im Hauptspeicher gehalten.

Bevor wir den Ableitungsalgorithmus im einzelnen vorstellen, wollen wir noch kurz auf die Überprüfung der Datenbasisrechte eingehen. Sobald ein Subjekt eine Datenbasis öffnet, werden die für dieses Subjekt vergebenen Datenbasisrechte ermittelt und im Hauptspeicher gehalten, solange die Datenbasis geöffnet bleibt (aufgrund der Ordnung auf den Operationsklassen muß nur *das* mächtigste Recht gepuffert werden). Die Überprüfung von Datenbasisrechten kostet somit nur wenige Hauptspeicherzugriffe.

Obwohl wir ihn in der Programmiersprache C implementiert haben, wollen wir den Ableitungsalgorithmus in PROLOG-Notation vorstellen, da dies eine kompakte Darstellung erlaubt.

Die in den Schutzinformationen gespeicherten Rechte werden durch PROLOG-Fakten dargestellt. Die Vergabe des Rechts (system.D, Read, Complex) an das Subjekt (Programmiergruppe, Tools) ergibt zum Beispiel foldendes Faktum: *right("Codiergruppe", "Tools", "system.D", read, complex)*.

Zur Simulation des Algorithmus müssen die Benutzer-, Programm- und Objekthierarchien mit PROLOG-Fakten ausgedrückt werden. Entsprechendes gilt für die Besitzer der jeweiligen Objekte und die Ordnung auf den Operationsklassen. Die resultierenden Darstellungen für das Autorisierungsbeispiel sind in der Abbildung 6 beschrieben.

```
user_stru("König",   "Codiergruppe").        data_stru(au_spec, au_mod).
user_stru("Keller",  "Codiergruppe").        data_stru(au_body, au_mod).
user_stru("Ziegler", "Codiergruppe").        data_stru(th_spec, th_mod).
user_stru("Legler",  "Codiergruppe").        data_stru(au_mod, system).
                                             data_stru(th_mod, system).
prog_stru("Editor",  "Tools").
prog_stru("Compiler","Tools").               owner(system, "Ziegler").
prog_stru("Linker",  "Tools").               owner(system, "Ziegler").
                                             owner(au_spec, "Ziegler").
oper_hier(exist, read).                       owner(au_body, "Ziegler").
oper_hier(read, write).                       owner(th_mod, "Keller").
oper_hier(write, delete).                     owner(th_spec, "Keller").
```

Abb. 6: Fakten zur Darstellung der Hierarchien, Besitzverhältnisse und Operationsklassen

Zur Überprüfung eines Zugriffsrechts wird versucht, das Prädikat *check(...)* mit den entsprechenden Variableninstanzen abzuleiten (siehe Abbildung 7). Falls der Benutzer *user_1* mit dem Programm *prog_5* mit der Operation *oper_2* auf das Schutzobjekt *data_4* zugreifen möchte, muß das Prädikat right(user_1, prog_5, data_4, oper_2) erfüllt werden. Während der Ableitung wird der Besitzer des Schutzobjekts benötigt. Deshalb wird mit *owner(...)* zunächst der Objektbesitzer ermittelt und versucht, das Prädikat *check_right(...)* zu erfüllen.

Die Ableitung eines Zugriffsrechts erfolgt in mehreren Schritten, die logisch bestimmten Ebenen zugeordnet werden können. Jede Ebene entspricht einem Schutzmerkmal:
– Ebene der Objekthierarchie
– Ebene der Benutzerhierarchie
– Ebene der Programmhierarchie
– Ebene der Rechterepräsentationen
Die Berechnung startet auf der Ebene der Rechterepräsentationen und endet auf der Ebene der Objekthierarchie. Jede Ebene wird während der Ableitung durch Rekursionen in die darunterliegenden Ebenen vollständig abgearbeitet, bevor die nächsthöhere logische Ebene bearbeitet wird.

Auf der Ebene der Objekthierarchie wird versucht, das Prädikat *exist_right(...)* mit den gelieferten Variableninstanzen zu erfüllen. Vorher werden jedoch die Besitzverhältnisse mit dem Prädikat *data(...)* überprüft, weil Rechte des Typs *komplex* nur auf eigene Objekte vererbt werden können. Falls dieser Versuch zu keinem Ergebnis führt, wird mit *data_vers(...)* geprüft, ob das spezifizierte

```
check(USER, PROG, DATA, CLASS) :-
            owner(DATA, OWNER),
            check_right(OWNER, USER, PROG, DATA, CLASS, simple).
```

Abb. 7: Überprüfung eines Exemplarrechts

Exemplar eine Version ist. Falls die Prüfung positiv verlief, wird das dazugehörige generische Objekt geliefert und *check_right(...)* wird rekursiv aufgerufen, um ein entsprechendes komplexes Recht für das gefundene generische Objekt zu suchen (siehe Abbildung 8).

Falls das spezifizierte Exemplar keine Version ist oder kein entsprechendes komplexes Zugriffsrecht für das generische Objekt ableitbar ist, wird in einem dritten Schritt getestet, ob das Exemplar Unterexemplar in einem strukturierten Objekt ist. Für alle gefundenen strukturierten Objekte wird versucht, *check_right(...)* rekursiv zu erfüllen, indem ein komplexes Zugriffsrecht für ein strukturiertes Oberobjekt gesucht wird. Siehe dazu die Regel in Abbildung 8.

```
check_right(OWNER, USER, PROG, DATA, CLASS, TYPE) :-
            owner(DATA, OWNER),
            exist_right(USER, PROG, DATA, CLASS, TYPE).
check_right(OWNER, USER, PROG, DATA, CLASS, TYPE) :-
            data_vers(DATA, GENE),
            check_right(OWNER, USER, PROG, GENE, CLASS, complex).
check_right(OWNER, USER, PROG, DATA, CLASS, TYPE) :-
            data_stru(DATA, STRU),
            check_right(OWNER, USER, PROG, STRU, CLASS, complex).
```

Abb. 8: Rechteableitung auf der Ebene der Objekthierarchie

Mit dem Versuch, das Prädikat *exist_right(...)* zu erfüllen, gelangt die Ableitung in die Ebene der Benutzerhierarchie. Dabei wird zunächst versucht, das Prädikat *exist_right(...)* mit den gelieferten Instanzenvariablen abzuleiten. Falls dies nicht gelingt, werden mit *user_stru(...)* die Benutzergruppen ermittelt, in denen der spezifizierte Benutzer Mitglied ist. Siehe dazu die Regeln in Abbildung 9. Es wird dann versucht, das Prädikat *exist_right(...)* rekursiv zu erfüllen, indem ein adäquates Zugriffsrecht für eine Benutzergruppe abgeleitet wird.

```
exist_right(USER, PROG, DATA, CLASS, TYPE) :-
            seek_right(USER, PROG, DATA, CLASS, TYPE).
exist_right(USER, PROG, DATA, CLASS, TYPE) :-
            user_stru(USER, GROUP),
            exist_right(GROUP, PROG, DATA, CLASS, TYPE).
```

Abb. 9: Rechteableitung auf der Ebene der Benutzerhierarchie

In Abbildung 10 sind die Regeln für die Ebene der Progammhierarchie dargestellt. Falls die direkte Ableitung mit dem spezifizierten Programm zu keinem Ergebnis führt, werden die Programmgruppen ermittelt, in denen das Programm Mitglied ist. Für die Programmgruppen wird dann versucht, ein adäquates Recht abzuleiten, indem in der Faktenbasis eine entsprechende Rechterepräsentation gesucht wird.

```
seek_right(USER, PROG, DATA, CLASS, TYPE) :-
            right(USER, PROG, DATA, CLASS, TYPE).
seek_right(USER, PROG, DATA, CLASS, TYPE) :-
            prog_stru(PROG, GROUP),
            seek_right(USER, GROUP, DATA, CLASS, TYPE).
```

Abb. 10: Rechteableitung auf der Ebene der Programmhierarchie

Auf der untersten Ebene der Rechteableitung wird berücksichtigt, daß ein komplexes Zugriffsrecht auch ein einfaches Zugriffsrecht ist. Außerdem gibt es auf den Operationsklassen eine Ordung, die eine implizite Rechtevergabe gestattet. Die Regeln zur Realisierung dieser Randbedingungen werden in Abbildung 11 dargestellt.


```
right(USER, PROG, DATA, CLASS, simple) :-
            right(USER, PROG, DATA, CLASS, complex).
right(USER, PROG, DATA, CLASS, TYPE) :-
            oper_hier(CLASS, HIGH),
            right(USER, PROG, DATA, HIGH, TYPE).
```

Abb. 11: Rechteableitung auf der untersten Ebene

Auch wenn mit der benutzten PROLOG-Notation einige Einzelheiten des Ableitungsalgorithmus übergangen wurden, ist deutlich geworden, daß die Berechnung von Zugriffsrechten zur Überprüfungszeit in mehreren Schritten durchgeführt wird. Diese Schritte können als logische Ebenen interpretiert werden, die sich an den Hierarchien der Schutzmerkmale Benutzer, Programm und Schutzobjekt orientieren.

5. Zusammenfassung

Strukturell objektorientierte Datenbanksysteme zeichnen sich dadurch aus, daß sie auf einfache und effiziente Weise komplexe Objektstrukturen bearbeiten und speichern können. Dazu werden im Vergleich zu Standard-Datenbanksystemen zusätzliche Konzepte wie strukturierte Objekte, allgemeine Beziehungen und Versionen angeboten, die den Entwurf eines Schutzkonzeptes beeinflussen.

In diesem Papier haben wir die wichtigsten Eigenschaften und Mechanismen des Schutzsystems von DAMOKLES beschrieben. Unter Berücksichtigung des Datenmodells wurden Objekte und Beziehungen in kleinere Schutzobjekte aufgespalten, um differenzierte Schutzmaßnahmen zu ermöglichen. Neben diesen atomaren Schutzobjekten sind auch strukturierte Objekte als Ganzes Einheit der Autorisierung. Komplexe Rechte gestatten die Berücksichtigung von Änderungen in der Struktur der komplexen Objekte. Das Pass-Through-Problem konnte einer einfachen Lösung zugeführt werden.

Die Unterscheidung zwischen Datenbasis- und Exemplarrechten, die Unterstützung von Entwurfstransaktionen und privaten Datenbasen, sowie die Möglichkeit, für bestimmte Datenbasen die Rechteüberprüfung auf Exemplarebene auszuschalten (*ohne* Beeinträchtigung des Schutzes), tragen den besonderen Anforderungen des Anwendungsszenariums von DAMOKLES Rechnung.

Geplant ist die Erweiterung des Schutzkonzeptes um transitive Rechteweitergabe und weitere Mechanismen, die zunächst nicht berücksichtigt wurden, um sich auf die wesentlichen aus der strukturellen Objekt-Orientierung resultierenden Fragestellungen konzentrieren zu können.

Im DAMOKLES-Prototyp sind mittlerweile das gesamte Datenmodell, sowie Verteilung und Entwurfstransaktionen implementiert; Recovery und geschachtelte Transaktionen werden bis Anfang 1989 integriert sein. Die vorgestellten Schutzmechanismen sind in einer separaten Version von DAMOKLES implementiert und getestet. Sie werden nun in den Prototypen integriert; ferner sind Optimierungen hinsichtlich der komplexen Rechte vorgesehen.

Da objekt-orientierte Datenbanksysteme noch am Anfang ihrer Entwicklung stehen, überrascht es nicht, daß sich bisher nur wenige Arbeiten mit Schutz bei solchen Systemen beschäftigen. Lösungsansätze sind kaum bekannt. Intensiv diskutiert werden Schutzprobleme im Zusammenhang mit Objekt-Verwaltungssystemen für den Einsatz in Software-Produktionsumgebungen [PCTE88, LyTe87]. Praktische Erfahrungen im Umgang mit vorgeschlagenen Schutzkonzepten wären für weitere Arbeiten auf diesem Gebiet besonders wertvoll.

6. Literaturverzeichnis

[Abra87]   Abramowicz, K. et al.:
            Datenbankunterstützung für Software-Produktionsumgebungen.
            Proc. Datenbanksysteme in Büro, Technik und Wissenschaft, Springer 1987.

[Banc88]   Bancilhon, F.:
            Object-oriented database systems.
            Proc. 7th ACM Symposium on Principles of Database Systems, March 1988.

[DAMO88]   The DAMOKLES Data Manipulation Language - User Manual.
            FZI Karlsruhe, March 1988.

[Date83]   Date, C.J.:
            An Introduction to Database Systems, Volume II.
            Addison-Wesley 1983.

[DBH87]   Lockemann, P.C.; Schmidt, J.W.:
            Datenbank-Handbuch.
            Springer Verlag 1987.

[Denn82]   Denning, D.E.:
            Cryptography and Data Security.
            Addison-Wesley 1982

[DiDa86]   Dittrich, K.R.; Dayal, U.:
            Proc. 1986 International Workshop on Objekt-Oriented Database Systems.
            IEEE Computer Society Press 1986.

[DiGL87]   Dittrich, K.R.; Gotthard, W.; Lockemann, P.C.:
            DAMOKLES - The Database System for the UNIBASE Software Engineering Environ-
            ment.
            IEEE Database Engineering, March 1987, pp 37-47.

[DiKL89]   Dittrich, K.R.; Kemper, A.; Lockemann, P.C.:
            Databases for Planning und Manufacturing.
            In: Rembold, U.: Robot Technology and Applications.
            Marcel Dekker Inc., New York 1989.

[Ditt83]   Dittrich, K.R.:
Ein universelles Konzept zum flexiblen Informationsschutz
in und mit Rechensystemen.
Springer Verlag 1983.

[Ditt87]   Dittrich, K.R.:
Object-oriented database systems.
In: Spaccapietra, S.: Entity-Relationship Approach.
North-Holland 1987.

[HsKM79]   Hsiao, D.K.; Kerr, D.S.; Madnick, S.E.:
Computer Security.
ACM Monograph Series, Academic Press 1979.

[Hsia87]   Hsiao, D.K.:
Database Security.
Naval Postgrade School, Montery, California.

[Lock85]   Lockemann, P.C. et al.:
Database requirements of engineering applications - an analysis.
Research Report, Forschungszentrum Informatik, Karlsruhe 1985.

[LyTe87]   Lyons, T.; Tedd, M.:
Technical overview of PCTE and CAIS.
Ada UK Conference, Ada User, Vol. 8 Supplement, January 1987.

[PCTE88]   PCTE+ Functional Specifications, issue 1, February 1988.

[RaWK88]   Rabitti, F.; Woelk, D.; Kim, W.:
A Model of Authorisation for Objekt-Oriented and Semantic Databases.
Proc. Extending Database-Technology, Italy, March 88.

[Rehm88]   Rehm, S. et al.:
Support for Design Process in a Structurally Object-Oriented Database System.
 Proc. 2nd Int. Workshop on Object-Oriented Database Systems.
Lecture Notes in Computer Science 334, Springer Verlag 1988.

[Schi81]   Schilling, A.:
Der Einsatz von Betriebssystemmechanismen
zum Schutz in Datenbanksystemen.
Universität Karlsruhe, Fakultät für Informatik 1981.

[Sidl80]   Sidle, T.W.:
Weaknesses of commercial database mangagement systems in engineering applications.
Proc. 17th Design Automation Conference 1980.

Konsistenzsicherung durch Verwaltung von Konsistenzverletzungen

Peter Leikauf
ETH Zürich
Institut für Informatik
ETH Zentrum
8092 Zürich

Zusammenfassung

Konsistenzbedingungen gehören zum konzeptionellen Schema einer Datenbank. Aus dem Datenbank-Grundsatz, dass die Daten von ihren Anwendungen getrennt zu verwalten sind, folgt unmittelbar, dass die Gewährleistung der Datenkonsistenz eine zentrale Aufgabe des Datenbankverwaltungssystems sein muss. Diese Forderung wird in heutigen Systemen erst ansatzweise erfüllt. SoftRDS ist ein Datenbankkern, welcher die Datenkonsistenz durch Speicherung und Verwaltung von Konsistenz-verletzungen indirekt gewährleistet. Verletzungen von Konsistenzbedingungen werden nämlich in SoftRDS vorerst beliebig zugelassen, aber zu 100% registriert und nachträglich wenn möglich eliminiert. Dadurch ergibt sich die grösstmögliche Flexibilität für den Benutzer. Ziel des Projektes ist es, Erfahrungen mit solch einem liberalen System zu sammeln, Rückschlüsse auf den Konsistenzbedingungs-Entwurf zu gewinnen und zu zeigen, dass ein solches System trotz seiner hohen Anforderungen softwaremässig einfach und regelmässig gestaltet werden kann.

Abstract

Consistency constraints belong to the conceptual schema of a database. One of the database principles is the separate management of the data and their applications which means that the guaranty of the database consistency must be a central task of the database management system. This postulate is, if at all, only partially respected in today's systems. SoftRDS is a database kernel which guarantees the data consistency indirectly by tolerating, but completely storing and managing consistency violations. In SoftRDS, violations of consistency constraints are permitted in any order and combination for the time being, but are fully registrated and - if possible - eliminated subsequently. This results in full flexibility for the user in spite of strict consistency control. The goal of the project is to get experience with such a liberal system, to draw conclusions for the design of consistency constraints, and to show that such a system, in spite of its high requirements, can be kept simple and regular as for the underlying software.

1 Die Bedeutung der Konsistenzbedingungen

Eine der *charakteristischen Eigenschaften* von Datenbanken ist die *Datenintegrität*. Diese zerfällt in die Aufgabenbereiche Datensicherung, Datenschutz sowie Datenkonsistenz. *Konsistenzbedingungen* (im folgenden KB genannt) sind Vorschriften über die Daten und ihre datenbankinternen Beziehungen [Zehnder 87]. In einer relationalen Datenbank können sie aufgefasst werden als eine Einschränkung der möglichen Datenbankzustände, allenfalls auch der möglichen Reihenfolge der Zustände.

Wird eine Datenbank nicht gegen die Aufnahme von Daten geschützt, die den Konsistenzbedingungen widersprechen, so kann diese innert kürzester Zeit wertlos werden. Im praktischen Betrieb einer Datenbank bildet die Erhaltung dieser lebenswichtigen Datenkonsistenz oftmals das grösste Problem.

1.1 Einteilung der Konsistenzbedingungen

Da KB sehr allgemeine Vorschriften sein können, gibt es dafür eine ganze Reihe von Klassifizierungskriterien [Rebsamen 83, Fernandez et al. 81]. So etwa: Anzahl zu prüfende Objekte, Fehlerreaktion, Zeitpunkt der Überprüfung usw. Für die nachfolgenden Überlegungen ist es zweckmässig, die KB in folgende Kategorien einzuteilen:

modellinhärente - modellexterne KB

modellinhärente KB sind all jene, welche bereits durch die Verwendung eines bestimmten Datenmodells sichergestellt sind. Betrachten wir *als Beispiel* ein Schema in Form eines Entitätenblockdiagramms im erweiterten Relationenmodell [Thurnherr/Zehnder 79]:

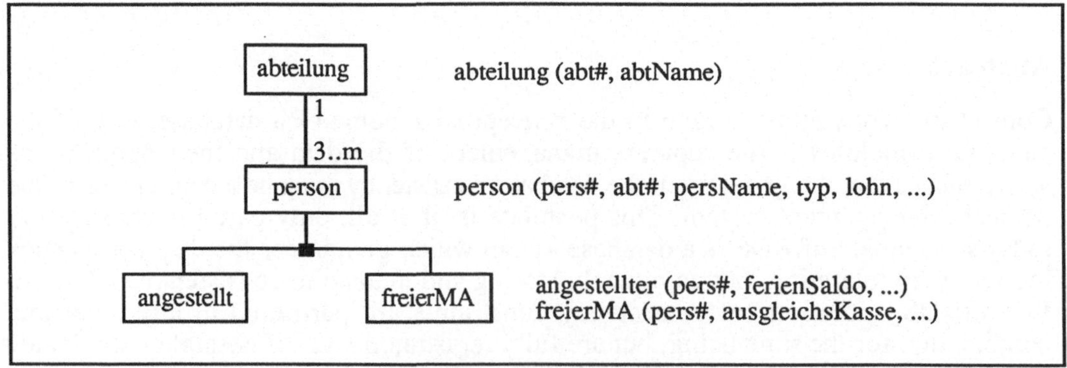

Fig. 1: Ausschnitt aus einer Personaldatenbank

In diesem einfachen Beispiel besteht eine Abteilung aus mindestens 3 Personen, jede Person gehört zu genau einer Abteilung, und jede Person ist entweder ein Angestellter oder ein freier Mitarbeiter.
Im erweiterten Relationenmodell, welches zur Klasse der Entitäten-Beziehungsmodelle (ER models) gehört, aber bewusst einfach gehalten ist (typisches

Merkmal ist, dass als direkte Beziehungstypen nur hierarchische zugelassen sind), existieren relativ wenige modellinhärente KB: Eindeutigkeit des Identifikationsschlüssels, Datentypen, referentielle Integrität, Einhaltung der Beziehungskardinalitäten und der Generalisierungen.

Alle weiteren Bedingungen, die nicht in eine dieser fünf Kategorien fallen, müssen in diesem Modell als *modellexterne KB* definiert und geeignet festgehalten werden. In unserem Beispiel könnte solch eine KB lauten: "In der Abteilung für Informatik darf kein freier Mitarbeiter pro Monat mehr verdienen als ein Fest-Angestellter".

starke - schwache KB

KB schützen einen Datenbestand vor widersprüchlichen Eingaben, aber dieser Schutz bildet auch eine Belastung, die vor allem auf Kosten der Flexibilität geht. Gerade bei Problemen der Unvollständigkeit (z.B. referentielle Integrität) kann eine nicht umgehbare KB den Betrieb unnötig erschweren, da besonders in einer Aufbauphase der Datenbestand oft temporäre Lücken aufweist. Um solchen Situationen besser gerecht werden zu können, entstand der Begriff "schwache KB", womit man eine KB meint, welche im Normalfall zwar einzuhalten ist, in Ausnahmefällen aber umgangen werden darf. Bei Verletzungen schwacher KB reagieren heutige Datenbanksysteme typischerweise mit einer Warnung (anstelle Fehlermeldung und Zurückweisung der Eingabe), wobei es dann dem Anwender überlassen bleibt, wie auf diese Warnung eingetreten wird.

primäre - sekundäre KB

Eine KB heisst primär, wenn sie nach jeder elementaren Datenbankoperation (insert, delete, modify) auf einem Tupel einer konzeptionellen Relation erfüllt sein muss (Beispiel: Eindeutigkeit des Identifikationsschlüssels). Eine KB S heisst sekundär, wenn für einen Übergang von einem bezüglich S konsistenten Datenbankzustand zu einem anderen hinsichtlich S konsistentem Zustand mehr als eine elementare Datenbankoperation erforderlich ist (Beispiel: Die 1:3..m-Beziehung im vorherigen Abschnitt; beginnt man die leere Datenbank zu füllen, so kann man gar nicht anders, als diese Bedingung temporär zu verletzen).

Dieses Problem leitet über zum Transaktionsbegriff: Eine *Transaktion* ist eine Folge von Elementaroperationen, welche die Datenbank von einem konsistenten wiederum in einen konsistenten Zustand führt, und die immer entweder vollständig oder gar nicht ausgeführt wird [Zehnder 87].

Zustandsbedingungen - Übergangsbedingungen

Zustandsbedingungen sind solche, die an keine bestimmte Operation gebunden sind, und die also die Menge der zulässigen Zustände einer Datenbank einschränken. Im Gegensatz dazu stehen die Übergangsbedingungen, welche an eine Operation (häufig: modify) gebunden sind und somit die Folge der erlaubten Zustände einschränken. Beispiel: Der Zivilstand einer Person kann nicht von "verheiratet" auf "ledig" geändert werden.

Einteilung nach der Menge der bei der Prüfung einzubeziehenden Objekte

Dieses Kriterium ist ein Mass für den Aufwand, der zur Überprüfung der KB bei Laufzeit geleistet werden muss. Gemäss [Zehnder 87] lassen sich sechs Klassen mit wachsenden Objektmengen (in Klammern jeweils ein konkretes Beispiel) unterscheiden:

1) einzelnes Attribut. (statischer Datentyp, z.B. Alter = [0..110])

2) einzelnes Tupel. (Alter = [18..65], falls Zivilstand <> ledig)

3) Tupel als Teil einer Relation. (Die Personennummer muss eindeutig sein)

4) Tupel als Teil einer Datenstruktur. (Eine Person muss eine Abteilungsnummer einer existierenden Abteilung haben)

5) ganze Relation. (Die Summe aller Gehälter darf einen bestimmten Betrag nicht übersteigen)

6) mehrere Relationen. (Die Durchschnitte der Gehälter der Abteilungen 1 und 2 dürfen sich höchstens um X % unterscheiden)

1.2 Konventionelle Methoden für Formulierung und Gewährleistung von Konsistenzbedingungen

Die Aufgabe der Sicherstellung und Prüfung von KB zur Laufzeit wird von den einzelnen Datenbanksystemen ganz unterschiedlich angegangen [Lockemann/Schmidt 87, Zehnder 87]. Allen heutigen Systemen sind dabei zwei Dinge gemeinsam:

a) Die Mächtigkeit der Gesamtheit von KB, die seitens des Entwurfssystems formulierbar sind und vom Laufzeitsystem überprüft werden, ist begrenzt.

b) Die Reaktion auf eine KB-Verletzung ist entweder eine Fehlermeldung mit Zurückweisung der Eingabedaten oder eine Warnung, also eine Ja/Nein-Antwort.

Aus den beiden Datenbank-Grundsätzen "Datenintegrität" und "Unabhängigkeit der Daten von ihren Anwendungen" folgt, dass die Konsistenz-Gewährleistung eine Aufgabe des Datenbankverwaltungssystems und nicht irgend eines Anwendungsprogrammes sein muss. Oder anders ausgedrückt: KB, die zwar irgendwo, aber nicht unter zentraler Kontrolle geprüft werden, können nicht sicher zur Datenkonsistenz gerechnet werden.

Variante 1: Unterprogramm-Bibliotheken

Sammlungen von parametrisierbaren Überprüfungsprogrammen, um einfache Konsistenztests zentral durchführen zu können (formale Prüfungen, Plausibilitätstests). Alle schwierigeren Konsistenzprüfungen bleiben dem Anwenderprogramm überlassen.

Variante 2: Datenbank-Module

Die Idee besteht darin, eine zusätzliche Software-Schicht zwischen das Anwendungsprogramm und das Datenbankverwaltungssystem zu schieben, und auf dieser Schnittstelle nur konsistenzerhaltende Transaktionen anzubieten. Der Datenbank-Administrator ist in diesem Fall zusätzlich noch für die Definition dieser Transaktionen verantwortlich. Dies ist eine sehr gute Methode, um mit sekundären KB (siehe 1.1) fertig zu werden. Ferner gibt es Datenbanksysteme, welche besagte

Software-Schicht automatisch generieren oder den Transaktions-Entwerfer zumindest unterstützen.

Variante 3: Datenbankverwaltungssystem mit Konsistenz-Unterprogrammen

Hier muss das Datenbankverwaltungssystem bei jeder Datenmanipulation selbst herausfinden, welche KB verletzt worden sein könnten, und die entsprechenden Prüfungen vornehmen. Ein solches Datenbankverwaltungssystem erfüllt zwar die Forderung nach zentraler KB-Prüfung unmittelbar, wird aber, falls es mächtige KB unterstützen will, sehr komplex und tut sich insbesondere mit sekundären KB enorm schwer. Ein solches Integritäts-Subsystem war für das System R geplant [Eswaran/Chamberlin 75], wurde aber später wieder aufgegeben. Das Projekt SoftRDS geht im Prinzip von diesem Ansatz aus.

Variante 4: Modifikation der Datenmanipulationen

Hier erfolgt der Einbau von Konsistenztests in die Anwenderprogramme durch einen DML-Compiler, welcher die DML-Befehle in bedingte Anweisungen einkleidet oder - wiederum bei sekundären KB - sie sogar zu konsistenzerhaltenden Transaktionen ergänzt.

In der Praxis kommen in der Regel Kombinationen dieser Varianten vor, z.B eignet sich Variante 3 gut für KB, welche auch für die physische Datenorganisation von Belang sind, wie Eindeutigkeit des Identifikationsschlüssels.

1.3 Die Probleme der Konsistenz-Gewährleistung

Die Gewährleistung von KB fristet in kommerziellen Datenbanksystemen ein unangebrachtes Mauerblümchendasein, ähnlich wie gewisse Bereiche der Datensicherheit (Stichworte: Transaktions-Mechanismuns, Recovery). Dafür gibt es zwei Gruppen von Ursachen:

Typische Probleme kommerzieller Systeme

Kommerzielle Hersteller haben ständig mit Effizienzproblemen bzw. hohen Effizienzanforderungen zu kämpfen. Die bekannten relationalen Datenbanksysteme (wie DB2, Oracle, Ingres) standen diesbezüglich von Anfang an - ob zu Recht oder Unrecht, sei dahingestellt - in einem schlechten Ruf, und sämtliche Forderungen der Datenintegrität stehen dem Wunsch nach Effizienzverbesserung diametral entgegen. Die Forderung nach Sicherstellung der Daten-Konsistenz ist nun ganz offensichtlich diejenige, mit der sich die Datenbanksysteme am schwersten tun. Die Erfüllung dieses Postulates ist nämlich aus zweierlei Gründen unattraktiv: Einerseits belastet sie das Laufzeitsystem besonders stark, zum anderen ist ein solches Datenbanksystem naturgemäss schwer zu vermarkten. Während beispielsweise eine mächtige oder benutzerfreundliche Abfragesprache auf einen potentiellen Benutzer unmittelbar attraktiv wirkt, lösen sauber integrierte Massnahmen zur Gewährleistung der Datensicherheit oder gar der Konsistenz für einen unerfahrenen Kunden kaum Bewunderung aus (ganz im Gegensatz natürlich zu jemandem, der selbst schon im Betrieb auf diese Probleme gestossen ist!).

Die Folge ist, dass die kommerziellen Hersteller den Anwender bezüglich Konsistenz mehr oder weniger im Stich lassen. Bei einer schweizerischen Grossbank schätzt man die Zahl der heute irgendwo einprogrammierten KB auf etwa 50'000, systemmässig weder zentral verwaltet noch überprüft, sondern in unzähligen Anwenderprogrammen verstreut [Gähler 87]. Programmgeneratoren wie etwa das System Oracle [Oracle 87] mit der Möglichkeit, komplexe Trigger-Prozeduren zu definieren, können zwar einzelne konsistenzerhaltende Anwendungen erzeugen, was aber die Datenkonsistenz noch nicht zentral sicherstellt.

Grundsätzliche Probleme

Unabhängig von Effizienzüberlegungen, sogar unabhängig vom Datenmodell, sind bisher folgende Probleme nicht zufriedenstellend gelöst:

- Die Frage, ob bestimmte Datenmanipulationen konsistenzerhaltend und damit zulässig seien, lässt sich in wichtigen Fällen nicht einfach mit Ja oder Nein beantworten. Zum einen möchte man, etwa während des Aufbaues eines Datenbestandes, *temporäre Inkonsistenzen* (oft Unvollständigkeiten) bewusst zulassen, um Flexibilität zu gewinnen. Zum anderen gibt es Fälle, wo bestehende plus neu hinzukommende Daten zusammen zwar die Konsistenz verletzen, wobei aber keinesfalls die neuen Daten "daran schuld" sind. Man denke etwa an eine KB der Art: "Das Duchschnittseinkommen einer Abteilung darf 5000 Franken nicht überschreiten". Eine neu eingegebene Person verdient 6000 Franken; der Durchschnitt wird zu hoch. Verdient jetzt die neue Person zu viel oder eine bereits bestehende mit 7000 Franken Lohn?

- Bei *schwachen KB*, die umgangen wurden, fehlt die Möglichkeit, temporäre Inkonsistenzen als solche zu kennzeichnen. Geschieht dies nicht, ist die Datenbank genauso inkonsistent, als wenn anstelle der schwachen KB gar keine vorgesehen gewesen wäre.

- *"Ausnahmen"* sind Konsistenzverletzungen schwacher KB, die nachträglich legalisiert werden. Für die Legalisierung sollte ein Mechanismus seitens des Datenbanksystems zur Verfügung stehen. Wenn eine Firma mit 1000 Angestellten einen einzigen über 65 Jahre hat, so soll dieser sicher auch als Ausnahme geführt werden (er ist ja auch in der realen Welt eine Ausnahme!); auf keinen Fall soll seinetwegen die KB abgeschwächt oder entfernt werden.

- Oft wird beklagt, es gäbe kein Datenbankverwaltungssystem, welches echt auf einem *ER-Modell* basiert. Einen Hauptgrund hierfür bilden die Beziehungen als modellinhärente KB, welche bereits eine ansehnliche Komplexität aufweisen. Während sich die Beziehungen bei Abfragen problemlos in die Funktionalität einbauen lassen (wie etwa "alle Söhne des Tupels X entlang der Beziehung Y"), sprengt die Datenmanipulation hier den üblichen Rahmen einer DML. Bezogen auf das Beispiel in Figur 1: Wie müsste eine Prozedur aussehen, welche das "Einfügen einer Person" erlaubt? Hier kommt in aller Deutlichkeit das Problem der *Fortpflanzungspfade* [Rebsamen 83] zum Ausdruck: Man kann zum voraus nicht einmal sagen, wieviele Parameter eine solche Prozedur (ganz im Gegensatz zur entsprechenden Elementaroperation) hätte. Je nach Datenvorkommen hätte das Einfügen einer Person im Extremfall das Einfügen einer Abteilung und zweier weiterer Personen zur Folge, und diese Daten müsste sich die Prozedur irgendwie "beschaffen", um konsistent zu bleiben. Falls dies möglich wäre (wie im System LIDAS), entsteht eine unglückliche Vermischung von Datenbank-Operationen und Benutzerdialog (inklusive vielfältigen Fehlermöglichkeiten!). Mit anderen Worten: Eine solche Prozedur würde die wichtigste Regel der Wiederverwendbarkeit von Software verletzen - und schon deshalb gibt es bisher keine vollständige, integrierte ER-Schnittstelle für Mutationen.

- Die *freie Mutation* ist zwar eine seltene Art der Datenbank-Benützung, stellt aber ein ausserordentlich effizientes Mittel zur Fehlerkorrektur dar, weil Fehlerkorrekturen von Natur aus a) selten und b) schwer vorhersehbar sind und es sich meist nicht lohnt, speziell dafür Transaktionsmodule zu entwickeln. Bei solchen Ausnahmen dürfen "verheiratete Personen wieder zu Ledigen werden", aber eben nur mit entsprechenden Schutzvorkehrungen.

Im folgenden soll ein System vorgestellt werden, das viele dieser Probleme auf unkonventionelle Weise löst, und das die übrigen wenigstens vom Datenbankverwaltungssystem fernhält.

2 Eine neue Methode der Konsistenzsicherung

Das Projekt SoftRDS wurde unter drei Zielsetzungen angegangen: Es soll ein Pilot-Datenbanksystem entwickelt werden, welches

- die Datenbank in jeder Betriebsart zu 100% vor *unbemerkten* Konsistenzverletzungen schützt,

- dabei die Einfachheit und Flexibilität einer Ein-Tupel-Schnittstelle anbietet, welche keinerlei Konsistenzbedingungen berücksichtigt, und

- dennoch eine einfache, überschaubare, reguläre Software-Architektur aufweist.

Ein Datenbankkern, der diese Anforderungen voll erfüllt, ist natürlich in gewisser Hinsicht eine Maximallösung. Die mit ihm gemachten Erfahrungen sollen deshalb dazu dienen, Rückschlüsse auf das Mass an Komplexität (bezüglich KB) zu ziehen, das einer relationalen Standard-Datenbank sinnvollerweise zugemutet werden kann.

2.1 Entwurf von Konsistenzbedingungen

Zur *Definition* von Konsistenzbedingungen sind in der Literatur verschiedene Ansätze vorgeschlagen worden, die sich sowohl hinsichtlich ihrer semantischen Mächtigkeit als auch bezüglich der verwendeten Formulierungstechniken stark unterscheiden [Rebsamen 83, Lockemann/Schmidt 87]. Da das primäre Ziel des SoftRDS-Projektes nicht die Definition, sondern die *Gewährleistung* der KB ist, soll hier nicht näher darauf eingegangen werden. Wir nehmen einfach an, dass zur Formulierung von KB eine Sprache mit gleicher Mächtigkeit wie die Abfragesprache des Datenbanksystems zur Verfügung steht. Dagegen stellt sich die Frage, wie Zustands/Übergangsbedingungen bzw. primäre/sekundäre KB unterschieden werden sollen. Das zweite Problem löst sich bei SoftRDS von selbst (siehe 2.3). Eine echte

Beschränkung bildet hingegen die Tatsache, dass alle KB als *Übergangsbedingungen* formuliert werden müssen. Dies hat zur Folge, dass der Entwerfende die Zustandsbedingungen mit allen Elementaroperationen verknüpfen muss, die eine Verletzung der betreffenden KB bewirken könnten. Dies erhöht den Aufwand beim Entwurf, falls man es nicht einfach vorzieht, die KB an alle drei Elementaroperationen zu binden.

Damit ergibt sich für den Entwurf folgende Definition einer KB: Eine KB besteht aus einer oder mehrerer *Elementaroperationen*, einer *Relation*, einer *Bedingung*, eines *Prüfzeitpunktes* (vor oder nach der Operation), einer *Reaktion* sowie der Angabe, ob es sich um eine starke oder *schwache* KB handelt.

Beispiel ("Eine verheiratete Person muss mindestens 3000 Franken verdienen"):

```
BEFORE INSERTION, MODIFICATION of PERSON assert STRONG:
(person.zivilstand <> ledig) or (person.lohn >= 3000)
ELSE Error("zu tiefer Lohn für verheiratete Person")
```

Mit diesem Schema lassen sich nun sämtliche Arten von externen KB gemäss Abschnitt 1.1 formulieren. Als Reaktion kann auch eine *Triggerprozedur* definiert werden, beispielsweise zur Nachführung redundanter Attribute.

2.2 Konsistenzverletzungen und Ausnahmen

Wir kommen jetzt zum Kern der Sache. Im System SoftRDS wird bei auftretenden Konsistenzverletzungen die auslösende Transaktion nicht zurückgesetzt, sondern ausgeführt; dazu wird der Tatbestand der Konsistenzverletzung vom Datenbankverwaltungssystem akzeptiert und in der Datenbank abgespeichert. Damit erhält der Begriff "Konsistenzverletzung" eine neue Bedeutung:

> *Def: Eine* Konsistenzverletzung *(im folgenden KV genannt) besteht aus einer (modellinhärenten oder modellexternen) Konsistenzbedingung sowie aus einem Paar von Verletzungsauslösern, nämlich einem Tupel einer Relation und einer Elementaroperation*

Nehmen wir als Beispiel eine einstufige Hierarchie. Das Einfügen eines Sohnes ohne zugehörigen Vater bewirkt eine KV, bestehend aus den drei Teilen

a) verletzte referentielle Integrität (modellinhärente KB),

b) "fehlbares" Tupel, welches jetzt (noch) keinen Vater hat,

c) insert-Elementaroperation

Wird nun diese KV (in einer Metadatenbank) abgespeichert, so befindet sich die Benutzer-Datenbank zwar nicht in einem konsistenten, die Datenbank als Ganzes jedoch in einem *semikonsistenten* Zustand, denn die Benutzerdatenbank enthält keine *unbemerkten* Inkonsistenzen.

> *Def: Eine Datenbank befindet sich in einem* semikonsistenten *Zustand, wenn sie keine unbemerkten Inkonsistenzen enthält*

Wie geht es nun weiter? Offenbar gibt es zwei Möglichkeiten, die Inkonsistenz auf Benutzerdaten-Ebene zu beheben: Entweder wird das fehlende Tupel in der Vater-Relation später nachgeliefert, oder das konsistenzverletzende Sohn-Tupel wird später wieder gelöscht. Bei komplexeren KB (man denke an den Durchschnittslohn!) gibt es in der Regel sogar viele Möglichkeiten, eine Inkonsistenz wieder zu beheben.

Interessant ist jetzt die Frage, ob das zweifelhafte Sohn-Tupel als zu den Benutzer-Daten gehörend betrachtet werden darf. SoftRDS kann diese Frage, wie wir im folgenden sehen werden, weitgehend offen lassen und sich darauf beschränken, der nächsthöheren Software-Schicht bei einem Zugriff auf dieses Tupel dessen unsicheren Zustand zu melden (siehe dazu 3.2).

Aber gehen wir noch einen Schritt weiter. Angenommen, das fehlende Tupel der Vater-Relation wird zwar eingefügt, verletzt aber seinerseits etwa eine modellexterne KB. Wird dadurch die erste KV behoben? Natürlich nicht, denn das Vater-Tupel ist ja selber noch nicht sicher und die Behebung der ersten KV hängt jetzt (nur noch) von der Behebung der zweiten ab.

Somit gibt es drei Arten von KV: a) Verletzungen modellinhärenter KB, b) Verletzungen modellexterner KB und c) abhängige KV. Zwischen a) und b) besteht bezüglich Handhabung kein Unterschied, wohl aber müssen die Fälle gemäss c) speziell behandelt werden.

Ein Problem ergibt sich hier natürlich sofort: Wenn trotz bestehender KV weiterhin alle Elementaroperationen gestattet sind, könnte doch die Komplexität leicht ins Unermessliche wachsen, vor allem im Hinblick auf abhängige KV! Bevor wir dieses Problem näher untersuchen, müssen wir noch den Begriff der Ausnahme einführen:

> *Def:* *Eine* Ausnahme *ist ein Tupel, das einmal eine Verletzung einer schwachen Konsistenzbedingung bewirkte, und das später legalisiert wurde.*

Dabei bedeutet "legalisiert", das die Daten des betreffenden Tupels trotz Kenntnisnahme der KV als konsistent erklärt werden. Man beachte, dass "Ausnahmen" im Gegensatz zu KV *keine* Inkonsistenzen (mehr) bewirken und dass das Etikett "Ausnahme" nur aus Gründen der Information (für die höheren Software-Schichten) mitgeführt wird.

2.3 Verwaltung von Konsistenzverletzungen und Ausnahmen

Zurück zur Frage, wie eine Menge von abhängigen und unabhängigen KV und Ausnahmen überhaupt verwaltet werden kann. Dies hätte wenig Sinn, wenn dadurch das Laufzeitsystem zu einem Mammut-Programm anwachsen würde.

Die Verwaltung der Datenbeschreibungen (=Metadaten) erfolgt bei SoftRDS in einem relationalen Data Dictionary (=Metadatenbank). Dazu gehören Beschreibungen der Relationen, Attribute, Konsistenzbedingungen etc. Die KV werden nun analog in einer erweiterten Metadatenbank abgespeichert (obwohl es sich hier streng genommen um Benutzer-Daten handelt). Figur 2 zeigt einen vereinfachten Ausschnitt aus der erweiterten Metadatenbank. Die KV selber wird in der Relation "violation" gespeichert; sie ist, wie man an der Generalisierung sieht, entweder modellinhärent, modellextern oder abhängig. Jede KV bezieht sich auf ein Tupel (diese Beziehung ist grafisch nicht darstellbar) und die zugehörige Relation. Falls die KV von einer anderen abhängig ist, existiert noch diese zusätzliche Beziehung.

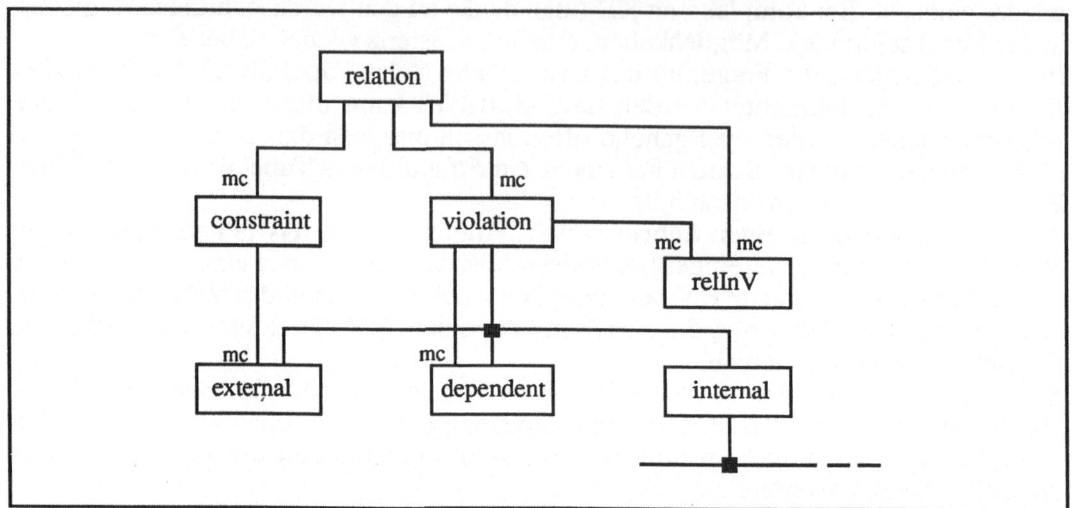

Figur 2: Ausschnitt aus der Konsistenzverletzungs-Metadatenbank

Zur Beschreibung einer KV würde dies genügen, aber zur Behebung fehlt noch eine wichtige Information: Zu jeder KV müssen diejenigen Relationen und Elementaroperationen festgehalten werden, die eine Behebung der KV bewirken könnten. Bezogen aufs vorherige Beispiel mit dem fehlenden Vater-Tupel würde dies heissen, dass die KV "fehlender Vater" durch eine Einfüge-Transaktion in der Vater-Relation oder durch eine Lösch- oder Modifikationsoperation in der Sohn-Relation behoben werden könnte. Diese Information steht in der Relation "relInV".

Woher nimmt das Laufzeitsystem diese Information beim Auftreten einer Verletzung? Hier gibt es nun einen wesentlichen Unterschied zwischen modellinhärenten und modellexternen KV. Bei ersteren "kennt" das Laufzeitsystem die Semantik und kann sich die Relation "relInV" selber ergänzen (so wird es auch technisch gemacht). Die externen KB hingegen sind für das Laufzeitsystem "black boxes", da sie rein textuell abgespeichert sind. Hier muss nun das Entwurfssystem etwas nachhelfen, indem es die externen KB semantisch analysiert und herausfindet, welche Relationen in irgend einer Form bei einer KB involviert sind - das sind dann genau diejenigen, die eine spätere Behebung der Verletzung bewirken könnten!

Übrigens könnte man den Unterschied zwischen externen und modellinhärenten KB zum Verschwinden bringen, indem man die modellinhärenten explizit in externe umwandelt, in der Form, wie sie in 2.1 beschrieben wurde. Doch damit würde das Laufzeitsystem das Semantikwissen über die modellinhärenten KB verlieren, was gewichtige Nachteile hätte, beispielsweise für die Erklärungskomponente. Daher sind die modellinhärenten KB nicht in der Metadatenbank gespeichert.

Der Algorithmus zur Nachführung von KV und zur Behebung derselben (dazu gehört die Auflösung von zyklisch abhängigen KV) wird im Kapitel 3 skizziert; er ist nicht trivial, aber einfach genug, um das Laufzeitsystem nicht ins Uferlose wachsen zu lassen. Insbesondere genügt es, pro Tupel nicht alle, sondern immer nur eine KV zu speichern.

Natürlich entsteht eine grosse Komplexität, wenn man in einer von Inkonsistenzen "verseuchten" Datenbank beliebig operieren darf. Aber, und das ist hier das Entscheidende: Einfacher geht es gar nicht, da ja in diesem Fall der Sachverhalt in der realen Welt genauso komplex ist, und diese Komplexität schlägt sich nicht in einem verwickelten Laufzeitsystem, sondern im Inhalt der KV-Metadatenbank nieder, von wo aus sie in eine beherrschbare Form gebracht werden kann.

Interessant ist in diesem Zusammenhang, dass E. F. Codd sich bereits 1970 bei der Frage der Konsistenzsicherung ganz ähnliche Überlegungen gemacht hat [Codd 70]: *"In one approach the system cheks for possible inconsistency whenever an insertion, deletion or update occurs. Naturally, such checking will slow these operations down. If an inconsistency has been generated, details are logged internally, and if it is not remedied within some reasonable time interval, either the user or someone responsible for the security and integrity of the data is notified."*

2.4 Vorteile und Grenzen der Methode

Ein Datenbankverwaltungssystem in der vorhin beschriebenen Form ist eine Maximal- und keine Universallösung, trotz auf den ersten Blick bestechender Eigenschaften. Mögliche Einsatzgebiete ergeben sich aus der Abwägung der Vor- und Nachteile.

Vorteile

Diese ergeben sich direkt durch die Behebung der in Abschnitt 1.3 angetönten Mängel konventioneller Datenbankverwaltungssysteme.

* Saubere und vollständige Trennung von Fehlerbehandlung und Dialogführung. Die Antwort auf die Frage, wie erfolgreich die letzte Elementaroperation durchgeführt werden konnte, kann in ihrer vollen Komplexität beantwortet werden, nämlich durch Beschreibung in einer Metadatenbank. Keine Reduktion auf Ja/Nein.

* Schwache Konsistenzbedingungen erhalten den ihnen zustehenden Stellenwert indem nach deren Umgehung das Wissen um die Inkonsistenz nicht einfach verschwindet. Dies geschieht erst durch explizite Umwandlung einer KV in eine Ausnahme.

* Bezogen auf Datenmanipulationen, bietet SoftRDS eine Entity-Relationship-Schnittstelle, da die im Vergleich zum reinen Relationenmodell zahlreicheren modellinhärenten Konsistenzbedingungen alle überwacht werden.

* Der Unterschied zwischen primären und sekundären Konsistenzbedingungen verschwindet. KB, deren Einhaltung mehrere Elementaroperationen erfordern, werden gewährleistet, wobei unterdessen ein KV-Baum in der Metadatenbank wächst und bei korrekter Operationsfolge wieder auf Null schrumpft. Dadurch wird der Transaktionsbegriff in gewisser Weise überflüssig gemacht (aber durch die nächsthöhere Software-Schicht nach Belieben wiederhergestellt).

Datenmanipulationen sind beliebig möglich und sicher, ohne dass sich der Benutzer in das Korsett eines Transaktionsmoduls zwängen muss.

- Als Nebenprodukt entsteht ein Mechanismus zur Handhabung von "langen Transaktionen".

- Nullwerte kommen zwar nicht explizit vor, können aber bequem simuliert werden.

- Trigger-Prozeduren können sauber implementiert werden. In üblichen Systemen dürfen Trigger selber keine Transaktionen auslösen (wegen Verschachtelung), und wenn ein Trigger selber Inkonsistenzen auslöst, kann dies nicht überprüft werden. In SoftRDS unterliegen auch die Trigger der Konsistenzprüfung, da sie auf Elementaroperationen aufbauen.

Nachteile und Grenzen

- Der grösste Nachteil besteht ohne Zweifel in der sehr starken Belastung für das Laufzeitsystem. Während die Konsistenz*prüfung* ohnehin, auch in konventionellen Systemen, gemacht werden muss, verschlingt hier die Suche nach möglichen Konsistenz-*Behebungen* enorme Ressourcen. Eine komplexe KV (wie etwa diejenige mit dem Durchschnittslohn) kann zur Folge haben, dass jede Operation auf den mitbetroffenen Relationen eine aufwendigen Konsistenz-Prüfung auslöst. Eine stark inkonsistente Datenbank wird dadurch sehr schwerfällig. Inkonstenzen, auch temporäre, sollten jedoch ohnehin nicht im Übermass vorkommen dürfen. SoftRDS bietet die Möglichkeit, dieses Problem etwas zu entschärfen (siehe 3.4).

- SoftRDS erlaubt eine völlig freie Datenmanipulation, unabhängig von bestehenden Inkonsistenzen; insbedondere kann die Behebung von temporären Inkonsistenzen beliebig lange verzögert werden. Wird diese Flexibilität aber allzusehr missbraucht, kann in der KV-Metadatenbank eine Komplexität entstehen, die der Benutzer selber nicht mehr durchschauen kann.

Daraus ergeben sich für die Praxis zumindest *drei mögliche Einsatzgebiete* für solch ein Maximal-System:

a) für die freie Datenmanipulation im Falle von Fehlerkorrekturen im System

b) für alle Anwendungen, bei denen das Laufzeitverhalten eine geringe Rolle spielt oder spielen kann, wie etwa bei der Datenerfassung (häufig, nicht immer) oder bei zeitunkritischer Stapel-Verarbeitung

c) für Testzwecke - etwa, um Transaktionsmodule (gemäss Variante 3 in Abschnitt 1.2) auf Vollständigkeit bezüglich Konsistenz zu prüfen

2.5 Rückwirkung auf den Konsistenzbedingungs-Entwurf

Wie bereits angetönt, soll SoftRDS unter anderem dazu dienen, Erfahrungen für den Konsistenz*entwurf* zu sammeln, indem ein solches System widersprüchliche oder überlappende oder allzu aufwendige Konsistenzbedingungen sehr rasch aufdeckt. Es stellt sich auch die Frage, wo genau die Grenzen zwischen verschieden strengen

Konsistenzbedingungen gezogen werden sollen. Eine Erweiterung der Kategorisierung stark/schwach könnte etwa wie folgt aussehen:

- "Super"-starke KB dürfen überhaupt nie, auch nicht temporär, verletzt werden und können sehr frühzeitig abgefangen werden

- Starke KB dürfen zwar temporär verletzt werden, müssen aber schlussendlich erfüllt sein, wenn die Datenbank konsistent genannt werden soll

- Schwache KB dürfen grundsätzlich bewusst verletzt werden, ohne die Existenz der Datenbank zu gefährden, und können auch in Ausnahmen umgewandelt und somit legalisiert werden

- "Sehr schwache" KB sind diejenigen unter den schwachen, die derart aufwendig zu prüfen sind, dass man auf eine (zentrale) Gewährleistung von Anfang an verzichtet

Die Tatsache, dass in einer Datenbank inkonsistente Tupel vorkommen können, hat auch eine Rückwirkung auf den Konsistenzbedingungs-Entwurf. Dies betrifft die Abfrage-Operationen, bei denen ein bestimmtes Tupel nicht mehr eindeutig gefunden oder nicht gefunden wird, sondern auch "unsicher" sein kann, provisorisch eingefügt oder provisorisch gelöscht. Ein Beispiel möge dies verdeutlichen:
Eine Fluggesellschaft fliege einen Flughafen in einem Krisengebiet an; der Flug muss jedesmal von einer amtlichen Stelle genehmigt werden; ohne Genehmigung fällt der Flug aus. Das Reservationssystem erlaubt Reservationen wie gewöhnlich vorbehaltlich der (modellexternen) Konsistenzbedingung, dass genügend Plätze frei sind. Diese Bedingung muss nun, damit sinnvoll gearbeitet werden kann, mehr ausdrücken als nur erfüllt/nicht erfüllt; denn es gibt jetzt drei Fälle: a) Flug genehmigt, genügend Plätze: alles ok. b) zu wenig Plätze: Reservation unmöglich. c) genügend Plätze, aber Flug (noch) nicht genehmigt: Reservation provisorisch ok (abhängige KV, denn der Flug selber verletzt eine KB!).
Der KB-Entwurf wird dadurch in gewissen Fällen komplizierter. Man kann natürlich auf der sicheren Seite bleiben, indem man beim Vorkommen auch nur eines zweifelhaften Tupels die Konsistenzbedingung als nicht erfüllt betrachtet, doch ist damit die volle Funktionalität nicht ausgeschöpft.

3 Das System SoftRDS

SoftRDS ist hervorgegangen aus dem LIDAS-Projekt [Zehnder 83] und besteht momentan aus einem Datenbank-Entwurfssystem, einem Datenbankkern mit Ein-Tupel-Schnittstelle für die Sprache Modula-2 sowie einer Erklärungskomponente. Völlig ausgeklammert wurde der Bereich Abfragesprache, da die Formulierung von Abfragen die Konsistenz nicht beeinflusst.

3.1 Die Ein-Tupel-Schnittstelle des Systems RDS

RDS ist ein Datenbankverwaltungssystem, das (mit Ausnahme der Eindeutigkeit des Identifikationsschlüssels) keinerlei Konsistenztests durchführt. Relationen und Zugriffsschlüssel sind als abstrakte Datentypen definiert. Angeboten werden für die Manipulation die drei Elementaroperationen sowie eine Prozedur zur Navigation. Done() gibt nach jedem Prozeduraufruf an, ob dieser ordnungsgemäss durchgeführt werden konnte. Zusätzlich gibt es drei Prozeduren für die Transaktionsverwaltung: Alle Manipulationsoperationen zwischen den Aufrufen von "BeginTransaction" und "CommitTransaction" bilden eine Transaktion im klassischen Sinn; mit "AbortTransaction" kann eine laufende Transaktion zurückgesetzt werden.

```
DEFINITION MODULE RDS;   (* Auszug *)
...
TYPE
  Relation;
  Key;
  Mode = (first, next, prior, nextequal, ...);
...
PROCEDURE Obtain(r: Relation; a: ADDRESS; k: Key; m: Mode);
PROCEDURE Insert(r: Relation; a: ADDRESS);
PROCEDURE Delete(r: Relation; a: ADDRESS);
PROCEDURE Replace(r: Relation; a: ADDRESS);
...
PROCEDURE BeginTransaction;
PROCEDURE CommitTransaction;
PROCEDURE AbortTransaction;
...
PROCEDURE Done(): BOOLEAN;
...
END RDS.
```

3.2 Die Schnittstelle des Systems SoftRDS

Um die volle Flexibilität beizubehalten, möchte man obige sehr einfache Schnittstelle auch für SoftRDS weitmöglichst beibehalten. Dies ist in der Tat möglich; eine bereits funktionierende, aber noch nicht sehr komfortable Minimallösung sähe folgendermassen aus:

```
DEFINITION MODULE SoftRDS;   (* Auszug *)
...
TYPE
  Relation;
  Key;
  Mode = (first, next, prior, nextequal, ...);
...
PROCEDURE Obtain(r: Relation; a: ADDRESS; k: Key; m: Mode);
PROCEDURE Insert(r: Relation; a: ADDRESS);
PROCEDURE Delete(r: Relation; a: ADDRESS);
PROCEDURE Replace(r: Relation; a: ADDRESS);
...
PROCEDURE BeginTransaction;
PROCEDURE CommitTransaction;
PROCEDURE AbortTransaction;
...
```

```
PROCEDURE Done(): INTEGER;
...
PROCEDURE OverrideViolation(vNr: INTEGER);
...
END SoftRDS.
```

Der wesentliche Unterschied liegt hier darin, dass die Prozedur "Done" mehr liefert als nur *TRUE/FALSE*, sondern eine ganze Zahl n, welche folgende Werte annehmen kann:

a) n = 0: Operation ok;

b) n = -1: Operation konnte nicht durchgeführt werden (z.B. Tupel nicht gefunden)

c) n > 0: Die Operation hat eine KV bewirkt (bei *Insert/Delete/Replace*) bzw. das gelieferte Tupel ist mit einer KV behaftet (bei *Obtain*), wobei n der Identifikationsschlüssel der KV ist (in der Meta-Relation "violation", siehe 2.3)

Alle weiteren Informationen stecken jetzt in der KV-Metadatenbank, auf die mittels der gleichen Schnittstelle zugegriffen werden kann. Behebungen von KV werden von SoftRDS selbständig durchgeführt. Mit *OverrideViolation* kann eine schwache KV in eine Ausnahme umgewandelt werden.

Die Einfachheit dieser Schnittstelle ist, verglichen mit der Funktionalität des darunterliegenden Datenbankkernes, geradezu frappant. Allerdings ist dazu zu sagen, dass die Konsistenzsicherungs-Probleme gewissermassen nur in die Metadatenbank "abgeschoben" wurden, wo sie von höheren Software-Schichten adäquat behandelt werden müssen - beispielsweise von der Erklärungskomponente. Darin liegt aber ein grosser Fortschritt: Die völlige Entflechtung von Fehler-Erkennung und Fehler-Behandlung. Die Erkennung ist ganz klar eine zentrale Aufgabe des Datenbank-verwaltungssystems. Die Behandlung liegt vollständig im Aufgabenbereich der jeweiligen Anwendung.

Die SoftRDS Schnittstelle wird nun noch mit drei Prozeduren ergänzt, welche die Benützung etwas komfortabler gestalten:

```
PROCEDURE Install(on: BOOLEAN);
PROCEDURE AutoRevert(on: BOOLEAN);
PROCEDURE ResetOperation(vNr: INTEGER);
```

Install erlaubt das Ein- und Ausschalten des Konsistenzprüfers. *AutoRevert* ermöglicht, das automatische Suchen nach KV-Behebungen bei jeder Elementaroperation zu unterdrücken. Dadurch kann die Erkennung einer KV-Behebung verzögert werden, was die Konsistenz nicht gefährden, aber das Laufzeitsystem stark entlasten kann und dadurch den in 2.4 gezeigten Nachteil etwas entschärft. *ResetOperation* schliesslich setzt eine Elementaroperation zurück, welche die KV *vNr* bewirkt hatte.

3.3 Entwurfssystem und Generierungsteil

Das Datenbank-Entwurfssystem für SoftRDS ist im wesentlichen eine Variante des Systems Gambit [Brägger 85]. Es lassen sich Relationen, Typen, Beziehungen, Attribute, Schlüssel und Konsistenzbedingungen z.T. grafisch formulieren, die

Beschreibungen werden in einer Metadatenbank abgelegt. Nach beendetem Entwurf generiert das System zwei Module:

- Das Datenbank-Definitionsmodul beschreibt die definierten Relationen und Schlüssel in Modula-2-Form; dabei werden die Attribute in RECORD-Felder transformiert. Die einzelnen Relationen werden somit als RECORD-Typen exportiert und als solche den Elementaroperationen von RDS/SoftRDS übergeben.

- Das Konsistenzprüfmodul enthält alle modellexternen Konsistenztests. KB können mit Gambit unter Benützung des Datenbank-Definitionsmoduls objektabhängig als Modula-2-Prozeduren definiert werden, während die Schnittstelle des Konsistenzprüfmoduls selber unveränderlich ist. Gambit generiert nur das Implementationsmodul, welches problemlos mit dem SoftRDS-System gelinkt werden kann. Das Konsistenzprüfmodul exportiert im wesentlichen nur eine Prozedur mit den drei Parametern Relation, Elementaroperation und Tupel. Diese Prozedur ermittelt die tiefststufige KV (Definition siehe nächster Abschnitt), die bei der betreffenden Operation entsteht.

In einer späteren Variante von SOftRDS soll es möglich sein, neue KB zu definieren bzw. bestehende zu löschen, auch wenn die Datenbank bereits in Betrieb ist. Dazu muss im ersten Fall ein Teil der Datenbank völlig neu überprüft werden, während im zweiten Fall lediglich KV wegfallen könnten.

3.4 Laufzeitsystem

In Abschnitt 1.1 wurde von der Klassifizierung der KB aufgrund der bei der Überprüfung involvierten Objekte erwähnt. Analog kann man auch die KV einteilen:

> *Def: Die* Stufe *einer Konsistenzverletzung X ist gleich der Anzahl von Relationen, welche die Behebung von X bewirken könnten, wenn auf ihnen eine Elementaroperation ausgeführt wird. Abhängige KV gehören immer zur höchsten Stufe.*

Nehmen wir als Beispiel das Schema aus Figur 1. Wenn wir eine neue Abteilung einfügen, so entsteht vorerst eine modellinhärente KV der Stufe 2. Die KV könnte nämlich behoben werden, indem entweder diese Abteilung trivialerweise wieder gelöscht würde oder indem 3 passende Personen eingefügt würden. Deshalb müssen die entsprechenden Elementaroperationen von *zwei* Relationen auf KV-Behebung geprüft werden; Operationen beispielsweise auf die Relation "angestellt" bleiben hingegen ohne Einfluss auf diese KV.
Zum Glück haben viele in der Praxis wichtige KV eine tiefe Stufe, oftmals sogar die Stufe 0 (dies sind Verletzungen der KB der Klassen 1) und 2) gemäss Abschnitt 1.1).

Es würde den Rahmen dieses Berichtes sprengen, den genauen Algorithmus der KV-Verwaltung zu beschreiben. Ganz wichtig dabei ist die Tatsache, dass es genügt, pro Elementaroperation nur jeweils eine (nämlich die tiefststufige) KV zu speichern, auch wenn diese Operation mehrere KB gleichzeitig verletzt. Sonst wäre der Versuch, die

Komplexität zu bewältigen, zum Scheitern verurteilt. Dies kann zur Folge haben, dass eine KV-Behebung zwar eine neue KV, aber *nur* von einer gleichen oder höheren Stufe, verursacht.

Damit ist auch das Problem der zyklisch abhängigen KV gelöst: Da eine abhängige KV gemäss obiger Definition immer zur höchsten Klasse gehört, bedeutet dies, dass ein Tupel mit einer abhängigen KV keine andere KB mehr verletzen kann - womit man zyklische Abhängigkeiten eliminieren und die betreffenden KV löschen kann.

Die Beziehung zwischen einer KV und dem betreffenden Tupel wird durch ein zusätzliches, aber für den SoftRDS-Benutzer verstecktes Attribut hergestellt. Dieses Attribut (und noch ein zweites, welches Ausnahmen als solche kennzeichnet) wird dabei bereits vom Entwurfssystem generiert. Die Erklärungskomponente, welche selber nicht SoftRDS, sondern RDS benutzt, hat auch auf dieses Attribut Zugriff.

3.5 Die Erklärungs-Komponente

Wenn eine Datenbank nach mehreren Manipulationen zwar in einem semi-konsistenten, nicht aber in einem konsistenten Zustand ist, möchte der Benutzer manchmal wissen, welche Konsistenzverletzungen vorliegen, wie diese behoben oder in Ausnahmen verwandelt werden können usw. Fragen sind möglich nach allen KV einer KB, oder allen KV einer Relation, oder nach der Abhängigkeitskette mehrerer KV. All dies kann als eine freie Abfrage auf der vereinigten Meta- und Benutzerdatenbank betrachtet werden.

Die Erklärungskomponente von SoftRDS ist ein vom Anwendungsprogramm unabhängiges Dienstprogramm, welches dem Benutzer ermöglicht, durch seine Datenbank zu navigieren. In der jetzigen Version ist sie auf den KB-Entwerfer, also den geübten Benutzer, zugeschnitten, da sie ja vor allem auch gebraucht wird, um die Implementation des Kernes zu unterstützen.

	Daten	Konsistenz
Beschreibung	**I** Datenbeschreibung	**II** Konsistenzregeln
Vorkommen	**III** Daten	**IV** Konsistenzverletzungen

Figur 3: Inhalt der Erklärungskomponente mit ihren Quadranten

Die Navigation in der Meta- und Benutzerdatenbank findet so statt, dass der Benutzer sich in einen der vier Quadranten (Figur 3) begibt und dort ein Objekt (Relation oder Tupel) auswählt. Die beiden oberen Quadranten sind Beschreibungen, die beiden unteren Vorkommen, die beiden linken beziehen sich auf die Daten selbst, die beiden rechten auf die Konsistenz. Bezogen auf das Beispiel vom Angestellten mit zu hohem

Alter: Im Quadrant I stünde dann die Beschreibung der Relation *Angestellter*, im Quadrant II die Konsistenzbedingungen dieser Relation, im Quadrant III die einzelnen Tupel, im Quadrant IV die Konsistenzverletzungen. Die Navigation erfolgt nun im Wesentlichen durch Wechsel des Quadranten; so erhält man beispielsweise das konsistenzverletzende Tupel, wenn man vom Quadrant IV in den Quadrant III wechselt.

4 Ausblick

Das hier vorgestellte System erfüllt die Idealanforderungen an ein Integritäts-Subsystem einer relationalen Datenbank in kompromissloser Weise, und das, ohne dem Anwender auch nur im geringsten Flexibilität zu nehmen. Der Preis dafür ist doppelt: Erstens ein stark belastetes Laufzeitsystem, und zweitens eine leichte Komplizierung des Konsistenzbedingungs-Entwurfes, indem die Frage nach der Existenz eines Datensatzes nicht mehr nur mit ja oder nein beantwortet werden kann. SoftRDS ist ein Datenbankkern, der - ohne eigene Viertgenerationsabfragesprache - nicht sehr nahe beim Benutzer ist. Das vorgeschlagene Integritäts-Subsystem bezieht sich auf das konzeptionelle Schema und auf Konsistenzbedingungen, gebunden an Elementaroperationen. Ein Gebiet für weitere Untersuchungen ist deshalb sicher die Transformation von Konsistenzbedingungen höherer Stufe - formuliert in einer KB-Sprache wie CSCL [Gähler 87] - in solche Elementar-KB. Ebenso offen ist die Behandlung von konsistenzverletzenden Tupeln in einer Viertgenerationssprache; ein Problem, das sich auch bei Nullwerten stellt. Da ist etwa das "Durchschnittsalter aller Angestellten" gesucht, während drei Angestellte eine KB verletzen: Einer ist zu alt, einer hat einen zu hohen Lohn, ein dritter hat eine (durch eine Übergangsbedingung verbotene) Lohnsenkung erfahren. Welche dieser drei Spezial-Tupel zählen nun mit zum Durchschnittsalter?
Auf die eine oder andere dieser Fragen Antworten zu finden, ist ein wichtiges Ziel des Projektes SoftRDS.

Literatur

[Borgida 85]
Borgida, A.: Language Features for Flexible Handling of Exceptions in Information Systems. In: ACM TODS. 10:4. 1985. 565-603

[Brägger 85]
Brägger, R.: Gambit Handbuch. ETH Zürich, Institut für Informatik. 1985

[Codd 70]
Codd, E.F.: A Relational Model for Large Shared Data Banks. Comm. ACM, Vol. 13, No. 6, 1970, p. 377-387

[Eswaran/Chamberlin 75]
Eswaran, K.P., Chamberlin, D.D.: Functional specification of a subsystem for database integrity. In: Proc. 1st Int. Conf. VLDB 1975. 48-68

[Fernandez et al. 81]
Fernandez, E.B., Summers, R.C., Wood, C.: Database Security and Integrity. Addison-Wesley Publishing Company. Reading. MA. 1981

[Gähler 87]
Gähler, F.: Externe Konsistenzbedingungen: Formulierung und Überwachung. ETH Zürich, Institut für Informatik. Bericht 83. 1987

[Lockemann/Schmidt 87]
Lockemann, P.C., Schmidt, J.W. (Hrsgg.): Datenbank-Handbuch. Springer-Verlag. 1987

[Oracle 87]
Oracle: SQL*Forms Designer's Tutorial, Version 2.3. Oracle Corporation. 1987

[Rebsamen 83]
Rebsamen, J.: Datenbankentwurf im Dialog - Integrierte Beschreibung von Strukturen, Transaktionen und Konsistenz. ETH Zürich. Dissertation 7325. 1983

[Zehnder 83]
Zehnder, C.A. (Hrsg.): Database Techniques for Professional Workstations. ETH Zürich, Institut für Informatik. Bericht 55. 1983

[Zehnder 87]
Zehnder, C.A.: Informationssysteme und Datenbanken. Verlag der Fachvereine. Zürich. 1983

Die Spezifikation von Nullwerten als Problem einer wissensbasierten Büroautomatisierung

Hans W. N a u ; Hartmut W e d e k i n d

Universität Erlangen–Nürnberg
Institut für mathematische Maschinen und Datenverarbeitung (VI),
Martensstr. 3, D–8520 E r l a n g e n , West Germany
e–mail: nau @ derdbs5.BITNET / wedekind @ derdbs5.BITNET

Zusammenfassung:

Die Bestimmung von *Nullwerten in Datenbanksystemen* ist der Gegenstand problemorientierter Büroarbeit. Die Behandlung von Nullwerten wird aus den Aspekten der Datenbanksysteme und aus der juristischen Perspektive analysiert. Es wird eine *wissensbasierte Blackboard–Architektur* zur Nullwertspezifikation in einem Auftragsbearbeitungssystem beschrieben.

Specification of Null–Values As a Problem of Knowledge–Based Office Automation

Abstract:

The specification of *null–values in database* systems is subject to problem–oriented office work. Handling null–values is considered from a database and a juridical point of view. To specify null–values a *knowledge–based blackboard architecture* for an order processing system is proposed.

1 Einführung

In der Sprache der Relationalen Datenbanksysteme sind Nullwerte *unbestimmte Attributausprägungen*. Nullwerte können Werte sein, die durch eigenes Handeln unbeeinflußbar sind. Man kann die Werte durch *Prophetie* zu bestimmen versuchen, was sich in der Regel nicht bewahrheitet, oder sich um ein Verlaufsgesetz bemühen, mit dessen Hilfe dann wenigstens im systematischen Teil eine Vorhersage gewagt werden kann. Wir sprechen hier nicht von Nullwerten, deren Ausprägungen wie das zukünftige Wetter oder das Datum bei natürlichem Tode ein *Widerfahrnis* als Bezug haben. Zur Debatte stehen durch *Handlungen zu bestimmende Nullwerte* wie offene Liefertermine oder auf Abruf zu haltende unbestimmte Bestellmengen. Diese Nullwerte bedürfen der *Spezifikation* und sind ein wesentlicher Teil der Bürotätigkeiten als *asynchron* ablaufende, *terminorientierte*, *sprachgebundene* und *problemlösende* Gemeinschaftsaufgaben. Datenbanksysteme, in denen Nullwerte dargestellt und zuweilen auch u. a. mit einer mehrwertigen Logik manipuliert werden können, unterscheiden nicht zwischen *Widerfahrnis–* und *spezifikationsbedürftigen Nullwerten*. Datenbanksysteme sind somit zu erweitern um eine Komponente zur Nullwertbestimmung. Es ist eine grundsätzliche Frage, ob diese Erweiterung durch Einbeziehung oder durch Anlagerung zu erfolgen hat. Da Datenbanksysteme durch ihr formales Transaktions- und Schemakonzept mit einigem Erfolg universelle Geltung beanspruchen können, erscheint es zweckmäßig, solche anwendungsspezifischen Probleme auszulagern, die nicht datenschemagesteuert sind, für die also das Anwendungsziel und nicht eine erfolgreiche konfliktbereinigende *Ressourcenverwaltung* im Mittelpunkt steht.

Die Nullwert–Problematik in ihrer Darstellung in der Literatur und in ihrer Systemimplementierung zeigt deutlich, daß ein *offen* gehaltenes Spezifikationsproblem vorliegt und daß eine anwendungsneutrale Instanz wie die Datenbanksysteme gar nicht "ausbrechen" darf, wenn sie nicht ihre Universalität verlieren will. Was den Betriebssystemen als Großvätern "widerfuhr", als Datenbanksysteme "geboren" wurden, um die Unmenge von Daten als knappe Ressourcen zu verwalten, das kommt nun auf die Väter nieder. Wie soll man einer Vielzahl von Anwendungen durch ein bloßes Verwalten und durch ein elementar–logisches Manipulieren von Nullwerten gerecht werden können? Jeder unversorgte Nullwert, d. h. jedes bloße Hoffen auf ein günstiges Widerfahrnis, ist eine Kapitulation vor den Problemen der Anwendung.

Wir gliedern unsere Ausführungen in drei Teile. Zunächst wird ein kurzer Bescheid über den Stand der *Nullwertbehandlung in der Datenbankliteratur* und in der Systemimplementierung gegeben. Da Nullwerte oftmals auch Leistungen und Gegenleistungen zwischen Vertragspartnern bedeuten, für die ein "Muß" zum Handeln auch nach internationalem Recht erforderlich ist, wird im zweiten Teil über die *juristische Problematik* unseres Gegenstandes berichtet. Im dann folgenden Hauptteil wird eine *Blackboard–Architektur für ein Auftragsbearbeitungssystem* beschrieben. Das Blackboard als Nullwert–Bestimmungssystem ist einem Datenbanksystem vorgelagert und arbeitet in einem inhaltlich bestimmten Lösungs– und nicht in einem formalen Transaktionszyklus. Auf implementierungstechnische Details muß verzichtet werden, da hierzu gesonderte Darstellungen erforderlich sind.

2 Überblick

2.1 Ansätze zur Behandlung von Nullwerten in der Literatur

Betrachtet man die Diskussion über die Behandlung von Nullwerten in Relationalen Datenbanken, so kann man zwei prinzipielle Ansätze zur Nullwertbehandlung feststellen:

- keine spezielle Darstellung und Behandlung von Nullwerten auf Datenbanksystemebene (**[DATE86]**) und

- Behandlung von Nullwerten durch das Datenbanksystem (**[CODD86]**).

Zum ersten Ansatz ist zu sagen, daß die Behandlung von Nullwerten damit ausschließlich in der Hand des Benutzers liegt, der mit Hilfe von ausgewählten Attributwerten (*default values*) Nullwerte darstellen und behandeln kann.

CODD (**[CODD86]**) schlägt die Erweiterung der relationalen Theorie vor, um Nullwerte zu behandeln. Er führt statt der klassischen zweiwertigen Logik eine mehrwertige Logik (drei– bzw. vierwertige) ein, um Anfragen an eine Datenbank mit Nullwerten auszuwerten. Unsere Auffassung ist, daß die Prädikatenlogik ungeeignet ist, Nullwerte adäquat zu beschreiben. Nullwerte sind Leerstellen für mögliche Werte, die in der Zeit erst entstehen. Es gibt in der Prädikatenlogik für *Zeit* und *Möglichkeit* keine Ausdrucksmittel. Der pragmatisch geeignetere Weg, Nullwerte logisch zu rekonstruieren, ist die Einführung weiterer Partikel in die Logik, die diesen Sachverhalt adäquat repräsentieren. Dies führt zur Verwendung der *Modallogik* ([**WEDE83**]), die eigens für solche Zwecke definiert wurde. Das Einbeziehen von *unmöglichen* Sachverhalten (*inapplicable* information [**CODD87**]) in eine Datenbank ist durch entsprechenden Schemaentwurf zu verhindern. In [**WEDE83**] wird eine *modallogische Normalform* vorgeschlagen, die Unmöglichkeiten a priori vermeidet.

Weitere Vorschläge für die Nullwertbehandlung verlassen mehr oder weniger die CODD'sche Theorie, speziell die klassische Logik und die Relationenalgebra, und verwenden die Theorie der *denotationellen Semantik* ([**VASS79**]), der *Produktionensysteme* [**WILL88**] oder gehen zur *Beweistheorie* über *(deduktive Datenbanken)* ([**REIT84**]). Dabei werden zum einen die theoretischen Grundlagen zur Nullwertbeschreibung und zum anderen prototypische Realisierungen von Datenbanksystemen jenseits der kommerziell durchgesetzten relationalen Datenbanksysteme betrachtet. Die Ansätze in [**WILL88**] und [**REIT84**] ermöglichen Nullwerte, deren Unbestimmtheit eingegrenzt werden kann, z. B. durch Beschränkung auf eine Teilmenge des gesamten Wertebereichs. Damit unterscheiden sich diese Vorgehensweisen erheblich von den Ansätzen in [**CODD86**] und [**VASS79**].

2.2 Behandlung von Nullwerten in Datenbanksystemen

Bei den hier betrachteten Relationalen Datenbanksystemen haben wir uns auf Systeme beschränkt, die *kommerziell* verfügbar sind und auf Grund ihrer Verbreitung einen entsprechenden Bekanntheitsgrad aufweisen. Zunächst untersuchen wir die beiden Datenbanksysteme *DB2* von IBM und *INGRES* von Relational Technology, bevor wir uns mit der Nullwertbehandlung im *SQL-Standard* auseinandersetzen.

2.2.1 Nullwertbehandlung in INGRES

Bis *Release 5.0* unterstützt INGRES keine Nullwertbehandlung. Die Nullwertbehandlung obliegt dem Benutzer. Attribute, denen keine Werte zugewiesen werden, belegt das System mit Standardwerten (sog. *default values*). Diese default-values sind abhängig von den Wertebereichen der Attribute und sind Elemente aus diesen. *Numerischen* Attributbereichen werden als default-value 0 (*zero*) und *alphanumerischen* Wertebereichen eine Leerzeichenkette (*blanks*) bzw. keine Zeichenkette (*empty string* bei Zeichenketten variabler Länge) zugeordnet. Ab *Release 6.0* unterstützt INGRES Nullwerte ([**DATE87**]). Die Behandlung entspricht der im SQL-Standard definierten Vorgehensweise (siehe 2.2.3).

2.2.2 Nullwertbehandlung in DB2

Da sich die Standardisierung von SQL auf Basis von SQL für DB2 vollzogen hat, entspricht die Nullwertbehandlung von DB2 ([**DATE84**]) dem ISO-Standard, den wir nachfolgend beschreiben.

2.2.3 Nullwertbehandlung im SQL-Standard

Für die Handhabung von Nullwerten in der Datenbanksprache SQL werden die *Relationen-* und *Boolesche Algebra* erweitert, um Nullwerte zu unterstützen ([**ISO87**]). Die Wahrheitstafeln umfassen neben den klassischen Wahrheitswerten *true* und *false* noch den dritten "Wahrheitswert" *unknown* (dreiwertige Logik). Die Vergleichsoperatoren werden um Definitionen für die Vergleiche mit Nullwerten modifiziert. Vergleiche von Konstanten oder Variablen mit Nullwerten (z. B. in einer WHERE-Klausel) ergeben den "Wahrheitswert" *unknown*. Bei Vergleichen von Tupeln untereinander dagegen ergibt die Gleichheitsrelation zwischen zwei Nullwerten den Wahrheitswert *true* — eine inkonsequente Verwendung der dreiwertigen Logik! Solche ein- oder mehrstelligen Tupelvergleiche treten immer dann auf, wenn identische Tupeleinträge (*duplicates*) bestimmt werden müssen, z. B. im Zusammenhang mit einer Anweisung zur Teilmengenbildung (GROUP BY-Klausel), der Forderung nach Mengeneigenschaft (DISTINCT) oder der Sortieranweisung (ORDER BY). Der Test von Attributen auf Nullwerte wird mit Hilfe einer Spracherweiterung (IS NULL) spezifiziert.

Ergänzend bleibt noch festzustellen, daß der SQL-Standard nur sehr eingeschränkt die Vorschläge übernommen hat, die in [CODD86] zur Nullwertproblematik gemacht wurden. Insbesondere werden keine *maybe-joins* unterstützt.

3 Nullwerte und Rechtsgeschäfte — die juristische Perspektive

In der Literatur über Nullwerte in Datenbanksystemen ist es bisher versäumt worden, herauszustellen, daß Nullwerte eine zentrale Bedeutung im Zuge der Vorbereitung, des Abschlusses und der Durchführung von Rechtsgeschäften haben. So werden z.B. zwischen Kunde und Unternehmung (Verkauf) sowie zwischen Lieferant und Unternehmung (Einkauf) Rechtsgeschäfte durch Verträge abgeschlossen, die ein Schuldverhältnis begründen. Die sachgerechte Behandlung von Nullwerten ist dann nicht das "Privatvergnügen" eines Datenbankbetreibers, sondern u. a. die Angelegenheit einschlägiger Vorschriften des bürgerlichen Rechts, das sich in diesen Grundtypen international nur in Nuancen unterscheidet. Für die Anpassung der Schuldverhältnisse an spätere Bedingungen wird ein rechtsverbindlicher Rahmen vorgegeben. Die Vertragsparteien können durch entsprechendes Offenhalten der näheren Bestimmungen von *Leistungsinhalt, -zeit* und *-ort* Vorsorge für künftige Entwicklungen treffen. Unversorgte Nullwerte, d. h. der technische Status quo marktüblicher Datenbanksysteme, können aus der Perspektive des Vertragsrechts der Ausgangspunkt für spätere Leistungsstörungen, evtl. sogar Vertragsverletzungen, sein. "Nullwerte" — so lautet die allgemeine Regel — müssen nach *billigem Ermessen* bestimmt werden (§ 315, Abs. 1 Bürgerliches Gesetzbuch, BGB). Den passiven Terminus "Nullwerte", der eine Übersetzung des amerikanischen "null-value" ist, kennt das Gesetz selbstverständlich nicht; der *handlungsvorschreibende* Begriff "Bestimmung der Leistung" wird vornehmlich benutzt. In Verbindung mit dem ebenfalls wichtigen § 375 Handelsgesetzbuch (HGB, das BGB des Kaufmanns) sprechen einige Lehrbuchautoren auch vom *Spezifikationskauf*. Der Gesetzgeber verfügt in § 375 HGB, daß beim Spezifikationskauf einer beweglichen Sache und bei einer entsprechenden vertraglichen Fixierung "dem Käufer die nähere Bestimmung über Form, Maß oder ähnliche Verhältnisse vorbehalten ist" und daß er dazu verpflichtet wird. Kann er das nicht, wobei das Gebot des billigen Ermessens gemäß § 315 BGB gilt, so ist er zu Schadensersatz wegen Nichterfüllung (§ 326 BGB) verpflichtet. An den zentralen Paragraphen § 315 BGB und § 375 HGB erkennt auch der Nicht-

Rechtskundige sofort den Grundtenor: Im Rahmen der Vertragsfreiheit können die Partner festlegen, wer bestimmt. Ist einer von beiden Kaufmann, so gelten die prägnanteren Vorschriften des HGB. Die Bestimmung des Nullwerts muß im Zweifel nach billigem und nicht nach freiem Ermessen erfolgen und dem anderen gegenüber erklärt werden (§ 315, Abs. 2 BGB). Wenn keine Billigkeit vorliegt, d. h. eine ungerechtfertigte Spezifikation, so ergeht u. U. die Bestimmung durch *Urteil*, d. h. durch den Richter von außen (§ 315, Abs. 3 BGB). In technischer Terminologie heißt das: Es gibt einen *Nullwert–Spezifikation–Sender* und einen *Nullwert–Spezifikation–Empfänger*. Der Sender hat als Nullwert–Bestimmer nach billigem Ermessen zu planen und seine Planungen dem Empfänger — im Zweifel natürlich umgehend — zu erklären. Der Gesetzgeber will die Einigung. Kommt sie nicht zustande, entscheidet der Richter als "übergeordnetes System" ebenfalls nach billigem Ermessen. "Ergänzung des Vertragsinhalts durch richterliche Gestaltung" nennt das die Jurisprudenz.

Zu einem berühmten "Nullwert–Fall" ist das Beispiel von FIKES und HENDERSON ([**FIKE80**]) geworden. Die Situation soll hier in zwei Varianten diskutiert werden, um daran die Wirkungen von § 375 HGB bei Leistungsstörungen darzutun:

Die Firma Xerox verkauft ihre Kopierer über Auftragssachbearbeiter (*customer order entry clerk*), die in der Regel Aufträge über Telefon entgegennehmen. Während eines Verkaufgesprächs füllt der Sachbearbeiter ein Formular aus, das später die Grundlage für Lieferung und Rechnungsschreibung wird. Liefer- und Rechnungsadresse werden u. a. erfaßt. In einem besonderen Fall nun konnte ein Kunde die Lieferadresse nicht angeben, weil der bestellte Kopierer auf einem Hochseeschiff aufgestellt werden sollte, dessen Anlaufhäfen und –zeiten zum Zeitpunkt der Bestellung noch unbekannt waren.

Dem Kunden als Käufer kommt nun die Bestimmung der Lieferadresse als Nullwert zu. In der ersten Version kümmert sich der Kunde (*Nullwert–Spezifikation–Sender*) nicht um die fehlende Angabe. Als das Gerät geliefert werden kann, liefert Xerox den Kopierer an die Rechnungsadresse aus, was beim Kunden zu einer Annahmeverweigerung führt. Die Frage, ob Xerox das durfte, ist bedingt mit "ja" zu beantworten, denn: Kommt der Käufer nach § 375, Abs. 2 HGB in Verzug, so kann der Verkäufer die Bestimmungen (des Nullwertes) dem Kunden gegenüber erklären und nach einer Frist die Bestimmung selbst vornehmen. Xerox kann darüber hinaus sogar gemäß § 326 BGB Schadensersatz wegen Nichterfüllung verlangen, falls der Kunde Annahme und Zahlung weiterhin verweigern sollte.

Im Falle einer Leistungsstörung, die die andere Seite zu vertreten hat, bekommt der *Nullwert–Spezifikation–Empfänger* nach HGB somit eine starke Stellung. Er wird vom Gesetz nach einer erklärten, angemessenen Frist zum Sender gemacht, d. h. die Positionen kehren sich um.

In der zweiten Version hinterläßt der Kunde im Felde "Lieferadresse" einen Hinweis auf eine Telefonnummer, über die die laufende Position des Schiffes und seine vermutlichen Anlaufhäfen und –zeiten in Erfahrung zu bringen sind. Das

Geschäft kann einwandfrei als eine Sequenz von Büroprozeduren abgewickelt werden. KRATZER und SCHREIER ([KRAT85]) behandeln Anmerkungen zu einem Nullwert-Feld, wie oben die Telefonnummer, als *Legenden*. Wer einen Nullwert zu spezifizieren hat, dem kommt nach dem Gesetz eine Erklärungspflicht zu (§ 315, Abs. 2 BGB). Verlangt wird somit datentechnisch ein Dialog zwischen Sender und Empfänger. Bloße Anmerkungen zu Nullwerten reichen hier nicht aus.

4 Eine Blackboard–Architektur zur Behandlung von Nullwerten

4.1 Büroarbeit als Spezifikation von Nullwerten

Eine zentrale Aufgabenstellung für Büros ist die Spezifikation von Nullwerten. Nullwerte sind Indikatoren dafür, daß *Daten im Werden* sind. Es hängt nun vom verlangten Aktualitätsstand und vom Einsatzfeld einer Datenbank ab, ob das Werden der Daten verfolgt und unterstützt wird oder ob nur fertige Daten zu registrieren sind. Die generelle Frage, wann Objekte der Büroarbeit in welchem Spezifikationszustand einer Datenbank für eine größere Benutzergemeinschaft verfügbar gemacht werden, soll hier nicht interessieren. Von Bedeutung ist für uns die Betrachtungsweise, daß Nullwerte als die noch unspezifizierte Spitze eines großen "Planungseisberges" anzusehen sind. Wir betrachten zur Erläuterung das Gerüst eines Auftrags–Bearbeitungssystems, z. B. einer Getriebefabrik. Zweck dieses Systems ist es, Tupeln der Relation

AuftragsPosten (Auftrag#, Position#, Artikel#, Kunden#, Datum, Menge, LieferDatum,...)

zu erzeugen. Ein Auftrag mit seinen Positionen, der an die Firma in noch nicht durchspezifizierter Form herangetragen wird, muß im Büro diversen Prüfungen unterzogen werden. Rein identifizierende Einträge, wie *Auftrag#* oder *Kunden#*, sind dabei problemlos. Sie konstituieren aber das Nullwertproblem. Denn erst nach dem Identifizieren wird deutlich, daß etwas fehlt. Wesentlich sind Attribute, mit denen Durchführbarkeitsfragen verbunden sind, d. h. Fragen, *ob* überhaupt, in *welchen* Mengen, *wann* und *wo* zu liefern ist? Daß noch etwas fehlt, darf einer Datenbankwelt, die weiß, daß etwas Vollständiges selten ist, zugemutet werden. Wenn angenommen wird, daß *Artikel#* ein sprechender Schlüssel ist, aus dem eine Erzeugnisvariante entnommen werden kann, dann ist *Artikel#* ein Nullwert, da die Nummer erst über eine Variantenprüfung und –auswahl aufgebaut werden kann. In einer ersten Phase sind im Zweifel alle technischen, organisatorischen und kaufmännischen Attributausprägungen unbestimmt. Es existieren allenfalls Wunschvorstellungen oder Vorschläge, die im allgemeinen einen unverbindlichen und ungeprüften Charakter haben. Man bleibt auf jeden Fall zunächst im Modus der Möglichkeit ([WEDE83]). Vorschläge und Wunschvorstellungen ändern an der unbestimmten Situation nur insofern etwas, als man nun weiß, daß Meinungen vorgetragen werden, nach denen etwas "erreichbar" sein müßte. Daß Fragen der Macht, d. h. die Prioritäten bei der Einplanung, zu berücksichtigen sind, versteht sich von selbst.

Die *technischen, organisatorischen* und *kaufmännischen* Spezifikationsarbeiten an Nullwerten lassen sich in entsprechende Funktionsbereiche gliedern. Wir wollen es hier dabei belassen, nur die oberste Stufe einer Hierarchie aufzuzeigen.

1. Technische Durchführbarkeit	2. Organisatsorische Material- und Zeitbedarfsermittlung	3. Kaufmännische Prüfung und Rechnungswesen
1.1 Aufbau einer Artikelstückliste aus einer Variantenstückliste.	2.1 Sofortauftrag, Verfügfügbarkeitsprüfung im Fertigwarenlager.	3.1 Preiskalkulation.
1.2 Stücklistenauflösung (Teilebedarfsermittlung).	2.2 Termin- und Abrufaufträge, Grobterminplanung.	3.2 Bonitätsprüfung des Kundens.
1.3 Materialverfügbarkeitsprüfung.		3.3 Finanzierungsprüfung.
		3.4 Prüfung der politischen Sicherheit bei Exportaufträgen.

Im übernächsten Abschnitt wird exemplarisch eine weitere Vertiefung des Bereichs 1.1 vorgenommen. Die Auflistung an dieser Stelle soll nur verdeutlichen, daß Nullwertspezifikationen die Koordinierung heterogener, asynchroner Tätigkeiten verlangen und eine umfangreiche Systemanalyse voraussetzen ([WEDE76]). Systemtechnisch muß einer Datenbank, in der Nullwerte indiziert werden, ein Spezifikationssystem vorangestellt werden. Innerhalb der Arbeiten zum Thema "Wissensbasierte Systeme" mit ihrer strikten Trennung von *Regelwerk, Kontrollogik* und *Datenbank* sind Blackboard-Architekturen entwickelt worden, die auch einen allgemeinen Rahmen für die Büroarbeit darstellen. Ein Blackboard-System muß einer Datenbank, die auch für Daten, die im Werden sind und somit nur den Status des Möglichen haben, vorgeschaltet werden. In dieser Applikation sind Blackboard-Systeme neuartig. Bekannt geworden sind Anwendungen im Bereich der Sprachverarbeitung, hier ist vor allem das Blackboard-System *Hearsay* ([ERMA80]) zu nennen. Im Bereich der Sonardatenverarbeitung zur Verfolgung von Schiffsbewegungen in einem Seegebiet ist das System *HASP/SIAP* ([NII86a]) entstanden. In Erlangen wurde bisher im Rahmen des *KONTUR*-Projekts (*KON*figurierung von Klein*TUR*binen) ein Blackboard-System implementiert, das in einem allgemeinen Zusammenhang die Konfigurierung technischer Systeme zum Gegenstand hat ([SPER88]). Die Erfahrungen bei dieser Systementwicklung bilden eine Grundlage für das Folgeprojekt *OPS* (*Order Processing System*).

4.2 Elemente einer Blackboard-Architektur

Blackboard-Systeme in ihrer allgemeinsten Struktur werden in der bedeutenden Arbeit von HAYES-ROTH ([HAYE85]) dargestellt. Eine Blackboard-Architektur ist nichts anderes als eine Rahmenanordnung für *wissensbasierte Systeme*. Das eigentliche Problem liegt darin, diesen Rahmen auszufüllen. Dieser Abschnitt dient der *terminologischen* Einführung. Die bildhafte Sprache der Blackboard-Systeme ist recht nützlich und keineswegs verzerrend.

Eine Blackboard-Architektur besteht aus den folgenden *Komponenten* (*Abb. 4-1*):

a) Die Wissensquellen (*knowledge sources*)

Sie beinhalten das *Fachwissen* zur Problemlösung. Das "Wissen" ist so auf die Wissensquellen aufgeteilt, daß diese funktional und logisch unabhängige Teilprobleme eigenständig lösen können.

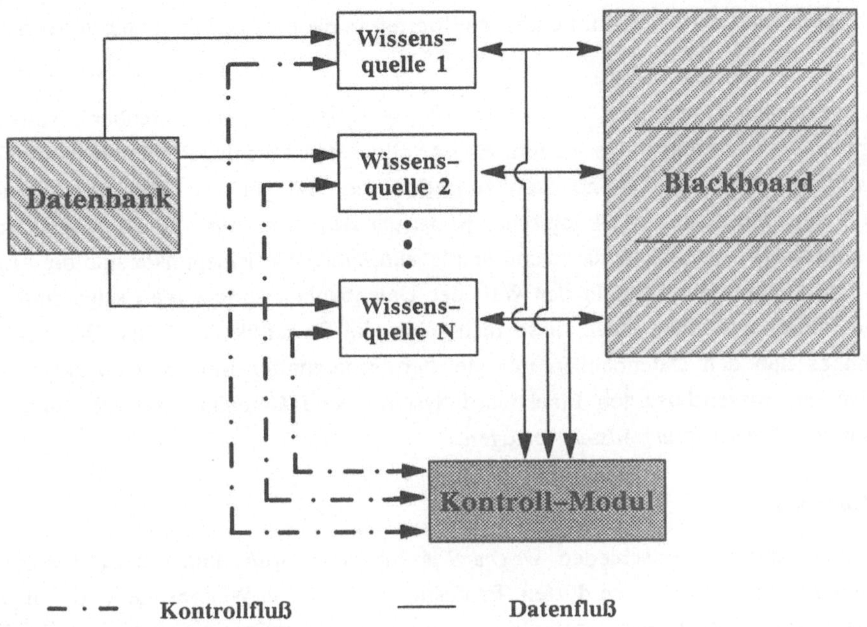

Abbildung 4–1: *Architektur eines Blackboard-Systems*

Unabhängigkeit bedeutet, daß keine Quelle weiß, wie Daten von anderen Wissensquellen verarbeitet werden. Es liegt also keine Prozedurhierarchisierung vor. Eine Wissensquelle weiß nicht, welche und ob überhaupt andere Wissensquellen existieren. Eine Wissensquelle besteht aus einem *Bedingungsteil*, der prüft, ob die Anwendbarkeitsbedingungen erfüllt sind, und einem *Ausführungsteil*, der die Lösungselemente erzeugt. Man kann eine Wissensquelle als eine "große Regel" ansehen.

b) Das Blackboard

Das Blackboard ist eine globale Datenstruktur und kann als das *"Kurzzeitgedächtnis"*, besser als das "Aufbaugedächtnis" des Systems betrachtet werden. Es enthält alle Daten und Lösungselemente für *Teillösungen, Zwischenlösungen* und *Alternativlösungen*.

Im Blackboard werden alle *transistenten* Daten gespeichert, während die Datenbank aus der Sicht des Problemlösens *permanente* Daten enthält. Das Blackboard ist leer, wenn es keine Probleme gibt. Die Wissensquellen holen sich permanente Daten aus der Datenbank und transistente Daten vom Blackboard-Speicher. Ist der Problemlösezyklus beendet, so werden die als permanent erachteten Daten in die Datenbank übertragen. Wissensquellen kommunizieren während eines Problemlösezyklus ausschließlich über den Blackboard-Speicher. Die Elemente eines Blackboards sind *anwendungsspezifisch* strukturiert. Ein Aufbau entsprechend einer disziplinierenden *Abstraktions-* bzw. *Teil-/Ganzes*-Hierarchie erscheint jedoch zwingend. Sicherlich

gehören Tupeln von Relationen mit Sender–Nullwerten in die oberste Hierarchiestufe eines Blackboards.

Sind permanente Daten noch nicht vollständig, so entstehen in der Datenbank Nullwerte, die
auf einen weiteren Lösungszyklus warten. Es ist völlig unangebracht, Problemlösungszyklen auf
den *Transaktionsbegriff* von Datenbanken zu reduzieren und gar von *Langzeittransaktionen* zu
sprechen. Eine Transaktion ist als logisches Konstrukt *zeitfrei, atomar* und *extensional* eingeführt
worden. *Intensionale, problemorientierte* und damit *zeitbehaftete* Gesichtspunkte sind die Angelegenheit von Problemlösungszyklen. In der Welt der Datenbanken spricht man scherzhaft von den
"dummen Betriebssystemen", weil diese nicht über die Semantik der Daten Bescheid wissen.
Man kann es nun den Datenbanken mit gleicher, scherzhafter Münze heimzahlen. Aus der
Perspektive der wissensbasierten Blackboard–Systeme sind Datenbanksysteme "dumm", weil
diese über kein *Problemlösungswissen* verfügen.

c) Die Kontrolle

Im Kontroll–Modul wird entschieden, *welche* Wissensquellen *wann* und mit *welchen* transienten
Daten eines Blackboards arbeiten dürfen. Er bestimmt damit die Wissensquelle, die als nächstes
einen Beitrag zur Lösung leisten soll. Im allgemeinen sind mehrere Quellen bereit, Transformationen auf dem Blackboardzustand durchzuführen, nämlich alle Quellen deren Bedingungen
erfüllt sind. Die aktivierte Wissensquelle erzeugt weitere Einträge im Blackboard, die wiederum
die Anwendbarkeitsbedingungen weiterer Wissensquellen befriedigen können. Nach jeder
Ausführung einer Wissensquelle wird dann erneut entschieden, welche Wissensquelle ausgeführt
wird. Ein *elementarer Kontrollzyklus* umfaßt die *Auswahl* einer Wissensquelle aus den bereiten
Wissensquellen und die *Ausführung* dieser Quelle. In einem erweiterten Blackboard–Modell
(**[HAYE85]**) kann das Kontroll–Modul ebenfalls nach dem Blackboard–Prinzip arbeiten und auf
diese Weise das *Kontrollproblem* lösen. Neben dem eigentlichen Blackboard zur Lösung des *An-
wendungsproblems* (*domain* blackboard) wird dann noch ein Blackboard zur Lösung des
Kontrollproblems (*control* blackboard) unterschieden. Es dürfte klar sein, daß der Entwurf eines
Systems von Kontrollstrategien ein zentrales Problem eines jeden komplexeren Blackboard–Systems ist. Kontrollstrategien für das Variantenbestimmen sind z. B. substantiell anders als
Strategien für die Lieferterminfestlegung. Hier kann u. U. die Aktivierung einer Wissensquelle,
die eine einfache Datenbankabfrage durchführt, ausreichend sein.

In unserem Zusammenhang kann man sich leicht vorstellen, daß das Erscheinen eines zu
Aktivitäten verpflichtenden Nullwerts auf der Tafel eine oder mehrere Wissensquellen anstößt (z.
B. auch Menschen, die eine Telefon–Nr. wissen, um zu erfahren, wo ausgeliefert werden kann),
damit Veränderungen auf einer der Ebenen der Blackboard–Hierarchie erzeugt werden.

Wir fassen zusammen: Blackboard–Systeme unterstützen *kooperative* Prozesse beim
Entstehen, d. h. bei der *Konstruktion von Daten*. Der Entwickler einer Wissensquelle ist frei von
dem Zwang, das zu entwickelnde Modul an andere Module anzupassen zu müssen. Die Vorgehensweise in Blackboard–Systemen ist von Nii (**[NII86]**) in treffender Weise mit dem Lösen
von Puzzlespielen verglichen worden. Ein Puzzle wird auf einer Tafel von mehreren Personen

(Wissensquellen) zusammengesetzt, wobei jeder von ihnen einen Teil der notwendigen Puzzlestücke bereithält. Eine Person beginnt und legt "vielversprechende Puzzlestücke" als Lösungsinseln auf die Tafel (z. B. Eckstücke und Randstücke). Die Mitspieler sind nun aufgefordert, passende Puzzlestücke zu finden. Hat jemand eins gefunden, geht er zur Tafel und fügt es hinzu. Das führt dazu, daß wieder neue Puzzlestücke hinzukommen können. Die Spieler sehen immer einen neuen Lösungsstand auf der Tafel und können nach ihrem Vermögen zur Lösungsentwicklung beitragen. So entsteht *inkrementell*, Schritt für Schritt die Gesamtlösung. Die Lösung entwickelt sich *opportunistisch*, d. h., eine Einzelperson tut in einem Augenblick das, was sie kann. Es gibt kein höheres, übergreifendes Zusammensetzverfahren, was von der klassischen Vorgehensweise verlangt wird. Benötigt wird jedoch eine Kontrollperson, die entscheidet, wer zur Tafel gehen darf. Die Personenauswahl geschieht nach einer bestimmten Strategie, die durchaus situationsabhängig wechseln kann.

d) Die Datenbank

Betrachtet man die unvollständige Spezifikation von Daten in der Datenbank als den Stimulus für einen Problemlösezyklus, so ist noch offen, wie das Zusammenwirken zwischen Datenbank und Blackboard erfolgt. Dazu kann man sich eine Wissensquelle vorstellen, die in der Lage ist, Zustände in der Datenbank, die einer Lösung bedürfen, zu erkennen, um entsprechende Einträge ins Blackboard zu erzeugen. Die im Rahmen eines Problemlösezyklus gefundenen Lösungen bzw. Teillösungen werden dann wieder in die Datenbank von einer Wissensquelle eingebracht. Die Entscheidung, was ein adäquater Lösungsbeitrag ist, liegt bei der Wissensquelle. Wann ein Eintrag in die Datenbank erfolgt ist abhängig von der zugrundeliegenden Kontrollstrategie. So kann eine Strategie prinzipiell die "Eintragswissensquelle" bevorzugen, womit sichergestellt wird, daß Teillösungen sofort in die Datenbank übernommen werden. Eine alternative Strategie wäre, erst am Ende eines Lösungszyklus die Gesamtlösung in die Datenbank einzubringen.

Untersucht man nun, welche der *Transaktionskonzepte*, die für *non-standard*-Datenbanken vorgeschlagen werden, geeignet sind, die verschiedenen Strategien bzgl. dem Einbringen von Lösungen in die Datenbank zu unterstützen, so kann man folgendes feststellen. Alle Transaktionskonzepte unterstützen nur einen *extensionalen* Transaktionsbegriff. Welche dieser Konzepte sind nun im Rahmen des Problemlösens verwendbar? Die Strategie, bei der am Anfang des Problemlösezyklus der betreffende Zustand der Datenbank in das Blackboard abgebildet wird, um am Ende des Zylus die Lösung wieder in die Datenbank zu übertragen, entspricht einem einfachen CHECKOUT/IN-Vorgehen, bei dem zu Beginn einer Design-Transaktion die entsprechenden Objekte aus der Datenbank ausgelesen werden (CHECKOUT), zum Zwecke der Manipulation in einer lokalen Umgebung, um sie dann am Ende der Design-Transaktion wieder in die allen zugängliche Datenbank auszubringen (CHECKIN) ([**HASK81**]) . Für den Fall, daß nicht nur zu Anfang eines Lösungszyklus Daten aus der Datenbank benötigt, bzw. am Ende des Zyklus Daten in die Datenbank eingebracht werden, ist ein einfacher CHECKOUT/IN-Mechanismus ungeeignet. Dafür sind Transaktionsmodelle entwickelt worden, die es gestatten, während einer Design-Transaktion, was in unserem Fall einem kompletten Problemlösezyklus entspricht, wiederholt Objekte aus der Datenbank zu entnehmen (mehrfaches CHEKOUT), um sie danach geändert wieder in die Datenbank einzubringen (ein- oder mehrfaches CHECKIN) ([LORI83]). Transaktionskonzepte, die dem intensionalen Aspekt des Problemlösens gerecht werden, sind nicht bekannt.

4.3 Aufbau eines wissensbasierten Auftragsbearbeitungssystems

Für das im Abschnitt 4.1 umrissene Auftragsbearbeitungsproblem wird eine Blackboard–Architektur vorgeschlagen. Damit sollen die mit einem Auftrag zusammenhängenden Probleme der Durchführbarkeitspüfung, Materialbedarfs– und Terminplanung sowie der Debitorenabrechnung in einer Gesamtarchitektur beschrieben werden. Im folgenden Abschnitt wird dann auf die Variantenbestimmung als Teilproblem der Auftragsbearbeitung detaillierter eingegangen. Das Blackboard als Lösungsbereich wird zunächst in *Ebenen* unterteilt, die einer Teil–/Ganzes–Hierarchie entsprechen. Die Wissensquellen, die zu (Teil–)Lösungen auf der entsprechenden Ebene beitragen, bezeichnen wir als *ebenenspezifische* Quellen. Orthogonal zu den Ebenen unseres Blackboards unterteilen wir den Lösungsbereich in *Funktionsbereiche* und ordnen diesen die dafür zuständigen Wissensquellen (*funktionsspezifische*) zu. Der Lösungsbereich wird somit in neun Teillösungsbereiche gegliedert (*Abb. 4–2*).

4.4 Aufbau einer Artikelstückliste als Teillösung des Auftragsbearbeitungsproblems

Das im Abschnitt 4.1 skizzierte Auftragsbearbeitungssystem verlangt im Teilproblem 1.1 "Technische Prüfung" die genaue, verbindliche Produktspezifikation. Als Nullwert tritt die Artikel– bzw. Erzeugnis–Nr. (*Artikel#*) auf. Um das Beispiel einfach zu halten, gehen wir von der *Variantenstückliste* eines hypothetischen Zahnradgetriebes aus (*Abb. 4–3*).

Variantenstücklisten können, wie in *Abbildung 4–3*, mit Hilfe des *Knotentypen*–Ansatzes dargestellt werden ([WEDE81a]). *Konjunktivknoten* (K) repräsentieren Baugruppen als logische Zusammenfassung von *Alternativknoten* (A) und von *Teileknoten* (T). Gerichtete und mit Mengenangaben bewertete Kanten bedeuten üblicherweise in Stücklistendarstellungen "geht–ein–in". Alternativknoten sind als exklusives *Oder* das Zentrum einer spezifikationsbedürftigen Stückliste, denn hier kann zwischen *Baugruppen* (K), *Teileknoten* (T) und *Leerknoten* (L) ausgewählt werden. Alternativknoten bilden Entscheidungsbereiche. Tritt ein untergeordneter Leerknoten (L) auf, so handelt es sich um eine *Kann*–Variante, d. h., man wählt wie im Falle "Sonderausstattung" (A_2) zwischen dem "Nichts" und dem "Etwas". Bei den Knoten A_1 und A_3 bzw. in den Entscheidungsbereichen "Leistungsklasse" und "Stufenzahl" ist konkret zu entscheiden. Es liegen *Muß*–Varianten vor. Ein bloßes Unterlassen wie im Falle des Leerknotens zählt nicht. Die dritte Form von Varianten, die sog. *Mengen*–Variante, wurde weggelassen. Bei Mengen–Varianten geht ein Teileknoten über zwei unterschiedlich bewertete Kanten in einen Alternativknoten ein.

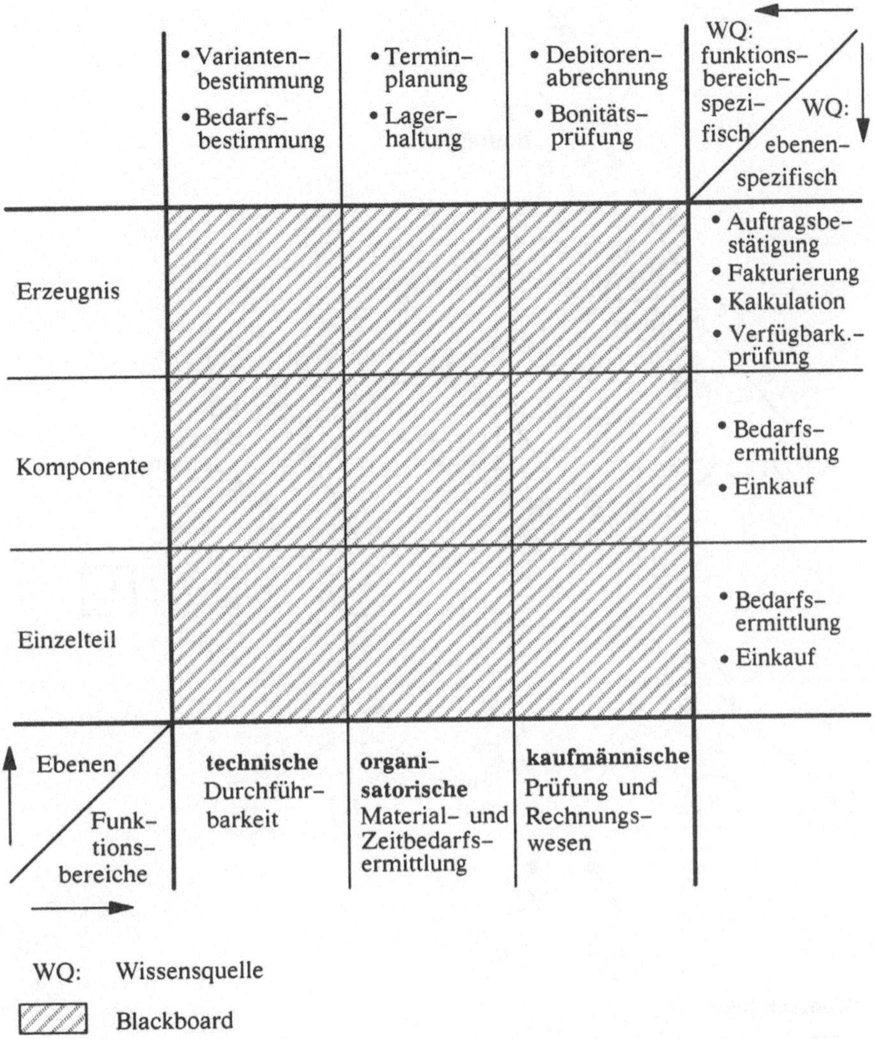

Abbildung 4-2: *Blackboard-Architektur für das Auftragsbearbeitungsproblem*

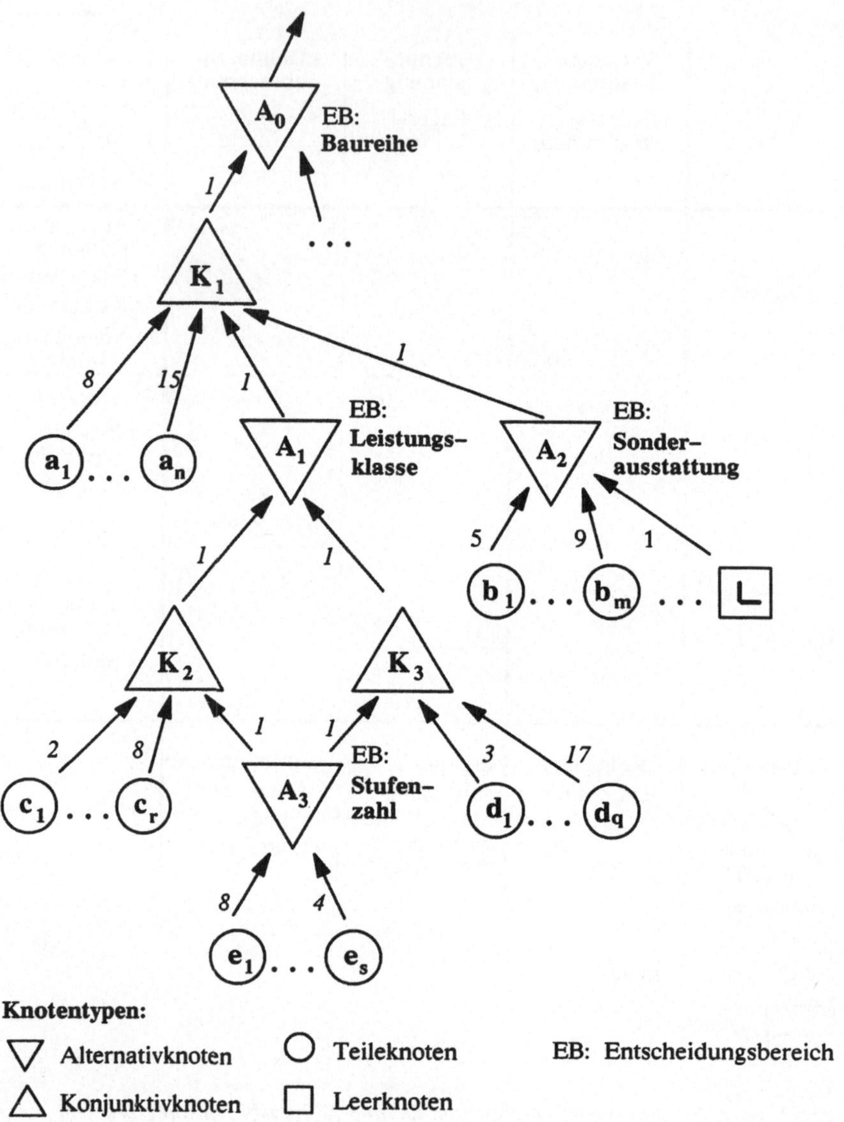

Abbildung 4–3: *Graph einer Variantenstückliste*

Erzeugnisnummern für Varianten werden zweckmäßig nach der Methode der Parallel-verschlüsselung aufgebaut. Ein Identifikationsteil mit einer *Id#* als laufende Nummer wird einem Klassifikationsteil, der die Varianten spezifiziert, vorangestellt:

Id# (xxxx)	A_0 (xx)	A_1 (xx)	A_2 (xx)	A_3 (xx)	Aufbau
4711	–	–	–	–	vor Nullwertbestimmung
4711	*K1*	*K3*	*b1*	*e1*	nach Nullwertbestimmung

In **[WEDE81a]** wird ein *sequentielles Dialogverfahren* mit der Kontrollstrategie *"von oben nach unten, Breite zuerst"* im Stücklistengraphen dargestellt. Diese Vorgehensweise wird dem Problemlösen im allgemeinen nicht gerecht. Wo steht z. B. geschrieben, daß über die Leistungs-klasse (A_1) eines Getriebes eher entschieden werden muß als über die Stufenzahl (A_3)? Die Blackboard–Architektur erlaubt hier eine viel liberalere, d. h. *problem–* und *situationsgerechtere Strategie*. Es hängt davon ab, in welcher Sequenz die zur Lösung beitragenden Wissensquellen der einzelnen Entscheidungsbereiche in den Problemlösezyklen abgearbeitet werden.

Die Variantenbestimmung mit Hilfe eines Blackboards wird in *Abbildung 4–4* schematisch gezeigt. Ausgangspunkt für die Bestimmung sind die mehr oder weniger vollständigen Spezifikationen des Kundenauftrags in Bezug auf Bauteil-, Baugruppen- und Baureihenbestim-mung. Diese fragmentarische Beschreibung einer Produkt–Stückliste wird durch die entsprechen-den Wissensquellen auf den einzelnen Ebenen ergänzt. Eine Lösung liegt vor, wenn die vor-gegebenen Fragmente zu einer zusammenhängenden Stückliste ohne Alternativknoten komplet-tiert werden können. Nicht verbindbare Teile bedeuten Produktwünsche, die nicht mit anderen Wünschen zu vereinbaren sind. Diese Diskrepanzen sind durch Rücksprache mit dem Kunden zu klären.

An diesem Beispiel wird deutlich, daß im Rahmen dieses hochdurchorganisierten Problemlösens eine einfache Kontrollstrategie zumindest in einem ersten Ansatz ausreichend ist. Unter den vier *Scheduling*-Klassen, die in der Literatur (z. B. **[HAYE85]**) erörtert werden, es handelt sich um

- solution based focusing,

- sophisticated scheduler,

- meta level architecture und

- blackboard control architecture,

ist das einfache "solution based focusing" auch schon wegen des geringsten Implemen-tierungsaufwands vorzuziehen. Es gibt dann keine komplizierte *Heuristik* bezüglich "konkurrieren-der Wissensquellen". Im wesentlichen gilt die *last-in-first-out* Regel. Man ist damit der klassi-schen Programmierung und ihrem "Stack-Prinzip" am nächsten, dennoch bleiben die Wis-sensquellen als Programmteile unabhängig und können beliebig ergänzt werden.

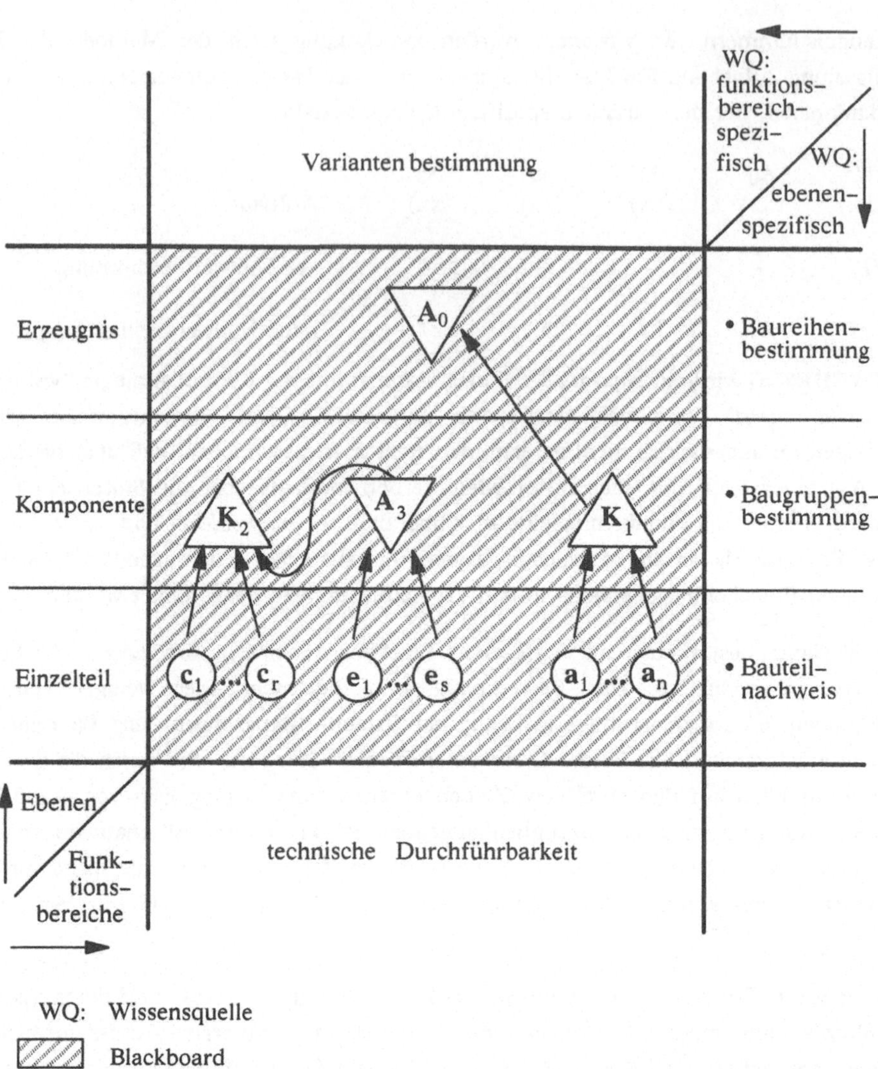

Abbildung 4–4: *Blackboard–Architektur für die Variantenbestimmung*

5 Zusammenfassung und Ausblick

Die bloß "buchhalterische" Verwaltung von Nullwerten in Datenbanken war für uns der Ausgangspunkt für eine Auseinandersetzung mit dem Problem der unbestimmten Information im Büro. Den pragmatischen Aspekt von Nullwerten haben wir am Beispiel von Rechtsgeschäften diskutiert. Die Gesetzgebung und Rechtssprechung hat sich schon immer mit Unbestimmtheiten befassen müssen. Eine rechtliche Würdigung zeigt, daß unversorgte Nullwerte in Rechtsgeschäften zu einem Verschulden führen können, das Schäden verursacht. Derjenige, der das Verschulden zu vertreten hat, muß für den Schaden aufkommen. Ein erster Rahmen für die Nullwertbehandlung ist also durch die Gesetzgebung abgesteckt. Die Spezifikation von Nullwerten kann ein einklagbares Gebot sein. Zur Bestimmung von Nullwerten in einer Büroumgebung haben wir eine Architektur vorgeschlagen, die geeignet ist, unbestimmte Werte zeitgerecht festzulegen.

Erfahrungen mit Blackboard–Systemen auf dem Gebiet der Konfigurierung von technischen Systemen lassen erwarten, daß Blackboard–Systeme auch zur Lösung des Auftragsbearbeitungsproblems erfolgversprechend eingesetzt werden können. Die Adäquatheit des Ansatzes muß sich in prototypischen Anwendungen in Rahmen der Auftragsbearbeitung erst noch zeigen.

6 Literaturverzeichnis

[BROX88] BROX, H.: *Allgemeines Schuldrecht*. C. H. Beck Verlag, München, 1980, 8. Aufl.

[CODD70] CODD, E. F.: *A Relational Model of Data for Large Shared Data Banks*. in: Comm. ACM, Vol. 13, No. 6, June 1970, S. 377–387.

[CODD86] CODD, E. F.: *Missing information (applicable and inapplicable) in relational databases*. in: ACM SIGMOD RECORD, Vol. 15, No. 4, Dec. 1986, S. 53–78.

[CODD87] CODD, E. F.: *More commentary on missing information in relational databases (applicable and inapplicable information)*. in: ACM SIGMOD RECORD, Vol. 16, No. 1, March 1987, S. 42–50.

[DATE84] DATE, C. J.: *A Guide to DB2*. Addison–Wesley, Reading, MA., 1984.

[DATE86] DATE, C. J.: *Relational Databases: Selected Writings*. Addison–Wesley, Reading, MA., 1986.

[DATE87] DATE, C. J.: *A Guide to INGRES*. Addison–Wesley, Reading, MA., 1987.

[ERMA80] ERMAN, L. D.; LONDON, P. E.; FICKAS, S. F.: *The Design and an Example Use of HEARSAY–III*. in: Proceedings of the 7th International Joint Conference on Artificial Intelligence, 1980, S. 409–415.

[FIKE80] FIKES, R. E.; HENDERSON, D. A., JR.: *On Supporting the Use of Procedures in Office Work*. in: BALZER, R. M. (Hrsg.): *Proceedings of the 1st Annual AAAI Conference*. American Association for Artificial Intelligence, Stanford, August 1980.

[HASK80] HASKIN, R. L.; LORIE, R. A.: *On Extending the Functions of a Relational Database System*. Research Report, RJ 3182, IBM Research Laboratory, San Jose, CA., 1981.

[HAYE85] HAYES-ROTH, B.: *A Blackboard Architectures for Control*. in: Artificial Intelligence Journal, Vol. 26, No. 3, 1985, S. 251–321.

[ISO87] *Information processing systems — Database language SQL*. International Organization for Standardization, ISO 9075, 15.6.1987.

[KRAT85]   KRATZER, K.; SCHREIER, U.: *Behandlung von Ausnahmesituationen mit einer Datenbank*. in: BLASER, A.; PISTOR, P. (Hrsg.): *Tagungsband BTW I*. Karlsruhe, 1985, S. 177–198.

[LIPS79]   LIPSKY, W., JR.: *On Semantic Issues Connected with Incomplete Information Databases*. in: ACM TODS, Vol. 4, No. 3, Sept. 1979, S. 262–296.

[LORI83]   LORIE, R. A.; PLOUFFE, W.: *Complex Objects and Their Use in Design Transactions*. in: *Engineering Design Application*, Proceedings of the Annual Meeting, Database Week, San Jose, CA., May 1983.

[NII86]   NII, P. H.: *Blackboard Systems: The Blackboard Model of Problem Solving and the Evolution of Blackboard Architectures*. in: The AI Magazine, Vol. 7, No. 2, 1986, S. 38–58.

[NII86a]   NII, P. H.: *Blackboard Systems: Blackboard Application Systems, Blackboard Systems from a Knowledge Engineering Perspective*. in: The AI Magazine, Vol. 7, No. 3, 1986, S. 82–106.

[REIT84]   REITER, R.: *Towards a Logical Reconstruction of Relational Database Theory*. in: BRODIE, M. L.; et al. (ed.): *On Conceptual Modelling*. Springer–Verlag, New York, 1984, S. 191–238.

[SPER88]   SPERBER, H. M.: *Eine Blackboard–Architektur zur Konfigurierung technischer Systeme*. Diplomarbeit, IMMD VI, Universität Erlangen–Nürnberg, Erlangen, 1988.

[VASS79]   VASSILIOU, Y.: *Null Values in Data Base Management, A Denotational Semantics Approach*. in: Proceedings of the Int. Conf. on Management of Data, May 30 – June 1, 79, Boston, MA, ACM SIGMOD, 1979, S. 162–169.

[WEDE76]   WEDEKIND, H.: *Systemanalyse — Die Entwicklung von Anwendungssystemen für Datenverarbeitungsanlagen*. Carl–Hanser–Verlag, München, 1976, 2. Aufl.

[WEDE81]   WEDEKIND, H.: *Datenbanksysteme I*. Bibliographisches Institut, Mannheim, 1981, 2. Aufl.

[WEDE81a]   WEDEKIND, H.; MÜLLER, T.: *Stücklistenorganisation bei großer Variantenzahl*. in: Angewandte Informatik, Heft 9, Sept. 1981, S. 377–383.

[WEDE83]   WEDEKIND, H.: *Nullwerte in Datenbanken aus modallogischer Sicht*. in: Softwaretechnik-Trends, Heft 3-3, Dez. 1983, S. 44–55.

[WEDE85]   WEDEKIND, H.: *Büroautomation — eine anthropotechnische Aufgabe*. in: WEDEKIND, H.; KRATZER, K. (Hrsg.): *Büroautomation '85*. Teubner, Stuttgart, 1985.

[WEDE88]   WEDEKIND, H.: *Nullwerte in Datenbanksystemen*. in: Informatik–Spektrum, Band 11, Heft 2, April 1988, S. 97–98.

[WILL88]   WILLIAMS, M. H.; NICHOLSON, K. A.: *An Approach to Handling Incomplete Information in Databases*. in: THE COMPUTER JOURNAL, Vol. 31, No. 2, April 1988, S. 133–140.

Zugriffskontrolle in einer Standarddatenbank für Software-Entwicklungsumgebungen

Erwin Petry
(Im Namen der Deutschen PCTE-Initiative)

Nixdorf Computer AG, Abt. EG ST 2
Berliner Str. 95, D-8000 München 40
email: {uunet,mcvax}!unido!nixpbe!petry.muc

Zusammenfassung:

Derzeit werden in Europa und den USA große Anstrengungen unternommen, um einen Standard als Basis für Software-Entwicklungsumgebungen zu etablieren. Die Deutsche PCTE-Initiative arbeitet an Verbesserungen zu bestehenden Vorschlägen. Die Einführung von komplexen Objekten in das Datenmodell im Zusammenhang mit objektorientierter Zugriffskontrolle hat sich als besonders schwer zu lösendes Problem herausgestellt. Hierfür wird eine Lösung vorgestellt, die widerspruchsfreie Zugriffskontrolle auf überlappenden Datengranulaten ermöglicht.

Summary:

In Europe and the USA big efforts are made to establish a standard as a basis for software engineering environments. The German PCTE Initiative is working on improvements to existing proposals. The introduction of complex objects into the datamodel together with object-oriented access control turned out to be a hard problem. We present a solution for this problem, realizing non contradictory access control on overlapping data granules.

1. Standardisierungsbemühungen für die Softwareentwicklung

Seit einiger Zeit setzt sich immer mehr die Einsicht durch, daß Standardschnittstellen für Software und Hardware wichtig sind und Vorteile für Anbieter und Anwender mit sich bringen. Eine Standardschnittstelle erhöht die Anzahl der Anwendungen, die darauf einsatzbereit sind, und bietet einem Anwender Unabhängigkeit. Um für die Softwareentwicklung zu Standards zu kommen, versucht man seit geraumer Zeit, eine Schnittstelle zu konzipieren, die das Betriebssystem für Werkzeuge und Softwareentwickler einkapselt ("portable tool interface"). Die entsprechenden Aktivitäten laufen u.a. in den USA unter dem Kürzel CAIS (Common APSE Interface Set [CAIS 86]) und in Europa als PCTE (Portable Common Tool Environment, ein ESPRIT Projekt). Zu PCTE gibt es derzeit Standardisierungsvorschläge [PCTE 88, PCTE+ 88] und erste Implementierungen. Das Ziel ist es, PCTE zu einem ECMA-Standard zu machen.

Die PCTE-Spezifikationen finden aber noch nicht überall Zustimmung für eine Normierung. Insbesondere in Deutschland haben sich vor einem Jahr 11 Forschungsinstitute und Industrieunternehmen (s.u.) unter der Federführung von Nixdorf zur Deutschen PCTE-Initiative (German PCTE Initiative; GPI) zusammengeschlossen. Politisches Ziel der GPI ist es, Verbesserungsvorschläge in den Standardisierungsprozeß einzubringen. Die Erfahrungen aus den Verbundprojekten POINTE, PROSYT, RASOP und UNIBASE fließen in die Arbeit ein.

Die Spezifikation des PCTE-Interface [PCTE 88] umfaßt als wohl wichtigste Komponente das Objekt-Management-System (OMS). Es ist verantwortlich für die Verwaltung aller Information, die in einer Software-Entwicklungsumgebung permanent zur Verfügung stehen soll. Es kann grob gesehen sowohl als Dateisystem als auch als Datenbanksystem bezeichnet werden. Als Dateisystem, weil Daten als Inhalt in disjunkten, hierarchisch angeordneten Objekten abgelegt werden, der Zugriff über Pfadnamen erfolgt und

Gruppen Zugriffsrechte zugeteilt werden. Als Datenbanksystem, weil Objekte Attribute haben und Beziehungen zwischen Objekten bestehen. Außerdem wird zwischen einer Schema- und Ausprägungsebene unterschieden. Das System ist ein Mehrbenutzersystem und hat einen Transaktionsmechanismus.

Neben dem OMS bietet PCTE Leistungen an, zur Ausführung von Programmen, zur Kommunikation zwischen Prozessen, zum User Interface und zur Verteilung des Systems auf Workstations in einem lokalen Netz.

Die GPI verfolgt bei Ihrer Arbeit das technische Ziel, die OMS-Spezifikationen von PCTE zu verbessern. Das Datenmodell soll um die drei neuen Konzepte komplexe Objekte, n-stellige Beziehungen und Versionen erweitert werden. Hinzu kommen eine Anzahl von Änderungen an vorhandenen Konzepten [GPI 88].

Wir wollen uns im folgenden mit einem schwierigen, konkreten Problem auseinandersetzen, das die GPI bei Ihrer Arbeit zu lösen hatte. Es geht um das Zusammenspiel von komplexen Objekten und Zugriffskontrolle. Beide Probleme können heute zwar einzeln als in hohem Maße gelöst angesehen werden, erhebliche Probleme ergeben sich aber aus ihrem Zusammentreffen.

2. Zugriffskontrolle

Mit Hilfe der Zugriffskontrolle wird in einem System geregelt, welcher Benutzer auf welchen Daten welche Rechte hat.

Zugriffskontrolle hat also drei Komponenten: Erstens Benutzer, die mit dem System arbeiten. Diese können außerdem Gruppen zugeordnet sein, wie beispielsweise in UNIX(*). Zugriffskontrolle bezieht sich dort auf Benutzer, Gruppen und "Sonstige". Zweitens bezieht sich Zugriffskontrolle immer auf bestimmte Datengranulate. In einer relationalen Datenbank ist etwa eine Relation ein Granulat, in einem Dateisystem typischerweise eine Datei. Drittens werden immer mehrere Zugriffsmodi unterschieden. Jeder Zugriffsmodus steht dabei i.a. für eine Gruppe von Operatoren und macht auf bestimmten Arten von Datengranulaten Sinn. Es wird immer mindestens zwischen lesendem und schreibendem Zugriff unterschieden, wobei beispielsweise alle Retrievaloperatoren das Leserecht voraussetzen. UNIX unterscheidet zusätzlich ein Ausführungsrecht. Daran wird deutlich, daß ein Recht nicht auf allen Daten sinnvoll ist.

Außerdem ist es sinnvoll, einen "Eigentümer" für jedes Granulat zu haben, dem die Daten "gehören", und der das spezielle Recht hat, die Zugriffsrechte der Benutzer auf "seinem" Granulat zu definieren.

Schließlich ist jeder Modus auf jedem Datengranulat für jeden Benutzer zu einem Zeitpunkt entweder gewährt oder nicht. ("Der Benutzer hat ein Recht oder er hat es nicht.") Wir sprechen hierbei von dem "Wert" eines Modus. Somit läßt sich Zugriffskontrolle auffassen als Funktion:

$$\text{Rechte:} \quad \text{Granulat x Benutzer x Zugriffsmodus} \quad \text{-->} \quad \text{Wert}$$

3. Komplexe Objekte

Verschiedene Konzepte für die Zugriffskontrolle variieren die genannten Parameter. Die Unterscheidung weiterer Rechte oder ein anderes Gruppenkonzept bringen dabei wenig Probleme mit sich. Schwierig wird allerdings die Einführung von komplexen Objekten.

Bisher sind wir implizit von der Annahme ausgegangen, daß die Datengranulate disjunkt sind, sich also nicht überlappen. Komplexe Objekte haben diese Eigenschaft nicht. Im GPI-Datenmodell besteht ein Objekt aus Komponenten, Attributwerten und internen Beziehungen. Jede Komponente ist wieder ein Objekt. Das Datenmodell erlaubt außerdem, daß eine Komponente in mehreren Objekten enthalten ist (Sharing von Objekten). Wählt man also als Datengranulat bezüglich Zugriffskontrolle das Objekt (was sehr sinnvoll ist), so sind Zugriffsrechte sowohl auf dem Objekt als auch auf der Komponente definiert. (Unterschiedliche Rechte auf einem Objekt und seinen Komponenten gewährt zu haben, ist beispielsweise sinnvoll, wenn einzelne Personen eines Projektteams verschiedene Komponenten eines Programmsystems entwerfen.) Hinzu kommt, daß ein komplexes Objekt nicht nur aus Datenwerten besteht, sondern auch eine innere Struktur hat, die selbst Gegenstand der Zugriffskontrolle sein sollte.

Probleme ergeben sich hauptsächlich aus der Überlappung der Datengranulate komplexer Objekte. Was bedeutet ein für ein Objekt gewährtes Recht, das an einer seiner Komponenten entzogen ist? Ist ein Recht an einem Objekt implizit durch die Rechte an allen seinen Komponenten bestimmt oder wird es explizit definiert? Wenn ein Benutzer eine Komponente in einem seiner Objekte haben will, die einem anderen Benutzer gehört, kann er dann noch Eigentümer seines Objekts sein? Gibt es Rechte, die sich nur auf das Objekt ohne seine Komponenten beziehen? Diese und ähnliche Fragen müssen von einem Konzept für Zugriffskontrolle auf komplexen Objekten beantwortet werden. Im folgenden wird das von der GPI definierte Konzept vorgestellt.

4. Zugriffskontrolle und komplexe Objekte

Im GPI-Datenmodell werden folgende **Datengranulate** bezüglich Zugriffskontrolle unterschieden:
- Objekte,
- n-stellige Beziehungen,
- Attributwerte von Objekten und Beziehungen.

Alle diese Granulate können mit eigenen Zugriffsrechten versehen werden! Bei diesen Datengranulaten ist zu berücksichtigen, daß sowohl Objekte als auch Beziehungen Attributwerte assoziiert haben können, insbesondere auch die Beziehungen zwischen Objekten und ihren Komponenten. Datengranulate sind hierarchisch ineinander geschachtelt, wie das folgende Bild zeigt:

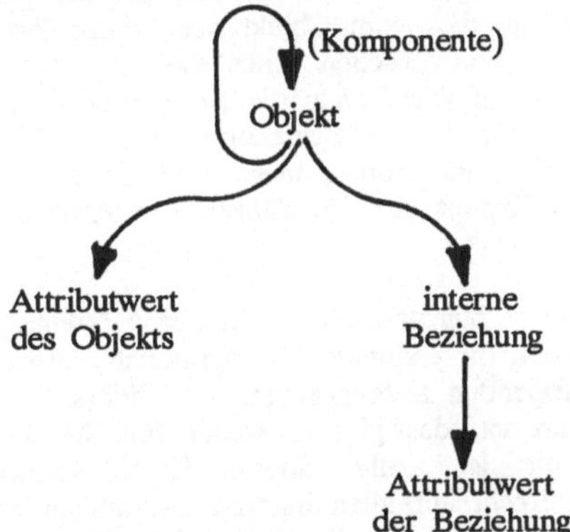

Ein Pfeil weist von einem "äußeren" auf ein "inneres" Granulat.

Eine OMS-Datenbank kennt Benutzer, Benutzergruppen und Programmgruppen, (die wir alle zusammen kurz als **Gruppen** bezeichnen,) die Rechte an Granulaten erhalten können. Ausgeführt werden OMS-Operatoren von Prozessen, die eine oder mehrere Gruppen "angenommen" haben. Für eine der angenommenen Gruppen müssen die für die Operation benötigten Rechte gewährt sein, damit die Ausführung erlaubt wird.

GPI-OMS unterscheidet 8 verschiedene **Zugriffsmodi**, die klassifiziert werden können nach solchen, die sich auf Datenwerte und solchen, die sich auf die Struktur beziehen. Hinzu kommt der Kontrollmodus für die Rechteänderung. Welche Rechte gibt es, auf welchen Granulaten sind sie anwendbar und zu welchen Operationen werden sie benötigt? Die folgende Tabelle gibt darüber Auskunft:

Zugriffsmodus	Attributwert	Beziehung	Objekt
		Granulat	
Navigate	-	Navigieren	
Component	-	-	Einfügen einer Komponente
Relationship	-	-	Anhängen einer Beziehung, Verwenden als Komponente
Read	Lesen		Kopieren
Write	Ändern	Löschen	Löschen
Append	Erweitern		
Exploit	Ausführen		
Control	Recht ändern	Recht ändern	Recht ändern

Manche Zugriffsmodi sind auf bestimmten Granulaten nicht anwendbar (z.B. Component auf Attributwerten; gekennzeichnet durch "-"). Ist aber ein Recht auf ein Granulat anwendbar, ist es auch auf alle äußeren Granulate anwendbar. Ist ein Recht auf einem Granulat gewährt, für das keine Operationen in der Tabelle angegeben sind, so ist dies nur das Recht auf allen inneren Granulaten. Hinzu kommt, daß die Rechte sich teilweise implizieren.

Um zu einem Objekt über Beziehungen zu navigieren, wird an allen betroffenen Beziehungen das Navigate-Recht benötigt. Über den Component-Modus wird kontrolliert, ob eine neue Komponente zu einem Objekt hinzugefügt werden darf. Das Relationship-Recht an einem Objekt benötigt eine Gruppe, die eine Beziehung an ein Objekt anhängen oder das Objekt als Komponente in einem (komplexeren) Objekt verwenden will. Es ist wichtig, dies vom Objekt aus kontrollieren zu können, da referenzielle Integrität gewährleistet werden soll. Das Löschen eines Objekts, das in einer Beziehung zu einem anderen Objekt steht, ist nämlich nicht möglich, ohne die Beziehung auch zu entfernen. (Die Tatsache, Komponente eines Objekts zu sein, ist auch eine Beziehung zwischen Objekten.) Das Read-Recht wird zum Lesen und Kopieren benötigt, Write zum Ändern und Löschen, Append zum Erweitern von Attributwerten (z.B. "longfield") und Exploit zum Ausführen von Attributwerten (z.B. ein Programm in einem "longfield").

GPI-OMS garantiert, daß alle Zugriffsrechte immer **"widerspruchsfrei"** vergeben sind. Widerspruchsfreiheit ist immer gegeben für disjunkte Datengranulate. Jedes Recht kann beliebig gewährt sein oder nicht. Anders bei überlappenden Datengranulaten. Widersprüchlich sind Zugriffsrechte, wenn für ein Granulat ein Recht gewährt ist, das gleiche Recht für die gleiche Gruppe auf irgendeinem inneren Granulat aber nicht gewährt ist. Alle anderen Kombinationen sind widerspruchsfrei, also insbesondere die Situation, daß ein Recht auf allen inneren Granulaten gewährt ist, nicht aber auf dem äußeren Granulat. Bei allen Änderungen an Rechten wird diese Widerspruchsfreiheit garantiert. Homogene Zugriffsrechte auf komplexen Objekten sind sichergestellt. Auf Teilen eines komplexen Objekts können mehr Rechte gewährt werden, als auf dem gesamten Objekt. Ein nicht gewährtes Read-Recht (z.B.) an einem Objekt besagt nicht, daß *kein* Teil des Objekts gelesen werden kann. Ein gewährtes Read-Recht dagegen besagt, daß *alle* Teile gelesen werden können. Was würde es auch bedeuten, wenn eine Gruppe auf einem komplexen Objekt (z.B.) das Read-Recht hat, nicht jedoch auf irgendeiner Komponente davon?

Der **Kontrollmodus** ("Eigentümer") ist notwendig, um die Rechte-Funktion zu ändern. Sonderregelungen gibt es für das Ändern von Werten des Kontrollmodus. Ist eine Gruppe Eigentümer eines Granulats, so darf sie auch andere Gruppen zu Eigentümern machen. Sie darf sich den Kontrollmodus entziehen, nicht aber einer anderen Gruppe. Dies darf sie für andere Gruppen nur für innere Granulate. Man beachte, daß dies aufgrund der Widerspruchsfreiheit nur möglich ist, falls diese anderen Gruppen nicht Eigentümer des äußeren Granulats sind. Auf jedem innersten Granulat muß es immer einen Eigentümer geben. Für alle anderen Granulate ist es möglich, daß es keinen Eigentümer gibt. Damit Änderungen an Zugriffsrechten dann überhaupt noch möglich sind, ist es in einer solchen Situation einem Eigentümer aller inneren Granulate erlaubt, sich selbst zum Eigentümer des äußeren Granulats zu machen.

Es gibt in GPI-OMS **Operatoren,** um Zugriffsrechte zu ändern, und um sie für Gruppen und Prozesse abzufragen. Konzeptionell wird ein Wert eines Zugriffsmodus für genau ein Granulat geändert. Der Operator zum Ändern der Werte hat aber einen Parameter, um zu steuern, ob (1) der Wert nur auf dem Granulat geändert wird, (2) auf dem Granulat und allen inneren Granulaten, (3) auf dem Granulat und allen äußeren Granulaten oder (4) auf allen Granulaten zusammen. Zu beachten ist, daß bei allen Änderungen auf dem entsprechenden Granulat natürlich der Kontrollmodus erforderlich ist. Zugriffsrechte werden von äußeren oder inneren Granulaten nicht implizit bei Änderungen an einem Granulat "aktualisiert".

5. Schlußbemerkungen

Ein komplexes Objekt eines Benutzers A soll eine Komponente enthalten, die einem Benutzer B gehört und deren alleiniger Eigentümer und Schreibberechtigter B bleiben will. Da die Komponente inneres Granulat des komplexen Objekts ist und A auf ihr weder das Kontroll- noch das Schreibrecht hat, kann A auf seinem komplexen Objekt insgesamt diese Rechte auch nicht erwerben. Er muß mit einer Vielzahl von gewährten Rechten auf anderen inneren Granulaten arbeiten. Für solche Situationen wäre es wünschenswert, zwischen "stärker" und "schwächer gebundenen komplexen Objekten" unterscheiden zu können. Komponenten, die in einem komplexen Objekt *nur benutzt* werden, sind dann "schwächere Komponenten", für die es auch weniger (!) Rechte geben kann.

Das Datenbankschema wird in GPI-OMS in einer Metadatenbank abgelegt. Diese Metadatenbank unterliegt ebenfalls der Zugriffskontrolle. Die Zugriffsmodi sind für die Metadatenbank mit einer angepaßten Bedeutung definiert, da Operatoren auf der Metadatenbank ebenfalls besondere Auswirkungen haben.

[PCTE+ 88] kennt neben einem gewährten und nicht gewährten Recht für jeden Zugriffsmodus einen dritten Wert, nämlich das explizit entzogene Recht (3-wertige Rechtelogik). Damit soll gezielt einzelnen Benutzern ein Recht entzogen werden und verhindert werden, daß sie den Zugriff dennoch erhalten, weil ihr Prozeß weitere Gruppen angenommen hat. Diese 3-wertige Rechtelogik ist nicht ohne weiteres auf komplexe Objekte übertragbar.

Literatur:
[CAIS 86]: U.S. DoD: Military Standard Common Ada Programming Support Environment (APSE) Interface Set (CAIS), DOD-STD-1838, October 9, 1986.
[GPI 88]: Deutsche PCTE-Initiative (GPI): Requirements, Specifications, Rationale. Nixdorf, München, 1988.
[PCTE 88]: PCTE Interface Control Group: PCTE - A Basis for a Portable Common Tool Environment, Functional Specifications, Version 1.5, 1988.
[PCTE+ 88]: Inter-European Procurement Group (IEPG) TA-13: PCTE+ Functional Specifications, C Binding, Issue 3, 1988.

Die Deutsche PCTE-Initiative wird vom Bundesministerium für Forschung und Technologie gefördert. Folgende Firmen und Institute arbeiten zusammen in der GPI:

FZI Forschungszentrum Informatik (Karlsruhe), GEI Gesellschaft für Elektronische Informationsverarbeitung mbH (Aachen), IABG Industrieanlagen-Betriebsgesellschaft GmbH (Ottobrunn), IITB Fraunhofer Institut für Informations- und Datenverarbeitung (Karlsruhe), mbp Software & Systems GmbH (Dortmund), Nixdorf Computer AG (München), PSI Gesellschaft für Prozeßsteuerungs- und Informationssysteme mbH (Berlin), Siemens AG (München), Softlab GmbH (München), Universität Dortmund, FB Informatik, Institut für Informatik X (Dortmund), VDI/VDE Technologiezentrum Informationstechnik GmbH (Berlin).

(*) UNIX ist ein eingetragenes Warenzeichen der Bell Laboratories.

LILOG–DB:
Database Support for Knowledge–Based Systems *

Th. Ludwig, B. Walter, M. Ley, A. Maier, E. Gehlen

Aachen University of Technology (RWTH)
Lehrstuhl für Informatik III
Ahornstraße 55
D–5100 Aachen

LILOG is an interdisciplinary project for developing an experimental system performing the acquisition of knowledge by analyzing documents written in a natural language (German). Part of the experimental system is LILOG–DB, a backend database system, that supports a variety of knowledge structures as well as inferential processing. An overview of the architecture of LILOG–DB is given, focussing on the Feature Term based data model and the corresponding Feature Term Algebra (FTA). It is demonstrated how queries stated in a language based on first–order feature–logic are translated to expressions of the FTA. Finally, it is shown how LILOG–DB supports the inferential processing in the other parts of the LILOG experimental system by sophisticated rule management.

1 Introduction

LILOG is an interdisciplinary project for developing an experimental system for knowledge acquisition by document analysis. Since the documents in question are written in a natural language (in German), a large amount of linguistic and applicational knowledge is needed to perform the analysis task. The building of the experimental system requires the integration of techniques from the areas of computational linguistics (feature logic, unification grammar), artificial intelligence (knowledge representation, automated deduction), and database management (efficient and reliable storage of large amounts of persistent data) as well as the development of some new mechanisms.

Letting linguistic problems aside, an ideal system would consist of

- a knowledge representation method based on classical first order logic (e.g. in the sense of the A–Box mechanism of KRYPTON /BrL87/ or other KL–ONE followers) enhanced by several features from non–classical logics (non–monotonic logic, modal logic, ...) and by powerful conceptual structuring concepts (e.g. in the sense of the T–Box mechanism of KRYPTON), suitable for representing linguistic as well as applicational knowledge,
- a powerful inference engine supporting standard techniques like forward and backward reasoning as well as is–a hierarchies and the non–classical features of the representation method,
- a fully integrated database system supporting inferential processing on a large body of persistent knowledge, preferably in a multi–user environment.

However, it is not yet possible to directly implement such a system. Considering the current state of the art, there do not exist representation methods or inference engines of comparable power, nor are there any database systems, suitable for a direct support of knowledge representation and inference engines. Thus, an objective of the LILOG project is to perform some steps from the current state of the art towards such an ideal system. As a consequence, the experimental system will not provide a single omnipotent representation and inference method, but a variety of methods each one more suitable for some tasks and less suitable for some other tasks. Currently, mainly two representation methods are provided, STUF /BPU88/ for representing linguistic knowledge and L₁₁₀₀ /BDP88/ for representing applicational knowledge. Both are moving targets and hence are investigated in different flavors. In the same way, the inference engine is currently a tool box usable for modelling different kinds of inferencing.

In the following an overview of the architecture of LILOG–DB will be given. LILOG–DB is a backend database system, able to store a variety of knowledge structures directly (e.g. STUF, L₁₁₀₀ and Prolog–Terms) and to perform some standard deductions on behalf of the inference engine. We will first give an informal overview of the various subsystems of LILOG–DB and then discuss some of the aspects in more detail.

---

* This research was supported by IBM Deutschland GmbH as part of the LILOG project.

LILOG–DB has to fulfill several requirements that are quite different from existent database systems:

- In traditional database systems files/relations usually consist of sets of identically structured data elements. In AI applications, knowledge is generally less well structured, such that the LILOG–DB equivalent to relations consists of sets of data elements which are structured just similarly.
- Some existing database systems provide rudimentary forms of rules (sometimes called view definitions) for deriving new facts from existing ones. LILOG–DB must be able to manage large amounts of full first oder rules.
- The architecture of most existent DBS is tuned for the processing of rather short transactions (of the 'debit/credit' type). LILOG–DB must handle with rather longish transactions. Assume for instance the analysis of a single page document.Then several hundreds of interactions with the backend DBS are necessary just to check the meaning of the words, to analyze the syntax, to construct the semantical contents in the context of the stored application knowledge, and to update the knowledge base. This also differs considerably from CAD–DBS since the dynamic nature of knowledge processing does not allow the usage of checkout/checkin mechanisms.
- The intended users of LILOG–DB are inference engines. So, inferential processing is the primary usage pattern to be supported.

LILOG–DB uses the so–called **Feature Term Data Model (FTDM)**. Feature Terms are built from integers and symbols by successive aggregations. Admissible constructors are *functor*, *list*, *set*, and *tuple* with the latter being a collection of feature–name/feature–value pairs. A database consists of a collection of sets (**Feature Term Sets, FT–Sets**) and each set consists of a collection of similarly structured feature terms.

The **Feature Term Algebra (FTA)** defines the possible retrieval operations on a database of the Feature Term Data Model. FTA is comparable to other attempts to extend or modify Relational Algebra to cope with complex objects, set valued attributes, etc., but extends these proposals to an open–world–assumption for the processing of incomplete knowledge. In order to define an algebra as an intermediate language for the compilation of Feature Logic database queries (see below), FTA has been enhanced by a closure operator for covering recursive queries as well, thus yielding an **Extended Feature Term Algebra (EFTA)**.

The **Feature Logic Language (FLL)** is a first–order predicate–logic language for the deductive retrieval of sets of feature terms. FLL uses a variant of the FTDM, which additionally allows for variables, order–sorted Feature Terms, and feature inheritance.

Since FLL is located at a higher level of abstraction than EFTA, and since nothing like rules, sorts, and variables is supported by EFTA, rules and sorts are mapped to separately handled 'Rule Systems' and 'Sort Lattices', whereas variables are mapped to null values of EFTA.

The architecture of LILOG–DB (sketched in Fig. 1) has been designed around these basic concepts (FLL, EFTA, Rule Systems, and Sort Lattices).

The **Fact Manager (FM)** is an enhanced relational database management system with a one–element–at–a–time interface. The FM implements unary operations on feature terms as well as all operations concerned with the definition of FT–Sets. Because of the heterogeneous structure of feature terms belonging to the same FT–Set, less schema information can be stored in a common catalog and more supplemental information is needed in the individual records. The efficient retrieval of records representing feature terms also requires more sophisticated access paths to handle heterogeneous record structures as well as complex search criteria.

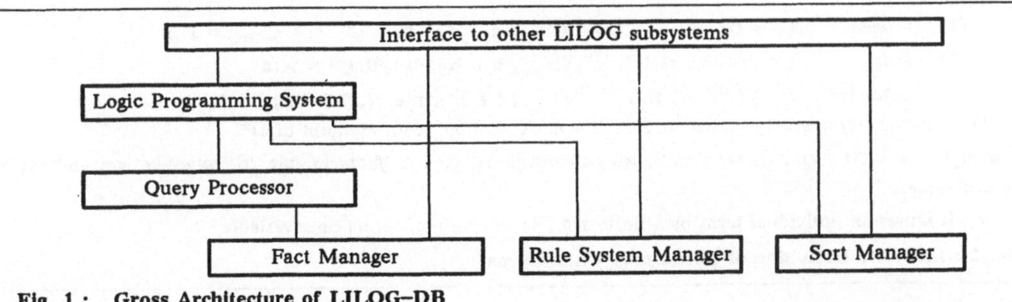

Fig. 1 : Gross Architecture of LILOG–DB

The **Logic Programming System (LPS)** is an experimental front end consisting of an enhanced Prolog-interpreter and FLL. Both support the same data model.

The **Query Processor (QP)** executes queries generated by the LPS. Unary operations on feature terms are forwarded to the FM, binary operations like joins are performed by the QP.

The **Rule System Manager (RSM)** stores rules as **rule goal graphs (RGG)**. In an RGG the rules are linked together in a way as they will probably be used by the inference engine. Thus, the RSM is able to perform a prefetching of rules by transferring RGG (or parts of RGG) into its local buffer instead of transferring just single rules.

The **Sort Manager (SM)** is responsible for storing, retrieving and manipulating the is-a relations defined over the knowledge base. The is-a relations of a program form a sort lattice that is usually stored and retrieved as a whole and kept in a special buffer.

All interactions between LILOG-DB and the inference engine are channelled through the **Interface Module**. It is possible to directly address lower level services of the FM, and the SM, as well as to request the standard inferences which can be performed by the LPS (currently either Prolog-style or set-oriented).

The paper is organized as follows. At first the LPS and the QP will be discussed, which also includes the definition of our data model and of the corresponding feature term algebra. It follows a short discussion of the lower level modules, especially the RSM and the FM.

2 The Logic Programming System

2.1 The Logic Data Model

Terms

The terms of our data model basically are the terms of an extended (first order) predicate-calculus. That means that we use atomic terms like **integers** (i.e. *5*) and **symbols** (i.e. *daisy*), further **variables, functors** (i.e. $f(a,X)$) and **lists** (i.e. [1,2,3]). One can see that these terms are denoted in Prolog-style.

Since for the sake of efficiency we want to process set-oriented instead of tuple-oriented queries in our database, our model includes FT-Sets like $\{1, 2, 3\}$. In Prolog-style, we could write a set-oriented query *?-findall(condition(X),Y)*. meaning that the variable Y should be instantiated to the set of all X satisfying the predicate *condition(X)*. The sets of our implementation are sets in a mathematical sense, they define no order of their elements and do not contain duplicates.

Definition *(FLL-Terms)* :

Let Σ be a non-empty alphabet. We define the universe $\mathfrak{U}_{fll}$ of *FLL*-terms as follows.

An *individual term* is an atomic term or a complex term.

A term t is *atomic* iff

    (1) t is an integer ($t \in \mathfrak{Z}$),

    (2) t is a symbol ($t \in \Sigma^+$).

A *complex term* t is either

    (1) a *tuple* $t = < \alpha_1 : \tau_1 , .., \alpha_n : \tau_n >$, $n \in N_0$, $\alpha_i \in \Sigma^+$, $\tau_i \in \mathfrak{U}_{fll}$, i = 1..n

    (2) a *list* $t = [\tau_1 , .., \tau_n]$, $n \in N_0$, $\tau_i \in \mathfrak{U}_{fll}$, i = 1..n

    (3) a *functor* $t = f (\tau_1 , .., \tau_n)$, $f \in \Sigma^+$, $n \in N$, $\tau_i \in \mathfrak{U}_{fll}$, i = 1..n

Let Ω be another non-empty alphabet, $\Sigma \cap \Omega = \emptyset$. A *variable* is an element of Ω^+

In a tuple $t = < \alpha_1 : \tau_1 , .., \alpha_n : \tau_n >$, we call the pairs $\alpha_i : \tau_i$ *features*, the α_i *feature-names* and the τ_i *feature-values*.

A *term* is either an individual term or a finite *set* $\{ \tau_1 , .., \tau_n \}$ of terms or a variable. □

Fig. 2 : Inductive Definition of (Unsorted) FLL-Terms

$$SORTDEFINITION \quad ::= \quad SORTNAME$$
$$| \quad integer$$
$$| \quad symbol$$
$$| \quad term$$
$$| \quad set\ of\ SORTDEFINITION$$
$$| \quad list\ of\ SORTDEFINITION$$
$$| \quad <\ (NAME\ :\ SORTDEFINITION\ )^+\ >$$
$$| \quad functor\ NAME\ of\ (\ SORTDEFINITION\ ^+\ )$$

Fig. 3 : Sort–Definition in FLL

In analogy to sets, **feature–tuples** (tuples for short) do not define any order of their elements either. We will call the elements of a tuple **features**, suggesting a strong connection to feature logic /KaR86, Smo88, AitK86a, AitK86b, Usz88/. Features contain a feature–name and a feature–value, and these are separated by a colon. *<name:albert,profession:mayor>* is an example for a tuple.

Sorts

There are two reasons for the introduction of order–sorting into our system. At first, a sort–concept imposes structure on knowledge bases by saying what kinds of terms are treated by a rule and how they are related to other classes of terms. An example is the program of Fig. 4 . The *singing_bird* rule only fires when X is a *bird*, so it is satisfied only by *nightingale* and *mocking_bird*. We see that a complete term in our model (an **FLL–term**) has the form

    unsorted_term.sort

A declaration of the sort *SORTNAME* is of the form

    sort SORTNAME [= *SORTDEFINITION*] [*with CONSTRAINTS*] [*isa SORTNAMELIST*].

For the syntax of *SORTDEFINITION* see Fig. 3. *CONSTRAINTS* impose semantic restrictions on the terms of the sort, e.g. in the sample sort–declaration

    sort teeny = < name: atom, age: integer > with age < 20 and age > 10 isa person.

SORTNAMELIST allows the enumeration of the supersorts of the specified sort.

We require our sorts to form an is–a–lattice (see Fig. 4c) with the most general sort TERM and the overspecified sort NIL. Terms with no sort–specification are assumed to be of the sort TERM, which in the example is the least upper bound of the sorts *person* and *bird*.

The second reason for the introduction of the sort–concept is the capacity of speeding up reasoning about the structured knowledge by exploiting it in unification and sort–inference. A slightly more complex unification procedure can save many logical inference steps /AitK86b, HuV87, Mon87/.

2.2 Tuples, Inheritance and Unification in the FLL Data Model

In the is–a–sort–lattice mentioned above inheritance of features is defined for sort–declarations based on tuples. A "tuple–sort" inherits all attributes from all of its supersorts (if this is a tuple–sort too !). I.e. for the sort–declarations

    sort person = < name: atom, age: integer >.
    sort worker = < salary: integer > isa person.

---

a) *singing_bird (X.bird) :– troubadour(X).*

    troubadour(jerry_lee_lewis).

    troubadour(erich_gehlen).

    troubadour(mocking_bird).

    troubadour(nightingale).

b) *sort person = { jerry_lee_lewis, erich_gehlen }*

    sort bird = { mocking_bird, nightingale}

c)

$$person \diagup^{TERM}\diagdown bird$$
$$\diagdown_{NIL}\diagup$$

Fig. 4 :   Sample Program (a), Sort–Declarations (b) and Sort–Lattice (c)

sort husband = < partner: husband > isa person.
sort married_worker = person isa husband, worker.

the sort *worker* inherits the features *name* and *age* from its supersorts *person*.

Unification

While the standard unification algorithm of Robinson treats the terms of first–order predicate–logic, we have to define unification for sets and tuples too, in the presence of a sort–lattice. Sets can only be unified iff they are ground and equal, e.g. set–unification fails in the presence of free variables (for instance: what should be the meaning of $\{W,X,Y,3\} = \{1,2,Z\}$?).

Unification of tuples is defined as elementwise unification of the features whose names are equal, so that for example the most general unifier of   *< name: alfred, partner: sheila>* and *< name: X, salary: 20000 >* is *< name: alfred , partner: sheila, salary: 20000>* and unification produces the variable–binding *X = alfred*.

The example shows that we treat tuples as open structures in the sense that we consider missing features as not specified instead of seeing them as not present.

As far as the sort–lattice is concerned, our kind of unification is **glb–unification** /AitK86a, AitK86b/. Therefore the sort of the most general unifier (mgu) of two typed terms is the greatest lower bound (glb) of their sorts in the is–a–lattice. With the sort–declarations of the example above the most general unifier of *< name: alfred, salary: 20000 >.worker*   and   *< name: X, partner: sheila >.husband*   is *< name: alfred , salary: 20000, partner: sheila>.married_worker* because in the sort–lattice

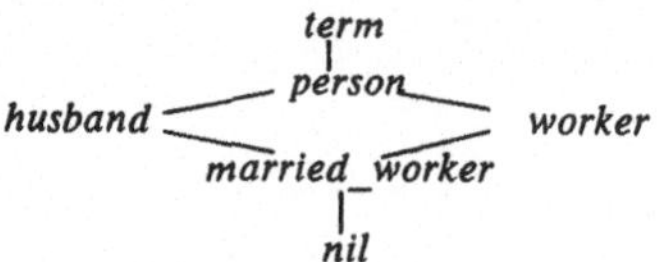

married_worker is the glb of the sorts *worker* and *husband*.

2.3 Inferences on FLL–Programs

FLL–Programs

A term *t* of the FLL data model (see Fig. 2) is a **positive literal**. If it is negated (*not t*), we call it a **negative literal**. A **clause** $g :- sg_1, .. , sg_n$ is a definite clause in the FLL data model. That means that it consists of a positive literal *g* on the left–hand side and a possibly empty conjunction of (positive or negative) literals $sg_1, .. , sg_n$ on the right–hand side. Iff there is no literal on the right, we will call the clause a **fact**. An example of an FLL–clause is

> *young_and_poor (X.worker) :-   X = <age: AGE, salary: SALARY> , AGE < 30 , SALARY < 20000.*

An **FLL–program** is a collection of clauses.

Note that until now we have assigned no meaning to FLL–programs; we can interpret them in Prolog–style as well as by assigning them a bottom–up semantics etc.

Various Inference Engines

Based on our notion of glb–unification, various inference engines can run. We can do forward–chaining inferences on our knowledge base to derive and store further knowledge as well as database style bottom–up–evaluation of set–oriented queries against a large knowledge base.

We feel the need to provide a group of adequate inference tools instead of one inflexible superpower–inference–mechanism. We will at first implement a Prolog–style resolution–machine for our model with a "findall"–interface to the database query processor based on a full Prolog–implementation called TLPROLOG that we wrote for experimental work, and a bottom–up–evaluator for database queries which will be discussed later. A forward–chaining capability will be provided too.

At this point of the presentation it should be stressed again that our system is an experimental one with a design that is open for extensions. It is likely that we will implement and study variants of our unification– and

way(X,X).
way(X,Y) :– street(X,Y).
way(X,Y) :– street(X,Z), way(Z,Y).

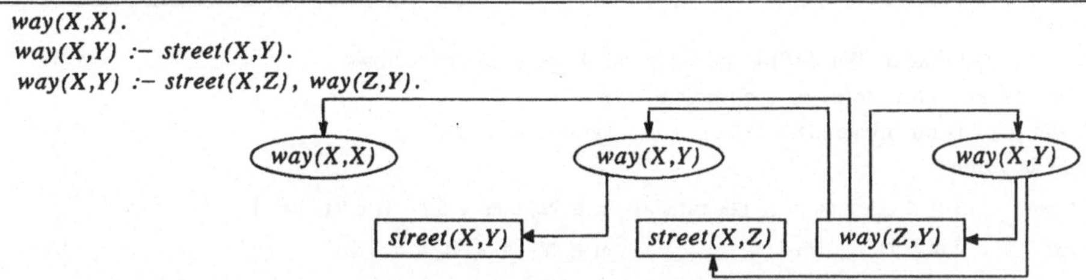

Fig. 5: A Sample Program and its Representation as a Rule Goal Graph

inference–procedures. We cannot yet say what set of unification variants, inference engines and sub–data–models will be the result of our studies, but we claim that our initial design is an adequate starting point.

2.4 Representation of Logic Programs

While our internal representation of feature terms with sorts is rather conventional, our method of representing intensional rules requires some remarks. It is a representative of a wide variety of methods of modeling rule systems as graphs /ChS79, Kow75, McKS81, Ull85/.

For a Horn–clause–program of our data model, the RGG contains a rule node for each rule of the program and a goal node for each subgoal of a rule. Rule nodes contain the head of their rule (a term!), goal nodes contain the goal itself (a term too!). For every subgoal of a rule, there's an edge from the corresponding rule node to the corresponding goal node. A goal node has a link to a rule node iff the head of the rule can be unified with the goal. An example is given in Fig. 5.

We chose RGGs as a representation structure because they allow the application of various program–manipulation (optimization !) techniques, are very suitable intermediate structures for the compilation of logic programs into operator–DAGs of our Feature Term Algebra /Lud88a/ and are a very efficient form of representing logic programs. This efficiency results from the fact that the possibly matching rule heads for a goal in resolution need not be searched at runtime (e.g. in a rule table) but have been explicitly linked to the goal at construction time.

2.5 Related Work

Concluding our presentation of the LPS, we make some remarks on its relation to other work in the field of knowledge based systems. It has become clear that when eliminating sets and feature tuples of the data model and applying SLDNF–resolution to definite clauses of this restricted model, one obtains Prolog.

It is obvious too that STUF–terms /BPU88/ can be transformed to our feature tuples in a straightforward manner.

The integration of functors and tuples of our model yields the functor tuples (i.e. functors with attributes as arguments) of languages like LOGIN /AitK86b/. Where our data model forces you to write

    priest(<name: JR, religion: money>)   */* a functor with a tuple as an argument */*

you can write in LOGIN

    priest(name: JR, religion: money)   */* a functor tuple with two arguments */.*

3 The Query Processor

From the LPS the query processor receives a set–oriented ("findall–") logical query. This is compiled and processed by the query processor, which returns the set of answers for the query to the LPS.

3.1 FTA

FTA /Lud88a/ is the language of the query processor. It has the same data model as our logic language presented above, except that variables are replaced by universally quantified null values and some other kinds

---

Definition *(Terms)* :

Let Σ be a non–empty alphabet. We define the universe $\mathcal{U}$ of terms as follows.

An *individual term* is an atomic term or a complex term.

A term t is *atomic* iff t is an integer ($t \in \mathcal{Z}$) or t is a symbol ($t \in \Sigma^+$).

A *complex term* t is either

    (1)   a *tuple* $t = \langle \alpha_1 : \tau_1 , .., \alpha_n : \tau_n \rangle$, $n \in \mathbf{N_0}$, $\alpha_i \in \Sigma^+$, $\tau_i \in \mathcal{U}$, $i = 1..n$

    (2)   a *list* $t = [\ \tau_1 , .., \tau_n\ ]$, $n \in \mathbf{N_0}$, $\tau_i \in \mathcal{U}$, $i = 1..n$

    (3)   a *functor* $t = f\ (\ \tau_1 , .., \tau_n\ )$, $f \in \Sigma^+$, $n \in \mathbf{N}$, $\tau_i \in \mathcal{U}$, $i = 1..n$

A *null value* is an element of the set $\mathcal{N} = \{\ O_e,\ O_f,\ O_{none},\ O_{nfs}\ \}$, $\mathbf{N} \cap \Sigma^+ = \emptyset$.

In a tuple $t = \langle \alpha_1 : \tau_1 , .., \alpha_n : \tau_n \rangle$, we call the pairs $\alpha_i : \tau_i$ *features*, the α_i *feature–names* and the τ_i *feature–values*.

A *term* is either an individual term or a finite *set* $\{\ \tau_1 , .., \tau_n\ \}$ of terms or a null value. $\square$

Fig. 6 : Feature Term Data Model

---

of null values are introduced. Before defining it informally, we want to characterize it in comparison to the well–known Relational Algebra (RA).

1)   The first basic difference of our Feature Term Algebra to RA is that it supposes its data containers to be potentially heterogeneous sets of terms instead of (first normal form) fixed–arity relations.

2)   FTA assumes incomplete and variant schemas of database "relations" instead of the fully specified ones of Relational Algebra. *Incomplete* here means that schema restrictions on terms do not necessarily describe the whole structure of the term, *variant* stands for the permission of disjunctive descriptions.

3)   It supports the open–world–assumption of feature logic by its introduction of exists–, forall–, no–feature–specified– and feature–not–present null values (a discussion of null values, schemas and updates is beyond the scope of this paper) and by allowing questions whether a feature is present/specified in the schema or not.

The three differences mentioned above refer to the fact that in the presence of "complex objects", feature logic terms and incomplete information in knowledge bases we cannot assume as much global structural knowledge in the database(–schema) as in Relational Algebra. Thus the efficient evaluation of conditions at query processing time becomes even more important in FTA than in RA. We evaluate very complex conditions with the γ–operator (which is a generalization of selection and projection in RA, see below).

Besides the **conditions** (Fig. 8), applications of **paths** (Fig. 7) and **constructors** (Fig. 8) are the other basic operations of FTA. Path–applications extend the possibility of accessing an attribute of a relation in RA to the access of arbitrary parts of a complex object in FTA. E.g. the path *1.2.*$\square$ applied to the term $f(a(1,2),b)$ evaluates to the term *2*.

Definition *(Paths and their Application):*

Let $\square \notin (\mathcal{Z} \cup \Sigma^+ \cup \mathcal{N})$ be the *empty–path symbol*.

ρ is a *path* $:\Leftrightarrow \rho \in \mathcal{P} :\Leftrightarrow$ (1) $\rho = \square$ or (2) $\rho = \nu . \rho_1$, $\nu \in (\mathbf{N_0} \cup \Sigma^+)$, $\rho_1 \in \mathcal{P}$

The *length* $\| \rho \|$ of ρ is defined as usual by

$$(1) \quad \| \square \| = 0 \qquad (2) \quad \| \nu . \rho \| = \| \rho \| + 1 \ , \text{if} \ \nu \in (\mathbf{N_0} \cup \Sigma^+)$$

Let ρ be a path, τ a term. Then the *path–application* τ/ρ of ρ on τ is defined as follows:

$$
\tau/\rho \ = \
\begin{cases}
\tau & \text{if} \quad \rho = \square \\[4pt]
\tau_i /\rho_1 & \text{if} \quad \rho = i . \rho_1 \ , i \in \mathbf{N} \quad \text{and} \quad \tau = [\ \tau_1 , ... \tau_i , ..] \\[4pt]
\tau_i /\rho_1 & \text{if} \quad \rho = \alpha_i . \rho_1 \ , i \in \mathbf{N} \ , \alpha_i \in \Sigma^+, \ \text{and} \quad \tau = \langle \alpha_1 : \tau_1 , ..., \alpha_i : \tau_i , .. \rangle \\[4pt]
f & \text{if} \quad \rho = 0.\square \quad \text{and} \quad \tau = f\ (\tau_1 , ... \tau_i , ..) \\[4pt]
\tau_i /\rho_1 & \text{if} \quad \rho = i . \rho_1 \ , i \in \mathbf{N} \quad \text{and} \quad \tau = f\ (\tau_1 , ... \tau_i , ..) \quad \square
\end{cases}
$$

Fig. 7 : Paths in FTA

Definition *(Constructors and their Application):*

Let $\mathcal{IC} = \mathcal{P} \cup \mathcal{U}$ be the set of *simple constructors*. Let further $\alpha_1, \alpha_2.. \in \Sigma^+$ be feature–names, $pc_1, pc_2.. \in \mathcal{IC}$ paths or terms, $f \in \Sigma^+$ a symbol. Then exactly all expressions of the forms

(1) pc_1 *arith–op* pc_2 , *arith–op* $\in \{ +, -, *, / \}$ (2) $f (pc_1, .., pc_n)$, $n \in \mathbf{N}$

(3) $< \alpha_1 : pc_1, .., \alpha_n : pc_n >$, $n \in \mathbf{N_0}$ (4) $[pc_1, .., pc_n]$, $n \in \mathbf{N_0}$

(5) $\{ pc_1, .., pc_n \}$, $n \in \mathbf{N_0}$

are called *constructors* The set of constructors is denoted by $\mathbf{CO}$. With $\quad pc'(\tau) = \begin{cases} pc, & \text{if } pc \in \mathcal{U} \\ \tau / pc, & \text{if } pc \in \mathcal{P} \end{cases}$

we define the *constructor–application* as the partial function *cons* with the weakest domain for which the following conditions hold:

(1a) $cons\,(pc_1 + pc_2, \tau) = pc_1'(\tau) + pc_2'(\tau)$ (1b) $cons\,(pc_1 - pc_2, \tau) = pc_1'(\tau) - pc_2'(\tau)$

(1c) $cons\,(pc_1 * pc_2, \tau) = pc_1'(\tau) * pc_2'(\tau)$ (1d) $cons\,(pc_1 / pc_2, \tau) = pc_1'(\tau) / pc_2'(\tau)$

(2) $cons(\, f(pc_1, .., pc_n), \tau\,) = f(\, pc_1'(\tau), .., pc_n'(\tau))$

(3) $cons(\, [pc_1, .., pc_n], \tau\,) = [\, pc_1'(\tau), .., pc_n'(\tau)]$

(4) $cons(< \alpha_1 : pc_1, .., \alpha_n : pc_n >, \tau\,) = <\alpha_1 : pc_1'(\tau), .., \alpha_n : pc_n'(\tau)>$

(5) $cons(\{ pc_1, .., pc_n \}, \tau\,) = \{ pc_1'(\tau), .., pc_n'(\tau)\}$

and all path–applications pc_i' in (1a) – (5) are defined . $\square$

Definition *(Conditions and their Value):*

Let $pc, pc_1, pc_2 \in \mathcal{IC}$ be paths or terms, $f \in \Sigma^+$ a name. We inductively define the set $\mathbf{C}$ of *conditions* as the set of terms having one of the following forms :

(1) pc_1 *op* pc_2 , $op \in \{ =, \neq, >, \geq, \leq, <, \text{in}\}$

(2) *arity*$(pc) = i$, $i \in \mathbf{N_0}$

(3) *type*$(pc) = x$, $x \in \{integer, symbol, list, tuple, functor, set \}$

(4) pc *feature_op* f , *feature_op* $\in \{ has, hasnot \}$

(5) *not* C , $C \in \mathbf{C}$

(6) C_1 *and* C_2 , $C_1, C_2 \in \mathbf{C}$

(7) C_1 *or* C_2 , $C_1, C_2 \in \mathbf{C}$

(8) *true, false*

Let OP= be the equality–relation on terms, OP!= its complement, OP> the union of the lexicographic greater–relation on Σ^+ and the numeric greater–relation on $\mathbf{R}$, OP>= $= ($OP> $\cup$ OP=$)$, OP< the complement of OP>= , OP<= $= ($OP< $\cup$ OP=$)$ and OP*in* the set–element–relation on terms.

The *value* $\omega(c, \tau)$ *of a condition* c applied to a term τ is

(1) $\omega(pc_1$ *op* $pc_2, \tau) = $ TRUE $\Leftrightarrow$ $(\, pc_1'(\tau), pc_2'(\tau)\,) \in $ OP*op*

(2) $\omega(arity(pc) = i, \tau) = $ TRUE $\Leftrightarrow$ $i = \#(\{\, j \mid \tau/j \text{ defined}, \| j \| = 1, j \neq 0.\square\})$

(3) $\omega(type(pc) = x, \tau) = $ TRUE $\Leftrightarrow$ $pc'(\tau)$ is of type x

(41) $\omega(pc$ *has* $f, \tau) = $ TRUE $\Leftrightarrow$ $f \in $ Def$(\lambda\alpha.\ pc'(\tau)/\alpha)$

(42) $\omega(pc$ *hasnot* $f, \tau) = $ TRUE $\Leftrightarrow$ $\omega(pc$ *has* $f, \tau) = $ FALSE

(5) $\omega(not\ C, \tau) = $ TRUE $\Leftrightarrow$ $\omega(C, \tau) = $ FALSE

(6) $\omega(C_1$ *and* $C_2, \tau) = $ TRUE $\Leftrightarrow$ $\omega(C_1, \tau) = $ TRUE and $\omega(C_2, \tau) = $ TRUE

(7) $\omega(C_1$ *or* $C_2, \tau) = $ TRUE $\Leftrightarrow$ $\omega(C_1, \tau) = $ TRUE or $\omega(C_2, \tau) = $ TRUE

(8) $\omega(true, \tau) = $ TRUE , $\omega(false, \tau) = $ FALSE

where all path–applications have to be defined if the value of the condition should be defined and all defined evaluations which are not TRUE are FALSE. $\square$

Definition *(Conditional Constructors and their Application):*

The set Γ of *conditional constructors* is the set of expressions cc satisfying one of the following conditions:

(1) $cc \in \mathbf{CO}$ (cc is a constructor)

(2) $cc = $ *if cond then* cc_1 *else* cc_2, $cond \in \mathbf{C}$, $cc_1, cc_2 \in \Gamma$ (cc is an *if–then–else*-expression)

Let $\tau \in \mathcal{U}$ be a term, $cc \in \Gamma$ a conditional constructor. We define the *application* of the γ–operator by a function *eval* as follows: (1) $eval(cc, \tau) = cons(cc, \tau)$, if $cc \in \mathbf{CO}$

(2) $eval(\,$ *if cond then* cc_1 *else* $cc_2, \tau\,) = \begin{cases} eval(cc_1, \tau) & , \text{if } \omega(cond, \tau) = \text{TRUE} \\ eval(cc_2, \tau) & , \text{else} \end{cases}$ $\square$

Fig. 8 : Constructors, Conditions and Conditional Constructors in FTA

Constructor-applications allow the composition of complex objects from simpler ones. By applying the constructor $f(1.\square)$ to the term 2 we obtain the term $f(2)$.

Operators of FTA

For the sake of brevity, a discussion of the FTA-operators $\setminus$ (set difference), $\cup$ (set union) and X (cross product) will be omitted here. What follows is a discussion of the really "new" (w.r.t. to RA) operators γ and *nest/unnest* (see /ScP81/ for a similar construction) and of enlarging FTA to EFTA by *E*xtending it by a powerful **closure-operator**.

The γ-operator is written (see Fig. 9 for details)

$\qquad \gamma$ *conditional_constructor F*

For instance the evaluation of

$$\gamma \ (\ if \ 1.\square > 5 \ \ then \ f(1.h,2.\square) \ else \ \ f(5,2.\square)) \ \{ \ g(3,4), \ g(4,5), \ g(9,6), \ g(7,2) \ \}$$

produces the result $\ \{ \ f(5,4), f(5,5), f(9,6), f(7,2) \ \}$.

The γ-operator provides the possibility to trigger path- and constructor-applications by complex conditions including negation ("else"-case). If we follow the convention to omit trivial parts of an if-statement in the γ-operator (condition is constant TRUE or else-part is empty), we can write "selections", "projections" and simple constructor-applications informally as

---

Definition *(FTA-Expressions and their Semantics):*

Let $\mathcal{R}$, $\mathcal{R} \cap (\Sigma^+ \cup \mathcal{P} \cup \mathcal{N}) = \emptyset$ be the set of all valid names for *EFTA*-sets. We define the set $\mathcal{F}$ of valid *fta-expressions* as the smallest set for which the following conditions hold:

    (1)   All finite sets of ground terms are in $\mathcal{F}$.

    (2) $\mathcal{R} \subset \mathcal{F}$

    (3)   For $f_1, f_2 \in \mathcal{F}$:

$\qquad\qquad f_1 \ X \ f_2 \ \ \in \mathcal{F} \qquad$ (cross product)

$\qquad\qquad f_1 \cup f_2 \ \ \in \mathcal{F} \qquad$ (union)

$\qquad\qquad f_1 \setminus f_2 \ \ \in \mathcal{F} \qquad$ (difference)

    (4)   Let cc be a conditional constructor. For $f \in \mathcal{F}$

$\qquad\qquad \gamma \ cc \ f \ \in \mathcal{F} \qquad$ (γ-Operator)

    (5)   Let ρ be a path and $f \in \mathcal{F}$.

$\qquad\qquad nest \ \rho \ \ f \in \mathcal{F} \qquad$ (nest- operator)

$\qquad\qquad unnest \ \rho \ \ f \in \mathcal{F} \qquad$ (unnest- operator)

    (6) $f \in \mathcal{F} \ \Rightarrow \ (f) \in \mathcal{F}$

We define the *substitution* for a term τ at path ρ by a term τ_1 by the equivalence

$subst \ (\ \tau, \ \rho, \ \tau_1) = \tau_2 \ :\Leftrightarrow \qquad$ (i) $\forall \ \rho_1$ with $(\neg \exists \ \theta \in \mathcal{P}: \rho = \rho_1.\theta) : \tau_2/\rho_1 = \tau/\rho_1$

$\qquad\qquad\qquad\qquad\qquad\qquad\qquad$ (ii) $\tau_2/\rho = \tau_1 \qquad\qquad$ (iii) Def $(\ \lambda \ \rho. \ \tau_2/\rho \ )$ is minimal.

The semantics of *FTA*-expressions are given by a function $[\![\ ]\!]$ with

(1) $[\![\ M \ ]\!] = M \ $, iff M is a finite set of ground terms.

(2) $[\![\ N \ ]\!] = M \ $, iff N denotes the set M.

(3) $[\![\ f_1 \ X \ f_2 \ ]\!] = \{ \ <\tau_1, \tau_2> \ | \ \tau_1 \in [\![\ f_1 \ ]\!], \ \tau_2 \in [\![\ f_2 \ ]\!] \ \}$

(4) $[\![\ f_1 \cup f_2 \ ]\!] = [\![\ f_1 \ ]\!] \cup [\![\ f_2 \ ]\!]$

(5) $[\![\ f_1 \setminus f_2 \ ]\!] = [\![\ f_1 \ ]\!] \setminus [\![\ f_2 \ ]\!]$

(6) $[\![\ \gamma \ cc \ f \ ]\!] = \{ \ eval \ (cc,\tau) \ | \ \tau \in [\![\ f \ ]\!], \ if \ eval \ (cc,\tau) \ is \ defined \ \}$

(7) $[\![\ nest \ \rho \ f \ ]\!] = \{ \ subst \ (\tau,\rho,M) \ | \ M = \{ \ \tau/\rho \ | \ \exists \mathcal{M}: \tau \in \mathcal{M} \in [\![\ f \ ]\!]\rho \ \} \ \}$

(8) $[\![\ unnest \ \rho \ f \ ]\!] = \{ \ subst \ (\tau,\rho,x) \ | \ \tau \in [\![\ f \ ]\!], \ \tau/\rho \ is \ a \ set \ of \ terms, \ x \in \tau/\rho \ \}$

(9) $[\![\ (f) \ ]\!] = [\![\ f \ ]\!] \qquad \square$

Fig. 9 : FTA-Expressions and their Semantics

(i)   *"select"* c $= \sigma$ c R $= \gamma$ (if c then $\square$) R

(ii)   *"project"* p R $= \pi$ p R $= \gamma$ (if true then p) R $= \gamma$ p R

(iii)   *"construct"* cons R $= \gamma$ (if true then cons) R $= \gamma$ cons R

Nest and unnest are needed for explicit (dis–)aggregation of sets. The unnest–operator *unnest p F* decomposes an element of *F* with a set–valued attribute *s* at path *p* into a set of tuples with the elements of *s* at position *p*: *unnest* $1.\square$ { $f(\{1,2\})$, f($\{2,3\}$) } = { $f(1)$, $f(2)$, $f(3)$ }.

nest works in the opposite direction: *nest* $1.\square$ { $f(1)$, $f(2)$, $f(3)$ } = { $f(\{1,2,3\})$ } .

As can be seen in the example, nest and unnest are not inverse to each other!

EFTA : Extend FTA by a closure–operator

FTA satisfies our needs as far as the treatment of complex objects and open features is concerned, but we do not yet have enough power to cope with recursive queries. Thus we extend FTA to EFTA by adding a closure–operator ϕ_e I. As will be shown below, this enables us to process an arbitrary (recursive) query in our data model if it can be proved safe by our safety–checker (what is in general undecidable so that we can only capture a subclass of recursive queries).

The closure–operator ϕ_e I is defined by an *n*–ary **tuple** (!) of initialisations I and a tuple of *EFTA–templates e*. An *EFTA–template* is an *incomplete EFTA–expression* where the arguments are replaced by *position–numbers p* (i. e. paths of length 1) ($1 <= p <= n$) as in the following examples:

EFTA–template	Incomplete Efta–exp.	position(s)
unnest 1.$\square$ 1	*unnest 1.$\square$*	*1*
1 X 2	*X*	*1, 2*

The semantics of ϕ_e I is that the closure under *e* is built from I. That (operationally) means that an *intermediate–result–tuple imr* is initialized with I and then for each *i* imr_i /p is constructed from imr_{i-1} by applying *e/p* to imr_i until $imr_i = imr_{i-1}$.

An example: If we consider the evaluation of

$$\text{RES} = \phi < \gamma \text{ if } (1.2.\square = 2.1.\square) \text{ then ancestor}(1.1.\square, 2.2.\square) \ (1 \ X \ 1) > <R>$$

R = { *ancestor(peter,george)* , *ancestor(george,harry)* , *ancestor(george,paul)* , *ancestor(paul,david)* }

we obtain

Definition *(Closure–Operator):*

Let $e_1,..,e_n$ be *EFTA*–operators and $f_1,..,f_n,f_{11},..,f_{1n},f_{21},..,f_{2n}$ *EFTA*–templates. We define the semantics of ϕ_e I by:

     apply (e, f) = apply (<e_1,e_2, ..,e_n>, <$f_1,..,f_n$ >)

         = < eval–template(e_1,f), .., eval–template(e_n,f) >

     eval–template(incomplete–expr pos–num,f) = ⟦ *incomplete–expr (f / pos–num)* ⟧

     $f_1 \cup_t f_2 =$ <$f_{11},..,f_{1n}$> $\cup_t$ <$f_{21},..,f_{2n}$> $=$ <$f_{11} \cup f_{21}$, .., $f_{1n} \cup f_{2n}$>

     $imr_0 = I$

     $imr_{i+1} = apply(e, imr_i) \cup_t imr_i, \ i \geq 0$

     $\phi_e I = \lim\limits_{i->\infty} imr_i$ $\square$

Fig. 10 : The Closure–Operator in EFTA

$$imr_0 = \; < \{ \; ancestor(peter,george), \; ancestor(george,harry), \; ancestor(george,paul), \; ancestor(paul,david) \; \} \; >$$

$$imr_1 = \; < \{ \; ancestor(peter,harry), \; ancestor(peter,paul), \; ancestor(george,david) \; \} \; > \; \; \cup_t \; imr_0$$

$$RES = imr_2 = \; < \{ \; ancestor(peter,david) \; \} \; > \; \; \cup_t \; imr_1$$

EFTA and the Open-World-Assumption

An example might illustrate how EFTA supports the open-world-assumption on tuples. If we got the FT-Set

$$R = \{ \; <name: \; alfred, \; job: \; scientist, \; salary: \; 20000> \; , \;\; <name:peter, \; salary:30000> \; \},$$

the query

$$\gamma \; if \; (job = scientist) \; then \; \Box \quad R \tag{1}$$

will have the answer R since we do not suppose R to contain all information (closed-world-assumption), but suppose it to contain all known information (open-world-assumption). The query should be read as

"Give me all the people who may be scientists !"

instead of

"Give me all the people who are definitely known to be scientists !".

The possibility to state *has*-conditions in the γ-operator allows the CWA-query too:

$$\gamma \; if \; (\Box \; has \; job \;\; and \; job = scientist) \; then \; \Box \quad R \tag{2}$$

While the query (1) assumes the second tuple of R to possibly be an underspecified scientist and lets it pass, the second query checks whether the feature job is really specified in the tuple, and the result is

$$R' = \{ \; <name: \; alfred, \; job: \; scientist, \; salary: \; 20000> \; \}$$

3.2 Query Compilation from Logic to EFTA

The input structure for our query compiler is the RGG of the logic program. The main idea of translating recursive queries is to recognize recursive cliques in the RGG of the rule system and translate them to a bundle of simultaneous transitive-closure-computations written as tuple argument of the ϕ-operator.

In the following we want to sketch our query translation by example. For reasons of simplicity, our example is given in abbreviated and somehow imprecise form. Let's use our *way*-program again: As highlighted in (a) of Fig. 11, it contains a recursive clique that has to be transformed to a ϕ-operator of EFTA. Suppose we got the query *?- way (ac, X).* , our initial RGG for query compilation is built by adding the query as a goal (b).

We eliminate our recursive clique by writing it as a ϕ-operator (c).

Since we can always push a constant into the rule heads of a recursive clique, we do so with *ac* (and push *ac* into the base relation STREET too!) and replace the original goal by a γ-operator realizing a projection (d).

The initialisation of the ϕ-operator can be transformed to a union with a set-constant { *way(ac,ac)* } and an application of the γ-operator to the relation STREET (e).

Finally, we translate the complex rule on the right by using the same γ-operator-application inserted in the step above as an argument to a join (f). Note that the intermediate result in the cyclic part of the Φ-operator is accessed via the position-number *1* .

That completes our translation from the FLL-program above to an EFTA-expression which can now be further optimized.

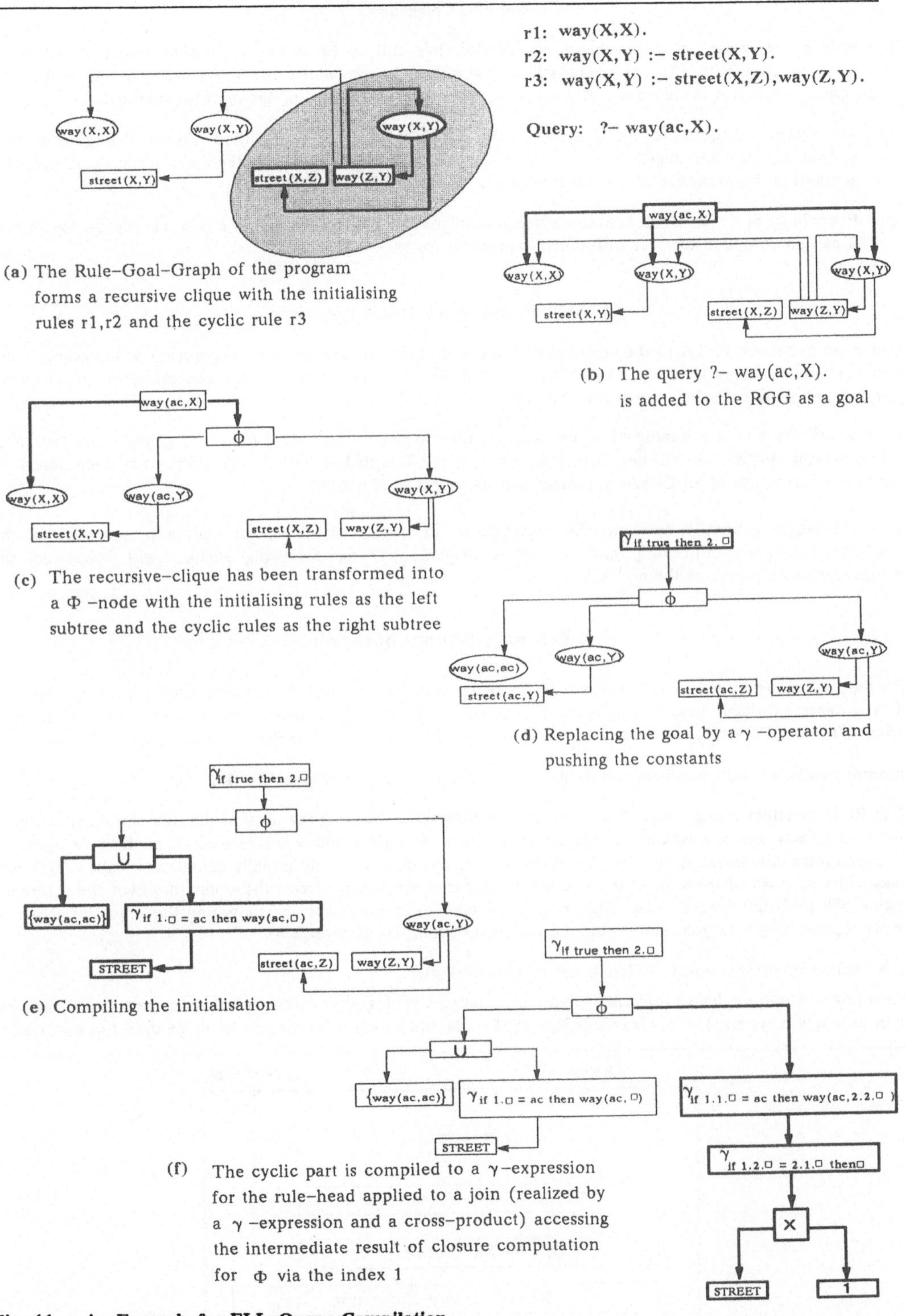

(a) The Rule–Goal–Graph of the program forms a recursive clique with the initialising rules r1,r2 and the cyclic rule r3

(b) The query ?- way(ac,X). is added to the RGG as a goal

(c) The recursive–clique has been transformed into a Φ –node with the initialising rules as the left subtree and the cyclic rules as the right subtree

(d) Replacing the goal by a γ –operator and pushing the constants

(e) Compiling the initialisation

(f) The cyclic part is compiled to a γ –expression for the rule–head applied to a join (realized by a γ –expression and a cross–product) accessing the intermediate result of closure computation for Φ via the index 1

Fig. 11 : An Example for FLL–Query–Compilation

Compiling Negation

Since detailed research on the problem of negation has still to be done, we currently make two naive restrictions on its use in FLL–programs which guarantee the possibility of compiling negation in FLL to set–difference in EFTA but do not really decrease the expressive power of set–oriented queries:

1)   We require our query program (i.e. FLL–rule–system + query) to be stratified. That basically means that it does not contain negation in recursive cliques. Expressed in model–theoretic terms, this property guarantees the existence of a unique minimal model of our query program.

2)   Every body of a rule which contains a negated subgoal $not\ sg_n$ has to contain a positive one sg_p too so that it can be compiled to a set–difference expression for $sg_n - sg_p$.

3.3 Architecture of the Query Processor

Having yet presented EFTA as the language of the query processor and given an impression of the compilation from our Feature Logic Language to EFTA, it's time for us to take a look at the general architecture of the query processor as a whole as shown in Fig. 12.

We currently have only a bundle of vague ideas on how to organize a rule rewriter for global optimization of FLL–programs, so that we will not further discuss it here. The FLL–to–EFTA translation has been described above, a presentation of an EFTA–optimizer can be found in /Lud88b/.

Since this paper primarily describes the upper levels of our architecture, we omit a presentation of the nonalgebraical query processing and storage management. The following section will focus on the administration of programs themselves.

4 The Rule System Manager

The purpose of the Rule System Manager (RSM) is the persistent storage of a collection of rules. Rules are part of the intensional database and support the deduction of new facts from existing ones, that is the derivation of virtual FT–Sets. Currently, all rules must be given as definite clauses over the universe of FLL–Terms.

Internally rules are not stored separately in a table, but in rule goal graphs (**RGGs**).

If an RGG describes a single rule, it consists of a rule node representing the head of the rule and a collection of goal nodes each one representing a subgoal of the rule. The goal nodes are connected to the rule node via so–called **intra rule links**. If an RGG describes more than one rule, it additionally contains so–called **inter rule links**. The purpose of these links is to connect rules in a way that reflects the order in which the inference engine will probably request rules. Currently, only such inter rule links are supported that connect a pair of nodes representing a subgoal and a unifying rule head (compare section 2.4).

A collection of rules stored in RGGs is called **rule system**.

Assuming a resolution–based inference engine (e.g. using a Prolog–style backward chaining or forward chaining as in production systems) – RGGs enable the RSM to decide which rules may probably be used together during

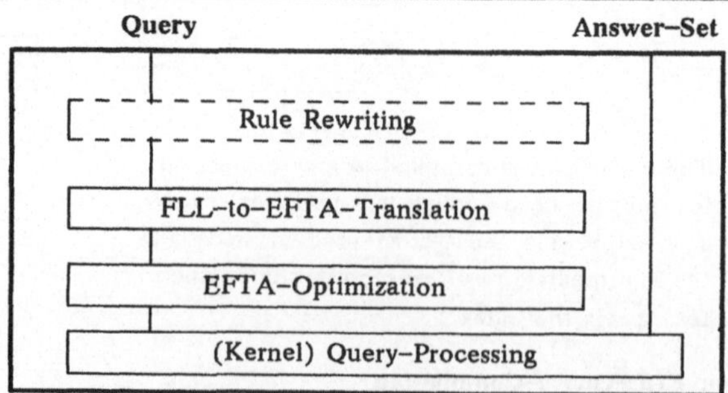

Fig. 12 : Architecture of the Query Processor

the inference process. Hence, the RSM is able to perform a prefetching of rules and to apply sophisticated clustering– and buffering–techniques in order to avoid expensive I/O overhead during inferential processing (see below).

In the following we shortly discuss the representation of the rule system and sketch the interface to the inference engine as well as strategies for buffering large RGGs.

4.1 Representation of Rule Systems

The RSM represents rules as collections of RGGs. RGGs restrict the search space for finding that rule which is used next during the inference process.

Sophisticated inference strategies as used in the LILOG inference machine work with information such as the *default value* of a rule or *vagueness*– and *uncertainty*–values of literals. Information about the complexity of rules and literals (i.e. *maximal term depth* or *number of variables*) can be relevant too. Therefore the RSM allows the specification of arbitrary attributes whenever a new rule is inserted. Each attribute has to be named and its value has to be an FLL–Term.

Attributes are also distinguished according to the fact whether they are *functional* or *additional*. Functional attributes (i.e. *number of variables*) can be computed by analyzing the rule respectively the literal, whereas additional attributes must be specified when inserting a rule.

The utilization of attributes leads to an attribution of RGG nodes. The RSM additionally uses internal attributes, for example to store whether there exist facts to a subgoal.

4.2 Interface to the Logic Programming System

The RSM has to support two kinds of access paths, one for finding the rules needed to start an inference process and one for finding the succeeding ones, i.e. for navigating in an RGG along inter rule links (e.g. *get_first_rule_unifying_with_goal*, *get_next_rule_unifying_with_goal*). For finding starting rules the RSM allows set–oriented access to the stored rules by specification of search conditions. The rules satisfying a search condition can be passed "one rule at a time" or "a list of n rules at a time". In principle, search conditions are conditons like those described in Fig. 8. Additionally one can specify whether a part of a rule (i.e. the rule head, a subgoal, an attribute or a subterm specified by a path) *unifies with a given term, has a given attribute* or *has a given sign* and one can specify that all subgoals of a rule have to fulfill a search condition or that there exists a subgoal fulfilling a search condition. The search condition

rule_head_unifies_with goal   and   rule_has_attribute default–value

is satisfied by a *default* rule whose head unifies with the given *goal*.

Furthermore the RSM supports the access to information about single rule/subgoal–features (i.e. the value of a functional attribute), the deletion/insertion of complete rules and the modification of arbitrary subterms and features of a rule/subgoal.

One problem at the interface RSM / inference engine is the size of the rule system granules to be transfered, that is, it is not clear if an inference engine should preferably access single subgoals/rules, a list of rules or larger granules (a recursive clique, a graph relevant for a given query). The usage of smaller granules leads to an increasing number of RSM calls whereas the usage of larger ones can lead to swapping in of rules not really needed. However, it is obvious that for inference engines closely coupled to the RSM, i.e. inference engines using the same internal term representation as the RSM, the number of RSM–calls plays a minor part since expensive transformations are avoided.

4.3 Graph Buffer

In the applications of interest it is not guaranteed that the RGG can be kept completely in main storage. That does not only lead to more complex addressing (rule and goal nodes cannot be identified by an address relative to a starting point of an RGG any longer) but also calls for strategies for a suitable clustering of an RGG and for swapping in/out of RGG–parts into/out of a graph buffer.

In order to decide which rules are preferably to be stored in a cluster, the RSM does not only consider the existence of inter rule links (if considering two rules, no one can be reached via inter rule links by the other one, they need not to be stored together in a cluster). Taking inference engine features like *set–oriented*, *tuple–oriented*, *goal–directed*, *data–directed* into account the RSM already tries at compile time to find the most probable respectively the most suitable order of inference steps and uses this information as a criterion for the decision which rules should preferably be stored together.

Our actual research is concentrated on resolution–based inference engines freeing the user from specifying the order in which the subgoals of a rule and the rules of a rule system are processed. The most suitable order of the steps of such an inference engine is currently determined by heuristics that could still be improved. Especially the presence of recursive cliques complicates the determination process. Although we can present but partial solutions to this problem, we consider it important to compute information about depth and breadth of proof trees. This information can be used by the inference engine too and has to influence the clustering– and prefetching–strategies, thus avoiding expensive disk accesses.

Finally we will sketch some ideas for finding the most suitable order of resolution operations and for prefetching.

If an inference engine has the features *goal driven* and *processing the subgoals of a rule in arbitrary order* the RSM proceeds as follows: First it examines what orders of subgoal processing are preferable when considering information passing between the subgoals of a rule /vGe85/. The RSM determines one out of the resulting orders according to a classification of the selectivity of the subgoals. For the classification of the selectivity of a subgoal the RSM uses criteria such as *degree of instantiation of a subgoal* and *does there exist facts to a subgoal*, assuming that proofs can be ended quicker the more a subgoal is instantiated and the more there exist facts to a subgoal. The selected order of processing the subgoals of a rule leads to cluster criteria, i.e. the rules whose heads unify with the first subgoal of this order are stored in the same cluster as the rule with a higher priority than those only unifying with the last one.

If the RSM notices (by looking ahead for inter rule links in the RGG) that rules not yet in the buffer are needed during one of the next inference steps, these are swapped into the buffer. In order to reduce the number of expensive disk accesses no single rules are swapped in, but always the whole cluster containing the demanded rule.

On request of a whole graph relevant for a given query all clusters containing a starting rule are swapped in first. Taking the constants of the query into account, the RSM tests whether rules can be reached via inter rule links whose clusters are not yet in main storage. If so, these clusters are also swapped in and the test continues.

As the rules of a recursive clique are always computed together, they are swapped in/out as a whole.

5 The Fact Manager

At a first sight, the Fact Manager (FM) can be characterized as being an enhanced Relational Database Manager (RDBM) providing an interface for defining and managing FT–Sets and access paths as well as a scan interface for accessing one term at a time. However, as already stated in the introductory chapter, the data model supported by the FM is more complex than the usual Relational Model, it allows FT–Sets to be composed of heterogeneous feature terms.

In the following the interface provided by the FM as well as the storage representation of variably structured complex terms will be shortly discussed. Then, an overview of the FM's internal architecture is given, followed by a discussion of some aspects of access paths for FT–Sets. A more detailed description of the FM can be found in /Ley88/.

5.1 The Fact Manager Interface

As usual, the FM interface consists of a schema manipulation part and a data update and retrieval part.

TYPE_DECLARATION	::=	type *TYPE_NAME* = *TYPE_DESCRIPTION*
	|	type *TYPE_NAME* = *TYPE_DESCRIPTION* with *CONSTRAINT*
TYPE_DESCRIPTION	::=	*TYPE_CALL* | *ENUMERATION*
	|	set of *TYPE_DESCRIPTION* | list of *TYPE_DESCRIPTION*
	|	< *FEATURE_DESCRIPTIONS* >
	|	functor *SYMBOL* (*TYPE_DESCRIPTIONS*)
	|	*TYPE_DESCRIPTION* or *TYPE_DESCRIPTION*
CONSTRAINT	::=	not *CONSTRAINT* | *CONSTRAINT* and *CONSTRAINT*
	|	*CONSTRAINT* or *CONSTRAINT*
	|	*PATH_OR_TERM OPERATOR PATH_OR_TERM*
	|	type(*PATH*) = *TYPE_CALL* | arity(*PATH*) = INTEGER
	|	*QUANTOR VARIABLE IN_OR_ARGOF PATH* : *CONSTRAINT*
QUANTOR	::=	forsome | forall
IN_OR_ARGOF	::=	in | argof
OPERATOR	::=	= | == | ≠ | < | > | ≤ | ≥ | in
BUILTIN_TYPE	::=	nil | term | integer | symbol
TYPE_CALL	::=	*BUILTIN_TYPE* | *TYPE_NAME*
ENUMERATION	::=	{ *TERMS* }
FEATURE_DESCRIPTIONS	::=	*SYMBOL* : *TYPE_DESCRIPTION*
	|	*SYMBOL* : *TYPE_DESCRIPTION* , *FEATURE_DESCRIPTIONS*

Fig. 13 : Type Definitions in the Logical Schema

The schema manipulation part supports the definition of types and FT–Sets and their corresponding access paths. The logical schema defines the type of those terms, that may be stored in a given FT–Set. Fig. 13 gives an idea of the type definition language which is compatible with the FLL sort definitions shown in Fig. 3. Unlike traditional database managers the FM supports the definition of recursive, variant and incomplete types, e.g. features may be optional, terms may include substructures not defined at the type level. Thus, the schema can only be stored partially in a common catalog, whereas the rest must be stored in the corresponding individuals. Optionally the catalog includes hints for the decomposition of complex objects. Since the FM is constructed as an experimental tool box, various decompositions can be implemented and tested. A slighty more detailed discussion on the definable access paths is given later on.

The data update and retrieval part is a scan interface supporting the navigational access to feature terms. Since the scan definition allows the usage of FTA's γ–operator, the scan interface supports the selective delivery of qualified subterms and the construction of new terms. The intended applications of LILOG–DB and thus of the FM do not require the navigational access to subterms. Hence, unlike NF²–implementations our first prototype does not support hierarchical scans, i.e. scans for navigation within complex (feature) tuples.

5.2 Representation of Complex Terms

Feature terms are directed trees. The nodes are attributed with the corresponding type identifier (integer, symbol, functor, tuple, set, list) and some additional values (e.g. field length). Edges starting at a tuple node are attributed with the corresponding feature name.

Throughout LILOG–DB, different internal representations of feature terms are used (see Fig. 14). LPS, Query Processor, and the FM interface of our prototype implementation use representation a), where tuples are represented as collections of main memory records connected by pointers. In the Interface Module, that connects LILOG–DB and other LILOG components, this representation is currently converted to meet the individual needs (e.g. conversion into Prolog clauses); however, a tighter integration with the LILOG inference engine will eliminate the conversion overhead.

Since the FM has been designed as a tool box, it supports different storage representations of feature terms. The general mapping strategy includes the following steps:

- If the user knows the type of queries to be applied to an FT–Set, it may be appropriate to decompose the complex terms of this FT–Set and allocate the subterms into different files (an optional step, see Fig. 14b).

- Mapping of the subgraphs into linear address spaces (Fig. 14c).

- Mapping of variable sized address spaces to fixed sized pages (Fig. 14d). This is currently done using a technique based on B*–trees, in a similar way as in EXODUS /CaD86, CDR86/ and OMS /FrB89/.

Modules, which transform the feature terms between this different representations are the central part of the internal FM architecture. Other important FM modules are the Data Dictionary Manager, the Scan Manager, and the Access Path Manager. Buffer management, free memory management, and secondary storage access are the main tasks of the File Manager, a module which isolates the FM from operating system and hardware dependencies.

5.3 Access Paths for FT–Sets

The variably structured complex feature terms of our data model lead to new requirements for indices. In conventional relational databases an index is defined over a subset A_I of the attribute set $A = \{ a_1, ..., a_n \}$. Queries using an exact match index have to specify values for all attributes in A_I, partial match indices can deal with queries which define values only for a subset of the attributes used to build the index. Indices supporting search conditions of the form $l_i \leq value(a_i) \leq u_i$ are called range indices.

A first simple step to generalize indices for our data model is to define them over a set of paths P_I. For all tuples stored in the indexed feature relation the paths of P_I have to end in atomic values. For the FT–Set

> { *<name: <first: alfred, last: smith>, address: <city: london>>,*
> *<name: <first: marc, last: miller>, salary: 40000>,*
> *<name: <first: sheila, last: smith>, salary: 30000, address: <city: london, street: 'new square'>>*
> }

we can define exact match indices over P_I = {name.last} or P_I = {name.last, name.first} to facilitate the search of tuples of persons known by name. If we define an index over P_I = {address.city} we can not include the second tuple because it has no address feature. A term is only considered for an index, if it contains atomic values at all positions specified in P_I, that is an index may point only to a subset of the terms in a FT–Set.

The LILOG applications working on the top of LILOG–DB require the retrieval of terms which match with a given term or which contain subterms matching with a given term. Hence, LILOG–DB must additionally support the retrieval of feature terms, that do not only contain certain values but additionally have these values arranged in a certain pattern, i.e. the given values must form a given (sub)term. Thus LILOG–DB currently supports two indexing mechanisms:

More traditional value oriented search is supported by exact match indices over path sets. We use a hybrid index of B*–trees and extendible hashing based on the bounded disorder method of Litwin and Lomet /LiL87/.

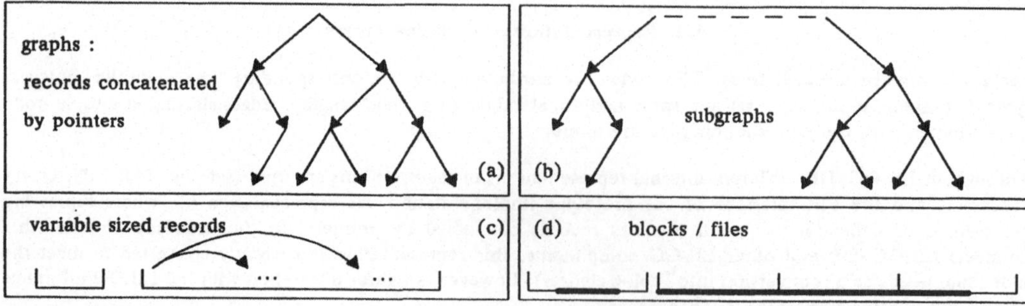

Fig. 14: Term Representations

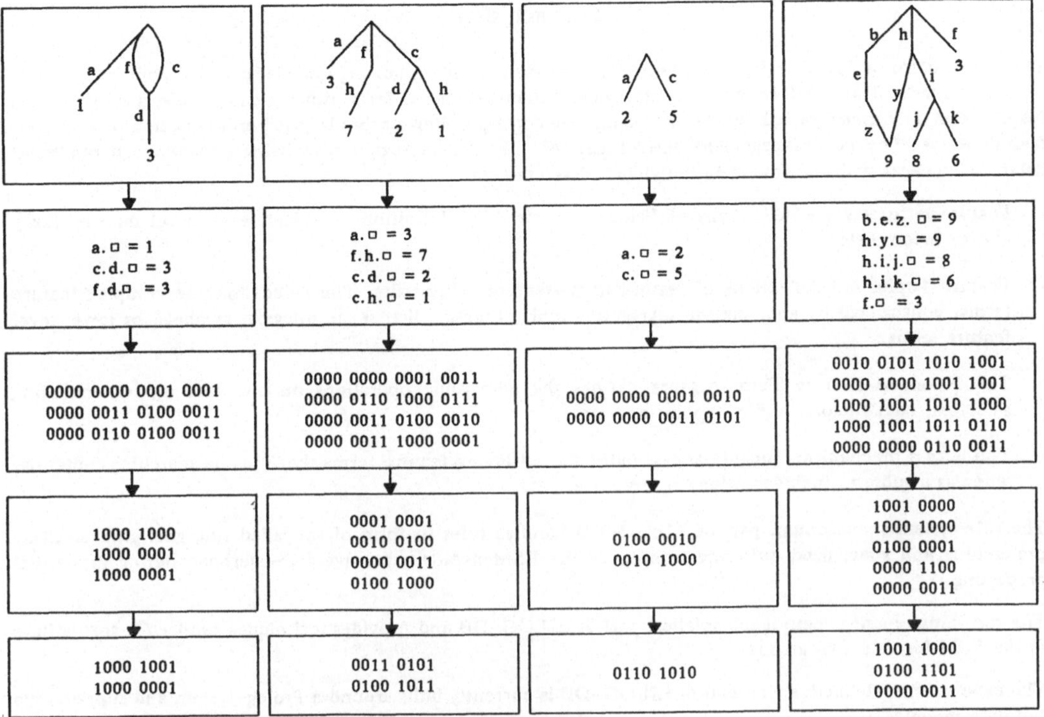

Fig. 15: Signature Extraction for Complex Feature Tuples

We have selected this method because it promises to combine the benefits of hashing and tree indexing, high performance and the ability to answer range queries efficiently, which is essential for fast join algorithms.

The second indexing mechanism supports pattern matching search operations. It is based on a new signature file method appropriate for complex feature terms. Signature files are a well known indexing technique used for text retrieval /Fal85/ and databases /FaC87/. The main idea is quite simple: For each feature term a compact code word of the properties, we are interested in when searching, is calculated. These code words are stored in the signature file. If a query is to be answered, the signature file is searched for code words matching the query pattern. Only the terms which are associated with matching code words have to be loaded and examined. Because the coding methods are usually entropy reducing transformations, there may be terms with matching code words, which are no members of the required answer set. This terms are called false matches or false drops. For very large databases it may become prohibitive to search the signature file sequentially. Several methods to organize signature files are proposed in the literature, for example bit sliced representation /Rob79/, multilevel signature files /SaR83/, or multiple block descriptor files /KSR88/.

We have developed a signature extraction method appropriate for complex feature terms. The term properties suitable for indexing are a subset of the FTA-conditions defined in Fig. 8 :

(1)	$p = v,$	$p \in \mathcal{P},\ v \in \mathcal{Z} \cup \Sigma^+$
(2)	$arity(p) = i,$	$p \in \mathcal{P},\ i \in \mathbf{N_0}$
(3)	$type(p) = x,$	$p \in \mathcal{P},\ x \in \{integer,\ symbol,\ list,\ tuple,\ functor,\ set\}$
(4)	$p\ has\ f,$	$p \in \mathcal{P},\ f \in \Sigma^+ \cup \mathbf{N}$

The user or database administrator may select one or more of these conditions for indexing. Fig. 15 shows the signature extraction of property (1) for a small FT-Set. In this example a word signature is calculated for each path ending in an atomic value. The word signatures are combined by a superimposed coding method to term signatures shown in the bottom boxes of Fig. 15. Details of the signature extraction method are described in /Ley88/.

6 Conclusion

The architecture of LILOG–DB, a backend database system for supporting knowledge based applications, has been presented. LILOG–DB supports the storage and management of facts, rule systems, and sort lattices. The feature term data model of LILOG–DB as well as the corresponding algebra is based on the notion of so–called feature terms. The fact management part of LILOG–DB can be regarded as being an enhanced relational database manager with the following individual characteristics:

- Feature term sets are collections of Feature Terms. The definition of a feature term set may be fuzzy and/or incomplete.

- Feature Tuples are collections of feature name/feature value pairs. The values may be complex feature terms, constructed by applying the aggregators tuple, functor, list, set to integers, symbols, or lower level feature terms.

- The Extended Feature Term Algebra defines the admissible operations on our data model, including selectors, constructors, and a fixpoint operator.

- The access mechanisms include access paths for retrieving feature terms that include matching subterms, whereas a subterm includes values as structure.

The rule system management part of LILOG–DB handles rules in form of so–called rule goal graphs. Using prefetching and specialized buffering techniques the RSM avoids expensive I/O–overhead during inferential processing.

The sort lattice management is the smallest part of LILOG–DB and provides techniques similar for sort lattices as the RSM for rule goal graphs.

The experimental deductive frontend of LILOG–DB is currently built around a Prolog–system and supports the full data model.

Literature

AitK86a   H. Ait–Kaci: An Algebraic Semantics Approach to Effective Resolution of Type Equations. Theoretical Computer Science 45, 1986, 293–351.

AitK86b   H. Ait–Kaci, R. Nasr: LOGIN: A Logic Programming Language with Built–In Inheritance. JLP 1986, 3, 185–215.

BDP88   C. Beierle, J.Dörre, U.Pletat, C. Rollinger, P.H. Schmitt, R. Studer: The Knowledge Representation Language LILOG. LILOG Report 41, 1988.

BPU88   C. Beierle, U. Pletat, H. Uszkoreit: An Algebraic Characterization of STUF. LILOG Report 40, IBM Stuttgart, 1988.

BrL87   R.J. Brachman, H.J. Levesque: Tales from the Far Side of KRYPTON. In: Expert Database Systems. Ed. L. Kerschberg, Expert Database Systems, First Int. Conf., Benjamin/Cummings, 1987, 3–43.

CaD86   M.J. Carey, D.J. DeWitt, D. Frank, G. Graefe, M. Muralikrishna, J.E. Richardson, E.J. Shekita: The Architecture of the EXODUS Extensible DBMS. Int. Workshop on Object–Oriented Database Systems, 1986, IEEE Computer Society Press, 52–65.

CDR86   M.J.Carey, D.J. DeWitt, J.E. Richardson, E.J. Shekita: Object and File Management in the EXODUS Extensible Database System. Proc. of the 12th VLDB Conf., Kyoto 1986, 91–100.

ChS79   C.L. Chang, J.R. Slagle: Using Rewriting Rules for Connection Graphs to Prove Theorems. Artificial Intelligence 12, 1979, 159–180.

FaC87   C. Faloutsos, S. Christodoulakis: Describing and Performance Analysis of Signature File Methods for Office Filing. ACM Transactions on Office Information Systems, Vol. 5, No. 3, July 1987, 237–257.

Fal85   C. Faloutsos: Access Methods for Text. Computing Surveys, Vol. 17, No. 1, March 1985, 49–74.

FrB89   J. Freitag, Th. Bode: Ein allgemeiner Speicherobjektmanager als Implementierungsbasis für komplexe Objekttypen in einem Objektmanagementsystem. BTW'89, Zürich, Informatik Fachberichte.

HuV87   M. Huber and I. Varsek: Extended Prolog for Order–Sorted Resolution. Symposium on Logic Programming, San Francisco 1987, 34–43.

KaR86   R.T. Kasper, W.C. Rounds: A Logical Semantics for Feature Structures. Proceedings of the 24th Ann. Meeting of the Ass. for Computational Linguistics. Columbia University, New York 1986, 257–265.

Kow75   R. Kowalski: A Proof Procedure Using Connection Graphs. JACM Vol. 22, No. 4, 1975, 572–595.

KSR88   A. Kent, R. Sachs–Davis, K. Ramamohanarao: A Superimposed Coding Scheme Based on Multiple Block Descriptor Files for Indexing Very Large Data Bases. Proc. of the 14th VLDB Conf., Los Angeles 1988, 351–359.

Ley88   M. Ley: Ein Fact–Manager zur persistenten Speicherung variabel strukturierter komplexer Objekte. LILOG Report 60, IBM Stuttgart, Oktober 1988.

LiL87   W. Litwin, D.B. Lomet: A New Method for Fast Data Searches with Keys. IEEE Software, March 1987, 16–24.

Lud88a   Th. Ludwig: EFTA: An Algebra for Deductive Retrieval of Feature–Terms. LILOG Report 58, IBM Stuttgart, October 1988.

Lud88b   Th. Ludwig: Algebraical Optimization of FTA–Expressions. LILOG Report 59, IBM Stuttgart, October 1988.

McKS81   D.P. McKay, S.S. Shapiro: Using Active Connection Graphs for Reasoning with Recursive Rules. IJCAI 1981, 368–374.

Mon87   G. Montini: Efficiency Considerations on Built–In Taxonomic Reasoning in Prolog. IJCAI, Mailand 1987, 68–75.

Rob79   C.S. Roberts: Partial–Match Retrieval via the Method of Superimposed Codes. Proceedings of the IEEE, Vol. 67, No. 12, December 1979, 1624–1642.

SaR83   R. Sachs–Davis, K. Ramamohanarao: A Two Level Superimposed Coding Scheme for Partial Match Retrieval. Information Systems, Vol. 8, No. 4, 1983, 273–280.

ScP81   H.–J. Schek, P. Pistor: Data Structures for an Integrated Data Base Management and Information Retrieval System. Proc. of the 8th VLDB Conf., Mexico City 1982, 197–207.

Smo88   G. Smolka: A Feature Logic with Subsorts. LILOG Report 33, 1988.

Ull85   J.D. Ullman: Implementation of Logical Query Languages for Databases. ACM Transactions on Database Systems, Vol. 10, No. 3, September 1985, 289–321.

Usz88   H. Uszkoreit: From Feature Bundles to Abstract Data Types: New Directions in the Representation and Processing of Linguistic Knowledge. In: Natural Language at the Computer. Proc. of the Scientific Symposium on Syntax and Semantik for Text Processing and Man–Machine–Communication. Ed. Blaser, Heidelberg, February 1988, 31–64.

vGe85   A. v. Gelder: A Message Passing Framework for Logical Query Evaluation. Stanford University, Report No. STAN–CS–85–1088.

DBA*:
Solving Combinatorial Problems
with Deductive Databases

Helmut Schmidt [1],   Werner Kiessling [1],
Ulrich Güntzer [2],   Rudolf Bayer [2]

[1]   MAD Intelligent Systems GmbH
Prinzregentenplatz 10
D-8000 München 80
West-Germany

[2]   Institut für Informatik
Technische Universität München
Arcisstrasse 21
D-8000 München 2
West-Germany

Abstract:

The evolution of database (DB) technology, with its origins in hierarchical databases, has currently reached the stage of matured relational DB systems and is about to grow into deductive DB systems, where logic programming - originated by the artificial intelligence (AI) community - plays a central theoretical role. Until now, however, no smooth integration of another important part of AI, namely that of heuristic search and intelligent planning, into DB technology was known. This paper contributes a first step beyond deductive DB systems towards intelligent DB systems. We describe the well-known A*-algorithm in terms of a general theoretical framework for deductive DB systems, the sloppy delta-iteration scheme, and give a generalized algorithm, called DBA*-algorithm. As an immediate consequence, heuristic search strategies for combinatorial problems become now feasible in the DB environment in a natural and efficient way. We also present a prototype implementation of the DBA*-algorithm, with the 15-Puzzle and the Traveling Salesman Problem as sample combinatorial problems. The benchmark results gained from this testbed demonstrate the applicability and efficiency of our approach for heuristic search in deductive DB systems.

1. Introduction

The purpose of this paper is to provide theoretically sound and practically feasible, efficient algorithms, which contribute to narrow down the still significant technological gap between AI and DB technologies by effectively amalgamating the virtues of both areas. Concretely, we present solutions for the following challenge: to show how deductive DB systems, which have a least fixpoint semantics, can be extended towards intelligent DB systems (or expert DB systems or knowledge base management systems) by adapting well-known algorithms from AI for heuristic search, which incorporate problem-dependent knowledge into the deduction process. As a matter of fact, this instantly opens up new application areas for DB technology, like - e.g. - intelligent planning methods for real-life applications, requiring complex reasoning on huge amount of data.

Before we shall present the technical details, some more general remarks seem appropriate to put our ideas into the right context. Historically, AI and DB technology progressed in almost total isolation of each other until not long ago. It is generally agreed that one of the strengths of current DB technology is the efficient management of large and even shared or distributed amount of data. On the other hand, despite 4th generation languages like SQL, DB query languages enormously lack of deductive power. Concerning both mentioned aspects, the strengths and weaknesses of AI systems are just dual. The obviously desirable integration of the respective advantages of AI and DB was shown to be theoretically feasible about 10 years ago in the landmark paper of [vEK76]. There, the least fixpoint semantics was identified as the crucial piece that allows to smoothly integrate logic programming with those relational DB systems that are extended by a least fixpoint operator (cp. also results in [AhU79]). It was not until recently that the practical feasibility of this theoretical affinity was demonstrated; see, e.g., [BaR86], [Bay85], [BaR87], [GKB87], [SaZ86], [Ull85], [Vie88], [Zan85].

So to date the know-how to build an efficient deductive DB system based on its natural least fixpoint semantics is available. However, as it was recognized and well investigated in AI for a long time, those increased deduction capabilities are still not sufficient to solve many important practical problems (see, e.g., [Nil80]), especially those generating a combinatorial explosion. Additional major deduction speed-ups can only be gained by the use of problem-dependent knowledge, which helps to guide the deduction process intelligently. This led to the well-known A*-algorithm (see [Nil80]). No question, it would be very promising, if one succeeded in integrating such heuristic search methods into deductive DBs. Then obviously, we had a clear perspective how to extend deductive DB systems into truly intelligent DB systems, which would be a powerful tool for future, novel DB-applications.

We provide a first successful step in this direction. The theoretical framework for the integration of heuristic search in deductive DB systems is the so-called **sloppy delta-iteration scheme**, which is described in detail in [SKGB87] and [GKB87]. The rest of this paper is organized as follows:

Section 2 describes the A*-algorithm in terms of the sloppy delta-iteration scheme. Because now the A*-algorithm can be executed efficiently in a DB environment, the name **DBA*-algorithm** was chosen for this particular representation. Section 3 describes generalizations of the DBA*-algorithm, which allow us to implement even more flexible search strategies. In section 4 we report on benchmark results for the 15-Puzzle and the Traveling Salesman Problem, which we used as test vehicles. Finally, section 5 summarizes our results and provides an outlook for future extended DB systems.

2. The A*-Algorithm as Sloppy Delta-Iteration

In the AI literature, several strategies for searching or-graphs can be found. In the following we want to show how these concepts carry over to the DB environment. Since for large real-life problems huge amount of data must be processed, passing these AI concepts into the DB environment is undoubtedly necessary. The classification, which has the greatest effect on the performance of the search, distinguishes between breadth-first search, depth-first search, and heuristic search:

Breadth-First Search:

Breadth-first search expands all nodes appearing on one level of the graph before any of the nodes on the next level is expanded. Breadth-first search is naturally performed by deductive DB systems that have a least fixpoint operator. Let us assume that the relation *Edge* contains the edges of the search graph. If the constant *Start* is the start node of the search graph, the following (Horn clause) rules describe the search that has to be performed.

$$\begin{aligned} &\rightarrow && \text{Reached (Start)} \\ \text{Reached (x), Edge (x, y)} \;\; &\rightarrow && \text{Reached (y)} \end{aligned}$$

The meaning of these two rules is:

o The search has already reached the node *Start*.

o If the search has already reached the node x and if there exists an edge from x to y, then the search has also reached the node y.

These two rules can be translated into a function defined by a relational algebra expression. The least fixpoint of this function will contain all the nodes, which can be reached from *Start*. If the least fixpoint is computed by semi-naive evaluation (see, e.g., [Bay85], [Ban86]), a breadth-first search on the graph is performed. (If the user is only interested in one solution, computing the entire least fixpoint can be avoided by stopping the iteration when the first solution is produced.)

If more information is necessary (like - e.g. - the path from *Start* to some node x reached by the search), then further attributes, which record this information, can be added to *Reached*.

Depth-First Search:

Depth-first search pursues a single branch of the search graph until an end node or a node that cannot be expanded is reached. Only in the latter case, the search procedure backtracks and explores other branches. This sort of search can easily be programmed within Prolog systems, which use SLD-resolution ([Llo87]). But since depth-first search implies a tuple-at-a-time processing, depth-first search can be coupled with a set-oriented database environment only with major difficulties and a loss of efficiency.

Heuristic Search:

Heuristic search basically takes an intermediate stand between the two extremes of breadth-first search and depth-first search. Its integration into the database environment will be explained in the following paragraphs.

2.1 The A*-Algorithm

The advantage of breadth-first search is that always a path from the start node to one of the end nodes is found, if such a path exists and if there is only a finite number of edges starting at each node in the graph. The disadvantage of breadth-first search is that an exhaustive search is performed; i.e., all paths shorter than the optimal path are explored. Thus, if the branching factor is high, a "combinatorial explosion" happens.

The advantage of depth-first search is that the search proceeds in greater depth very quickly. But depth-first search spends a lot of time exploring fruitless paths. Moreover, if an infinite path is entered, the search procedure does not terminate (unless there is a depth cut-off, which often must be programmed by the user in a cumbersome way). This is a classical problem for SLD-resolution based systems.

But for problems with combinatorial explosion of the search space, both methods often fail, because they expand too many nodes before a solution is found. The reason for this deficiency is that both search procedures (breadth-first and depth-first) are "uninformed methods", which lack a possibility to control the search in a more intelligent way by utilizing problem-dependent knowledge. But it is often possible to specify a heuristics that reduces the search effort. Then a heuristic search procedure, known as A*-algorithm, can be used.

If the A*-algorithm is used, the edges of the search graph are assigned a positive number representing the cost of this edge. The objective of the search is not only to find a path from a start node to an end node, but also to find the cheapest path (resp. a path that is approximately the cheapest one). Moreover,

In the beginning, only the start node is in the set of unexpanded nodes. Until an end node should be expanded, the search continues with expanding that unexpanded node n that has the minimal value $f(n)$ in the set of unexpanded nodes. (If there are several nodes having the same value, anyone of them is expanded.) The nodes generated by this expansion are processed as follows:

Case 1: If the node is new (that is, if it is neither in the set of expanded nodes , nor in the set of unexpanded nodes), it is inserted into the set of unexpanded nodes.

Case 2: If the node is already in the set of unexpanded nodes, the g-value of this node is set to the minimum of the new and the old g-value. (The f-value is updated accordingly.)

Case 3: If the node is already in the set of expanded nodes, the g-value of this node is set to the minimum of the new and the old g-value. If the g-value changes, this change is (recursively) propagated to the successors of this node that are already generated. (All f-values are updated accordingly.)

As shown in [Nil80], the cheapest path from the start node to an end node is always found by the A*-algorithm, if the function h is admissible; that is, if the estimated cost $h(n)$ of an optimal path from node n to an end node is less than or equal to the actual cost of such a path.

2.2 Sloppy Delta-Iteration

To integrate the A*-algorithm into the database environment, we first must introduce a new method for efficient evaluation of recursion in deductive databases, called sloppy delta-iteration (see also [SKGB87], [GKB87]). Sloppy delta-iteration is a general framework offering flexible control for computing the least fixpoint or part of the least fixpoint of a continuous function F defined by a relational algebra expression.

The principal characteristics of fixpoint iterations is that the least fixpoint of a function F is approximated by subsequent iteration steps. Let S be that part of the least fixpoint that is computed until now. During the standard delta-iteration (see [GKB87]), the next iteration-step entirely computes $F(S)$. The main idea of the sloppy delta-iteration scheme is to compute only some part of $F(S)$.

Definition: An iteration producing the sequence $(S_t)_{t \geq 0}$ is called
> **systolic,** if $S_{t+1} = F(S_t)$ for all t.
> **sloppy,** if $S_t \subseteq S_{t+1} \subseteq F(S_t)$ for all t.

We also use an analogous distinction for iteration-steps.

The sloppy delta-iteration scheme consists of several sloppy sub-iterations approximating the least fixpoint intelligently, and - if necessary - one systolic sub-iteration that finally computes the entire least fixpoint. In each iteration-step of a sloppy sub-iteration, the tuples newly generated by this iteration-step are divided into a NICE-part and a REST-part. The NICE-part will be processed in the next iteration-step of the current sub-iteration, whereas the REST-part is accumulated and will be processed in one of the following sloppy sub-iterations or in the completing systolic sub-iteration. Since the REST-part is disregarded for the current sub-iteration, consequences, which can be deduced from the REST-part will not be computed. Hence the current sub-iteration normally is a sloppy one.

A sloppy sub-iteration starts by selecting a NICE-part from all the accumulated REST-parts. Since the sloppy delta-iteration scheme consists of several sloppy sub-iterations, intelligent backtracking to previously disregarded tuples is easily possible by starting another sloppy sub-iteration from these tuples. Backtracking may be necessary, if the search has entered a dead end or if tuples that were previously disregarded seem to be more promising than the current ones.

The completing systolic sub-iteration finally starts from all accumulated REST-parts and performs systolic iteration steps until the least fixpoint is computed.

For showing the completeness of the sloppy delta-iteration scheme, it is required that the number of sloppy sub-iterations is finite, that each sloppy sub-iteration only executes a finite number of iteration-steps, that the last sub-iteration is a systolic sub-iteration and that - for each sloppy iteration-step - the union of the NICE-part and the REST-part is equal to the set of tuples newly generated by this iteration-step. With these restrictions, we can guarantee that, ultimately, the completing systolic sub-iteration computes the entire least fixpoint; that is, all answers are deduced by the sloppy delta-iteration scheme. If the user does not need all answers, these restrictions can be dropped.

Let F be the continuous function gained by translating the rules, which define a recursive predicate R, into a relational algebra expression. If F is applied to a set S, containing tuples for the recursive predicate R, it produces all consequences of R that can be deduced by applying all the rules to S once (if all the other relations appearing in these rules are assumed to be base relations).

Let Aux be an auxiliary function for F; that is,

$$Aux(S, \Delta) \setminus F(S) = F(S + \Delta) \setminus F(S) \quad \text{for all sets } S, \Delta \text{ with } S \cap \Delta = \varnothing.$$

The auxiliary function efficiently computes all new consequences, which can be deduced from $S + \Delta$ and which cannot already be deduced from S. As shown in [Ban86], such an auxiliary function can easily be found by formal differentiation.

Let k be the number of sloppy sub-iterations.

For each i in $\{1, \cdots, k\}$ let n_i be the number of iteration-steps of the i-th sloppy sub-iteration.

For each t in $\{0, \cdots, n_i\}$ let $N_{i,t}$ and $R_{i,t}$ be two functions that partition the tuples generated in the t-th step of the i-th sloppy sub-iteration into a NICE-part and a REST-part. That is, let $N_{i,t}$ be a function with $N_{i,t}(S) \subseteq S$ for all S (i.e., $N_{i,t}$ is a selection function), and let $R_{i,t}$ be a function defined by $R_{i,t}(S) := S \setminus N_{i,t}(S)$ for all S (i.e., $R_{i,t}(S)$ is the complement of $N_{i,t}(S)$ with respect to S).

The following iteration scheme computes the least fixpoint of F (which is returned in the variable S):

Iteration Scheme Sloppy-Δ :

```
S := Ø;
Σ := F(Ø);
for i := 1 to k do                      (* k sloppy sub-iterations *)
   begin
      NICE := N_{i,0}(Σ);               (* initialization of a sloppy sub-iteration *)
      REST := R_{i,0}(Σ);
      Δ := NICE;
      Σ := REST;

      for t := 1 to n_i while Δ ≠ Ø do  (* n_i sloppy iteration-steps *)
         begin
            AUX := Aux(S, Δ);
            S := S + Δ;
            AUX := AUX \ (S + Σ);
            NICE := N_{i,t}(AUX);
            REST := R_{i,t}(AUX);
            Δ := NICE;
            Σ := Σ + REST
         end;

      AUX := Aux(S, Δ);                  (* epilogue of a sloppy sub-iteration *)
      S := S + Δ;
      AUX := AUX \ S;
      Σ := Σ + AUX;
   end;

Δ := Σ;                                 (* completing systolic sub-iteration *)
while Δ ≠ Ø do
   begin
      AUX := Aux(S, Δ);
      S := S + Δ;
      Δ := AUX \ S;
   end;
```

The advantage of this sloppy iteration scheme is that all tuples, which are not processed in a sloppy sub-iteration, are not thrown away, but are accumulated in Σ. Thus, the next sloppy sub-iteration (or the completing systolic sub-iteration) can start over by selecting the relevant tuples from Σ (by applying the selection $N_{i,0}$ to Σ). There is no need to apply F to S in order to get a starting point. Moreover, Σ is needed for the efficient and correct use of the auxiliary function, since $Aux(S, \Delta) \setminus F(S) = Aux(S, \Delta) \setminus (S + \Delta + \Sigma)$.

The power of this iteration scheme comes from the degrees of freedom provided by the parameters k and $n_1, \cdots, n_k$ and by the functions $N_{i,t}$ and $R_{i,t}$, which allow an arbitrary control of the deduction process. Moreover, the above restrictions were only made for guaranteeing the completeness of the iteration scheme. If the user is only interested in a part of the least fixpoint, these restrictions can be dropped and much greater freedom is achieved.

2.3 Sloppy Delta-Iteration adjusted to Heuristic Search

In order to perform heuristic search in the DB environment, we first have to enlarge the information stored in the relations *Reached* and *Edge*. We add two attributes to the relation *Reached* with the following meaning: The second attribute of *Reached* contains the g-value, the third attribute contains the f-value of the node in the first attribute. (Since the h-value is the difference of the f-value and the g-value, it is omitted.) Additionally, the relation *Edge* obtains a third attribute containing the cost of the edge determined by the nodes in the first and second attribute. Then these two relations have the form

Reached (node, g-value, f-value),

Edge (start, end, cost).

The resulting Horn clause program (that also changes the g- and f-values) has the following form:

$$\longrightarrow \quad \text{Reached (Start, 0, h(Start))}$$
$$\text{Reached}\,(x, g, \_\,), \text{Edge}\,(x, y, z) \quad \longrightarrow \quad \text{Reached}\,(y, g + z, g + z + h(y))$$

Here the underscore denotes an anonymous variable.

This program can be translated into a function defined by an extended relational algebra expression ([Zan85]), which also handles the functions appearing in the above program. The least fixpoint (resp. some relevant part of the least fixpoint) of this function can be computed by a sloppy delta-iteration scheme adjusted to heuristic search. Before we describe the necessary adjustments, we give the correspondences between the terms of the A*-algorithm and those of the sloppy delta-iteration scheme:

o S will contain the expanded nodes.

o Σ will contain the unexpanded nodes.

o Δ and NICE will contain the nodes that have to be expanded, resp. the nodes, which are already expanded and whose g-value has changed. Note, that in the latter case the change of the g-value has to be propagated to the successors of these nodes.

o REST will contain the unexpanded nodes that will not be considered for the current sub-iteration.

o AUX will contain the nodes that are immediate successors of the nodes in Δ .

DBA*-Algorithm:

In each sloppy sub-iteration the following is done:

1. During the initialization phase that tuple of Σ that has the minimal f-value of all tuples in Σ is selected into the NICE-part. (If there are several tuples with the same f-value, anyone of them is chosen.)

2. Then the NICE-part is expanded according to the above program. This expansion produces a set AUX of tuples that are the immediate successors of the tuple in the NICE-part.

3. Then AUX is divided into a NICE-part and a REST-part as described in the sequel (see also the above description of the A*-algorithm). For each tuple $t \in$ AUX, the following is done:

Let n be $t.node$ (that is, n is the value of the *node*-attribute of the tuple t).

Case 1: If n is a new node, insert it into the set of unexpanded nodes:

$$\begin{aligned} &\text{if} \quad not\,(\exists\, s \in (S \cup \Sigma): \quad n = t.node = s.node\,) \\ &\text{then} \quad \text{insert}\,(t, \text{REST}). \end{aligned}$$

Case 2: If n is already in the set of unexpanded nodes, then set the g-value of this node in the set of unexpanded nodes to the minimum of the new and old value.

$$\begin{aligned} &\text{if} \quad (\exists\, s \in \Sigma: \quad n = t.node = s.node \text{ and } t.g-value < s.g-value) \\ &\text{then} \quad \text{delete}(s, \Sigma);\ \text{insert}\,(t, \text{REST}). \end{aligned}$$

Case 3: If n is already in the set of expanded nodes, then set the g-value of this node in the set of expanded nodes to the minimum of the new and old value.

$$\begin{aligned} &\text{if} \quad (\exists\, s \in S: \quad n = t.node = s.node \text{ and } t.g-value < s.g-value) \\ &\text{then} \quad \text{delete}\,(s, S);\ \text{insert}\,(t, \text{NICE}) \end{aligned}$$

4. If the NICE-part (and hence Δ) is empty, the sloppy sub-iteration stops and another sloppy sub-iteration starts. Otherwise, the sloppy sub-iteration continues with step 2.

Assuming that only one solution is required, we stop the sloppy delta-iteration as soon as an end node should be expanded; i.e., the completing systolic sub-iteration is not executed.

$$\circ$$

Remarks:

o In each sloppy sub-iteration only the first iteration step expands unexpanded nodes whereas the remaining iteration steps only propagate updates of the g-values from already expanded nodes to their successors. In the sequel, we therefore distinguish between expansion and update phase.

o Since $S \cap \Sigma = \emptyset$, the above algorithm is deterministic.

o The recursive propagation of an update to all the successors of a node n is **automatically** done by the sloppy sub-iteration (by putting the tuple t in case 3 into the NICE-part.) This is possible because the expansion and the update phase both use the same rules.

o If - for the cases 2 and 3 - the tuple s has a greater g-value than the tuple t, then s can be deleted from Σ, resp. S, because it will never produce better results than the tuple t.

o Analogously, if the g-value of a tuple t in AUX is greater than or equal to the g-value of a corresponding tuple s in S or Σ, then the tuple t need no longer be considered; that is, t is neither in the NICE-part nor in the REST-part.

If the sloppy delta-iteration scheme is adjusted to heuristic search as described above, it performs the same processing as the A*-algorithm. Since the sloppy delta-iteration scheme is a database framework, we call the adjusted iteration scheme **DBA*-algorithm**.

3. Generalizations of the DBA*-Algorithm

In the following, we give some generalizations of the DBA*-algorithm that normally improve the performance of the algorithm in a DB environment. By the description of the DBA*-algorithm in terms of fixpoint theory, the correctness and completeness of these generalizations are obvious. This flexibility in tailoring the DBA*-algorithm to the special situation at hand is another important advantage of our approach.

3.1 Tuning by Set-Oriented Expansion

The classical A*-algorithm performs a depth-first-like search with intelligent backtracking. The optimization we propose here adds a breadth-first component to the A*-algorithm. Instead of expanding only one tuple in the expansion phase (namely that tuple of the set of unexpanded tuples that has the minimal f-value within this set), several tuples are expanded at the same time, i.e., those tuples of the set of unexpanded tuples that have a value near to the minimal f-value of this set. By using this strategy, one proceeds from a **tuple-at-a-time** processing to a **set-at-a-time** processing. Since databases support well the processing of sets, this strategy will normally gain efficiency.

Expansion of several tuples should especially be done at the beginning of the search, because here it is more likely to enter an impasse. By exploring several paths simultaneously the decision which path to continue can be taken at a later time if more information is available.

On the other hand, if only one path is explored, it is necessary to backtrack from impasses. Therefore, the tuple-at-a-time approach requires more expansion-steps than the set-at-a-time approach. If the cost of one expansion-step depends only marginally on the number of tuples expanded in this step, expanding several tuples is better than expanding only one.

The DBA*-algorithm conveniently allows the user to find the optimal balance between depth-first and breadth-first by introducing a tuning parameter **breadth,** which controls the number of tuples in the NICE-part selected for expansion. Appendix 2 shows performance results for this optimization.

3.2 Tuning by Exploiting Locality

Until now, the expansion phase of a sloppy sub-iteration consists of one iteration step expanding the tuple with the minimal f-value. The new tuples generated by this expansion-step are inserted into the set Σ and the next sloppy sub-iteration continues with expanding that tuple that has the minimal value within the entire set Σ. If there are several paths, which are approximately equally good, it is possible that the search jumps from one path to another expanding every path only by one edge. A much more local processing can be achieved, if each sloppy sub-iteration consists of several expansion steps, each one expanding all or only the best tuples produced by the preceding expansion step. This optimization will in general save disk accesses, if the DBA*-algorithm is implemented on a secondary memory DB system.

3.3 Adaptable Heuristic Search

At the beginning of the search, only uncertain knowledge about the optimal path is available; i.e., the estimation values of the tuples are rather vague. Since, at this time, impasses are easily entered, a breadth-first-like search should be done. This can be achieved by using the first optimization. If the search continues, information grows and entering impasses becomes more unlikely. Therefore, promising paths should be explored in greater depth; i.e., the second optimization should be used. By changing the two parameters

— number of tuples expanded by one expansion-step (*breadth*) and

— number of expansion-steps of a sloppy sub-iteration (*depth*)

in the course of the search, a heuristic search evolves that adapts itself to the growing information during the search. Since the two optimizations given in the previous sections are orthogonal, both of the above parameters can - at the same time - be greater than 1.

A possible heuristics for changing the above parameters is as follows:

The product of *breadth* and *depth* is always equal to a constant c. (This constant should be problem-dependent or resource-dependent.)

At the beginning, *breadth* is set equal to c; that is, as many paths as possible are explored, but only the first edge of each path is explored. During the search, *breadth* is diminished and *depth* is increased. If - e.g. - the f-values of some tuples are very low or much better than the f-values of the other tuples, *breadth* is set to the number of these tuples; that is, only the promising paths are explored, but these paths are pursued as deeply as possible.

3.4 Heuristic Search for Several Start Nodes

Until now we assumed that there is one start node and an optimal path from that start node to one of the end nodes has to be found. (There may be several end nodes. But the iteration stops if one end node is reached.) In the following we describe how the restriction on one start node can be dropped:

We add an additional attribute, namely the start node, to the predicate *Reached*. If there are n start nodes $Start_1, \cdots, Start_n$, we get the following rules:

$$\longrightarrow \quad \text{Reached}\,(Start_1, Start_1, 0, h(Start_1))$$
$$\cdots$$
$$\longrightarrow \quad \text{Reached}\,(Start_n, Start_n, 0, h(Start_n))$$
$$\text{Reached}\,(start, x, g, \_), \text{Edge}\,(x, y, z) \quad \longrightarrow \quad \text{Reached}\,(start, y, g+z, g+z+h(y))$$

These rules explicitly record the start node and the third attribute of the relation *Reached* gives the cost of the (so far) optimal path between the nodes of the first and second column.

The NICE-part of the expansion phase is constructed as follows: From each group of tuples with the same start node that tuple is chosen that has the minimal f-value within this group. Then, the expansion is done for the set of selected tuples.

The result is for each start node an optimal path from that start node to one of the end nodes (if there exists one). Since a set-at-a-time processing is reached now, this computation is much more efficient than applying the DBA*-algorithm to all start nodes one after another.

If only an optimal path from one of the start nodes to one of the end nodes should be found, the original DBA*-algorithm can be used. Let *Start* be the name of an artificial start node. Then, we only have to add the following facts to the relation *Edge*:

$$\longrightarrow \quad \text{Edge}\,(Start, Start_1, 0)$$
$$\cdots$$
$$\longrightarrow \quad \text{Edge}\,(Start, Start_n, 0)$$

But also the modified DBA*-algorithm (with recording the start node) can be used. We only have to choose that unexpanded tuple for expansion that has the minimal f-value among all unexpanded tuples (i.e., no distinction between start nodes is made).

3.5 Heuristic Search for Several End Nodes

Besides a search starting from several start nodes, a search for paths to several end nodes can easily be implemented, too. An additional attribute, namely the end node, is added to the predicate *Reached* and the function h gets two parameters, the node that is already reached by the search and the end node that should be reached. If there are m end nodes $End_1, \cdots, End_m$, we get the following rules:

$$\rightarrow \quad \text{Reached}(\text{Start}_1, \text{Start}_1, \text{End}_1, 0, h(\text{Start}_1, \text{End}_1))$$

$$\vdots \qquad\qquad\qquad\qquad\qquad\qquad\qquad\qquad\qquad (n * m \text{ facts})$$

$$\rightarrow \quad \text{Reached}(\text{Start}_n, \text{Start}_n, \text{End}_m, 0, h(\text{Start}_n, \text{End}_m))$$

$$\text{Reached}(\text{start}, x, \text{end}, g, \_), \text{Edge}(x, y, z) \rightarrow \text{Reached}(\text{start}, y, \text{end}, g + z, g + z + h(y, \text{end}))$$

The NICE-part of the expansion phase is constructed as follows: From each group of tuples that have the same start node and the same end node that tuple is chosen for expansion that has the minimal f-value within this group.

The result is, for each pair of start node $Start_i$ and end node End_j, an optimal path between these nodes (if there exists one).

4. Implementation and Performance Results

In this section, we want to exemplify the performance of our DBA*-algorithm. For this purpose, we chose the familiar 15-Puzzle problem ([Nil80]) as an academic AI exercise and the Traveling Salesman Problem ([Pea84]) as a practical DB problem.

The prototype-implementation of the DBA*-algorithm was done on the Declare™ Expert Database System which is the core of MAD Intelligent Systems' Smart Data System™. The Declare system has a deductive database language, which is compiled by the novel optimizing rule compiler ORC into RelationalLisp®. This language is similar to the logic data languages LDL1 ([BNRST87]) and NAIL! ([MUvG86]). As an extended Horn-clause language with least fixpoint semantics, it is completely declarative and features recursion, function-terms, negation, explicit all-quantifiers in the premise of a rule, and aggregation. RelationalLisp is a relational database system with an extended relational algebra, implemented on top of a UNIX-based COMMON LISP environment. It also includes a general database adaptor, giving applications access to heterogeneous local and remote databases (like - e.g. - Oracle, Informix). By using the database adaptor, relations used by the Declare system can reside on external databases. Therefore the DBA*-algorithm can also be applied to base relations stored on external databases.

For the DBA*-algorithm, we have implemented a further straightforward optimization that we could not find anywhere in the AI literature: instead of implementing Σ by a sorted list - to retrieve the minimum - a heap (see [AHU74]) must be the data structure of choice for this purpose. A heap has the following properties: finding the minimum can be done in constant time; insertion and deletion of elements can be done in logarithmic time.

4.1 The 15-Puzzle

The 15-Puzzle consists of fifteen numbered, movable tiles set in a 4 x 4-frame. One cell of the frame is always empty thus making it possible to move an adjacent numbered tile into the empty cell - or, we could say, to move the empty cell (see also [Nil80]). Representing puzzle states by lists of lists (with indices starting form 0) we can describe the possible moves by the following Declare program (in Lisp notation).

```
(def-virt-rel  Puzzle
   ((state  :type list)                              ;;; schema definition
    (row    :type integer)
    (column :type integer))

   (ASSERT ((  (( 5  3 12  8)                         ;;; a start position
               ( 4  0  1  6)
               (10  2 13  7)
               (11 15  9 14)) 1 1)))

   (IF   (Puzzle ?p (?row (/= 0)) ?col)              ;;; rule to move blank up
    THEN (Puzzle (up ?p ?row ?col) (- ?row 1) ?col))

   (IF   (Puzzle ?p (?row (/= 3)) ?col)              ;;; rule to move blank down
    THEN (Puzzle (down ?p ?row ?col) (+ ?row 1) ?col))

   (IF   (Puzzle ?p ?row (?col (/= 0)))              ;;; rule to move blank left
    THEN (Puzzle (left ?p ?row ?col) ?row (- ?col 1)))

   (IF   (Puzzle ?p ?row (?col (/= 3)))              ;;; rule to move blank right
    THEN (Puzzle (right ?p ?row ?col) ?row (+ ?col 1))))


(defun up (p row col)                                ;;; function to move blank
                                                     ;;; on position p_row,col up
  (let ((cp (copy-tree p)))                          ;; cp := copy of p
     (setf (elt (elt cp row) col)
           (elt (elt cp (- row 1)) col))             ;; cp_row,col := cp_row-1,col
     (setf (elt (elt cp (- row 1)) col)
           0)                                        ;; cp_row-1,col := 0
  cp))                                               ;; result is cp

;;; down, left and right are defined analogously.
```

The natural reading for the first of the above rules is:

If in *puzzle ?p* the blank is in position *?row, other than 0,* and *?col,*

then move the blank *up* from *?p* with blank position *?row* and *?col,* and the blank is now in position *?row - 1* and *?col.*

Heuristics and Performance Results:

For our benchmark, we used the "snail"-heuristics, an improved heuristics combining the Manhattan distance heuristics and the sequencing score. This snail-heuristics proved effective for our goal state, being the following position:

<pre>
1   →   2   →   3   →   4
                        ↓
12 → 13 → 14   5
↑   ↓   ↓
11   0   15   6
↑   ↓
10 ←   9   ←   8   ←   7
</pre>

The Manhattan distance $M(n)$ of a position n is computed as follows (see [Kor85]): For each tile, the number of grid units between the current position of the tile and its goal position are computed, and these values are summed for all tiles. We changed the Manhattan distance heuristics in the following way: If the Manhattan distance of a tile is 1, we do not take into account its value. This heuristics proved more efficient because it is often necessary to temporarily move a tile from its goal position in order to reach the goal state.

The sequencing score $S(n)$ is obtained by checking around the fringe squares allotting 2 for every tile not followed by its proper successor, allotting 0 for every other tile (see [Nil80]).

Manhattan distance $M(n)$ and sequencing score $S(n)$ are combined to the "snail"-heuristics by the formula $h(n) = M(n) + 3 * S(n)$ (see also [Nil80]).

Additionally, for emphasizing depth-first search, we used the weighted combination $f(n) = g(n) + 2 * h(n)$. (The exact choice was - of course - intuition guided.) This combination prefers tuples with low h-values; that is, nodes that are (or are assumed to be) close to the end node (see [Pea84]).

By using all these optimizations, we achieved to solve randomly generated puzzles. We ran our algorithm on the problem instances 1 - 32 given in [Kor85]. The average time for solving a puzzle was about 81 seconds. The exact time results are given in the appendix. There, we also show the number of generated tuples, the number of union-queries and the number of select-project queries.

4.2 The Traveling Salesman Problem

The Traveling Salesman Problem consists of finding the cheapest tour (that is, the cheapest path that visits each node exactly once and returns to the initial node) in a symmetric graph with each edge assigned a non-negative cost. Note, that for this problem the search graph is different from the original graph. A node in the search graph consists of a partial tour (which can be traveled in the original graph).

For using the A*-algorithm, we have to provide an estimation function f, which estimates for a given partial tour the minimal cost of a complete tour containing that partial tour. Since we want to find an optimal tour, we will use an admissible estimation function, which guarantees finding an optimal solution. The estimation functions that have received the greatest attention in the literature use (see - e.g. - [Pea84]):

o the cheapest second degree graph going through the remaining nodes, or

o the minimum spanning tree through all remaining nodes.

The first is obtained by solving the so-called optimal assignment problem using on the order of N^3 computational steps, whereas the second requires on the order of N^2 steps (if N is the number of remaining nodes). We have used a computationally simpler estimation function which only requires a constant number of computational steps.

For each node n, let b_n (resp. s_n) be the cost of the best (resp. second-to-best) edge adjacent to node n. Let c_{ij} be the cost of the edge from node i to node j. For a partial tour $(n_0, \cdots, n_k)$, let M denote the set of nodes, which are not part of that partial tour. Then our estimation function f for that partial tour is

$$f((n_0, \cdots, n_k)) = \sum_{i=1}^{k} c_{n_{i-1}, n_i} + b_{n_k}/2 + \sum_{m \in M} (b_m + s_m)/2 + b_0/2 .$$

Let us briefly explain why this estimation function is admissible: A lower bound f for the cost of any complete tour containing a given partial tour is the sum of the cost of the partial tour (g-value) and a lower bound for all cycle-free paths going from the actual end node of the partial tour through all the remaining nodes to the start node of the partial tour (h-value). For each such cycle-free path p (which starts in n_k and ends in n_0) the sum of the two edges adjacent to some inner node m of p are no less than the sum of the two edges of least cost adjacent to m. The cost of the edge starting at n_k (resp. ending in n_0) is no less than the cheapest edge adjacent to n_k (resp. to n_0).

As mentioned above, the advantage of this estimation functions is that $f((n_0, \cdots, n_k, n_{k+1}))$ can be computed from $f((n_0, \cdots, n_k))$ in constant time, if $c_{n_k, n_{k+1}}$, $s_{n_{k+1}}$ and b_{n_k} are known. Since these values are independent from the partial path under consideration, they can be precomputed before the A*-algorithm starts. Then

$$f((n_0, \cdots, n_k, n_{k+1})) = f((n_0, \cdots, n_k)) + c_{n_k, n_{k+1}} - (b_{n_k} + s_{n_{k+1}})/2$$

Moreover $f((n_0))$ can also easily be computed by

$$f((n_0)) = b_{n_0} + \sum_{m \neq n_0} (b_m + s_m)/2$$

Due to space limitations we omit the rules describing the Traveling Salesman Problem. But we want to give some typical application:

Assume that the traveling salesman uses a database containing a base relation that stores the distances between the cities he might want to visit. From this distance relation, he selects the distances between those cities he actually wants to visit into a view *Edge*. Then he can run - **without** having to leave the database environment - the DBA*-algorithm on the view *Edge* and gets the optimal tour.

In the appendix, we give three figures showing the time for finding the best solution vs. the number of tuples that are expanded in one expansion-step (*breadth*). These figures indicate that performance gains can be achieved by choosing *breadth* greater than 1.

For a larger problem size one probably still needs to apply specialized Operations Research algorithms. However using the DBA*-algorithm has the advantage that it offers a general purpose mechanism to quickly solve a large class of combinatorial problems on deductive DB system with a reasonable efficiency.

5. Summary and Outlook

The evolution from relational DB systems to expert DB systems requires at least two things: more deductive power (like recursion) and a rich environment for knowledge representation, where the rule-based programming paradigm is one instance, and inheritance mechanisms, frames, semantic nets are others. Extending current relational DB technology towards deductive DB systems is a necessary, but not sufficient step. Starting from deductive DB systems we have shown a promising approach towards expert DB systems by efficiently integrating heuristic search in the form of the A*-algorithm into the DB environment. The theoretical foundation for this integration is the framework of the sloppy delta-iteration scheme. Within this framework, several interesting generalizations of the A*-algorithm can be recognized and proved correct easily. It can be expected that more classes of algorithms, which relate to heuristic and intelligent search, can be described in terms of sloppy delta-iteration and hence be readily transferable to a database context.

We have demonstrated the usefulness of this approach by the academic 15-Puzzle problem and the Traveling Salesman Problem as real-life DB-application. More practical applications can be identified in the following areas: travel business (e.g., airlines or travel agency), where large databases already exist. Inquiries typically involve some form of heuristic or expert knowledge to find a satisfactory answer to a customer's request. Another application is the overland travel problem, as described and likewise treated with a DB approach in [KHISSS84]. Also typically here, large amount of road map data are stored on external databases, which can be accessed right away by our DBA*-implementation. Finally, since uncertainty reasoning can be integrated into deductive databases with least fixpoint semantics equally smoothly ([SSGK89]), we expect that the DBA*-algorithm can be applied successfully to this important class of DB-applications, too.

Literature

[AHU74] Aho, A.; Hopcroft, J.; Ullman, J.: *The Design and Analysis of Computer Algorithms*, Addison Wesley, 1974.

[AhU79] Aho, A.; Ullman, J.: *Universality of Data Retrieval Languages*, 6th ACM Symposium on Principles of Programming Languages, 1979, pp. 110 - 120.

[Ban86] Bancilhon, F.: *Naive Evaluation of Recursively Defined Relations*, in *On Knowledge Base Management Systems*, Brodie and Mylopoulos, eds, Springer, 1986, pp. 120 - 129.

[BaR86]   Bancilhon, F.; Ramakrishan, R.: *An amateurs introduction to recursive query processing strategies*, ACM SIGMOD, Washington, May 1986, pp. 16 - 52.

[Bay85]   Bayer, R.: *Database Technology for Expert Systems*, Internationaler GI-Kongress 85, Wissensbasierte Systeme, Informatik Fachberichte 112, Springer Verlag, 1985, pp. 1 - 16.

[BNRST87] Beeri, C.; Naqvi, S.; Ramakrishnan, R.; Shmueli, O.; Tsur, S.: *Sets and Negation in a Logic Database Language (LDL1)*, 6th ACM Symposium on Principles of Database Systems, San Diego, March, 1987, pp. 21 - 37.

[BaR87]   Balbin, J.; Ramamohanarao, K.: *A Generalization of the Differential Approach to Recursive Query Evaluation*, Journal of Logic Programming, Vol. 4, No. 3, Sept. 1987, pp. 259 - 262.

[GKB87]   Güntzer, U.; Kiessling, W.; Bayer, R.: *On the Evaluation of Recursion in (Deductive) Database Systems by Efficient Differential Fixpoint Iteration*, 3rd International Conference on Data Engineering, Los Angeles, Febr. 1987, pp. 120 - 129.

[KHISSS84] Kung, R.; Hanson, E.; Ioannidis, Y.; Sellis, T.; Shapiro, L.; Stonebraker, M.: *Heuristic Search in Data Base Systems*, 1st International Workshop on Expert Database Systems, Kiawah Island, Oct. 1984, pp. 96 - 107.

[Kor85]   Korf, R.: *Depth-First Iterative-Deepening: An Optimal Admissible Tree Search*, Artificial Intelligence 27, 1985, pp. 97 - 109.

[Llo87]   Lloyd, J.W.: *Foundations of Logic Programming*, Springer Verlag, 1987.

[MUvG86]   Morris, K.; Ullman, J.; van Gelder, A.: *Design Overview of the NAIL! system*, 3rd International Conference on Logic Programming, London, 1986, pp. 554 - 568.

[Nil80]   Nilsson, N.: *Principles of Artificial Intelligence*, Tioga, 1980.

[Pea84]   Pearl, J.: *Heuristics*, Addison-Wesley, 1984.

[SaZ86]   Sacca, D.; Zaniolo, C.: *On the Implementation of a Simple Class of Logic Queries for Databases*, ACM SIGMOD, Washington, May 1986, pp. 16 - 23.

[SKGB87]   Schmidt, H.; Kiessling, W.; Güntzer, U.; Bayer, R.: *Compiling Exploratory and Goal-Directed Deduction into Sloppy Delta-Iteration*, 4th IEEE Symposium on Logic Programming, San Francisco, Sept. 1987, pp. 234 - 243.

[SSGK89]   Steger, N.; Schmidt, H.; Güntzer, U.; Kiessling, W.: *Semantics and Efficient Compilation for Quantitative Deductive Databases*, 5th International Conference on Data Engineering, Los Angeles, Febr. 1989.

[Ull85]   Ullman, J.: *Implementations of Logical Query Languages for Databases*, ACM Transactions on Database Systems, Vol. 10, No. 3, Sept. 1985, pp. 289 - 321.

[vEK76]   van Emden, M.; Kowalski, R.: *Semantics of Predicate Logic as a Programming Language*, Journal ACM, 23, 4, Oct. 1976, pp. 733 - 742.

[Vie88]   Vieille, L.: *From QSQ to QoSaQ: Global Optimization of Recursive Queries*, 2nd International Conference on Expert Database Systems, Tysons Corner, April 1988, pp. 421 - 436.

[Zan85]   Zaniolo, C.: *The Representation and Deductive Retrieval of Complex Objects*, VLDB 85, Stockholm, 1985, pp. 458 - 469.

Appendix 1

Benchmark results for the 15-Puzzle (for *breadth* = 1 and *depth* = 1). The instance numbers in the following table refer to the problem instances given by [Kor85]. The measurements were obtained on MAD's Series 3000 Intelligent Workstation, which is a 80386-based system. Declare, RelationalLisp and the DBA*-algorithm were implemented on Lucid CommonLisp, under UNIX V.3.

instance	time in sec.	number of gene-rated tuples	number of select-project queries	number of union queries
1	34.4	885	2251	451
2	57.4	1193	3276	656
3	70.3	1444	3756	752
4	58.3	1224	3136	628
5	77.9	1582	4216	844
6	38.4	977	2566	514
7	23.2	645	1706	342
8	19.0	548	1451	291
9	258.9	3715	9586	1918
10	175.0	2835	7636	1528
11	21.3	605	1586	318
12	18.6	540	1431	287
13	23.4	644	1751	351
14	40.7	1022	2651	531
15	243.4	3521	9311	1863
16	9.5	295	776	156
17	39.6	1006	2566	514
18	14.6	436	1146	230
19	13.0	397	1006	202
20	356.0	4332	11581	2317
21	11.0	339	896	180
22	210.9	3158	8196	1640
23	81.9	1629	4176	836
24	138.7	2351	6366	1274
25	74.2	1551	3856	772
26	57.1	1203	3146	630
27	7.8	250	636	128
28	173.2	2790	7511	1503
29	100.9	1939	5066	1014
30	32.8	864	2301	461
31	37.2	952	2521	505
32	78.8	1590	4241	849

Appendix 2

Benchmark results for the Traveling Salesman Problem (for *depth* = 1).

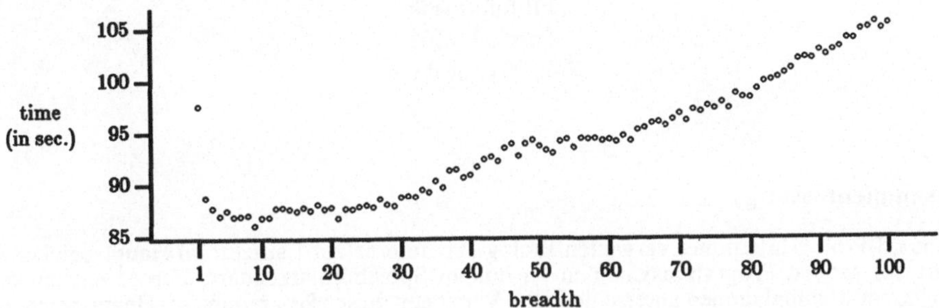

Figure 1. time vs. breadth for 12 cities

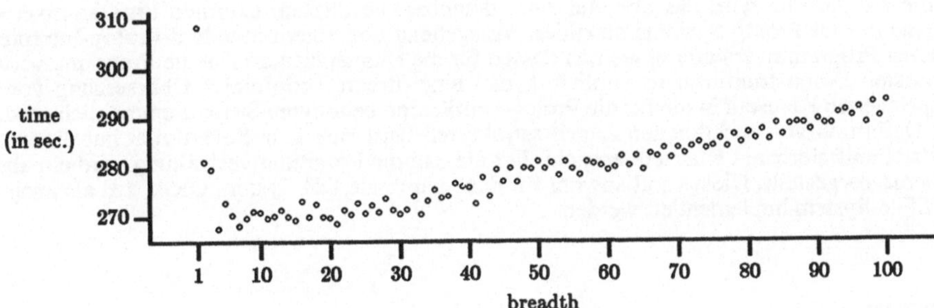

Figure 2. time vs. breadth for 13 cities

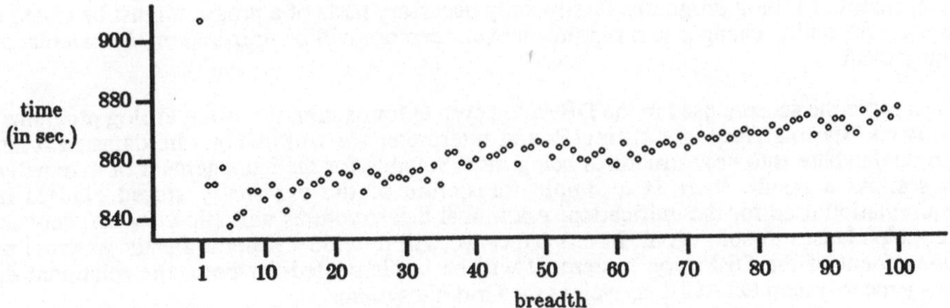

Figure 3. time vs. breadth for 14 cities

Prolog und Datenbanken: Ein Schema für die externe Verwaltung von Prolog-Programmen

Heinrich Jasper
Universität Oldenburg
FB Informatik
Postfach 2503
D-2900 Oldenburg

Zusammenfassung

Standard-Prolog-Interpreter verwalten Prolog-Programme zur Laufzeit im Hauptspeicher. Dieses führt bei großen Programmsystemen zu hohem Speicherplatzbedarf. Ferner entstehen durch Programm-Manipulationen unterschiedliche Versionen dieser Programme im Hauptspeicher und in den externen Dateien. Eine datenbankgestützte Prolog-Programmierumgebung vermeidet diese Nachteile dadurch, daß nur die für eine aktuelle Abfrage relevanten Teile der Prolog-Programme im Hauptspeicher vorgehalten und Veränderungen an den Programmen sofort in der Programmdatenbank nachgehalten werden.

In diesem Aufsatz wird das Schema einer datenbankgestützten, externen Programmverwaltung anhand des DBProlog-Systems diskutiert. Ausgehend von einem Standard-Prolog-Interpreter mit interner Programmverwaltung werden dessen für die hauptspeicherresidente Programmverwaltung benutzten Datenstrukturen so verändert, daß eine direkte (minimale) Übersetzung von extern gespeicherten Klauseln in die für die Prolog-Unifikation benötigten Strukturen möglich wird. Durch die Definition von zusätzlichen Zugriffsstrukturen wird eine gute Selektivität auf die mit einem Teilziel unifizierbaren Klauseln erreicht. Für die externe Programmverwaltung wird ein abstraktes Schema vorgestellt. Dieses soll sowohl für das relationale DB-System ORACLE als auch für das GridFile-System implementiert werden.

Abstract

Standard Prolog interpreters store the programs in main memory at run time. This results in a huge amount of main memory that is necessary for interpreting large programs. Furthermore, manipulating programs with built-in predicates leads to different versions of these programs in main memory and on external files. These deficiencies will be overcome by using a database for the management of Prolog programs. Firstly, only necessary parts of a program must be stored in main memory. Secondly, changes to programs in main memory will be mirrored on the external program management.

In this paper the schema used in the DBProlog system for externally storing Prolog programs will be discussed. Starting from an existing Prolog interpreter we will change the datastructures of the internal database into new structures being more suitable for the management of externally stored clauses. As a result, there is a simple translation of the externally stored clauses into the representation used for the unification. Additional datastructures will allow for efficient access of unifyable clauses to some goal. In this paper we will provide a schema for the external program management of the DBProlog system. It will be implemented for both, the relational database management system ORACLE as well as the GridFile system.

1. Einleitung

Standard-Prolog-Interpreter verwalten Prolog-Programme zur Laufzeit im Hauptspeicher, was bei großen Programmsystemen zu einem entsprechend hohen Speicherplatzbedarf führt. Ferner entstehen durch die Benutzung eingebauter Prädikate zur Manipulation von Programmen unterschiedliche Versionen dieser Programme im Hauptspeicher und in den externen Dateien.

Eine datenbankgestützte Prolog-Programmierumgebung vermeidet diese Nachteile dadurch, daß

1. nur die für die Beantwortung der aktuellen Anfrage notwendigen Teile der Prolog-Programme in den Hauptspeicher geladen werden. Dadurch wird nicht nur der benötigte Speicherplatz reduziert, sondern durch geeignete Zugriffsmechanismen wird auch der Suchraum für die Unifikation kleiner. Somit können sehr große Prolog-Programme effizient bzgl. Speicherplatz und Zeit bearbeitet werden.

2. Prolog-Programme dynamisch verwaltet werden können, d.h. die durch eingebaute Prädikate vorgenommenen Änderungen an Prolog-Programmen werden permanent in der für die Programmverwaltung benutzten Datenbank gespeichert.

In dieser Arbeit werden die Speicherung von Prolog-Programmen in Datenbanken und der Zugriff auf diese gespeicherten Programme während der Beantwortung einer an das Prolog-System gestellten Anfrage untersucht. Eine solche datenbankgestützte Prolog-Programmierumgebung soll im System DBProlog realisiert werden.

Das Thema "Prolog und Datenbanken" hat in den letzten Jahren ein breites Interesse gefunden, wie Veröffentlichungen in den entsprechenden Tagungsbänden (siehe z.B. die speziellen Tagungen EDS'84, EDS'86, EDS'88, LPDB´86, sowie die SIGMOD-, VLDB- und BTW-Bände) zeigen. Die meisten Arbeiten beziehen sich auf eine Integration einer externen Daten- bzw. Faktenverwaltung in die jeweilige Prolog-Umgebung, d.h. für in Prolog geschriebene Anwendungen wird der Zugriff auf (i.a. relationale) Datenbanken ermöglicht.

In der Literatur gibt es vergleichsweise wenig Arbeiten, die sich mit der Speicherung von kompletten Prolog-Programmen in Datenbanken befassen. Nussbaum'88 und Sellis/ Roussopoulos'88 ermöglichen zwar beide die Speicherung (einer Teilmenge) von Prolog-Programmen, aber durch die jeweils benutzte Berechnungsregel für Ableitungen wird die z.B. in Clocksin / Mellish'87 beschriebene Semantik von Prolog verletzt.

Zwei weitere Ansätze (siehe Appelrath'85 bzw. Bocca'85) realisieren explizit jeweils ein Prolog-System, das die Programme in einer Datenbank verwaltet. Der in Bocca'85 beschriebene Ansatz erlaubt, eine Teilmenge der Regeln in einer Relation zu speichern. Ein modifizierter Prolog-Inferenzmechanismus lädt die zu einer Anfrage relevanten Regeln, bevor auf die ebenfalls in der Datenbank gespeicherten Fakten zugegriffen wird. Dieser Ansatz bewahrt jedoch nicht die Semantik von Prolog, da dazu die gemischte Abarbeitung von Fakten und Regeln in der Reihenfolge ihrer Eingabe notwendig ist.

Der Ansatz in Appelrath'85 garantiert zwar die Semantik von Prolog, die dort vorgenommene Speicherung von Prolog-Programmen, bei der die Argumente der Literale der Klauseln bis auf Symbolebene aufgebrochen und in einer Relation abgelegt werden, ist jedoch nicht sehr effizient.

Die Probleme, die bei der externen Prolog-Programmverwaltung mittels Datenbanken auftreten, betreffen generell folgende Themenbereiche:

1. Speicherung komplexer Objekte dynamischer Größe

   Prolog-Programme bestehen aus Klauseln, die jeweils aus einer Liste von Literalen aufgebaut sind. Jedes Literal kann als Baum repräsentiert werden. Diese Bäume können eine beliebige Höhe und einen beliebigen Verzweigungsgrad besitzen.

2. Definition von Zugriffsstrukturen

   Um während der Beantwortung einer Anfrage effizient auf die mit einem Teilziel unifizierbaren Klauseln zugreifen zu können, sollte die externe Programmverwaltung geeignete Zugriffsmechanismen bereitstellen.

3. Unterschiedliche Semantik von Prolog-Ableitungsstrategie und DB-Manipulationssprache

Die Reihenfolge der Abarbeitung von Prolog-Klauseln ist durch deren Eingabereihenfolge definiert. Ferner wird im Prolog-Ableitungsmechanismus immer nur eine Klausel zu einem Zeitpunkt untersucht. Da diese Eigenschaften von Prolog im DBProlog-System bewahrt werden sollen, müssen die notwendigen Umsetzungen in einer Schnittstelle zwischen Prolog-System und Datenbanksystem vorgenommen werden.

Das DBProlog-System baut auf einen Interpreter auf, der die in Clocksin/Mellish'87 beschriebene Funktionalität (insbesondere bezüglich Umfang der eingebauten Prädikate) und zusätzlich ein Modulkonzept besitzt. Die Klauseln der Module werden so in der Datenbank gespeichert, daß keine größere Umsetzung der externen Klauselrepräsentation in die vom Unifikationsmechanismus benötigte Klauselrepräsentation notwendig wird. Zu den Klauseln werden teilweise redundante Zugriffsinformationen gespeichert, die den Zugriff auf eine möglichst minimale Obermenge der zu einem Literal unifizierbaren Klauseln ermöglichen. In dieser Arbeit konzentrieren wir uns auf die ersten beiden Probleme der obigen Aufzählung, das im dritten Punkt angesprochene Problem wird durch das in Jasper'87 beschriebene Modell gelöst.

Die nachfolgende Arbeit gliedert sich wie folgt: nach der Architekturübersicht in Abschnitt 2 wird in Abschnitt 3 die bisher übliche, hauptspeicherresidente Klauselverwaltung beschrieben. In Abschnitt 4 wird diese modifiziert und ein Schema für die externe Speicherung von Klauseln gegeben. Die Struktur der Zugriffsinformationen zu den Klauseln wird in Abschnitt 5 vorgestellt. In Abschnitt 6 wird die Abbildung des Schemas in eine ORACLE-Datenbank und in GridFiles (siehe Nievergelt et.al.'84) diskutiert. Ein Überblick über den Stand der Realisierung und eine kurze Zusammenfassung schließen die Arbeit ab.

2. Architektur des DBProlog-Systems

Abb. 1 veranschaulicht die drei Schichten der Architektur des DBProlog-Systems:
- DBProlog-Interpreter (I),
- DBProlog-Kopplungssystem (II) und
- DBProlog-Basissystem (III).

Der DBProlog-Interpreter (Schicht I) entspricht einem Standard-Prolog-Interpreter, jedoch ohne eine eigene Klauselverwaltung. Er besteht aus den sechs Modulen
- DBProlog-User-Interface: hier werden die Benutzeroberfläche und ein Programm-Editor realisiert,
- Parser: übersetzt textuell repräsentierte Prolog-Klauseln in eine interne Repräsentation und umgekehrt,
- Proof-Tree-Traverser: verwaltet den Ableitungsbaum,
- Built-In-Predicates: realisiert die eingebauten Prädikate,
- Fine-Filter: liefert zu einem Teilziel (einem Literal) unifizierbare Klauseln einschließlich der Bindungen,
- Unifier: unifiziert zwei Literale und liefert die entsprechenden Bindungen.

Das DBProlog-Kopplungssystem (Schicht II) bildet die für die Klauselverwaltung des DBProlog-Interpreters notwendigen Funktionen auf die vom Basissystem exportierten Funktionen ab. Dafür werden die folgenden Module benötigt:
- Scan-Manager: verwaltet eine Obermenge der unifizierbaren Klauseln für jedes Teilziel, und liefert diese einzeln und geordnet dem Fine-Filter (ein Funktionsmodell ist in Jasper'87 beschrieben),
- DB-Access: greift auf Relationen existierender Datenbanken zu,
- Clause-Translator: bildet die interne Repräsentation von Prolog-Klauseln auf DB-Relationen ab und verwaltet Zugriffsstrukturen,
- Virtual Scan-Manager: unterstützt virtuell die Verwaltung der Klauselmengen des Scan-Managers.

Das DBProlog-Basissystem (Schicht III) besteht aus
- dem für die Klauselverwaltung benutzten Datenbanksystem (DBMS),
- dem Kernel-Modul, das allgemein benutzte abstrakte Datentypen für das DBProlog-System zur Verfügung stellt,

- und der Modula-2-Bibliothek HOST, die eine Portabilität des DBProlog-Systems garantiert (z.Zt. ist HOST auf Sun, IBM RT, PCS Cadmus und Macintosh implementiert).

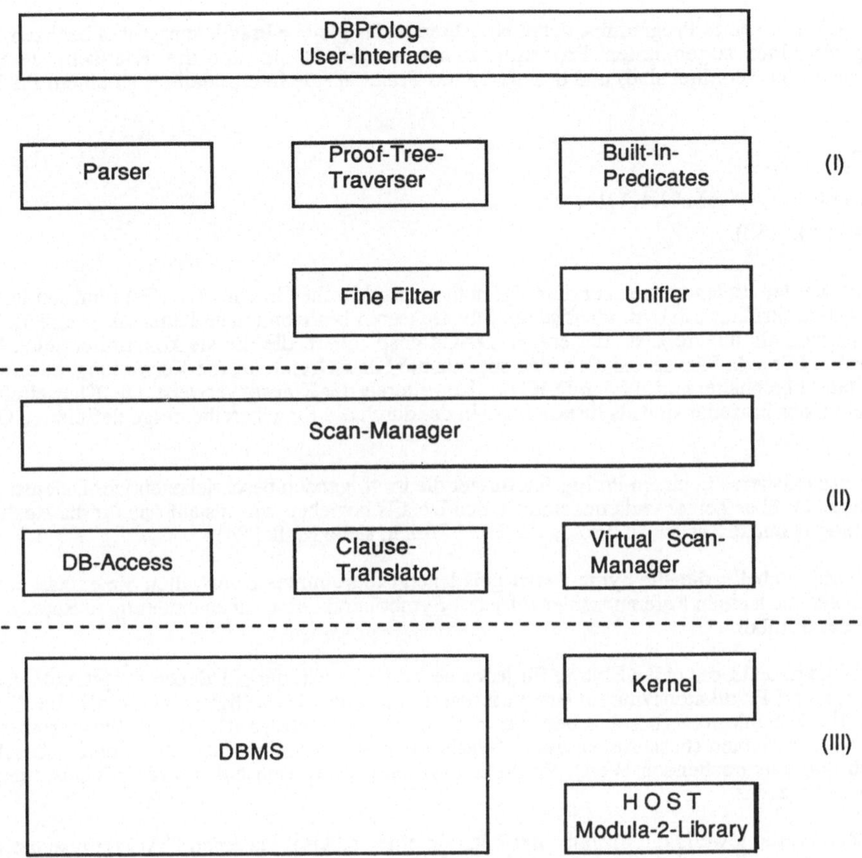

Abb. 1: DBProlog-Schichtenarchitektur

3. Prolog-Programmverwaltung im Hauptspeicher

Ein Standard-Prolog-Interpreter verwaltet die geladenen Programme im Hauptspeicher. Dazu wird i.a. eine (unten beschriebene) komprimierte Darstellung des Programmtextes benutzt. Der Programmtext ist eine Folge (geordnete Menge) von Klauseln, die jeweils aus einer nicht-leeren Folge von Literalen bestehen. Das erste Literal einer Klausel ist das Kopfliteral, die Elemente der (evtl. leeren) Restfolge heißen Rumpfliterale.

Ein Literal besteht aus einem Prädikatensymbol (Name und Stelligkeit) sowie aus einer gemäß dessen Stelligkeit definierten Anzahl von Argumenten. Der Name des Prädikatensymbols wird als alphanumerische Zeichenkette, beginnend mit einem kleinen Buchstaben geschrieben. Die Argumente sind entweder Konstante (unterschieden in Atome und Zahlen) Variablen oder Terme.

Prolog-Atome sind alphanumerische Zeichenketten einschließlich Sonderzeichen wie "!", "." etc., normalerweise beginnend mit einem kleinen Buchstaben oder in Hochkommata geschrieben. Zahlen werden in Ganzzahlen und Realzahlen unterschieden und sind i.a. maschinenabhängig definiert.

Variablen sind alphanumerische Zeichenketten, die mit einem Großbuchstaben oder einem Unterstrich beginnen. Anonyme Variablen bestehen nur aus einem Unterstrich. Mittels Funktoren (syntaktisch identisch mit Prädikatensymbolen) werden aus Konstanten bzw. Variablen rekursiv komplexe Strukturen, Terme genannt, gebildet, die eine Baumstruktur besitzen.

Diejenigen Klauseln eines Programms, deren Kopfliterale das gleiche Prädikatsymbol besitzen, werden in Prolog zu einer sogenannten Prozedur zusammengefaßt (in der die Klauseln gemäß der Eingabereihenfolge geordnet sind) und definieren das Prädikat (die Interpretation) zu einem Prädikatensymbol.

Beispiele für Klauseln:

> (i) $p(X) :- q(Y), r(s(X,Y), t(Y))$.

> (ii) $r(s(a, b), t(X))$.

Die Literale werden im Hauptspeicher durch gerichtete, azyklische Graphen (DAGs) repräsentiert, da sie eine baumartige Struktur mit evtl. identischen Substrukturen besitzen (siehe Kluzniak et.al.'85). Prolog-Klauseln werden als lineare Liste derjenigen DAGs gespeichert, die die sie konstituierenden Literale repräsentieren. Für jede Klausel existiert eine sogenannte Klauselreferenz, die Verwaltungsinformationen über die Klausel beinhaltet und auf den DAG des Kopfliterals der Klausel verweist. Die Klauselreferenzen der Klauseln einer Prozedur sind als lineare Liste in der durch die Eingabereihenfolge definierten Ordnung gespeichert.

Üblicherweise existieren in einem Prolog-Interpreter die im folgenden beschriebenen vier Datenstrukturen, die untereinander über Zeiger verkettet sind (in den Details beziehen wir uns auf das für die Realisierung von DBProlog benutzte System M2Prolog der ETH Zürich, siehe Muller'84) :

(i)   Die Symboltabelle, die alle Symbole der geladenen Programmtexte verwaltet. Sie enthält neben den Symbolen auch einen Referenzzähler für jedes Symbol und liefert einen eindeutigen Repräsentanten für jedes Symbol.

(ii)   Die Objekttabelle, die einen Eintrag für jedes benannte Objekt der geladenen Programme verwaltet. Objekte sind Prädikatensymbole (beschrieben durch Symbol, Stelligkeit und evtl. eine Operator-definition), Funktoren (beschrieben durch Symbol und Stelligkeit), Atome (beschrieben durch Symbol), Variablen (beschrieben durch Symbol und Variablennummer) und Zahlen (beschrieben durch den entsprechenden Wert). Prädikatensymbole verweisen auf die erste Klausel der zuge-hörigen Prozedur.

(iii)   Die Zellen, die jeweils die Struktur der Literale einer Klausel als einen DAG repräsentieren. Der "Inhalt" der Zellen wird durch Verweise auf die entsprechenden Objekte in der Objekttabelle definiert. Die zu einer Klausel gehörenden Zellen sind untereinander verkettet.

(iv)   Die Klauselreferenzen, die für jede gespeicherte Klausel den Verweis auf die erste Zelle der zugehörigen Liste der DAGs, die Anzahl der Zellen und der verschiedenen Variablen der Klausel sowie einen Verweis auf die nächste Klausel mit demselben Prädikatensymbol repräsentieren.

Die Extensionen dieser Datenstrukturen werden von einem Parser (siehe Abb. 1) erzeugt. Aus der internen Darstellung der Programme kann eine (normierte) textuelle Repräsentation zurückgewonnen werden. Als Beispiel für diese Datenstruktur sei die interne Repräsentation des Fakts "author('KOFIS', jasper)" in Abb. 2 visualisiert. (In der Darstellung wurde die vereinfachende Annahme gemacht, daß außer diesem Fakt keine anderen Objekte gespeichert sind.)

Die Abb. 3 zeigt den Zusammenhang zwischen den Datenstrukturen in einem vereinfachten Entity-Relationship-Modell nach Zehnder'87. Ellipsen bezeichnen dabei Enitätsmengen, zu den Beziehungen werden i.a. nur die Assoziationstypen gespeichert.

Aus der Abb. 3 wird ersichtlich, daß zu jeder Zelle genau ein Objekt existiert. Dieses beschreibt den Inhalt der Zelle, nämlich das zugehörige Symbol (bzw. dessen Wert, falls das Objekt eine Zahl ist) sowie bei einem Funktor bzw. Prädikatensymbol die Stelligkeit. Diejenigen Objekte, die Prädikatensymbole repräsentieren, verweisen über eine Klauselreferenz auf die erste Klausel der zugehörigen Prozedur.

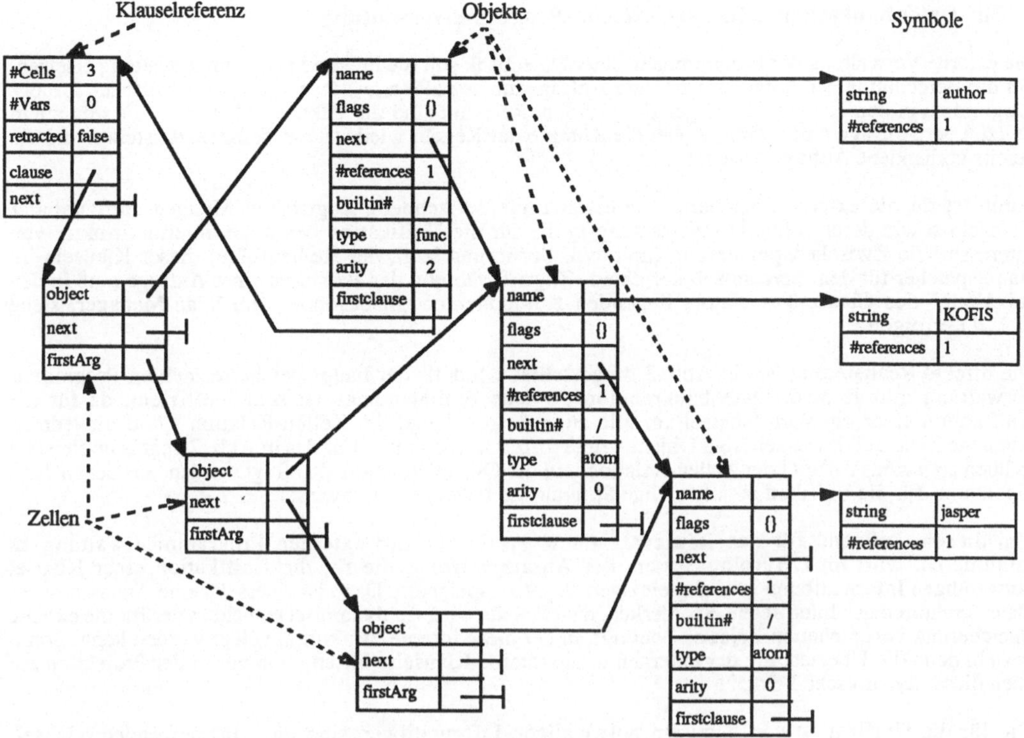

Abb. 2: Beispiel für eine hauptspeicherresidente Programmverwaltung

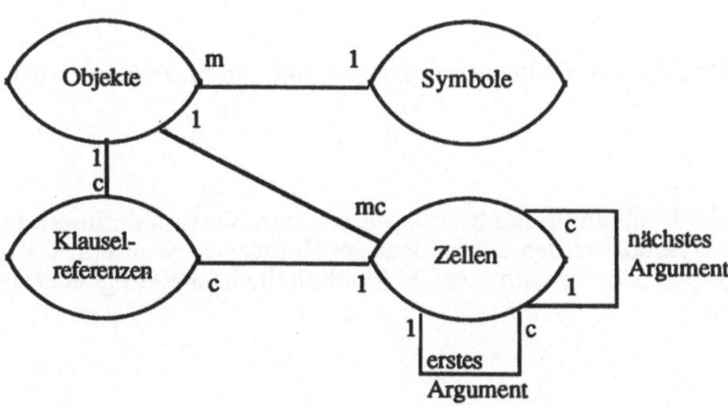

Abb. 3: Schema zur hauptspeicherresidenten Programmverwaltung

Während des Ableitungsprozesses wird für jedes Teilziel (entspricht einem Literal der aktuellen Anfrage) auf diejenigen Klauseln zugegriffen, deren Kopfliterale mit diesem Teilziel unifizieren. Eine Unifikation kann dann erfolgreich durchgeführt werden, wenn die Substrukturen der beiden Literale bis auf die in ihnen enthaltenen Variablen identisch sind.

4. Ein Datenbankschema für die externe Programmverwaltung

Die externe Verwaltung der Programme in einer Datenbank soll die interne Programmverwaltung ersetzen. Für die Berechnung der Antworten zu einer Anfrage müssen alle relevanten Teile der betroffenen Prolog-Programme in den Hauptspeicher geladen werden. Relevant sind die Fakten und Regeln, die mit einem Teilziel der Anfrage unifizieren, wobei die Rümpfe der Regeln wieder neue Teilziele darstellen und die bereits vorhandene Anfrage erweitern.

Somit ist für die externe Speicherung in erster Linie der schnelle Zugriff auf Mengen unifizierbarer Klauseln sowie deren schnelle Übersetzung in die für die Unifikation benötigte, interne Struktur von Interesse. Die Zwischenspeicherung (und evtl. Sortierung bzgl. der Reihenfolge) dieser Klauseln im Hauptspeicher für den "semantisch korrekten" Zugriff während des Beweises einer Anfrage muß in den "oberhalb" des Clause-Translators liegenden Komponenten (insbesondere im Scan-Manager, siehe Abb. 1) erfolgen.

Die direkte Realisierung des in Abb. 3 dargestellten Modells der hauptspeicherresidenten Programmverwaltung mittels einer Datenbankrelation für jede Entitätsmenge ist sehr ineffizient, da für die Unifikation einer einzigen Klausel auf alle zugehörigen Tupel der Zellen-Relation - und für jede so erhaltene Zelle auf das zugehörige Objekt - zugegriffen werden muß. Für das in Abb. 2 gegebene Beispiel müßten so jeweils 3 Tupel der Zellen-Relation und der Objekt-Relation abgefragt werden, aus denen dann die interne, für die Unifikation notwendige Struktur des Fakts generiert wird.

Um diesen Aufwand für das Retrieval von Klauseln aus der externen Programmverwaltung zu minimieren, wird im DBProlog-System der Ansatz verfolgt, die für die Unifikation einer Klausel notwendigen Informationen in einem einzigen Tupel zu speichern. Dazu ist einerseits eine Anpassung der Datenstrukturen des Interpreters erforderlich, andererseits wird ein dynamisches Feld in der für die externe Speicherung vorgesehenen Relation benötigt, in der diese interne Struktur abgelegt werden kann. Somit besteht dann die Übersetzung der externen in die interne Klauselrepräsentation nur in der Projektion auf eben dieses dynamische Feld.

Die für die Unifikation von Klauseln notwendigen Informationen sind die entsprechenden Klauselreferenzen, die zugehörigen Zellen und ein Teil der in den Objekten gespeicherten Informationen. Die Einträge in der Objekttabelle, die für die Unifikation benötigt werden, sind Objekttyp, Objektname (definiert durch den Symbolidentifikator) und bei Funktoren die Stelligkeit. Die anderen in den Objekten gespeicherten Informationen (z.B. Operatorvereinbarungen und Spy-Points) sind nur für die Darstellung der Objekte an der Interpreteroberfläche von Interesse. Sie werden in einer zusätzlichen Repräsentationstabelle abgelegt.

Im folgenden werden die im DBProlog-System benutzten Datenstrukturen im einzelnen diskutiert.

Symboltabelle

In der Symboltabelle werden alle Symbole (in der hier beschriebenen Version definiert durch Name und Stelligkeit) verwaltet. Für jedes Symbol werden ein eindeutiger Repräsentant und die Anzahl der Zellen, die das Symbol referenzieren, gespeichert. Die Struktur der Symboltabelle sieht folgendermaßen aus:

symbolId	NUMBER
string	STRING
arity	NUMBER
#references	NUMBER

Zellen

In den Zellen werden alle Informationen gespeichert, die für die Unifikation relevant sind. Je nach Typ des Objekts (die Menge der Typen "DBTypes" ist definiert als {atom, number, variable, functor, builtin, userdefined}), werden entweder die entsprechende symbolId (bei atom, variable oder functor), der Wert einer Zahl (bei number) oder die Nummer der entsprechenden Prozedur (bei builtin oder userdefined) gespeichert. Über firstArg und next werden die Zellen verkettet, im Falle einer Variablen wird statt firstArg die Variablennummer gespeichert.

type	DBPTypes						
symbolId	NUMBER	number	NUMBER	builtin#	NUMBER	uproc	NUMBER
firstArg	^Cell	varNum	NUMBER				
next	^Cell						

Repräsentationstabelle

Für einige Symbole existieren zusätzliche Informationen, die insbesondere die Darstellung dieser Symbole oder das Verhalten der Symbole während des Ableitungsprozesses betreffen. Dieses wird in der Repräsentationstabelle gespeichert, deren Einträge folgendermaßen aussehen:

symbolId	NUMBER
flags	FlagSet
opSpecifier	opSpecifiers
precedence	NUMBER

Der flags-Eintrag kennzeichnet verschiedene Eigenschaften, z.B. ob das Symbol für ein eingebautes Prädikat reserviert ist, oder ob die spy-Option für Klauseln zu diesem Symbol eingeschaltet ist. Eine Menge dieser Eigenschaften können einem Symbol zugewiesen werden. Für ein Symbol, das einen ein- oder zweistelligen Funktor repräsentiert, kann eine Operatordefinition vorgenommen werden. Dies wird in den Einträgen für opSpecifier und precedence festgehalten.

Klauselreferenzen

Die Klauselreferenzen sind wie in der alten Datenstruktur (siehe Abb. 2) definiert: es werden zu jeder Klausel die Anzahl der Zellen und Variablen gespeichert. Das "retracted"-Flag gibt an, ob eine Klausel aus dem hauptspeicherresidenten Auszug der aktuellen Datenbank gelöscht wurde. Der clause-Eintrag verweist auf die Zelle des Kopfliterals der Klausel, die nächste Klausel der Prozedur wird über den next-Zeiger referenziert.

#Cells	NUMBER
#Vars	NUMBER
retracted	BOOLEAN
clause	^Cell
next	^DB-node

In der so neu definierten internen Datenstruktur werden durch die Zusammenfassung von Objekt- und Klauselinformationen einige der in der alten Datenstruktur vorhandenen Einträge überflüssig. Das sind die Zeiger zur Verbindung von Objekten und Zellen sowie der Referenzzähler für die Objekte.

Abb. 4 zeigt das obige Beispielfakt in dieser neuen Datenstruktur.

Diese neue Datenstruktur benötigt mehr Speicherplatz als die alte, da die Tabellen weniger "normalisiert" sind. Der Mehrbedarf kann folgendermaßen abgeschätzt werden: Messungen mit verschiedenen Klauselmengen (Regelbasis mit ca. 150 Regeln eines Informationssystems und die Faktenbasis desselben Informationssystems mit ca. 3000 Fakten sowie eine Anwendung aus der Produktionsplanung) ergaben eine Häufigkeit von ca. 8 Zellen pro Objekt in der alten Datenstruktur.

In der neuen Datenstruktur wird für eine Zelle ein Speicherwort mehr (insgesamt jetzt 4 Worte) benötigt als in der alten Tabelle. Dafür fallen in der neuen Struktur die Objekteinträge weg, die je 8 Worte Speicherplatz benötigten. Somit entspricht der Speicherplatzbedarf für Objekte und Zellen in der alten Struktur (für jede Zelle 3 Worte plus ein Achtel der Größe eines Objekteintrags, insgesamt also 4 Worte) genau dem Speicherplatzbedarf für die Zellen in der neuen Datenstruktur.

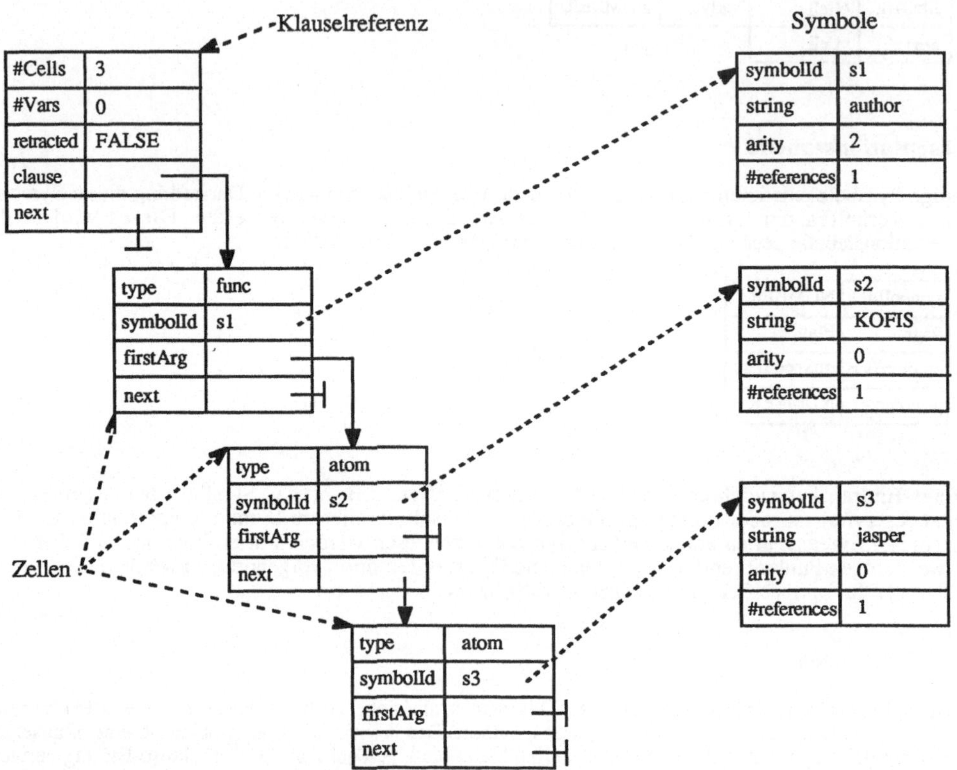

Abb. 4: Beispiel der neuen internen Datenstruktur

Da die Größe der Klauselreferenzen unverändert bleibt, müssen nur noch die Symboltabelleneinträge und die Repräsentationsinformationen betrachtet werden. In der Symboltabelle muß pro Symbol ein weiteres Wort gespeichert werden. Nur für bestimmte Symbole, für die zusätzliche Informationen gehalten werden müssen, werden Repräsentationsinformationen verwaltet.

Der Mehrbedarf M in Speicherworten wird also folgendermaßen berechnet:

$$M = M_{neu} - M_{alt} = \#\text{Symboltabelle} + (4 * \#\text{Repräsentationstabelle}),$$

wobei #Symboltabelle die Anzahl der Einträge in der Symboltabelle und #Repräsentationstabelle die Anzahl der Einträge in der Repräsentationstabelle bezeichnet.

Das Entity-Relationship-Schema für diese Datenstruktur ist in Abb. 5 dargestellt. Dieses Schema wird folgendermaßen auf DB-Relationen bzw. GridFiles abgebildet: die Entitätsmengen der Datenbankeinträge und Zellen werden zusammen in einer Klauseltabelle verwaltet, sodaß alle Informationen zu einer Klausel in einem Tupel abgelegt werden. Dies geschieht in der Form, daß die zu einer Klausel gehörenden Entitäten in einem Attribut mit dynamischem Wertebereich gespeichert werden. Diese Entitäten sind die zu der Klausel gehörende Klauselreferenz, die Zelle, auf die dieser Klauselreferenz verweist sowie die transitive Hülle der Nachfolgerzellen bzgl. "nächstes Argument" und "erstes Argument" zu dieser Zelle.

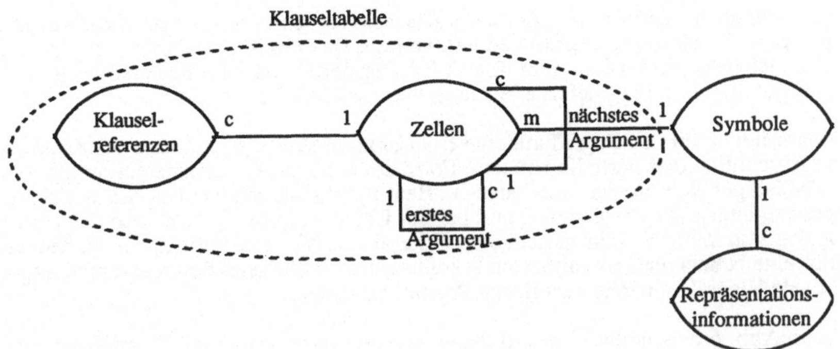

Abb. 5: Schema der neuen Datenstruktur

In der externen Datenbank werden die Zellen nicht miteinander verkettet, sondern sequentiell abgelegt. Die Linearisierung der Datenstruktur einer Klausel erfolgt in der Reihenfolge erst "erstes Argument"- und dann "nächstes Argument"-Zeiger (entspricht einem leftmost depth-first Durchlauf in der Baumdarstellung einer Klausel). Dadurch wird für jede Zelle nur noch der Speicherplatz von 2 Worten benötigt, da die Verzeigerung entfällt, jedoch muß das Ende der Argumentliste eines Funktors durch ein Sonderzeichen ("end-functor") definiert werden, da die Stelligkeit eines Funktors nicht explizit in der SymbolId codiert ist.

Das oben genannte Beispiel sieht dann als Eintrag in der Klauseltabelle wie in Abb. 6 veranschaulicht aus, wobei zu beachten ist, daß das Tupel nur in einem Attribut (mit dynamischen Wertebereich) gespeichert ist. Die interne Struktur des Tupels bleibt gegenüber dem benutzten Datenverwaltungssystem verborgen und wird "nur" von dem Unifikationsmechanismus bzw. Übersetzungskomponente "erkannt":

| 0 | 3 | functor | s1 | atom | s2 | atom | s3 | end-functor |

Abb. 6: Beispiel eines Tupels der Klauseltabelle

Die Belegungen in der Abb. 6 bedeuten das folgende: die beiden ersten Einträge entstammen der Klauselreferenz, die 0 steht für die Anzahl Variablen und die 3 definiert die Anzahl der Zellen (das retracted-Flag wird nicht gespeichert; es gibt eine hauptspeicherresidente Liste aller gelöschten Klauseln, die nach dem Ende einer Ableitung auf die externe Datenverwaltung übertragen wird). Jeder Eintrag, der eine Zelle repräsentiert, besitzt an der ersten Stelle den Typ des dargestellten Objekts. Die Verweise s1, s2 und s3 zeigen auf (unterschiedliche) Einträge in der Symboltabelle, der "end-functor"-Eintrag klammert die Argumente des Funktors "s1".

Durch das hier definierte "weniger normalisierte" Schema können keine zusätzlichen Probleme bei Änderungsoperationen auf Prolog-Programmen auftreten, da die in der DBProlog-Programmierumgebung definierten Änderungsoperationen, Transaktionen auf vollständigen Klausel sind. Von einer Änderung ist immer nur eine Klausel betroffen.

5. Zugriffsunterstützung für unifizierbare Klauselmengen

Wie in Abschnitt 3 beschrieben, ist für die Selektion (Unifikation) einer Klausel in einem Ableitungsschritt nur das Kopfliteral relevant. Zugriffsstrukturen (z.B. Indizes) mit einer guten Selektivität können die Anzahl der für eine Unifikation zu untersuchenden Klauseln reduzieren, und zwar werden im günstigsten Fall zu einer Anfrage genau die unifizierbaren Klauseln aus der externen Datenbank geliefert.

Für den Zugriff auf die zu einem Teilziel unifizierbaren Klauseln sollte mindestens das Prädikatensymbol (Name und Stelligkeit) als Selektionskriterium benutzt werden. Das Prädikatensymbol ist gemäß des in Abb. 6 beispielhaft gegebenen Schemas in dem dritten Eintrag der Klausel-Repräsentation gespeichert. Eine Identitätsabfrage auf diesen Eintrag liefert alle Klauseln einer Prozedur.

Als weitere Selektionskriterien für den Zugriff auf eine Klausel kommen die Argumente des Kopfliterals in Betracht. Für die in Abschnitt 4 definierte linearisierte Form der externen Klauselspeicherung gilt nun: da das Kopfliteral von beliebiger Komplexität sein kann - in Baumrepräsentation kann es eine beliebige Höhe und beliebigen Verzweigungsgrades besitzten -, und bei der Unifikation die beiden betrachteten Literale nicht syntaktisch gleich sein müssen - falls in dem einen Literal eine Variable auftritt, darf in dem anderen "an derselben Stelle" eine beliebiger Term auftreten -, können die für die Selektion relevanten Argumente der Kopfliterale für jede Klausel an unterschiedlichen Positionen stehen.

Somit kann für die in Abb. 6 beispielhaft beschriebene Klauselspeicherung eine Zugriffsunterstützung mittels indexierter Felder nur dann definiert werden, wenn unterschiedliche Relationen für die Klauseln definiert werden, deren Kopfliterale unterschiedliche Strukturen besitzen. Dieses würde jedoch zu einer Vielzahl von verschiedenen Relationen führen, da i.a. die Kopfliterale in den Prolog-Programmen sehr unterschiedliche Strukturen aufweisen.

Ferner ist es nicht möglich, alle Informationen der Kopfliterale in den Zugriffsstrukturen abzulegen, da die Kopfliterale als Bäume dynamischer Größe definiert werden können, und die Zugriffsstruktur eine statisch definierte Größe besitzen muß. Die Speicherung aller Informationen der Klauselköpfe einer Prozedur kann bei vielen Anwendungen zudem zu einem unnötigen Mehraufwand bzgl. der Dateiorganisation führen, da die meisten Prozeduren nur aus wenigen (ca. 1 bis 5) Klauseln bestehen.

Es ist ersichtlich, daß die bisher definierte, aus einem Attribut bestehende Klauseltabelle für eine Zugriffsunterstützung nicht ausreichend ist. Um die unterschiedlichen Strukturen verschiedener Kopfliterale auf für relationale Datenbanken geeignete Zugriffsstrukturen abzubilden, benutzen wir das in Rothermel'88 beschriebene Verfahren. Dazu ist ein Adressierungsschema für die in einem Literal auftretenden Symbole (identifiziert durch Name und Stelligkeit) notwendig, sowie eine gesonderte Behandlung von Variablen. Das Adressierungsschema ist wie folgt definiert:

- Das Prädikatensymbol hat die Adresse 1.
- Die n Argumente des Prädikatensymbols haben die Adressen 1.1, . . ., 1.n.
- Die Argumente eines n-stelligen Funktors mit der Adresse k haben die Adressen k.1, . . ., k.n.

Mit diesem Schema werden nun diejenigen Stellen der Kopfliterale der Klauseln definiert (sogenannte Zugriffsadressen) definiert, die mit einer Indexierung unterstützt werden sollen. Diese Argumente werden auf Attribute der Klauseltabelle abgebildet. Die Anzahl der repräsentierten Stellen muß nicht mit der Anzahl der Attribute übereinstimmen, durch entsprechende Zuordnungsvorschriften und eine Kollisionsbehandlung kann dieser Fall auf Kosten der Selektivität realisiert werden (siehe Rothermel'88). Die Attribute für die Zugriffsunterstützung werden vor dem dynamischen Feld für die Klauselrepräsentation gespeichert, da einige Datenverwaltungssysteme, wie das GridFile, ein dynamisches Feld nur am Ende der Datensätze zulassen.

Die Zugriffsadressen müssen nicht für alle Klauseln in der Klauseltabelle identisch sein, sondern kann z.B. für jedes Programm oder jede Prozedur (der letzte Fall wird im DBProlog-Ansatz realisiert) anders definiert werden. Dann muß jedoch zu einem Programm bzw. einer Prozedur (in diesem Fall z.B. in den Repräsentationsinformationen) die Information über die Zugriffsadressen gespeichert werden.

Die Beispiele in Abb. 7 verdeutlichen diesen Abbildungsprozeß. Es sei eine Klauseltabelle unterstellt, die Attribute A1 und A2 für die Zugriffsunterstützung sowieein dynamisches Nichtschlüsselfeld A3 für die Klauselrepräsentation habe. Die Zugriffsstruktur sei (1, 1.1, 1.2), das sind das Prädikatsymbol und die ersten beiden Argumente des Kopfliterals.

Die Abbildung der drei Adressen der Zugriffsstruktur auf die beiden Attribute erfolgt folgendermaßen: 1 -> A1, 1.1 -> A2 und 1.2 -> A2. Zur Vereinfachung wird die Klausel symbolisch repräsentiert, "V" bedeutet Variable, "*" bedeutet Kollision.

(i)   p(X) :- q(Y), r(s(X,Y),t(Y)).   => | p/1 | V | p(X) :- q(Y), r(s(X,Y),t(Y)) |

(ii)   r(s(a,b)).   => | r/2 | s/2 | r(s(a,b)) |

(iii) author('KOFIS', jasper).   => | author/2 | * | author('KOFIS', jasper) |

Abb. 7: Beispiele für die Repräsentation von Klauseln mit Zugriffsinformationen

Die Zugriffsinformationen sind somit redundant zur Klausel und in weitere Attribute untergliedert, während die Klauselrepräsentation weiterhin in einem Attribut gespeichert wird. Die Zugriffsadressen zusammen mit der Abbildung auf die Attribute der Klauseltabelle wird im folgenden Zugriffsstruktur genannt.

Die Verwaltung der Reihenfolge der Klauseln wird mittels eines systemdefinierten Attributs durchgeführt, das die Position einer Klausel in der Menge der bekannten Klauseln definiert und eindeutig ist. Dieses Attribut wird ferner im Scan-Manager (siehe Abb. 1) für die Identifizierung von bestimmten Instanzen einer Klausel benutzt.

Die Zugriffsstruktur wird für jede Prozedur eines Programms extra generiert, um eine möglichst gute Selektivität zu erhalten. Sie wird, wie in Rothermel'88 beschrieben, sowohl für die Speicherung der Klauseln als auch für die Generierung von Anfragen zu einem Teilziel während des Ableitungsprozesses genutzt. Die Antwort zu einer solchen Anfrage ist eine Obermenge der unifizierbaren Klauseln, da einerseits nicht in jedem Fall alle Terme der Kopfliterale dargestellt werden können, und andererseits bei der Abbildung der Adressen auf weniger Attribute Informationen verloren gehen. Diese Zugriffsstruktur wird im DBProlog-System in der Repräsentationstabelle abgelegt (diese ist i.a. klein und kann im Hauptspeicher gehalten werden).

Für die Generierung der Zugriffsstrukturen sind verschiedene Verfahren denkbar, die in Zukunft noch weiter untersucht werden müssen. Stichworte in diesem Zusammenhang sind z.B. minimale Anzahl derjenigen Argumente, die Eindeutigkeit einer Klausel einer Prozedur definieren, Häufigkeit des Zugriffs auf bestimmte Klauseln einer Prozedur etc.

6. Abbildung des Schemas auf ORACLE- und GridFile-Datenbanken

In diesem Kapitel wird unterstellt, daß das ORACLE (SQL)- bzw. das GridFile-System soweit bekannt sind, daß die untenstehenden Definitionen der Relationen bzw. GridFiles nachvollziehbar sind. Es wird in beiden Fällen eine Zugriffsstruktur definiert, die eine Speicherung von 2 Argumenten der Kopfliterale der Klauseln erlaubt. Zuerst werden die Tabellen einer ORACLE-Datenbank für die Speicherung von DBProlog-Programmen anhand der Befehle zur Generierung der Datenbank vorgestellt.

Diese generieren die folgenden 3 Relationen:

Symboltabelle:

```
CREATE TABLE Symbols
    SymbolId     NUMBER(10),
    HValue       NUMBER(10),
    Arity        NUMBER(5),
    References   NUMBER(5),
    Name         LONG;
```

SymbolId definiert einen eindeutigen Bezeichner für jedes Symbol. Das Feld HValue wird mittels einer Hashfunktion aus dem Namen des Symbols berechnet und dient dem Zugriff über den Namen eines Symbols, da über LONG-Felder kein Zugriff möglich ist. Der Name selbst (dargestellt als eine Sequenz von Buchstaben) kann sehr unterschiedliche Längen annehmen und wird daher in einem LONG-Feld dargestellt.

Klauseltabelle:

```
CREATE TABLE Clauses
    TID            NUMBER(10),      (* TID für die Klausel *)
    FirstSymbol    NUMBER(10),      (* erstes relevantes Argument, i.a. Prädikatensymbol *)
    SecondSymbol   NUMBER(10),      (* zweites relevantes Argument *)
    Clause         LONG RAW.        (* Code der Klausel in interner Repräsentation *)
```

Veränderungen der Klauseltabelle, wie z.B. Einbeziehung eines weiteren Attributes für die Zugriffsunterstützung, führen nicht zu einer Neuorganisation der bisher gespeicherten Klauseln, sofern die neuen Attribute mit einem DUMMY-Symbol belegt werden. Der Zugriff wird über die Zugriffsstruktur definiert, die die Abbildung auf die "alten" Attribute beibehält.

Repräsentationstabelle:

```
CREATE TABLE RepresentationInfo
    SymbolId    NUMBER(10),
    Flags  RAW(4),
    OpSpecifier    RAW(4),
    Precedence    NUMBER(2),
    AccessStr    LONG RAW.
```

Die Repräsentationstabelle beinhaltet Informationen über Prädikatensymbole und Funktoren (Flags, OpSpecifiers, Precedence) und Vorschriften für die Zuordnung der Kopfliteral-Informationen zu den Attributen der Zugriffsstruktur (AccessStr). Diese Tabelle ist i.a. klein und kann im Hauptspeicher verwaltet werden.

Entsprechend werden 3 GridFiles zur Speicherung der oben angegebenen Datenstrukturen definiert, wobei hier nur die interne Struktur der GridFile-records angegeben wird, sowie ein Hinweis, ob ein Eintrag ein Schlüsselfeld ist:

Symboltabellen-GridFile:

```
0..3:     HValue (Schlüsselfeld),
4..7:     SymbolId (Schlüsselfeld),
8..9:     Arity (Schlüsselfeld),
10..13:   References,
14..xx:   Symbol (dynamisch langer String als ARRAY OF BYTE).
```


Klauseltabellen-GridFile:

```
0..3:     TID für die Klausel (Schlüsselfeld)
4..7:     SymbolId für das erste relevante Argument, i.a. Prädikatensymbol (Schlüsselfeld)
8..9:     SymbolId für das zweite relevante Argument (Schlüsselfeld)
10..xx:   Code der Klausel in interner Repräsentation gem. der Definition in Abschnitt 4.
```


Repräsentationstabellen-GridFile:

```
0..3:     SymbolId (Schlüsselfeld),
4..7:     Flags,
8..9:     OpSpecifier,
10..13:   Precedence,
14..xx:   AccessStr (dynamisch langer String als ARRAY OF BYTE).
```

7. Stand der Arbeit

Die hier beschriebene externe Prolog-Programmverwaltung wird zur Zeit im Rahmen eines EUREKA-Projektes (siehe Appelrath'87) an der Universität Oldenburg realisiert. Eine erste Version, die das Datenverwaltungssystem GridFile nutzt, ist für das Frühjahr 1989 geplant.

Aufbauend auf der HOST-Schnittstelle und dem GridFile werden zur Zeit die Module Kernel und Clause-Translator (siehe Abb. 1) implementiert. Dabei werden die in dieser Arbeit beschriebenen Datenstrukturen in die abstrakten Datentypen des Kernel-Moduls integriert. Die Algorithmen zur Übersetzung von Klauseln aus der internen Datenstruktur in die Datenbankrepräsentation und umgekehrt werden im Clause-Translator-Modul realisiert.

Zur ersten Version des DBProlog-Systems gehört ebenfalls der Scan-Manager, der das in Jasper'87 beschriebene Modell für eine prologkonforme Verwaltung von Antwortmengen enthält. Weiterhin werden in diesem Modul die Anfragen vom Fine-Filter-Modul mittels der Zugriffsstruktur der zugehörigen Prozedur auf die Attribute der Klauseltabelle abgebildet.

Die Module aus der Schicht I der DBProlog-Architektur (siehe Abb. 1) werden von dem vorhandenen M2Prolog-Interpreter übernommen und an die neuen Datenstrukturen entsprechend angepaßt.

Die Module DB-Access und Virtual Scan-Manager werden erst in einer späteren Version des DBProlog-Systems berücksichtigt.

8. Zusammenfassung und Ausblick

Wir haben ein Schema für die externe Speicherung von Prolog-Programmen vorgestellt. Dieses entstand durch Änderung der Datenstrukturen für die hauptspeicherresidente Verwaltung von Prolog-Programmen. Durch die Benutzung von Attributen mit dynamischen Wertebereichen ist es möglich, komplexe Objekte dynamischer Größe extern zu verwalten. Die Speicherung der für die Unifikation benötigten Informationen einer Klausel in einem einzigen Tupel liefert zusammen mit den parametrisierbaren Zugriffsstrukturen für Klauselmengen eine effiziente Unterstützung beim Zugriff auf extern gespeicherte unifizierbare Klauseln.

Derzeit gibt es weitere Überlegungen zur Minimierung der Anzahl der Zugriffe auf extern gespeicherte Klauseln. Diese betreffen die Punkte

- geeignete Definition relevanter Zugriffsadressen für die Klauseln einer Prozedur. Hierbei ist die Selektivität der an bestimmten Adressen eines Kopfliterals vorhandenen Symbole zu berücksichtigen.

- Ausnutzung von z.B. Teilmengenbeziehungen zwischen Antwortmengen.

- Übersetzung von mehr als einem Teilziel einer aktuellen Anfrage in eine Datenbankanfrage, um den Join-Operator der externen Datenverwaltung nutzen zu können (siehe z.B. Venken'84).

Das Laufzeitverhalten des DBProlog-Systems wird vermutlich stark von der Strategie der Klauseleinlagerung beeinflußt. Bei der vollständigen Einlagern aller zur Beantwortung einer Anfrage benötigten Klauseln vor der Ausführung der entsprechenden Berechnungen entspricht die Laufzeit derjenigen des M2Prolog-Systems. Wie sie sich bei einer interaktiven Einlagerungsstrategie verhält, müssen umfangreiche Tests zeigen.

Bei der Diskussion der externen Verwaltung von Prolog-Programmen tritt auch immer wieder die Frage nach einem Wissensbasis-Managementsystem auf. Zur Realisierung solcher Systeme müssen der hier vorgestellte Ansatz erweitert und die Eignung z.B. des GridFiles im Rahmen einer Mehrbenutzerumgebung untersucht werden.

Literatur

Appelrath'85 — Appelrath, H.-J.: "Von Datenbanken zu Expertensystemen", Informatik Fachberichte Nr. 102, Springer Verlag, 1985.

Appelrath'87 — Appelrath, H.-J.: "PROTOS- Prolog Tools for Building Expert Systems", in "GI-Kongress 1987, Wissensbasierte Systeme", Informatik Fachberichte Nr. 155, Springer Verlag, 1987.

Bocca'86 — Bocca, J.: "On the Evaluation Strategy of EDUCE", in ACM SIGMOD '86, 1986.

Clocksin/ Mellish'87 — Clocksin, W. F.; Mellish, C. S.: "Programming in Prolog", 3rd edition, Springer Verlag, 1987.

EDS'84 — Kerschberg, L. (ed.): "Expert Database Systems", proceedings of the 1st intern. workshop on Expert Database Systems, Addison Wesley, 1986

EDS'86 — Kerschberg, L. (ed.): "Expert Database Systems", proceedings of the 1st intern. conference on Expert Database Systems, Benjamin/Cummings Publ. Inc., 1986.

EDS'88 — Kerschberg, L. (ed.): "Expert Database Systems", proceedings of the 2nd intern. conf. on Expert Database Systems, George Mason Univ., Fairfax, Virginia, 1988.

Jasper'87 — Jasper, H.: "Interfacing Prolog and External Data Management Systems: A Model", in GWAI-87, Proc. of the 11th German Workshop on Artificial Intelligence, Geseke, 1987.

Kluzniak et.al.'85 — Kluzniak, F.; Szpakowicz, S.; Bien J.S.: "Prolog for Programmers", Academic Press, London, 1985.

LPDB'86 — Proceedings of the "Workshop on Integration of Logic Programming and Data Bases", Commission of the Europ. Com., Esprit Project 530, Venice, December 1986.

Muller'84 — Muller, C.: "A Prolog Front End To The GridFile", Diplomarbeit, ETH Zürich, 1984.

Nievergelt et.al.'84 — Nievergelt, J.; Hinterberger, H.; Sevik, K.C.: "The GridFile: An Adaptable, Symmetric Multikey File Structure", ACM TODS, Vol. 9, No. 1, pp. 38 - 71, 1984.

Nussbaum'88 — Nussbaum, M.: "Delayed Evaluation in Logic Programming: An Inference Mechanism for Large Knowledge Bases", Dissertation 8542, ETH Zürich, 1988.

Rothermel'88 — Rothermel, K.: "An Effective Method for Storing and Retrieving PROLOG Clauses from a Relational Database", 3rd Int. Conf. on Data and Konwledge Bases, Jerusalem, 1988.

Venken'84 — Venken, R.: "A Prolog Meta-Interpreter for Partial Evaluation and its Application to Source to Source Transformation and Query-Optimization", in proceedings ECAI '84, "Advances in Artificial Intelligence", T. O'Shea (ed.), North-Holland, 1984.

Zehnder'87 — Zehnder, C.A.: "Informationssysteme und Datenbanken", Teubner, Stuttgart, 1987.

Making the Partial Transitive Closure
an Elementary Database Operation

Bin Jiang

Technical University of Darmstadt

Computer Science Department

Alexanderstrasse 24

D-6100 Darmstadt, West-Germany

e-mail: jiang at ddadvs1.bitnet

Abstract

A framework for processing recursive queries is briefly described. In this framework, computation of partial transitive closures (PTC's) is considered as an elementary and essentially new database operation which deals with the recursion. To
realize this operation, a breath-first searching algorithm is proposed which works on
a successor-list representation of the directed graph representating a base relation.
The usage of these searching strategy and data structure leads to a very efficient
database PTC algorithm. Since the algorithm processes each relevant successor-list
only once, we show that it is not only computationally very efficient ($O(e')$ where
e' is the number of the relevant tuples to the query), but also most suitable in the
context of databases (I/O's). The locality of the computation allows a fairly simple
implementation on top of the DASDBS kernel.

1   Introduction

Generally, a (*deductive*) *database* contains two sorts of relations, so-called *base relations*,
and *derived relations*. Tuples in base relations are explicitly stored, whereas those of
derived relations are not. For each derived relation there is a set of rules in the database,
according to which the relation, i.e. data, is derived.

For *definite deductive databases* [GMN85] such rules are normally represented with
Horn-clauses which have the following form:

$$P_0(t_{01}, ..., t_{0n}) :- P_1(t_{11}, ..., t_{1r}), ..., P_m(t_{m1}, ..., t_{ms})$$

where $P_i(0 \leq i \leq m)$ are predicates with corresponding arities and t_{ij} are arguments of
the predicates, i.e. constants, variables or functions (but in our discussion no functions
are used as the arguments). P_0 is the *head* predicate of the clause and $P_1, ..., P_n$ are
body predicates. Each body predicate represents a relation in the database, either

base relation or derived relation while the head predicate represents only a derived relation. This rule means that if there are tuples $(t_{11},...,t_{tr})$ in the relation P_1 and ... and $(t_{m1},...,t_{ms})$ in the relation P_m, then there is a tuple $(t_{01},...,t_{0n})$ in the derived relation P_0. We also say that predicates $P_1,...,P_m$ imply P_0, respectively. If there is at least one body predicate in a rule which is implied directly or indirectly by its head predicate P_0 and vice versa, e.g. P implies Q, Q implies R and R implies P, then we say predicate P_0 (the relation) is *recursively defined*, the rule is a *recursive rule* and the queries on the relation are *recursive queries*.

As mentioned above, a derived relation can be defined by several rules. If at least one of them is recursive and only one of the body predicates in each recursive rule is implied by the head predicate, the derived relation is said *linear* and the recursive rules are called *linearly recursive*.

Essentially, one of the key problems in the implementation of deductive databases is efficient processing of recursive queries. Therefore, in the last years much effort has been made in searching for efficient approaches [AD88,AJ87,Ban85,BR86,BR87,GKB87] and [GSS87,HH87,HQC88,Ioa86,IR88,JAN87,Lu87,Nau87,RHDM86,SZ87,SS88,Vie86] and [YHH88].

Recently, based on the work in [Ioa85,Nau86], a promising framework has been developed. With this framework, every linearly recursive rule can be analyzed by using a graphical model, and then translated into so-called compiled formulas according to this analysis [YHH88]. Observing such compiled formulas, it can be seen that computing partial transitive closures is a reasonable computational unit and a new elementary database operation for recursive query processing[1].

This paper will follow this observation. To realize this new operation, a breath-first searching algorithm in graph theory is proposed [Baa83,Eve79,Tar83]. Unlike most other algorithms, this algorithm works on a successor-list representation of the directed graph representating a base relation and the access to the base relations is carried out at the very end of the processing. The usage of these searching strategy and data structure leads to a very efficient database PTC algorithm. Since the algorithm processes each relevant successor-list only once, we show that it is not only computationally very efficient ($O(e')$ where e' is the number of the relevant tuples (to the query) in the relation), but also most suitable in the context of databases (I/O's). It is also shown that the locality of the computation allows a fairly simple implementation on top of the DASDBS kernel.

The paper is organized as follows. In section 2 the compiled formulas of linear recursive rules are briefly described. It is shown that partial transitive closure is an elementary and new operational unit for recursive query processing. The algorithm proposed for computing partial transitive closures is described in section 3. In section 4, the complexity analysis of the algorithm and some comparisons with related work are given. In section 5 some implementation aspects are discussed. The last section gives a conclusion.

---

[1] It is considered as a new *computational* operation, not a new relational *algebraic* operation as the least fix-point operation in [AU79].

2 Compiled Formulas of Linearly Recursive Rules

The *compiled formula* of a linear recursive rule is a relational expression describing which operations will be made if the corresponding derived relation is computed.

Here we assume that each recursive predicate has only one non-recursive rule, i.e. the *exit rule*, with a single base predicate in its body, e.g. E_i, having the same arities i as the recursive predicate (If the arity is not given explicitly, binary is assumed). We call operations in $R \cdot S$ or shortly RS, P^l and P^* *composition*, i.e. the natural join followed by projection on the non-joined attributes, where R, S, P are relations and P is binary.

Now, the compiled formula of rule (1), for instance, is formula (2) given in the following:

$$ANC(x,y) : -par(x,z), ANC(z,y). \tag{1}$$

$$ANC = \bigcup_{l=0}^{\infty} (par^l \cdot E) = par^* \cdot E \tag{2}$$

In fact, this compiled formula can be obtained by *expanding* rule (1) gradually, and then the derived relation ANC contains the following components[2]:

$$
\begin{aligned}
&E(x_0, y_0); &&(= par^0 \cdot E)\\
&par(x_0, z_1), E(z_1, y_0); &&(= par^1 \cdot E)\\
&par(x_0, z_1), par(z_1, z_2), E(z_2, y_0); &&(= par^2 \cdot E)\\
&par(x_0, z_1), par(z_1, z_2), par(z_2, z_3), E(z_3, y_0); &&(= par^3 \cdot E)\\
&\vdots
\end{aligned}
$$

Here we will not repeat the results and details of the investigation in [YHH88]. We only give some examples of compiled formulas and discuss the issues of their computation.

Example 1: The compiled formulas of rules (3) and (4) are formulas (5) and (6), respectively:

$$SG(x,y) : -up(x,w), SG(w,z), down(z,y). \tag{3}$$

$$GSG(x,y,z) : -a(x,u), b(y,v), c(z,w), GSG(u,v,w). \tag{4}$$

$$SG = \bigcup_{l=0}^{\infty} (up^l \cdot E \cdot down^l) = \bigcup_{l=0}^{\infty} ((up^l \mid down^l) \cdot E) \tag{5}$$

---

[2]Since all base relations are assumed finite, as the case in the real databases, the derived relations are also finite.

234

$$GSG = \bigcup_{l=0}^{\infty}((a^l \mid b^l \mid c^l) \cdot E_3) \tag{6}$$

where $((P \mid Q) \cdot R)$ means that relations P and Q are separetedly composed with the relation R on corresponding attributes. []

It is important to point out that quite a lot of the compiled formulas obtained with this approach can be transformed into the similar formulas by applying unions or compositions on their non-powered partitions first. For example, the compiled formula of rule (7) (from [YHH88])

$$P(x_1, x_2, x_3) : -a(x_1, y_3), b(x_2, y_1), c(y_2, x_3), P(y_1, y_2, y_3). \tag{7}$$

is

$$P = \bigcup_{l=1}^{\infty}(((acb)^l \mid (abc)^l \mid (cab)^l) \cdot (E_3 \cup (a \mid b \mid c) \cdot E_3 \cup ((ac) \mid (bc) \mid (ab)) \cdot E_3))$$

which, obviously, can be transformed into the form of compiled formula (6).

As a matter of fact, in the rest of the paper we are not interested in the whole relations but rather in queries on them. That is, a selection on the corresponding compiled formula, or only a partition of the compiled formula is desired. The simplest example is the recursive query $ANC(k, ?)$ on the relation ANC. It can be described by the following formula:

$$ANC(k, ?) = \sigma_{a_1=k} \bigcup_{l=0}^{\infty} par^l \cdot E = \bigcup_{l=0}^{\infty} \sigma_{a_1=k} par^l \cdot E$$

where "$\sigma_{a_1=k}$" means that all tuples in the operand relation whose first attribute value is equal to k are selected. The partion of the formula without composition with exit relation E, i.e. "$\bigcup_{l=1}^{\infty} \sigma_{a_1=k} par^l$", is the so-called *partial transitive closure (PTC)(of the relation par) from k* which is obviously the main computation of the whole processing of the query. The same consideration can also be applied to other kinds of compiled formulas. For example, the recursive query $SG(k, ?)$ can be described as

$$SG(k, ?) = \bigcup_{l=0}^{\infty} \sigma_{a_1=k}(up^l \cdot E \cdot down^l)$$

and processed by computing two so-called *level-numbered* PTC's with respect ot *up-part* and *down-part*, respectively[3].

As we consider these kind of PTC queries very frequent, we propose to support it within the database as an elementary operation. In the following section we shall describe an algorithm which carries out the computation of PTC's so efficiently that it shows considering PTC as an elementary computational operation is reasonable.

---

[3]However, the computation is more complicated than the case above. For the sake of space limitation, in this paper we only discuss the computation of the simplest case. The techniques utilized here can be applied to process those more complicated queries. The interested readers are referenced to [Jia88a].

3 An Algorithm for Computing Partial Transitive Closures

As is well known, a binary relation like $par(x, y)$ can be represented as a directed graph in the way that each node in the graph stands for a constant in the relation and each directed edge from node i to node j presents a tuple (i, j) in the relation. With this graphical representation in mind, the computation of the PTC from node k is reduced to the search for all nodes which can be reached from node k by some way through the graph.

In graph theory, there are quite a lot of algorithms which carry out such a task [HNC65,Kno69,Meh84,Nol76,Pra76,Sed84]. However, the algorithm proposed here seems to be the most suitable one in the context of database. The basic idea of the algorithm is: *From the starting node k one visits breath-first all reachable nodes exactly once.* Here *visiting a node* means a traversal of the part of the graph from this visited node.

If the directed graph is represented with a $n \times n$-matrix *par* where n is the number of the nodes in the graph, and for all i and j with $1 \leq i, j \leq n$: $par[i, j] = 1$, if there is an edge from node i to node j, else $par[i, j] = 0$, the following is the algorithm:

```
procedure PTC ( k: integer; var par: array[1..n, 1..n] of integer );
        var i, j, l : integer;
        begin
            for l := 1 to n − 1 do
                for i := 1 to n do
                    if par[k, i] = l then
                        for j := 1 to n do
                            if par[i, j] = 1 and par[k, j] = 0 then
                                par[k, j] := l + 1;
        end.
```

It works as follows. For node k in the query, the following computation is carried out $n - 1$ times (the outmost loop), regarding with a certain length l of path[4] each time. For each node i the following will be done: If there is a *shortest* path of length l which leads from node k to node i $(par[k, i] = l)$, then node i will be *visited*. That is, for each node j it is tested whether there is an edge leading from node i to node j $(par[i, j] = 1)$, and whether no path is known yet between node k and node j $(par[k, j] = 0)$. If it is the case, it is evident that there is a shortest path of length $l + 1$ which leads from node k to node j. This fact is kept $(par[k, j] := l + 1;)$ and node j will be visited in the next loop with regard to $l + 1$.[5]

---

[4]A *path* in a directed graph is a list of directed edges $< e_1, \ldots, e_i, \ldots, e_n >$ where the incoming node of edge e_{i-1} is the outgoing node of edge e_i $(1 < i \leq n)$. The outgoing node of e_1 is the starting node, and the incoming node of e_n is the end node of the path, respectively. The *length* of the path is n, the number of the edges. If $e_1 = e_n$ here, the path builds a *cycle* with length n. In a directed graph without cycles, the longest path is of length $n - 1$.

[5]The idea of exploiting the path length to mark the visited nodes, according to [Tar83], was discovered by [Moo57] and independently by [Bel58]. Recently, it has been suggested, independently once again, for deadlock detection in the transaction management [Jia88b].

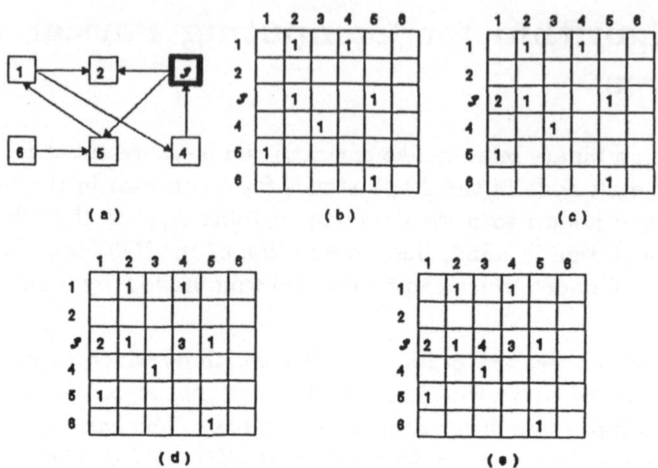

Figure 1: Computing the PTC from Node k

Obviously, the algorithm terminates in any case, no matter whether there are cycles in the graph, and row k of the matrix gives the answer to the query, i.e. all reachable nodes from node k in the graph *par*.

Example 2: In Figure 1, a simple example is given to show how the algorithm works and what the output is.

In (a) a "*par*" graph is given with nodes $\{1, 2, 3, 4, 5, 6\}$ and directed edges $\{(1, 2), (1, 4), (3, 2), (3, 5), (4, 3), (5, 1), (6, 5)\}$. Note that such directed edges can be regarded as tuples in a binary relation, e.g. the *relation par* with tuples $\{par(1, 2), par(1, 4), \ldots, par(6, 5)\}$, accordingly. The matrix representation of the graph is given in (b) which is the input of the algorithm.

(c) gives the state of the matrix after the first loop. Row 3 of the matrix means that nodes 1, 2, 5 are reachable from node 3 and there is a path of length 2 from node 3 to node 1 because there is a path of length 1 from node 3 to node 5 and a path of length 1 from node 5 to node 1. After the second computation loop, row 3 in (d) says that there is also a path of length 3 from node 3 to node 4 since there is a path of length 2 from node 3 to node 1 and a path of length 1 from node 1 to node 4. As a matter of fact, there is also a path of length 3 from node 3 to node 2. However, since node 2 has already been visited with regard to path length 1, it is not necessary to visit it once more: No new information will be obtained from this duplicate visiting. Thus, this fact has been ignored.

After the third loop the state of the matrix remains constant (e). Row 3 says that all reachable nodes from node 3 are nodes 1, 2, 3, 4, 5 with paths of minimum length 2, 1, 4, 3, 1, resprectively[6]. Because the longest path in a directed graph with n nodes is at most of length $n - 1$ if it does not form a cycle, the algorithm terminates after $n - 1$ loops. []

---

[6]The fact that there is a path from node 3 to node 3 means that there exists a cycle in the graph. This can be exploited to detect deadlocks [Jia88b].

4 Complexity of the Algorithm and Comparison with Related Work

At first glance one could get the impression that the algorithm in the matrix version, i.e. the procedure PTC, has time complexity $O(n^3)$ since it has three nested **for**-loops (for l, i and j, respectively). But in fact its time complexity is $O(n^2)$.

Obviously, the following part is of $O(n)$:

```
for j := 1 to n do
    if par[i, j] = 1 and par[k, j] = 0 then
        par[k, j] := l + 1;
```

But note that the execution of this piece is restricted by the condition "$par[k, i] = l$" above it, i.e. if there is a shortest path of length l leading from node k to node i. That means that its execution is independent of the first two nested **for**-loops (with time complexity $O(n^2)$).

There could be several paths form node k to another node. But the minimum length of these paths is unique for each node. Thus, there are at most n such minimums with regard to n nodes respectively, i.e. the marked elements in row k. Since for each of these minimums the above part is executed only once, a computational upper bound is $n \times$ "above part". That means that the whole computation is $O(n^2)$.

Because the algorithm visits every reachable node from the starting node k only once, each of the *relevant edges* to the PTC from node k in the graph, i.e. the edges building paths from the starting node to its reachable nodes, is visited exactly once. Thus, the time complexity of the algorithm shoud be $O(e')$ where e' is the number of the relevant edges in the graph, or the *relevant tuples* to the query in the corresponding relation. As we shall see in the following, with proper data structures, it can be really made as efficient as that.

In order to present and discuss the algorithm and its data organization easily and clearly, we used a matrix as the basic data structure. However, it is obviously unrealistic to solve our problem really with a matrix as the underlying data structure because matrices representing binary relations are generally very sparse. (Representing a binary relation as a matrix has space complexity $O(n^2)$ where n is the number of disjoint constants in the relation.) Therefore, we use a sparse matrix representation by a set of *successor-lists*. Each such list represents a row of the matrix and each element of the list stands for a marked element of the matrix and contains the node number and a pointer to the next element of the the list. The list representing row i is called the *i-th-list*, or the *list of node i*.

Since row k is the only one which has to be changed during the computation, we use an array of size n for it (the *array-k* below). Each element of the array is a bit marking whether the corresponding node has already been reached. Besides, we use a special list, the *current-list*, each element of which contains the node number and a pointer to the next element in the list which will be visited after having visited this node. (This node corresponds to the node marked with l and the next node corresponds to the node marked with l or $l+1$ in the procedure PTC.) It is initiated with node k. Based on this data organization and modifying the procedure PTC, we obtain the procedure PTC' (the kernel part) as follows which is of complexity $O(e')$: (The *current-list* is empty and the *array-k* is zero at the beginning)

```
procedure PTC'(k):
        begin
            current-list:= k;  array-k[k] := 1;
            foreach i in current-list do
                foreach j in i-th-list do
                    if array-k[j] = 0 then
                    begin
                        array-k[j] := 1;
                        current-list:=current-list • j;
                    end
    end.
```

Here, i and j present nodes i and j, respectively, and $\bullet$ in the last statement means that node j is concatenated to the *current-list* (at the end of the list). Besides, it is assumed that the nodes in a list are processed sequentially and only once.

Proposition: *The procedure PTC' is of time complexity $O(e')$ where e' is the number of the relevent edges to the computed PTC in the graph, and each relevant successor-list is fetched during the computation only once.*

Proof: A node j is put into the *current-list* only when it has be reached from node k first ($array\text{-}k[j] = 0$). Thus, there are no duplicates and at most n nodes in the *current-list*. Therefore, for each such node and only for them, the corresponding list is *fetched* and processed *only once*. With regard to each node in these lists, the test "$array\text{-}k[j] = 0$" is carried out exactly once. So the time complexity of the procedure is proportional to the number of nodes in all such processed lists.

For each list of node i, the *i-th-list*, each node j in it corresponds to an edge from node i to this node j in the graph. A list of node i is processed only if it is relevant, or in other words, only if all edges represented by this list are relevant to the computed PTC. That is, node i has been reached from node k and with this list, i.e. through the corresponding edges represented by the list, (new) nodes can be reached, i.e. the corresponding edges build paths from node k to these (new) nodes.[]

It is important to point out that a more efficient algorithm is impossible since without visiting all relevant edges in the graph the answer can not be said complete.

Usually, e', the number of the relevant edges to a PTC in the graph for database relation is much less than e, the number of all edges in the graph. It is, in turn, much less than n^2 where n is the number of nodes in the graph: $e' \ll e \ll n^2$.

Now, let us consider the space complexity and I/O cost of the procedure PTC' briefly. For storing all lists in the database, $O(e)$ space is required. For the computation in the

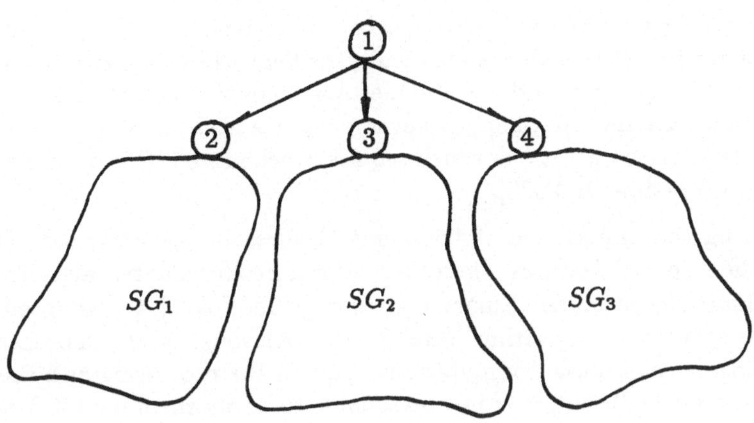

Figure 2: A Depth-First Traversal from Node 1

main memory without any unnecessary I/O's, i.e. without swappings (because of too small main memory), $O(n + list)$ main memory space is necessary where *list* is the space for a (part of) list being processed and n is, in fact, the size of the *array-k*. This complexity is called the *main memory space complexity*. Since during the computation each relevant list is fetched from the database to the main memory exactly once, the number of the I/O's with respect to *fetching lists* is minimal. This is the very merit of the algorithm which make it most suitable for the database application.

Obviously, algorithms working depth-first can also be used to traverse directed graphs and compute PTC's, as has been done in [IR88], which usually have a simple implementation and a complexity of $O(e')$, theoretically. In fact, the depth-first seaching strategy is used as the base of many very efficient and elegant algorithms. Some examples are given in [Tar72]. However, in the context of database applications such algorithms are generally not suitable because their accesses to elements are rather random which would cause too many unnecessary redundant I/O's. For instance, if successor-lists are used as underlying data structure, as in [IR88], it can be necessary to fetch relevant successor-lists from the database to the main memory more than once, as demostrated by the following example.

Example 3: A depth-first traversal is started from node 1, as shown in Figure 2. For the visiting of node 2, the list consisting of nodes 2, 3 and 4 is fetched. After having processed node 2, instead of processing node 3 immediately the subgraph SG_2 is traversed depth-first. Such subgraphs can be very large. After having traversed the subgraph SG_2 completely, node 3 now should be processed. However, during the traversal of SG_2 the list consisting of nodes 2, 3 and 4 has already been driven out from the main memory. Therefore, it must be fetched *once more* and node 3 will be processed. The same will happen with regard to node 4. Note that this situation can also arise with regard to many of the nodes in the subgraphs SG_2, SG_3 and SG_4, respectively.[]

Essentially, most known algorithms used to compute PTC's in database applications are breath-first traversers. For example, the Naive-algorithm with initiation, the Wavefrond algorithm (the both are identical), the Semi-Naive algorithm with initiation, the δ-Wavefrond algorithm and the Δ-Operator algorithms (essentially, they are also identical) [Ban85,GKB87,HQC88]. However, they use traditional joins, unions and differences as elementary operations which require much more I/O's, or much larger main memory and CPU-time [HQC88].

Considering the importance of transitive closures in the recursions [JAN87] and to exploit their special features, there are several newly adapted algorithms, such as the Logarithmic algorithm and Smart algorithm [VB86,Ioa86], the adapted Warschall's algorithm and Warren's algorithm [AJ87,Lu87]. Although these approaches consider transitive closures as a basic computational unit in the processing and the algorithms themselves are very efficient, it is not reasonable to apply them for PTC computation, because these algorithms are invented mainly for computing complete transitive closures, i.e. the cost is not reduced if they are used to compute PTC's. In other words, using them to compute PTC's is just as using Floyd's algorithm (for the *all-pairs shortest paths problem*) for the computation of the *single-source shortest paths problem* instead of using Dijkstra's algorithm [AHU85]. Furthermore, queries about complete transitive closures are atypical in database practice.

Even if the computation of the complete transitive closure is reqired, we can use our algorithm trivially by calling it once with requard to each node in the graph. The computation takes $O(n \times e')$ time where e' is always less than n^2, as mentioned above, and at the same time, the time complexity of Warshall's algorithm is $O(n^3)$ and the main memory space complexity is $O(n^2)$ [War62]. Besides, the procedure PTC is not more complicated than the simplest representation of Warshall's algorithm.

5 Implementation Aspects

As we have seen, our algorithm works with a sparse representation of the directed graph which corresponds to the base relation and is much smaller than it. The accesses to the base relations are carried out only at the very end of the whole computation. Thus, quite a lot of database accesses are avoided. Obviously, we need an encoding schema from values to node numbers. For such encoding, hashing approaches or B-tree method can be applied.

As we have seen, one of the important merits of the algorithm is the *locality* of the computation: Almost all computing activity is carried out at the *array-k* or row k. We can exploit this merit even further to cope with extremely large base relations as sketched in the following where the buffer in main memory can not hold even a single list. The lists now will be partitioned into several parts, respectively and the buffer in main memory in three blocks. One block is for the part of the *current-list*, where the current working element is contained in, i.e. node i in the procedure PTC'. The second block is for the part of the list corresponding to node i where node j is. The last block is for the part of the *array-k* where the test "*array-k*$[j] = 0$" is executed. Now assume that the buffer in main memory has q pages ($3 \leq q$). It reduces I/O's considerably if we use one page for the first part, one page for the second part and all the rest, i.e. $q - 2$ pages, for the last part. We call this the *"3-blocks strategy"*. With such a data organization, we can compute PTC's of arbitrarily large base relations effectively and efficiently.

We plan to implement these algorithm and data organization by using an NF^2 relation based database kernel system, *DASDBS* [PSSWD 87]. One of the important characteristics of the kernel utilized here is the so-called *tuple clustering*. That means that all data belonging to a tuple, e.g. atomic attributes, subrelations and subtuples of the tuple, are stored clustered in physical proximity to the tuple.

We use an NF^2 relation for each base relation to store its corresponding directed graph in the following way. Each tuple of the NF^2 relation presents a node having incoming and/or outgoing edges in the graph in the way in which the tuple contains an atomic attribute *NodeId* for the number of the constant corresponding to this (current) node, and two subrelations, **Incomings** and **Outgoings**, corresponding to the column and row of the node in the matrix, respectively. Each subtuple of the subrelation **Outgings** contains an atomic attribute *OutNodeId* holding the number of one of successor-nodes of the current node and all other attributes of the corresponding tuple in the base relation (which is now replaced by the NF^2 relation). Each subtuple of the subrelation **Incomings**[7] contains an atomic attribute *InNodeId* holding the number of one of predecessor-nodes of the current node and perhaps some other redundant attributes for the selections mentioned above.

This scenario, however, is only one possible schema. Many variants can be derived from it. For instance, if necessary, we can store information like successor-lists and/or predecessor-lists separatedly from other information (attributes), as reasoned above, as special access paths to make the processing faster. Now, all subtuples in subrelations of a tuple are sorted according to the numbers, and all tuples can be accessed directly by some usual access path, e.g. a B-tree, indexing on the attribute *NodeId*. The mechanism offered by the kernel is very suitable for the processing sketched above. For example, all subtuples of a tuple are stored in one or several pages, sorted and clustered. If the buffer is not large enough to hold the whole tuple at a time, the pages are loaded one after other. The NF^2 relation schema for storing the directed graph is given in Figure 3.

In practice, the building of a transitive closure itself can be restricted by some conditions. For example, to the query "Is it possible driving a truck of 50 tons from city A to city B?", we must know not only whether city B is reachable from city A, but also wether the both cities are connected by at least one road-list, each part of which the truck can drive on. Thus, the possibility of selections during the computation of transitive closures is desirable. On one side, it gives correct answers to the query as mentioned above, on the other side, intermediate results of each composition can be considerably reduced which implicits a significant reduction of unnecessary I/O's in turn. Similar can also be found in [AD88,AU79,LH87].

---

[7]The information in this subrelation is used to process queries like $ANC(?, k)$, i.e. all decendants of node k.

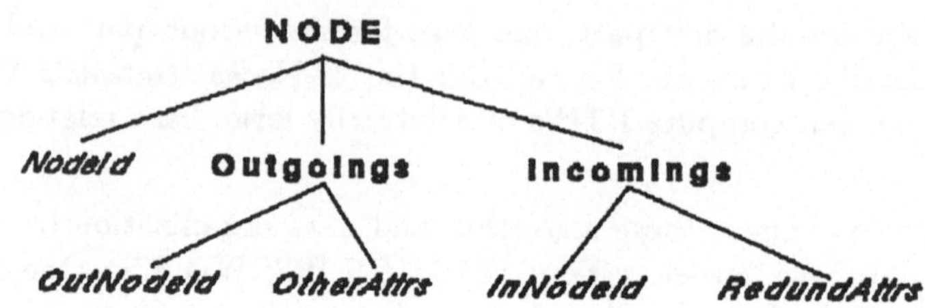

Figure 3: The NF^2 Relation Schema

Our algorithm can be easily extended to perform such selections. We give selection conditions in the form of a predicate as a parameter to the algorithm. Then, for each processed list the nodes in it are tested whether they satisfy the condition. If not, it will not be concatenated to the *current-list*. Clearly, database access is necessary here to test the corresponding tuples in the base relation. However, if the relevant attributes or their signatures [Fal85] are redundantly stored in the successor-lists, no other accesses to the base relations may be necessary.

6 Conclusion

Based on the observations that (1) processing queries on the compiled formulas of linear recursive rules can be considered as computing partial transitive closures and (2) special merits of partial transitive closures can be exploited for their efficient computation, an breath-first searching algorithm for computing partial transitive closures in a database environment was proposed. It was shown that the algorithm is most suitable for the database application. That is, it is not only with optimal CPU-time complexity ($O(e')$), but also with minimal list-fetchings. Besides, its main memory space complexity is $O(n + list)$ and the implementation is fairly simple.

Recently, we have minimized the page-fetchings by adapting a bit-vector technique, suggested by [Qad88,HQC88], to optimize the buffer utilization. Unfortunately, space limitations prevent us from presenting such techniques and from completing the proposal at all, i.e. from discussing how to extend the algorithm to efficiently compute *multi-source PTC's*, i.e. the nodes in the directed graph which are reachable from a set of starting nodes, and *level-numbered PTC's*, i.e. PTC's that are related to the computation of queries on compiled formulas like given in formula (5) or formula (6). The interested readers are referenced to [Jia88a]. An implementation and practical evaluation is underway.

7 Acknowledgments

I would like to thank Prof. Hans-Jörg Schek for critical reading of the early drafts, many helpful discussions and constructive suggestions.

References

[AD88]   R. Agrawal and P. Devanbu. Moving selection into linear least fixpoint queries. In *Proceedings of the IEEE International Conference on Data Engineering*, pages 452–461, 1988.

[AHU85]   A. V. Aho, J. E. Hopcroft, and J. D. Ullman. *Data Structures and Algorithms*. Addison-Wesley, 1985.

[AJ87]   R. Agrawal and H. V. Jagadish. Direct algorithms for computing the transitive closure of database relations. In *Proceedings of the International Conference on Very Large Databases*, pages 255–266, 1987.

[AU79]   A. Aho and J. Ullman. Universality of data retireval languages. In *Proceedings of the ACM Symposium on Principles of Programming Languages*, pages 110–117, 1979.

[Baa83]   S. Baase. *Computer Algorithms: Introduction to Design and Analysis*. Addison-Wesley, 1983.

[Ban85]   F. Bancilhon. Naive evaluation of recursively defined relations. In *On Knowledge Base Management Systems*, pages 165–178, Spring-Verlag, 1985.

[Bel58]   R. E. Bellman. On a routing problem. *Quart. Appl. Math.*, 16:87–90, 1958.

[BR86]   F. Bancilhon and R. Ramakrishnan. An amateur's introduction to recursive query processing strategies. In *Proceedings of the ACM SIGMOD Conference on Management of Data*, pages 16–52, 1986.

[BR87]   C. Beeri and R. Ramakrishnan. On the power of magic. In *Proceedings of the ACM Symposium on Principles of Database Systems*, pages 269–283, 1987.

[Eve79]   S. Even. *Graph Algorithms*. Computer Science Press, 1979.

[Fal85]   C. Faloutsos. Access methods for text. *ACM Computing Surveys*, 17(1):49–74, January 1985.

[GKB87]   U. Güntzer, W. Kiessling, and R. Bayer. On the evaluation of recursion in (deductive) database systems by efficient differential fixpoint iteration. In *Proceedings of the IEEE International Conference on Data Engineering*, 1987.

[GMN85]   H. Gallaire, J. Minker, and J.-M. Nicolas. Logic and databases: a deductive approach. *ACM Computing Surveys*, 16(2):153–185, 1985.

[GSS87]   G. Grahne, S. Sippu, and E. Soisalon-Soininen. Efficient evaluation for a subset of recursive queries. In *Proceedings of the ACM Symposium on Principles of Database Systems*, pages 284–293, 1987.

[HH87]   J. Han and L. J. Henschen. Handling redundancy in the processing of recursive database queries. In *Proceedings of the ACM SIGMOD Conference on Management of Data*, pages 73–81, 1987.

[HNC65]   F. Harary, R. Z. Norman, and D. Cartwright. *Structural Models: An Introduction to the Theory of Directed Graphs*. John Wiley/Sons, Inc., 1965.

[HQC88]   J. Han, G. Qadah, and C. Chaou. The processing and evaluation of transitive closure queries. In *Proceedings of the International Conference on Extending Database Technology*, pages 49–75, 1988.

[Ioa85]   Y. Ioannidis. A time bound on the materialization of some recursively defined views. In *Proceedings of the International Conference on Very Large Databases*, pages 219–435, 1985.

[Ioa86]   Y. Ioannidis. On the computation of the transitive closure of relational operators. In *Proceedings of the International Conference on Very Large Databases*, pages 403–411, 1986.

[IR88]   Y. Ioannidis and R. Ramakrishnan. Efficient transitive closure algorithms. In *Proceedings of the International Conference on Very Large Databases*, pages 382–394, 1988.

[JAN87]   H. V. Jagadish, R. Agrawal, and L. Ness. A study of transitive closure as a recursion mechanism. In *Proceedings of the ACM SIGMOD Conference on Management of Data*, pages 331–344, 1987.

[Jia88a]   B. Jiang. Computing partial transitive closures as an elementary operation for processing linearly recursive queries. 1988. In preperation.

[Jia88b]   B. Jiang. Deadlock detection is really cheap. *ACM-SIGMOD Record*, 17(2):2–13, June 1988.

[Kno69]   W. Knödel. *Graphentheoretische Methoden und ihre Anwendungen*. Springer-Verlag, 1969.

[LH87]   S. Lee and J. Han. Semantic query optimization in recursive databases. In *Proceedings of the IEEE International Conference on Data Engineering*, pages 444–451, 1987.

[Lu87]   H. Lu. New strategies for computing the transitive closure of a database relations. In *Proceedings of the International Conference on Very Large Databases*, pages 267–274, 1987.

[Meh84]   K. Mehlhorn. *Data Structures and Algorithms 2: Graph Algorithms and NP- Completeness*. Springer-Verlag, 1984.

[Moo57]   E. F. Moore. The shortest path through a maze. In *Proceedings of the International Symposium on the Theory of Switching*, pages 285–292, 1957. Also in *Annals of the Computation Laboratory of Harvard University*, 30, Harvard Uni. Press, Cambridge, MA, 1959.

[Nau86]   J. F. Naughton. Data independant recursion in deductive databases. In *Proceedings of the ACM Symposium on Principles of Database Systems*, pages 267–279, 1986.

[Nau87]   J. F. Naughton. One-sided recursions. In *Proceedings of the ACM Symposium on Principles of Database Systems*, pages 340–348, 1987.

[Nol76]   H. Noltemeier. *Graphentheorie mit Algorithmen und Anwendungen*. Walter de Gruyter, 1976.

[Pra76]   R. E. Prather. *Discrete Mathematical Structures for Computer Science*. Houghton Mifflin Company, 1976.

[Qad88]   G. Qadah. An efficient algorithm for the processing of transitive closure queries. 1988. In preperation.

[RHDM86] A. Rosenthal, S. Heiler, U. Dayal, and F. Manola. Traversal recursion: a practical approach to supporting recursive applications. In *Proceedings of the ACM SIGMOD Conference on Management of Data*, pages 155–165, 1986.

[Sed84]   R. Sedgewick. *Algorithms*. Addison-Wesley, 1984.

[SS88]   S. Sippu and E. Soisalon-Soininen. An optimization strategy for recursive queries in logic databases. In *Proceedings of the IEEE International Conference on Data Engineering*, pages 470–479, 1988.

[SZ87]   D. Saccà and C. Zaniolo. Magic counting methods. In *Proceedings of the ACM SIGMOD Conference on Management of Data*, pages 49–59, 1987.

[Tar72]   R. Tarjan. Depth-first search and linear graph algorithms. *SIAM Journal on Computing*, 1(2):146–160, June 1972.

[Tar83]   R. E. Tarjan. *Data Structures and Network Algorithms*. SIAM, 1983.

[VB86]   P. Valduriez and H. Boral. Evaluation of recursive queries using join indices. In *Proceedings of the International Conference on Expert Database Systems*, pages 197–208, April 1986.

[Vie86]   L. Vieille. Recursive axioms in deductive databases: the query/subquery approach. In *Proceedings of the International Conference on Expert Database Systems*, pages 179–193, 1986.

[War62]   S. Warshall. A theorem on boolean matrices. *Journal of the ACM*, 9(1):11–12, January 1962.

[YHH88]   C. Youn, L. J. Henschen, and J. Han. Classification of recursive formulas in deductive databases. In *Proceedings of the ACM SIGMOD Conference on Management of Data*, pages 320–328, 1988.

The Implementation of the Cell Tree:
Design Alternatives and Performance Evaluation

Oliver Günther and Jeff Bilmes***

** Department of Computer Science, University of California, Santa Barbara, CA 93106*
*** International Computer Science Institute, 1947 Center St., Suite 600, Berkeley, CA 94704*

Abstract

The cell tree is a new dynamic object-oriented index structure for geometric databases. All data objects in the database are represented as unions of convex point sets (*cells*). The cell tree is a balanced tree structure whose leafs contain the cells and whose interior nodes correspond to a hierarchy of nested convex polyhedra. This index structure allows quick access to the cells (and therefore to the data objects) that occupy a given location in space. Furthermore, the cell tree is designed for paged secondary memory to minimize the number of disk accesses occuring during a tree search. Point locations and range searches can therefore be carried out very efficiently using the cell tree. This paper reports our experiences with the implementation of the cell tree and presents the results of a performance evaluation.

Kurzfassung

Der Zellbaum ist ein neuer dynamischer, objektorientierter Datenbankindex für geometrische Daten. Sämtliche Datenobjekte in der Datenbank werden als Vereinigung konvexer Punktmengen (*Zellen*) dargestellt. Der Zellbaum ist ein ausgeglichener Baum, in dessen Blättern die Zellen abgespeichert sind. Die inneren Knoten entsprechen einer Hierarchie geschachtelter konvexer Polyeder. Diese Struktur erleichtert den schnellen Zugriff auf Zellen (und damit auf Datenobjekte) in Abhängigkeit von ihrer Position im Raum. Zudem ist der Zellbaum als Hintergrundspeicherstruktur konzipiert, um die Anzahl der Datenseiten zu minimieren, die für eine Suchoperation in den Hauptspeicher gebracht werden müssen *(Externzugriffe).* Punkt- oder Bereichsanfragen lassen sich mit Hilfe des Zellbaumes daher sehr effizient durchführen. Diese Arbeit berichtet über unsere Erfahrungen mit der Implementierung des Zellbaums und über die Ergebnisse einer experimentellen Laufzeitanalyse.

1. Introduction

Modern database systems are no longer limited to business applications. Non-standard applications such as robotics, computer vision, CAD/CAM, and geographic data processing are becoming increasingly important, and geometric data play a crucial role in many of these areas. To support these new applications efficiently, it is necessary to utilize the special properties of geometric data. A geometric database needs to make use of data structures and algorithms designed specifically for the management of geometric data objects.

For example, a retrieval query on a geometric database typically requires the fast execution of a geometric search operation such as a point or range search. Given a set of geometric objects in d-dimensional Euclidean space $\mathbf{E}^d$, stored in a geometric database, a *range search* computes those objects in the database that overlap a given search space $S \subset \mathbf{E}^d$. In the *point search* problem, which can be viewed as a degenerate range search, one determines all objects in the database that contain a given point $A \in \mathbf{E}^d$. Both operations require fast access to the data objects in the database that occupy a given location in space.

In order to facilitate such search operations on large geometric databases, the use of suitable index structures is a practical necessity. Indices for the computation of (one-dimensional) search operators play an important role in conventional database systems [Baye72, Come79]. Indices should be dynamic with respect to updates of the database, i.e. it should be possible to perform insertions and deletions without having to reorganize the index completely. Furthermore, an index should minimize the number of disk accesses occuring during a search operation.

Earlier proposals for geometric (i.e. multi-dimensional) index structures did not account for paged secondary memory and are therefore unsuited for very large geometric databases. An early example for such a method is the *binary space partitioning (BSP)* tree by Fuchs et al. [Fuch80, Fuch83]. BSP-trees are binary trees that represent a recursive subdivision of a given space into subspaces by means of $(d-1)$-dimensional hyperplanes. Each subspace is subdivided independent of its history and of the other subspaces. Each hyperplane corresponds to an interior node of the tree, and each partition corresponds to a leaf. Figure 1 gives an example of a BSP and the corresponding BSP tree. BSP trees can adapt well to the distribution of the data in the database. However, they are typically very deep, which has a negative impact on tree performance.

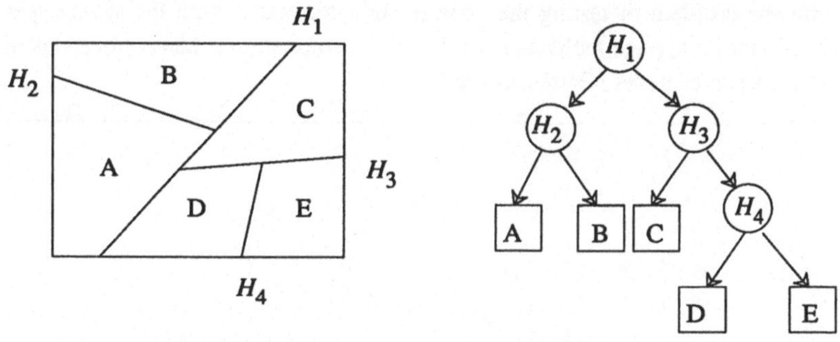

Figure 1: A binary space partitioning with BSP tree.

The first geometric index structure that has been designed specifically for paged secondary memory is Robinson's *k-d-B-tree* [Robi81], a generalization of Bayer's B-tree [Baye72] to higher dimensions. k-d-B trees are designed for indexing points in arbitrary dimensions; a generalization to extended geometric objects (such as polyhedra) is not immediately obvious. The same restriction holds for three non-hierarchical point indices that are based on address computation or hash techniques: Tamminen's *EXCELL* [Tamm82], Nievergelt's *gridfile* [Niev84], and for an access method devised by Kriegel and Seeger [Krie86]. All of these index structures are dynamic, i.e. insertions and deletions of objects can be interleaved with searches and no periodic reorganization is required.

A direct generalization of these point index structures to handle extended geometric objects is not possible. However, there are approaches to utilize these structures for extended objects as well. If the objects are d-dimensional intervals (*boxes*), they can be represented as points in $2d$-dimensional space (the *point space*) [Hinr85]. Then the search operators can be formulated as point queries in point space and computed by means of a point index. Note however, that the formulation of search queries in point space is much more complicated than it is in the original space. Also, the images of two intervals that are nearby in original space may be arbitrarily far apart from each other in point space [Falo87]. In the case of the k-d-B-tree these problems do in fact cause serious performance penalties [Gree89]. Non-hierarchical index structures such as the gridfile or EXCELL, which are based on address computation techniques, seem to suffer much less from these disadvantages [Niev87].

Another approach to use point indices for the management of extended geometric objects has recently been proposed by Six and Widmayer [Six86]. It can not only be used for the management of d-dimensional intervals, but for arbitrary extended d-dimensional geometric objects as well. The objects are indexed by means of a *layering* of several point indices. Six and Widmayer use a three-layer gridfile to demonstrate the advantages of this approach.

There are also several index structures that have been designed a priori as secondary storage indices for extended objects. The first such structure was Guttman's *R-tree* [Gutt84], also a generalization of the B-tree to higher dimensions. R-trees are balanced trees that correspond to a nesting of d-dimensional intervals (fig. 2). Each node N corresponds to a disk page $D(N)$ and an interval $I(N)$. If N is an interior node then all intervals corresponding to the immediate descendants of N are subsets of $I(N)$ and stored on the disk page $D(N)$. If N is a leaf node then $D(N)$ als٠ contains a number of intervals that are subsets of $I(N)$. Each of these *data intervals* is wrapped tightly around a data object. For data objects that are not intervals themselves, the R-tree can therefore not solve a given search problem completely. One rather obtains a set of intervals whose enclosed objects *may* intersec٠ the search space. One is left with the problem of testing the *objects* for intersection with the search space. This step, which may cause additional page faults and considerable computations, has not been taken into account by existing performance analyses [Gutt84, Gree89].

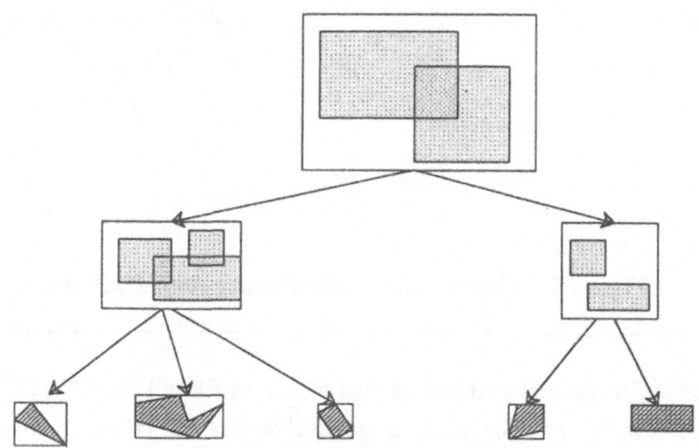

Figure 2: An R-tree with data objects (shaded).

As in the case of the B-tree, the R-tree has an upper and lower bound for the number of descendants of an interior node. The lower bound prevents the degeneration of trees and leads to an efficient storage utilization. Nodes whose number of descendants drops below the lower bound are deleted and its descendants are distributed among the remaining nodes (*tree condensation*). The upper bound can be derived from the fact that each tree node corresponds to exactly one disk page. Once a node requires more than one disk page, it is split and its descendants are distributed among the two resulting nodes. Each splitting may propagate up the tree, i.e. it may be necessary to split the ancestor node as well, and so on.

Furthermore, it should be noted that sibling nodes, i.e. nodes whose ancestor nodes are identical, may correspond to overlapping intervals. This property of the R-tree facilitates the insertion and deletion of data objects, but it may lead to performance losses during search operations. In the case of point locations, one may have to traverse several search paths. Even for range searches, the number of nodes to be inspected tends to be higher with overlaps. Moreover, the overlap tends to increase as objects are inserted into the R-tree. These problems led to the development of techniques to minimize the overlap [Rous85] and to the R^+–$tree$ [Ston86a, Sell87] where no overlaps are allowed (see fig. 3). For the reasons mentioned above, the R^+-tree allows the fast computation of search operators. However, the insertion and deletion of data objects may be much more complicated in turn [Gunt89a]. In particular, the insertion of one data object may require the extension of *several* sibling intervals. Also, node splitting now propagates not only up the tree, but also *down* the tree.

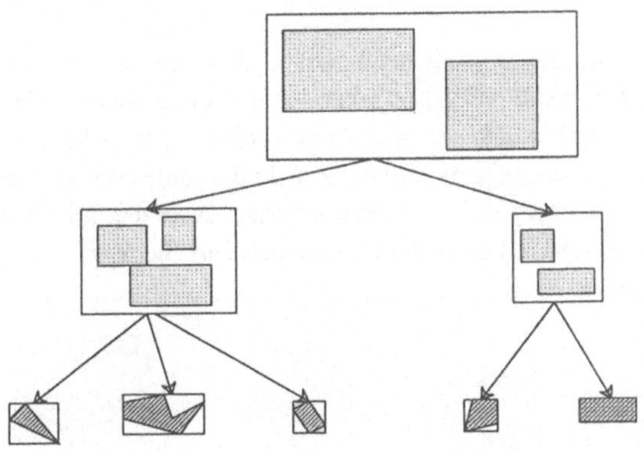

Figure 3: An R^+-tree with data objects (shaded).

The main goal during the design of the *cell tree* was to facilitate searches on data objects of arbitrary shapes, i.e. especially on data objects which are not intervals themselves. Especially in robotics and computer vision, intervals are not necessarily a good approximation of the data objects enclosed. Each cell tree node corresponds not necessarily to an interval, but to a convex polyhedron. In order to minimize the number of disk accesses occuring during a search operation, the leaf nodes of a cell tree contain all the information that may be required to answer a given search query; no pages other than those containing the cell tree will be needed. This is an important advantage of the cell tree over the R-tree and related structures, where data objects may have to be retrieved from secondary memory, thereby causing additional page faults. To optimize search performance, we decided to avoid overlaps between sibling polyhedra. In subsequent sections, it will be shown how the resulting disadvantages can be partly compensated by restricting the polyhedra to be partitions of a BSP (binary space partitioning) (see fig. 1). Therefore the cell tree can be viewed as a combination of a BSP- and an R^+-tree.

Section 2 is a brief review of the cell tree design, as presented in [Gunt88, Gunt89a]. Section 3 reports our experiences with the implementation of the cell tree and discusses the parameters we have been using. Section 4 presents the results of an experimental performance evaluation of the cell tree, and section 5 contains our conclusions.

2. The Cell Tree

2.1. Tree Structure

Consider a database consisting of a collection of d-dimensional point sets in Euclidean space $\mathbf{E}^d$. In order to support search and set operations efficiently, we represent the data objects as unions of convex cells. Formally, each data object D is represented as a convex chain [Whit57, Gunt87a, Gunt89b] in $\mathbf{E}^d$,

$$x_D = \sum_{k=1}^{m} z_i$$

The cells z_i are d-dimensional convex closed point sets that are not necessarily bounded. Note that we do not require the cells to be mutually disjoint; the cells form a *convex cover* of the data object. A point $t \in \mathbf{E}^d$ is considered inside D if and only if it is inside any of the cells, i.e. $t \in D \iff t \in z_i$ for some $i=1 .. m$.

Convex chains are a simple and powerful tool to describe various kinds of geometric objects, including objects that have holes or consist of several disjoint components (fig. 4). Unlike simple point sets, convex chains are closed under set operations (union, intersection, difference). Although the decomposition of the original data objects into cells will take some computation time, we believe that it will pay off by making search operations simpler and faster. Note that this decomposition is completely transparent to the user; cells need not be seen or manipulated by the user.

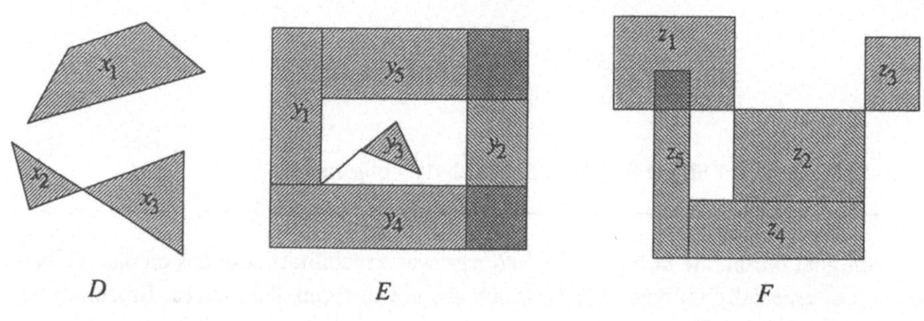

Figure 4: $x_D = x_1+x_2+x_3$, $x_E = y_1+y_2+y_3+y_4+y_5$, $x_F = z_1+z_2+z_3+z_4+z_5$.

A cell tree indexes the cells in a geometric database based on their location in space. In analogy to the R-tree, a cell tree is a height-balanced tree and each tree node corresponds to exactly one disk page. Therefore the computation of a search operator requires only a small number of disk accesses. The cell tree is a fully dynamic index structure; insertions and deletions can be interleaved with searches and no periodic reorganization is required.

Each leaf node entry E represents a cell $E.Z$. In addition to a description of the cell geometry, it contains the ID $E.D$ of the data object whose convex chain $x_{E.D}$ contains the cell $E.Z$. Moreover, E contains all attributes of the data object $E.D$ which may be required to answer a query in the given application. Examples for such attributes are the color of $E.D$ or its convex chain $x_{E.D}$.

Interior (non-leaf) nodes contain entries of the form

$$(cp, P, C)$$

Here, cp is the child pointer, i.e. the address of the corresponding descendant node. P is a convex, not necessarily bounded d-dimensional polyhedron. All cells in the database that are subsets of P are in the subtree under the descendant node. The *container* C is a convex subset of P, which also contains each cell z in the subtree, i.e. $z \subseteq C$. C provides a more accurate localization of these cells, which may speed up search queries. In the following, $E.cp$, $E.P$, and $E.C$ denote the corresponding attributes of an interior node entry E. m is a parameter specifying the minimum number of entries in an interior node. Finally, given a node N, its entry in its ancestor node is denoted by E_N, and the entries in N are denoted by $E_i(N)$.

A cell tree satisfies the following properties.

(1)   The root node has at least two entries unless it is a leaf.

(2)   Each interior node has at least m entries unless it is the root.

(3)   For each entry (cp, P, C) in an interior node, the subtree that cp points to contains a cell z if and only if $z \subseteq P$.

(4)   For each entry (cp, P, C) in an interior node, the container $C \subseteq P$ is a convex polyhedron that can be specified as the intersection of P with at most k halfspaces in E^d. For each cell z in the subtree pointed to by cp, it is $z \subseteq C$.

(5)   For each interior node N, the polyhedra $E_i(N).P$ form a binary space partitioning (BSP) of $E_N.P$.

(6)   All leaves are on the same level.

(7)   Almost every node requires no more than one disk page of storage space.

Figure 5 shows an example cell tree.

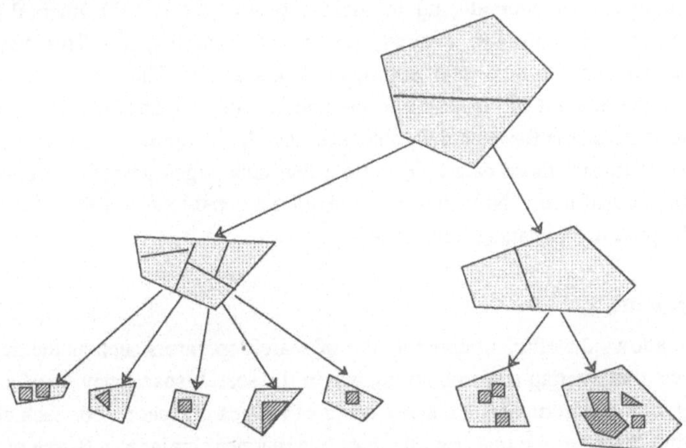

Figure 5: A cell tree with cells (shaded) for $m=2$. For simplicity, the containers $E.C$ are omitted.

Property (5) has two interesting consequences. First, the polyhedra $E_1.P$ and $E_2.P$ corresponding to two entries E_1 and E_2 on the same tree level cannot overlap. Second, the entries of an interior tree node N can now be stored in a very compact manner: rather than describing the polyhedra $E_i(N).P$ explicitly, one only stores the BSP of $E_N.P$.

Note that the cell tree (in analogy to the R$^+$-tree) does not put any upper bounds on the number of node entries. Nevertheless it is attempted to limit the storage requirements for each node to one disk page. If a node requires more storage space after one or more insertions, it is attempted to split that node such that both subnodes can be stored on one disk page each. In most cases this is in fact possible: the node is split and the split may propagate up the tree. If the splitting does not succeed then the node is stored using overflow pages; these cases are the only ones that the word *almost* in property (7) refers to. One can show [Gunt89a] that the maximum number of entries of an interior node is roughly proportional to the page size. The choice of the right page size therefore has a significant impact on the performance of the cell tree and will be evaluated extensively in section 4. A similar statement about the maximum number of leaf node entries is not possible as the storage requirements per leaf node entry may vary considerably, depending on the complexity of the corresponding cell.

Note that, other than the R^+-tree, the cell tree has a *lower* bound m for the number of entries of an *interior* node. Of course, it is also possible to define the cell tree with a lower bound for the number of *leaf* entries. To keep insertions and deletions simple, however, we have decided not to impose such a bound.

The height of a cell tree containing n index records is bound by $\lfloor \log_m n \rfloor + 1$, because the branching factor of each node is at least m. Except for the root and for overloaded nodes, the worst-case space utilization is m/M for interior nodes.

Note that in the cell tree, clustering of the data objects corresponding to their location in space is intrinsic: each leaf node corresponds to a convex partition in space and all the cells in that partition are actually stored on the corresponding disk page. This is not necessarily the case for the R- and R^+-tree. Earlier work on these structures [Gutt84, Sell87] has not addressed this problem because in those papers all search algorithms are restricted to the retrieval of the data intervals, i.e. the bounding rectangles of the data objects. In most applications, however, this is not sufficient to answer a given search query. If a search space overlaps a data interval (and the data object is not just the interval itself), one has to retrieve the actual data object and test it for overlap with the search space. This may require considerable computations and a certain number of additional disk accesses. The actual number of disk accesses depends heavily on the amount of clustering in the underlying geometric database. Without clustering, one may incur one disk access for each data object retrieved. To optimize the search performance, it is therefore desirable to cluster those data objects on a few disk pages whose data intervals are stored in the same R- or R^+-tree leaf node. Note that it may require a considerable effort to maintain this amount of clustering in the presence of database updates.

2.2. Search Operations

The cell tree allows the efficient computation of search operators such as the general range query: find all data objects that overlap a search space, where the search space may be of arbitrary shape. To answer this query, one first computes a convex cover of the search space. For each convex component, the search algorithm descends the tree from the root in a manner similar to a B-tree or an R-tree. At each interior node the search space is decomposed further into several disjoint convex subspaces, and a not necessarily convex remainder space. The remainder space is insignificant to the search and therefore eliminated. The convex subspaces are each passed to one of the subtreees to be decomposed recursively in the same manner. Note that this algorithm differs from the equivalent R-tree algorithm where the subspaces are allowed to overlap, thereby decreasing the search efficiency.

Algorithm **Search**(T,S). Given a cell tree with root T, find all data objects that overlap a given search space S.

S1. [Decompose S.] If S is not convex, find a (small) set of convex polyhedra S_i such that $\sum_i S_i = S$. For each S_i, **Search**(T,S_i) and stop.

S2. [Search subtree.] If T is not a leaf, check each entry $E_i(T)$ to determine whether S overlaps the container $E_i(T).C$. If yes, **Search**(T',$S \cap E_i(T).C$) where T' denotes the node $E_i(T).cp$ points to.

S3. [Search leaf node.] If T is a leaf, check each entry $E_i(T)$ to determine whether the cell $E_i(T).Z$ overlaps S. If yes, return the data object $E_i(T).D$.

Other than step S1, the main effort in this algorithm is to detect and compute overlaps between the search space S on one hand and the containers $E_i(T).C$ or the cells $E_i(T).Z$ on the other hand. A very efficient method to perform these computations is based on a dual representation for the search space, the containers $E_i(T).C$ and the cells [Gunt87b]; see section 3.2.

Other search queries can be computed in a similar fashion.

2.3. Update Operations

To insert a new data object, one first computes a convex cover of the object. Then each component in the cover is inserted separately into the cell tree. The number of components per data object is highly data-dependent. If all data objects are convex (as it is actually the case for CAD layout data, for example), of course there would be only one component per data object. Note that a convex component may have to be split and inserted into several subtrees because it overlaps several sibling polyhedra. Therefore the insertion of *one* component into the cell tree may cause the creation of *several* new leaf node entries (i.e. cells). This is a general property of index structures based on a partitioning of space into non-overlapping subspaces.

Inserting index records for new cells is similar to insertion into a B- or R-tree. Index records are added to the leaves, nodes that overflow are split, and splits may propagate up the tree (see also section 3.3). This insertion algorithm is currently also used for the construction of a cell tree from a given geometric database: the data objects in the database are inserted consecutively into a cell tree that is initially empty.

In order to delete a data object D from a cell tree that indexes the object, one also first computes a convex cover of D. For each component D_i in the cover, one performs a range search using D_i as search space. Each cell overlapping D_i is checked if it belongs to D's convex chain x_D. If that is the case, the cell is deleted. To avoid empty leaves, a tree condensation is performed where necessary. The tree condensation eliminates empty leaves and propagates the elimination up the tree. Interior nodes with less than m entries are also deleted and the entries under these nodes are reinserted into the cell tree.

3. Implementation Issues

3.1. Tree Structure

The cell tree has been implemented at the International Computer Science Institute in Berkeley on a SUN 3/60 workstation with a 68020 processor and a 68881 floating point coprocessor. So far, the implementation is in two dimensions. As explained above, there are three parameters to tune the performance of the cell tree: m, k, and l.

m is the minimum number of entries of an interior node. A large m will increase space efficiency and decrease the height of the tree, which might in turn improve the search performance. On the other hand, a large m may cause updates to become very expensive, as tree condensations will occur more frequently and become more complex. In particular, the probability that the splitting of an interior node may fail is directly related to the size of m [Gunt89a]. In fact, the probability of failure in a typical two-dimensional setting would only be about 1 : 500,000 for $m=2$. For $m=10$, however, one obtains a probability of about 1 : 3. For $m=2$, we never encountered a single case in our experiments where the splitting of an interior node had failed. Therefore, it was never necessary to use overflow pages for the storage of interior nodes. Experiments with higher values for m lead to overflow pages without yielding an improvement in space requirements or search performance. We have therefore chosen m to be 2.

k denotes the maximum number of hyperplanes that may be used to specify the container $E.C$ of an entry E if the partition $E.P$ is known. A large value for k allows a more accurate localization of the cells in the subtree under E, which might improve the search performance. On the other hand, k is inversely proportional to the maximum number of entries that can be stored in an interior node. A large k will therefore increase the tree height and decrease the search performance. Furthermore, a large k makes searches and updates computationally more complicated. Our current implementation uses no containers at all (i.e. $k=0$).

We are also experimenting with an approach that combines the cell tree with the advantages of the *bounding box* approach used in the R-tree, for example. Here, the $k := 2d$ halfspaces corresponding to an entry E define a minimum interval I that contains all cells under E, i.e. I is a bounding box for the cells under E. The container $E.C$ is then defined as the intersection of I with the partition $E.P$, i.e. $E.C = E.P \cap I$, and therefore $z \in E.C$ for all cells z under E (fig. 6). This kind of container can be updated very easily in the case of insertions and deletions. So far, however, we could not achieve any improvements in search performance using this bounding box approach. It seems that an even more detailed container $E.C$ will be even less advantageous. The advantage of having a better localization of the cells will be offset by higher space requirements (which leads to a higher number of disk accesses in turn) and higher computation requirements during searches and updates.

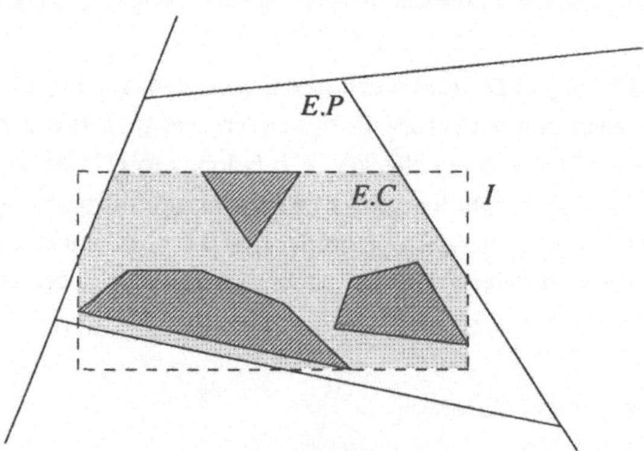

Figure 6: A partition $E.P$ and container $E.C$ corresponding to an entry E. The cells under E are shaded.

3.2. Search Operations

The main effort in the search algorithm **Search** (see previous section) is to *detect* and *compute* overlaps between the (convex) search space on one hand and the (convex) containers or the cells on the other hand. A very efficient method to perform these operations is based on a dual representation for the convex polyhedra involved [Gunt87b, Gunt88]. This scheme is based on a geometric duality transformation in d-dimensional Euclidean space $\mathbf{E}^d$ that is an isomorphism between points and hyperplanes [Prep79, Brow79, Lee84]. Each convex polyhedron P is represented by a set of two functions in the dual space, TOP^P, BOT^P: $\mathbf{E}^{d-1} \to \mathbf{E}^1$, such that a hyperplane H intersects P if and only if the dual of H lies between TOP^P and BOT^P. It can be shown that TOP^P is convex, while BOT^P is concave. In two dimensions ($d=2$), one obtains two functions which map the slope b_1 of a straight line into the minimum (BOT^P) and maximum (TOP^P) intercept b_2 such that the line denoted by $y=b_1x+b_2$ intersects the polyhedron P (fig. 7).

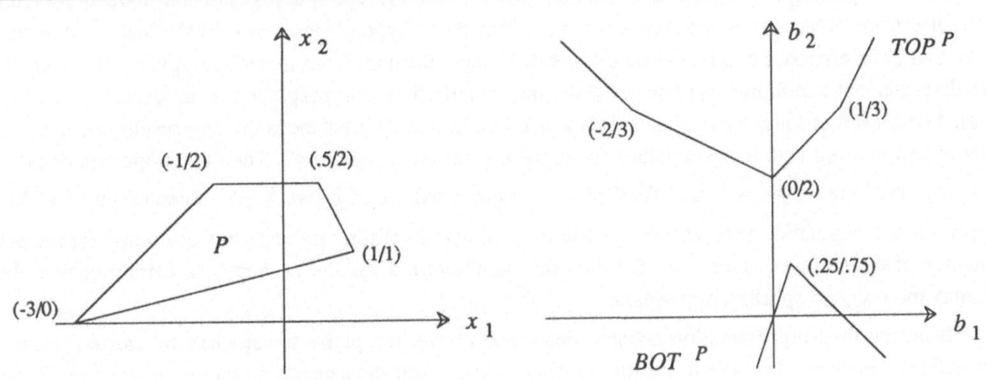

Figure 7: A cell P with dual representation.

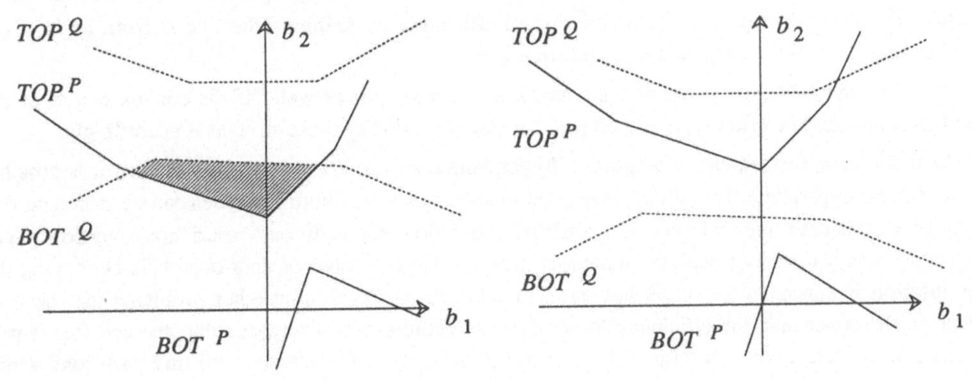

(a) no intersection: the points in the shaded area are the duals of the separating hyperplanes.

(b) intersection

Figure 8

Two polyhedra P and Q intersect if and only if for all $x \in \mathbf{E}^{d-1}$, we have $TOP^P(x) \geq BOT^Q(x)$ and $TOP^Q(x) \geq BOT^P(x)$. Otherwise, there will be a separating hyperplane which means that the two polyhedra do not intersect (fig. 8). As shown in [Gunt87b], the time complexity to check the above condition is polylogarithmic in the number of vertices of the polyhedra P and Q.

In step S2 of algorithm **Search** it becomes necessary to *compute* the intersection of the search space with a container. To compute the intersection of two convex polyhedra P and Q in the dual representation scheme, one has to perform two convex hull computations on the graphs of TOP^P, BOT^P, TOP^Q, and BOT^Q. In two and three dimensions, the time complexity of these computations is linear in the number of vertices of the polyhedra.

3.3. Update Operations

Whenever a leaf node becomes too full, it will be attempted to split that node. An efficient way to find a suitable splitting hyperplane is to conduct plane sweeps [Prep85] across the leaf node along l different directions. Our current algorithm first identifies those hyperplanes that split the leaf node in such a way that both subnodes can be stored on one disk page. Second, from those hyperplanes it selects the ones that intersect a minimum number of cells (one usually finds a hyperplane that intersects none of the cells). Third, each of these hyperplanes is evaluated on how well it balances the two resulting subleaves. After experimenting with various values for l, we are currently using $l=7$. Then the slope angles of the sweeping lines are $\dfrac{i \cdot 180}{l} = i \cdot 25.7$ for $i=1 \dots 7$. Larger values of l (we tried values of up to $l=360$) require more computation time without yielding much better splitting hyperplanes or improving the performance of the cell tree otherwise. On the other hand, with a smaller l, there is a certain chance that one may miss a good splitting hyperplane.

Using the dual representation scheme described above, the plane sweeps can be carried out in a very efficient manner. In order to perform a plane sweep with the sweep line having a slope of $\overline{m}$, one fetches the values $TOP^{P_i}(\overline{m})$ and $BOT^{P_i}(\overline{m})$ for all cells P_i in the leaf node to be split. Then each cell P_i can be represented by a line segment $(TOP^{P_i}(\overline{m}), BOT^{P_i}(\overline{m}))$ on the real line L (fig. 9). Associated with each line segment is a byte count that indicates how much storage space the representation of P_i requires. The plane sweep can then be conducted efficiently by scanning the line L from left to right while keeping track of the byte balancing information.

Note that the splitting of leaf nodes may cause cells to split as well. If the convex chains of the data objects are stored explicitly, it is therefore necessary to modify these structures accordingly.

As mentioned, the search for a splitting hyperplane does not always succeed. In fact, it is possible that there is no hyperplane that splits a leaf node in such a way that both subnodes can be stored on one disk page. In this case, the leaf node is stored using overflow pages. In our experience, overflow pages only occur in very densely populated databases where a large number of data objects is occupying the same location in space. In that case, however, the cell tree is developing other problems that become critical much sooner than the efficiency losses due to overflow pages. In particular, the cell tree is performing a lot of leaf node splittings. As a result, the universe is fragmented into tiny partitions which correspond to one leaf node each. If a new convex object is now inserted into such a tree, it will be partitioned into a large number of cells and cause the creation of a correspondingly large number of leaf node entries. Figure 10 shows how the number of cells per convex object depends on the size of the objects in the database. The larger the objects are, the more densely populated is the universe, which causes a lot of leaf node splitting. As a consequence, each new convex object will be partitioned into a larger number of (smaller) cells. If the size of the objects is relatively small compared to the size of the universe, then the number of cells per objects does not increase too heavily with the size of the geometric database. For a description of the benchmark database used, see section 4.1.

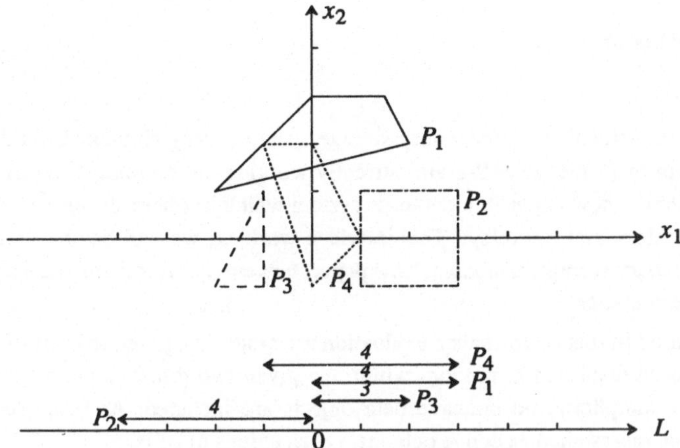

Figure 9: A set of cells P_i and their representation on the real line L for the sweep line slope $\overline{m}=1$. The numbers in italics indicate the space requirements of each cell.

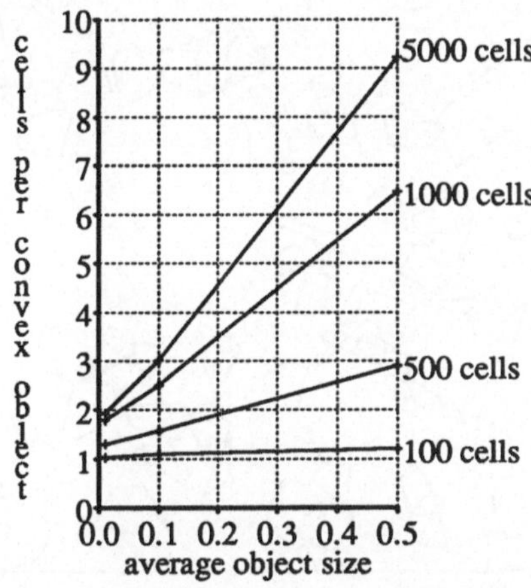

Figure 10: Average number of cells per convex object vs. average size of the objects in the database (measured in percent of the size of the universe). The four plots represent the situation after the insertion of 100, 500, 1000, and 5000 convex objects into an initially empty cell tree. Page size is 2048 bytes.

When splitting interior nodes, one needs to maintain the condition that the number of partitions on each side of the splitting hyperplane is at least m. Furthermore, the splitting hyperplane should intersect a minimal number of containers $E_i(N).C$ because each such intersection has to be propagated down the tree. A large number of such intersections may cause the split to become very costly. The hyperplane $H^*(N)$ corresponding to the root node of N's BSP-tree does not intersect *any* of the polyhedra $E_i(N).P$ (or $E_i(N).C$). Therefore a split using $H^*(N)$ would not have to be propagated down the tree. For that reason, in the cell tree an interior node will *only* be split if the hyperplane $H^*(N)$ is suitable for splitting, i.e. if the number of partitions on both sides of $H^*(N)$ is at least m. If that is not the case, N will not be split. It will rather be stored using overflow pages. Whenever another entry is added to N, however, another attempt will be made to split N along the hyperplane $H^*(N)$.

4. Performance Evaluation

4.1. Tree Structure

In our current implementation, secondary storage access is only simulated; all databases used are small enough to fit in main memory. We are currently working on the integration of the cell tree with POSTGRES [Ston86b], a new extensible database system which has been designed and implemented at the University of California at Berkeley. This interface working, we will be able to test our structures with very large secondary storage databases. This paper, however, only reports our experiences with the main memory implementation.

All databases used in this performance evaluation are randomly generated sets of convex polygons. Each polygon has been displaced at random within the given two-dimensional universe; see figure 11 for an example. For simplicity, no concave data objects are included. As discussed above, concave objects can always be represented as convex chains, i.e. as unions of cells.

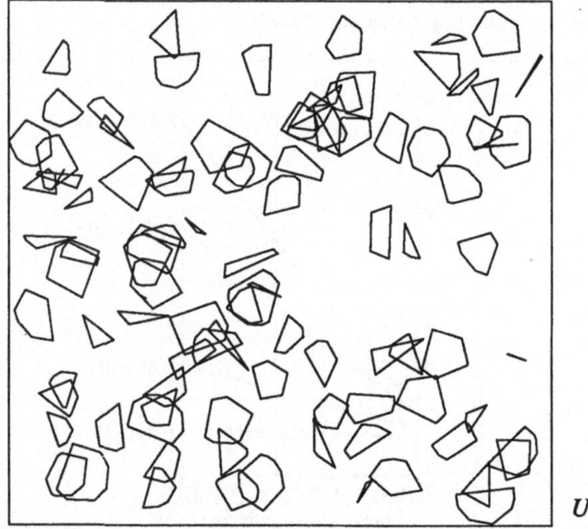

Figure 11: An example database with 100 convex two-dimensional data objects of average size 0.5 in a universe U.

There are two major parameters that characterize such a geometric database: the number N of data objects (the *database size*) and their *average size S*, measured in percent of the size of the universe. From there, various other parameters can be computed: the product $N \times S/100$, for example, yields the *coverage* of the universe, which often is a good indicator for the overlap between data objects. We took measurements for five different databases containing 100, 500, 1000, 5000, and 10000 convex polygons. Unless noted otherwise, the average data object size S is chosen to be 0.01, i.e. 0.01 % of the size of the universe.

Three page sizes have been tested: 512, 1024, and 2048 bytes. Each page size corresponds to a different value for the maximum branching factor of an interior node. It can easily be shown [Gunt89a] that for a two-dimensional implementation ($d=2$) without containers ($k=0$), the corresponding branching factors are 26, 52, and 103, respectively.

The first thing measured is the depth and the space requirements of the cell tree tree for various database sizes. Our results are presented in table 12 and figure 13. In this section, CPU times are measured in seconds, database sizes in number of data objects, page sizes in bytes, and space requirements in megabytes. Note that the space requirements of the cell tree decrease as the page size increases. Smaller disk pages cause more splits and therefore more tree nodes with associated overhead. Furthermore, the data objects are partitioned into a higher number of cells.

For comparison purposes, we also include some figures for the R- and R+-tree. A major comparative performance study is currently in preparation. It is apparent that both R- and R+-tree require less storage space than a cell tree for the same geometric database.

database size	100	500	1000	5000	10000
Cell tree, page size = 512	3	3	4	5	6
Cell tree, page size = 1024	2	3	3	4	4
Cell tree, page size = 2048	2	2	3	3	3
R-tree, page size = 2048	1	2	2	2	3
R+-tree, page size = 2048	2	2	2	2	3

Table 12: Tree depths for various database and page sizes.

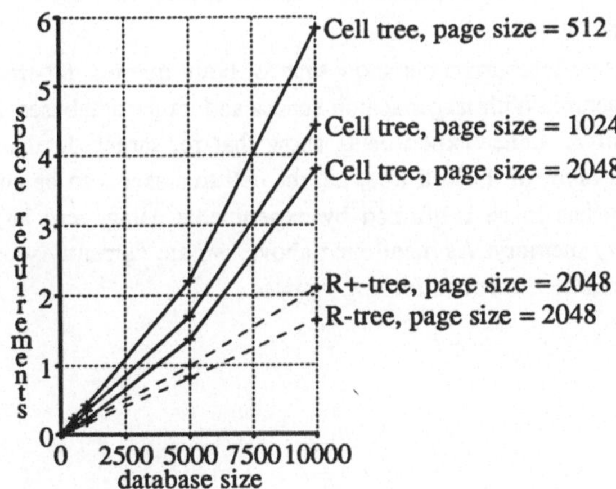

Figure 13: Space requirements [MBytes] vs. database size.

All cell trees were constructed by means of a consecutive insertion of the data objects into an initially empty tree. The average insertion time for an additional data object increases with the size of the database; see figure 14. Larger page sizes cause an increase in performance. The smaller the page size, the more CPU time has to be spent on the insertion of a new data object into the tree.

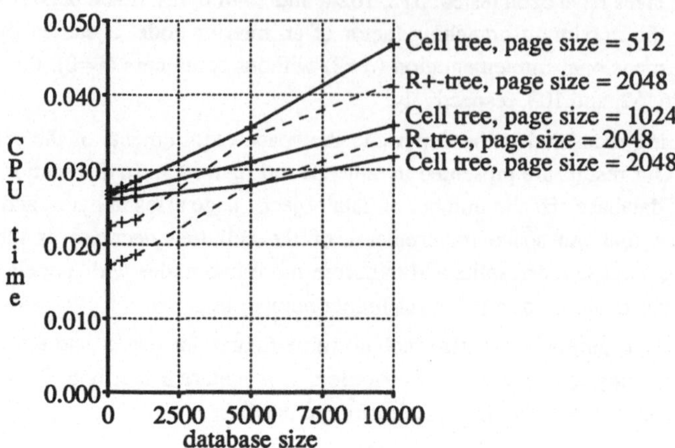

Figure 14: Average CPU time per insertion vs. database size.

4.2. Search Operations

In order to measure the search performance of the cell tree, we defined a benchmark of point and range search operations. The size of the search space for the range search has been chosen as 1 (measured in percent of the size of the universe). For both point and range search, 400 random queries have been generated. Using the dual approach described in section 3.2, we obtained average CPU times per search operation, as shown in fig. 15a-b. While for point queries smaller page sizes are better, the situation changes for larger search spaces. For search spaces of size 1 or larger, larger page sizes are definitely advantageououss.

Our comparative measurements show that for point queries, R+-trees clearly seem to be the most efficient index structure. With larger search spaces and larger databases, however, cell trees are becoming more competitive. Other experiments show that for larger databases the balance seems to shift somewhat more in favor of the cell tree, i.e. the cell tree seems to be superior even for smaller search spaces. This claim has to be confirmed by experiments using very large databases that are actually stored on secondary memory. As mentioned above, we are currently working on a POSTGRES implementation of these index structures for that purpose.

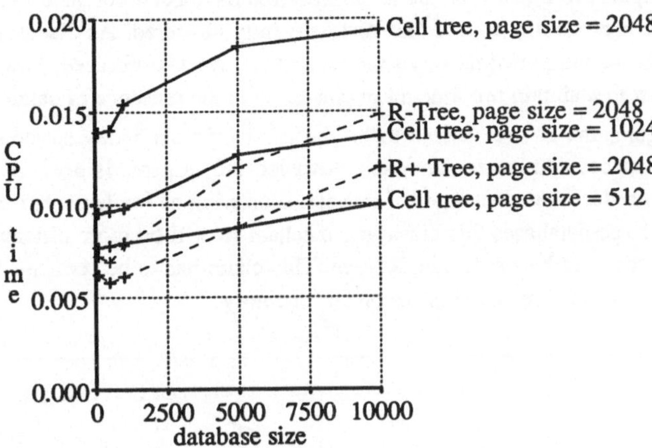

Figure 15a: Average CPU time per point query vs. database size.

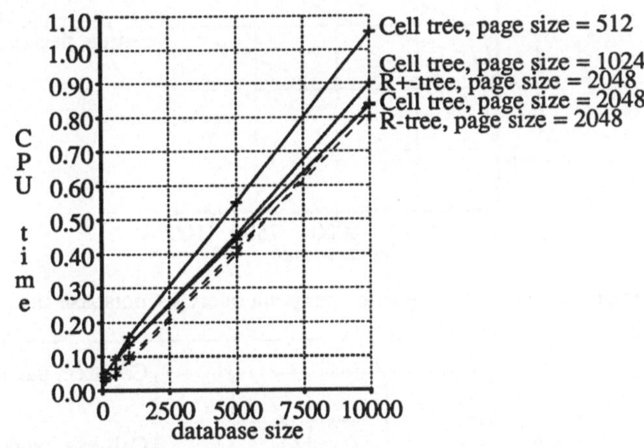

Figure 15b: Average CPU time per range query vs. database size. The size of the search space is 1.

More important than the average *CPU time* per search, however, is the number of *nodes visited* during a search operation. Each node corresponds to one disk page, and therefore each visited node may cause a page fault. As most search operations are I/O-bound rather than CPU-bound, the number of disk accesses is the crucial factor in evaluating the performance of index structures. Although it is virtually assured that the cost of large main memories will drop at a remarkable rate over the next few years, we believe that the average size of industrial databases will grow accordingly. It therefore seems somewhat unlikely that a switch to main memory databases and a corresponding emphasis on CPU-bound search operations will occur in the near future.

Figures 16a-b show the average number of nodes visited during a point and range search operation. The usage of smaller page sizes is clearly a disadvantage: the average number of visited nodes decreases with increasing page size.

The comparative figures for the R- and R+-tree have been obtained under the assumption that the data objects corresponding to one leaf node are fully clustered. As discussed in section 2.1, with this assumption the search performance of the R- and R+-tree is optimized; however, it may require a considerable effort to maintain this amount of clustering in the presence of database updates.

Once again, the R+-tree seems to be the most efficient index structure for point queries. With larger search spaces and larger databases, however, the cell tree is becoming much more competitive. This seems to reflect the advantages of intrinsic clustering as implemented by the cell tree. We suspect that for very large databases this clustering mechanism will be more efficient than the explicit clustering, which is required by the R- and R+-tree. This claim has to be confirmed by experiments with very large databases, which are stored on secondary memory.

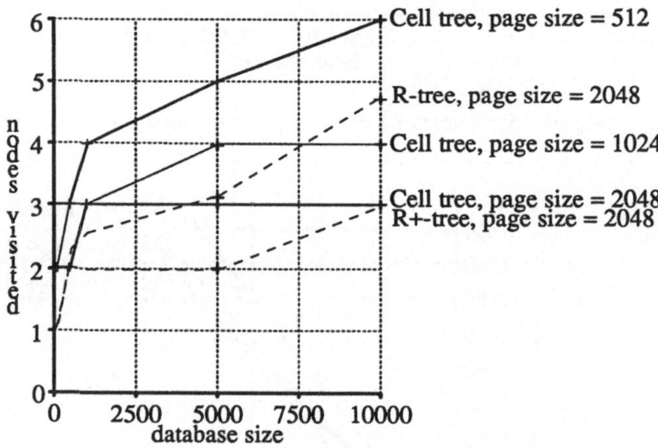

Figure 16a: Average number of nodes visited per point query vs. database size.

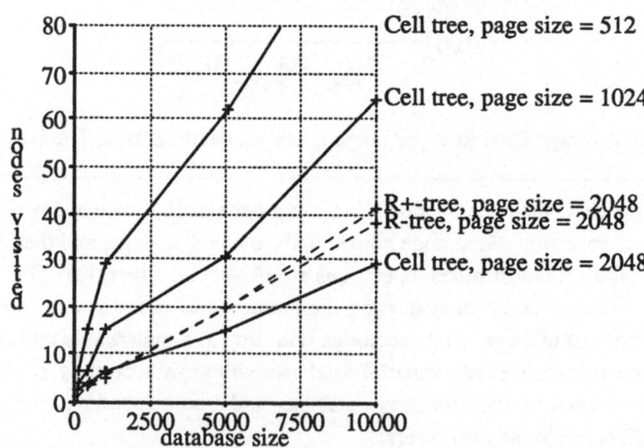

Figure 16b: Average number of nodes visited per range query vs. database size. The size of the search space is 1.

5. Conclusions

The cell tree is a new dynamic index structure for geometric databases. All data objects in the database are represented as unions of convex point sets (cells). The cell tree is a balanced tree structure whose leafs contain the cells and whose interior nodes correspond to a hierarchy of nested convex polyhedra. This index structure allows quick access to the cells (and therefore to the data objects) that occupy a given location in space. Furthermore, the cell tree represents an attempt to minimize the number of disk accesses per search operation. Each tree node corresponds to a disk page, and no pages other than those containing the cell tree will be required to answer a given search query. This is an important advantage of the cell tree over the R-tree and related structures, where data objects may have to be retrieved from secondary memory, therefore causing additional disk accesses. Point locations and range searches can therefore be carried out very efficiently using the cell tree.

In this paper, we reported our experiences with the implementation of the cell tree and presented the results of a performance evaluation. It became clear that a large page size should be chosen to optimize the performance of a cell tree. We are currently working on the integration of the cell tree with POSTGRES [Ston86b], a new extensible database system which has been designed and implemented at the University of California at Berkeley. The cell tree will be integrated using POSTGRES' planned facility for user-defined access methods. Furthermore, we will also implement the R-tree by Guttman [Gutt84] and the R+-tree by Sellis et al. [Sell87] under POSTGRES. This implementation will enable us to run a series of benchmarks on very large geometric databases and to compare the performance of these three index structures. Our experiments with smaller databaes indicate that the cell tree may require more storage space and more CPU time to answer a given search query. In return, however, the cell tree should obtain the results with a lower number of disk accesses than the two rival structures.

References

[Baye72] Bayer, R. and McCreight, E. M., Organization and maintenance of large ordered indices, *Acta Informatica* **1**, 3 (1972), pages 1-21.

[Brow79] Brown, K. Q., *Geometric transformations for fast geometric algorithms*, Ph.D. dissertation, Carnegie-Mellon University, Pittsburgh, Pa., Dec. 1979.

[Come79] Comer, D., The ubiquitous B-tree, *Computing Surveys* **11**, 2 (1979), pages 121-138.

[Falo87] Faloutsos, C., Sellis, T., and Roussopoulos, N., Analysis of object oriented spatial access methods, in *Proc. of ACM SIGMOD Conference on Management of Data*, San Francisco, Ca., June 1987.

[Fuch80] Fuchs, H., Kedem, Z., and Naylor, B., On visible surface generation by a priori tree structures, *Computer Graphics* **14**, 3 (June 1980).

[Fuch83] Fuchs, H., Abram, G. D., and Grant, E. D., Near real-time shaded display of rigid objects, *Computer Graphics* **17**, 3 (Summer 1983), pages 65-72.

[Gree89] Greene, D., An implementation and performance analysis of spatial data access methods, in *Proc. IEEE Fifth International Conference on Data Engineering*, Los Angeles, Ca., to appear, Feb. 1989.

[Gunt87a] Gunther, O. and Wong, E., A dual space representation for geometric data, in *Proc. 13th International Conference on Very Large Data Bases*, Brighton, England, Sept. 1987.

[Gunt87b] Gunther, O. and Wong, E., A dual approach to detect polyhedral intersections in arbitrary dimensions, in *Proc. 25th Annual Allerton Conf. on Comm., Control and Comp.*, Oct. 1987.

[Gunt88] Gunther, O., *Efficient structures for geometric data management*, Lecture Notes in Computer Science No. 337, Springer-Verlag, Berlin, 1988.

[Gunt89a] Gunther, O., The cell tree: An object-oriented index structure for geometric databases, in *Proc. IEEE Fifth International Conference on Data Engineering*, Los Angeles, Ca., to appear, Feb. 1989.

[Gunt89b] Gunther, O. and Wong, E., Convex polyhedral chains: A representation for geometric data, *Computer-Aided Design*, to appear, 1989.

[Gutt84] Guttman, A., R-trees: A dynamic index structure for spatial searching, in *Proc. of ACM SIGMOD Conference on Management of Data*, Boston, Ma., June 1984.

[Hinr85] Hinrichs, K. H., *The grid file system: Implementation and case studies of applications*, ETH Zürich, Dissertation No. 7734, 1985.

[Krie86] Kriegel, H. P. and Seeger, B., Multidimensional order preserving linear hashing with partial expansions, in *Proc. International Conference on Database Theory*, Lecture Notes in Computer Science, Springer, Berlin, 1986.

[Lee84] Lee, D. T. and Preparata, F. P., Computational geometry - a survey, *IEEE Trans. on Computers* **C-33**, 12 (Dec. 1984), pages 1072-1101.

[Niev84] Nievergelt, J., Hinterberger, H., and Sevcik, K. C., The grid file: An adaptable, symmetric multikey file structure, *ACM Trans. on Database Systems* **9**, 1 (March 1984), pages 38-71.

[Niev87]   Nievergelt, J. and Hinrichs, K., Storage and access structures for geometric data bases, in *Proc. International Conference on Foundations of Data Organization 1985*, S. Ghosh, Y. Kambayashi, K. Tanaka (eds.), Plenum Press, New York, 1987, pages 441-455.

[Prep79]   Preparata, F. P. and Muller, D. E., Finding the intersection of a set of N half-spaces in time $O(N \log N)$, *Theoret. Comput. Sci.* **8** (1979), pages 45-55.

[Prep85]   Preparata, F. P. and Shamos, M. I., *Computational geometry*, Springer, New York, NY, 1985.

[Robi81]   Robinson, J. T., The k-d-b tree: A search structure for large multidimensional dynamic indexes, in *Proc. of ACM SIGMOD Conference on Management of Data*, April 1981.

[Rous85]   Roussopoulos, N. and Leifker, D., Direct spatial search on pictorial databases using packed R-trees, in *Proc. of ACM SIGMOD Conference on Management of Data*, Austin, Tx., June 1985.

[Sell87]   Sellis, T., Roussopoulos, N., and Faloutsos, C., The R+-tree: A dynamic index for multi-dimensional objects, in *Proc. 13th International Conference on Very Large Data Bases*, Brighton, England, Sept. 1987.

[Six86]   Six, H.-W. and Widmayer, P., Hintergrundspeicherstrukturen für ausgedehnte Objekte, in *Tagungsband GI - 16. Jahrestagung*, Informatik-Fachberichte No. 126, Springer, Berlin, Oct. 1986.

[Ston86a] Stonebraker, M., Sellis, T., and Hanson, E., An analysis of rule indexing implementations in data base systems, in *Proc. of the 1st International Conference on Expert Data Base Systems*, April 1986.

[Ston86b] Stonebraker, M. and Rowe, L., The design of POSTGRES, in *Proc. of ACM SIGMOD Conference on Management of Data*, Washington, DC, June 1986.

[Tamm82]   Tamminen, M. and Sulonen, R., The EXCELL method for efficient geometric access to data, in *Proc. 19th ACM Design Automation Conf.*, 1982, pages 345-351.

[Whit57]   Whitney, H., *Geometric integration theory*, Princeton University Press, Princeton, NJ, 1957.

Adding Inferencing to a Relational Database Management System

R. Marti, C. Wieland, B. Wüthrich

Institut für Informationssysteme, ETH-Zentrum, 8092 Zürich

Abstract

The LogiQuel System is a deductive DBMS which supports the management of clauses expressed in LogiQuel, a language with the expressive power of extended Datalog with negation. The inference mechanism used to evaluate LogiQuel queries is both sound and complete under the tight-tree semantics. The system is implemented on top of a commercial relational DBMS. After a brief overview of LogiQuel we show how a LogiQuel statement is translated into SQL for subsequent evaluation by the DBMS.

Kurzfassung

Das LogiQuel System ist ein deduktives Datenbanksystem, das die Verwaltung von Klauseln unterstützt. Dazu wird die Sprache LogiQuel, die erweitertem Datalog mit Negation entspricht, verwendet. Der Inferenzmechanismus, der zur Evaluation von LogiQuel Abfragen verwendet wird, ist korrekt und vollständig bezüglich der "Tight-Tree" Semantik. Das System wurde auf der Basis eines kommerziellen relationalen Datenbanksystems implementiert. Nach einem kurzen Überblick über LogiQuel wird gezeigt, wie LogiQuel Anweisungen in entsprechende SQL Anweisungen übersetzt und anschliessend vom Datenbanksystem ausgewertet werden.

1. Introduction

The merging of services provided by expert system shells, (i.e., high-level knowledge representation models, inferencing, and explanation facilities) with those offered by DBMS products, (i.e., semantic integrity checking, authorization, concurrency control, and recovery) appears highly desirable since it allows the sharing of the knowledge between different "intelligent" applications. Therefore, we have decided to design and implement a deductive DBMS [Gallaire et al. 84] as a first step toward the goal of a truly integrated knowledge base management system. Our system, called the LogiQuel system, extends the capabilities of a relational DBMS by allowing the storage of multiple facts together with multiple, potentially recursive rules in a uniform manner.

2. LogiQuel

LogiQuel is an attempt to combine the best of two worlds, namely, relational database query languages and logic programming languages. The language is entirely declarative, set-oriented and strongly typed[1]. Its syntax is similar to that of Prolog [Clocksin &Mellish 87].

Informally, a LogiQuel knowledge base consists of a set of *clauses*, each of which has a head consisting of a predicate, the symbol : – denoting logical implication, and a body consisting of a (possibly empty) set of literals connected by logical conjunctions (denoted by the symbol &) and disjunctions (denoted by |). A *literal* is either a predicate or a negated predicate. A *predicate* is either declarative, that is, declared explicitly by the user, or evaluable. Evaluable predicates, such as = or >, are pre-defined. As usual, a clause with an empty body is called a *fact* and a clause with a non-empty body is called a *rule*.

A LogiQuel *query* consists of the symbol ?– and a collection of literals connected by conjunctions and disjunctions. If a query contains no variables, its answer is yes if the clause representing the query can be inferred from the clauses in the knowledge base and no otherwise. Alternatively, if one or more variables occur in a query, its answer is the set of all variable substitutions for which the clause representing the query is true.

---

[1] To some degree, strong typing was a consequence of our decision to store knowledge in a relational database. However, we believe that strong typing is desirable in order to protect the semantic integrity of the knowledge base.

In order to guarantee the soundness and completeness of the inference process, all clauses must fulfil the allowedness property as defined below:

Def.: A variable is *secure* if it occurs in the body of a clause[2], either as an argument of a non-negated declarative predicate or in an equality predicate within which it can be computed from constants and other secure variables.

Def.: A clause is *allowed* if and only if every variable occurring in the clause is secure.

The set of values which a secure variable can assume at each step of the query evaluation is finite and each value can be computed from values stored in the knowledge base. For example, in the clause

```
Ancestor('Adam', x).    /* Adam is everybody's ancestor */
```

the variable x is not secure and, as a result, some queries about ancestors have infinitely many answers. However, the following modified clause fulfils the property of allowedness as defined above:

```
Ancestor('Adam', x) :- Person(x).
```

The expressive power of LogiQuel is equivalent to that of extended Datalog with negation. The extensions to Datalog we support are assigment of values and arithmetic within equalities. By negation we mean that we are not restricted to Horn clauses. The semantics of a LogiQuel knowledge base is the tight tree semantics [Van Gelder 88] which is equivalent to the iterated fixed-point semantics for stratified knowledge bases (see also [Lloyd 87]). The semantics of negation is defined by the closed world assumption [Reiter 78]. As a result, it is possible to prove that our inference process is both sound and complete.

3. Translating LogiQuel to SQL

Facts are represented in a LogiQuel knowledge base as rows of a base table while (non-recursive) rules are represented as views. This representation determines the translation of LogiQuel statements into the database query language of the underlying DBMS, i.e. SQL [Date 87]:

A declaration DECLARE p(...) is translated into CREATE TABLE p_ext(...). Moreover, the LogiQuel system catalog (see Chapter 5) is updated accordingly. The assertion of a fact with predicate symbol p results in the insertion of a tuple into the base table p_ext. Similarly, a retraction is translated into an SQL DELETE-statement. Assertions and retractions of rules are more difficult to handle. Essentially, these operations involve the following two steps: The body of the rule must be translated into an SQL SELECT-statement (see below). Moreover, the LogiQuel system catalog must be updated to reflect the addition or removal of a rule. This involves the manipulation of a directed graph which describes the evaluation dependencies between declarative predicates (see Chapter 4).

The translation of a LogiQuel query (or the body of a LogiQuel rule) is done in three steps:
1. The query is transformed into disjunctive normal form
2. Each normalized sub-expression is checked for the allowedness property. Subsequently, an SQL SELECT-statement is generated according to the algorithm outlined below.
3. The SELECT-statements constructed in step 2 are concatenated into a single SELECT-statement using the SQL UNION-operator.

The basic algorithm for translating a sub-expression without disjunctions (step 2) works as follows:

```
FOR each predicate p in the sub-expression DO
  IF p is declarative THEN
    IF p is not negated THEN
      FOR each argument a of p DO
        IF a is a variable THEN
          IF a occurred before THEN
            generate join condition "WHERE column_name = join_column_name";
          END;
        ELSE  (* a is a constant *)
          generate selection condition "WHERE column_name = constant";
```

---

2   In these definitions, it is assumed that all clauses are in disjunctive normal form.

```
           END;
         END;
       ELSE  (* p is negated *)
         generate join condition involving a sub-query
           "WHERE (...) NOT IN (SELECT ... FROM p WHERE ...)"
       END;
     ELSE  (* p is evaluable, i.e., one of the operators =, #, <, <=, >, >= *)
       IF both operands are variables THEN
         generate join condition "WHERE column_name_1 operator column_name_2";
       ELSE
         generate selection condition "WHERE column_name operator expression";
       END;
     END;
   END;
```

The following simple examples illustrate how the algorithm works. For the sake of simplicity, we assume that for all tables, the name of the first column is $c1$, the name of the second column is $c2$, and so forth.

```
?- P(x,y,z) & Q(z,w) & Q(w,3) & y > 5.    SELECT  A1.c1, A1.c2, A1.c3, A2.c2
                                          FROM    P A1, Q A2, Q A3
                                          WHERE   A2.c1=A1.c3 AND A3.c1=A2.c2
                                          AND     A3.c2=3 AND A1.c2>5.
?- P(x,y,z) & ~Q(y,0).                    SELECT  A1.c1, A1.c2, A1.c3
                                          FROM    P A1
                                          WHERE   A1.c2 NOT IN (SELECT A2.c1
                                                               FROM   Q A2
                                                               WHERE  A2.c2=0)
```

4. Query Evaluation

The key principle of our query evaluation strategy is that as much work as possible is left to the underlying DBMS. Thus, we hope to profit from previous work in database query optimization. A somewhat related principle is that the number of calls issued to the DBMS should be as small as possible. There are two reasons for this principle: First, each DBMS call incurs overhead in parsing, catalog lookup, optimization, etc. Moreover, the DBMS should be able to apply certain global optimizations on a single complex query which it could not do on a collection of several simple queries producing the same result. Therefore, in the absence of recursion, query evaluation is left up to the DBMS.

The interesting cases are those involving recursive predicates. In order to formally define the notion of recursion, we have to look at the evaluation dependencies between the predicates involved in rules: For example, if the knowledge base contains a rule of the form $p()\ :-\ q()$ then the answer of a query involving p obviously depends on the answer of a query involving q. (The same were true if q were negated.) We denote such a dependency between two predicates q and p as $q\ ->\ p$. Moreover, the transitive, non-reflexive closure of the $->$ relation is denoted by $->^*$. This is used in the following definitions:

Def.: A declarative predicate p is *recursive* if and only if there exists a declarative predicate q such that both $p\ ->^*\ q$ and $q\ ->^*\ p$ hold. The predicate q is said to be *recursive with respect to* p and vice versa.

Def.: A declarative predicate p is *linearly recursive* if and only if it is recursive and in each (normalized) rule with p in its head, there is at most one declarative predicate in the body of that rule which is recursive to p.

Def.: A declarative predicate q is *strongly connected* to the declarative predicate p if both $p\ ->^*\ q$ and $q\ ->^*\ p$ hold. Moreover, each declarative predicate p is strongly connected to itself.
The *strongly connected component* of p, denoted by [p], is the set of all to p strongly connected declarative predicates.

A LogiQuel query is evaluated as follows: First, the graph describing the evaluation dependencies between declarative predicates, which is kept in the system catalog, is extended with a node representing the query and edges which lead from the predicate symbols which occur in the query toward the node representing the query. For example, for the query `?-p(.)` the single edge `p -> query` is added to the graph. Then, this graph is transformed by collapsing strongly connected components to a single node. The resulting graph is acyclic and has a single root node[3], namely the node which represents the query. The constructed graph is traversed starting at an arbitrary leaf node and gradually working its way toward the root of this graph. Different actions are taken depending on what an inspected node represents:

- If the node represents a single, non-recursive predicate, a view representing the union of all facts (stored in a table) and all rules (represented as view or as temporary table) for that predicate is defined.
- If the node represents a collection of n mutually recursive predicates which are all linearly recursive then the extensions of the n temporary relations corresponding to the n predicates are computed according to the semi-naive evaluation strategy [Bancilhon & Ramakrishnan 86].
- In all other cases, the node represents n mutually recursive predicates, at least one of which is not linearly recursive. In this case, the extensions of the n temporary relations are computed using the naive strategy [Bancilhon & Ramakrishnan 86] since, in general, the semi-naive strategy cannot handle non-linear forms of recursion.

The basic idea of both the naive and the semi-naive strategy is to handle recursion by repeatedly issuing join queries and adding the newly generated tuples to a temporary table until the join queries produce no new tuples. The naive strategy requires two temporary tables and two views for each mutually recursive predicate[4]. For a recursive predicate with name p, the temporary tables are named `p_delta` and p where `p_delta` is an used to store the facts derived in one iteration and p is used to store all facts derived so far. The two auxiliary views are named `p_init` and `p_rec`. `p_init` is defined as the union of all rules with head p which do not have a recursive predicate in their body. This view is used to initialize table p. `p_rec` in turn is defined as the union of all rules with head p and at least one recursive predicate in their body. This view is used at each iteration step to compute the tuples for `p_delta`.

For example, the four rules

```
p(.) :- q(.).   q(.) :- p(.).   p(.) :- r(.).   p(.) :- s(.) & t(.).
```

require the following view definitions for the mutually recursive predicates p and q:

```
CREATE VIEW p_init (...) AS SELECT ... FROM p_ext
                          UNION SELECT ... FROM r WHERE ...
                          UNION SELECT ... FROM s, t WHERE ...
CREATE VIEW q_init (...) AS SELECT ... FROM q_ext
CREATE VIEW p_rec (...) AS  SELECT ... FROM q
CREATE VIEW q_rec (...) AS  SELECT ... FROM p
```

The algorithm for naive query evaluation of all predicates belonging to the strongly connected component SCC works as follows:

```
FOR each predicate p in SCC DO p := "SELECT * FROM p_init" END;
REPEAT
   FOR each predicate p in SCC DO p_delta := "SELECT * FROM p_rec" END;
   unchanged := TRUE;
   FOR each predicate p in SCC DO
     "INSERT INTO p SELECT * FROM p_delta";
     IF tuples were inserted into p THEN unchanged := FALSE END;
   END;
UNTIL unchanged;
```


5. LogiQuel System Architecture

The current implementation of the LogiQuel System is based on the relational database management system Oracle [Oracle 87]. On top of Oracle, we have implemented a front-end to support the additional features of LogiQuel. This front-end is implemented entirely in Modula–2. Its module structure is shown below:

---

3   A root node is defined as a node with no outgoing edges. Similarly, a leaf node is defined as a node with no incoming edges.

4   Semi-naive query evaluation works similarly but is more efficient in that it avoids some unnecessary work inherent in the naive strategy. Our implementation of the semi-naive strategy requires three auxiliary tables and two views.

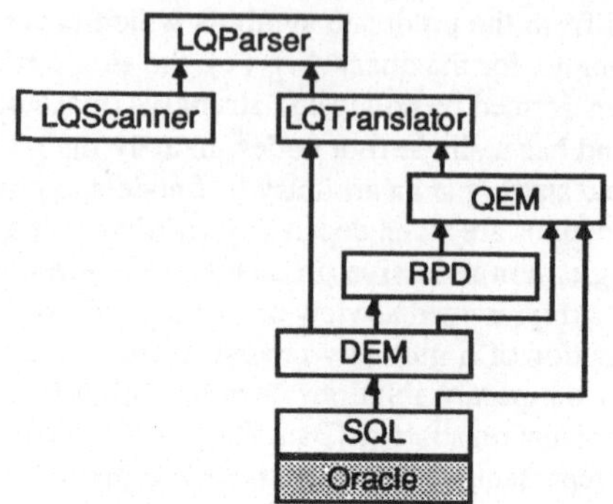

Modules `LQParser` and `LQScanner` handle the syntactical and lexical analysis of LogiQuel using the technique of recursive descent. The transformation of LogiQuel into SQL statements (see Chapter 3) is performed by the `LQTranslator` module. The query evaluation algorithm of Chapter 4 is implemented in module `QEM` (**Q**uery **E**valuation **M**anager) with the help of module `RPD` (**R**ecursive **P**redicate **D**etector). Module `DEM` (**DE**scription **M**anager) provides procedures to manage the LogiQuel system catalog which keeps track of predicate declarations and dependencies (see below). Finally, module `SQL` serves as interface to the underlying Oracle DBMS.

The LogiQuel system catalog consists of a collection of tables which are under system control. Some of these tables belong to the Oracle system catalog (e.g., tables `SYSTABLE` and `SYSCOLUMN`). In addition to these, the LogiQuel system catalog consists of the following tables:

```
Predicate (predName)
Argument (predName, argName, argType, argLength, nullAllowed)
Rule (ruleNr, headPredName, lqBody, sqlBody)
RulePredDep (ruleNr, bodyPredName, numOccurrences)
```

The tables `Predicate` and `Argument` are used to store information about user-declared predicates. The dependency graph introduced in Chapter 4 is represented in the tables `Rule` and `RulePredDep`. For each rule, the `Rule` table contains an entry consisting of the predicate name appearing in the rule head (column `headPredName`) and two strings representing the body of the rule in both LogiQuel and SQL source form (columns `lqBody` and `sqlBody`). The `RulePredDep` table contains multiple entries per rule, one for each declarative predicate occurring in the body of the rule (column `bodyPredName`).

6. Conclusion

We have described a way to extend a relational DBMS such that it supports the representation of (potentially recursive) rules. We have shown how the query evaluation provided by the DBMS can be extended to provide an inference mechanism similar to the mechanisms found in Prolog and expert system shells. We see the resulting deductive DBMS as a first step toward an integrated knowledge base management system serving multiple applications which display various degrees of intelligence.

References

[Bancilhon & Ramakrishnan 86] F. Bancilhon and R. Ramakrishnan: An Amateur's Introduction to Recursive Query Processing Strategies. *Proc. ACM SIGMOD Int. Conf. on Management of Data*, pp.16–52, 1986.

[Clocksin & Mellish 87] W.F. Clocksin and C.S. Mellish: *Programming in Prolog*. 3rd Edition. Springer Verlag, 1987.

[Date 87] C.J. Date: *A Guide to the SQL Standard*. Addison Wesley, 1987.

[Gallaire et al. 84] H. Gallaire, J. Minker and J.-M. Nicolas: Logic and Databases: A Deductive Approach. *ACM Computing Surveys, Vol. 16, No. 2*, 1984.

[Lloyd 87] J.W. Lloyd: *Foundations of Logic Programming, 2nd Edition*. Springer Verlag, 1987.

[Oracle 87] Oracle Corporation: *Oracle Overview and Introduction to SQL*. Oracle Part No. 3801, 1987.

[Reiter 78] R. Reiter: Deductive Question Answering on Relational Databases. *Logic and Databases*, pp. 149–177, Plenum Press, 1978.

[Van Gelder 88] A. Van Gelder: Negation as Failure Using Tight Derivations for General Logic Programs. *Foundations of Deductive Databases and Logic Programming*, J. Minker (Ed.), Morgan Kaufmann, pp. 149–176, 1988.

Ein Geschichts- und Versionsmodell für komplexe Objekte

Wolfgang Käfer
Universität Kaiserslautern

Überblick

Nicht-Standard-Datenbanksysteme (NDBS) werden zur Verwaltung komplex strukturierter Objekte, wie sie beispielsweise in Ingenieur- oder Büroanwendungen vorkommen, entwickelt. Die Integration der Zeit in das Datenmodell ist eine inhärente Forderung, wenn zusätzlich Entwurfsabläufe oder Büroprozeduren unterstützt werden sollen. Die heterogenen Anwendungen führen zu unterschiedlichen Zeitmodellen, die durch Begriffe wie "Version" oder "Geschichte" gekennzeichnet sind.

Das vorgestellte TeMA-Datenmodell erlaubt die Definition und Verarbeitung von zeitbehafteten oder versionsbehafteten Entities. Der gemeinsame Kern der Zeitmodelle und dessen Grundstrukturen und -operationen sowie deren Implementierung als Zusatzebene des NDBS PRIMA /Hä87/ werden aufgezeigt.

1. Das Geschichtsmodell

Das Geschichtsmodell basiert auf den in /Hä84/ und /Kl81/ vorgestellten Überlegungen und ist in /Kä88/ beschrieben. Die Geschichte eines Entities wird als *zeitlich geordnete Folge von charakteristischen Aussagen*, den sog. *Geschichtsausprägungen*, zusammen mit einer Auswertefunktion gesehen. Damit lassen sich sowohl zustandserhaltende (z.B. Kontostand), ereignisorientierte (z.B. Ein-/Auszahlungen auf/von einem Konto) als auch kontinuierliche (z.B. Fieberkurve) Geschichten abbilden. Der Ablauf der Geschichte wird dabei durch die *Gültigkeitszeit* geprägt, die angibt, zu welchem Zeitpunkt die Aussage in der realen Welt zu wirken beginnt. Die *Aufzeichnungszeit* beschreibt den Zeitpunkt, zu dem die Aussage in der Datenbank abgespeichert wurde und wird somit im Gegensatz zur Gültigkeitszeit vom DBS automatisch bestimmt (Revision). Sie ist von der primär interessierenden Gültigkeitszeit unabhängig (z.B. rückwirkende Lohnerhöhungen). Dies hat zur Folge, daß für die Aktualisierung von Geschichten neben den Operationen zum Erzeugen und Anfügen von Aussagen auch das Einfügen und aus praktischen Erwägungen auch das Ändern und Löschen benötigt werden. Weiterhin müssen neben den einfachen Wiedergewinnungsoperationen, die "AS-OF"- und "WALK-THRU-TIME"-Anfragen auf Geschichten realisieren, auch Operationen zur Unterstützung komplexer Anfragen (z.B. zeitbehafteter Verbund) vorgesehen werden. Die Relevanz der Gültigkeitszeit in CIM-Umgebungen wird schon in /BI87, MS83/ aufgezeigt. Sie resultiert aus der Tatsache, daß CIM die Schnittstelle zwischen den "internen" Produktionsunterlagen (Miniwelt) und dem fertigen Produkt (Welt) etabliert.

In CAD-Umgebungen wird die Gültigkeitszeit wenig beachtet, da die Miniwelt stark in sich abgeschlossen ist. Bei der Entwicklung eines "Objektes" werden meist nur Abhängigkeiten innerhalb des Objektes verwaltet.

2. Das Versionsmodell

Das Versionsmodell wurde im wesentlichen aus den in /BK85, DL88, KAC86/ und /KSW86/ vorgestellten Anforderungen entwickelt. Analog zum Geschichtsmodell müssen die Veränderungen der Entities als zunächst *ungeordnete Menge von Versionen* (= unterschiedliche Beschreibung des gleichen Entity) aufgezeichnet werden. Die *Entstehungsreihenfolge* wird meist durch eine fortlaufende Numerierung, die *Abstammungsbeziehungen* (welche Version wurde aus welcher Version entwickelt) meist in Form von azyklischen, gerichteten Graphen dokumentiert. Auch eine Darstellung wichtiger Entwurfsentscheidungen (diese Version beschreibt einen alternativen Lösungsweg) wird gefordert (*Klassifizierung* von Versionen eines Entities, beispielsweise als "Alternativen").

Die Verwaltung der Versionsmengen und der Entstehungsreihenfolge wird durch das Geschichtsmodell in natürlicher Weise unterstützt. Im folgenden wird deshalb auch nicht mehr zwischen Versionen und Aussagen bzw. Versionsmengen und Geschichtsausprägungen unterschieden. Innerhalb der Versionsverwaltung müssen zusätzlich Operationen zur Manipulation von azyklischen, gerichteten Graphen und Klassen bereitgestellt werden.

Weiterhin müssen *Beziehungen zwischen Versionsmengen* (und nicht zwischen Aussagen wie im Geschichtsmodell) behandelt werden können. Diese Forderung ergibt sich aus dem Entwurfsvorgang, bei dem erst in einer späteren Verfeinerung entschieden wird, welche der Versionen eines Entities konkret verwendet werden soll. Diese sog. *generischen Referenzen* sind den Geschichtsmodellen nicht inhärent.

Zusammenfassend läßt sich festhalten, daß in unserem Geschichts- und Versionsmodell ein Entity durch folgende Begriffe beschrieben wird:

- Aussage/Version: dient zur Beschreibung eines Entities zu einem Änderungsstand
- Graph: spezifiziert Beziehungen zwischen Versionen eines Entities
- Klasse: faßt Versionen (mit gleichen Eigenschaften) eines Entities zusammen
- Referenz: wird zur Bildung von generischen und direkten Beziehungen herangezogen

Der folgende Abschnitt befaßt sich mit der Implementierung dieser Objekte im Molekül-Atom-Datenmodell (MAD-Modell, /Mi87, Mi88/). Dabei werden die Objektstrukturen durch das MAD-Modell beschrieben und die Objekte selbst als die Grundeinheiten des Temporalen MAD-Modells (TeMA-Datenmodell) vorgestellt.

3. Integration in das MAD-Modell

3.1 Skizzierung des MAD-Modells

Beim MAD-Modell handelt es sich um eine Relationenmodell-Erweiterung, deren Ziel der konsistente Übergang der Verarbeitung von homogenen zu heterogenen Satzmengen ist. Die Grundelemente des MAD-Modells sind die *Atomtypen*. Sie sind vergleichbar mit den Relationen des Relationenmodells, d.h., sie fassen *Attribute* unterschiedlichen Typs zusammen. Aus diesen Atomtypen können dynamisch *Molekültypen* gebildet werden. Ein Molekültyp ist die Zusammenfassung von Atomtypen, zwischen denen definierte *Beziehungstypen* existieren. Die Spezifikation dieser Beziehungstypen basiert auf einem vom *System unterstützten Primärschlüssel-Fremdschlüssel-Konzept*, welches durch speziell dafür eingeführte Attributtypen (IDENTIFIER und REFERENCE) realisiert wird. Jeder Beziehungstyp wird immer symmetrisch (d.h. als bidirektionale Beziehung) dargestellt, wobei sowohl (1:1) als auch (1:n)- bzw. (n:m)-Beziehungen direkt und als Teil des Atomtyps beschrieben werden können. Damit können auf Atomebene beliebige Netzstrukturen aufgebaut werden. Molekültypen können selbst wieder zum Aufbau noch komplexerer, insbesondere rekursiver Molekültypen benutzt werden.

Die Datenmanipulationssprache des MAD-Modells (MQL, Molecule Query Language) erlaubt die Verarbeitung von Molekülmengen, wobei jedes Molekül wiederum aus einer Menge von Atomen potentiell verschiedener Typen besteht. Der Typ der Moleküle entspricht dabei entweder einem bereits vordefinierten Molekültyp oder er wird dynamisch in der Anweisung festgelegt. MQL ist an SQL angelehnt und besteht analog aus einer FROM-Klausel (zur Spezifikation und Definition der für die Anweisung relevanten Molekültypen), einer WHERE-Klausel (zur Spezifikation der Restriktionen / Qualifikationsbedingungen) und einer SELECT-Klausel (zur Spezifikation der Projektionen).

3.2 Realisierung der Geschichtsausprägungen bzw. der Versionsmengen

Die Geschichtsausprägungen bilden die Einheit der Verarbeitung der Geschichts- und Versionsverwaltung und entsprechen aus dieser Sicht den Atomen des MAD-Modells. Die Darstellungsmächtigkeit der Atome ist jedoch zu gering, um zeitlich geordnete *Folgen von Aussagen* modellieren zu können. Deshalb werden die Aussagen bzw. Versionen als Atome, die Folge derselben als (generische) Moleküle gebildet. Jeder versionsbehaftete Atomtyp wird durch genau einen Molekültyp realisiert, der aus zwei Atomtypen aufgebaut ist, um zugunsten eines schnellen Zugriffs auf die aktuellen Daten, eine Trennung von aktuellen und historischen Daten zu erreichen. Die Atome eines solchen Molekültyps werden zeitlich geordnet, d.h., beginnend von den aktuellen Daten wird eine zeitlich sortierte Liste von historischen Daten (mittels Rekursion) aufgebaut. Aus diesen Anforderungen läßt sich das MAD-Schema-Diagramm aus Bild 1 ableiten.

Der Atomtyp **?_topic** umfaßt dabei die aktuellen Daten. Über den Beziehungstyp **hist** können die nächst älteren Daten erreicht werden. Durch den Beziehungstyp **later** wird dieser Vorgang rekursiv in die Vergangenheit fortgesetzt. Nach diesem Prinzip wird jeder zeitbehaftete Atomtyp im Anwenderschema in einen entsprechenden Molekültyp umgesetzt. Bild 2 zeigt dies an einem Beispiel.

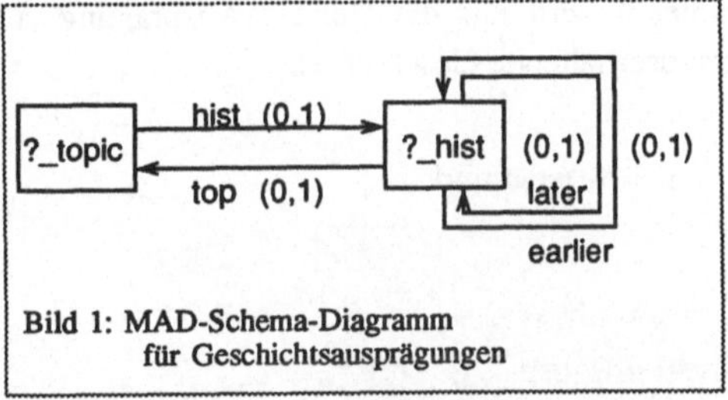

Bild 1: MAD-Schema-Diagramm
für Geschichtsausprägungen

Die Beschreibung des versionsbehafteten Atomtyps **bsp** (mit einem baumartigen Abstammungsgraphen **extraction**, ohne Klassen) im TeMA-Datenmodell wird im MAD-Modell durch eine Molekültypdefinition ersetzt. Die in der DEFINE MOLECULE_TYPE-Anweisung angegebene FROM-Klausel gibt die Struktur des Moleküls an. Es wird eine "lineare Liste" erzeugt, deren Anker durch ein Atom des Typs **bsp_topic** und deren folgende Elemente durch Atome des Typs **bsp_hist** gebildet werden. Die Kardinalitätsrestriktion "(0,1)" besagt, daß 0 oder 1 **bsp_hist**-Atom über die Beziehung **hist** erreicht werden kann. Die RECURSIVE-Klausel bewirkt, daß die Liste solange in die Vergangenheit expandiert wird, bis keine weiteren Elemente mehr erreichbar sind. Die Angabe "(0,*)" hätte eine Struktur in Art eines "Pointer-Array" definiert, dessen Reihenfolgeinformation aber innerhalb der MQL nicht effizient einzusetzen gewesen wäre.

<table>
<tr><td>TeMA-Datenmodell</td><td></td><td>MAD-Modell</td></tr>
</table>

```
CREATE TEMPORAL_ATOM_TYPE  bsp
  (extraction : TREE; NO_CLASSES)
  (bsp_id  : IDENTIFIER,
    . (* benutzerdefinierte Attribute *)
              );
```

Abbildung
⟹

```
DEFINE MOLECULE_TYPE bsp : ALL

  FROM   bsp_topic.hist-bsp_hist

  RECURSIVE   bsp_hist.later-bsp_hist
```

Definition der den Molekültyp konstituierenden Atomtypen im MAD-Modell:

```
CREATE   ATOM_TYPE bsp_topic
(bsp_id           : IDENTIFIER,
valid             : TIME,
alive             : BOOLEAN,
extraction_succ   : REFERENCE (bsp_topic.extraction_pred) (0,*),
extraction_pred   : REFERENCE (bsp_topic.extraction_succ) (0,1),
hist              : REFERENCE (bsp_hist.top) (0,1),
                  :
                  : (* benutzerdefinierte Attribute *)
                  :           );
```

```
CREATE ATOM_TYPE bsp_hist
(bsp_v_id  : IDENTIFIER,
valid      : TIME,
top        : REFERENCE (bsp_topic.hist) (0,1),
later      : REFERENCE (bsp_hist.earlier) (0,1),
earlier    : REFERENCE (bsp_hist.later) (0,1),
           :
           :
           : (* benutzerdefinierte Attribute *)
           :           );
```

Bild 2: Definition eines versionsbehafteten Atomtyps

Die vordefinierten Molekültypen, die als Makros gesehen werden können, sind innerhalb der MQL wie Atomtypen verwendbar. Bei der Übersetzung der MQL-Anweisungen werden zunächst die Makros expandiert und anschließend die Projektions- und Selektionsklausel angewendet. In /Kä88/ wird diese Vorgehensweise auf die Selektionsklausel übertragen: es werden spezielle Prädikate zur Formulierung zeitbehafteter Anfragen bereitgestellt, die zur Übersetzungszeit auf Selektions- und Projektionsbedingungen auf den konstituierenden Atomen der Geschichtsausprägungen expandiert werden. Analog können spezielle Operatoren zur Verwaltung der Graphen und Klassen gebildet werden. In Bild 3 wird die Expansion für den Fall aufgezeigt, daß der Zustand von Geschichtsausprägungen zu einem bestimmten Zeitpunkt (in der Vergangenheit) ermittelt werden soll (der Zugriff auf eine bestimmte Version ist ein Sonderfall dieser Anfrage). Durch die UNTIL-Klausel wird die Evaluierung des Rekursivmoleküls bei Erreichung der benötigten Aussage abgebrochen. PREVIOUS bewirkt, daß diese Aussage noch zum Ergebnismolekül hinzugenommen wird. Von diesem gebildeten Rekursivmolekül wird nur die "letzte" Ausprägung (LAST) zur Bildung des Ergebnisses herangezogen (zustandserhaltende Geschichte).

TeMA-Datenmodell   **MAD-Modell**

```
SELECT *

FROM  bsp                 Expansion

WHERE (bsp_v_id = "?")      ===>

     AT  06.12.1988
```

```
SELECT bsp_hist (LAST)

FROM  bsp_topic.hist-bsp_hist

   RECURSIVE  bsp_hist.later-bsp_hist

   UNTIL bsp_hist.valid (PREVIOUS) <= 1988/12/06

WHERE (bsp_hist.bsp_v_id = "?") AND (alive = TRUE)
```

Bild 3: Expandierung einer Anfrage zur Bestimmung einer bestimmten Version

3.3 Realisierung direkter und generischer Referenzen

Die Bildung von Molekültypen geschieht im MAD-Modell durch die Definition von Beziehungstypen zwischen Atomtypen. Die Erweiterung der Atomtypen zu versionsbehafteten Atomtypen, die als Molekültypen realisiert sind, bewirkt, daß sich auch die Qualität der Referenzen ändert: an Stelle von Atomen müssen jetzt Moleküle (in ihrer Gesamtheit) referenziert werden. Eine Realisierung dieser Molekülreferenzen als Atomreferenzen auf das Wurzelatom des Moleküls genügt nicht. Bild 4 zeigt einen versionsbehafteten Molekültyp **ABC**, der durch drei versionsbehaftete Atomtypen **A**, **B** und **C** gebildet wird. Jeder versionsbehaftete Atomtyp wird gemäß Kapitel 3.2 durch einen entsprechenden Molekültyp realisiert, der aus je einem **topic**- und einem **hist**-Atomtyp gebildet wird. Bild 4 zeigt die Abbildung sowie eine mögliche Ausprägung, die nur aktuelle Daten enthält. Wegen der besseren Übersichtlichkeit werden die bidirektionalen Referenzen im Gegensatz zum MAD-Schema-Diagramm aus Bild 1 im folgenden durch ungerichtete Kanten dargestellt.

versionsbehafteter Molekültyp mit einer möglichen Ausprägung   **Abbildung im MAD-Modell**   **eine mögliche Ausprägung**

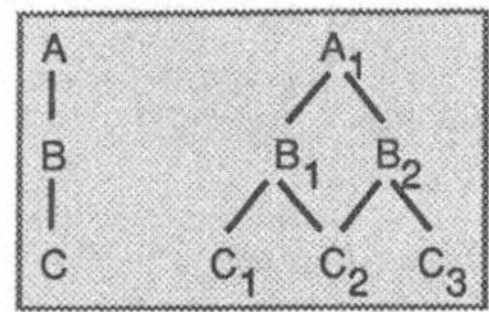
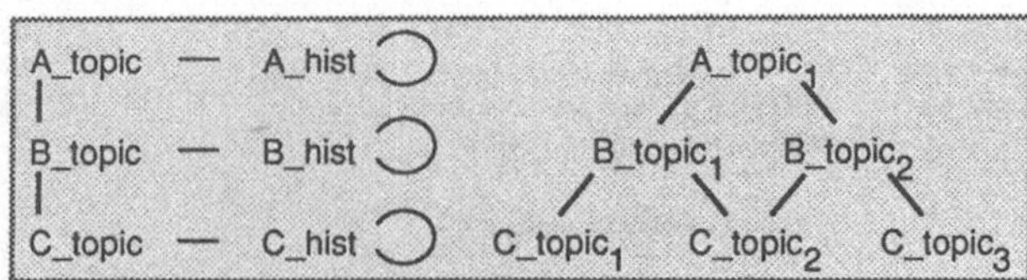

Bild 4: Beispiel eines versionsbehafteten Molekültyps zusammmen mit einer Ausprägung

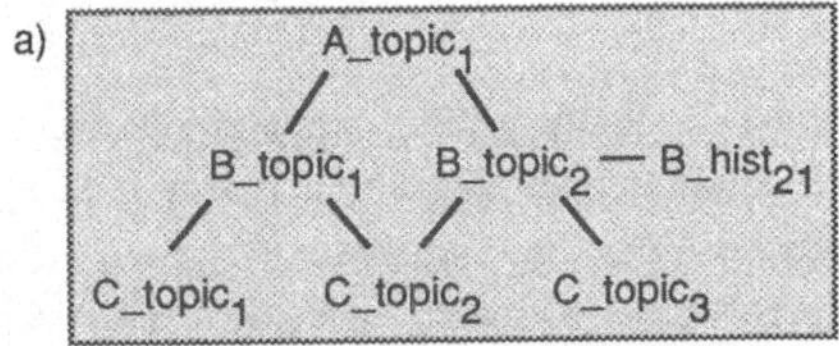
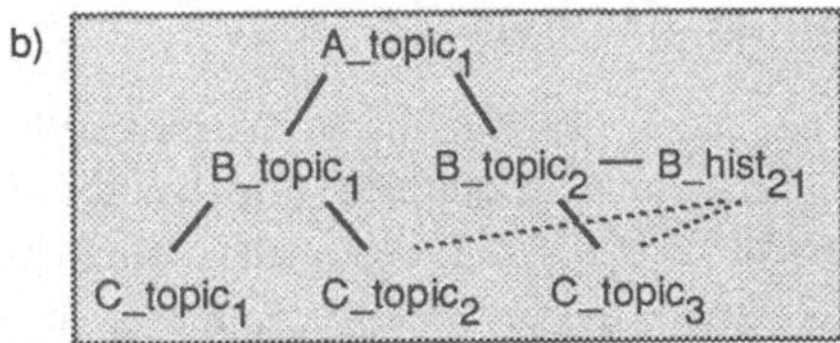

Bild 5: Änderung eines nicht-strukturbildenden und eines strukturbildenden Attributs in B_topic$_2$

Werden nicht-strukturbildende Attribute beispielsweise in **B_topic**$_2$ geändert, so ergibt sich die in Bild 5a dargestellte Änderung der Molekülausprägung. Wird allerdings ein strukturbildendes Attributpaar geändert, so daß beispielsweise die Beziehung zwischen **C_topic**$_2$ und **B_topic**$_2$ aufgelöst wird, so zeigt sich, daß die Referenzen auf die Wurzelatome nicht ausreichend sind. Im vor der Änderung aktuellen Atom **B_hist**$_{21}$ müssen Referenzen auf C_2 und C_3 enthalten sein, die auf die jeweiligen Wurzelatome **C_topic**$_2$ und **C_topic**$_3$ abgebildet werden. Wegen der Symmetrie der Referenzen müssen somit auch Referenzen von **C_topic**-Atomen auf **B_hist**-Atome möglich sein. Damit ergibt sich die Darstellung aus Bild 5b. Bei dieser Art der Referenzen handelt es sich um generische Referenzen. Soll eine konkrete Version verwendet werden, so muß sie noch innerhalb der Versionsmenge bestimmt werden, beispielsweise durch die Versionsnummer, durch eine bestimmte Eigenschaft usw. Zur Realisierung der direkten Referenzen wird eine weitere Beziehung zwischen den **hist**-Atomtypen benötigt. Damit ergibt sich das in Bild 6 dargestellte MAD-Schema-Diagramm.

Die molekülbildenden Referenzpaare zwischen **A**, **B** und **C** bzw. zwischen **A_topic**, **B_topic** und **C_topic** realisieren Beziehungen zwischen Entities, d.h. Mengen von Versionen und damit also generische Referenzen. Die Referenzpaare zwischen den **topic**- und den **hist**-Atomtypen sowie die rekursive Beziehung auf den **hist**-Atomtypen werden zur Bildung der versionsbehafteten Atomtypen benötigt. Das Referenzpaar zwischen den **hist**-Atomtypen realisiert direkte Referenzen.

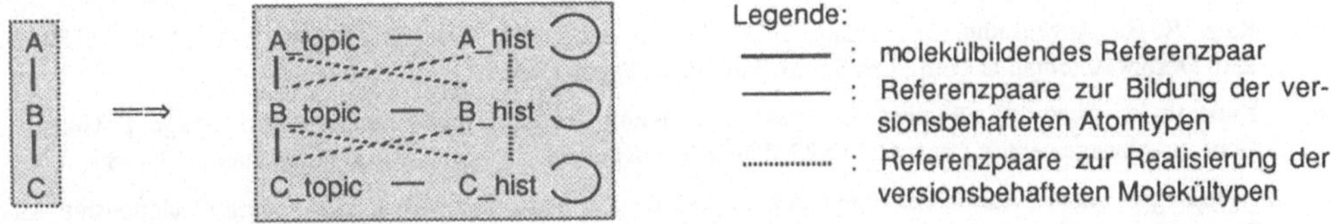

Bild 6: Realisierung von Molekülreferenzen

Anfragen auf versionsbehafteten Molekültypen werden analog den Anfragen auf versionsbehafteten Atomtypen behandelt:

1. Expansion der Molekültypdefinitionen (rekursiv).

2. Expansion der Prädikate (rekursiv) und Zuordnung zu den entsprechenden Atomtypen.

3. Die expandierte Anfrage entspricht einer herkömmlichen MQL-Anweisung. Das Ergebnis muß ggf. entsprechend den Vorgaben des Geschichts- oder Versionsmodells aufbereitet werden.

Eine exakte Beschreibung der Implementierung der Graphen und Klassen muß aus Platzgründen unterbleiben. Beide Konzepte können jedoch leicht mit dem Beziehungskonzept des MAD-Modells ausgedrückt werden. Ähnlich dem Rekursivmolekültyp zur Bildung der versionsbehafteten Atomtypen kann ein Rekursivmolekültyp für Graphen angegeben werden. Das Auffinden aller Vorgänger oder Nachfolger eines Graphknotens läßt sich auf eine elementare MQL-Anweisung zur Selektion des Referenzattributes (vgl. **extraction_pred** bzw. **extraction_succ** in Bild 2) abbilden. Klassen können analog behandelt werden.

Zusammenfassung

Die Integration der Zeit in ein Datenmodell für Non-Standard-Datenbanksysteme stellt einen wichtigen Schritt zur Unterstützung der Handhabung von Entwurfsobjekten dar. Dazu wurde ein Konzept vorgestellt, das die auf den ersten Blick heterogenen Bereiche "Zeit in Datenbanksystemen" und "Versionsmodelle zur Unterstützung von Ingenieuranwendungen" gleichermaßen befriedigt. Das vorgestellte Geschichts- und Versionsmodell, das auf einer gemeinsamen Struktur zur Verwaltung zeitbehafteter Daten beruht, wurde in das MAD-Modell, das die Beschreibung komplex strukturierter Objekte erlaubt, integriert.

Danksagung:

Ich möchte mich bei Herrn Prof. Dr. Härder für die Anregung bedanken, mich mit dieser Thematik zu befassen.

Literatur

Ar86:   Ariav, G.: A Temporally Oriented Data Modell, ACM TODS, Vol. 11, No. 4, Dec. 1986, Pages 499-527

BI87:   Blanken, H., Ijbema, A.: Storage of Versioned Objects in a CIM Environment, Int. Conf. on Data and Knowledge Systems for Manufactoring and Engineering, Hartford, Connecticut, 1987, Pages 65-74

BK85:   Batory, D.-S., Kim, W.: Modeling Concepts for VLSI CAD Objects, ACM TODS, Vol. 10, No. 3, Sept. 1985, Pages 322-346

DL88:   Dittrich, K.-R., Lorie, R.-A.: Version Support for Engineering Database Systems, IEEE TOSE, Vol. 14, No. 4, April 1988, Pages 429-437

Hä84:   Härder, Th.: Überlegungen zur Modellierung und Integration der Zeit in temporalen Datenbanksystemen, Forschungsbericht Nr. 19/84, SFB 124, Universität Kaiserslautern, 1984

Hä87:   Härder, Th., Meyer-Wegener, K., Mitschang, B., Sikeler, A.: PRIMA A DBMS Prototype Supporting Engineering Applications, Proc. of the 13th Int. Conf. on VLDB, Brighton, Great Britain, 1987, Pages 433-442

Kä88:   Käfer, W.: Ein Modell zur Integration der Zeit in relationalen Datenbanksystemen, SFB-Bericht Nr. 27/88, SFB 124, Universität Kaiserslautern, 1988

KAC86:   Katz, R.-H., Anwarrudin, M., Chang, E.:A Version Server for Computer-Aided Design Data, ACM IEEE 23rd Design Automation Conf., Las Vegas, June 1986, Pages 27-33

KCB86:   Katz, R.-H., Chang, E., Bhateja, R.: Version Modeling Concepts for Computer-Aided Design Databases, Int. Conf. on Management of Data, ACM SIGMOD RECORD, Vol. 15, No. 2, Washington, Pages. 379-386

Kl81:   Klopprogge, M.-R.: TERM An Approach to Include the Time Dimension in the Entity-Relationship Model, Proceedings of the 2nd Int. Conf. on Entity-Relationship Approach, 1981, Pages 477-512

KSW86:   Klahold, P., Schlageter, G., Wilkes, W.: A General Model for Version Management in Databases, Informatik Berichte Nr. 58, Fern-Universität, Hagen, März 1986

Lu84:   Lum, V., Dadam, P., Erbe, R., Guenauer, J., Pistor, P., Walch, G., Werner, H., Woodfill, J.: Designing DBMS Support for the Temporal Dimension, Proc. of the SIGMOD Int. Conf. on Management of Data, 1984, Pages 115-130

Mi87:   Mitschang, B.: MAD - ein Datenmodell für den Kern eines Non-Standard-Datenbanksystems, GI-Fachtagung "Datenbanksysteme für Büro, Technik und Wissenschaft", Darmstadt, IFB Nr. 136, Springer-Verlag, Berlin, Heidelberg, 1987, S. 180-195

Mi88:   Mitschang, B.: Das Molekül-Atom-Datenmodell für Non-Standard-Anwendungen - Anwendungsanalyse, Datenmodellentwurf, Implementierung -, Diss., Universität Kaiserslautern, IFB Nr. 185, Springer-Verlag, Berlin, Heidelberg, März 1988

MS83:   Müller, Th., Steinbauer, D.: Eine Sprachschnittstelle zur Versionenkontrolle in CAM Datenbanken, in: Schmidt, J.-W.: Sprachen für Datenbanken, IFB Nr. 72, Springer-Verlag, Berlin, Heidelberg, 1983, S. 76-95

Sn87:   Snodgrass, R.: The Temporal Query Language TQuel, ACM TODS, Vol. 12, No. 2, June 1987, Pages 247-298

DB++ – persistent objects for C++

Duri Schmidt, Kurt Bauknecht
Institut für Informatik der Universität Zürich
Winterthurerstr. 190
CH-8057 Zürich
e-mail: schmidt@unizh.UUCP

Motivation

Most object-oriented programming languages (OOPL) are designed without regard to data base aspects and do not support persistent objects or mechanisms to share objects. Experiences with the combination of C++ [STR86] and a relational database system (RDBS) in the development of a toolset based on the prototyping paradigm [POM88] have shown that the relational data model is not adequate to model the complex objects of the tools.In addition it has been found that the concepts like inheritance and encapsulation realized in the implementation language C++ do not go together well with the concepts incorporated in the RDBS, as for example, the set oriented data manipulation language. This has led to the decision to build persistent objects for C++ as basis for new CASE-tools.

Related work

A number of research projects have recently begun to address the problem of building object-oriented database systems, e.g. GemStone [MAI86], ENCORE [SKA86], Iris[FIS87] or VISION [CAR88]. In contrast to these efforts, DB++ tries to provide persistent objects for a compiled object-oriented language using the existing features of this language.

Goals

The goals of this project and the reasons for these goals are:

- Provide persistent objects for C++: C++ was chosen as the target language because it satisfies many of the requirements a programming language should meet from a software engineering point of view, like information hiding, inheritance, and efficiency. A further reason was that C++ is used as the implementation language for other tools of the prototyping project and other projects at our institute, as for example, ET++ [WEI88].

- Offer persistent objects as a service of an object-oriented database system (OODBS) by means of a library of specialized classes. There are different possibilities of offering the services of an OODBS in an OOPL like C++:

  - extending the definition of the OOPL so that it incorporates persistent objects,

  - formulating the data base interactions in a special data manipulation language and embedding these in the source code of the OOPL similar to the concept of embedded SQL, or

  - providing the services of the OODBS by means of a library of specialized classes.

  In our project we have choosen the last possibility because this approach prevents the programmer from working with more than one programming language and because any unmodified C++ compiler may be used for software development.

- Base the persistent objects on a simple yet powerful data model and build more complex concepts on top of this simple data model. The advantages of this approach are manifold:

  - it is easier to experiment with different design alternatives if the additional features for concepts like versions are contained by special classes and if the underlying base system is kept in a stable state.

  - not every application requires the same features of an OODBS. With this layered approach, applications not using higher concepts like versions do not have to pay for these unneeded features, e.g. with reduced efficiency.

  The cost of this approach may be that some optimizations might be harder to implement than in a more monolithic approach.

- Integrate the persistent objects in the application framework ET++: the development of applications with a graphical user interface using overlapping windows and a mouse is facilitated greatly by the use of an application framework. Therefore it is very attractive to combine the advantages of persistent objects with the advantages of an application environment to get an even more productive software development tool.

- Specify the requirements for an object server: in order to have a working system after a short period of time, a RDBS is used as the object server. In addition to the persistent storage management it offers the possibility of doing associative queries and to define fast access paths. The price that has to be paid for this solution is limited performance. Another reason for this solution is that it was not possible to define an optimal set of features for the object server at the start of the project. With the OODBS using a RDBS as the object server we expect to get enough experience and insight to be able to specify the requirements for a fast and convenient object server.

Basic concepts

Properties of persistent objects in DB++

C++ objects have a maximum life span of one program execution. Persistent objects are objects that survive the end of a program execution. The next time a program is started, they still exist and can be reused. Persistent objects in DB++ are instances of normal C++ classes inheriting directly or indirectly from the base class of all persistent object classes.

of all persistent objects `DBObject` and has as persistent data two strings, `name` and `firstname`, and a persistent pointer to an address object called `homeaddress`, which is also a persistent object. As transient data `Person` has the instance variable `currentMode` which keeps information about how to draw the `person`. The fields `name`, `firstname`, and `homeaddress` are persistent because they are instances of a persistent field class. Syntactically they do not differ form other C++ instance variables.

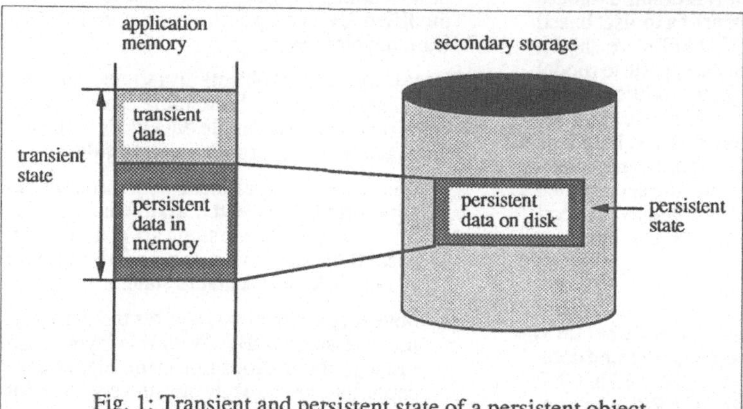

Fig. 1: Transient and persistent state of a persistent object

Until now only the definition of the state of persistent objects has been discussed, but the goal is not only to model the state of objects of the real world but also their behaviour. In order to achieve this goal, methods have to be defined for the persistent object class in the same way as for any other C++ class. The methods of the objects are not stored in the database but in the executable files of the programs using these classes.

A further concept of the data model of DB++ is the database. A database is the common repository of the persistent data of the instances of a group of persistent object classes. This group of classes forms the schema of the database. In contrast to schemas of conventional databases, a schema of DB++ not only defines the structure of the persistent data but also the behaviour of the entities modeled by these classes. Classes in C++ are not objects and cannot be created during runtime. Therefore the schema of a database defined by the persistent object classes cannot be changed during runtime.

Persistent objects can be either active or passive. Active means that an object has a copy in one or more applications, that it can execute its methods, and that messages can be sent to it. Passive means that an object has no copy in any application. It therefore exists only on secondary storage, it can neither execute its methods nor can messages be sent to it. The only thing one can do with passive objects is to query their state as held on disk by means of the query facilities of the object manager and to activate it.

The data of a passive object consist of the persistent data held on secondary storage which is called its persistent state (Fig. 1). The data of an active object consist of its persistent state together with its transient state, i.e. the persistent and the transient data held in memory.

Every persistent object gets a unique identifier at creation time. This identity is immutable and can be used to refer to an object. The scope of the uniqueness is one database.

Modelling power

The data model of DB++ is extensible and allows the user to define databases with arbitrary persistent object classes with partly persistent and partly transient data. The data model is similar to the data model of the C++ class construct. Persistent objects hold their persistent data in fields which are instances of subclasses of the basic persistent field class. An example of a definition of a persistent object class is shown in Fig. 2. The class `Person` inherits from the base class

In the current version persistent fields and persistent objects can only be pointer members of another persistent object, since their initialization is handled partly by their C++ constructor and partly by a special factory object. Persistent fields shared by all instances of a class with persistent objects are not supported. Because persistent objects are instances of normal C++ classes, only single inheritance is provided.

```
class Person: public DBObject {

    ShortStr * name;
    ShortStr * firstname;
    PointerField * homeaddress;
    DrawingMode currentMode;
    //...
}
```

Fig. 2: example of a persistent object class

Architecture

DB++ uses a client-server model as its basic architecture. The clients and the server are workstations connected through a local area network (Fig. 3). The object server receives the persistent data from the persistent objects in the programs that are running on the workstations and stores them on secondary storage. It also retrieves the persistent data from there and trans-

example is the class associated with DBObject. The purpose of these associated classes is that their instances assist as factory objects in the creation of new objects of the corresponding class. Another purpose is to provide access to the instances of the corresponding class.

In DB++ persistent objects keep the persistent data in instances of the persistent field classes. DBField is the abstract base class of all persistent field classes. Associated with every persistent field class is another class whose instances are factory objects for the corresponding field class objects. DBFieldClass for example is the class associated with DBField. The naming convention is the same as for the persistent object classes.

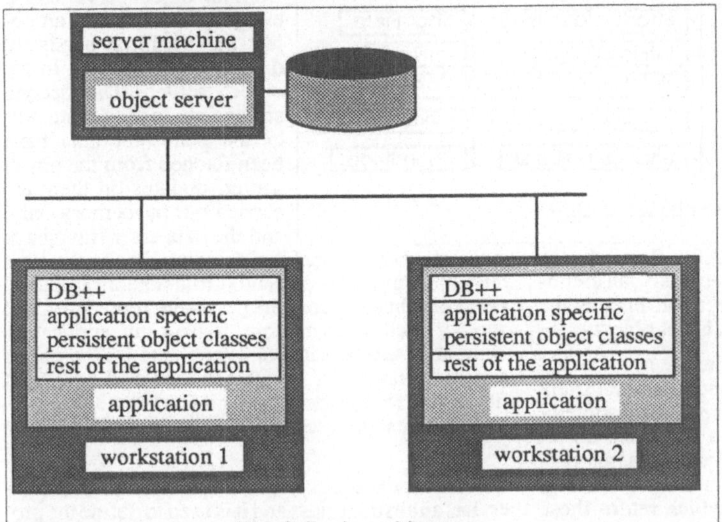

Fig. 3: Basic architecture

Base classes

Instances of the class DBase provide the necessary functionality to open or close a database. Further, DBase defines methods of checking the existence of an object, of checking whether an object is active in the current application or not, and of activating a persistent object. For each database a subclass of DBase must be defined. Its purpose is to install and register at opening time every instance of the so-called Class-class of each persistent object class of the database, as for example DBObjectClass.

mits them to the persistent objects in the programs on the workstations. Computations on the data, i.e. applying the methods of the persistent objects to their respective data, are carried out on the transient state. The server can only do associative queries on the persistent state. As mentioned above, the object server is currently a RDBS.

A program on a workstation con-sists of the following classes:

- the classes implementing the generic behaviour of the persistent objects, i.e. the classes DB++ consists of,
- the classes implementing the application specific persistent objects, and
- the classes implementing the rest of the application.

The structure of DB++

Overview

The most important classes of DB++ are DBase, DBObjectClass, DBObject, DBFieldClass and its subclasses, and DBField and its subclasses (Fig. 4). DBase implements the concept of the database. DBObject is the base class of all persistent object classes and implements the behaviour common to all persistent objects. Associated with every persistent object class is another class which has by convention the same name as the corresponding class, concatenated with the suffix "Class". DBObjectClass for

As stated above, for each persistent object class an associated class inheriting directly or indirectly from DBObjectClass has to be defined. DBObjectClass is the class associated with DBObject. DBObjectClass and its subclasses are called Class-classes. Their purpose is:

- To registrate every active object of the class it is associated with: every instance of the corresponding persistent object class of a Class-class is registered during its activation. This registration guarantees that a persistent object is activated at most once per application. This mechanism is further used to synchronize the transient and the persistent state of all active persistent objects either upon user request or upon closing the database.

- To create new and activate existing persistent objects of the corresponding class: during the creation or the activation of a persistent object, the corresponding Class-object serves as the factory object. By means of the services of DBase it checks whether the object to be created or activated already exists, and it consults its own register to see wether the object in question

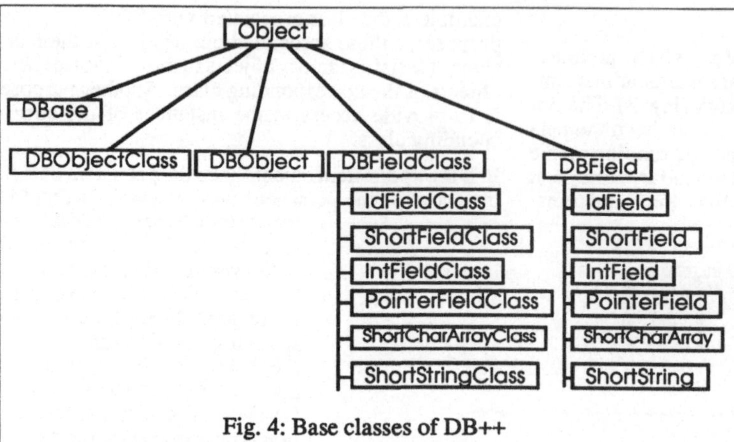

Fig. 4: Base classes of DB++

has been activated earlier. After these checks the Class-object fetches, if necessary, an identifier from the database object and installs the new field objects in the persistent object.

* To provide iterators which iterate over the active instances of the corresponding persistent object class: it can be very useful to do something with every instance of a persistent object class. DBObjectClass and its subclasses provide iterators which simply enumerate the registered objects and others which return those objects that have passed a filter only.

* To provide iterators which iterate over all instances of the corresponding class: the iterators operating on the active objects use their transient state. The iterators iterating over all instances use a service of the object server which is based on the persistent state. These iterators allow sequential access to all persistent objects of a class, iteration over a set of objects selected by a query formulated in the query language of the object server, and access to persistent objects not only by identity but also by content via fast access paths, such as BTrees defined on the persistent data on the object server. These iterators return either the identifiers of the persistent objects or their memory addresses, activating them automatically if necessary. This feature called object faulting is very useful for activating all objects of a class, having fast access to objects through the content of their persistent state, or activating a group of objects selected by the content of their persistent state.

DBObject is the base class of all persistent object classes. As mentioned above, the instantiation of persistent objects is handled partly by the associated Class-class and partly by the object. Therefore DBObject provides a constructor which carries out the part of the initialization the persistent object has to do. Reading and writing of persistent objects are other methods of this class. They are implemented in such a manner that subclasses with any number of persistent

fields do not have to reimplement them. Writing is optimized so that only modified data is written back to the object server. Two storage modes are offered: in the first mode, at every read access of an object the data are fetched from the object server and at every write access of an object the modified persistent data are written back to the object server. The second storage mode is caching: after the persistent data have been fetched from the object server, updates on them are carried out in memory only, and the data are written back to the object server only on demand. Finally the class DBObject provides a method to delete an instance, i.e. to eliminate it from the persistent repository, and another method to remove it from an application without destroying its persistent state on the object server. Instances of DBObject have two persistent fields, one for the identifier and one for a class number which can be used for typechecking during activation.

DBField is the base class of all persistent field classes. It is an abstract class and it is used to define the protocol of the persistent field classes. All the persistent data is kept in instances of subclasses of DBField. Subclasses of DBField have an instance variable for the value and two methods to get the current value and to assign a new value. This means that the access to the value is controlled and that this control can be easily used to do consistency checks or to trigger another action during access of the value. In the current version of DB++ persistent field classes for persistent shorts, integers, short character arrays i.e. less then 256 characters, short strings i.e. less then 256 characters, and persistent pointers are defined. Furthermore, a persistent field class for identifier fields is defined having in contrary to the other persistent fields only read access to its value. Other persistent field classes can be derived from these existing ones.

The persistent pointer field is based on object identity. Beyond the normal methods to access its value i.e. the identifier of the object referred to, persistent pointers have a method which returns the memory address of the object referred to. If the object referred to is not active, it is activated automatically. This mechanism, called object faulting, allows easy following of persistent pointer chains without having to worry about the activation of the object that is being referred to.

Similar to Class-classes of the persistent object class, each persistent field class has its own associated Class-class, too. The instances of the Class-classes serve as the factory for the construction of the persistent field objects.

Other classes

Beyond the classes discussed in the previous part, DB++ contains the following classes:

- Classes defining the iterators which have been mentioned in the discussion of the DBObject-Class and its subclasses.

- Persistent collection classes: in many applications it will be necessary to collect a group of persistent objects of one or more classes, e.g. in a list. Therefore DB++ contains classes for persistent object lists and for sorted persistent object lists. These classes provide methods for adding and removing persistent objects to a list, for replacing elements, and for selecting a group of the elements satisfying a given condition. Moreover, iterators with or without filters to iterate over the elements are provided, as well as methods for applying a method to all elements of a list.

State of the project

At the time of writing the implementation of the concepts and classes presented above has nearly been completed and a running version of DB++ exists.

Current work

There are different areas in which DB++ is being extended:

- Persistent field classes: it is planned to implement other persistent field classes, e.g. floating point numbers, long text fields and binary fields. The long text field will have as its value a string of arbitrary length and the binary field a byte stream of arbitrary length.

- Collection classes: currently only the persistent object list and the sorted persistent object list are implemented. We plan to enhance the persistent object classes with persistent object arrays, persistent bags, persistent sets and persistent dictionaries.

- Integration with the application framework ET++: in this area it is planned to extend the features of DB++ so that DB++ and ET++ can be smoothly integrated. In order to get more knowledge of the implications of using an application framework together with an OODBS, we plan to modify some CASE tools based on ET++ and to develop some new CASE tools using DB++.

- Definition of a sharing and a versioning concept: at the moment sharing is only supported through simple locking of objects and nothing is done to support versioning. Because DB++ is intended to be used in software development where group work and cooperative sharing as well as the production of different versions of a product is common, a sharing and a versioning concept is being developed.

Future work

There are different directions we would like follow:

- As soon as C++ allows for multiple inheritance, we will include it in DB++. Further we will redesign DB++ so as to benefit from this new feature.

- We would like to construct a design tool to simplify the definition of new persistent objects and we would like to integrate a database browser in DB++ to better support the development of applications using DB++.

- Finally, as stated in the goals we want to formulate a specification for an object server based on our experiences with the current object server which is a RDBS.

Literature

[GOL83]   Adele Goldberg, D. Robson, Smalltalk-80: The Language and Its Implementation, Addison Wesley, 1983.

[MAI86]   David Maier, Jakob Stein: Development of an Object-Oriented DBMS, OOPSLA Conference Proceedings, Oregon, 1986.

[SKA86]   Andrea H. Skarra, Stanley B. Zdonik: The Management of Changing Types in an Object-Oriented Database, OOPSLA Conference Proceedings, Oregon, 1986.

[FIS86]   D.H. Fishman et al., Iris: An OBject-Oriented Database Management System, ACM Transaction on Office Information Systems, Vol. 5, No. 1, Jan. 1987.

[CAR88]   Michael Caruso: The VISION Object-Oriented Database Management System, OOPSLA Tutorial 4A, San Diego, 1988.

[STR86]   Bjarne Stroustrup: The C++ Programming Language, Addison-Wesley, 1986.

[WEI88]   André Weinand, Erich Gamma, Rudolf Marty: ET++ – An Object-Oriented Application Framework in C++, OOPSLA Conference Proceedings, San Diego, 1988.

[POM88]   Gustav Pomberger et. al.: TOPOS - A Toolset for Prototyping-oriented Software Development, Genie Logiciel / Software Engineering, Paris, 1988.

Extern definierte Datentypen und Prozeduren in DASDBS *

Andreas Wolf
Technische Hochschule Darmstadt
Fachgebiet DVS1 †

Kurzfassung

Um den Einsatz eines Datenbanksystems für die Lösung eines gegebenen Anwendungsproblems sinnvoll möglich zu machen, muß gewährleistet sein, daß Datenstrukturen und bewährte Operationen einfach und leistungsfähig auf das Datenbanksystem abgebildet werden können. Dies setzt ein für diese Anwendungen geeignetes Angebot an Datentypen und Operationen voraus. In diesem Beitrag soll dieser Problemkreis diskutiert werden und auf den Aspekt der automatischen Generierung der dazu nötigen Typkonvertierungsfunktionen eingegangen werden.

1 Einführung

Bestehende Datenbanksysteme haben trotz ihrer allgemein anerkannten Vorzüge nur ein relativ beschränktes Anwendungsfeld im Bereich kommerzieller Systeme (Banken, Versicherungen, Buchhaltungen) gefunden. Wenn man an den Einsatz in Ingenieurbereichen wie CAD/CAM, integrierte Büroumgebungen mit multimedialer Dokumentenverwaltung oder das von uns intensiver untersuchte Gebiet der Geo-Informationssysteme denkt, ist es vor allem das Fehlen geeigneter Datentypen im Datenbanksystem, das eine sinnvolle Abbildung der Anwendungsstrukturen behindert. Was wir uns wünschen ist, daß ein Datenbankanwender, zum Beispiel bei der Entwicklung eines Landinformationssystems, auf einer Benutzerrelation

```
Stadt = {   Bezeichnung      : Name
            Stadtteile       : set of Name
            Einwohnerzahl    : integer
            Grundfläche      : Polygon_Fläche }
```

mit verschiedenen komplexen Typen in einer Art embedded SQL eine Anfrage der Form

```
select Bezeichnung,Grundfläche
    from Stadt
    where Grundfläche innerhalb Planungsgebiet
```

in der gleichen Weise stellen kann, wie er dies für die Standardtypen gewöhnt ist. Dazu sind zwei Dinge neu im Datenbanksystem zu verankern. Der Datentyp *Polygon_Fläche* des Attributes *Grundfläche* muß an der Schnittstelle bekannt gemacht werden, damit die Ergebnisse der Anfrage korrekt in Benutzervariable eingetragen werden können [HSSW88]. Das gleiche gilt natürlich auch für den umgekehrten Weg im Falle des Datentyps der Variablen *Planungsgebiet*, zum Beispiel *Rechteck*, wo ein Wert aus dem Programm zur Auswertung ins Datenbanksystem transportiert werden muß. Auf der anderen Seite muß die Prozedur, die den Test für innerhalb implementiert, vom Datenbanksystem ausführbar sein.

Um mehr als nur eine schöne Schnittstelle zu erhalten, müssen diese Typen (Typ und Datentyp werden im Folgenden synonym verwandt) und ihre Operationen tief im Datenbanksystem eingebettet werden. Teilweise benötigt man zusätzlich auch innerhalb des Datenbanksystems weitere Operationen wie es [WWH88] für Zugriffspfade zeigt.

Erweiterung um neuartige Datentypen kann auf mehrere Arten geschehen. Ein Weg ist die Nutzung der für das Datenbanksystem vorhandenen Typkonstruktoren wie sie zum Beispiel in [LKD*] vorgeschlagen wird. Der Anwender kann in einer einheitlichen Definitionsumgebung sowohl die rein datenbankspezifischen Strukturen (das Schema der Datenbank), wie auch die programmierorientierten Typen entwickeln und zumindest teilweise auch Operationen implementieren. Natürlich sind so definierte Typen nicht direkt in einer Programmiersprache

---

*DArmStädter DatenBankSystem

†Diese Arbeit entstand im Forschungsprojekt GEO-Datenbankarchitektur des DFG Schwerpunktprogramms Datenstrukturen und effiziente Algorithmen

benutzbar. Zum Anschluß an Anwendungen muß daher eine äquivalente programmiersprachliche Darstellung aus der Datenbankdefinition abgeleitet werden [LKD*].

Ein zweiter Weg ist die Trennung zwischen den datenbankspezifischen und den programmierorientierten Definitionen. Alle Strukturen, deren exakte Kenntnis im Datenbanksystem benötigt wird, werden auch dort mit den üblichen Definitionsmechanismen der DDL deklariert. Typen, die aus programmiertechnischen Gründen, zum Beispiel für einen bestimmten Algorithmus, benötigt werden, werden dort deklariert, wo die Detailkenntnis nötig ist, also in der Anwendung und in der Anwendungsprogrammiersprache. Das Datenbanksystem stellt dann nur die nötigen Schnittstellen und Mechanismen zu deren Integration zur Verfügung.

Dieses Papier beschäftigt sich mit dieser zweiten Methode der Typ-Erweiterung. Es geht dabei speziell auf die Frage der Konvertierung zwischen den Datentypen und -Strukturen der Anwendungsumgebung und denen des Datenbanksystems ein. Nachfolgend wird unser Lösungsansatz für diese Form der Erweiterbarkeit präzisiert und speziell auf die Generierung von Typkonvertierungsroutinen eingegangen. Danach schließt sich ein kurzer Hinweis auf die bereits in DASDBS verwirklichten Komponenten an.

2 Lösungsansatz bei externer Erweiterung

Auch heutige Datenbanksysteme mit ihren fest integrierten Grundtypen kennen bereits das Problem der verschiedenen Umgebungen. Betrachten wir beispielhaft eine Sequenz in einer Art 'embedded SQL' [1]

```
EXEC SQL BEGIN DECLARE SECTION                    .
    DCL K_NR INTEGER                     .         .
EXEC SQL END DECLARE                     EXEC SQL
                     .                       SELECT Kontonummer
                     .                       INTO  :K_NR
                                             FROM  Buchung
                                             WHERE Betrag > 10000
```

so definiert der DECLARE Abschnitt eine Variable, die ein Bindeglied zwischen dem Datenbanksystem und der Programmiersprache darstellt. Diese *Hostvariable* wird in der Anwendungsumgebung deklariert, über den Precompiler der Datenbankumgebung bekannt gemacht, dort beim Retrieval gefüllt und anschliessend wiederum in der Anwendungsumgebung interpretiert. Dies ist bei heutigen Systemen kein Problem, da als Typen im Datenbanksystem nur solche bekannt sind, die auch in der Programmiersprache bekannt sind. Beide Umgebungen verstehen sich also a priori.

Anders sieht es dagegen aus, wenn man versucht einen beliebigen Typ der Programmiersprache zu übergeben. Übernimmt man das Einführungsbeispiel in 'embedded SQL' Notation, so ergibt sich

```
type Polygon_Flaeche = record
                    Eckenzahl : integer;
                    Koordinaten : array [maxsize] of record
                                        X,Y : real
                    end
        end ;
```

```
EXEC SQL BEGIN DECLARE SECTION                    .
    DCL STADTNAME  Name                  .         .
    DCL FLAECHE  Polygon_Flaeche         EXEC SQL
EXEC SQL END DECLARE                         SELECT Bezeichnung,Grundflaeche
                     .                       INTO :STADTNAME,:FLAECHE
                     .                       FROM Stadt
                                             WHERE Einwohnerzahl > 500000
```

Der Precompiler würde in diesem Fall jedoch das DECLARE Statement für FLAECHE zurückweisen, da kompliziertere Strukturen nicht mehr über das Interface zwischen Programmiersprache und Datenbanksystem transportiert werden können. Dabei ist die prinzipielle Vorgehensweise identisch mit der bei dem einfachen Beispiel anzuwendenden.

Der Precompiler muß bei der Analyse der DECLARE Section den Typ der Hostvariablen erkennen, und daraus eine Variablendefinition ableiten, die einerseits vom Datenbanksystem mit Werten gefüllt und andererseits im Anwendungsprogramm bearbeitet werden kann. Sollte es einen derartigen für beiden Seiten verständlichen Typ für eine Variable nicht geben, was heute zu der eben angesprochenen Zurückweisung führt, muß dafür gesorgt werden, daß für jede der Umgebungen ein eigener Typ definiert wird und für eine Konvertierung zwischen den Datenstrukturen beider Umgebungen gesorgt wird.

Im einfachsten Fall kann man fordern, daß das Datenbanksystem einen Grundtyp *Datencontainer* kennt, eine lineare Bytefolge, die jeden beliebigen Typ aufnehmen kann. Stellt dann ein Benutzer für jeden seiner

---

[1] Die Notation für Beispiele des Datenbankzugriffes orientiert sich an der PL/1 Einbettung des Systems SQL/DS [SQL,SQL1], programmiersprachliche Beispiele orientieren sich an PASCAL [JW79].

Anwendungstypen, den er im Datenbanksystem speichern will, die Konvertierungsfunktionen

IN : Anwendungstyp $\longrightarrow$ Datencontainer
OUT : Datencontainer $\longrightarrow$ Anwendungstyp

[HSSW88] dem Datenbanksystem zur Verfügung, so kann jeder dieser Typen in einer Anfrage verwendet werden. Der Precompiler muß dann nur für jede Hostvariable die entsprechende Konvertierungsroutine aufrufen, IN in INSERT Anfragen undbei der Übergabe von Werten an das Datenbanksystem und OUT in RETRIEVAL Anfragen (vgl. Abb. 1).

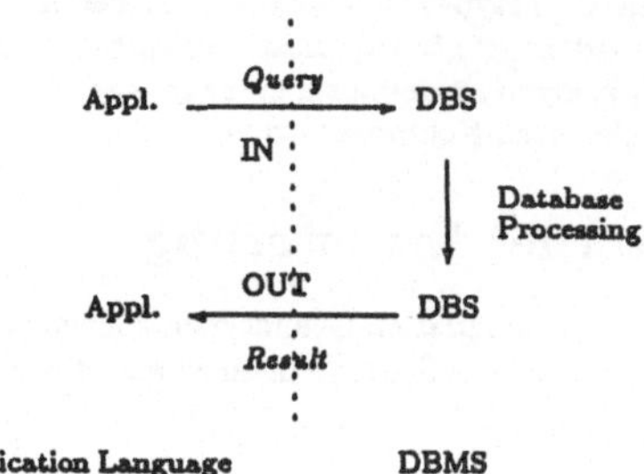

Abbildung 1: Abarbeitung einer Anfrage

Es gibt verschiedene Gründe, warum diese Konvertierungsprozeduren nicht von dem jeweiligen Anwender selbst zur Verfügung gestellt werden sollten. Selbstverständlich sollte der Aufwand einer solchen Implementierung nicht vernachlässigt werden. Das Hauptargument ist jedoch ein Sicherheitsgedanke. Die Konvertierungsprozeduren, ganz besonders natürlich OUT, erzeugen Datenstrukturen, die in einem anderen Typsystem interpretiert werden müssen. Dabei verlassen sie zwangsläufig die Wege, die normalerweise durch die sprachspezifischen Typ-Prüfungssysteme abgesichert werden. Es liegt also allein in der Verantwortung dieser Operationen, daß ihr Resultat in der jeweiligen Zielumgebung auch korrekt weiterverarbeitet werden kann. Aus diesem Grund muß der Transformationsmechanismus auch für komplexe Typen vom Datenbanksystem, also zum Beispiel vom Preprozessor übernommen werden. Eine mögliche Erweiterung seiner Kontrollstrukturen führt also zu einer Queryformulierung in der Form

```
EXEC EDT_SQL BEGIN TYPE SECTION
type Polygon_Flaeche = record
                    Eckenzahl : integer;
                    Koordinaten : array [maxsize] of record
                                            X,Y : real
                                    end
                end ;
type Rechteck = ...
predicate Inside( Polygon_Flaeche, Rechteck ) ;
EXEC EDT_SQL END TYPE


EXEC EDT_SQL BEGIN DECLARE SECTION                 .
    DCL STADTNAME  Name
    DCL FLAECHE  Polygon_Flaeche             EXEC EDT_SQL
    DCL PLANUNGSGEBIET  Rechteck               SELECT Bezeichnung,Grundflaeche
EXEC EDT_SQL END DECLARE                        INTO  :STADTNAME,:FLAECHE
        .                                       FROM  STADT
        .                                       WHERE Einwohnerzahl > 500000
                                                AND   Grundflaeche Inside :Planungsgebiet
```

Hier ist jetzt die komplette Anfrage des Eingangsbeispiels dargestellt. Sie enthält neben dem reinen Transport der extern definierten Typen auch den Aufruf eines typspezifischen Suchprädikates. Dieses unterscheidet sich für den Benutzer nicht von den Prädikaten, wie sie von den Basistypen des Datenbanksystems bekannt ist. Seine Implementierung wird dem Datenbanksystem durch Deklaration der entsprechenden externen Prozedur zusammen mit dem Typ bekanntgegeben [HSSW88]. Die Abarbeitung dieser Anfrage zeigt schematisch Abb. 2.

Die Bearbeitung findet jetzt in drei Umgebungen statt. Die Anwendung formuliert ihre Anfrage und konvertiert die Querykonstanten in einen von der Datenbank verarbeitbaren Datentyp. Dort kann die Ausführung der Anfrage für alle Basisstrukturen der Datenbank, also zum Beispiel INTEGER, REAL etc. gestartet werden. Erreicht die Bearbeitung eine benutzerdefinierte Operation, so muß das Datenbanksystem die Kontrolle an die

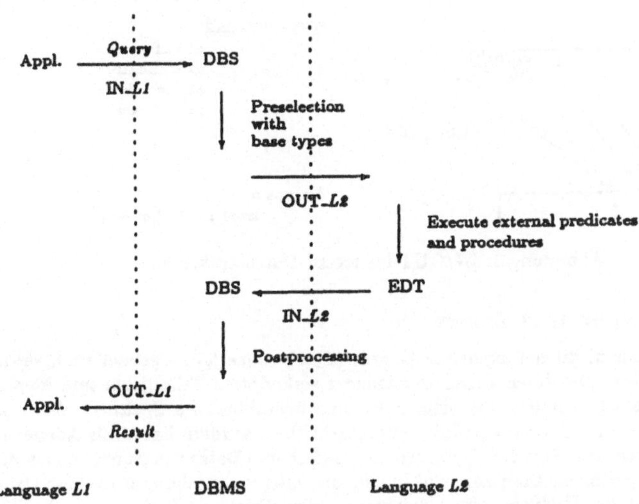

Abbildung 2: Anfragebearbeitung mit EDT-Funktionen

zugehörige externe Implementierung übergeben. Dabei werden die Parameter vor dem Aufruf in das Format der zugehörigen Umgebung konvertiert und die Resultate entsprechend wieder in das Datenbankformat transformiert. Der Mechanismus entspricht dem Umgebungswechsel am Anwendungsinterface, er ist jedoch nicht notwendig auf die gleiche Umgebung festgelegt. Nach der restlichen Bearbeitung werden dann Resultate der Anfrage in die Anwendung transferiert.

3 Generierung von IN/OUT Prozeduren

Die Wunschvorstellung ist sicherlich, daß jede Art von Datenstruktur als Eingabe in das Datenbanksystem und als Prozedurparameter im Datenbanksystem erlaubt ist. Um den Aufwand und die Grenzen einer automatischen Generierung der dafür nötigen IN/OUT Transformationsfunktionen zu erkennen, haben wir verschiedene Gruppen von Datenstrukturen, aufbauend auf den zur Deklaration üblicherweise zur Verfügung stehenden Basistypen und Typkonstruktoren, untersucht und angepaßte Lösungen erarbeitet.

3.1 Einfache Typen

Die erste Klasse von Typen sind die Skalaren. Im Prinzip existieren für diese bereits Lösungen in den bekannten Systemen, zum Beispiel für *integer, real, char* und *date* Sie sind durch zusammenhängende Speicherbereiche dargestellt und können so relativ leicht aus Anwenderbereichen in Systembereiche und wieder zurück transportiert werden. Das einzige, was hier beachtet werden muß ist die Ausrichtung der Speicherbereiche (Alignment). Dies ist jedoch unkritisch, da diese Typen, bis auf *date*, auch Grundtypen der Prozessoren sind und so automatisch ausgerichtet werden. *Date* arbeitet in den meisten Fällen auf einer Zeichendarstellung und ist so auch problemlos. Sollen diese Typen jedoch nicht direkt mit allen erlaubten Operationen im Datenbanksystem verdrahtet werden, so muß auch hier zwischen einer nicht ausgerichteten internen Bytedarstellung und einer ausgerichteten "Arbeitsrepräsentation" konvertiert werden.

Vergleichbar den skalaren Typen lassen sich die aggregierten wie *arrays* und *records* und deren Kombinationen behandeln. Im Prinzip stellen auch sie einen zusammenhängenden Speicherbereich dar, der aber im Falle von records durch verschiedene Komponentenausrichtungen Lücken aufweisen kann (vgl. Abb. 3). Entsprechend kann man auch hier bei Beachtung der Ausrichtung des ersten record-Elementes sehr schnell einen Transfer von einer Datenbankseite in den Arbeitsbereich realisieren, die Typanpassung ist dann auch hier eine triviale "Uminterpretation", ein *casting* beziehungsweise ein Strukturoverlay. Ist der Ausrichtungsverlust innerhalb eines records nicht tragbar, so kann nicht auf eine echte Transformation verzichtet werden. Sie ist jedoch sehr einfach und der entsprechende Code kann problemlos aus der Datenstruktur abgeleitet werden.

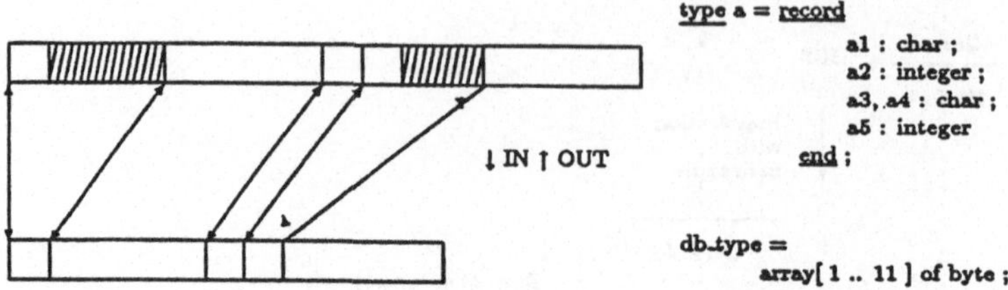

Abbildung 3: IN/OUT für record-Datenstrukturen

3.2 Dynamische Typen und Zeiger

Spätestens bei Datenstrukturen, die auf expliziten Zeigern (Typ *pointer to*) aufgebaut sind, versagen die einfachen Überlagerungsstrategien. Die durch Zeiger miteinander verknüpften Teilobjekte sind im allgemeinen Fall dynamisch erzeugt und stehen deshalb nicht mehr notwendig benachbart im Speicher. Auch die Zeiger sind normalerweise nicht als Wert durch Überlagerung weiterbearbeitbar, sondern haben als Adressen eine spezielle Bedeutung nur in ihrer Umgebung. Durch Zeigerstrukturen aufgebaute Datenstrukturen können daher nur durch geeignete Traversierungsalgorithmen analysiert und in eine neutrale, verschiebungsinvariante Darstellung transformiert werden. Dabei ist das Problem, einen geeigneten Algorithmus zu finden, nicht trivial, da mit sehr einfachen Deklarationen sehr viele verschiedene und unterschiedlich komplexe Datenstrukturen aufgebaut werden können (vgl. Abb. 4).

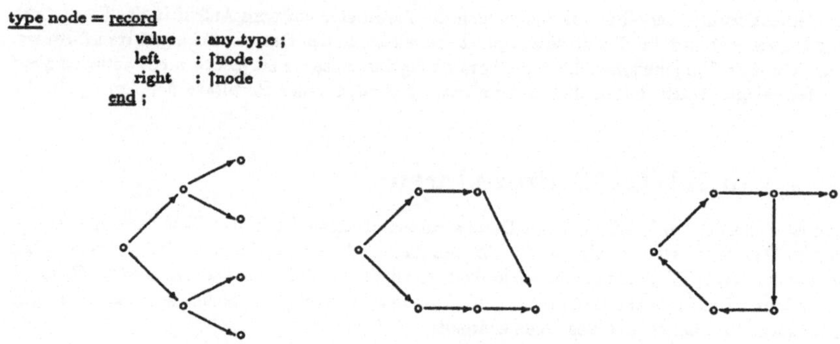

Abbildung 4: Beispiele für Zeigerstrukturen

Eine automatische Definitionsanalyse würde für jeden record-Typ mit Zeiger-Feldern einen allgemeinen Graph-Traversierungs Algorithmus nach Abb. 5 generieren, der eine Zyklen- und Querverweiserkennung enthalten muß. Im Falle einfacher Strukturen wie linearer Listen oder binärer Bäume sind aber weitaus effizientere Umsetzungsalgorithmen denkbar. Ohne Hilfsinformationen sind sie jedoch aus der Typdeklaration allein nicht ableitbar.

3.3 Automatische Generierung und ihre Grenzen

Bereits bei den Zeigerstrukturen zeigt sich, daß der effizienteste Ansatz nicht immer erkennbar ist. Viele Programmiersprachen erlauben oder erzwingen jedoch auch Deklarationen die überhaupt keine Datenstruktur beschreiben können. So enthält die nachfolgende Fortran-Deklaration

```
       SUBROUTINE INTERSECT(L1,POL_1,L2,POL_2,LR,POL_R)
C                 INTERSECTS TWO GIVEN POLYGONES
C                 ALL PARAMETER-ARRAYS VARYING LENGTH
       INTEGER L1,L2,LR
C                 LENGTH OF EACH COORDINATE ARRAY
       INTEGER POL_1(*,2),POL_2(*,2),POL_R(*,2)
C                 COORDINATE ARRAYS
C
C                 CODE OF PROCEDURE INTERSECT
```

```
global : list_of_known_nodes, internal_representation
proc traverse_graph( current_node )
begin
   id := lookup( current_node, list_of_known_nodes )      /* Knoten schon bekannt? */
   if id = not_found_id                                    /* nein, */
      id := add( current_node, list_of_known_nodes )       /* dann bearbeite ihn */
      space := internal_lenght( type_of( current_node ) )
      reserve( space, internal_representation )
      move( current_node, internal_representation )        /* Speichere Inhalt */
      /* the following sequence has to be repeated */
      /* for every pointer son */
      son_id := traverse_graph( pointer_son )              /* Bearbeite Nachfolger */
      move( son_id, internal_representation )
      /* end of repeated sequence */
   end_if
   return(id)                                              /* Liefere Knotenkennung zurück */
end_proc
```

Abbildung 5: Generisches Schema eines Graphtraversierungs-Algorithmus

gleich zwei implizite Vereinbarungen, die nur mit Hilfsinformationen sichtbar werden. Zum einen stellen die jeweiligen L_i und POL_i eigentlich records dar, was aber in FORTRAN nicht ausdrückbar ist. Das Datenbanksystem muß diese Variablenpaare aber immer als Einheit behandeln. Zum anderen bestimmen die Längenvariablen die jeweiligen Ausprägungen der Array-Variablen. Auch dieser Zusammenhang ist bei der Bereitstellung von Speicherbereichen wichtig und muß dem Datenbanksystem bekannt gemacht werden.

4 Die Implementierung in DASDBS

Unsere derzeitige DASDBS Systemumgebung [PSSWD87] ist ein Drei-Schichten Ansatz nach Abbildung 6. Es besteht aus einem Speichersubsystem für hierarchische komplexe Objekte (NF^2-Tupel) das nur die notwendigsten Typen für atomare Attribute unterstützt. Derzeit sind dies neben dem Standardtyp Bytestring, Zahlen (*integer* und *real*) für Standard-Anwendungen, Bitlisten für Textsignaturen und Punkte und Rechtecke (Quader) für GEO-Anwendungen.

Auf diesem Kern baut das Zugriffspfadsystem auf, das die Bildung und Wartung von Clusterung und Zugriffstrukturen nach beliebigen Attributen und Eigenschaften erlaubt.

Die oberste Ebene implementiert das Datenmodell an der Benutzerschnittstelle. Sie enthält die entsprechenden Definitionsmechanismen einer Querysprache und die Komponenten zur Querybearbeitung.

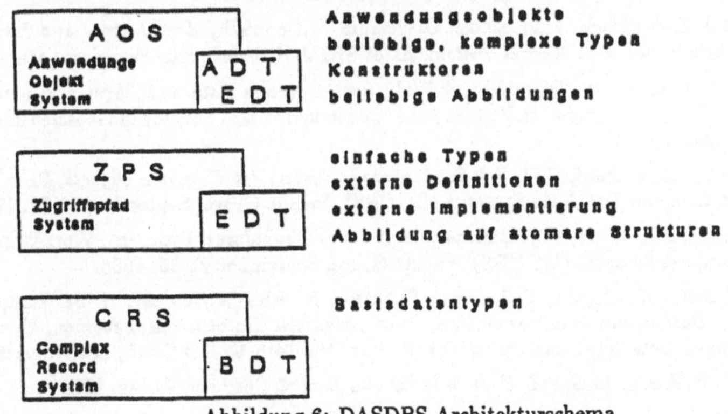

Abbildung 6: DASDBS Architekturschema

Entsprechend der unterschiedlichen Anforderungen der verschiedenen Systemebenen kommen für die externe Typerweiterung verschiedene Techniken zum Einsatz.

Im Kern (CRS [DPS86]) ist das vorrangige Entscheidungskriterium selbtverständlich die Arbeitsgeschwindigkeit, da hier alle Daten angefasst werden müssen. Es sind daher bewußt nur die Datentypen zugelassen, die eine triviale IN/OUT-Abbildung also ein Overlay erlauben, wobei wir eventuelle Lücken durch Alignments in Kauf nehmen. Außerdem muß aufwendiger Schutzcode hier unbedingt vermieden werden. Im Moment ist dies noch unkritisch, da wir die Typen selbst implementieren. Auch die Prüfung fremder Implementierungen bereitet keine Probleme, da der Kern als Basis-Speichersystem nur ein elementares Typangebot zur Verfügung stellt.

Auf der Ebene der Zugriffspfade [HSWW87] werden derzeit nur einfache aggregierte Typen benutzt. Hier werden aber schon verschiedene Programmiersprachen eingesetzt (PASCAL,. FORTRAN, C). Das System ist damit jedoch für den Einsatz von IN/OUT-Funktionen vorbereitet und kann so auch mit beliebigen anderen Datenstrukturen arbeiten. Hier werden wir auch komplexere Typen von fremden Entwicklern einbinden. Die Datenbank-Zieldatenstruktur ist jedoch derzeit nur ein variabel langes, atomares Attribut. Die Umsetzung auf mehrere Attribute oder Mengen ist zwar möglich, es muß jedoch noch untersucht werden, ob sich diese Technik entscheidende Vorteile bringt. Ein Generator für Teile des benötigten Hilfscodes ist zur Zeit getrennt im Test und wird bald mit den ersten IN/OUT Generatoren gekoppelt in das System eingebunden.

5 Zusammenfassung und Ausblick

Die gezeigte Methode zur Erweiterung von Datenbanksystemen um neue Typen erweist sich als ein flexibles Instrument zur Anpassung an Anforderungen beliebiger Anwendungen. Erste Untersuchungen haben gezeigt, daß zumindestens eine teilweise Automatisierung der Typanpassung erreicht werden kann. Für komplexere Strukturen muß die Effizienz der gewählten Methode noch nachgewiesen werden.

Das langfristige Ziel ist sicher die weitgehende Automatisierung aller Entscheidungsprozesse und aller Hilfscodeentwicklung bei der Konfiguration. Dies betrifft unter anderem die Entscheidung, ob eine Datenstruktur die strengen Anforderungen für die Einbettung in den Kern erfüllt.

Der zweite wichtige Bereich bei der Datenstrukturanalyse ist die automatische Generierung von IN/OUT-Transformationsfunktionen für die nichttrivialen Fälle mit Pointervariablen, verschiedenen Sprachumgebungen und komplexeren Datenbank-Zieldatenstrukturen.

Für beide Bereiche muß auch intensiver über eine eigene Deklarationssprache nachgedacht werden, die eine vollständige Automatisierung aller Teilaufgaben erlaubt. Sie soll jedoch nie die eigentliche programmiersprachliche Deklaration ersetzen sondern nur ergänzen. Wie diese Sprache aussehen kann und wie die beiden nebeneinander stehenden Deklarationen abgeglichen werden können, muß noch untersucht werden.

Literaturverzeichnis

[HSSW88] L.M. Haas, H.-J. Schek, P.M. Schwarz, P.F. Wilms, *Incorporating Data Types in an Extensible Database Architecture*, in Proc. 3rd Int. Conf. on Data and Knowledge Bases, C. Beeri, U. Dayal (eds.) Jerusalem, June 28-30, Morgan Kaufman Publishers, Los Altos CA, 1988

[WWH88] W. Waterfeld, A. Wolf, D. Horn, *How to Make Spatial Access Methods Extensible*, in Proc. 3rd Int. Conf. on Spatial Data Handling, Sydney, August 22-24, 1988

[PSSWD87] H.-B. Paul, H.-J. Schek, M.H.Scholl, G.Weikum, U.Deppisch, *Architecture and Implementation of the Darmstadt Database Kernel System*, ACM SIGMOD Conf., San Francisco, May 27-29, 1987

[HSWW87] D.Horn, H.-J. Schek, W. Waterfeld, A.Wolf, *Spatial Access Path and Physical Clustering in a Low-Level Geo-Database System*, R.Vinken (ed.), Construction and Display of Geoscientific Maps Derived from Databases, 1987

[DPS86] U. Deppisch, H.-B. Paul, H.-J. Schek, *A Storage System for Complex Objects*, Proc. Int. Workshop on object Oriented Database Systems (OODBS), Pacific Grove, September 23-26, 1986

[St86] M. Stonebraker,L. Rowe, *Object Management using Prozedures*, Proc. Int. Workshop on object Oriented Database Systems (OODBS), Pacific Grove, September 23-26, 1986

[LKD*] V. Linnemann, K.Küspert, P. Dadam, P. Pistor, R. erbe, A.Kemper, N. Südkamp, G.Walch, M. Wallrath, *Design and Implementation of an Extensible Database Management System Supporting User Defined Data types and Functions*, Proc. of the 14th VLDB Conf., Los Angeles, 1988

[JW79] K.Jensen, N.Wirth, *PASCAL User Manual and Report*, Springer Verlag, 1979

[SQL] SQL Data System, Programmprodukt der Firma IBM

[SQL1] SQL Data System - Application Programming

Eine objektorientierte Datenbankmodellierung für den VLSI-Entwurf

Ernst Siepmann
Universität Kaiserslautern
Fachbereich Informatik
D-6750 Kaiserslautern

Überblick

Mit steigender Komplexität der VLSI-Chips müssen neue Entwurfsverfahren gefunden werden. Im PLAYOUT System werden die Entwurfsaufgaben wie Logikentwurf, Flächenabschätzung, Layoutgenerierung usw. auf CAD-Toolboxen verteilt, die rekursiv über mehrere Hierarchieebenen eingesetzt werden. Die zwischen den Toolboxen ausgetauschten Daten wie Funktionsbeschreibungen, Schaltpläne, Layouts usw. werden mit ihren Hierarchie- und Erzeugungsbeschreibungen als komplexe Objekte in einem objektorientierten Datenbankmodell beschrieben. Das Modell unterstützt außerdem Klassifikationen, Alternativen, Konfigurationen sowie Versionen und entspricht damit wesentlichen Forderungen der Praxis.

1. Die PLAYOUT-Architektur

Beim PLAYOUT-System /Zi86, Zi88, Sm88/ wird der Entwurf in einem zweidimensionalen Entwurfsraum (Abb. 1.1) durchgeführt, der von den vier **Entwurfsbereichen** Verhalten, Struktur, Flächenplan und Layout und beliebig vielen **Hierarchieebenen** innerhalb jedes Entwurfsbereiches aufgespannt wird. Die Einzelaufgaben werden jeweils von einer **CAD-Toolbox** wahrgenommen. Diese besteht aus einer Anzahl von Tools (Algorithmen), die Teilaufgaben wie Partitionieren und Orientieren der Modulflächen, Plazieren der I/O-Pins, Flächenmodellberechnung, globale Verdrahtung usw. lösen. Die Tools verwenden eine gemeinsame interne Datenstruktur, die am zweckmäßigsten als ADT (abstrakter Datentyp) implementiert ist. Der Entwurfsablauf innerhalb der Toolbox erfolgt statusgesteuert.

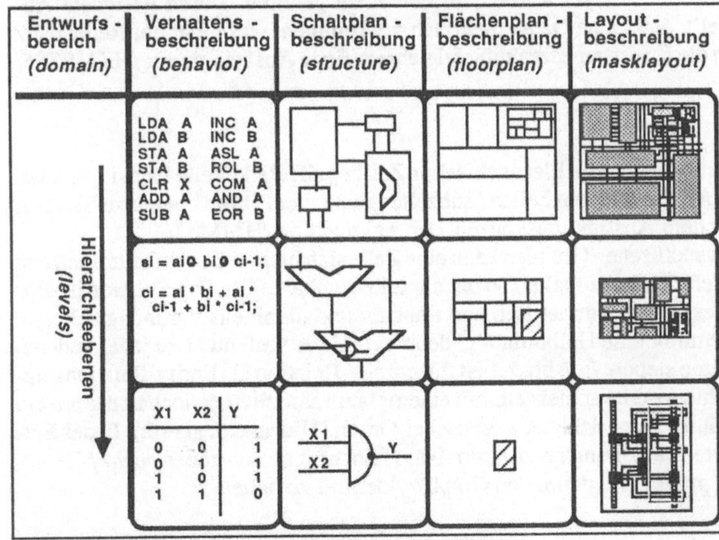

Abb. 1.1 Entwurfsbereiche und Hierarchieebenen

Alle Toolboxen außer dem Repartitionierer führen einen Entwurfsteilschritt durch, der den Übergang von einem Entwurfsbereich in den nächsten bewirkt, und zwar immer in Richtung Verhalten zu Layout. So erzeugt ein Logikentwurfssystem aus einer Verhaltensbeschreibung einen Schaltplan, der *Chip Planner* aus einem Schaltplan einen Flächenplan, das *Chip Assembly* aus einem Flächenplan ein Layout usw. Gleichzeitig findet dabei ein Hierarchieübergang statt.

Die meisten Toolboxen sind so entworfen, daß man sie **rekursiv** einsetzen kann, d.h. für alle Hierarchieebenen wird dieselbe Toolbox verwendet. Zum Beispiel können alle Rahmen der Subzellen, die beim Planen einer Zelle entstehen, als Eingabedaten für den gleichen *Chip Planner* verwendet werden, wenn er auf einer Hierarchieebene tiefer die Planung der entsprechenden Subzellen ausführt.

Es findet jedoch kein direkter Datenaustausch zwischen den Toolboxen statt, die Kommunikation erfolgt nur über die **Entwurfsdatenbank**, siehe Abb. 1.2. Der Grund dafür ist, daß die Toolboxen ihre Daten nicht

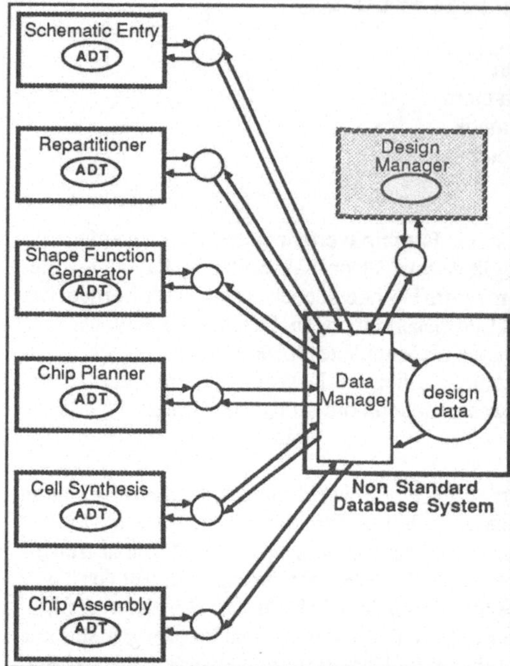

Abb. 1.2 PLAYOUT - Systemarchitektur

nur jeweils von einer anderen Toolbox erhalten, sondern von mehreren. So erhält der *Chip Planner* die Netz- und Modulliste (Subzellen) vom Logikentwurfssystem oder vom *Repartitioner*, die Flächenmodelle vom *Shape Function Generator* und den Rahmen der Zelle vom *Chip Planner* auf der Hierarchieebene darüber. Andererseits werden die gleichen Flächenmodelle, die gleichen Netz- und die gleiche Modulliste auch für den Flächenfunktionsgenerator benötigt, so daß bezüglich des Datenaustausches zwischen den Toolboxen eine komplexe n : m-Beziehung besteht. Bei direkter Kommunikation würde also ein komplizierter Graph entstehen, was eine konsistente Haltung der Entwurfsdaten, insbesondere wenn noch verschiedene Alternativen, Versionen und Konfigurationen existieren, erheblich erschweren würde. Der Datentransport zwischen der Datenbank und den Toolboxen erfolgt über Files im PLIF-Format /Si88a/.

2. Das PLAYOUT-Datenbankmodell

In den folgenden Unterkapiteln wird das Modell ausgehend von einem Hierarchiemodell schrittweise hergeleitet. Dabei soll das objektorientierte Paradigma gelten, nach dem die Daten bei den Objekten abgelegt werden, zu denen sie gehören. Durch geeignete Abstraktionskonzepte wird sichergestellt, daß keine Daten mehrfach vorkommen, was nicht nur Redundanz vermeidet, sondern ganz wesentlich die Konsistenzerhaltung erleichtert. Erste Ansätze sind in /HKMSZ85/ zu finden.

2.1. Hierarchiemodell

Der Ausgangspunkt des Datenbankmodells ist ein **hierarchischer Zellbegriff**. Jede Zelle kann in anderen Zellen (Superzellen) enthalten sein und kann andere Zellen (Subzellen) enthalten. Diese komplexe Relation wird *part-of* genannt und entspricht dem Abstraktionskonzept der Aggregation /HMM87/.

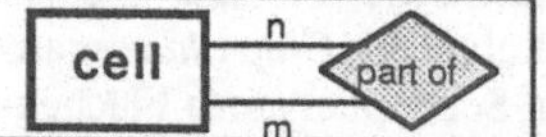

Abb. 2.1 Hierarchiegraph

Aus physikalischen Gründen kann eine Zelle sich nicht selbst enthalten und erst recht nicht Zellen enthalten, in der sie selbst enthalten ist. Die Relation ist also antireflexiv, antisymmetrisch und transitiv und damit eine Ordnungsrelation. Sie beschreibt eine Halbordnung, denn eine Zelle muß nicht zu jeder anderen Zelle in einer Enthaltenseinsbeziehung stehen. In Abb. 2.1 ist die *part-of*-Relation als Entity-Relationship-Diagramm dargestellt. Eine Hierarchie wird zwar meistens mit einem Baum assoziiert, jedoch ist das nur ein Sonderfall der allgemeinen Darstellung als gerichteter azyklischer Graph (**Hierarchiegraph**). In der Entwurfsdatenbank wird diese kompakte Darstellung benutzt, um beim Hinzufügen von neuen *part-of*-Relationen diese auf ihre Zulässigkeit zu prüfen und damit den Graph zyklenfrei zu halten.

2.2. Klassifikation

In einem Schaltplan wird eine Subzelle (z.B. ein nand-Gatter) typischerweise mehrfach verwendet; dabei müssen die Verwendungen voneinander unterscheidbar sein, da die Verbindungsrelationen (Netze) von verschiedenen Verwendungen unterschiedlich sind. Eine Modellierung, die für jede Subzelle eine neue Zelle vorsieht, würde dem objektorientierten Paradigma widersprechen. Mit dem Abstraktionskonzept der Klassifikation werden die Zelle als Typbeschreibung mit allen Zelldaten und ihre Verwendungen, die Zellinkarnation (*cell instance*), eingeführt. Jede Zellinkarnation verweist eindeutig auf ihre Zelle (Relation *instance-of*) und wird nur in einer Zelle

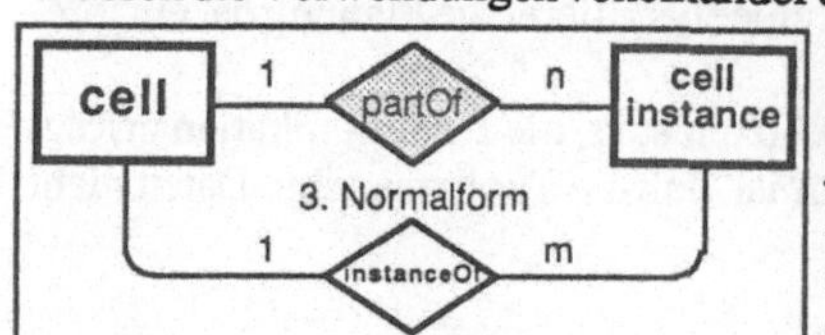

Abb. 2.2 Hierarchiebaum

als Subzelle verwendet (Relation *part-of*). Damit wird die komplexe Relation aus Abb. 2.1 in zwei funktionale Relationen (Abb 2.2) aufgelöst, und aus dem Hierarchiegraph wird ein **Hierarchiebaum**. Dieses Hierarchiemodell ist die Grundlage der Datenstrukturen von vielen CAD-Tools. Alternativen werden dabei als neue Zellen modelliert. Das hat den Nachteil, daß man sich schon beim Entwurf einer Zelle für die Alternativen der Subzellen entscheiden muß, z.B. ob in dem Schaltplan einer ALU1 der Addierer1 oder der Addierer2 verwendet wird. Eine spätere Änderung dieser Entscheidung macht den Entwurf einer zweiten Zelle ALU2 erforderlich, wenn diese wiederum in einer Zelle Prozessor verwendet wird, muß diese auch neu entworfen werden usw.

2.3. Realisierungsalternativen

Die ungünstige Modellierung von Alternativen im letzten Unterkapitel macht eine Erweiterung des Modells notwendig. Dazu müssen die Begriffe Zelle und Alternative genauer definiert werden.

Eine **Zelle** ist charakterisiert durch ihre Funktion (z.B. nand-Gatter mit 2 Eingängen, nand-Gatter mit 3 Eingängen, 1-bit-Volladdierer, Prozessor vom Typ xyz, ein spezieller OPS-Interpreter usw.). Für die Realisierung dieser Funktion kann es mehrere Alternativen innerhalb der Zelle geben. Die Zelle kann sich hierarchisch aus Subzellen zusammensetzen.

Eine **Realisierungsalternative** zu einer Zelle beschreibt eine mögliche Realisierung der Funktion der Zelle; die Realisierungsalternativen sind alle gleichzeitig gültig.

Für die weiteren Überlegungen betrachten wir vorerst nur einen Entwurfsbereich. In Abb. 2.3 ist die Zelle in ein *interface* und ein *contents* aufgeteilt. Ähnliche Ansätze finden sich auch in /BBN85, MDK87/. Jedes *contents* entspricht einer Realisierungsalternative und verwendet die Daten von seinem *interface* (Relation *realization*). Bei hierarchischem Aufbau der Zelle setzt sich jedes *contents* aus *instances* der Subzellen zusammen (Relation *part-of*). Ein *instance* ist nicht mehr die Verwendung einer Zelle mit ihrer Realisierung, sondern die Verwendung des *interface* einer Zelle. Das *interface* enthält bereits alle Informationen, die bei der Verwendung der Zelle benötigt werden. Um einen Schaltplan zu entwerfen, muß von den Subzellen nur die Zahl und Funktion der Anschlüsse, aber nicht der innere Aufbau (die Realisierung) der Subzelle bekannt sein.

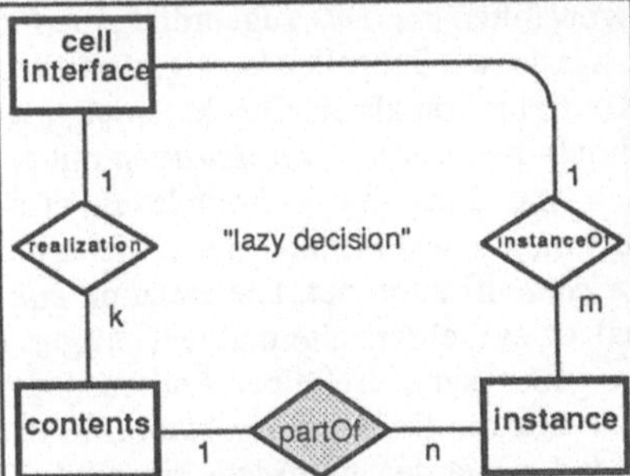

Abb. 2.3 Realisierungsalternativen

Das hat den entscheidenden Vorteil, daß beim Entwurf (einer Realisierung von) einer Zelle nicht die Realisierungen der Subzellen ausgewählt werden müssen (**Prinzip der spätestmöglichen Entscheidung**). Der Entwerfer hat dadurch erst die Möglichkeit, einen hierarchischen *top-down*-Entwurf mit Alternativen durchzuführen; es genügt, wenn er beim Entwurf einer Zelle die Funktionen und die *interfaces* der Subzellen spezifiziert.

2.4. Entwurfsbereiche

In Abb. 2.4 ist das Datenmodell aus Abb. 2.3 auf die Entwurfsbereiche aus Abb. 1.1 erweitert. Eine Zelle ist nun ein komplexes Objekt, das selbst keine Entwurfsdaten mehr enthält, sie setzt sich aus einem oder mehreren *interfaces* pro Entwurfsbereich (Relation *domain*) mit den jeweiligen realisierenden *contents* zusammen (Abstraktionskonzept der Aggregation).

Alle in Abb. 2.3 beschriebenen Relationen gelten zwischen Objekten innerhalb eines Entwurfsbereiches, doch muß es auch Relationen zwischen den Entwurfsbereichen geben, denn der Entwerfer will z.B. wissen, welcher Schaltplan und welcher Flächenplan für ein Layout ursächlich waren. Im Modell aus Abb. 2.4 werden diese Beziehungen zwischen den Entwurfsbereichen als eindeutige *generated*-Relation dargestellt. Interessanterweise befindet sich diese Relation zwischen einem *contents* des realisierungsferneren Entwurfbereiches und einem *interface* des realisierungsnäheren Entwurfbereiches, denn alle Flächenpläne, die zu einem Schaltplan entworfen werden können, haben das gleiche

Abb. 2.4 Zelle als komplexes Objekt

Flächenmodell (*floorplan interface*), das direkt aus dem Schaltplan errechnet wird. Ebenso gilt, daß alle Layouts, die zu einem Flächenplan entworfen werden können, das gleiche *ghost* (*masklayout interface*) haben, denn durch den Flächenplan ist der Rahmen mit den Positionen der I/O-Pins vorgegeben.

2.5. Konfiguration

Auch beim Prinzip der spätestmöglichen Entscheidung von Realisierungsalternativen muß sich der Entwerfer vor der Maskengenerierung für eine der Alternativen entschieden haben; dieser Vorgang wird **Konfigurieren** genannt. Dies kann explizit durch ein Konfigurationswerkzeug oder implizit durch die CAD-Toolboxen geschehen, indem diese aus mehreren angebotenen Alternativen die für sie günstigste auswählen.

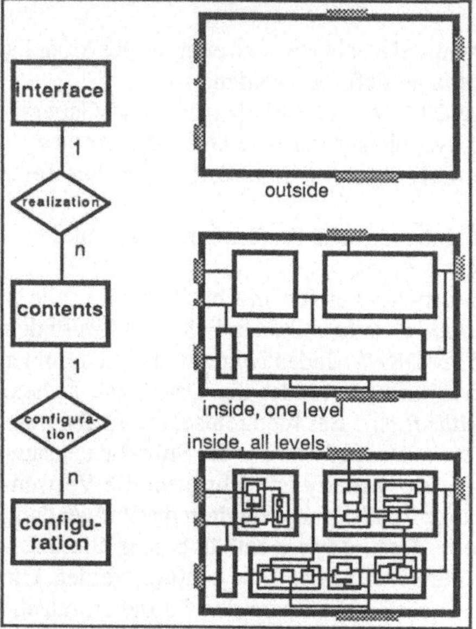

Abb. 2.5 Alternativenentscheidung

Beim Konfigurieren wird für jedes *instance* aus der Menge der *contents*, die das *interface* des *instance* realisieren, eins ausgewählt. Damit liegt die Realisierungsalternative fest. Diese Auswahl wird **Vorkonfiguration** genannt, denn es wird keine Entscheidung bezüglich der Konfigurationen der *instances* in dem ausgewählten *contents* getroffen. Mit der Zuweisung eines *contents* zu jedem *instance* läßt sich also die Alternativenauswahl bei einer aus mehreren Hierarchieebenen aufgebauten Zelle nicht eindeutig bestimmen.

Deshalb wird bei der **Endkonfiguration** dem *instance* eine Konfiguration des ausgewählten *contents* zugeordnet, die für dieses *contents* angibt, wie dessen Subzellen konfiguriert sind. In Abb. 2.6 wird die Konfiguration als ein Objekt (*configuration*) modelliert, das durch die Relation *configuration* mit einem *contents* verbunden ist und das mit der komplexen, dreistelligen Relation *association* jedem *instance* des *contents* ein *configuration* oder ein *contents* zuordnet. Die Relation *configuration* ist funktional, da es mehrere alternative Konfigurationen für ein *contents* geben kann. Bei einer Änderung der Konfiguration muß also nur die Relation *association* in der Entwurfsdatenbank geändert werden und nicht ein *contents* (z.B. ein Schaltplan) neu entworfen werden.

In Abb. 2.5 sind die drei Beschreibungsstufen für eine Zelle, die sie in jedem ihrer Entwurfsbereiche hat, dargestellt. Mit der Angabe des *interface* wird noch keine Aussage über die Realisierung gemacht, mit der Angabe des *contents* wird die Realisierung für eine Hierarchieebene und mit der Angabe des endkonfigurierten *configuration* für alle Ebenen entschieden.

Wenn die *instances* des zu konfigurierenden *contents* selbst nicht mehr aus Zellen bestehen, sondern die Primitiven der Zellhierarchie sind, kann natürlich weder ein *contents* noch ein *configuration* zugeordnet werden. In diesem Fall erfolgt eine Endkonfiguration durch die Angabe des *interface* eines realisierungsnäheren Entwurfsbereiches (Flächenplan oder Layout) dieser Subzelle (**primitive Konfiguration**).

In Abb. 2.6 ist das erweiterte Datenbankmodell angegeben. Mit der Relation *association* (schwarz für Endkonfiguration, grau für Vorkonfiguration) stößt man an die Grenzen der Darstellungsfähigkeit des Entity-Relationship-Modells.

Abb. 2.6 läßt auch eine andere Interpretation der Relation *association* zu: als hierarchieübergreifende zweistellige Relation auf der Menge der *configurations* korrespondiert sie mit der Relation *part-of* aus Abb. 2.1. Wie jene bei den Zellen bildet sie mit den Konfigurationsobjekten einen gerichteten azyklischen Graphen, den **Konfigurationsgraph**. Dieser ist ein Teilgraph

Abb. 2.6 Konfigurationsgraph

des Hierarchiegraphen. Während im Hierarchiegraphen die Hierarchiebeziehungen aller Alternativen vorhanden sind, gibt der Konfigurationsgraph die konfigurierte Auswahl an. Operationen zur Ausgabe einer Konfiguration über alle Hierarchieebenen benutzen zweckmäßigerweise den Konfigurationsgraph.

2.6. Views

Die Entwurfsdaten, die von den CAD-Toolboxen bearbeitet und erzeugt werden, wie Schaltpläne, Flächenmodelle, Layouts usw. werden nicht direkt in den bisher vorgestellten Objekten des Datenmodells abgelegt, sondern in *views* gespeichert. Jede *view* ist eindeutig einem Objekt zugeordnet, das beliebige *views* haben kann. Jede *view* stellt eine Sicht auf die Daten des Objekts dar, z.B. eine graphische oder numerische Darstellung. Eine *view* kann auch nur eine Teilsicht enthalten, d.h. daß erst durch mehrere *views* die Objektdaten vollständig beschrieben werden können, z.B. ein Flächenplan durch die *views frame*, *iopins*, *slicingtree* und *fpnetlist*.

2.7. Versionen

Bisher enthält das Datenmodell noch keine Unterstützung für die Versionsverwaltung. Versionen sollen hier als zeitliche Versionen, von denen nur die jeweils letzte gültig ist, verstanden werden; im Gegensatz zu den Alternativen, die alle gleichzeitig gültig sind und unter denen der Entwerfer eine Auswahl treffen kann. Eine neue Version wird also üblicherweise nur erzeugt, wenn in der alten Version ein Fehler gefunden wurde. Trotzdem müssen alte Versionen aufbewahrt werden, damit die Änderungstransaktion, die die von der geänderten Version abhängigen Objekte anpaßt, zurückgesetzt werden kann.

Versionsobjekte sind für alle *interfaces* und *contents* und für manche *configurations* vorgesehen. *Instances* haben keine Versionsobjekte, denn eine Änderung der *instance*-Daten verursacht in der Regel eine Änderung der *contents*-Daten, so daß es genügt, wenn die *instances* einer Version ihres *contents* zugeordnet werden (*part-of*-Relation). Die *views* und damit die Entwurfsdaten sind natürlich nicht mehr den *interfaces* und *contents*, sondern dessen Versionen zugeordnet.

2.8. Die vollständige Datenbankmodellierung

In Abb. 2.7 ist die vollständige Datenbankmodellierung als erweitertes Entity-Relationship-Modell /HKMSZ85/ angegeben. Auf die Darstellung der *views* wurde aus Gründen der Übersichtlichkeit verzichtet. Das Datenbankmodell besteht für jeden der vier Entwurfsbereiche aus dem Modell aus Abb. 2.6, wobei die Versionsobjekte ergänzt sind. Alternativen bei der Relation *association* werden durch überlappende Rauten dargestellt; die grau gedruckten Alternativen bezeichnen die Vorkonfiguration.

In den einzelnen Entwurfsbereichen ergeben sich Unterschiede bei der Modellierung der Konfiguration und der *generated*-Relation, die aus den entwurfsspezifischen Anforderungen resultieren. Alle Einzelheiten können im Rahmen dieses Artikels nicht beschrieben werden; insbesondere das *top-down*-Chipplanning stellt besondere Anforderungen an die Modellierung, siehe hierzu /Si88b/.

3. Literatur

/Zi86/ G. Zimmermann, "Top-down design of digital systems", in Logic Design and Simulation,
    E. Hörbst (Editor), Elsevier Science Publ. B.V., Amsterdam 1986
/Zi88/ G. Zimmermann, "PLAYOUT - A Hierarchical Layout System", GI-Jahrestagung 1988
/Sm88/ B.Schürmann,"Hierarchisches Top Down Chip Planning",Informatik Spektrum, Heidelberg 1988
/HKMSZ85/ T. Härder, W. Keller, B. Mitschang, E. Siepmann, G. Zimmermann, "Datenstrukturen und
    Datenmodelle für den VLSI - Entwurf", SFB 124 Bericht 26/85, Kaiserslautern 1985
/HMM87/ T. Härder, N. Mattos, B. Mitchang, "Abbildung von Frames auf neuere Datenmodelle",
    Proc. zur 11. GWAI, Schloß Eringerfeld bei Geseke 1987
/BBN85/ A. Beetem, J. Beetem, A. Nigam, "HDMS: A Hierarchical VLSI Design Data Management
    System", IBM Research Report, Yorktown Heights 1985
/MDK87/ J. Mülle, K. Dittrich, A. Kotz, "Design Management Support by Advanced Database Facilities"
    Proc. of the IFIP WG 10.2 Workshop on Tool Integration and Design Environm., Paderborn 1987
/Si88a/ E. Siepmann, "PLIF - Ein objektorientiertes Datenaustauschformat zur Kommunikation in
    PLAYOUT", SFB 124 Bericht 32/88, Kaiserslautern 1988
/Si88b/ E. Siepmann, "Eine objektorientierte Datenbankmodellierung für das integrierte VLSI-Entwurfs
    system PLAYOUT", SFB 124 Bericht 35/88, Kaiserslautern 1988
/Ka85/ R. Katz, "Information Management for Engineering Design", Berlin Heidelberg 1985

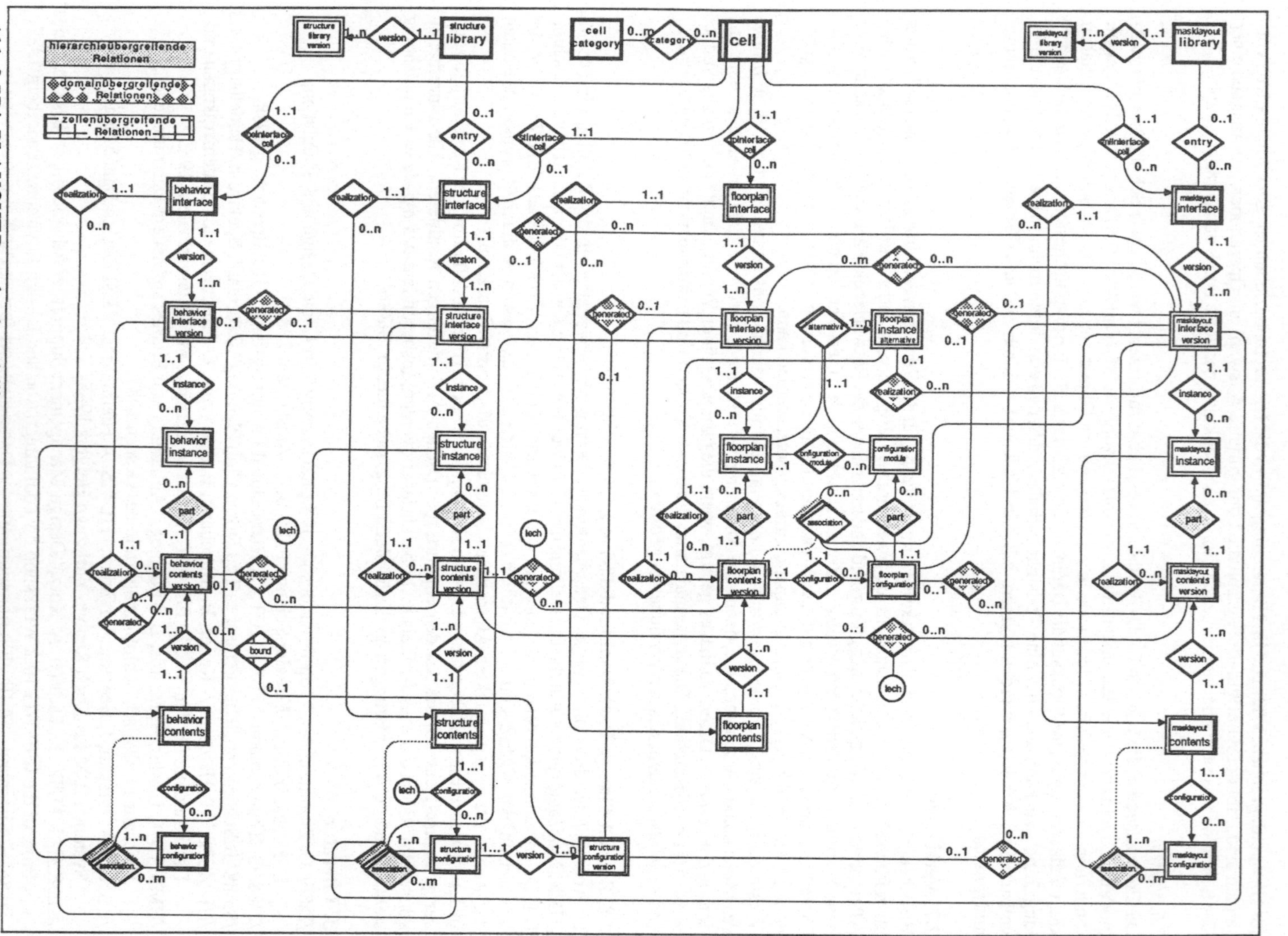

Abb. 2.7 Die PLAYOUT Datenbankmodellierung

REPRESENTING DIGITAL SYSTEMS AS COMPLEX OBJECTS *

L. G. Golendziner, F. R. Wagner, C. M. Dal Sasso-Freitas
V. Boklis & K. Becker
Universidade Federal do Rio Grande do Sul
Depto. de Informática e PG em Ciência da Computação
Porto Alegre, RS, BRAZIL

Abstract

AMPLO is an integrated design environment where the design objects, digital systems, are described by means of nets of agencies. Concepts like molecular objects, version generalization, instantiation and parameterized versions are present in the representation of agencies as complex objects. Graphical and textual hardware description languages incorporate these well defined modelling and management concepts. The objects are manipulated through the use of an object-oriented data base interface that allows the integration of all design tools around a unified data base.

Introduction

AMPLO (from portuguese "AMbiente para o Projeto LOgico de sistemas digitais") is an integrated CAD environment for digital systems design under development at UFRGS - Federal University of Rio Grande do Sul - at Porto Alegre, Brazil [WAG 88] . Integration is present in AMPLO due to the following features:

- all design information about systems descriptions and simulation models is stored in a unified data base;

- the description of the inteface of digital systems is uniformly done at all levels, allowig consistency checking between several representations of the same object;

- design tools (graphical editors, compilers, simulators) have homogeneous user interfaces. There is also a high-level user interface that gives access to all design tools and allows queries and updates to the data base;

- the same design management concepts are present in all design levels and tools, allowing the organization of data in several design alternatives and versions.

Digital systems are described in a modular and hierarchical way

---

* Work partially supported by CNPq and FINEP

as **nets of agencies** [WEN 80], where each agency can be further refined as another net (**composite description**) of agencies or described with primitives of a particular design level (**primitive description**). Three hardware description languages are available for primitive descriptions, corresponding to three design levels: system, register transfer and gate level. Composite descriptions are obtained using the REDES language, which is based on the CASCADE language [BOR 85]. All languages have equivalent textual and graphical forms.

Design validation is performed by a family of simulators. Since agencies are described in a hierarchical way, a **simulation model** is built by traversing the hierarchy of composite descriptions until obtaining a net where each agency is described with primitives of some desired level.

Concepts used in describing digital systems

Every digital system in AMPLO is represented as an agency. The designer can create several **alternatives** and **versions** for an agency. **Alternatives** for an agency represent different interface definitions, e.g. different number of signals, names or types of signals. Figure 1 shows a graphical description of an alternative for agency ALU_1_BIT. For the further example, we suppose that this description is that of the first alternative for this agency, i.e. it takes the identification ALU_1_BIT.1.

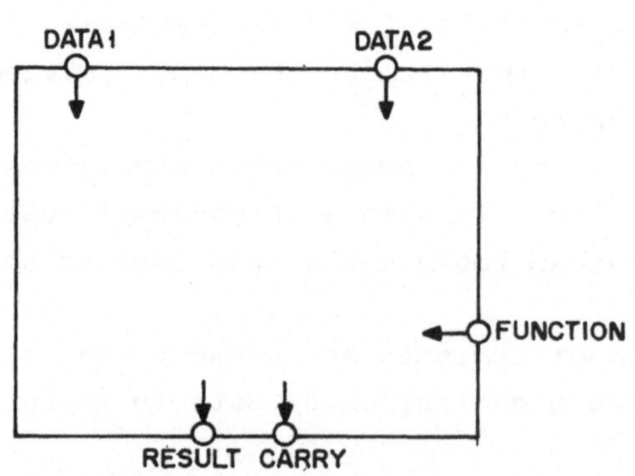

Fig.1: Graphical description of alternative 1 of agency ALU_1_BIT.

This interface comprises the definition of three input signals (DATA1, DATA2, FUNCTION) and two output signals (RESULT,CARRY). In a top-down design process, an agency can be described either in a composite way, as a net of agencies, or in a primitive way, by means of one of the hardware description languages mentioned before. These descriptions represent (composite or primitive)

versions of an alternative. All versions of an alternative share the same interface definition. Figure 2 shows a composite version (e.g.

version no. 1) for the alternative ALU_1_BIT.1.

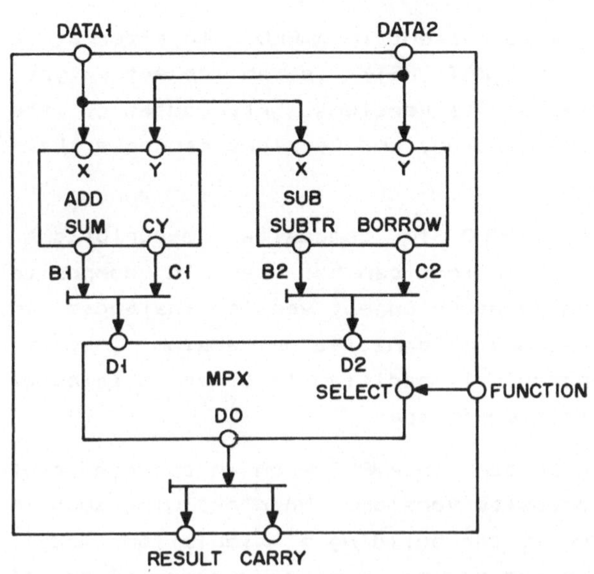

Fig.2: A composite version for
       alternative ALU_1_BIT.1

ADD, SUB and MPX are the names of the component agencies of ALU_1_BIT.1.1, that are connected through their interface signals. Each component agency in a composite version is an occurrence of either an alternative or a version of the referenced agency.Using occurrences of versions means that the composite version is completely defined and is ready to use for simulation purposes,for example. Its components are statically defined. Using occurrences of alternatives means that only the interfaces of the component agencies are defined in the composite description; later, the designer will have to choose one of the of the several versions that may exist for the alternatives in order to complete the description. For example, in the specification of a simulation model, the designer dinamically chooses the appropriate (or desired) versions. The use of occurrences of alternatives in a composite description provides a definition of a template [BAT 85], where the designer may change the selected versions, building a variety of configurations of the system to be analyzed.

The concepts used in AMPLO [BOK 88] have a straightforward relation with the concepts presented by Batory and Kim [BAT 85]. There, four concepts were recognized as necessary in modelling VLSI objects: molecular objects, version generalization, instantiation and parameterized versions.

Molecular objects [BAT 84] are objects that have two levels of description: an interface and an implementation. In AMPLO, this concept is present, in the sense that these two levels are clearly separated in the hardware description languages (figures ? and 3). To an interface (i.e. an alternative) the designer can associate many implementations (versions).

Version generalization is also present in AMPLO. An alternative (with another meaning than in [BAT 85]) is an object type, representing the common features of its versions. Attributes of the alternative are inherited by each version, and versions can have their own attributes.

Instantiation appears in AMPLO in composite descriptions. Occurrences of alternatives or versions can be used in composite versions, like object type instances or object version instances in [BAT 85]. An occurrence of an agency alternative or version inherits all the attributes of that agency, in addition to other attributes that are not inherited, e.g. position in space.

Parameterized versions are present in AMPLO when an occurrence of an alternative is used in a composite version. When refining such a composite version or when using it for building a simulation model, the designer has to replace this occurrence by an occurrence of one of the versions of the alternative.

Implementation

The unified data base is implemented upon the file system of the host machine. A set of access functions constitutes the object-oriented interface [BEC 88], hiding from the design tools the implementation of the objects. The access functions perform some consistency checks at design management level.

The objects in the data base are agencies, alternatives, versions, and occurrences of alternatives or versions. Composite descriptions are seen as complex objects through the access functions (operational object-orientation [DIT 87]). Primitive descriptions have an interface and an implementation part. The implementation part is not internally handled by the access functions, but retrieved as a whole.

All design tools use the object-oriented interface to perform functions like: creation of agencies, alternatives, composite or primitive versions; replacement of the last alternative or version by another one; removal of versions, alternatives or agencies; retrieval of textual or graphical descriptions of these objects, etc.

Consistency checking is done by these functions, for example, alternatives or versions that are referenced in composite descriptions cannot be removed.

Conclusions

The concepts used for modelling digital systems in AMPLO were presented. It has been pointed out the applicability of the concepts already recognized by Batory and Kim [BAT 85] in this type of design environment. The concepts of molecular objects, version generalization, instantiation and parameterized versions are present in the objects of AMPLO.

The objects are manipulated through an object-oriented interface that maintains object-related integrity constraints. This interface provides data independence, in the sense that tools only access data through the access functions. It is then easy to incorporate new tools to the environment, provided they use the defined access functions. Otherwise, new functions can be specified and incorporated to the system, with no influence to the existing ones.

References

[BAT 84] BATORY, D.S. and BUCHMAN, A.P. Molecular objects, abstract data types and data models: a framework. In: International Conference on Very Large Databases, 10, Singapure, 1984. Proceedings. pp. 172-182.

[BAT 85] BATORY, D.S. and KIM, W. Modelling concepts for VLSI CAD objects. ACM Transactions on Database Systems, 10(3):322-346, sept. 1985.

[BEC 88] BECKER, K. and GOLENDZINER, L.G. Database Support for a CAD Environment for Digital Systems Design. In: Conferencia Internacional de Ciencia de la Computacion de la SCCC, 8, Jul. 1988. Proceedings. Santiago, Pontificia Universidad Catolica de Chile, 1988. pp 231-243.

[BOK 88] BOKLIS,V. and GOLENDZINER, L.G. Data modelling in a digital systems design environment. In: Congresso Nacional de Informática, 21, Rio de Janeiro, Aug. 1988. Proceedings. (in portuguese)

[BOR 85] BORRIONE, D. The CASCADE Multilevel Hardware Description Language. Grenoble, IMAG-Artemis, march 1985. (RR 514)

[DIT 87] DITTRICH, K.R. Object-oriented database systems. In: Spaccapietra,S.(ed.) : Entity-Relationship Approach. North-Holland, 1987. pp. 51-66

[MER 85] MERMET, J. Several Steps Towards a Circuits Integrated CAD System: CASCADE. Grenoble, IMAG-Artemis, march 1985. (RR 515)

[WAG 88] WAGNER, F.R., DAL SASSO-FREITAS, C.M. and GOLENDZINER, L.G. The AMPLO System - an integrated environment for digital systems design. In: F.J. Rammig (ed.) Workshop on Tool Integration and Design Environment. Paderborn, 1987. Proceedings. Amsterdam, North-Holland, 1988. pp 221-232

[WEN 80] WENDT, S. On the partitioning of computing agencies into communicating agencies. In: GI-NTG Fachtagung - Struktur und Betrieb von Rechensystemen. Springer-Verlag, 1980. pp 194-204

R. Buhr
Hoechst AG
Pharma Forschung Informatik
D-6230 Frankfurt 80

Zusammenfassung: Dieser Beitrag beschreibt die Konzipierung eines Informationssystems für die Pharma Forschung der HOECHST AG. Das System verwaltet Forschungsergebnisse in Form strukturierter, unstrukturierter und grafischer Information und ermöglicht den gezielten schnellen Zugriff auf die gespeicherte Information. In diesem Zusammenhang werden der Einsatz eines semantischen Netzes in der Entwicklungsphase sowie einer natürlich sprachlichen Benutzeroberfläche diskutiert.

1. Zielsetzung

Für die Pharma Forschung der HOECHST AG ist ein Informationssystem zu schaffen mit dem Ziel:

- signifikante chemische und biologische Information, die bei der Synthetisierung chemischer Substanzen bzw. bei Testungen dieser Substanzen auf ihre pharmakologische Wirksamkeit anfallen, in großem Rahmen zu dokumentieren,
- den tätigen Wissenschaftlern einen gezielten und schnellen Zugriff auf den sich im Laufe der Zeit ansammelnden Wissensfundus zu gewähren.

Der Nutzen des Informationssystems ist offensichtlich strategischer Art.
Ein derzeit vorhandenes System auf Basis des Software Produkts IBM STAIRS® wird den zunehmend gestellten Recherchieranforderungen rein funktionell nicht mehr gerecht.

Der Wissensfundus umfaßt derzeit die Dokumentation von ca. 120 Tsd synthetisierten Substanzen mit den wesentlichsten physikalischen und chemischen Eigenschaften (inklusive der grafischen Darstellung der chemischen Strukturformel) in Form eines standardisierten Präparatebogens (Abb. 1) sowie die Dokumentation von 1,5 Mio Testprotokollen mit der exakten Beschreibung der Testbedingungen, den biologischen Testdaten (abgeleitete Daten - keine Rohdaten) und deren Beurteilung in Form eines Befundbogens (Abb. 2).

2. Problemstellung

Eine unter dem Aspekt der Arzneimittelentwicklung interessante chemische Substanz wird bestimmten Tests unterzogen mit dem Ziel:

- ein aussichtsreiches Indikationsfeld für diese Substanz zu spezifizieren (Screening) oder
- die biologische Wirkung der Substanz für ein vorgegebenes Indikationsfeld näher zu untersuchen und zu bestimmen.

In Abhängigkeit des Indikationsfelds gibt es vorgegebene Methoden, durch die der Rahmen für die Durchführung einzelner biologischer Tests (sogenannte Versuchseinheit) bis ins Detail beschrieben und festgelegt ist. Zu jeder der ca. 600 vorhandenen Methoden existieren methodenspezifische, komplex strukturierte Befundbögen zur Erfassung der zu dokumentierenden Einzeltest-bezogenen Daten.
Die gesamte Information über alle biologischen Tests und synthetisierten Wirksubstanzen ist als eine logische Einheit anzusehen, in der der Wissenschaftler unter sich ständig ändernden Suchkriterien frei recherchieren können soll.

<u>Beispiele:</u>
1. Selektiere alle Substanzen unter der Vorgabe von: das Bearbeitungsjahr, verschiedene
    Methoden, die erzielte Mindestwirkstärke (relativ zu Standardpräparat).
2. Selektiere alle Substanzen unter der Vorgabe von: der chemischer Grundkörper (gleiche
    Stammverbindung), das Indikationsgebiet (Text), die verwendete Methode, die erzielte
    Mindestwirkstärke.

Während der erste Recherchetyp als Ergebnis die Grafiken der gesuchten Substanzen liefert, werden im
zweiten Recherchetyp die Grafiken als Selektionskriterium für die gesuchten Substanzen verwendet.

<u>3. Daten- und Systemanalyse</u>

Die für eine detaillierte Anforderungs-Analyse und -Spezifikation notwendigen Angaben /KAH 85/
resultieren sowohl aus den einschlägigen Erfahrungen und Erkenntnissen, die anhand des bereits
existierenden Systems gesammelt wurden, als auch aus gezielten Befragungen einzelner Vertreter der
verschiedensten Benutzergruppen (Durchführung von Interviews). Um zu einer möglichst umfassenden
Definition der Informations- und Bearbeitungs-Anforderungen /VOS 87/ zu gelangen, werden als
praktikable Vorgehensweise der Analyse-Ansatz (bestehendes System) mit dem Synthese-Ansatz
(Befragungsergebnisse) /DAT 86/ kombiniert. Bei der Datenmodellierung wird parallel nach dem 'top-
down' und dem 'bottom-up' Prinzip vorgegangen.

In der konzeptionellen Entwurfsphase des Informationssystems ist es wichtig, möglichst viel Wissen und
Erkenntnisse über die Informationselemente des zu realisierenden Systems und ihrer Zusammenhänge
untereinander zu erfahren und geeignet zu organisieren, ohne bereits auf spezielle Beschränkungen oder
Charakteristika eines konkreten 'record-orientierten' Datenbankmodells Rücksicht nehmen zu müssen.
Auf dieser hohen Abstraktionsebene sind semantische Datenmodelle äußerst nützlich /KIN 85/: im
konkreten Fall wird zur objekt-orientierten Wissensrepräsentation eine Darstellungsform in Anlehnung an
KL-ONE /BRA 85/ verwendet, die gerade in Zusammenarbeit mit Mitarbeitern der Dokumentation die
Möglichkeit natürlicher und anwendungsnaher Ausdrucksmöglichkeiten bietet, ohne gleich Datenbank-
Expertenwissen vorauszusetzen.
Abbildung 3 zeigt das Ergebnis der Arbeiten. Die gewählte Darstellungsform erscheint für die Analyse
der Realität gefälliger als die nach dem klassischen Entity-Relationship-Modell /CHE 76/: neben der
Darstellung relevanter, einfacher Objekte und der Bildung von Objektklassen lassen sich komplex
strukturierte Objekte und vor allem Objektbeziehungen transparent abbilden. Innerhalb der vorliegenden
Datenstruktur ist die Modellierung folgender Hierarchiestufen von zentraler Bedeutung:

    <u>1. Hierarchiestufe:</u> die pro Versuchseinheit anfallenden Meßwerte, die in Abhängigkeit der
Versuchsparameter meist mehrdimensional strukturiert sind.
    <u>2. Hierarchiestufe:</u> eine aus wissenschaftlicher Sicht angebrachte logische Zusammenfassung von
Befundbögen verschiedener Versuchseinheiten zu einem Versuchsprotokoll, unter der
Voraussetzung, daß die gleiche Wirksubstanz mit der gleichen Methode untersucht wird und sich
dabei von Test zu Test die Ausprägung ausschließlich einer Methodenvariablen ändert.

Neben dem skizzierten top-down Vorgehen werden die benutzerseitig gewünschten Sichten auf den
Datenbestand in eine formale Darstellung einzelner Datenelemente und ihrer Beziehungen untereinander
überführt. Als Darstellungsmittel in dieser untersten Abstraktionsebene werden modifizierte bubble-
charts /MAR 87/ verwendet (Beispiel Abb. 4), die zur Definition genereller Recherchetypen dienen.
Diese Darstellungen werden anschließend im Prozeß der View Integration zu einem Gesamtschema
zusammengefaßt /MAR 83/, das dann mit weiterer Information über Integritätsbedingungen, funktionalen
Abhängigkeiten usw. die Basis für den logischen Entwurf des Systems bildet.

Die parallele Vorgehensweise ist nicht nur für das View-Modelling und View-Integration förderlich,
sondern umgekehrt auch für die Ableitung des semantischen Netzes, wo eine ausreichende Analyse

bestehender Informationssachverhalte aufgrund des hohen Abstraktionsgrads oft schwer zu realisieren ist. Durch diese Rückwirkung auf die jeweils andere Betrachtungsebene wird die Konsistenz und die Wirklichkeitsnähe des gesamten Entwurfprozesses wesentlich gesteigert.

4. Systemanforderung

An die 'multimediale Datenbank' sind folgende Anforderungen zu stellen:

1. Informationsverwaltung vom Typ 'strukturierte Daten':
   z.B. Versuchsdatum, Prüfername, Schmelzpunkt (Datum, alphanumerisch, numerisch)
2. Informationsverwaltung vom Typ 'strukturierte mehrdimensionale Datenfelder':
   z.B. Meßwerte (numerisch)
3. Informationsverwaltung vom Typ 'unstrukturierte Daten':
   z.B. Bemerkung zum Versuchsablauf, Beurteilung (Text)
4. Informationsverwaltung vom Typ 'grafische Daten':
   z.B. Darstellung der chemischen Strukturformel
5. Recherchen über die gesamte Datenbasis, wobei als Suchkriterium sowohl die Kombination von Vorgabewerten eines einzelnen Datentyps als auch die Kombination von Vorgabewerten aller genannten Datentypen in der Anfrage möglich sein muß
6. anwenderfreundliche Benutzeroberfläche mit den Eigenschaften:
   - minimaler Eingabeaufwand seitens des Benutzers,
   - automatisches Transformieren aller Anfragevarianten in effiziente Datenbank-Queries,
   - frei von Befehlselementen der verwendeten Datenbank-Anfragesprache,
   - benutzbar ohne Kenntnis der inneren Datenbankstruktur.

5. System-Softwarebasis

Rein von der Datenmodellierung her könnte der Einsatz von non-standard Datenbanksystemen /BLA 85/ zur besseren Wiedergabe der im Abschnitt Datenanalyse geschilderten Hierarchiestrukturen und der laut Systemanforderungen zu verwaltenden verschiedenen Informationsstrukturen gerechtfertigt sein. Doch sind folgende Aspekte abzuwägen:

- die Entwicklung von non-standard Datenbanksystemen ist in vollem Gang
- eingeschränkte Einsatzmöglichkeiten (z.B. als CAD- oder Büroinformationssystem) bedingt durch die Unterstützung der vom Einsatzgebiet abhängigen Datenstruktur-Erweiterungen
- bedingt durch den Entwicklungsstand meist nur in spezifischem DV-Environment lauffähig
- zur Verwaltung insbesondere chemischer Strukturformeln existieren bewährte dedizierte Systeme
- Universalität des Systems bezüglich Anwendungsbereich und Lauffähigkeit auf verschiedener Hardware als Unternehmen-spezifische Auflage.

Zur Verwaltung chemischer Strukturformeln wird in der HOECHST AG das Softwareprodukt MACCS® der Firma MDL (Molecular Design Limited) eingesetzt. Als Standard-Datenbanksystem hat sich ORACLE® bewährt. Zwischen beiden Produkten existieren Software-Schnittstellen. Unter Einbeziehung der genannten Kriterien werden beide Produkte als Basis für das Informationssystem gewählt.

6. Benutzeroberfläche

Datenerfassung: Die Sicherstellung der Datenintegrität und Datenkonsistenz des Gesamtsystems erzwingt eine Masken-gestützte methodenspezifische Datenerfassung mit Plausibilitätsprüfungen parallel zur Dateneingabe.

<u>Recherche:</u> Die Vielzahl der nachgefragten Recherchetypen erfordert eine einfach zu handhabende Benutzeroberfläche mit möglichst flexiblen Vorgabemechanismen für die Suchkriterien und die Ergebnisdatenfelder. Als mögliche Lösungsansätze kommen in Betracht:

- Kombination von Menü- und Window-Technik,
- natürlich sprachliche Oberfläche.

Bei der ersten Alternative spezifiziert der Benutzer in einer Bildschirmliste aller optionalen Vorgabewerte die ihn aktuell interessierenden Vorgabegrößen: durch diesen Vorgang ist der Recherchetyp und damit der Aufbau des zugeordneten SQL-Statements festgelegt. In einer zweiten Bildschirmliste, die ausschließlich zum spezifizierten Recherchetyp semantisch sinnvolle Ausgabedatenelemente umfaßt, markiert der Benutzer die Datenfelder, die er als Ergebnis der Recherche angezeigt haben möchte.

Die andere Alternative sieht zunächst die Formulierung der Anfrage in natürlicher Sprache vor, bevor systemseitig eine semantische Interpretation dieser Anfrage erfolgen /HAR 85/ und mit Hilfe einer Wissensbasis über das logische Datenbankschema ein entsprechendes SQL-Statement nach bestimmten Formalismen erzeugt werden kann. Das Rechercheergebnis wird schließlich über das Benutzerinterface zur Anzeige gebracht. Auf dem Markt werden bereits Softwareprodukte dieser Art angeboten: so das Produkt PARLANCE® von der Firma BBN (Bolt, Beranek and Newman Corp.) /BBN 88/.

Ein Vergleich beider Ansätze läßt Vorteile der zweiten Alternative erkennen:

- hohe Flexibilität bei der Anfrageformulierung in englischer Sprache,
- absetzen modifizierter bereits vorher verwendeter Recherchen,
- selbsterklärende Synonyme für ganze Anfragen,
- Historie über die gesamte Session.

Allerdings bietet diese Alternative einige Nachteile:

- keine Eingriffsmöglichkeiten für die Optimierung von SQL-Statements in Abhängigkeit spezifischer interner Datenbankstrukturen,
- keine Unterstützung, systemseitig einen Kontext-abhängigen Vorschlag für die als nächstes durchzuführende Recherche zu erzeugen (Anfragesequenz),
- bei komplexen oder unvorhersehbaren Recherchen relativ schwierige Anfrageformulierung und mühsame Eingabe des Wortlauts,
- Integration grafischer Information in die Anfrageformulierung bzw. Ergebnisdarstellung offen,
- durch das natürlich sprachliche KI-System zusätzlicher System-Overhead und Ressourcenbedarf,
- im Vergleich zur Dateneingabe aus Anwendersicht eine von der Handhabung her völlig anders gestaltete Benutzeroberfläche.

7. Systemkonzept

Die Abbildung 5 vermittelt eine Übersicht über das Konzept des Informationssystems. Das Intelligente Interface System, mit dem der Benutzer kommuniziert, besitzt die Module

- Benutzer-Interaktion-System,
- Recherchetyp-Manager,
- Dateneingabemasken-Manager,
- SQL-Generator,

mit folgenden Aufgaben:

- Reaktion auf unzureichend spezifizierte bzw. nicht unterstützte Recherchetypen,
- Unterstützung spezifischer Anfragesequenzen (Recherchestrategien),
- Zuordnung zu dem gemäß der Anfrage optimalsten vorgefertigten SQL-Statement,
- Zusammenfassen der vom Benutzer angegebenen Größen zu einem vollständigen SQL-Statement,
- Kommunikation mit dem Anfrage-Koordination-Systems,
- Kommunikation mit dem Informations-Darstellung-Systems.

Beim Vorliegen eines systemseitig nicht unterstützten Recherchetyps bleibt die manuelle Eingabe eines entsprechenden SQL-Statements.

Das Anfrage-Koordination-System ist Bindeglied zwischen den beiden Softwareprodukten ORACLE® und MACCS®. Im Bedarfsfall koordiniert es den Informationsaustausch zwischen beiden Subsystemen. Die Kopplung der relationalen Tabelle im MACCS® mit den ORACLE®-Tabellen erfolgt dabei über ein gemeinsam definiertes Schlüsselfeld. Betrifft die aktuelle Anfrage beide Subsysteme wird in Abhängigkeit der Vorgabegrößen (WHERE-clause) und unter Beachtung von Realisierungs- und Optimierungskriterien entschieden, in welchem Subsystem der Suchprozeß starten muß.

Das Ergebnis der durchgeführten Recherche, das sich aus Information aus beiden Subsystemen zusammensetzen kann, wird im Informations-Darstellung-System den spezifischen Benutzerwünschen entsprechend aufbereitet, formatiert und schließlich angezeigt.

8. Schlußbemerkung

Das skizzierte System soll zunächst von ca. 250 Personen benutzt werden. Als Hardware-Equipment ist ein DEC VAX®-Rechnersystem vorgesehen, die einzelnen Arbeitsplätze sind sowohl mit konventionellen Terminals als auch mit Personal Computern ausgestattet.

® registrierte Warenzeichen der zitierten Firmen

Literaturverzeichnis

/BBN 88/   The PARLANCE Interface: A Technical Overview; BBN Systems and Technologies Corp., Cambridge, Massachusetts, 1988
/BLA 85/   A. Blaser, P. Pistor: Datenbank-Systeme für Büro, Technik und Wissenschaft; Informatik-Fachbericht Nr. 94, Springer-Verlag, 1985
/BRA 85/   R.J. Brachmann, L.A. Schmolze: An Overview of the KL-ONE Knowledge Representation System; Cognitive Science, Vol 9, 1985
/CHE 76/   P.P-S. Chen: The Entity-Relationship Model - Towards a Unified View of Data; ACM Transaction on Database Systems, Vol 1, No 1, March 1976
/DAT 86/   C.J. Date: Relational Database: Selected Writings; Addison-Wesley, 1986
/HAR 85/   M.D. Harris: Introduction to Natural Language Processing; Reston Publishing, Reston, 1985
/KAH 85/   B.K. Kahn: Requirement Specification Techniques; in S.B. Yao: Principles of Database Design; Prentice-Hall, 1985
/KIN 85/   R. King, D. McLeod: Semantic Data Models; in S.B. Yao: Principles of Database Design; Prentice-Hall, 1985
/MAR 83/   J. Martin: Managing the Data Base Environment; Prentice-Hall, 1983
/MAR 87/   J. Martin: Recommended Diagramming Standards for Analysts and Programmers; Prentice-Hall, 1987
/VOS 87/   G. Vossen: Datenmodelle, Datenbanksprachen und Datenbankmanagement-Systeme; Addison-Wesley, 1987

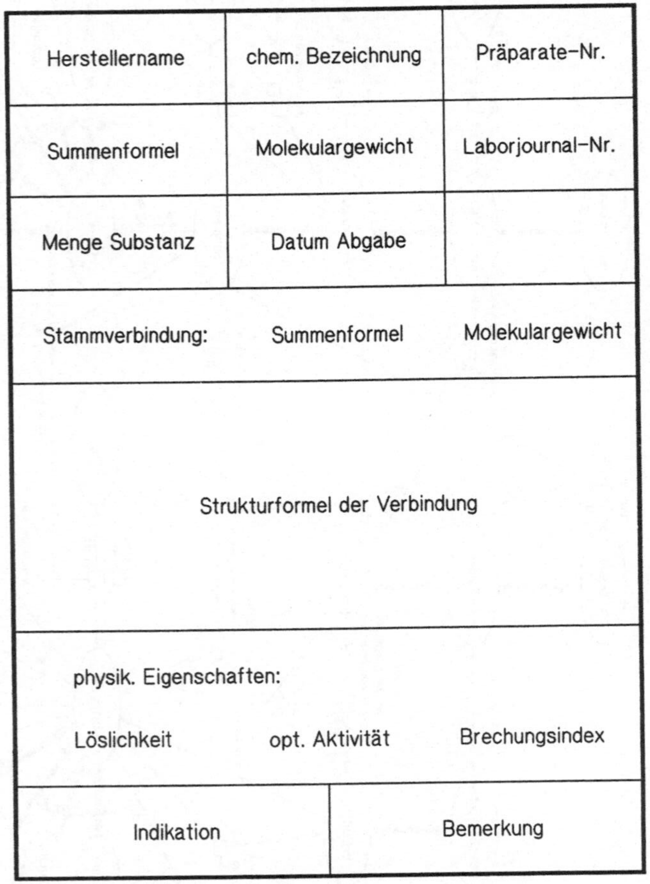

Herstellername	chem. Bezeichnung	Präparate-Nr.
Summenformel	Molekulargewicht	Laborjournal-Nr.
Menge Substanz	Datum Abgabe	
Stammverbindung:	Summenformel	Molekulargewicht
Strukturformel der Verbindung		
physik. Eigenschaften:		
Löslichkeit	opt. Aktivität	Brechungsindex
Indikation		Bemerkung

Abb. 1: Präparatebogen (schematisiert)

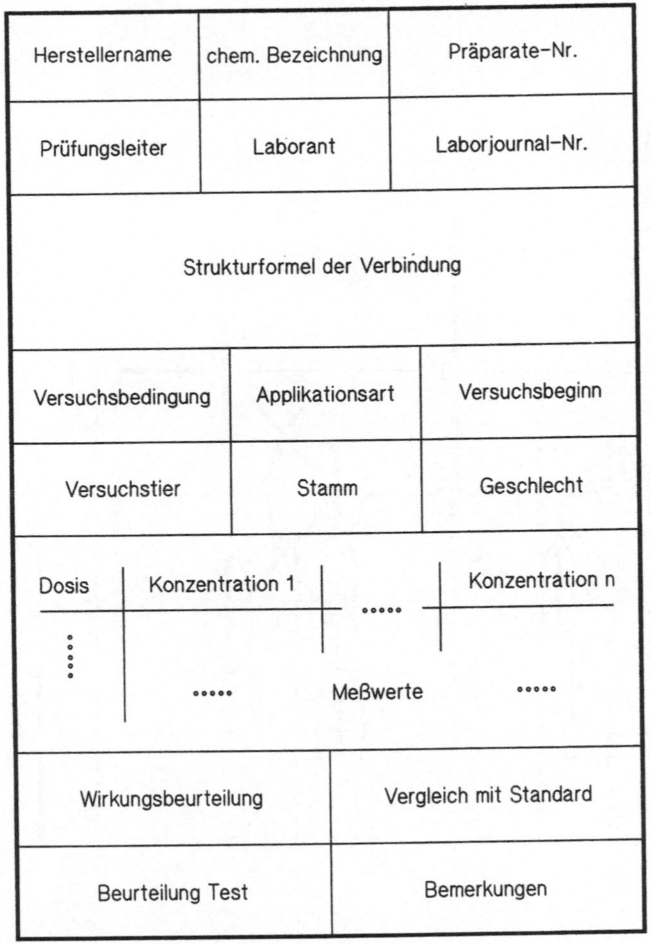

Herstellername	chem. Bezeichnung	Präparate-Nr.
Prüfungsleiter	Laborant	Laborjournal-Nr.
Strukturformel der Verbindung		
Versuchsbedingung	Applikationsart	Versuchsbeginn
Versuchstier	Stamm	Geschlecht
Dosis	Konzentration 1 ..... Konzentration n	Meßwerte
Wirkungsbeurteilung	Vergleich mit Standard	
Beurteilung Test	Bemerkungen	

Abb. 2: Befundbogen (schematisiert)

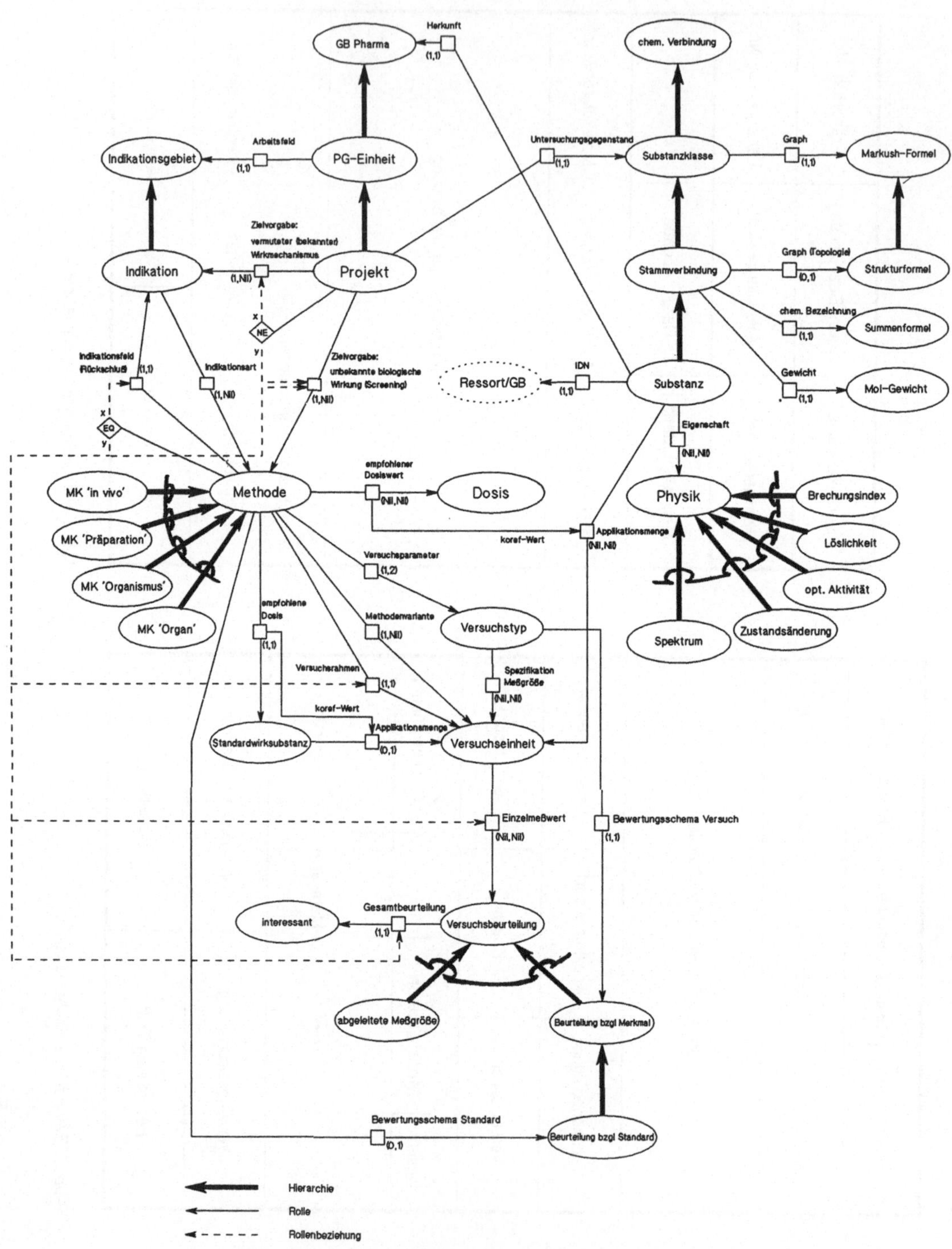

Abb 3: Darstellung in Anlehnung an KL-ONE (siehe Text)

DrRB 25/8/88

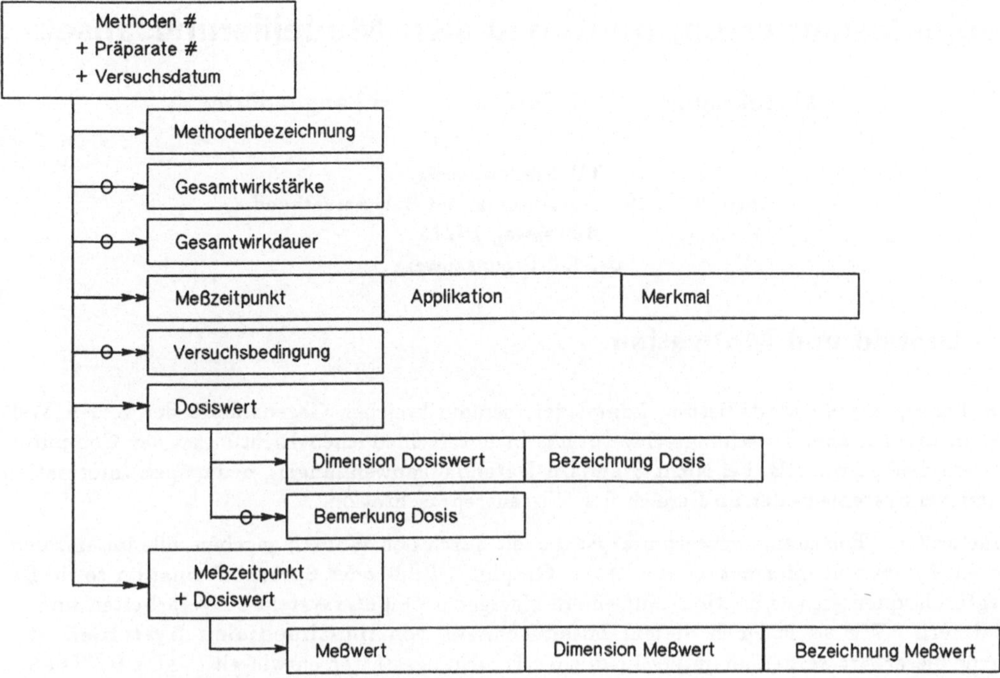

Abb. 4: Beispiel für einen modifizierten "bubble chart"

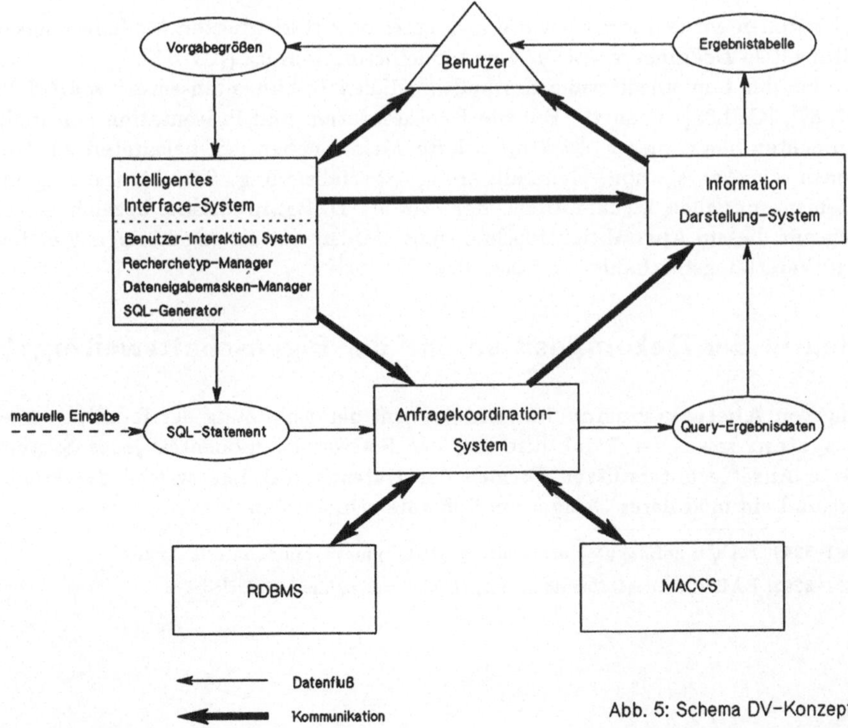

Abb. 5: Schema DV-Konzept

Dekomposition und Wertfortpflanzung

in einem

objektorientierten, multimedialen Modellierungsansatz

M.Hofmann[1]   R.Cordes[2]   H.Langendörfer

TU Braunschweig
Institut für Betriebssysteme und Rechnerverbund
Bültenweg 74/75
D-3300 Braunschweig

1   Umfeld und Motivation

Die konzeptionelle Modellierung komplexer, semantikreicher Gegenstände der realen Welt ist ein momentaner Forschungsschwerpunkt in unterschiedlichen Richtungen der Computerwissenschaften wie z.B. bei Nicht-Standard-Datenbankanwendungen, neuartigen Information Retrieval Systemen oder im Bereich der Wissensrepräsentation.

Eine weiterer Forschungsschwerpunkt ist derzeit durch den Wunsch gegeben, alle unterschiedlichen Typen von Information wie Text-, Graphik-, Bild- oder Sprachinformation sowie Bewegtbildsequenzen (Animation) auf einem einzigen Computersystem zu verarbeiten und zu speichern. Wir sprechen in diesem Zusammenhang von **multimedialen Systemen**. Systeme dieser Art werden an unterschiedlichen Forschungsstätten entwickelt (Vgl. z.B. [Ts+83], [CTHPP86], [Co+86], [BC+87], [WoKi87]).

Eine **strukturierte multimediale Informationseinheit** ist ein spezieller Typ eines komplexen Objekts, und es existieren eine Menge an unterschiedlichen Modellierungsansätzen für solche multimedialen Objekte (Vgl. z.B. [CTHPP86], [TFGN87], [WoKi87], [Hofm88]).

In diesem Papier stellen wir den formalen Rahmen eines objektorientierten Modellierungsansatzes für multimediale Dokumente vor. Dieser Modellierungsansatz ([CBHL87], [CHLB89]) wurde teilweise bei der Implementierung des multimedialen Dokumentenservers *MuBIS-Pro* ([LCB86], [BCL87], [CBL88]) benutzt. Für die Repräsentation und Präsentation von multimedialen Dokumenten bietet dieser objektorientierte Ansatz neben den bekannten Abstraktionsmechanismen wie Aggregation, Generalisierung, Spezialisierung, Schichtenbildung und Klassifikation einen speziellen Mechanismus, den wir als **Dekomposition** bezeichnen. In Zusammenhang mit diesem Abstraktionsmechanismus werden wir die zugehörigen Wertfortpflanzungs- und Vererbungsmechanismen vorstellen.

2   Zum Begriff der Dekomposition und der Eigenschaftsweitergabe

Die Anwendung von **Abstraktionsmechanismen** dient der Abbildung der Realität auf ein **Informationssystem** sowie der Strukturierung der Softwarekomponenten jenes Systems. Objektorientierte Ansätze unterstützen Formen der Datenabstraktion, welche die Wiederverwendbarkeit und ein modulares Design von Software ermöglichen.

---

[1]Tel.: 0531 / 391–3249, EARN: hofmann@dbsinf6.bitnet, UUCP: mcvax!unido!infbs!hofmann

[2]Tel.: 0531 / 391–3293, EARN: cordes@dbsinf6.bitnet, UUCP: mcvax!unido!infbs!cordes

Ziel dieses Abschnitts ist es, einen formalen Rahmen für derartige objektorientierte Modellierungstechniken vorzustellen, der die Definition unterschiedlicher Abstraktionsmechanismen und der mit diesen verbundenen Formen der Eigenschaftsweitergabe erlaubt.

Herkömmliche objektorientierte Sprachen (etwa Smalltalk) unterstützen nur bestimmte Mechanismen zur Abbildung der realen Welt auf ein Informationssystem, nämlich **Klassifikation** und **Spezialisierung** (bzw. **Generalisierung**). Besonders bei Design und Implementierung von Ingenieur-Datenbanken und anderen Nicht-Standard-Anwendungen sind jedoch weitere Mechanismen nötig, um den Weltausschnitt konsistent abbilden zu können. Hierzu zählen besonders **Aggregation** (part_of- oder has_a-Beziehung) und **Dekomposition** (consists_of-Beziehung). Hinweise darauf geben u.a. Blake und Cook in [BlCo87], Diederich und Milton in [DiMi87] sowie Cordes et al. in [CHLB89].

Während die Aggregation zur Bildung von komplexen Objekten dient, stellt die Dekomposition eine Abbildung zwischen unabhängigen, in getrennten **Schichten** liegenden Objekten dar. Die Schichtbildung ist beim Entwurf großer Softwaresysteme seit langem ein grundlegendes Prinzip; gemeinhin unterstützen objektorientierte Ansätze jedoch gerade diesen Mechanismus kaum.

Die folgende Beschreibung enthält zunächst eine Formalisierung der Begriffe Abstraktionsschicht, Klasse und Eigenschaften. Mit Hilfe der formalisierten Schreibweise werden dann einige Constraints bezüglich der Verwendung dieser Mechanismen in unserem Datenmodell angegeben; ferner werden Mechanismen der **Eigenschaftsweitergabe** definiert, die hinsichtlich der Dekomposition über die normale Vererbung hinausgehen müssen.

Def. 1a: $\mathcal{L}_{L_i} = \{\, O^{L_i}, \overset{L_i}{\sim} \,\}$ ist eine *Abstraktionsschicht*.

Def. 1b: L_i ist der *Index* der Abstraktionsschicht. Ist $L_i > L_k$, so ist L_i die tiefere Schicht der Abstraktion.

Def. 1c: O^{L_i} ist die Menge aller *Objekte* derselben Schicht L_i.

Def. 1d: $\overset{L_i}{\sim}$ ist die Menge der *Beziehungen*, nach der die Objekte in eine Schicht L_i angeordnet werden. Diese Menge hängt dabei von der Semantik des abzubildenden Weltausschnitts ab.

Def. 2a: In jeder Schicht werden Klassen von Objekten unterschieden. C ist eine *Klasse*, und C_k ($1 \leq k \leq n$) nennen wir *Subklassen*. $C_k^{L_i}$ ist eine Klasse in einer Schicht L_i. Klassen gehören i.allg. zu genau einer Schicht.

Def. 2b: Eine *Instanz (Exemplar, Ausprägung)* einer Klasse $C_k^{L_i}$ nennen wir $I_{C_k^{L_i}}$. Der j-te Teil eines *Aggregats* heißt $I_{C_k^{L_i},j}$.

Def. 2c: O_m ist dann eine allgemeine Bezeichnung für ein beliebiges *Objekt*.

Bemerkung: O^{L_i} läßt sich dann darstellen als $\bigcup_{k=1}^{n} C_k^{L_i} \cup \bigcup_{k=1}^{n} I_{C_k^{L_i}}$

Def. 3a: $P_{C^{L_i}}$ ist die Menge der *Eigenschaften* einer Klasse C aus Schicht L_i.

Def. 3b: $\mathrm{attr}(C_k^{L_i}) \subseteq P_{C^{L_i}}$ sind die *Variablen* einer bestimmten Klasse C_k in Schicht L_i.

Def. 3c: $\mathrm{meth}(C_k^{L_i}) \subseteq P_{C^{L_i}}$ sind die *Methoden* der Klasse.

Def. 3d: $\mathrm{attr}(I_{C_k^{L_i}}) \subseteq \mathrm{attr}(C_k)$ sind die *Attribute* einer Instanz, $\mathrm{meth}(I_{C_k^{L_i}}) \subseteq \mathrm{meth}(C_k)$ ihre *Methoden*.

Def. 3e: $V(\mathrm{attr}(I_{C_k^{L_i}}))$ ist der *Wert* einer Instanzvariablen.

	Abstraktions-mechanismus	Constraint
1	Spezialisierung	$P_{C^{L_i}} := \bigcap_{j=1}^{k} P_{C_j^{L_i}}; \quad 1 < k < n(C^{L_i}),$
2	Generalisierung	$P_{C^{L_i}} := \bigcup_{j=1}^{k} P_{C_j^{L_i}}; \quad 1 < k < n(C^{L_i}),$
3	Aggregation	$O_{C^{L_i}} := \biguplus_{j=1}^{\#(O_{C^{L_i}})} O_{C^{L_i},j}; \quad 1 < \#(O_{C^{L_i}}) \leq n(O_{C^{L_i}})$
4	Dekomposition	$O_{C^{L_i}} := \bigotimes_{i=1}^{\#(O_{C^{L_k}})} O_{C^{L_k},j}; \quad 1 < \#(O_{C^{L_k}}) \leq n(O_{C^{L_k}})$

Tab. 1: Constraints der Abstraktionsmechanismen

(1), (2): Bei der *Spezialisierung* können in Unterklassen neue Eigenschaften auftreten; bei der *Generalisierung* sind *alle* Eigenschaften der Subklassen in der gemeinsamen Oberklasse zu finden. $n(C^{L_i})$ ist die Anzahl der Klassen in Schicht L_i.

(3): *Aggregation* verbindet Objekte zu einem sie umfassenden Aggregat (komplexes Objekt). Objekt und abhängige Teilobjekte liegen in *derselben Schicht*; Aggregation schließt eine Semantik (z.B. die Anordnung einzelner Teile) ein. Wir stellen die Aggregation als Vereinigung von elementfremden Teilen dar ($\uplus$). $\mathcal{A} : O^{L_i} \longmapsto \mathcal{P}(O^{L_i})$.

(4): *Dekomposition* bildet Objekte einer höheren Schicht auf unabhängige Objekte einer tieferen Schicht ab. $\mathcal{D} : O^{L_i} \longmapsto \mathcal{P}(O^{L_k})$, $\quad L_i < L_k$. Zeichen für die Dekomposition sei $\otimes$.

	Eigenschafts-weitergabe	Constraint
1	Vererbung	$\iota : P_{C^{L_i}} \longmapsto P_{C_k^{L_i}},$ und $\ \mathrm{meth}(C_k^{L_i}) \subseteq \mathrm{meth}(C^{L_i}).$
2	Wertfortpflanzung	$\upsilon : P_{C^{L_i}} \longmapsto P_{C^{L_k}}; \ L_i < L_k,$ und $\{V(\mathrm{attr}(I_{C^{L_k}})) = V(\mathrm{attr}(I_{C^{L_i}})) \mid \mathrm{attr}(C^{L_k}) \subseteq \mathrm{attr}(C^{L_i})\}$
3	Derivation	$\delta : P_{C^{L_k}} \longmapsto P_{C^{L_i}}; \ L_i < L_k,$ mit $\mathrm{attr}(C^{L_i}) \subseteq \mathrm{attr}(C^{L_k})$ und $\ V(\mathrm{attr}(I_{C^{L_i}})) := f_D(\mathrm{attr}(I_{C^{L_k}}))$

Tab. 2: Formen der Eigenschaftsweitergabe

(1): Unter *Vererbung* verstehen wir die aus objektorientierten Sprachen bekannte Weitergabe von Methoden an Subklassen.

(2): *Wertfortpflanzung* ist eine top-down Weitergabe von Attributwerten.

(3): *Derivation* ist eine *berechnete* bottom-up Herleitung von Attributwerten.

3 Ein Anwendungsbeispiel: Das multimediale Büroinformationssystem *MuBIS*

Basierend auf der Kombination von laser-optischen und magnetischen Sekundärspeichertechnologien und der Verwendung eines objektorientierten Modellierungskonzeptes, das eine adäquate Repräsentation von multimedialen Bürodokumenten erlaubt, wurde in den letzten Jahren an unserem Institut der Prototyp eines multimedialen Bürodokumentationssystem *MuBIS-Pro* entwickelt und implementiert (Vgl. [BCL87], [CBL88])[3].

---

[3]Dieser Prototyp, es handelt sich um ein Einbenutzersystem, wurde während der CeBIT87 der Öffentlichkeit präsentiert. Die Implementierung ist im Rahmen mehrerer Diplomarbeiten in C bzw. Assembler unter MS/DOS vorgenommen worden.

Konzeptuell setzt sich *MuBIS* aus drei Schichten zusammen: dem **Anwendersystem** mit den Benutzerobjekten und Werkzeugen, dem **Objektmanager** zur Verwaltung der Objekte und Abbildung auf die Einheiten der physikalischen Schicht, und dem **Retrievalmodul** zur Verwaltung dieser Schicht (Zugriffspfade, Hardware-Treiber).

Abb. 1 zeigt die Aufteilung von Dokumentklassen in den Moduln gemäß den verwendeten Abstraktionsmechanismen, wobei der Objektmanager die Verwaltung des Dekompositions-vorgangs und der einzelnen Objekte übernimmt; die dabei verwendeten internen Objekte im Objektmanager werden hier nicht dargestellt.

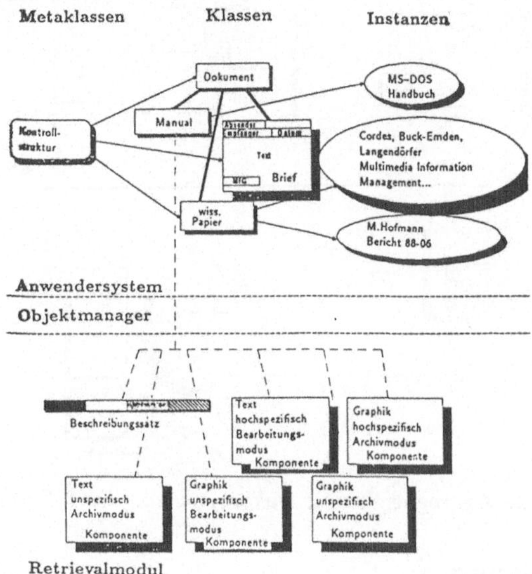

Abb. 1: *Beispiel für die Anwendung von Abstraktionsmechanismen*

Die Objektklasse **Dokument** besitzt die Subklassen **Manual, Brief** und **wiss. Papier.** Die Klasse **Brief** wird als Aggregat dargestellt; die Klasse **Manual** wird durch Dekomposition auf einen **Beschreibungssatz** und (mehrere) Typen von **Komponenten** abgebildet.

In Abb. 2 wird die Aggregation und die Dekomposition an der Objektklasse **Dokument** noch einmal verdeutlicht; die Abbildung soll als Beispiel für die Eigenschaftsweitergabe dienen.

Boxen besitzen eine Wichtigkeit[4]. Durch Wertfortpflanzung wird der Wert des Attributs auf die entsprechenden Attribute der Objekte in tieferen Schichten entlang der Dekompositions-pfade weitergegeben (**logische Blöcke → Komponentenbereiche → Komponenten**).

Umgekehrt wird aus dem Modus[5] von **Komponenten** eines **Dokuments** durch Derivation der Modus der **Boxen** errechnet; befindet sich mindestens eine **Komponente** im Bearbeitungsmo-dus, so muß das gesamte **Dokument** im Bearbeitungsmodus sein.

---

[4]Mit hoher Wichtigkeit (hochspezifisch) gekennzeichnete **Boxen** werden schnell zur Verfügung gestellt und auf speziellen, raschen Zugriff garantierenden Speichern gehalten.

[5]Es gibt die Modi Archivmodus und Bearbeitungsmodus (s. auch [CBHL87]). Objekte im Bearbeitungsmodus sind bearbeitbar; Objekte im Archivmodus sind nicht mehr veränderbar.

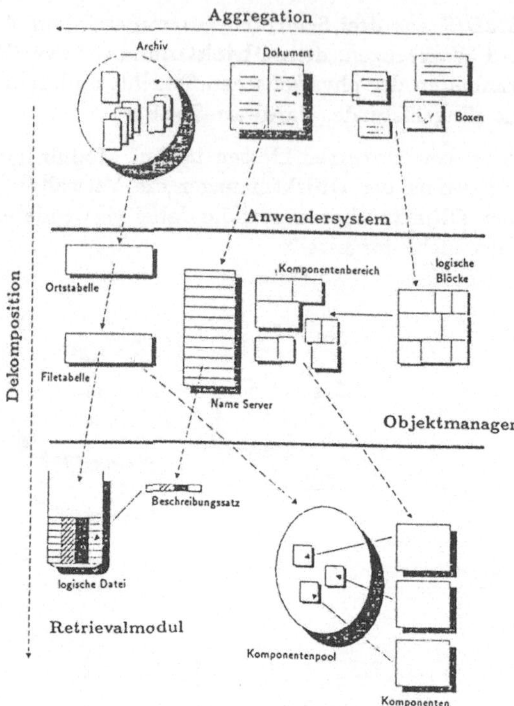

Abb. 2: *Aggregation* und *Dekomposition* eines **Dokuments**

4 Zusammenfassung

Wir haben unterschiedliche Abstraktionsmechanismen in einem objektorientierten Ansatz zur Modellierung von multimedialen, komplexen Informationseinheiten präsentiert. Speziell stellten wir die Dekomposition (als eine consists-of-Relation) vor und grenzten sie von der Aggregation (als eine has-a-Relation) ab.

Wir benutzen einen schichtenförmigen Modellierungsansatz für den Entwurf eines multimedialen Systems und zeigten, daß die Dekomposition als schichtenübergreifender Abstraktionsmechanismus zu sehen ist. Ebenso läßt dieser Ansatz jedoch bekannte schichtenspezifische Abstraktionsmechanismen zu und gestattet es, unterschiedliche Formen der Eigenschaftsweitergabe zu beschreiben und voneinander abzugrenzen.

Als Konsequenz zeigten wir, daß so eine spezielle Form von Information Hiding erlaubt wird, indem wir Objekte einer höheren Schicht in unabhängige Objekte einer tieferen Schicht abbilden können. Außerdem wurde der Prototyp eines multimedialen Dokumentservers vorgestellt, bei dem diese Mechanismen genutzt wurden.

5 Literatur

[BC+87]   J.Banerjee, H.-T.Chou et al., *Data Model Issues for Object-Oriented Applications*, in: [ToOIS87], pp.3–26

[BCL87]   R.Buck-Emden, R.Cordes, H.Langendörfer, *MuBIS-Pro: Ein System zur integrierten Erstellung und Online-Archivierung multimedialer Bürodokumente*, Proc. GI–17.Jahrestagung, München, Oktober 1987, pp.460–476

[BlCo87]   E.Blake, S.Cook, *On Including Part Hierarchies in Object-Oriented Languages with an Implementation in Smalltalk*, in: Proc. ECOOP87, Paris, Juni 1987, pp.41–50

[CBHL87]   R.Cordes, R.Buck-Emden, M.Hofmann, H.Langendörfer, *Objekt- und Kommunikationsmanagement im multimedialen Büroinformationssystem MuBIS*, Kurzbeitrag in: [ScSc87], pp.410–414

[CBL88]   R.Cordes, R.Buck-Emden, H.Langendörfer, *Multimedia Information Management and Optical Disk Technologies as a Basis for Advanced Information Retrieval*, in: Proc. RIAO88, M.I.T., Cambridge (MA), März 1988

[CHLB89]   R.Cordes, M.Hofmann, H.Langendörfer, R.Buck-Emden, *The Use of Decomposition in an Object-Oriented Approach to Present and Represent Multimedia Documents*,in: Proc. HICSS'89, angenommener Beitrag für die HICSS-22, Hawaii, Januar 1989

[Co+86]   P.Constantopoulos et al., *Office Document Retrieval in MULTOS*, in: Proc. 3rd ESPRIT Technical Week, Brüssel, 1986

[CTHPP86]   S.Christodoulakis, F.Theodoridou, F.Ho, M.Papa, A.Pathria, *Multimedia Document Presentation, Information Extraction and Document Formation in MINOS*, in: ACM ToOIS, Vol.4, No.4, Oktober 1986, pp.345–383

[DiMi87]   J.Diederich, J.Milton, *An Object-Oriented Design Shell*, in: Proc. OOPSLA'87, Orlando (FA), Oktober 1987, pp.61–77

[Ditt86]   K.R.Dittrich, *Object-Oriented Database Systems — A workshop report*, in: Proc. 5th ER-Conference 1986, Dijon, 1986, pp.51–66

[Hofm88]   M.Hofmann, *Objektorientierte Konzepte in Informationssystemen*, Informatikbericht 88-06, TU Braunschweig, März 1988

[LCB86]   H.Langendörfer, R.Cordes, R.Buck-Emden, *Multimedia Filing & Retrieval based on Optical and Magnetic Mass Storage Technologies*, Proc. Euromicro86, Venedig, September 1986

[ScSc87]   H.-J. Schek, G.Schlageter, *Datenbanksysteme in Büro, Technik und Wissenschaft*, GI-Fachtagung, Darmstadt, April 1987, Springer

[Ts+83]   D.Tsichritzis et al., *A Multimedia Office Filing System*, in: Proc. VLDB83, Florenz, pp.2–7

[TFGN87]   D.Tsichritzis, E.Fiume, S.Gibbs, O.Nierstrasz, *KNOs : KNowledge Acquisition, Dissemination and Manipulation Objects*, in: [ToOIS87], pp.96–112

[ToOIS87]   *Transactions of Office Information Systems*, F.H.Lochovsky (Ed.): *Special Issue on Object-Oriented Systems*, ACM ToOIS, Vol.5, No.1, Januar 1987

[WoKi87]   D.Woelk, W.Kim, *Multimedia Informationmanagement in an Object-Oriented Database System*, in: Proc. VLDB87, Brighton, pp.319–329

MACHINE LEARNING TECHNIQUES FOR PROGRESSIVE RETRIEVAL IN AN IMAGE DATABASE

M. Créhange, G. Halin

Centre de Recherche en Informatique de Nancy (CRIN) - UA 262 of CNRS

BP 239 . 54506-VANDOEUVRE lès NANCY CEDEX . FRANCE

Abstract

Use of interactive image storage devices will become more and more widespread in offices, and this incites to develop different ranges of friendly applications concerning image databases. The common point of the applications we deel with is that they focus on **progressive retrieval** in an **image database** (for instance on videodisk) coupled with an alphanumeric database. The paper is based on two main ideas : deep interactivity and considering a retrieval process as a machine learning process.

Deep interactivity, for us, means that man and machine share responsibility in pretty equal proportions. We briefly describe how this deep interactivity is realized in the EXPRIM system we have designed and prototyped (using Smalltalk language on SUN) ; deep interactivity is realized all along the three phases of the EXPRIM iterative process : before-visualization (request interpretation and retrieval), visualization (and image choices), after-visualization (choice analysis, and request reformulation). The user's feed back, thanks to image vision instantness, plays an essential role in the process.

Finally, we explain our way of implementing the retrieval process as a **machine learning process** where the concept to learn is the user's need. We adapt and mix existing methods, relying on examples (the chosen image descriptions) and negative examples (the rejected image decriptions), and using a taxonomy (thesaurus). This is processed through marking the terms in the thesaurus by "expressivity weights" which measure their power to express the user's need.

I . Image retrieval and machine-learning

Use of interactive image storage devices will become more and more widespread in offices, and this incites to develop different ranges of friendly applications concerning image databases [Sal 86] [Opt 87]. We are working about such systems, and we suppose to have an image base coupled with a database containing descriptions of the images (or various informations about them). The base of our interest is what we call a **deep interactivity**, where man and machine share responsibility in pretty equal proportions. In the system we propose, EXPRIM, the typical dialogue is as follows : the user asks a request, the system interpretes it and retrieves descriptions, then the user visualizes the corresponding images, makes choices among them, possibly gets ideas from this visualization, and in turn, the system analyses the user's choices and thus reformulates the request, and the cycle turns on... In this process, the fact that image vision is instant is essential. We are involved in three categories of applications of such a system :

- image retrieval and delivering [Esp 86]. A designer or an agent may look for images to suggest him some ideas of new models or to aid customers in discovering their needs or desire ; a tourist may look for ideas of places to visit in an area or in a museum ; ... In such applications, a system as EXPRIM may be of great help for him to progressively define what he wants.

- image based computer aided education. Many kinds of scenarios [Thi 87] can be imagined for education with a strong role given to images, especially in subjects where vision has an important impact, for instance in natural science or art or mode or trade. Pictures can be used for their illustrating power but also for their evocative or creative power as well as their power of recognition, ...

- computer and image aided identification or diagnosis [Fou 87]. This problem can be likened to the retrieval one, except that the expected result is not the set of images but the last version of the request. Actually, the user may give his first sketch of diagnosis as first request, to which the system gives a set of images as answer. Then the system gives a new formulation of the request (new diagnosis) after having analysed the user's choice of fitting images among proposed ones. And so on.

In these three kinds of applications, vision plays an essential role. Its role is linked with the user and also with the system. The role of vision towards the user is clear : information, evocation, creativity by "visual inference" [Hud 82], ... Let us explain its role towards the system : the system can analyse the choices the user made during visualization in order to improve its knowledge of what the user has in mind (for retrieval and CAE) or in hand (for identification). So, the system will apply a kind of machine-learning process to progressively learn a concept which consists in the user's needs.

After giving a brief description of the EXPRIM project our team is elaborating, we show that a learning by examples and negative examples, using a taxonomy, is a good possibility for this purpose. The idea of applying machine learning techniques to retrieval is not new in itself ; but first the fact we deel with images makes the machine learning approach much more fitting and effective thanks to the better feed back, and secondly the way we adapt and mix some existing techniques is new.

II . The EXPRIM project

The target of EXPRIM (EXPert to Retrieve IMages) is to aid a user, especially a "naive" one, in progressively retrieving images in an image database coupled with a descriptive database. The project has been supported by the European ESPRIT program and by the French PRC BD3 (Programme de

Recherches Coordonnées "Bases de données de 3ème génération"). It has been described in several papers ([Cre 85] [Cre 86] [Hal 88a] [Esp 87]). We give its main features below.

II . 1 . The objects :

The EXPRIM process deels with different "objects" ; the main ones are :
- the image base, for instance on a videodisk ; in the pilot application we are deeling with (for the French Ministry of Culture), Old Paris images, there are 1000 images but our present testbed only consists in 200 of them ;
- the data base (descriptive base) made of image descriptions, which, for the moment, are only sets of words (from the thesaurus) put into different "fields", as "main content", possibly "secondary containt", "photo author", "date", "connotation", "morphology", "circumstances",... ;
- the thesaurus, which is the set of words used in the descriptions, with semantic links, which for the moment are of two kinds : "generic-specific" and "see also". In the pilot application, the thesaurus contains 6000 terms ;
- the user demands or requests, which are made of terms from the thesaurus (descriptors) or not (no-descriptors, the links with descriptors of which are defined) ; they are split into "facets" which fit with the user's knowledge degree and may be less precise than description fields ; no logic connector is required (and the system will propose some).

II . 2 . The process :

The system is built as the iteration of three phases: "before-visualization", "visualization" and "after-visualization".

In the **before-visualization phase**, the system aids the user to formulate or reformulate his **demand**. The role of the system in this phase is to transform this primitive demand into a system query which can be carried out by a classic information retrieval system. The transformation may be much more than a translation and may include broadening or narrowing or other modulations. It uses rules, often heuristic (cf § II.3.). The result of this phase is an image set called : **selected image set.**

The **visualization phase** gives the user the ability of friendly displaying and manipulating the selected images, classifying them and finally making a choice. The result of this phase is 3 image sets called : **chosen image set, rejected image set, neutral image set.**

In the **after-visualization phase**, the system tries to understand the real user's needs, relying on the previous image sorting. To develop its reasoning, the system uses learning techniques and also heuristics. The result of this last phase is a new demand which may be, after the user's agreement or addition, submitted to a next before-visualization phase.

II . 3 . The prototype :

Presently, a prototype has been written in SMALLTALK on a SUN and begins to be a test bed for the different ideas put forward in the system, and particularly the numerous heuristic rules. These heuristics [Cre 88][Hal 88c] are invoked, for instance, to change the granularity of data in the user request by distributing the terms of the different facets into the different domains (fields) present in the image descriptions, to choose boolean connectors between the different terms, to transform a query when too wide or too restrictive, but also to manage the user's choice analysis, the request reformulation, ... ; they lean in particular on knowledge about the present kind of user and kind of use. Let us give 3 examples of heuristic :
- if in a request a term doesn't allow to attain more than few images and if the search strategy is a large search, then add to the request the disjunction of associated terms ("see-also" relation of the thesaurus);
- if the user is a specialist of some notion present in the request, then allow few derivations for this notion ;
- if a term is "often" present in the chosen image descriptions and nearly never in the rejected ones, then give it an expressivity weight produced by a certain formula F and give its generic terms expressivity weights produced by a certain formula F'.

III . Machine Learning techniques applied to the request reformulation

III . 1. Introduction to the approach :

Machine Learning techniques [Mic 83a] [Kod 86] offer methods allowing a certain understanding of the user's needs. In an information retrieval system the Machine Learning techniques can be applied at different levels [Smi 80] [Cre 85] and particularly :
     - at the scale of the system life to improve its way of retrieving ;
     - at a one-retrieval scale, where the system tries to learn the user's needs.

The method we propose takes place at this second level. Request reformulation is known in information retrieval systems as a problem of "relevance feedback" [Sal 86]. The existing methods propose to construct a new request including terms which are considered relevant depending on their presence in the relevant or no-relevant documents [Sal 84]. These methods have been tested on textual bases, with satisfying results [Sal 83]. But for this type of base, understanding the user's needs is pretty difficult, since quickly giving an opinion about a textual document (article, book, ...) is very hard. For an image base, where interaction with documents (images) is immediate and total, selection is easier and more suitable. Then trying to understand the user's needs from his image choices is really effective.

This attempt to interactively understand the user's needs requires a semantic approach in which the term meanings are taken into account. The symbolic learning techniques developed in AI seem to us to suit very well, since the concepts they point out gradually improve the understanding as the retrieval steps follow on. Interactivity is here particularly important since in image retrieval the user and the system are complementary : indeed the user sees the images and the system only "sees" their access means, the descriptions.

III . 2. Method principle :

The main originality of the method we propose [Hal 88b] is the combination of ideas and methods originating from different search domains, as Artificial Intelligence, Information Retrieval, Databases. There exists several forms of Machine Learning techniques [Mic 83a] ; the form used in the method we presently propose is close to a **learning from examples** approach [Mic 83b] where the "positive examples" are the chosen image descriptions and the "negative examples" the rejected image descriptions. By this approach, we want to understand the user's need by an interpretation of the choices he made during the visualization phase : the "concept to learn" is the user's needs.

The method we propose consists in representing the demand expression by an **expression level** built as a marking of terms within the thesaurus. The mark attached to a term measures its ability to express the demand. This representation of expression level within the thesaurus is inspired by the Space of Versions of Mitchell [Mit 83]. Learning proceeds in two steps, after a first marking of the thesaurus words (first expression level) has been set from the initial request :

- The first one consists in making the expression level of the demand concept evolve as the retrieval progresses. We shall more particularly study its evolution at the conclusion of a visualization phase.
- The second step consists in using the expression level written in the thesaurus to build a new expression of the concept, that is to say a new demand.

Let us give an idea about a possible calculation mode of this evolution ; it is heuristic and will have to be tested and no doubt improved.

III . 3. Expression level evaluation and use :

- <u>Before the visualization</u>

Initialization :
Each expressivity weight value is contained between -1 and 1. A term having a weight close to -1 is bad to express the demand concept ; on the other hand a term the weight of which is close to 1 is necessary to correctly express the demand. Given the initial ignorance of the user's real needs, every expressivity weight is initialized to zero.

After the demand formulation :
Each term present in the demand has its expressivity weight put to 1 as well as for its specifics of whatever level. The repercution towards the generics (not present in the demand) is done according such a formula that the expressivity weights will decrease as one climbs towards the thesaurus root.

While modulating the system request :
The modulation intervenes when the result of the image retrieval has not been judged as satisfactory. Each rule modifying the system request will then update the demand expression level by modifying the expressivity weights in the thesaurus.

- <u>After the visualization :</u>

To make the expression level evolve according to the user's choices, we calculate for each term present in the selected image descriptions a **relevance weight** computed in a way close to the relevance mesure of Salton and Dillon [Dil 80] [Sal 84]. Then the expressivity weights are updated by taking into account the relevance weights so as to obtain a new expression level closer to the user's needs.

Term relevance :
The relevance weights of the terms are caculated by analysing the descriptions of respectively the chosen and rejected images and associating to each present term a relevance weight calculated by such a formula that their values are close to 1 if the term characterizes well the chosen images and close to -1 if the term characterizes well the rejected ones.

Updating the expression level :
The repercussion of the relevance weights on the expression levels in the thesaurus is calculated from a formula which spreads their effects from the most specific terms (the leaves) to the most generic term (the root).

Formulation of the learned concept, new demand construction :
The new demand construction first requires scanning the thesaurus to extract the terms which characterize the concept well. A breadth-first scanning is made : for every node of the tree we compare its expressivity weight with a threshold ; if the weight is upper, the term is selected and the scanning stops for this tree part, if the weight is lower we go down the tree and apply the same treatment to the nodes of this level. A set of characteristic terms is then obtained. To correctly express the concept under the form of a demand, the terms must be distributed into the facets for which they are semantically suitable. A new user demand is then obtained and proposed to the user.

It is very important to notice that the method permits to propose to the user new search criteria which were completely absent from its first demand.

<u>Example</u> :

the thesaurus parts representative of the user's choices after an updating of the expressivity weights
(the initial demand was "photo content = boat") :

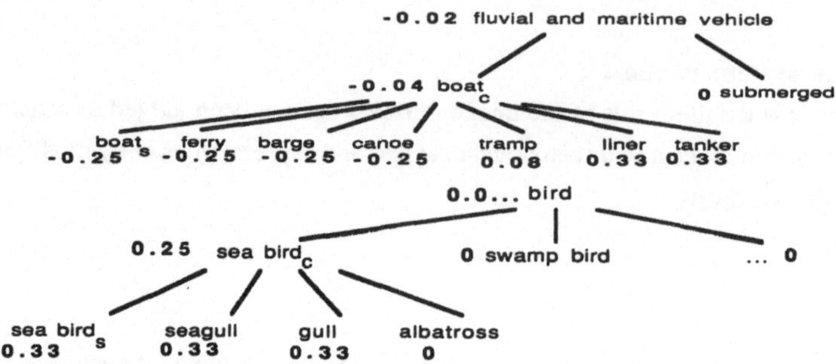

After a thesaurus scanning with a threshold of 0,20 we obtain the following new demand :

<u>Demand:</u>   *Photo content* = liner, tanker, sea bird$_c$.

Let us remark that a new search criteria, *sea bird* , which was absent from the first demand, has been
found.

Dialogue for a reformulation :

The demand then built is proposed to the user who can dialogue with the system to propose or modifie
some criteria or their distribution. As soon as the user has finished his actions and when he judges his
demand satisfactory, it is on turn submitted to the system as for an initial request. The process goes on
since the user and the system succeed in expressing clearly the user's need concept and in obtaining
fitting images.

III . Method implementation

The realization, we are getting going on, takes place in an integrated environment, Smalltalk. This
choice intends to eliminate the often insoluble problem of software communication and to privilege the
dialogue with the user by taking advantage of the reciprocal action facilities of Smalltalk. The object
oriented programming offers some qualities of modularity, of reusability and extendility induced from
the inheritance mecanisms and the dynamic binding. Indeed the inheritance mecanisms permit to share
and reuse code between representations of different types without reproducing or modifying this code.
Then it allows to develop modular and flexible programs. These caracteristics added to the interative
programming environment permit the development of an interactive prototype in a short time [Mey
88][Leo 88].

The facilities of programming in Smalltalk allowed to represent the thesaurus and its caracteristics
(inverted list of each term, expression level and all the links between terms) as one object with the

operations needed to use it (term access, browsing, updating...). The descriptive base is also represented as one object with its specific operations (description access, image visualization, consultation). Many other objects have been defined as for example : the user demand, the system request, ... All these objects are directly accessible in the programming environment and their structure can be modified at any time. We assume it is a good situation to experiment our method.

The data we deal with are extracted from the "Old Paris images" which is a real image collection of the "Ministère de la culture", stored on a videodisc and complemented by a thesaurus and descriptions [Hal 88a]. The thesaurus of the "Ministère de la culture", contains 6000 terms with their semantic links. We are testing our approach with this thesaurus and with only 50 images to make a first evaluation. After what we will progressively introduce up to 1000 images.

IV . Conclusion

We have just shown that image retrieval may be likened to a machine-learning problem where the system tries to learn and to formulate the user's needs during the search steps.

The learning technique applied consists to make explicit an expression level for each demand, to make this expression level evolve by learning, and to deduce a new demand from the final state of the expression level at the end of an evolution phase. The expression level is represented by attaching an "expressivity weight" to the nodes of the thesaurus. These expressivity weights are calculated at first by taking only into account the request, and then evolve in particular using the "relevance weights" calculated according to the user's choices among the images proposed by the system after a retrieval phase. The displayed learning technique inspired especially by the "Version Space" of Mitchell and by "INDUCE" of Michalski, analyses the user's choices regarding the chosen image descriptions as examples and the rejected image descriptions as negative examples. We are presently prototyping our ideas with Smalltalk and are going to carry on a decisive work which consists in putting to the test and improving the various above-mentioned formulas.

This kind of approach [Cre 88], with machine learning and deep interactivity, appears to us very suitable to be used in sophisticated office systems. In fact, it allows non specialist users to take advantage of computerized systems in an active and even creative and formative way. This is true as well at the scale of progressive image retrieval as for machine-learning in general.

Bibliography :

[Cre 85]   Créhange M., David J.M., Foucaut O., Heulluy B : **Le point sur EXPRIM**
CRIN 85-R-019, Nancy 1985.

[Cre 86]   Créhange M., David J.M., Foucaut O., Halin G., Thiery O : **Les structure de données dans le projet EXPRIM** . Congrès INFORSID May 1986.

[Cre 88]   Créhange M : **Bases d'images et Intelligence Artificielle**
In "Image et Vidéodisque", La Documentation Française, Sept 1988.

[Dil 80]   Dillon M., Desper J. : **Automatic relevance feedback in boolean retrieval systems** . Journal of Documentation 1980, 36, pp 197-208.

[Esp 86]   Delcroix J.C. (BMvD) : **Semantic relationships and general framework for expert information retrieval systems (state of the art and guidelines for specifications)** . Esprit (N°901) report T2/I. July 1986.

[Esp 87]   CRIN & BMvD : **Specifications of the functions of the dialogue and piloting module** . Esprit (N°901) report T2/J. February 1987.

[Fou 87]   Foucaut O., Mouaddib N.,Crehange M., Foucaut J.F. : **Les informations nuancées, une approche de leur gestion. Application à la mycologie**
Proceedings of Inforsid 87 Lyon, pp 1-20.

[Hal 88a]   Halin G., Mouaddib N., Foucaut O., Crehange M. : **Semantics of user interface for image retrieval : possibility theory and learning techniques applied on two prototypes** . Proceeding RIAO 88, pp 676-688, Boston, March 1988.

[Hal 88b]   Halin G., Créhange M. : **Request reformulation in an image database : a machine-learning problem** . CRIN Nancy 1988.

[Hal 88c]   Halin G. & al. : **Specification des fonctions de dialogue et du module de pilotage du projet EXPRIM.** Rapport CRIN n° 88-R-075.

[Hud 82]   Hudrisier H. : **L'iconothèque - Documentation audiovisuelle et banques d'images** . Thèse d'Etat, La Documentation Française, Paris 1982.

[Hud 85]   Hudrisier H. : **L'imageur documentaire**
Le documentaliste, vol 22, n°4-5. Juillet - Octobre 1985, pp 155-160.

[Kod 86]   Kodratoff Y. : **Leçons d'apprentissage symbolique**
Cepadues edition 1986.

[Leo 88]   Léonard D., Colnet D., Masini G., Napoli A., Tombre K. : **Les langages à objets**
Inter-Editions 1988.

[Mey 88]   Meyer B. : **Object-oriented software construction**
Prentice Hall 1988.

[Mic 83a]   Michalski R.S., Carbonell J.G., Mitchell T.M. : **Machine Learning, an Artificial Intelligence Approach** . Tioga Publishing Company, Palo Alto 1983.

[Mic 83b]   Michalski R.S., Diettrich T.G. : **A comparative review of selected methods for learning from examples** . In Machine Learning, an Artificial Intelligence Approach, 1983 pp41-81.

[Mit 83]   Mitchell T.M., Utgoff P.E., Banerji R. : **Learning by experimentation, acquiring and refining problem-solving heuristic** . In Machine Learning, an Artificial Intelligence Approach,1983.

[Opt 87]   OPTICA 87 : Proceedings of the international meeting for Optical Publishing & Storage Amsterdam April 1987.

[Sal 83]   Salton G., Mc Gill MJ : **Introduction to modern Information Retrieval**
Mc Graw-Hill, New-York 1983.

[Sal 84]   Salton G., Voorhees E. : **A comparison of two methods for boolean query relevancy feedback** . Information Processing & Mangement Vol 20, n°5/6 pp637-651, 1984.

[Sal 86]   Salton G. : **Recent Trends in Automatic Information Retrieval**
Proceedings of ACM Information Retrieval, Pisa 1986, pp 1-10.

[Smi 80]   Smith L.C. : **Artificial Intelligence, Application in Information Systems**
In Annual Review of Information Science and Technology, 15, Knowledge Industry Publications, Inc., White Plains, New York 1980. pp 67-105.

[Thi 87]   Thiery O., David AA. : **CAE + Image + intelligence**
Internal report - May 1987.

Ein wissensbasierter Ansatz zur Dokumentenverwaltung in einem Büro-Informationssystem.

Stephanie Schmidt, Kurt Bauknecht
Institut für Informatik
Universität Zürich-Irchel
Winterthurerstr. 190
CH - 8057 Zürich

Zusammenfassung: Modellierung und Entwicklung eines modernen Büro-Informations-system (BIS) können nicht mehr länger mit klassischen Methoden gelöst werden. Die Haupt-Informationsträger in einer Büroumgebung sind Dokumente, aus denen wir Wissen extrahieren müssen, um eine bestmögliche Dokumentenverwaltung zu gewährleisten. Hierzu sind Modelle und Techniken der künstlichen Intelligenz erforderlich. Basierend auf dem extrahierten Wissen wird im Projekt MARS ein Modell zur Wissensverarbeitung aufgestellt. MARS vermittelt einen Eindruck darüber, wie die Wissensstrukturen für eine spezielle Applikation, nämlich die Doku-menten Retrieval Komponente, angewandt werden.

1. Dokumente als operationale Grundelemente in einem BIS

Alle Tätigkeiten in einer Organisation benötigen bzw. produzieren Informationen, die sich in Form von Dokumenten als Haupt-Informationsträger und zentrales Hilfsmittel für die Integration von Büro-funktionen /KRÖN 88/ präsentieren. Unter einem 'Dokument' verstehen wir eine maschinenlesbare Information, welche für die Verwaltung und den Austausch auf Standardformate abgebildet werden kann. Die Dokumente können sich aus ver-schiedenen Medien zusammensetzen (Multimedia-Dokumente) und sie besitzen meist keine einheit-liche Struktur. Analog zu /BARB87/ können wir aber alle Dokumente in zwei Teile unterteilen:

den **Index** und den **eigentlichen Inhalt**.

Der Index selbst besteht aus zwei Teilen: der administrativen Beschreibung und der inhaltlichen Beschreibung. Unter administrativer Beschreibung werden Begriffe wie Dokumenten-Identifikation, Autor(en), Erstellungsdatum, Dokumentenart (z. B. Artikelbeschreibung, Mahnung, Auftrag) /ISO 86/ verstanden, während die inhaltliche Beschreibung aus einer Abstraktion des Dokumenteninhaltes besteht, die auf einer kontrollierten Informations-struktur, z.B. einem Thesaurus, basiert.

Jede Organisation besitzt eine eigene, wohl definierte Struktur, in deren Kontext die Dokumente zu sehen sind. Dies bedeutet, daß ein Dokument kein eigenständiges, unabhängiges Element in einer Organisation ist, sondern als operationales Grundelement gewissen Abteilung-en, Personen, etc. zugeordnet und mit Aktionen und Regeln behaftet ist. In Abb. 1 ist das generelle Organigram eines Fertigungsbetriebes aufgezeigt, worauf unsere weiteren Ausführungen beruhen.

Betrachten wir zum Beispiel die **Vertriebsabteil-ung** (s. Abb. 2) mit den 4 Unterabteilungen: Marketing/Akquisition, Auftragsbearbeitung, Ver-kauf und Versand. Jede dieser Unterabteilungen kann weitere Teilbereiche besitzen, deren jeder den Ausgangspunkt für eine Dokumentenklasse bildet; so gehören z.B. Versandpapiere der Vertriebsab-teilung in die Klasse *Vertrieb-Versand-Ausliefer-ung*. Dabei ist zu beachten, daß Dokumente exis-tieren, die bereichsübergreifend benötigt werden, was bei ihrer Ablage berücksichtigt werden muß.

Für die Bearbeitung einiger Dokumente werden zu-sätzliche Informationen benötigt. So ist es in

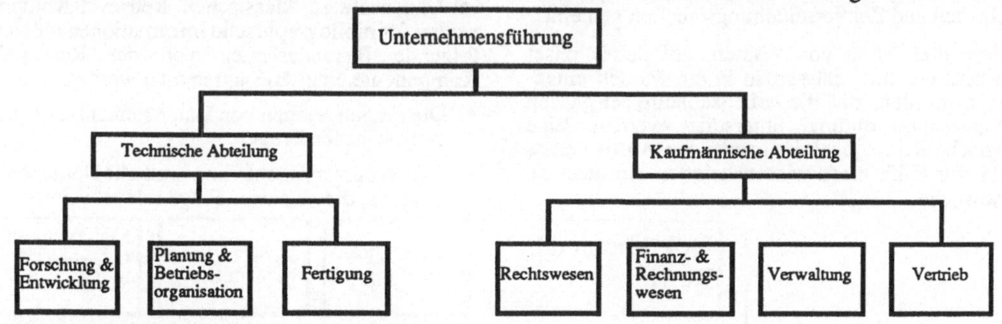

Abb. 1: Organigram eines Fertigungsbetriebes.

unserem Beispiel (Abb. 2) notwendig, die Export-vorschriften für ein Land, die Bestimmungsorte in diesem Land und die Umladestationen zu kennen, um Versandpapiere und Versandschein für das Produkt korrekt erstellen zu können.

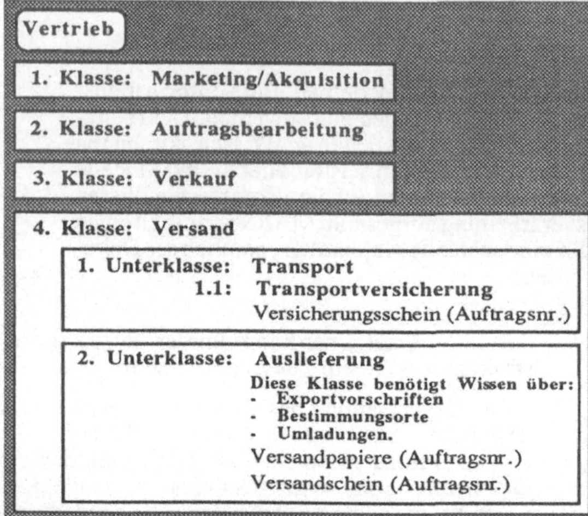

<u>Abb. 2:</u> Beispiel der Dokumentenklassifikation für die Vertriebsabteilung.

Aus den Dokumenten und deren Klassifikation müssen wir das Wissen so herauskristallisieren, daß die entstehende Wissenbasis das Fundament für eine bestmögliche Dokumentenverwaltung bildet (siehe auch /EIRU 88/). Dabei gewinnen wir aus den Dokumentenindexen Wissen, welches wir als *Dokumentenwissen* bezeichnen, während die Dokumentenklassifikation und Organisationsstruktur Wissen darstellt, welches wir *organisatorisches Wissen* nennen.

Zusätzlich zum Dokumentenwissen und organisatorischen Wissen benötigen wir Informationen, die zu unserer 'Welt' in Bezug stehen, um die Tätigkeiten der Büroangestellten zu unterstützen. Mit diesem *marginalem Wissen* sind z.B. Exportvorschriften und Zeitverschiebungstabellen gemeint.

Diese drei Arten von Wissen, auf denen unser System operiert, müssen so in ein Modell eingebracht werden, daß die Arbeitsabläufe der ganzen Organisation optimal unterstützt werden. Eine logische Konsequenz ist somit, den Aufbau eines BIS mit Hilfe eines wissenbasierten Ansatzes zu realisieren.

2. Das MARS-Projekt

Ausgehend von obigen Überlegungen und den Anforderungen an einen wissenbasierten Ansatz zur Dokumentenverwaltung in einem BIS wurde das Projekt MARS (Model and Retrieval System for an Office Information System) am Institut für Informatik der Universität Zürich initiiert. Mit Hilfe dieses Projektes sollen zwei Teile des BIS realisiert werden /SCHM 88/. Erstens soll ein Grundmodell für das Büro-Informationssystem modelliert und aufgebaut und zweitens die Dokumenten-Retrieval-Komponente basierend auf dem Grundmodell entwickelt werden.

Wir definieren ein Büro-Informationssystem entsprechend /LOCK 86/ als eine Ansammlung von menschlichen und computerisierten Agenten, die miteinander kooperieren im Erwerb, in Produktion, Bearbeitung, Speicherung, Benutzung und Verteilung von Informationen, um die ganze Organisation zu überwachen, zu beeinflußen und zu kontrollieren.

2.1. Das Grundmodell

Eine Organisation ist eine begrenzte Domäne, d.h. wir haben eine abgeschlossene Welt und das Wissen über diese Welt zu betrachten. In die Definition eines Modells für ein BIS muß daher dieses Wissen einfließen. Wir können kein generelles wissenbasiertes System für alle Büro-Applikationen aufbauen. Vielmehr müssen wir die Tätigkeiten, die in allen Büros ähnlich bzw. gleich sind (Routinetätigkeiten), herauskristallisieren und sie in das Grundmodell aufnehmen. Für eine spezielle Applikation müssen wir die individuellen Tätigkeiten dem Grundmodell hinzufügen. Weitere Werkzeuge, die die anderen Tätigkeiten in einem BIS unterstützen, bauen auf diesem Grundmodell auf (siehe Abb. 3) /BRAC 84/.

2.2. Die Dokumenten-Retrieval-Komponente

Im Gegensatz zu 'klassischen' Retrieval Komponenten für bibliographische Informationen müssen folgende Besonderheiten von der Retrieval-Komponente eines BIS unterstützt werden:

* Die Fragen reichen von Datenbankanfragen bis zu unscharfen Fragen.

* Der Benutzer möchte und muß **alle** Dokumente erhalten, die zu seiner Frage relevant sind.

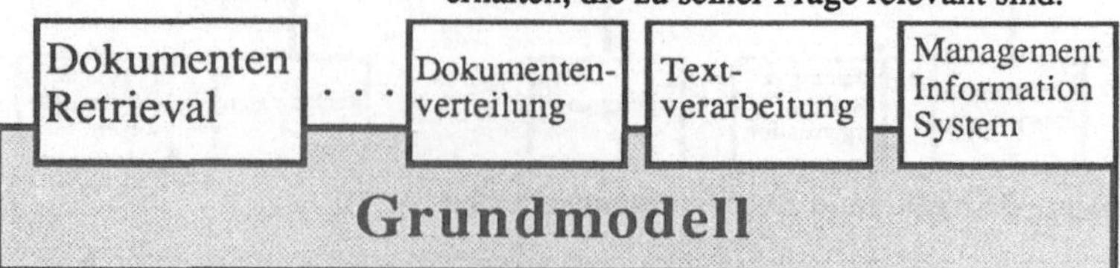

<u>Abb. 3:</u> Struktur eines Büro-Informationssystem

- Die Dokumente besitzen keine einheitliche Struktur und beinhalten verschiedene Medien.

- Die Anzahl der Dokumente verändert sich laufend.

In einer Büroumgebung ist im Prinzip ein Informations- und Wissensfluß wie in Abb. 4 gezeigt zu finden. Der Dokumenteninhalt wird dabei im Dokumentenspeicher abgelegt, während der Index des Dokumentes zum Aufbau der Wissensbasis benutzt wird. Der Retrievalprozeß, d.h. die Frageauswertung, benutzt die Wissensbasis, um die relevanten Dokumente zu finden.

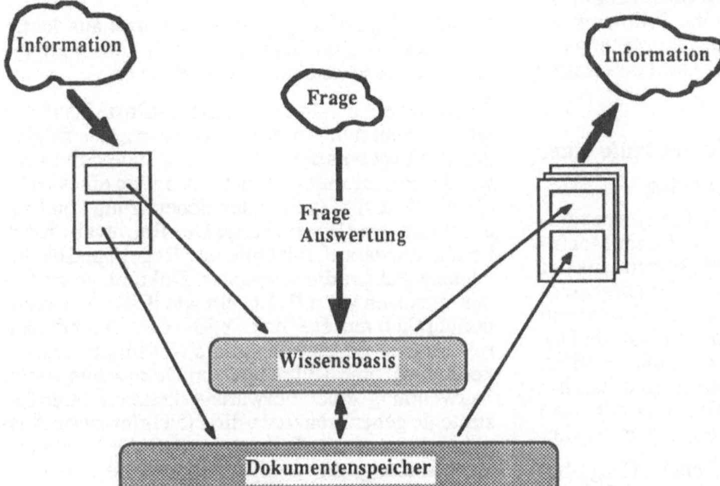

<u>Abb. 4:</u> Informations- und Wissensfluß.

Die Dokumenten-Retrieval Komponente besteht somit aus drei Hauptmoduln: Indexierung, Frageformulierung und Frageauswertung (Retrieval).

Indexierung

Die meisten Einträge in der administrativen Beschreibung können automatisch generiert werden. Zum Beispiel wird der Name des gerade im System arbeitenden Benutzers als Autor für ein neu erstelltes Dokument benutzt und das Erstellungsdatum des Dokumentes wird von der aktuellen Systemzeit abgeleitet. Einige Einträge dieser Beschreibung benötigen dennoch die Interaktion mit dem Benutzer (z.B. die Lebenszeit eines Dokumentes, Zugriffsberechtigung).

Der Inhalt des Dokumentes wird auf die inhaltliche Beschreibung abstrahiert, die bei natürlichsprachigen Dokumenteninhalt auf zwei Arten generiert werden kann: automatische Indexierung oder intellektuelle Indexierung. Für die automatische Indexierung natürlichsprachiger Dokumente existieren vielfältige Ansätze (z.B. /SALT 83/). Bei der intellektuellen Indexierung entscheidet der Benutzer über den Dokumentenindex, wobei dieses Vorgehen aber vom System unterstützt werden sollte. Zum Beispiel kann das System einen Vorschlag für die inhaltliche Beschreibung unterbreiten, den der Benutzer entweder akzeptieren oder verändern kann. In einer Büroumgebung muß eine kontrollierte Indexierung vorgenommen werden. Die administrative Beschreibung kann daher automatisch erstellt werden, während die inhaltliche Beschreibung intellektuell mit Systemunterstützung geschieht (semi-automatisch).

Das Resultat der administrativen und inhaltlichen Indexierung besteht in der Generierung von Fakten für unsere Wissensbasis.

Frageformulierung

Dokumente können mit Hilfe des Indexes wiedergefunden werden. Die oben vorgenommene Unterteilung des Indexes führt zu drei Fragearten. Wir haben Fragen bzgl. der administrativen Beschreibung (Datenbankanfragen), der inhaltlichen Beschreibung (unscharfe Fragen) und beider Beschreibungen (teilweise unscharfe Fragen). Wenn der Benutzer genau weiß welche(s) Dokument(e) er sucht, so stellt er eine Datenbankanfrage. Sucht der Benutzer Dokument(e) mit einem bestimmten Inhalt, so beschreibt er sein Informationsbedürfnis mit Hilfe von Begriffen der Informationsstruktur. Dies ist eine unscharfe Beschreibung. In der hier betrachteten Umgebung treten normalerweise Fragen auf, die nur teilweise unscharf sind. Der Benutzer weiß, was er im Prinzip sucht. Ein Beispiel hierfür wäre, wenn der Benutzer die Dokumentenart (Term aus der administrativen Beschreibung) kennt und gewisse Aussagen über den Dokumenteninhalt (Begriffe der inhaltlichen Beschreibung) machen kann. Solche Fragen sind vergleichbar mit sog. structure searches in Hypermedia-Systemen (vergl. /HALA 88/). Für jede dieser Fragearten muß der Benutzer bei der Formulierung seiner Informationsbedürfnisse unterstützt werden. Eine Unterstützungsart besteht darin, daß der Benutzer sich die Informationen und/ oder die organisatorischen Strukturen ansehen kann (browsing), um Begriffe und/oder Suchpfade für die Dokumente und damit für seine Frageformulierung zu finden.

Retrieval

Der Retrievalprozeß wird durch die verschiedenen Fragearten kontrolliert. Mit einer Datenbankanfrage ist das Informationsbedürfnis genau bestimmt, d.h. wir haben exakt eine mögliche Antwortmenge (Ausbeute =1). Die Benutzung unscharfer Fragen bedeutet vage Formulierung des Informationsbedürfnisses (Ausbeute < 1). Die Datenbankanfrage gibt als Antwort eine exakte Teilmenge aller Dokumente, während unscharfe Fragen eine unscharfe Teilmenge aller Dokumente ergeben. In Büchereisystemen ist der Benutzer bereit, einige 'falsche Antworten' zu tolerieren, in einem Büro-Informationssystem ist er dazu nicht bereit /BERT 86/. Die Ausbeute muß also nahe 1 sein.

Teilweise unscharfe Fragen werden in einem BIS folgendermaßen behandelt. Als erstes wird eine Vorauswahl von Dokumenten aus dem Dokumentenspeicher mit Hilfe der Datenbankschlüssel der Frage getroffen. Diese Auswahl ergibt eine Teilmenge aller Dokumente. Danach findet eine Auswertung des unscharfen Teils der Frage auf der wohl definierten Teilmenge statt.

3. Beispiel der Fragéerstellung mit Hilfe eines rudimentären Prototyps in Prolog

Die oben gemachten Aussagen sind in einem rudimentären Prototyp in LPA Prolog auf dem Macintosh II realisiert. Das Grundmodell besteht aus der groben Struktur des bereits als Beispiel aufgezeigten Fertigungsbetriebes und der damit verbundenen Dokumentenklassen; darauf aufbauend ist die Dokumenten-Retrieval-Komponente implementiert. Es wurde besonderen Wert darauf gelegt, daß die Gestaltung der Benutzungsoberfläche bereits von Anfang an in die Entwicklung einbezogen wurde.

Beispielhaft wird hier folgende Benutzerfrage betrachtet: *Finde alle Vertreterberichte seit 1985, die mit dem Verkauf der Produktklasse Autoersatzteile zu tun haben.*

Der Benutzer erhält in diesem Beispiel als erstes eine Übersicht über die Firmenstruktur. Nun kann er eine Abteilung aus dieser Firmenstruktur auswählen.

In unserem Beispiel die Abteilung **Verwaltung**. Daraufhin erscheint ein Fenster, in dem alle Dokumenten-Arten, die in dieser Abteilung existieren, aufgelistet sind. Wählt der Benutzer z.B. **Vertreterberichte** aus der Liste aus, so erscheint seine Frage im Fenster 'Ihre Frage' als natürlichsprachiger Text (Abb. 5).

Der Benutzer gibt nun weitere administrative Eigenschaften seiner gesuchten Dokumente an, z.B. die Erstellungsdaten (Abb.6).

In Abb. 7 wird gezeigt, wie der Benutzer aus der Informationsstruktur Begriffe, die sein Informationsbedürfnis beschreiben, auswählen kann.

Übertragen wir nun den Retrieval-Prozeß auf den wissensbasierten Ansatz, so bedeutet dies folgendes: das Ergebnis der Dokumenten-Indexierung sowie der Frageformulierung (Erzeugung eines virtuellen Indexes) besteht in der Generierung von Fakten für unsere Wissensbasis. Der Retrieval-Prozeß beruht nun darauf, mit Hilfe von Regeln und der erzeugten Fakten die relevanten Dokumente zu finden. Besitzen wir z.B. Regeln wie if X = Vertreterbericht then retrieve_dok (Y,id = cs . . .) für die administrative Beschreibung, die fest bindend ist, so können wir eine Teilmenge von Dokumenten unter Verwendung einer vorwärtsverketteten Inferenzstrategie generieren (data-directed inference). Ausgehend von dieser Teilmenge muß die inhaltliche Beschreibung, die weniger bindend ist, überprüft und die relevanten Dokumente müssen ausgewählt werden. Dies geschieht mit Hilfe einer rückwertsverketteten Inferenzstrategie (goal-directed inference).

Zusammenfassend kann man sagen, daß für ein modernes BIS zwei wichtige Voraussetzungen existieren. Erstens muß dem Benutzer eine geeignete Benutzungsoberfläche angeboten werden, mit deren Hilfe seine Aufgaben optimal unterstützt und gelöst werden können (Ikonen, Fenster- und Menütechnik, natürlichsprachige Anfragen, usw.). Zweitens muß das BIS auf einem wissensbasierten Ansatz beruhen. Es sind also Techniken und Methoden der künstlichen Intelligenz, auch im Bereich des Dokumenten-Retrievals, anzuwenden.

<u>Abb. 5</u>: Frageerstellung.

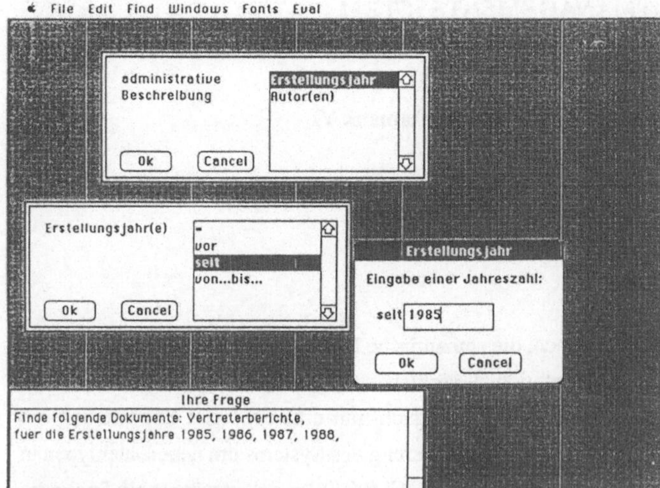

<u>Abb. 6:</u> Frageerstellung.

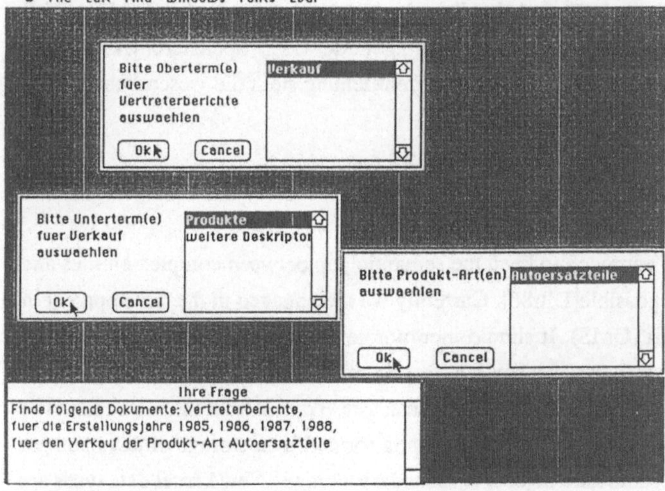

<u>Abb. 7:</u> Frageerstellung.

Referenzen

/BARB 87/
F. Barbic et al.: Semantics and Conceptual Modeling of Documents. Proc. IFIP WG8.4, Office Knowledge, Toronto, 1987.

/BERT 86/
E. Bertino et al.: Text Retrieval Techniques for Office Documents. Technical Report, Olivetti, Pisa, 1986.

/BRAC 84/
G. Bracchi, B. Pernici: The Design Requirements of Office Systems. ACM Transactions on Office Information Systems, Vol. 2, No. 2, 1984.

/EIRU 88/
H. Eirund, K. Kreplin: Knowledge Based Document Classification Supporting Integrated Document Handling. Proc. IFIP WG8.4 Office Information Systems, ed. R.B. Allen, Palo Alto, 1988.

/HALA 88/
F.G. Halasz: Reflections on Notecards: Seven Issues for the Next Generation of Hypermedia Systems. CACM, Vol. 31, No. 7, 1988.

/ISO 86/
ISO/DS 8613: Information Processing - Text and Office Systems-Document Structures. 1986.

/KRÖN 88/
G. Krönert: Genormte Austauschformate für Dokumente. Informatik Spektrum, No. 11, 1988.

/LOCK 86/
P. Lockemann, H. Mayr: Information System Design: Techniques and Software Support. Proc. IFIP Information Processing 86, ed. H.-J. Kugler, North Holland, 1986.

/SALT 83/
G. Salton, M. McGill: Introduction to Modern Information Retrieval, McGraw Hill, 1983.

/SCHM 88/
S. Schmidt: MARS - A Model and Retrieval System for an Office Information System. Interner Bericht, Institut für Informatik, Universität Zürich, Zürich, 1988.

EIN ALLGEMEINER SPEICHEROBJEKTMANAGER ALS IMPLEMENTIERUNGSBASIS FÜR KOMPLEXE OBJEKTE IN EINEM OBJEKTMANAGEMENTSYSTEM

J. Freitag, Th. Bode

Universität Dortmund, Lehrstuhl Informatik VI

Postfach 500 500

D-4600 Dortmund 50

Kurzfassung

Objektorientierte Datenbanksysteme sind ein Versuch, die semantische Lücke zwischen Anwendungen mit komplexen Objekten und deren Datenbankrepräsentation zu verkleinern [Ditt86]. Derzeit arbeiten wir an der Entwicklung eines Objektmanagementsystems (OMS), das nicht nur eine Frontend-Erweiterung um neue Datentypen sondern aus Effizienzgründen auch eine Anreicherung des Systems um neue Datentypen in tieferen Systemschichten erlauben soll. Ähnlich wie in EXODUS [CDFG86] wurde zunächst ein Speicherobjektmanager entwickelt, der den im Systemkern eingebetteten Objekttypen als Basis zur Implementierung ihrer Sekundärspeicherrepräsentation dient. Während der Speicherobjektmanager in EXODUS jedoch Bytestrings als Behälter für zusammengesetzte Objekte bereitstellt, geht der OMS-Speicherobjektmanager von der Idee hierarchisch aufgebauter Records aus. Diese Veröffentlichung stellt die wesentlichen Ideen der Realisierung dieses Speicherobjektmanagers vor.

Abstract

Object-oriented database systems are an approach to keep the semantic gap between complex entities and their database representation as small as possible[Ditt86]. Currently we are engaged in the development of an extensible object management system (OMS). It should incorporate features to introduce new object types by front end extensions of a database kernel system, but to gain efficiency it should also be capable to enrich the kernel itself by new basic types including type constructors. To deal with the introduction of new types into the kernel the bottom level of our kernel system is formed by a storage object manager which provides useful primitives to map composite objects to secondary storage. New kernel data types are implemented on top of these primitives. As far as the introduction of primitive storage objects is concerned our approach is similar to EXODUS. But whereas in EXODUS the basic abstraction of an storage object is an untyped bytestring, the notion of a OMS storage object is an hierarchically structured record. This paper discusses the main ideas of the implementation of the storage object manager.

Diese Veröffentlichung wurde im Rahmen des DFG-Schwerpunktprogammes "Objektbanken für Experten" erstellt.

1. Einordnung des OMS-Ansatzes

In der gegenwärtigen Entwicklung von Datenbanksystemen für "Nicht-Standard"-Anwendungen lassen sich hauptsächlich drei Architekturkonzepte unterscheiden:

Erweiterbare "General-Purpose" Datenbanksysteme sollen eine einheitliche Unterstützung aller oder zumindest der wesentlichsten "Nicht-Standard"-Anwendungen ermöglichen. Ihre Vielseitigkeit beruht auf der Einbettung spezieller Erweiterungsmechanismen, die es erlauben, das Datenbanksystem an die einzelnen Anwendungen anzupassen. So können zum Beispiel neue Datentypen und Funktionen (User Data Extensions [LPP87]) oder alternative Speicherungs- und Zugriffspfadstrukturen (Data Management Extentions [LPP87]) in das Datenbanksystem integriert werden. Beispiele für diese Entwicklungslinie sind die Systeme AIM-P [LKPD88], STARBURST [LPP87], PROBE [DMBC87], POSTGRES [RoSt87] und GRAL [Güti88].

Beim Datenbank-Toolkit Ansatz steht nicht die Entwicklung eines möglichst universellen Datenbanksystems im Vordergrund, sondern die Realisierung von besonders auf einzelne Anwendungsbereiche zugeschnittenen Spezial-Datenbanksystemen. Um die Entwicklungskosten für eine Vielzahl solcher Spezial-Datenbanksysteme zu reduzieren, werden Grundbausteine (z.B. Bibliotheken mit unterschiedlichen Zugriffsverfahren [CDFG86]) und Werkzeuge (z.B. Parser- und Optimierer-Generatoren [CDFG86]) bereitgestellt, mit denen Spezial-Datenbanksysteme effizient konfigurierbar werden. So erzeugte Spezial-Datenbanksysteme können durchaus wiederum User-Data-erweiterbar sein (vergl. EXTRA [CDV87]). EXODUS [CDFG86] und GENESIS [BBGS86] sind Beispiele für diese Entwicklungsrichtung.

Wie beim Datenbank-Toolkit- steht auch beim Datenbank-Kernsystem-Ansatz die effiziente Entwicklung von Spezial-Datenbanksystemen im Vordergrund. Anstatt aus einer Vielzahl vorgegebener bzw. generierter Bausteine bestehen die mit diesem Ansatz entwickelten Spezial-Datenbanksysteme aus lediglich zwei Komponenten (vergl. [HäRe85, PSSW87]):

- Ein universelles Basissystem, das ein anwendungsunabhängiges Zwischendatenmodell bereitstellt und somit für alle Anwendungen gleichermaßen geeignet ist. - Der KERN -
- Eine je nach Anwendungsklasse unterschiedliche Front-End-Erweiterung des Kerns, die ein anwendungsbezogenes Spezialdatenmodell realisiert. - Die MODELLABBILDUNG -

Im Vergleich mit Toolkit-Systemen geht so zwar Flexibilität verloren, dies wird aber durch eine ausgereifte Kernarchitektur/Kernimplementierung ausgeglichen (Der Kern selbst muß nicht konfigurierbar sein und wird von Spezialisten entwickelt).Entsprechende Kernsysteme werden zur Zeit in Darmstadt (DASDBS [PSSW87]) und Kaiserslautern (PRIMA [Härd88, HMMS87]) entwickelt.

Im OMS-Projekt arbeiten wir an der Entwicklung eines User-Data-erweiterbaren Datenbank-Kernsystems mit folgenden Erweiterungsmechanismen:

1. Anweisungen der Query-Sprache können zu parametrisierbaren Funktionen/Prozeduren zusammengefaßt werden. Nach der Definition sind sie genauso verwendbar wie die "Built-in" Funktionen des Kernmodells. Für solche Funktionen/Prozeduren ist Rekursion möglich. (vergl. EXESS-Functions and -Procedures in EXODUS [CDV87])
Anders als in POSTGRES [RoSt87] sollen diese Funktionen/Prozeduren nicht zum Aufbau von komplexen Objekten verwendet werden. Das Datenmodell enthält einen eigenständigen, hiervon unabhängigen Komplex-Objekt-Begriff.

2. Das Kerndatenmodell kann um extern definierte Datentypen (EDTs) erweitert werden. EDTs sind durch die Implementierung der auf ihnen ausführbaren Operationen definiert. Im Gegensatz zu den in EXTRA realisierten EDTs [CDV87] ist in OMS nicht nur die Einbettung atomarer, sondern auch die parametrisierter (polymorpher) EDTs in das System möglich. Diese erlaubt die Erweiterung des OMS Datenmodells um neue Typkonstruktoren, und wir streben an, so auch unterschiedliche Zugriffspfadstrukturen in OMS einzubetten.

Ein Beispiel für einen in OMS besonders wichtigen polymorphen EDT ist der Objekttyp MENGE[...]. Er ist parametrisiert mit dem Objekttyp der Mengenelemente und ermöglicht mit seinen Operationen Selektion und "Projektion" eine mengenorientierte Verarbeitung. Diese Selektions- bzw. Projektionsoperationen können als Verallgemeinerungen der entsprechenden Operationen der relationalen Algebra betrachtet werden:

> - Der Typ der Mengenelemente ist nicht auf "Tupel" beschränkt. Sie können jeden anderen im OMS-System bekannten Objekttyp besitzen.
> - Das Ergebnis einer "Projektion" ist eine Menge, deren Elementtyp jedoch von der konkret auszuführenden "Projektion" bestimmt ist. Die Ergebnismenge ensteht durch Anwendung einer Transformationsfunktion (der "Projektion") auf die einzelnen Elemente der Ausgangsmenge.

Ihre Semantik läßt sich leicht beschreiben:

> Sei M ein Objekt vom Typ MENGE[E], E ein in OMS bekannter Objekttyp, P eine boolsche Funktion auf Objekten vom Typ E, und T eine Transformationsfunktion, die Objekten vom Typ E Objekte vom Typ E´ zuordnet (T: E --> E´).
> Dann gilt:
> Selektion $(P,M) = \{ m \mid m \in M \text{ und } P(m) \}$
> "Projektion" $(T,M) = \{ T(m) \mid m \in M \}$

Außer Selektion und "Projektion" besitzt der Typ MENGE[...] natürlich noch eine Reihe weiterer Operationen.

3. Extern Definierte Funktionen/Prozeduren (EDFs) können in die Kern-Query-Sprache integriert werden. Sie dürfen Parameter beliebiger in OMS bekannter Typen (auch komplexester Struktur) besitzen, und sind, analog zu EDTs, durch ihre Implementierung in der Datenbankimplementierungssprache definiert (vergl. extern definierte Funktionen in AIM-P [LKDP88]). Für die Transformation der aktuellen Parameter von einer kerninternen Darstellung in Datenstrukturen der entsprechenden Programmiersprache (dies ist die Darstellung, die den EDF-Realisierungen zugrundeliegt) sind für die im OMS-Datenmodell fest vorhandenen "Built-in"-Datentypen entsprechende Operationen vorhanden. Bei der Implementierung von EDTs müssen sie allerdings explizit angegeben werden.

Aufgrund so vielfältiger Erweiterungsmechanismen und vor allem dank der Möglichkeit, neue Typkonstruktoren nachträglich in den Kern einzuführen, hoffen wir in OMS mit einem überaus schlanken Kern auszukommen (Mindestkonfiguration). Die für einzelne Anwendungen notwendigen Typen und Funktionen sind ja leicht auch später noch integierbar.

Das OMS-Kernsystem besitzt folgende (grobe) Systemarchitektur:

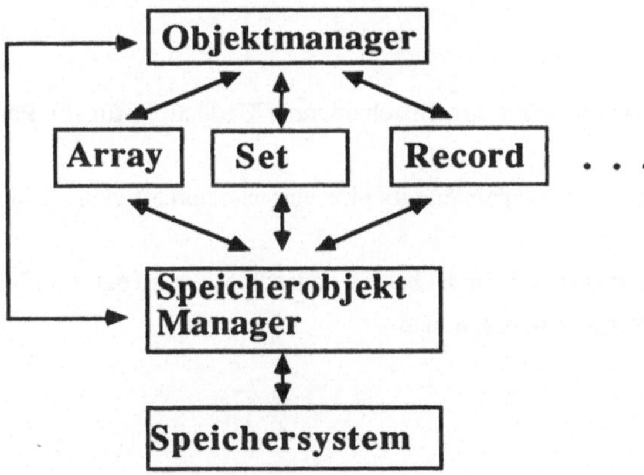

Abbildung 1: Die Systemarchitektur des OMS-Kernsystems

Der OMS-Objektmanager realisiert die Schnittstelle zur Modellabbildung. Er verwaltet die im System vorhandenen bzw. später hinzugefügten eingekapselten Objekttypen und Funktionen, deren Summe den jeweiligen OMS-Objektbegriff bildet. Hierin ist er vergleichbar mit dem im EXODUS-Projekt realisierten TYPE-MANAGER [CDFG86].

Die Realisierungen der einzelnen EDTs und EDFs bilden die Typebene des Kernsystems. Ihre Anzahl ist variabel. Die Implementierung der EDTs stützt sich zur Abbildung der Objekte auf den Hintergrundspeicher auf die vom Speicherobjektmanager bereitgestellten Operationen ab (Speicherungsstrukturabhängigkeit).

Der OMS-Speicherobjektmanager bildet die Basis für die Implementierung der in OMS bekannten Typen. Dies gilt sowohl für die fest im Kern vorhandenen wie auch für die später hinzugefügten atomaren und polymorphen Typen bzw. Typkonstruktoren. Damit ist er in Bezug auf die Performanz des OMS-Systems von entscheidender Bedeutung.

Obwohl beiden Systemen ein anderer Speicherobjektbegriff zu Grunde liegt, ist der OMS-Speicherobjekt-manager vergleichbar mit dem Storage-Object-Manager in EXODUS [CDRS86]. Im Gegensatz zu EXODUS entspricht ein OMS-Speicherobjekt nicht ausschließlich einem ungetypten, variabel langen Bytestring beliebiger Größe . Solche Strings repräsentieren in OMS lediglich ein atomares Speicherobjekt. Ein (komplexes) OMS-Speicherobjekt besteht aus hierarchisch strukturierten Kollektionen solcher atomaren Speicherobjekte. Dabei stehen zwei unterschiedliche Kollektionsmechanismen zur Verfügung (Mengen- und Listenbildung). Dank der im Gegensatz zum "flachen" EXODUS-Speicherobjekt komplexen Struktur der OMS-Speicherobjekte lassen sich viele in Datenbanksystemen gebräuchliche Objekttypen effizient modellieren (vergl. Kap.2).

In diesem Artikel konzentrieren wir uns auf die Beschreibung des OMS-Speicherobjektmanagers. Dies hat drei Gründe:

- Der Speicherobjektmanager ist wie erwähnt von entscheidender Bedeutung für die Performanz des OMS-Kernsystems.
- Erst die Flexibilität des Speicherobjektmanagers erlaubt eine einfache und effiziente Einbettung neuer Typkonstruktoren.
- Die Implementierung dieser Systemkomponente ist bereits abgeschlossen, so daß für diesen Statusbericht erste Erfahrungen berücksichtigt werden konnten.

2. Der Speicherobjektbegriff in OMS

Der Speicherobjektmanager in OMS ist als Versuch einer effizienten Implementierung komplexer physischer Records zu verstehen, deren Aufbau eine allgemeine hierarchische Kompositionsbeziehung bereits auf der Ebene der Sekundärspeicherzugriffe unterstützen soll.

Ein solches hierarchisch strukturiertes Speicherobjekt in OMS ist rekursiv beschrieben als

- ein Bytestring beliebiger Länge (atomares Speicherobjekt), oder

- eine Kollektion von Speicherobjekten, wobei die Identifikation eines Elementes dieser Kollektion wahlweise unterstützt werden kann über

   - seine Position in der physischen Anordnung, wir nennen diese Objekte dann Listenobjekte, oder
   - das erste im Element enthaltenen Atom(Bytestring), wir nennen diese Objekte dann Mengenobjekte.

Der Identifikationstyp muß für alle Elemente einer Kollektion einheitlich gewählt sein.

Netzwerkartige Beziehungen kennt der Speicherobjektmanager in seiner Rolle als Primitive zur Abbildung hierarchisch organisierter Records nicht. Sie sind beispielsweise durch die Einführung eines Objekttyps REFERENCE in der Typebene modellierbar.

Man kann den Speicherobjektbegriff als Verallgemeinerung der NF2-Speicherstrukturen [DGW85] betrachten, in der nun Mengenelemente nicht mehr zwingend einheitlich strukturiert sein müssen, und neben der Mengenbildung auch eine Listenbildung auf Ebene der Speicherungsstrukturen explizit zugelassen wird. Der Speicherobjektmanager stellt, will man einen Vergleich zur Architektur von DASDBS [DOPS85] ziehen, einen hinsichtlich seiner Funktionalität reduzierten Complex Record Manager dar, der Primitive zur Speicherung allgemeinerer hierarchischer Strukturen implementiert, dagegen aber noch keine vergleichbaren Selektionsfilter und Projektionsmöglichkeiten bietet. Eine entsprechende Ergänzung erfolgt durch die Implementierung von Objekttypen wie SET und RECORD in der übergeordneten Typebene. Der Speicherobjektmanager muß hierzu eine hinreichend effiziente Implementierungsbasis bieten.

Hinsichtlich der Zielsetzung kann zum Storage-Objekt-Manager in EXODUS [CDFG86] ein direkterer Vergleich gezogen werden. Wie bei diesem wird beabsichtigt, durch einen Speicherobjektmanager eine allgemeine Basis zur Implementierung der Sekundärspeicherabbildung zusammengesetzter Objekte zu liefern. Der Storage-Objekt-Manager in EXODUS kennt Bytestrings, die den übergeordneten Ebenen als Behälter für zusammengesetzte Objekte dienen, und unterstützt positionsorientierte Zugriffe auf Teile dieser Bytestrings. Darüberhinaus können Bytestrings zu Kollektionen, sogenannten Files, zusammengefaßt werden. Der direkte Zugriff auf Elemente dieser Kollektionen über einen Objektidentifikator sowie ihre sequentielle Verarbeitung werden unterstützt. Die innere Struktur der Bytestrings ist für den Storage-Objekt-Manager nicht sichtbar.

Der Speicherobjektmanager in OMS hingegen bietet durch seine Unterstützung hierarchisch strukturierter Records die Möglichkeit, eine feinere Unterteilung zusammengesetzter Objekte bereits auf der Ebene der Sekundärspeicherabbildung sichtbar zu machen. Durch das Angebot dieser einfachen Strukturbildungsmechanismen wird die Implementierung zusammengesetzter Objekttypen vereinfacht. So reicht zur Implementierung eines Tupelbegriffes eine feste Zuordnung von Attributidentifikatoren aus, um unter Inanspruchnahme des Speicherobjektmanagers die Tupelstruktur zu erkennen. Darüberhinaus können ohne Kenntnis der implementierten Typen auf der Ebene des Speicherobjektmanagers einfache Concurrency Control- und Recoverymechanismen angeboten werden, die beliebige Teilhierarchien der hierarchischen Recordstruktur als Einheit betrachten. Entsprechendes gilt für eine primitive Unterstützung von Versionen. [BoFr89]

Zielsetzung der Speicherobjektimplementierung in OMS ist es, diese Auffassung hierarchisch strukturierter Speicherobjekte zu unterstützen hinsichtlich

- ihrer Clusterung,
  d.h., jeder Teilbaum der Speicherobjekthierarchie ist aggregiert auf den Sekundärspeicher abgebildet,

- der relativen und absoluten Lokalisierung von Teilhierarchien,
  d.h., jeder Teilbaum der Speicherobjekthierarchie kann getrennt im Sekundärspeicher lokalisiert werden, sowohl relativ unter Bezug auf eine zuvor eingenommene Position (navigierender Zugriff) als auch absolut unter Angabe der Objektidentifikatoren (schlüsselorientierter Zugriff über die Position oder das identifizierende Atom),

- der atomaren Bereitstellung von Teilhierarchien,
  d.h., jeder Teilbaum der Speicherobjekthierarchie kann getrennt in einem Schritt im Kernspeicher bereitgestellt werden,
  und

- der atomaren Einfügung, Löschung, oder Ersetzung von Teilhierarchien,
  d.h., es können Teilbäume in einem Schritt eingefügt, ersetzt, und gelöscht werden.

Eine 1:1 - Abbildung von zusammengesetzten Objekten der Typebene auf Speicherobjekte ist natürlich nicht erforderlich und sicherlich auch nicht immer sinnvoll. Für die Wahl der Abbildung auf Speicherobjekte ist entscheidend, welche Objektbestandteile bereits auf Sekundärspeicherebene getrennt manipulierbar gehalten werden sollen. So kann zum Beispiel ein Tupel als Bytestring realisiert werden, aber auch als Kollektion von Listenobjekten, wenn ein separater Sekundärspeicherzugriff auf seine Attribute unterstützt werden soll. Der typische Identifikator für eine Kollektion von Tupeln wäre ein systemintern vergebener kurzer Schlüssel, der für die Lebensdauer des Tupels konstant bleibt.

Die Abbildung 2 zeigt eine mögliche Speicherobjektrepräsentation von in Datenbanksystemen üblichen zusammengesetzten Objekten. Läßt man in Beispiel 2.1 an den Plätzen der Attribute wieder Relationen zu, erhält man eine mögliche Speicherungsstruktur für NF2-Relationen. Das Beispiel 2.2 illustriert, daß prinzipiell eine komplette Datenbank in einem Speicherobjekt abgelegt werden kann. Da ein Speicherobjekt die Zusammenfassung von variabel strukturierten Objekten zu einer Kollektion zuläßt, kann eine unterschiedliche Tupelstruktur in den verschiedenen Relationen auf der Speicherobjektebene durchaus verwaltet werden.

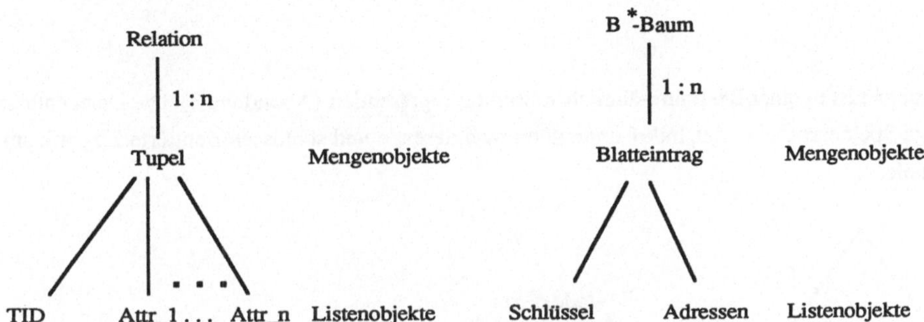

Beispiel 2.1: Relation als Speicherobjekt

Beispiel 2.3: Ein B*-Baum als Speicherobjekt

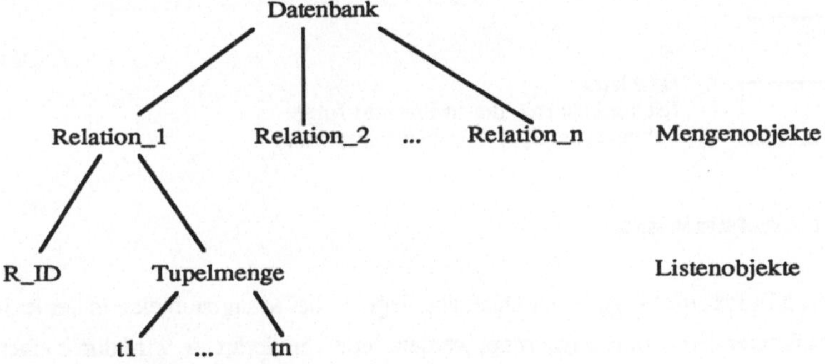

Beispiel 2.2: Eine einfache "Datenbank" als Speicherobjekt

Abbldung 2: Einige zusammengesetzte Objekte in Datenbanksystemen als Speicherobjekte

Das Beispiel 2.3 deutet zwei wesentliche Punkte an:

- Der Speicherobjektmanager soll nicht nur als Basis zur Implementierung zusammengesetzter Objekttypen dienen, die dann in einem übergeordneten Datenmodell verwendet werden, sondern er soll auch eine Basis zur Implementierung von Zugriffspfadstrukturen darstellen, und

- die Implementierung der Speicherobjekte stellt bereits unter einer Voraussetzung eine B*-Baum-Implementierung dar: Die Schlüssel müssen ordnungserhaltend auf Bytestrings abgebildet werden können.

3. Die Abbildung von Speicherobjekten auf den Sekundärspeicher

Jedes Speicherobjekt ist in einer B*-Baum-ähnlichen Struktur repräsentiert (Abbildung 3). Die Datei enthält das vollständige Speicherobjekt , der Index unterstützt navigierende und schlüsselorientierte Zugriffe auf Objektbestandteile.

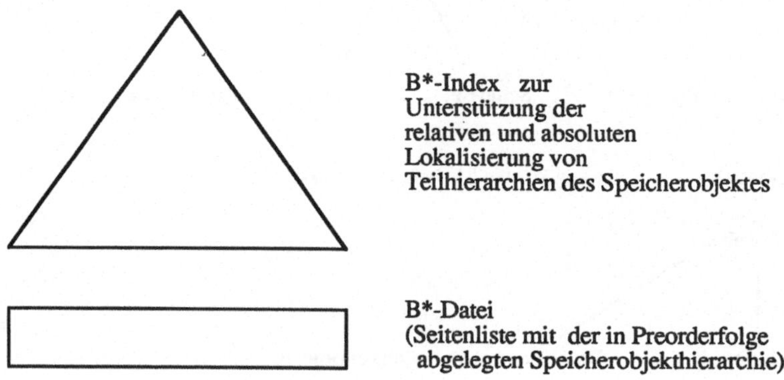

Abbildung 3: Die Zugriffspfadstruktur der Speicherobjekte

Die Speicherobjekthierarchie wird in Preorderfolge in der Datei abgelegt, wobei Mengenobjekte in der lexikographischen Folge ihrer identifizierenden Atome angeordnet werden. Jede Teilhierarchie wird durch einen Objektheader eingeleitet, der im wesentlichen drei Bestandteile enthält:

- die Ebene des Objektes in der Hierarchie,
- ein Identifikationsflag (Mengen- oder Listenobjekt), und
- ggf. die Länge des Bytestrings, wenn es sich um ein Atom handelt.

Das Speicherobjekt kann damit als (in der Regel sehr großer) Bytestring aufgefaßt werden, dessen Struktur in ihm selbst durch die Objektheader kodiert ist (Abbildung 4). Wir nennen diese Struktur physisches Record, und die Teilhierarchien repräsentierenden Bestandteile des Bytestrings (physische) Subrecords. Diese Subrecords bzw. das komplette Record sind die Übertragungseinheiten zwischen dem Speicherobjektmanager und den höheren Systemschichten. Aufgrund der Objektheader benötigt der Speicherobjektmanager keine Kataloginformationen, um in Bewältigung seiner Aufgaben die Zusammensetzung des physischen Records zu erkennen.

Im Vergleich zu gewöhnlichen B*-Baum-Dateien gibt es drei Abweichungen:

- Neben Mengenobjekten, die über einen Schlüssel identifiziert sind, gibt es Listenobjekte, die über ihre Position identifiziert sind. Diese Position wird nicht zusammen mit den Listenobjekten gespeichert. Die Schlüssel der Mengenobjekte sind die in Kapitel 2 erwähnten identifizierenden Atome, die damit extern, d.h. durch benutzende Module, festgelegt werden müssen.

- Statt einer "flachen" Relation von <Schlüssel, Information>- Paaren liegt eine geschachtelte Relation dieser Paare vor (wobei bei Listenobjekten der Schlüssel aus ihrer Anordnung in der Kollektion hervorgeht, s. oben): Die Information kann selbst wieder eine derartige Relation sein.

- Da Atome beliebig lang werden können, ist die Dateiknotengröße nicht fest, sondern ein beliebiges Vielfaches der Seitengröße: Seiten, in denen außer der "Fortsetzung" eines (langen) Atoms keine Information steht, werden mit der Seite des Atombeginns zu einem Knoten zusammengefaßt.

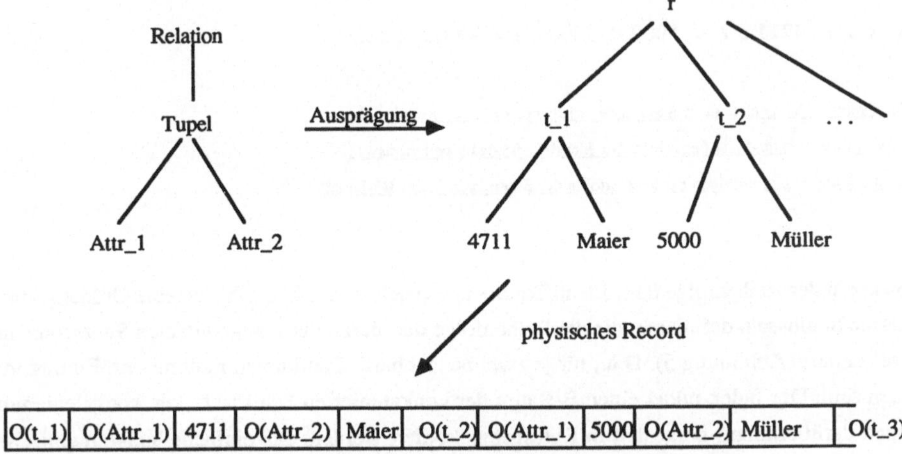

Abbildung 4: Der Aufbau des zu einem einfachen Speicherobjekt gehörenden physischen Record.
O (...) symbolisieren die Objektheader der Tupel bzw. Attribute.

Diese Repräsentation des Speicherobjektes als physisches Records in einer B*-Baum-Datei schafft die Voraussetzung zur einfachen Aufrechterhaltung der gewünschten Clusterung. Allerdings wird die physische Clusterung benachbarter Dateiseiten in der derzeitigen Implementierung des Speicherobjektmanagers unter UNIX noch nicht unterstützt.

Die genestete Struktur der Informationen in der B*-Datei erfordert eine besondere Indexierung, wenn der Index den Zugriff auf ein beliebiges Subrecord unterstützen soll. Erreicht wird dies durch konkatenierte

Schlüssel, die jedem Subrecord zugewiesen werden, ohne jedoch mit diesem zusammen abgespeichert zu werden. Diese setzen sich aus dem Identifikator (Position oder identifizierendes Atom) des Subrecords und der übergeordneten Subrecords zusammen. Für den Fall, daß die identifizierenden Atome systeminterne Identifikatoren sind, ist diese Art der Adressierung vergleichbar zum in DASDBS diskutierten HITID-Konzept[DGW85, De84].

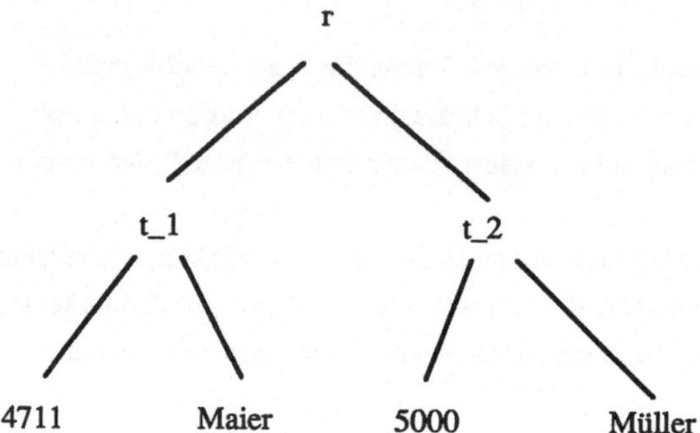

$$4711 \; < \; 4711 \, o \, 1 \; < \; 4711 \, o \, 2 \; < \; 5000 \; < \; 5000 \, o \, 1 \; < \; 5000 \, o \, 2 \; < \, ...$$

Abbildung 5: In der Ordnung der konkatenierten Schlüssel wird zuerst die .<. -Relation des ersten Schlüsselbestandteils betrachtet, bei Identität die des zweiten, usw. . Diese Ordnung entspricht dann der Reihenfolge der Subrecords in der B*-Datei.

Da Mengenobjekte in der Reihenfolge ihrer Identifikatoren gespeichert werden, läßt sich eine Ordnung über den konkatenierten Schlüsseln definieren, die die Reihenfolge der hierarchisch angeordneten Subrecords in der B*-Datei reflektiert (Abbildung 5). D.h., für je zwei benachbarte Blattknoten muß nur ein Eintrag im Index vorhanden sein. Der Index bildet einen B-Baum der konkatenierten Schlüssel . Die konkatenierten Schlüssel können darüberhinaus dergestalt in Bytestrings kodiert werden, daß einfache lexikographische Vergleiche bei der Suche über den Index ausreichen. Diese Möglichkeit macht die konkatenierten Schlüssel als mit einfachen Mitteln aufrechtzuerhaltende stabile Adressen attraktiv (s. Kapitel 4.3). Ein weiterer Vorteil ist die Eigenschaft, daß sich die Stellung zweier Subrecords zueinander in einer Speicherobjekthierarchie bereits anhand ihrer konkatenierten Schlüssel erkennen läßt, was die Implementierung eines Sperrverfahrens erleichtert[BoFr89].

Somit kann zu jedem Subrecord über den Index unter Angabe des konkatenierten Schlüssels der Blattknoten aufgesucht werden, in dem, wenn existent, das Subrecord beginnt. Wie bereits gesagt, wird die identifizierende Postition von Listenobjekten nicht zusammen mit dem Objekt gespeichert. Diese kann jedoch bei Bedarf beim Einstieg über den Index problemlos rekonstruiert werden. Ist das erste Subrecord im Knoten ein

Listenobjekt, so kann nämlich dessen identifizierende Position über den im Index eingetragenen konkatenierten Schlüssel bestimmt werden. Innerhalb der Blattknoten wird in der derzeitigen Implementierung sequentiell gesucht. Zur Abbildung der Knoten auf Seiten bedient sich der Speicherobjektmanagers eines derzeit nur provisorisch implementierten Speichersystems.

4. Die Funktionalität des Speicherobjektmanagers

Zur Implementierung mengenorientierter Verarbeitungen in höheren Systemschichten stellt der Speicherobjektmanager ein primitives Cursorkonzept zur Verfügung (s. 4.1), mit dem navigierend und/oder durch die Angabe von Identifikatoren Subrecords positioniert werden können.

Die Bereitstellung der Subrecords für höhere Systemschichten (s. 4.2) und die Modifikation eines Speicherobjektes (s. 4.3) bezieht sich auf eine mit diesem Cursor eingenommene Position. Von einer "one-tuple-at-a-time"-Schnittstelle hebt sich die Implementierung jedoch insofern ab, als, wie bereits gesagt, beliebige Teilhierarchien eines physischen Records die Übertragungseinheit zwischen dem Speicherobjektmanager und den höheren Systemschichten bilden. Das betrifft sowohl die Bereitstellung als auch die Modifikation eines Speicherobjektes. Natürlich sind dabei besondere Mechanismen notwendig, um beliebig große Objekte übertragen zu können (s. 4.2). Eine Zusammenfassung der wichtigsten derzeit implementierten Funktionen befindet sich im Anhang.

Erzeugt wird ein Speicherobjekt durch die Funktion create_storage_object. Es ist nach Ausführung dieser Funktion äquivalent zu einer leeren Kollektion von Listen- oder Mengenobjekten, oder zu einem Atom der Länge 0. Eine Unterscheidung dieser Objekte ist auf der Speicherobjektebene nicht notwendig. Der dabei vergebene Speicherobjektidentifikator bleibt konstant für die Lebensdauer des Objektes.

4.1 Die Lokalisierung der Speicherobjekte und ihrer Bestandteile

Bevor ein Subrecord bereitgestellt oder modifiziert werden kann, muß es über die Positionierungs-operatoren des Speicherobjektmanagers identifiziert werden. Dieses kann navigierend unter Bezug auf eine zuvor eingenommene Position oder schlüsselorientiert unter Angabe eines Subobjektidentifikators geschehen. Die Funktion open_storage_object startet die Manipulation eines Speicherobjektes und positioniert gleichzeitig das physische Record, so daß ein direkt nachfolgendes get_object das komplette Speicherobjekt liefern würde. Ferner wird die in der kommenden Verarbeitung benötigte Verwaltungs- information ("storage_object_handle") initialisiert. Identifiziert wird das Speicherobjekt durch den beim create_storage_object zugewiesenen Identifikator, der durch die übergeordneten Schichten geeignet zu katalogisieren ist.

Die weiteren Positionierungsoperatoren tragen dem hierarchischen Aufbau des physischen Records Rechnung. Mit einem positionierten Subrecord sind gleichzeitig alle umschließenden Subrecords bis hin zum kompletten physischen Record positioniert. Die Positionierungsoperatoren können sich auf irgendeines dieser positionierten Records beziehen, was über die Angabe der Ebene des Bezugsrecords im Speicherobjekt geschieht. Dabei identifiziert die Ebene 0 das komplette Speicherobjekt, die Ebene 1 die Subrecords dieser Kollektion, und so weiter.

Ist zur Identifikation eines Subrecords mehr als eine Positionierungsoperation notwendig, so kann seine physische Positionierung (d.h., die Suche nach den Seiten, die dieses Subrecord enthalten, und das Laden dieser Seiten in die Systempuffer) optional hinausgezögert werden. Durch diese verzögerte Ausführung ist der Speicherobjektmanager in der Lage, die Zahl der Knotenzugriffe auf den B*-Baum minimieren. So ist zum Beispiel in einer Folge von pos_sub_object-Aufrufen, die die Recordhierarchie "hinabsteigt", letztendlich nur ein Zugriff über den Index zur Einnahme der gewünschten Position notwendig. Die Funktionen get_object, exists, insert, replace und delete erzwingen, falls noch nicht geschehen, eine physische Positionierung in ihrer Ausführung.

Eine weitere Maßnahme zur Reduzierung der Seitenzugriffe stellen die im "storage_object_handle" eingetragenen Pfadinformationen zur zuletzt eingenommenen Position dar: Für jede Indexebene wird das Intervall der konkatenieren Schlüssel der über den Indexknoten erreichbaren Subrecords festgehalten. Bei der nächsten Postionierungsoperation wird diese Information ausgenutzt, um so tief wie möglich, ggf. auf Blattebene, die Suche zu beginnen. Natürlich erfordert diese Informationshaltung geeignete Synchronisationsmechanismen im Mehrbenutzerbetrieb. Im wesentlichen muß vor einem erneuten Zugriff auf einen Knoten festgestellt werden können, ob die zugehörige Pfadinformation noch gültig ist. Entsprechende Vorschläge finden sich in [BoFr89].

Die Funktion pos_sub_object führt den schlüsselorientierten Zugriff durch. Der Parameter subobject_id enthält entweder die Position des gewünschten Listenobjektes oder das identifizierende Atom des gewünschten Mengenobjektes. In Ausführung der Funktion wird zunächst eine logische Position durch Bildung des identifizierenden konkatenierten Schlüssels eingenommen. Optional kann, wie oben erwähnt, auf eine direkte Einnahme der physischen Position verzichtet werden.

Die Funktionen pos_first_subobject, pos_next_subobject und pos_encl_object positionieren das erste, das nächste bzw. ein umschließendes Subrecord. Pos_next_subobject verläßt dabei das umschließende Subrecord nicht. Auch für diese (hinauszögerbaren) navigierenden Zugriffe wird der B*-Index ausgenutzt. Da sich das bei einem pos_next_subobject zu überspringende Subrecord über beliebig viele Blattknoten erstrecken kann, ist das nur konsequent. Durch die im "storage_object_handle" gespeicherte Pfadinformation wird ein überflüssiger Zugriff auf den Index vermieden.

Bei einem pos_encl_object ist immer ein direkter Zugriff über den Index möglich, da der konkatenierte Suchschlüssel eindeutig bestimmt werden kann. Die Funktionen pos_first_subobject und pos_next_subobject bilden zunächst einen konkatenierten Schlüssel y mit der Eigenschaft x < y <= z, wobei x der konkatenierte Schlüssel des zuvor positionierten Subrecords und z der noch nicht bekannte Schlüssel des zu positionierenden Subrecords ist. Mit diesem Schlüssel kann in der Regel mit einem gewöhnlichen Zugriff über den Index das gesuchte Subrecord positioniert werden. Nur wenn das Subrecord das erste in einem Blattknoten ist, ist ggf. der irrtümliche Zugriff (y < z) auf den Vorgängerknoten zu korrigieren.

4.2 Die Bereitstellung der Speicherobjekte und ihrer Bestandteile

Um die Zahl der Schnittstellenüberquerungen zu minimieren, sind beliebige Teilhierarchien des physischen Records die Übertragungseinheit zwischen dem Speicherobjektmanager und den höheren Systemschichten, bis hin zum vollständigen physischen Record selbst. Nach Möglichkeit sollte das mit den Positionierungs-operatoren identifizierte Subrecord durch einen Aufruf der Bereitstellungsfunktion get_object komplett in den Systempuffern bereitgestellt werden. Da dieses beliebig groß werden kann, ist das aber nicht immer möglich. Wir kommen weiter unten auf dieses Problem zurück.

Ein zweites Problem ist die Darstellungsart, in der ein Subrecord den übergeordneten Systemschichten angeboten werden soll. In DASDBS [PSSW87,DOPS85] werden zur Lösung der beiden Probleme an "Database Portals" orientierte Übergabebereiche vorgeschlagen, in denen NF2-Relationen in einer Form übergeben werden, die sich an die zugehörigen Speicherstrukturen anlehnt.

Da OMS-Speicherobjekte jedoch als Behälter für beliebige in der übergeordneten Schicht implementierte (polymorphe) Typen dienen sollen, wurde in der Implementierung der Funktion get_object darauf verzich-tet, das Subrecord in eine eigene hauptspeicherinterne Darstellung zu überführen. Nach unserer Auffassung ist eine universelle, hinreichend effiziente Darstellung ohne Kenntnis der implementierten Typen nicht mög-lich, so daß durch diese Vorgehensweise ein Kopiervorgang eingespart wird.

Statt spezielle Übergabepuffer zu verwenden, liefert get_object daher eine Adresse, die den Beginn des Subrecords in einem Seitenpuffer referiert (bzw. den Beginn eines Teils des Subrecords, s. unten). Die speicherstrukturabhängig implementierten Typmodule sind dann dafür verantwortlich, das Subrecord in eine geeignete typisierte Darstellung zu überführen. Die Seitenpufferadresse wird dabei als "abstrakter Da-tentyp" angeboten und nur in den Kopieroperationen cp_buf_to_str und cp_buf_to_objh ausgewertet. Cp_buf_to_str kopiert eine vorgegebene Anzahl Bytes des physischen Subrecords in einen Hauptspeicher-bereich, der vom aufrufenden Modul zur Verfügung gestellt werden muß. Cp_buf_to_objh dekodiert einen durch die Seitenpufferadresse referierten Objektheader. Optional kann in den beiden Operationen die Seitenpufferadresse weiterbewegt werden.

Durch die beiden Kopieroperationen sind höhere Systemschichten unabhängig von der Art der Bereitstel-lung des physischen Records in den Seitenpuffern, insbesondere also auch davon, welcher Teil des (beliebig großen) positionierten Subrecords sich überhaupt in den Puffern befindet. Beim Aufruf von get_object signalisiert die aufrufende Instanz, welcher Bereich des positionierten Subrecords in nachfolgenden Kopieroperationen bearbeitet werden soll, und damit nach Möglichkeit in den Seitenpuffern gehalten werden soll. Der tatsächlich in den Seitenpuffern vorhandene Teil wird aber durch den Speicherobjektmanager unter Inanspruchnahme des Speichersystems bestimmt.

Das derzeit nur behelfshalber implementierte Speichersystem stellt keine Seitenmengen (s. [Härd88, DOPS85]) zur Verfügung, daher werden derzeit die zu ladenden Seiten einzeln in die Seitenpuffer gebracht. Mit der sicherlich sinnvollen Einführung eines Seitenmengenkonzeptes wäre es zum Beispiel möglich, die Blattknoten auf eine exklusiv zugeordnete Seitenmenge abzubilden, und so einen Performanzgewinn zu erzielen.

4.3 Die Modifikation eines Speicherobjektes

Wie schon bei der Bereitstellung von Subrecords referieren auch die Modifikationsoperatoren insert, replace und delete komplette Teilhierarchien des physischen Records. Während ein "delete" das zuvor durch die Positionierungsoperatoren identifizierte Subrecord entfernt, ist wie bei der Bereitstellung von Subrecords in der Implementierung der Operatoren insert und replace dafür Vorsorge zu treffen, daß die neue bzw. ersetzende Teilhierarchie nicht vollständig im Hauptspeicher bereitgestellt werden kann.

Die Funktionen insert und replace initiieren daher nur die entsprechende Modifikation. Durch die Kopieroperationen cp_str_to_buf und cp_objh_to_buf wird dann das neue Subrecord sequentiell in den Seitenpuffern aufgebaut. Bis zu einem Aufruf von end_of_modifikation, der die Änderung abschließt, läßt der Speicherobjektmanager nur noch Aufrufe der Kopierfunktionen unter dem zugehörigen "storage_object_handle" zu.

Für die abschließende Anpassung der in Kapitel 3 geschilderten Zugriffspfadstruktur reichen die B*-Baumüblichen Reorganisationsmechanismen aus. Die konkatenierten Schlüssel bilden unter Ausnutzung der B*-Baum-Struktur daher im Fall von Mengenobjekten und arrayartigen Listenobjekten (Beispiel: Tupel) stabile Adressen, die mit einfachen Mitteln aufrecht erhalten werden können, was einen herauszuhebenden Vorteil der gewählten Abbildung darstellt.

Die Modifikation von Listenobjekten ist eingeschränkt: das Einfügen bzw. Löschen von Listenobjekten ist nur am Ende der Kollektion zugelassen, da sich mit einer derartigen Modifikation gleichzeitig die konkatenierten Schlüssel aller nachfolgenden Listenobjekte ändern würden, was ggf. eine Anpassung von Schlüsseln im B*-Index nach sich ziehen kann.

In einer frühen Implementierung des Speicherobjektmanagers existierte diese Einschränkung nicht, und der notwendigen Indexanpassung wurde dadurch Rechnung getragen, daß für Kollektionen von Listenobjekten die konkatenierten Schlüssel im Index anders verwaltet wurden: Statt der Position eines Listenobjektes wurde die Anzahl der im jeweiligen B*-Teilbaum abgelegten Listenobjekte eingetragen, und der tatsächliche Schlüssel wurde dann beim Durchlaufen des Indexes berechnet . Nach Modifikationen notwendige Anpassungen beschränkten sich auf einen Pfad zur Wurzel des B*-Indexes. Diese Implementierung orientierte sich am bekannten Vorschlag von Stonebreaker zur Implementierung von Strukturen für geordnete Relationen [SSLK83], und eine entsprechend inspirierte Lösung findet man auch in EXODUS [CDRS86] zur Indexierung langer Bytestrings. In der derzeitigen Implementierung des OMS- Speicherobjektmanagers wurde auf diese Lösung zu Gunsten einer beträchtlichen Vereinfachung der Algorithmen verzichtet.

Es besteht aber in der derzeitigen Implementierung eine Möglichkeit, diese Einschränkung durch Inkaufnahme einer ineffizienteren Positionierung aufzuheben. Die Objektheader im physischen Record enthalten ein zusätzliches Flag, mit dem ggf. die Zugriffsunterstützung über den B*-Index für das durch den Objektheader eingeleitete Subrecord ausgeschaltet werden kann. Wie schon beim Identifikationsflag muß dieses Flag für alle Objekte einer Kollektion einheitlich gesetzt sein. Bezüglich der Blattknotenbildung wird dann eine derartige Kollektion wie ein Atom behandelt, daß heißt, sie wird komplett einem Blattknoten zugeordnet.

5. Zusammenfassung und Ausblick

Ziel der Speicherobjektimplementierung in OMS ist es, eine Primitive zur effizienten Abbildung hierarchisch zusammengesetzter Objekte auf den Sekundärspeicher zu schaffen, auf die dann Typimplementierungen in der nächsthöheren Systemschicht in geeigneter Art und Weise zurückgreifen. Die gewählte Implementierung liefert durch die Preorderspeicherung der Objekthierarchie in den Blättern einer B*-Baum-ähnlichen Struktur (mit variabler Blattknotengröße) die Möglichkeit einer einfachen Aufrechterhaltung der angestrebten physischen Clusterung.

Zur Lokalisierung beliebiger Teilhierarchien wird ein B*-Index ausgenutzt, der konkatenierte Schlüssel als eindeutige Identifikatoren beliebiger Subrecords enthält. Die Ordnung dieser konkatenierten Schlüssel reflektiert die Ordnung der Subrecords in der B*-Datei, so daß für je zwei benachbarte Blattknoten nur ein Indexeintrag existieren muß. Der Index kann sowohl für schlüsselorientierte als auch für navigierende Zugriffe auf Subrecords ausgenutzt werden. Die konkatenierten Schlüssel sind mit einfachen Mitteln (den B*-Baum-üblichen Underflow- und Overflowbehandlungen) aufrechtzuerhaltende stabile Adressen, so daß wenig Aufwand für Reorganisationen anfällt.

Die Übertragungseinheit zwischen Speicherobjektmanager und höheren Systemschichten sind beliebige Teilhierarchien des Speicherobjektes. Die Bereitstellung eines zuvor positionierten Subrecords erfolgt in den Seitenpuffern in seiner Darstellungsform in der B*-Datei. Durch diese Vorgehensweise wird ein Kopiervorgang eingespart, wenn man annimmt, daß eine hinreichend effiziente hauptspeicherinterne Darstellung

der Objekte für beliebige Typen nur in Kenntnis dieser Typen und damit auf der Ebene dieser Typimplementierungen erreicht werden kann. Größerer Objekte werden "portionsweise" bereitgestellt, wobei die
aufrufenden Module den zu bearbeitenden Bereich bei einem get_object signalisieren. Sie definieren damit
ein "Fenster", wobei das tatsächliche Vorhandensein des Fensterinhaltes in die Regie des Speicherobjektmanagers fällt, da das Fenster immer noch beliebig groß sein kann.

Wie erwähnt ist die Implementierung des Speicherobjektmanagers bereits abgeschlossen. Diese einsatzfähige Version unterstützt allerdings lediglich den Einbenutzerbetrieb. Bereits bestehende Erweiterungsvor-
schläge zum Mehrbenutzerbetrieb finden sich in [BoFr89]. Eine weitere Einschränkung bildet das durch den
Speicherobjektmanager verwendete Ordnungskriterium für Kollektionen von Mengenobjekten: die identifizierenden Atome können nur in lexikographischer Ordnung betrachtet werden. Ein allgemeinerer Ansatz ist
hier wünschenswert.

Diese Implementierung des Speicherobjektmanagers erfolgte auf SUN-Rechnern unter UNIX. Aufgrund
UNIX-spezifischer Probleme verwenden wir ein recht primitives Speichersystem, das mengenorientiertes
Seiten-I/O genauso wenig ermöglicht wie die Fixierung der vom Kern benutzten Seiten im Hauptspeicher.
Trotzdem zeigt das jetzige System bisher ein durchaus ansprechendes Leistungsverhalten, welches aber
noch intensiver untersucht werden muß. Im einzelnen arbeiten wir zur Zeit an folgenden Problemen, deren
Lösung unter Umständen wiederum Änderungen am Speicherobjektmanager nach sich ziehen kann:

1. Eine Reimplementierung des Speichersystems soll zur Abhilfe der beschriebenen betriebssystemab-
   hängigen Mängel führen.

2. Zur weiteren Erprobung der Funktionalität und Perfomanz des Speicherobjektmanagers implementieren wir zur Zeit eine größere Anzahl Datentypen (z.B. Menge, Record, Graph, Punkt, Linie, ...), die
   sich auf den Speicherobjektmanager abstützen. Wir hoffen diese Typimplementierungen später auch
   als EDT-Realisierungen wiederzuverwenden .

3. Im Hinblick auf die Realisierung des Objektmanagers und damit des OMS-Kernsystems überhaupt ist
   der Enwurf der Kernoberfläche bald abgeschlossen. Wir hoffen eine evtl. eingeschränkte Funktionalität bis Ende 1989 zu erreichen. Dabei stellen wir Optimierungsaspekte wie z. B. die Einführung von
   Redundanz zunächst bewußt zurück, um bereits frühzeitig Erfahrungen mit der Tauglichkeit des Kerns
   sammeln zu können.

Wir danken Herrn Prof. Dr. A.B.Cremers, Herrn Prof. Dr. R.H. Güting und den Referees für die
hilfreichen Anmerkungen und Verbesserungsvorschläge.

6. Literaturverzeichnis

BBGS86   D. Batory, J. Barnatt, J. Garza, K. Smith, K. Tsukuda, C. Twichell, T. Wise
GENESIS: A Reconfigurable Database Management System
Tech. Rep. 86-07, Dept. of Comp. Science, Univ. of Texas at Austin, 1986

BoFr89   Th. Bode, J. Freitag
Einige Primitive zur Implementierung von Concurrency Control- und
Recovery -Mechanismen in OMS auf der Basis von Versionen
In Vorbereitung.

CDFG86   M. J. Carey, D. J. DeWitt, D. Frank, G. Graefe, M. Muralikrishna, J. E. Richardson, E. J.
Shektia
The Architekture of the EXODUS Extensible DBMS
in: Proc. International Workshop on Object-Oriented Database Systems, 1986

CDV87   M. J. Carey, D. J. DeWitt, S. L. Vandenberg
A Data Model and Query Language for EXODUS
University of Wisconsin-Madison, Computer Sciences TR-734, December 1987

CDRS86   M. J. Carey, D. J. DeWitt, J. E. Richardson, E. J. Shekita
Objekt and File Management in the EXODUS Extensible Database System
in: Proc. VLDB 1986

De84   U. Deppisch
Hiierarchisches TID-Konzept und weitere Adressierungstechniken für die komplexen Tupel
des NF2-Relationenmodells
DVSI-1984-A7, TH Darmstadt

Ditt86   K. R. Dittrích
Object-oriented Database Systems: the Notion and the Issues
in: Proc. International Workshop on Object-Oriented Database Systems, 1986

DGW85   U. Deppisch, J. Günauer, G. Walch
Speicherungsstrukturen und Adressierungstechniken für komplexe Objekte des NF2-
Relationenmodells
in: Proc. BTW 1985

DMBC87   U. Dayal, F. Manola, A. Buchmann, U. Chakavarthy, D. Goldhirsch, S. Heiler, J. Orenstein, A. Rosenthal
Simplifying Complex Objects: The PROBE Approch to Modelling and Querying Them
in: Proc. BTW 1987

DOPS85   U.Deppisch, V. Obermeit, H.-B. Paul, H.-J. Schek, M. Scholl, M. Weikum
Ein Subsystem zur Speicherung versionenbehafteter, hierarchisch strukturierter Tupel
in: Proc. BTW 1985

Güti 88   R. H. Güting
Modeling Non-Standard Database Systems by Many-Sorted Algebras
Universität Dortmund, Fachbereich Informatik, Report 255, 1988

Härd88   T. Härder (ed.)
The PRIMA Project - Design and Implementation of a Non-Standard Database System
Universität Kaiserslautern, SFB 124, Report No. 26/88, 1988

HäRe85   T. Härder, A. Reuter
Architektur von Datenbanksystemen für Non-Standard Anwendungen
in: Proc. BTW 1985

HMMS87   T. Härder, K. Meyer-Wegener, B. Mitschang, A. Sikeler
PRIMA- a DBMS Prototype Suporting Engineering Applications
in: Proc. VLDB 1987

LKDP88   V. Linnemann, K. Küspert, P. Dadam, P. Pistor, R. Erbe, A. Kemper, G. Walch, M. Wallrath
Design and Implementation of an Extensible Database Management System Supporting User Defined Types and Functions
in: Proc. VLDB 1988

LPP87   B. Lindsay, J. McPherson, H. Pirahesh
A Data Management Extension Architecture
in: Proc. SIGMOD 1987, San Francisco, Mai 1987

PSSW87   H.-B. Paul, H.-J. Schek, M. H. Scholl, G. Weikum, U. Deppisch
Architecture and Implementation of the Darmstadt Kernel System
in: Proc. SIGMOD 1987, San Francisco, Mai 1987

RoSt87   L. A. Rowe, M. R. Stonebraker
           The POSTGRES Data Model
           in: Proc. VLDB 1987

SSLK83   M.Stonebreaker, H. Stettner, M. Lynn, J. Kalasch, A. Guttman
           Document Processing in a Relational Database System
           in: ACM Transactions on Office Information Systems 83/1

Anhang: Überblick über die wichtigsten derzeit implementierten Operatoren des Speicherobjektmanagers.

1. Erzeugen eines neuen Speicherobjektes

> **create_storage_object   (segment_id,   storage_object_id,   storage_object_handle)**
>
> IN: segment_id   Idenifikator des Segmentes (linearen Adreßraumes)
>
> OUT: storage_object_id   Identifikator des neuen Objektes
>   storage_object_handle   Verwaltungsinformation zur Manipulation des Objektes in
>   anschließenden Operationen (Cursor)

2. Lokalisierung der Speicherobjekte und ihrer Bestandteile

> **open_storage_object (storage_object_id,   storage_object_handle)**
>
> IN: storage_object_id   Identifikator des Speicherobjektes
>
> OUT: storage_object_handle   Verwaltungsinformation zur Manipulation des Objektes in
>   anschließenden Operationen (Cursor)
>
> **close_storage_object   (storage_object_handle)**
>
> IN: storage_object_handle   Cursor
>
> **pos_subobject (storage_object_handle, rel_to_olevel, subobject_id, force_stpos)**
>
> IN: storage_object_handle   Cursor
>   rel_to_olevel   Ebene des Bezugsrecords, zu dem ein Subrecord positioniert werden soll
>   subobject_id   Identifikator des Subrecords (Position oder identifizierendes Atom)
>   force_stpos   'true', wenn die Operation die zugehörige physische Position einnehmen soll
>
> **pos_first_subobject (storage_object_handle, rel_to_olevel, force_stpos)**
>
> IN: storage_object_handle   Cursor
>   rel_to_olevel   Ebene des Bezugsrecords, zu dem das erste Subrecord positioniert
>   werden soll
>   force_stpos   Erzwingen der physischen Position
>
> **pos_next_subobject (storage_object_handle, at_olevel, force_stpos)**
>
> IN: storage_object_handle   Cursor
>   at_olevel   Ebene des Bezugsrecords, zu dem das nächste Record positioniert werden soll
>   force_stpos   Erzwingen der physischen Position

```
pos_encl_object  (storage_object_handle,    at_olevel,  force_stpos)
```

IN:	storage_object_handle	Cursor
	at_olevel	Ebene des umschließenden Records, das positioniert werden soll
	force_stpos	Erzwingen der physischen Position

```
exists  (storage_object_handle)
```

IN:	storage_object_handle	Cursor
OUT:	<exists>	Statusmeldung zur Existenz des zuletzt positionierten Subrecords.

3. Bereitstellung der Speicherobjekte und ihrer Bestandteile

```
get_object  (storage_object_handle,  offset,  no_bytes,  buffer_address)
```

IN:	storage_object_handle	Cursor
	offset	Beginn des zu bearbeitenden Teils relativ zum Subrecordanfang
	no_bytes	Länge des zu bearbeitenden Teils (-1: bis zum Subrecordende)
OUT:	buffer_address	Adresse zum Lesen des Subrecordteiles in den nachfolgenden Kopieroperationen

```
cp_buf_to_str    (storage_object_handle,  buffer_address,  destination,  no_bytes,  move_addr)
```

IN:	storage_object_handle	Cursor
	buffer_address	Adresse des zu übertragenden Subrecordteiles.
	no_bytes	Länge des zu übertragenden Teiles.
	move_addr	TRUE, wenn die Pufferadresse entsprechend weiterbewegt werden soll.
	destination	Hauptspeicheraddresse zur Aufnahme des zu übertragenden Teiles.
OUT:	buffer_address	(wenn move_addr TRUE)

```
cp_buf_to_objh    (storage_object_handle,  buffer_address,  obj_type,  ...,  move_addr)
```

IN:	storage_object_handle	Cursor
	buffer_address	Adresse des zu übertragenden Subrecordteiles.
	move_addr	TRUE, wenn die Pufferadresse entsprechend weiterbewegt werden soll.
OUT:	buffer_address	(wenn move_addr TRUE)
	obj_type	Listenobjekt oder Mengenobjekt
	...	

4. Modifikation der Speicherobjekte

```
insert  (storage_object_handle,  buffer_address)
```

IN:	storage_object_handle	Cursor
OUT:	buffer_address	Seitenpufferadresse, ab der die Übergabe des Subrecords begonnen werden kann

```
replace  (storage_object_handle,  buffer_address)
```

IN:	storage_object_handle	Cursor
OUT:	buffer_address	Seitenpufferadresse, ab der die Übergabe des Subrecords begonnen werden kann

```
cp_str_to_buf  (storage_object_handle,  buffer_address,  source,  no_bytes)
```

IN:	storage_object_handle	Cursor
	buffer_address	Seitenpufferadresse; Ziel der Übertragung
	no_bytes	Länge des zu übertragenden Subrecordteiles.
	source	Hauptspeicheraddresse des zu übertragenden Teiles.
OUT:	buffer_address	neue Pufferadresse nach der Übertragung

cp_objh_to_buf   (storage_object_handle, buffer_address, obj_type, ...)

    IN: storage_object_handle   Cursor
              buffer_address   Seitenpufferadresse; Ziel der Übertragung des Objektheaders
              obj_type   Listenobjekt oder Mengenobjekt
              ...

    OUT: buffer_address   neue Pufferadresse nach der Übertragung

delete   (storage_object_handle)

    IN: storage_object_handle   Cursor

end_of_modification   (storage_object_handle)

    IN: storage_object_handle   Cursor

Erste Beobachtungen zum Leistungsverhalten von DASDBS

H.-Bernhard PAUL

TH Darmstadt, FB Informatik   Mannesmann Kienzle GmbH
FG Datenverwaltungssysteme I   Abt. 01.05
Alexanderstr. 10, D-6100 Darmstadt   Postfach 1640, D-7730 VS-Villingen
e-mail: PAUL @ DDADVS1.BITNET

Kurzfassung

Der Kern des erweiterbaren Datenbanksystems DASDBS liegt als Prototyp in einer UNIX- und einer VM-Version vor. Zur Realisierung der Mengenorientierung an der Kernschnittstelle wird das Konzept des Objektpuffers eingeführt und beschrieben. Erstmals wird dann über Erfahrungen mit dem System und über Ergebnisse einer Evaluierung berichtet. Dabei zeigen Messungen, daß gerade die Objektpuffer-Komponente maßgeblich an dem hohen CPU-Anteil des Systems beteiligt ist.

1 Architektur von DASDBS

Das DArmStädter DatenBankSystem DASDBS realisiert den Ansatz der erweiterbaren Kern-Architektur mit einem gemeinsamen Kernsystem und verschiedenen anwendungsspezifischen Schichten (s. Abbildung 1). Das Kernsystem hat u.a. folgende Eigenschaften (s.a. [PSSWD87]):

- Mengenorientierung an allen drei Schnittstellen

- Hierarchisch strukturierte Kernobjekte (Complex Records), die jeweils einen Speicher-Cluster bilden

Um die Mengenorientierung an der Kernschnittstelle zu realisieren, wird als Konzept ein neuer Puffer, der sog. **Objektpuffer**, eingeführt. Bei der Leseoperation wird z.B. dort die Ergebnismenge aufgefüllt. So wie mittels des Stable Memory Manager SMM die Daten zwischen externem Speicher und dem Seitenpuffer hin und her bewegt werden, transportiert der Complex Record Manager CRM die Daten zwischen dem Seiten- und dem Objekt-Puffer. Der Anwendungsspezifische Objekt Manager AOM bearbeitet die so ermittelten Daten weiter und führt dabei insbesondere auch Nicht-Kernoperationen aus. Ähnliche Konzepte wie unser Objektpuffer werden auch in der Architektur von anderen neueren Datenbanksystemen vorgeschlagen.

Das wesentliche Problem, das von der Objektpufferverwaltung gelöst werden muß, ist, eine Menge von strukturierten Objekten, die wiederum Mengen von gleichartigen Objekten enthalten können, zu verwalten. Jeder atomare Teil eines (Sub-)Objektes hat dabei variable Länge. Insgesamt wird also die wiederholte Anwendung des Konstruktes **set of record** benötigt, was in keiner der herkömmlichen Programmiersprachen in voller Allgemeinheit zugelassen wird. Eine Programmiersprache, die dieses Konstrukt anbietet, müßte

bei der Implementierung des Laufzeitsystems das lösen, was in DASDBS in der Objektpufferverwaltung realisiert ist.

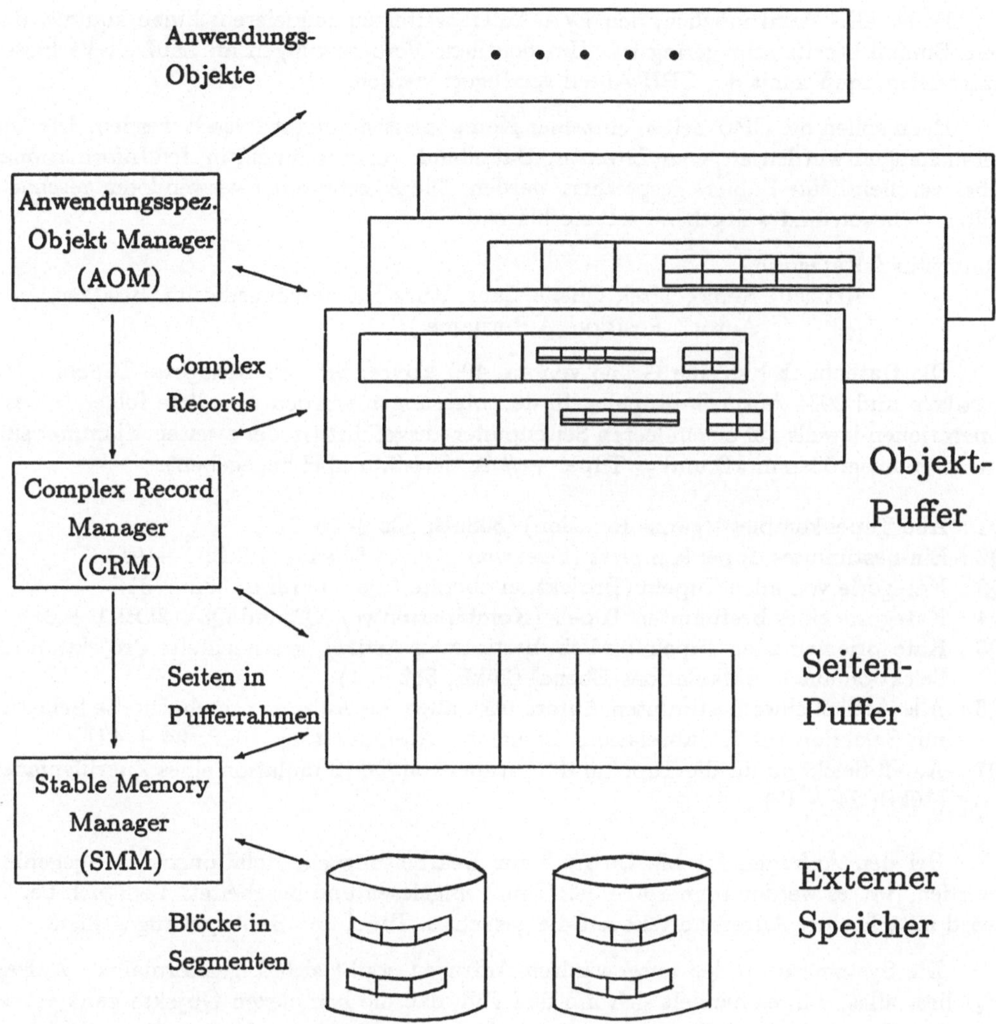

Abbildung 1: Seiten- und Objekt-Puffer zur Übergabe von Daten in verschiedenen
Abstraktionsebenen

2 Erste Beobachtungen zum Leistungsverhalten des Kernsystems

Die nachfolgenden Beobachtungen und Messungen wurden mit der PASCAL-Version des
Kernsystems von DASDBS gemacht, die auf dem Betriebssystem VM/CMS entwickelt
wurde. Details und genauere Analysen dieser Untersuchungen, die von Ende 1987 bis
Mitte 1988 durchgeführt wurden, finden sich in [Pau88].

Bei ersten Messungen stellte sich schnell heraus, daß es gelungen war, den Anteil
der Ein-/Ausgabe sehr niedrig zu halten. Dieser Erfolg wurde durch die Speicherungs-

strukturen (s. [DPSW88]) und der darauf aufbauenden Implementierung der linearen Kern-Operationen (s. [Pau88]) sowie durch den Einsatz von chained-I/O-Techniken an der Betriebssystem-Schnittstelle (s. [WNP87]) erreicht.

Es ist also kaum möglich, den E/A-Anteil weiter zu reduzieren; hinzu kommt, daß sein Einfluß bereits sehr gering ist. Um deutliche Verbesserungen im Laufzeit-Verhalten zu erzielen, muß somit der CPU-Anteil verringert werden.

Dazu sollen die CPU-Zeiten einzelner Komponenten aufgeschlüsselt werden. Die Untersuchungen wurden an einer Literatur-Datenbank vorgenommen, in der Informationen über veröffentlichte Papiere gespeichert werden. Die Attribute der verwendeten geschachtelten Relation sind weitgehend selbsterklärend:

Literatur (Kategorie,
        Artikel (Refno, Titel, Quelle, Jahr, Kürzel, Erfassungsdatum, Besitzer,
            Autor (Position, Autorname)))

Die Datenbank hat eine Größe von ca. 400 kByte, bei 382 Kategorie-Tupeln, 1506 Artikeln und 2934 Autor-Subtupeln. In den Messungen wurden vor allem folgende Leseoperationen jeweils auf einem leeren Seitenpuffer ausgeführt (in der zweiten Klammer sind die Ergebnisgrößen in kB und # Tupel + # Artikel-Subtupel angegeben):

Q1 : Alle Tupel komplett (ganze Relation) (308kB; 382 + 1506)
Q2 : Ein bestimmtes Tupel komplett (Selektion oberste Ebene) (16kB; 1 + 91)
Q3 : Kategorie von allen Tupeln (Projektion oberste Ebene) (18kB; 382 + 0)
Q4 : Kategorie eines bestimmten Tupels (Kombination von Q2 und Q3) (2kB; 1 + 0)
Q5 : Kategorie von allen Tupeln und ein bestimmter Artikel (geschachtelte Projektion mit
      Selektion auf 1. Subrelations-Ebene) (20kB; 382 + 1)
Q6 : Alle Artikel eines bestimmten Autors inkl. allen Ko-Autoren (geschachtelte Selektion
      mit Selektion auf 2. Subrelations-Ebene mit All-Operator) (10kB; 24 + 42)
Q7 : Adreß-Selektion für die Tupel und Subtupel von Q6 (Simulation eines Zugriffspfades)
      (10kB; 24 + 42)

Bei den Anfragen Q1 bis Q6 muß zur Bearbeitung ein Relationenscan ausgeführt werden, d.h. es werden immer alle 382 Tupel eingelesen und bearbeitet. Lediglich bei Q7 wird mittels einer Adresse direkt auf die gesuchten Tupel und Subtupel zugegriffen.

Die Systematik in den ausgewählten Anfragen ergibt sich folgendermaßen: Anfrage Q1 liest alles, d.h. es handelt sich um den Fall, daß die komplexen Objekte ganz gelesen werden. Das Datenbank-Kernsystem muß aber auch die Auswahl von Informationen gut unterstützen können. Als Beispiele dafür sind eine Selektion in Q2, eine Projektion in Q3 sowie die Kombination von beidem in Q4 angegeben. Diese Operationen betreffen die oberste Ebene der Relation. In Q5 und Q6 sind dagegen Selektionsbedingungen bei der 1. bzw. 2. Subrelations-Ebene angegeben. Da ein Kernsystem auch den direkten Zugriff auf einzelne Teile effizient ausführen soll, ist als Beispiel Anfrage Q7 angegeben. Sie hat dasselbe Ergebnis wie Q6, greift jedoch auf die Tupel und Subtupel direkt über die Adresse zu.

Anteile einzelner Komponenten an der Gesamtzeit

In Abbildung 2 sind die Anteile einzelner Kern-Komponenten an der Gesamt-CPU-Zeit angegeben. Die beiden Werte "Stable Memory Mgr. SMM" und "Objektpuffer-Verw. OBM" geben die gesamte CPU-Zeit aller Aufrufe in dem jeweiligen Modul an. Mit der Bezeichnung "Katalog & Anfrage-Baum" sind das Lesen des Katalogtupels inklusive dem Übertragen in einen Objektpuffer und das einmalige Bearbeiten des Anfragebaums gemeint. Der Wert "Complex Record Mgr. CRM" gibt die zur eigentlichen Verarbeitung der Complex Records benötigte Zeit an.

Messungen Literatur–Relation

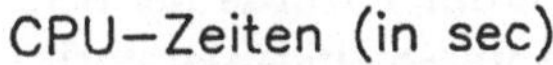

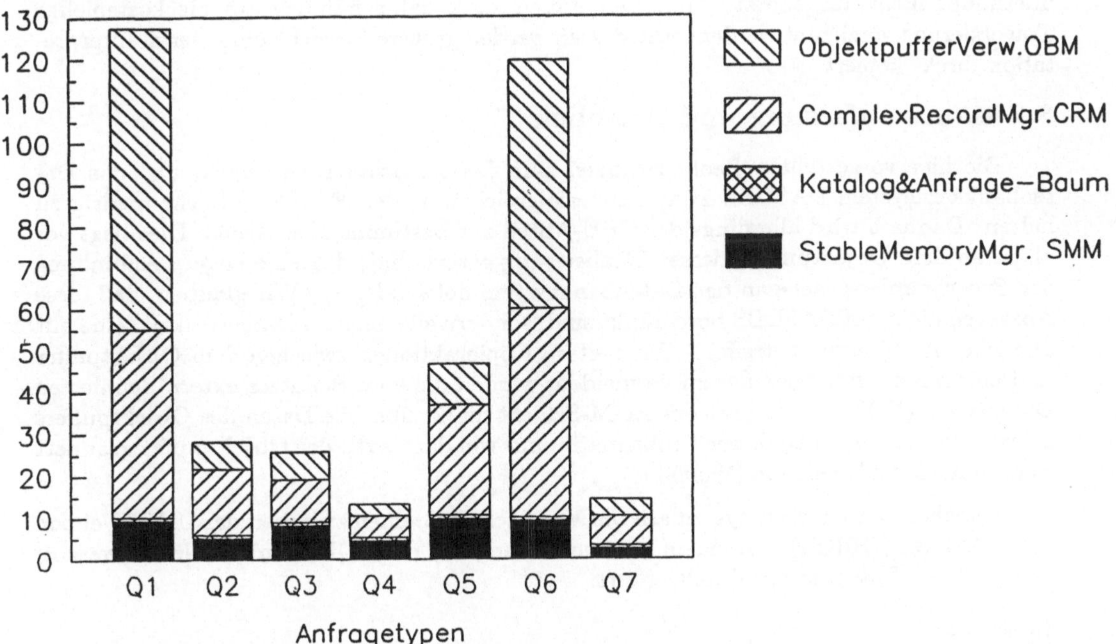

Abbildung 2: Meßergebnisse der einzelnen Anfragen

Während die Zahlen für SMM und Katalog relativ stabil sind, schwanken die anderen Werte beträchtlich. Dies liegt daran, daß die Zahl der zu interpretierenden Strukturen in den Seiten von der Anfrage und im Objektpuffer vom Ergebnis abhängen. Besonders auffallend ist der hohe Anteil des OBM, der teilweise über 50% liegt. Genauere Analysen dieses Verhaltens zeigen, daß der größte Teil der CPU-Zeit mit der Interpretation der internen Strukturen verbraucht wird. Diese Kosten entstehen dadurch, daß komplexe Objekte im Seitenpuffer analysiert und selektiert werden und anschließend evtl. in den Objektpuffer kopiert werden müssen. Dies ist wegen der Objektstruktur kein einfaches Kopieren, sondern erfordert eine Traversierung der komplexen Objekte. Dabei tritt gerade das oben dargestellte Problem der Einbettung von variabel großen Hierarchien in die Programmiersprache auf.

Da dies schon relativ früh als Problem erkannt wurde, sind verschiedene Alternativen zur Hauptspeicher-Repräsentation von Complex Records realisiert worden. In der ersten Variante werden die einzelnen Elemente eines Complex Records durch PASCAL-Zeiger miteinander verkettet. In der zweiten implementierten Variante besteht jeder Complex Record im Objektpuffer aus zwei variabel langen Bytestrings. In einem stehen die Datenwerte, in dem anderen Strukturinformationen mit Offsets in den ersten Bytestring. Bei der dritten Variante wird der Objektpuffer wie der Seitenpuffer in Kacheln oder Pufferrahmen aufgeteilt. Zur Darstellung der Tupel können dann die gleichen Verfahren wie bei den Seiten verwendet werden. Die durchgeführten Untersuchungen zeigen, daß zwischen einer Darstellung mit variabel langen Bytestrings und der mit den Seiten-Strukturen kein entscheidender Unterschied bzgl. der Performance besteht. Allerdings wurde bei bei der letzten Variante die Kenntnis über die Gleichheit der internen Tupel-Strukturen noch überhaupt nicht ausgenutzt. In vielen Fällen kann dabei nämlich auf die kostspielige Traversierung verzichtet werden; stattdessen werden größere Bereiche ohne deren Interpretation direkt kopiert.

3 Zusammenfassung und Ausblick

Die hier vorgestellten Beobachtungen zum Leistungsverhalten zeigen, daß das Datenbankkernsystem DASDBS zwar sehr erfolgreich war, den E/A-Anteil sehr niedrig zu halten. Dadurch wird allerdings der CPU-Anteil zur bestimmenden Größe. Dies liegt vor allem an dem Objektpuffer, dessen Realisierung gezeigt hat, daß eine engere Anbindung der Programmiersprache an das Datenbanksystem notwendig ist. Wir glauben, daß diese Aussagen nicht auf DASDBS beschränkt sind, sondern alle neueren Datenbanksysteme mit ähnlicher Architektur betreffen. Um weitere Kopieraktionen zwischen dem Objektpuffer und einem Anwendungspuffer zu vermeiden, werden die vom Benutzer extern definierten Datentypen (EDT's) innerhalb der AOM-Schicht direkt über die Daten des Objektpuffers gelegt. Überlegungen zu dieser Problematik und wie dazu evtl. der Objektpuffer geändert werden muß, finden sich in [Wol89].

Daneben werden z.Zt. systematische Vergleichsmeßreihen zwischen der UNIX-Version von DASDBS (DBKSI) und einem kommerziellen DBS mit SQL-Schnittstelle auf wesentlich größeren Datenbanken durchgeführt.

Literatur

[DPSW88] Deppisch, U., Paul, H.-B., Schek, H.-J., Weikum, G.: *Managing Complex Objects in the Database Kernel System*, to appear in: Buchmann, A., Dayal, U., Dittrich, K. (eds.): *Object-Oriented Database Systems*, Topics in Information Systems, Springer-Verlag, 1988

[Pau88] Paul, H.-B.: *DAS Datenbankkernsystem für Standard- und Nicht-Standard-Anwendungen, — Architektur, Implementierung, Anwendungen —*, Dissertation, Technische Hochschule Darmstadt, 1988

[PSSWD87] Paul, H.-B., Schek, H.-J., Scholl, M.H., Weikum, G., Deppisch, U.: *Architecture and Implementation of the Darmstadt Database Kernel System*, Proc. ACM SIGMOD Intl. Conf. on Management of Data, San Francisco, May 27-29, 1987, pp. 196-207

[WNP87] Weikum, G., Neumann, B., Paul, H.-B.: *Konzeption und Realisierung einer mengenorientierten Seitenschnittstelle zum effizienten Zugriff auf Komplexe Objekte*, in Schek, H.-J., Schlageter, G. (Hrsg.): Proc. GI-Fachtagung *Datenbanksysteme in Büro, Technik und Wissenschaft*, Darmstadt, 1.-3. April 1987, Informatik-Fachberichte 136, Springer-Verlag, 1987, S. 212-230

[Wol89] Wolf, A.: *Extern definierte Datentypen und Prozeduren in DASDBS*, in diesem Tagungsband

Anwendungsnahe Pufferung komplexstrukturierter Objekte - ein Erfahrungsbericht

Christoph Hübel, Martin Pick
Universität Kaiserslautern

1. Einleitung

Rechneranwendungen auf dem Gebiet der Ingenieursysteme bestimmen zunehmend neue Anforderungen an die Datenhaltung. Bereits frühzeitig wurden die in verfügbaren konventionellen Datenbanksystemen (DBS) angebotenen Konzepte als unzureichend erkannt. Ihr praktischer Einsatz resultierte in einem insgesamt sehr schlechten, nicht zu tolerierenden Leistungsverhalten. In der Datenbankforschung wurden daher in den vergangenen Jahren zahlreiche Ideen und Konzepte entwickelt, die eine angemessene Unterstützung von Ingenieuranwendungen durch sog. Nicht-Standard-Datenbanksysteme (NDBS) versprechen [Hä88, HR85, Lo85, LK84, Pa86, SS86]. Die vorgeschlagenen Ansätze betreffen in erster Linie die Architektur und die Datenmodellierungsmächtigkeit solcher Systeme. Neben der anwendungsneutralen und vor allem ganzheitlichen Beschreibung der häufig komplexstrukturierten Ingenieurobjekte sind Konzepte erforderlich, die eine einfache, direkte und möglichst effiziente Komplexobjektverarbeitung unterstützen.

Die dominierende Bedeutung des Verarbeitungsaspektes für das resultierende Leistungsverhalten wird klar, wenn man die Zugriffscharakteristik von Ingenieuranwendungen betrachtet. So sind Häufigkeiten zwischen 10^3 und 10^6 Referenzen im Rahmen einer einzigen Benutzerinteraktion nicht selten. Dabei sind oftmals über 90% der Datenreferenzen durch Zweit- oder Mehrfachzugriffe bedingt. Die in konventionellen DBS meist vorherrschende satz- oder tupelbezogene Verarbeitungsphilosophie [Co78, Da82] führt hier zu einem Verarbeitungsproblem: selbst wenn die Lokalität der Datenreferenzen auf DBS-Pufferebene ausgenutzt werden kann, resultiert die Pfadlänge des innerhalb des DBS auszuführenden Codes in einem unerträglich hohen Overhead. Eine mögliche Lösung sehen wir in der Nutzung der Verarbeitungslokalität nahe an ihrem Entstehungsort. Hierzu schlagen wir die anwendungsnahe Pufferung und damit verbunden eine stärkere Bindung der komplexstrukturierten Objekte an die Datenstrukturierungs- und Verarbeitungsmöglichkeiten der Anwendungsprogramme vor.

Im vorliegenden Beitrag sollen Erfahrungen aufgezeigt werden, die im Rahmen einer Prototypimplementierung basierend auf dem Konzept des anwendungsnahen "Objektpuffers" gemacht werden konnten. Ausgehend von dem 3D-Bauteilmodellierer KUNICAD [HHLM87], dessen Datenhaltung auf dem konventionellen DBS UDS [UDS88] aufbaut, wurde eine Objektpufferverwaltungskomponente (OPVK) realisiert und in das KUNICAD-System integriert. Das resultierende objektpuffergestützte System wird quantitativ bewertet und mit dem Ausgangssystem verglichen.

2. Integration einer anwendungsnahen Pufferverwaltung in das KUNICAD-System

In diesem Abschnitt wollen wir die entwickelte Objektpufferverwaltungskomponente und ihre Integration in den Bauteilmodellierer KUNICAD näher erläutern. Zunächst allerdings sollen die wesentlichen Eigenschaften sowie die Grobarchitektur des KUNICAD-Systems kurz zusammengefaßt werden. Eine detaillierte Systembeschreibung ist [HHLM87] zu entnehmen.

2.1 Das KUNICAD-System

Das KUNICAD-System ist ein datenbankgestütztes, volumenorieniertes Modellierungssystem für Werkstücke, das als Kernalgorithmus für die geometrische Modellierung ein volumenorientiertes Verfahren (CSG, constructive solid geometry [RV84]) einsetzt. Dabei werden Bauteile als Polyeder dargestellt, die aus Basiskörpern unter Anwendung zugelassener Operationen (u.a. Durchschnitt, Vereinigung, Differenz) gewonnen werden. Intern werden zusätzlich Strukturen nach dem Begrenzungsflächenmodell (BREP: boundary representation [RV84]) verwaltet, die automatisch aus den CSG-Strukturen abgeleitet und, falls erforderlich, nachgeführt

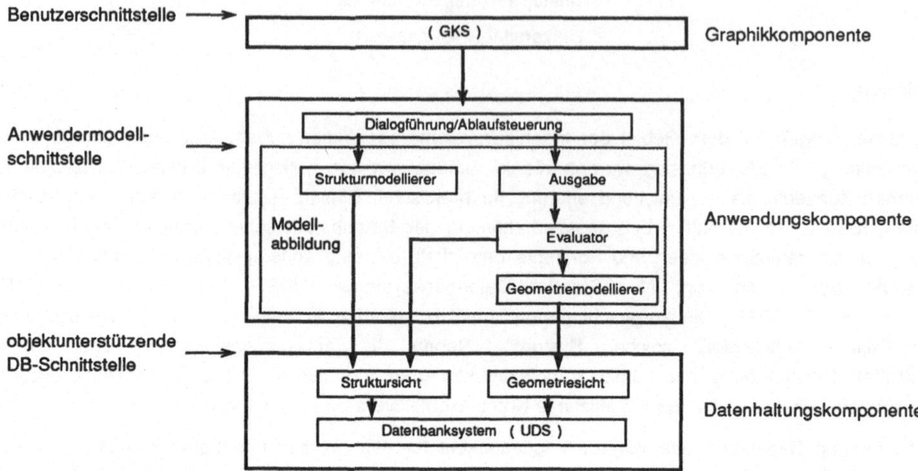

Bild 1 : Architektur des KUNICAD-Systems

werden. Das KUNICAD-System stellt ein sog. körperorientiertes "dual representation"-Modellierungssystem dar, da die rechnerinterne Darstellung der Konstruktionskörper einer CSG-BREP-Kombination entspricht. Die primäre, CSG-artige Darstellung erlaubt die direkte und einfache Abbildung des "Anwendermodells", während sich die optionale BREP-Darstellung, wegen ihrer Nähe zur Graphik-Repräsentation, u.a. sehr gut für Ausgabezwecke eignet.

Zu den Hauptkomponenten unseres datenbankbasierten 3D-Bauteilmodellierers gehört zum einen die Graphikkomponente, die Hilfsmittel zur Realisierung einer interaktiven, benutzerfreundlichen System-oberfäche zur Verfügung stellt. Ein anderer Teil des Systems, die Datenhaltungskomponente, verwaltet die rechnerinterne Darstellung der Konstruktionsdaten. Die dritte Schicht, die Anwendungskomponente, bildet die "Anwendersicht" auf die rechnerinterne "Datensicht" ab (vgl. Bild 1).

Die Graphikkomponente erlaubt der Anwendungskomponente die Ein- und Ausgabe graphischer und textueller Information. Die Funktionalität der Graphikschnittstelle entspricht der von GKS [GKS83]. Der Modul Dialogführung ist Bestandteil der Anwendungskomponente. Seine Hauptaufgabe besteht in der Vorverarbeitung der Ein- und Ausgabe sowie in der Entkopplung der implementierten Benutzerschnittstelle von der darunterliegenden Anwendermodellschnittstelle (auf der Ebene des Anwendermodells spielt es keine Rolle, ob die Benutzerschnittstelle menü- oder kommandogesteuert arbeitet bzw., ob eine Selektion durch eine "Pick"-Eingabe möglich ist oder nicht). Zusammen mit der Ablaufsteuerung werden die notwendigen Aktivitäten innerhalb der Modellabbildung angestoßen und kontrolliert. Die weiteren Moduln der Anwen-dungskomponente dienen der Modellabbildung, d.h. der Projektion der Anwendermodell-Objekte auf die Datenstrukturen und die damit assoziierten Operationen einer im System darunterliegenden Schnittstelle (Geometrie-/Struktursicht). Der Modul Strukturmodellierer verwaltet und aktualisiert die organisatorischen und strukturellen Konstruktionsdaten. Hierzu verwendet er Funktionen des Struktursichtmoduls an der Schnittstelle zur Datenhaltungskomponente. Der Modul Ausgabeaufbereitung übernimmt vorwiegend die Transformation der gespeicherten 3D-Information in eine 2D-Darstellung, die unmittelbar auf einem Graphik-Terminal sichtbar gemacht werden kann. In dem Modul Geometriemodellierer wird die eigentliche Verarbeitung der Geometriedaten durchgeführt. Geometrische Körperbeschreibungen können durch reguläre Mengenoper-ationen zu komplexeren Körperbeschreibungen aggregiert werden. Die Datenhaltungskomponente stellt im Modul Geometriesicht die hierzu erforderlichen Grundfunktionen bereit. Der Evaluator schließlich repräsentiert das Bindeglied zwischen der strukturellen (CSG) und der geometrischen (BREP) Interndar-stellung eines Werkstücks. Dieser Programmbaustein steuert die Berechnung der BREP-Darstellung eines Körpers aus seiner CSG-Repräsentation. Hiermit ist es möglich, vom Aufbau des CSG-Baumes ausgehend, erst zu einem späteren Zeitpunkt, zu dem eine geometrische Beschreibung tatsächlich benötigt wird, diese auch herzuleiten. Die Moduln Struktur- und Geometriesicht der Datenhaltungskomponente repräsentieren die sogenannte objektunterstützende DB-Schnittstelle und stellen die Implementierung einer "Zusatzebene" [HR85] auf dem zugrundeliegenden CODASYL DBS UDS [UDS88] dar. Sie stellen Objekte bereit, die von den Moduln der Modellabbildung auf vorteilhafte Art und Weise zu nutzen sind.

2.2 Die Objektpufferverwaltungskomponente

Der Objektpuffer dient zur "anwendungsnahen" Speicherung derjenigen Datenstrukturen, die in einem bestimmten Verarbeitungsabschnitt gerade den "Gegenstand der Verarbeitung" bestimmen. Das Ziel ist es, diese Daten im Vorfeld der eigentlichen Verarbeitung zu ermitteln, in den Objektpuffer einzulagern und möglichst eng an das Anwendungsprogramm zu binden, um dann in der anschließenden Bearbeitungsphase einen effizienten Zugriff zu erlauben. Nach der Verarbeitung durch die Anwendung kann der eventuell modifizierte Objektpufferinhalt wieder in den Datenbestand der Datenbank eingebracht werden. Die OPVK unterstützt demnach die ganzheitliche Handhabung der zur Repräsentation von Anwendungsobjekten erforderlichen komplexen Datenstrukturen.

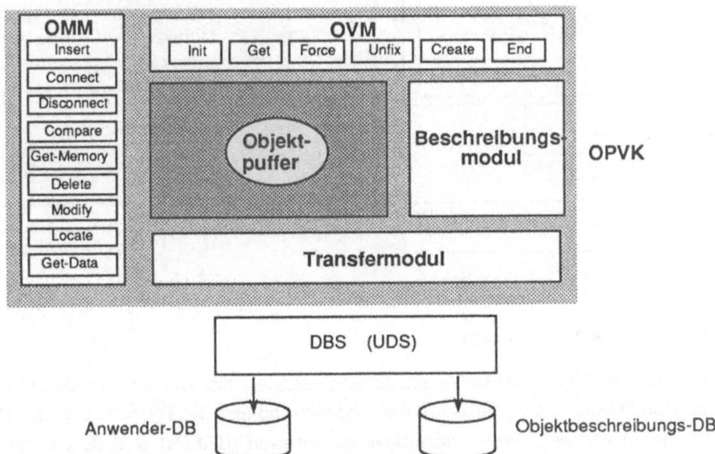

Bild 2 : Architektur der Objektpufferverwaltungskomponente

Bild 2 skizziert die Architektur der von uns realisierten OPVK, die wie das KUNICAD-System auf dem DBS UDS aufsetzt. Die Beschreibung der jeweiligen Verarbeitungsgegenstände erfolgt im wesentlichen durch Angabe der involvierten Satz- und Beziehungsarten und kann in einer speziellen Objektbeschreibungsdatenbank als Typinformation abgelegt werden. Die Generierung und der Zugriff auf diese Beschreibungsdaten obliegt dem Beschreibungsmodul, das dynamisch zur Laufzeit die zur Objektpufferverwaltung erforderlichen Informationen aus der Beschreibungsdatenbank extrahiert. Die konkrete Ausprägung eines Verarbeitungsgegenstandes wird durch den Identifikator eines ausgezeichneten Ankersatzes bestimmt, von dem ausgehend alle weiteren konstituierenden Satzausprägungen ermittelt werden können. Das Auffinden dieser Sätze in der Anwender-DB, das Aufbauen entsprechender Datenstrukturen im Objektpuffer sowie das Einbringen (Propagieren) von Änderungen aus dem Objektpuffer zurück in die Anwender-DB ist Aufgabe des Transfermoduls, das hierzu auf die vom Beschreibungsmodul extrahierten Informationen zurückgreift.

Die Schnittstelle zu den Anwendungsprogrammen ist durch das Objektmanipulationsmodul (OMM) und das Objektverwaltungsmodul (OVM) bestimmt. Das OMM stellt Funktionen zur navigierenden Verarbeitung der im Objektpuffer eingelagerten Datenstrukturen bereit. Die Funktionen des OVM ermöglichen dagegen die Kontrolle des Objektpufferinhaltes: neben der Initialisierung (Init) und der Terminierung (End) der objektpuffergestützten Verarbeitung können Beschreibungsdaten (Create) und Verarbeitungseinheiten (Get) angefordert bzw. wieder vollständig zum Verdrängen (Unfix) oder zum Propagieren von Änderungen (Force) freigegeben werden.

2.3 Das KUNICAD-OP System

Zur Validierung der realisierten Konzepte wurde die OPVK in das KUNICAD-System integriert. Die extrem aufwendige Geometriedaten-Verarbeitung sollte hierdurch im besonderen Maße unterstützt werden. Die Geometrie eines Bauteils, repräsentiert durch die Begrenzungsflächendarstellung (BREP), wurde daher als Verarbeitungseinheit bestimmt und in entsprechender Form in der speziellen Beschreibungs-DB abgelegt.

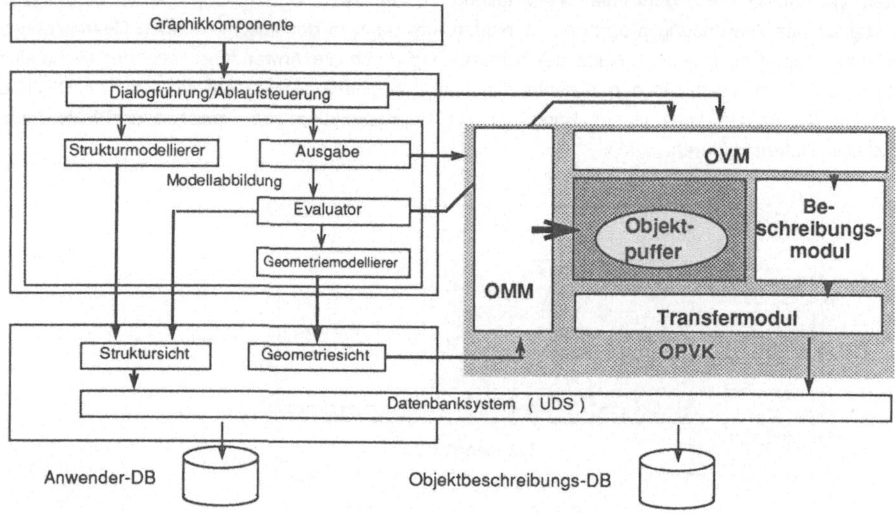

Bild 3: Architektur des KUNICAD-OP-Systems

Bild 3 zeigt die Architektur des KUNICAD-OP-Systems und illustriert die funktionalen Beziehungen zwischen den einzelnen Moduln. Das Dialogmodul übernimmt die Initialisierung und die Terminierung der OPVK. Das Einlagern bzw. das Propagieren von geänderten Verarbeitungseinheiten (BREPs) wird durch den Evaluator ausgelöst. Die eigentliche Verarbeitung, also der Zugriff auf die gepufferten Datenstrukturen erfolgt in den Moduln Geometriesicht und Ausgabeaufbereitung. Wie die Abbildung verdeutlicht, konnten wesentliche Teile des KUNICAD-Systems unverändert übernommen werden. Dialogsteuerung und Evaluator mußten geringfügig angepaßt werden (entsprechende OPVK-Steueranweisungen wurden eingebaut). Größere Änderungen waren dagegen in der Geometriesicht und der Ausgabeaufbereitung erforderlich. Besonders die Geometriesicht mußte wegen der von der DBS-Schnittstelle abweichenden Funktionalität des OMM entsprechend angepaßt werden.

3. Eine vergleichende Systembewertung

Die in Abschnitt 2.3 angesprochenen Anpassungen des KUNICAD-Systems an die OPVK betreffen im wesentlichen diejenigen Systemteile, die für die Datenversorgung verantwortlich sind, weniger dagegen die eigentlichen Verarbeitungsalgorithmen. Hieraus resultiert eine gute Vergleichbarkeit beider Systeme wodurch die Bewertung des eingeschlagenen Weges (also die anwendungsnahe Pufferung komplexstrukturierter Verarbeitungsgegenstände) anhand des erreichten Leistungsverhaltens ermöglicht wird.

Es wurden Zeit- und Häufigkeitsmessungen an den verschiedenen Systemebenen durchgeführt (die folgenden Zahlenangaben beruhen auf einem einfachen Anwendungsfall, nämlich der Vereinigung zweier sich durchdringender Basiskörper (Quader)). Unterschiedliche Aufrufhäufigkeiten treten verständlicher Weise nur an

DB-Operationen	KUNICAD	KUNICAD-OP
ACCEPT	5279	611
CONNECT	78	40
ERASE	36	-
GET	108	-
MODIFY	235	-
STORE	739	358
FIND/FETCH_KEY	5327	846
FIND/FETCH_ORDER	6456	403
FIND/FETCH_OWNER	3541	192
FIND/FETCH_7	700	-
OPVK-Operationen		
CONNECT	-	1316
DISCONNECT	-	260
DELETE	-	102
GET_DATA	-	3814
MODIFY	-	235
INSERT	-	257
LOCATE	-	6807
COMPARE	-	712
GET_MEMORY	-	871

ausschließlich durch das Transfermodul verursacht: 2455 Aufrufe

insgesamt 22511 Aufrufe

insgesamt 14374 Aufrufe

Tabelle 1: Aufrufhäufigkeiten bei der geometrischen Verknüpfung zweier Basiskörper (Quader)

der Schnittstelle zur OPVK und an der DBS-Schnittstelle auf. Tabelle 1 gibt hierüber näheren Aufschluß. Im KUNICAD-OP-System verursacht ausschließlich das Transfermodul Aufrufe an der DBS-Schnittstelle. Im vorliegenden Fall beträgt ihre Summe etwa 11% der in KUNICAD auftretenden DB-Operationen, was einem deutlichen Rückgang der unmittelbaren DB-Verarbeitung entspricht. Die markante Diskrepanz der Aufrufhäufigkeiten, die durch den Geometriemodellierer bzw. die Geometriesicht verursacht werden (22511/14374), erklärt sich aus der unterschiedlichen Funktionalität von DBS und OPVK. So ist es in der objektpufferbasierten KUNICAD-Variante z.B. nicht erforderlich, den Identifikator (DB-Key) einer Satzausprägung über eine spezielle Funktion (ACCEPT) zu beschaffen, da praktisch bei jedem OPVK-Aufruf eine Art "temporärer" Satzschlüssel mit zurückgeliefert wird. Dagegen ist die Aufrufhäufigkeit von Funktionen mit gleicher Semantik erwartungsgemäß dieselbe (z.B. MODIFY).

Bei den durchgeführten Zeitmessungen im KUNICAD-OP-System zeigte sich ein relativ hoher Anteil des Transfermoduls an den anfallenden Gesamtkosten (~38%). Dies sollte jedoch nicht verwundern, da für die Datenhaltung immer noch ein konventionelles DBS eingestetzt wird, das nur wenig auf die hier vorherrschenden Anforderungen zugeschnitten ist. Allerdings reduziert sich der Kostenanteill, da i.a. nicht jede BREP mo-

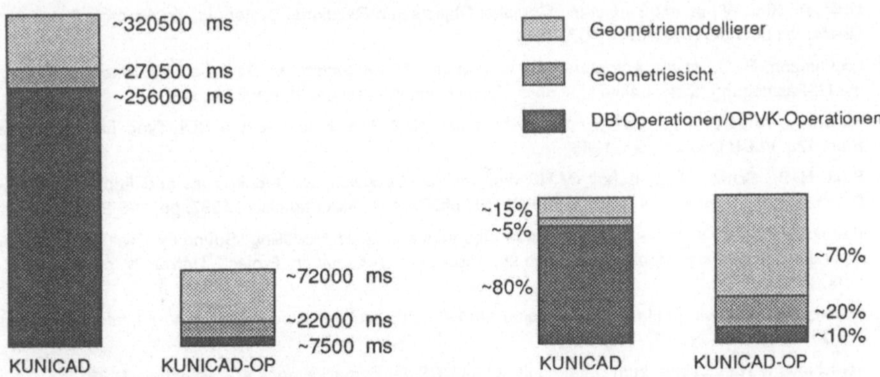

Bild 4: Verhältnis absoluter und relativer Ausführungszeiten

difiziert und damit in die Datenbank propagiert werden muß. Ebenso kann typischerweise eine höhere Lokalität vorausgesetzt werden, da eine einmal eingelagerte BREP meist von mehreren Benutzeraktionen betroffen ist. Dennoch muß festgestellt werden, daß die Datenbereitstellung auch weiterhin einen nicht unerheblichen Engpaß darstellt.

Zur Bewertung des realisierten Verarbeitungskonzeptes soll im folgenden der Kostenanteil für die Datenbereitstellung außer Acht gelassen werden. Bild 4 zeigt das Verhältnis der absoluten und der prozentualen Ausführungszeiten mit dem Anteil der einzelnen Systemebenen. Im vorliegenden Beispiel konnte die Antwortzeit auf 20% der ursprünglichen reduziert werden, wobei sich der auf die eigentlichen Datenzugriffe entfallende Anteil von 80% auf 10% verringerte. Es wird deutlich, daß durch Einsatz des Objektpuffers vor allem die Kosten für die Datenversorgung in der Verarbeitungsphase signifikant verringert werden konnte und sich damit eine "Normalisierung" bei der systeminternen Aufwandsverteilung eingestellt hat (vgl. Bild 4). Damit scheint insgesamt die prinzipielle Tauglichkeit des realisierten Konzeptes der anwendungsnahen Pufferung komplexer DB-Strukturen belegt, wenngleich zur weiteren Validierung noch umfassendere Anwendungsfälle in einem größeren Rahmen betrachtet werden müssen. Darüberhinaus ist eine Optimierung der Datenbereitstellung vorzunehmen, um eine realistische Gesamtbewertung zu ermöglichen.

Danksagung

Wir danken Herrn Prof. T. Härder für die hilfreichen Anmerkungen während der Entstehungsphase dieser Arbeit. Bei unseren Kollegen Herrn Dr. B. Mitschang und Herrn B. Sutter möchten wir uns für das sorgfälltige Korrekturlesen des Manuskripts bedanken.

Literatur

Co78   CODASYL Data Description Language Comittee Report, Information Systems, Vol. 3, No. 4, 1978, pp. 247-320.

Da82   Date, C.J.: An Introduction to Database Systems, third editon, Addison Wesley-Verlag, 1982.

GKS83   mehrere Artikel in: Informatik-Spektrum, Bd.6, Heft 2, Springer-Verlag, April 1983.

Hä88   Härder, T.: Overview of the PRIMA Project, in: The PRIMA Project, Design and Implementation of a Non-Standard Database System, Härder, T. (ed.), Forschungsbericht Nr. 26/88, SFB 124, Universität Kaiserslautern, 1988.

HHLM87   Härder, T., Hübel, Ch., Langenfeld, S., Mitschang, B.: KUNICAD - ein datenbankgestütztes geometrisches Modellierungsystem für Werkstücke, in: Informatik in Forschung und Entwicklung, Bd.2, Heft 1 , Springer-Verlag, 1987.

HR85   Härder, T., Reuter, A.: Architektur von Datenbanksystemen für Non-Standardanwendungen, in: Tagungsband der GI-Fachtagung "Datenbanken für Büro, Technik und Wissenschaft", Karlsruhe, 1985, pp. 253-286.

LK84   Lorie, R., Kim. W., et. al.: Supporting Complex Objects in a Relational System for Engineering Databases, IBM Research Laboratory, San Jose., CA, 1984.

Lo85   Lockemann, P. C., et al.: Anforderungen technischer Anwendungen an Datenbanksysteme, in: Tagungsband der GI-Fachtagung "Datenbanken für Büro, Technik und Wissenschaft", Karlsruhe, 1985.

PA86   Pistor, P., Anderson, F.: Designing a Generalized NF2 Data Model with a SQL-Type Language Interface, Proc. 12th VLDB Conf., Kyoto, 1986.

PSSWD87   Paul, H.-B., Schek, H.-J., Scholl, M.H., Weikum, G., Deppisch, U.: Architecture and Implementation of the Darmstadt Database Kernel System, in: ACM SIGMOD Conf., San Francisco, 1987, pp. 196-207.

RS82   Requicha, A.A.G., Voelcker, H.B.: Boolean Operations in Solid Modelling: Boundary Evaluation and Merging Algorithms. Technical Memorandum No.26, Production Automation Project, University of Rochester, New York, 1984.

SS86   Schek, H.-J., Scholl, M.H.: The Relational Model with Relation-Valued Attributes, in: Information Systems, Vol. 2, No. 2, 1986, pp. 137-147.

UDS88   verschiedene Handbücher zum Datenbanksystem UDS der Firma Siemens AG, München, 1988.

Parallelisierung von Anfragen auf komplexen Objekten durch Hash Joins

H. Zeller

Universität Stuttgart, Institut für Informatik, Azenbergstr. 12, D-7000 Stuttgart 1

Zusammenfassung. Relationale Datenbanksysteme sind von ihrer Leistungsfähigkeit her noch nicht für den Einsatz in technischen Datenbanken geeignet. Dieser Artikel befaßt sich mit Techniken zur Parallelisierung von Datenbankanfragen durch Hash Joins. Ein Schwerpunkt liegt auf der Untersuchung der Eigenschaften des Hash Join-Algorithmus' zur Verwendung für Anfragen auf komplexe Objekte. Neben Performanceaspekten werden auch Möglichkeiten zur Bearbeitung rekursiver Strukturen untersucht.

Abstract. Relational Databases currently do not provide the performance to be used in technical applications. This paper is concerned with methods for the use of hash joins for database queries. A major point in this paper is the application of hash join techniques in databases containing complex objects. Besides a discussion of performance aspects, the paper focuses on the usage of hash joins to process recursive joins.

1. Einführung

Im Datenbankbereich hat sich der Forschungsschwerpunkt mehr und mehr von den klassischen relationalen Systemen auf die sogenannten Nicht-Standard-Datenbanksysteme verlagert. Antrieb dieser Entwicklung ist der Wunsch, die Nutzung von Datenbanksystemen in neuen Anwendungsgebieten, wie z. B. CAD oder Expertensystemen, möglich zu machen [Haer85]. Bei herkömmlichen relationalen Datenbanksystemen scheitert dieses Vorhaben hauptsächlich an der nicht ausreichenden Verarbeitungsleistung. Im Rahmen des PROSPECT-Projektes (**PR**ocessor **O**rganizations **S**upporting **P**arallel **E**xecution of **C**omplex **T**ransactions) [Reut86, Dupp87] werden Methoden zur Parallelisierung von Datenbankoperationen auf Mehrprozessorrechnern entwickelt und geprüft. In diesem Artikel soll untersucht werden, wie sich Hash Joins zur Leistungssteigerung in DBS für komplexe Objekte einsetzen lassen. Ein Teil der vorgestellten Techniken ist aber ebenso auch auf konventionelle Anwendungen übertragbar.

Komplexe Objekte (Moleküle) sind aus Atomen verschiedenen Typs zusammengesetzt. In einem relationalen System entsprechen die Atome den Tupeln von Relationen. Ein Molekül muß daher durch einen Join verschiedener Relationen zusammengesetzt werden. Eine Möglichkeit, diesen Join zu beschleunigen, ist die Verteilung der Daten auf mehrere Platten, die eventuell von mehreren Prozessoren bedient werden. Durch paralleles Lesen der Platten erhöht sich die effektive I/O-Bandbreite des Systems. Die Verteilung von Atomen auf die Platten kann zufällig geschehen, üblicherweise wird aber der Ort der Speicherung eines Atoms durch dessen Primärschlüssel bestimmt.

Bei verteilten Ausgangsdaten bietet sich natürlich auch die Anwendung von verteilten, parallel arbeitenden Join-Algorithmen an. Zu dieser Klasse gehören die Hash Joins, die zunächst in Einprozessorsystemen verwendet wurden [DeWi84], dann aber wegen ihrer hervorragenden Eignung für parallele Systeme bald in Multiprozessorrechnern eingesetzt wurden [DeWi85, Gerb86].

2. Parallelisierung von Joins durch Anwendung von Hashfunktionen

2. 1. Konventionelle und auf Hashing basierende Joinverfahren

Das Ergebnis eines Joins besteht aus den Elementen des kartesischen Produkts der Ausgangsrelationen, die die Joinbedingung erfüllen. Eine Methode, einen Join auszuführen, ist daher die Bildung des kartesischen Produkts und die Selektion der durch die Joinbedingung qualifizierten Tupel. Dieses Verfahren entspricht dem sog. Nested-Loop-Join, wenn keine geeigneten Zugriffsstrukturen vorhanden sind. Die Kosten für dieses Verfahren wachsen mit $o(n^2)$ an, wenn n die Anzahl der Tupel in einer Ausgangsrelation ist[1]. Bild 1a zeigt den "Suchraum" für dieses Verfahren im Vergleich mit den Ergebnissen.

Eine Verbesserung der Kosten kann durch Verwendung von Indexstrukturen beim Nested-Loop-Join oder durch eine andere Methode, den Sort-Merge-Join, wie er z. B. in [Blas77] beschrieben ist, erzielt werden. Die Merge-Phase verursacht nunmehr nur noch Kosten, die mit $o(n)$ anwachsen (Bild 1b). In die Gesamtrechnung müssen allerdings auch die Sortierkosten ($o(n \log n)$) mit einbezogen werden. Es ergibt sich damit insgesamt ein Kostenmaß von n log n.

Mehrprozessor-Hash-Joins nutzen den vorhandenen Hauptspeicher wesentlich stärker aus als die anderen Verfahren und erzielen dadurch ein verbessertes Zeitverhalten. Dies wird durch folgende Maßnahmen erreicht:

- Eine Ausgangsrelation (üblicherweise die kleinere)[2] wird durch eine Hash-Funktion, die auf die Joinattribute angewendet wird, in p Partitionen, die auf p Prozessoren gehalten werden, aufgeteilt. Allein durch diese Maßnahme verringert sich der potentielle Suchraum für die Ergebnismenge (Bild 1c). Das entsprechende Kostenmaß würde

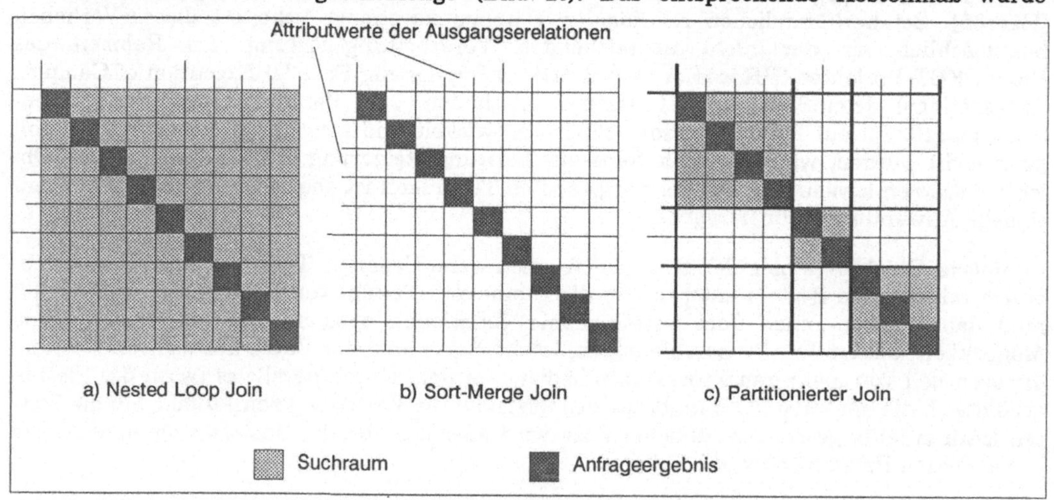

Bild 1: Vergleich von drei Joinverfahren

---

1)   Der Einfachkeit halber seien hier gleich große Ausgangsrelationen angenommen.

2)   Bei der Beschreibung wird zunächst von zwei Ausgangsrelationen ausgegangen, das Verfahren ist allerdings problemlos auf mehrere Relationen erweiterbar.

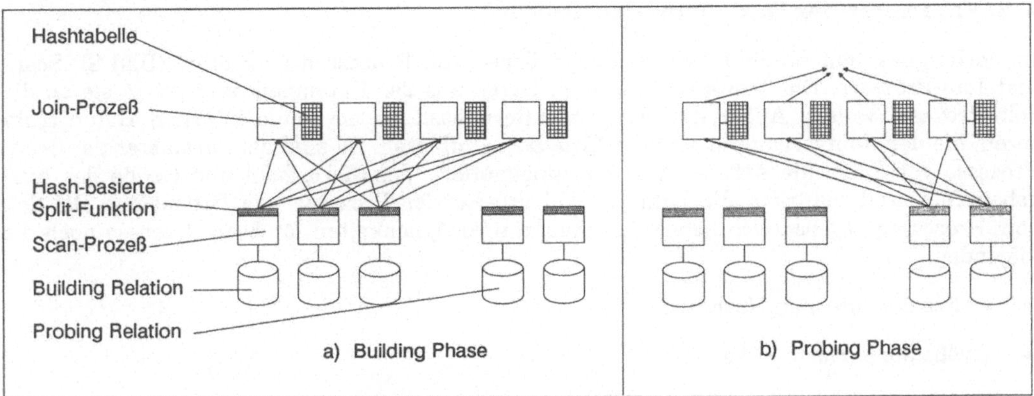

Bild 2: Phasen des Hash Join

$o((n/p)^2)$ betragen, wenn innerhalb der Partitionen ein Nested-Loop-Join ohne Indizes verwendet würde:

- Jeder Prozessor, der eine Partition zugeteilt bekommen hat, speichert deren Tupel in einer Hashtabelle im Hauptspeicher. Es wird davon ausgegangen, daß die Partition vollständig in den Hauptspeicher des Prozessors paßt. Andernfalls verringert sich die Effizienz des Verfahrens ganz erheblich. Diese erste Phase des Joinvorganges wird *Building Phase* genannt, die Relation die in dieser Phase verarbeitet wird, *Building Relation*. Der Ablauf der Phase ist in Bild 2a gezeigt.

- Nachdem die Hashstrukturen aufgebaut sind, kann in einer zweiten Phase (*Probing Phase*) die zweite Relation (*Probing Relation*) gelesen und nach den gleichen Kriterien (Anwendung der Hashfunktion auf die Joinattribute) verteilt werden (Bild 2b). Damit ist gewährleistet, daß Tupel der beiden Ausgangsrelationen, die gleiche Werte in den Joinattributen haben[1], auf demselben Prozessor verarbeitet werden. Das Ergebnis wird nun erzeugt, indem für jedes Tupel der zweiten Relation die entsprechenden Tupel der ersten in der Hashstruktur aufgesucht werden. Die zweite Relation verbraucht daher keinen Platz im Hauptspeicher, ihre Tupel wandern in p Strömen durch die Prozessoren.

Der Aufwand zur Erzeugung der Hashstrukturen wächst linear mit der Anzahl der Tupel, ebenso der Aufwand in der zweiten Phase, wenn die Menge der Ausgabetupel nicht quadratisch mit der Größe der Ausgangsrelationen wächst, was hier in keinem der Beispiele angenommen ist. Damit ergibt sich ein Kostenmaß, das nur mit o(n) (wie in Bild 1b) anwächst. Bei diesem günstigen Ergebnis ist allerdings zu berücksichtigen, daß die Ausgabetupel unsortiert sind. Ist eine Sortierung nach bestimmten Attributwerten verlangt, dann kann unter Umständen ein Sort-Merge-Join die effizientere Lösung sein. Liegt allerdings die zweite Ausgangsrelation bereits in der gewünschten Sortierreihenfolge vor und beziehen sich die Sortierkriterien nicht auf die erste Relation, dann kann mit nicht allzu hohem Aufwand diese Reihenfolge erhalten bleiben.

---

1)   Dies entspricht der Joinbedingung für einen sog. Gleichverbund. Joins anderer Art, die allerdings in der Praxis eher selten sind, können mit dem Verfahren nicht bearbeitet werden.

2. 2. Parameter des Hash Join-Algorithmus'

Im vorhergehenden Abschnitt wurden zwei Typen von Prozessen eingeführt (Bild 2): Scan-
und Join-Prozesse. Die Scan-Prozesse lesen Daten aus der Datenbank und geben sie an die
Join-Prozesse weiter. Außer den Ausgabepuffern besitzen sie keine internen Datenstrukturen, die den Joinvorgang in seiner Effizienz beeinflussen. So sind als Parameter der Scan-
Prozesse vor allem die Art der Ausgabe (ungepuffert, gepuffert, Zahl und Größe der Ausgabepuffer) und natürlich die Zahl parallel arbeitender Prozesse von Bedeutung. Bei den
Join-Prozessen ergeben sich neben den Steuerungsmöglichkeiten für Scan-Prozesse noch die
folgenden:

- Größe der internen Hashtabelle,

- Größe eines Hashblocks,

- Art des Hashverfahrens (Standardverfahren, Extendible Hashing),

- Art der Überlaufbehandlung.

Diese Parameter sind nicht ganz leicht zu bestimmen und beeinflussen den Algorithmus ganz
erheblich. Sendet ein Prozeß seine Ausgabetupel ungeblockt und synchron an seine Aus-
gabeprozesse, dann wird er einen großen Teil seiner Zeit im Wartezustand verbringen. Sollen
mehrere Tupel in einer Botschaft zusammen gesendet werden, dann muß pro Ausgabeprozeß
ein Puffer vorhanden sein.

Die Zahl der parallel arbeitenden Joins richtet sich natürlich in erster Linie nach der Anzahl
der vorhandenen Prozessoren und deren Hauptspeicherkapazitäten. Eine wichtige Forderung
ist, daß alle beteiligten Prozesse die Bearbeitung ihrer Partition ungefähr zur gleichen Zeit
abgeschlossen haben sollten, denn sonst bleiben die restlichen Prozessoren in der Wartezeit
auf den letzten Prozeß ungenutzt. Bei unterschiedlichen Belastungen der Prozessoren (CPU-
Auslastung, verfügbarer Hauptspeicher) durch andere Anwendungen kommen daher auch unterschiedlich große Partitionen in Betracht.

Die Größe der Hashtabelle bestimmt – wenn nicht geeignete Überlauftechniken vorgesehen
werden – die maximale Anzahl der Tupel, die die Tabelle aufnehmen kann. Ist die Größe der
Building Relation bekannt, dann ist diese Größe noch mit einiger Sicherheit bestimmbar. Zu
bedenken ist jedoch, daß die Größe für jede Partition angegeben werden muß und dadurch ein
gewisser Zuschlag für eventuelle Ungleichgewichte in der Partitionierung hinzukommen
muß. Schwieriger zu schätzen ist die Größe von Relationen, die als Zwischenergebnisse
auftreten. In diesem Fall muß entwender eine Überlaufstrategie entwickelt oder ein erweiter-
bares Hashverfahren [Enbo88] eingesetzt werden.

2. 3. Verwendung von Hash Joins für komplexe Objekte

Prinzipiell unterscheidet sich der für komplexe Objekte verwendete sog. *implizite* Join nicht
von üblichen relationalen Join-Operatoren. Er besitzt lediglich einige Eigenschaften, die An-
satzpunkte für eine Optimierung bieten. Da die Attribute, auf die sich implizite Joins
beziehen, bekannt sind, ist es dem Datenbanksystem möglich, wesentlich genauere Angaben
bzw. Schätzungen über deren Schlüsseleigenschaften, Werteverteilungen und Kardinalitäten
zu machen. Implizite Joins sind oft Mehrwege-Joins. Mehrwege-Joins führen eine weitere
Dimension bei den Parallelisierungsmöglichkeiten ein: die parallele Ausführung eines n-
Wege-Joins. Auch dafür eignen sich Hash Joins hervorragend. Beim Zugriff auf ein komplexes
Objekt wird von einem einzigen "Ankeratom" ausgegangen. Nur Atome, die mit diesem Anker
in Beziehung stehen, sind für das Anfrageergebnis interessant. Es kann daher ineffizient
sein, Joins ganzer Relationen durchzuführen, weil sich nur wenige Tupel qualifizieren. Unter

diesem Aspekt empfiehlt sich eine schrittweise Bearbeitung von Mehrwege-Joins ausgehend vom Ausgangstupel, so daß sich nicht qualifizierende Tupel bereits in den Zwischenergebnissen eliminiert werden. Diese Vorgehensweise steht allerdings im Widerspruch zum Versuch der Parallelisierung.

Bei der Berechnung rekursiver Joins (z. B. Stücklistenauflösung) werden Zwischenrelationen verwendet, die zu Beginn kreiert und teilweise nach jedem Iterationsschritt geleert werden müssen. Die dadurch entstehenden Kosten können beträchtliche Höhen erreichen. Auch der mehrmalige Anstoß des Join-Operators ist ein Kostenfaktor. Eine Lösung, die in einem logischen Auftrag die gesamte Hülle berechnet und keine Zwischenrelationen im Datenbanksystem kreiert, kann die Hüllenbildung effizienter machen. Im folgenden wird eine Modifikation des Hash Join-Algorithmus' vorgeschlagen, durch die diese Eigenschaften erreicht werden können.

Bei der Bearbeitung von n-Wege-Joins unterscheidet H. Gerber in seiner Arbeit [Gerb86] links-tiefe (left-deep) und rechts-tiefe (right-deep) Operatorbäume (Bild 3). Während ein n-Wege-Join in einem links-tiefen Baum in n Phasen abgearbeitet wird, benötigt er im rechts-tiefen Baum nur zwei Phasen. Das Problem des rechts-tiefen Baumes ist, daß in allen Knoten gleichzeitig die Hashtabellen gebildet werden und die Prozesse somit um die knappe Ressource Hauptspeicher konkurrieren. Beim links-tiefen Baum sind dagegen immer nur in zwei Knoten Hashtabellen angelegt. Bei Joins mit kleinen Selektivitäten hat der links-tiefe Baum ebenfalls Vorteile, da nur wenige Tupel in den Zwischenergebnissen enthalten sind, die in der Hashtabelle der nächsthöheren Stufe abgelegt werden müssen. Wenn dieser Effekt vorausberechenbar ist, kann die Hashtabelle entsprechend klein angelegt werden. Zusammenfassend ist daher zu sagen, daß sich rechts-tiefe Bäume nur dann lohnen, wenn genügend Hauptspeicher vorhanden ist, und daß bei Joins mit erwiesenermaßen kleinen Selektivitäten die Probing Relation eine Basisrelation sein sollte.

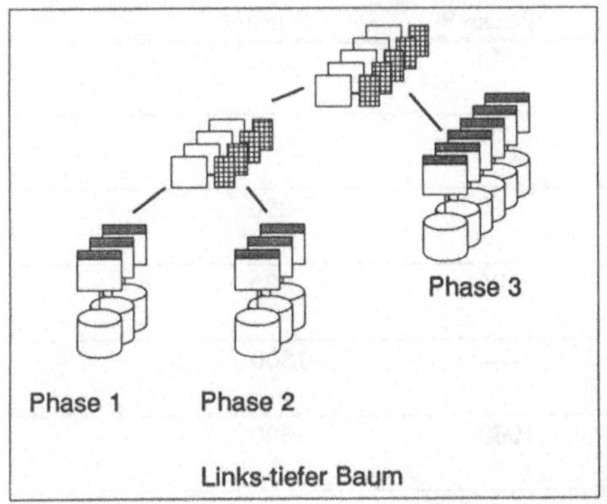

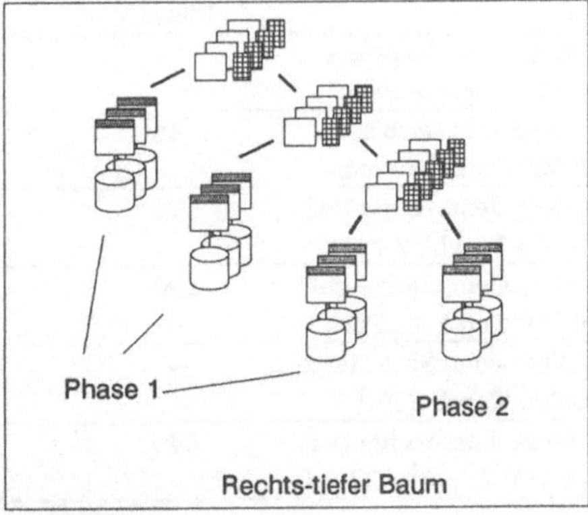

Bild 3: Links-tiefe und rechts-tiefe Bäume

Bei der Betrachtung des rechts-tiefen Baumes in Zusammenhang mit der Berechnung rekursiver Joins (z. B. von Stücklisten) liegt es nahe, die Rekursion auf einfache Weise durch Rückkopplung des Ergebnisstroms zur Basisrelation zu realisieren. Bei der hier verwendeten Anfragesprache leistet der rekursive Join die Aufgabe, die mit dem gesuchten Molekül zusammenhängeden Atome zu finden. Das Ende der Berechnung ist dann erreicht, wenn ein Iterationsschritt keine neuen Tupel mehr liefert. Um dies festzustellen kommen die folgenden Möglichkeiten in Betracht:

- Die Join-Ergebnisse werden ebenfalls in einer Hashtabelle gehalten. Tupel, die von einem Join-Prozeß als Ergebnis ausgegeben werden und schon in der Tabelle enthalten sind, werden verworfen. Durch eine Statusvariable wird angezeigt, ob in einem Iterationsschritt noch neue Tupel erzeugt wurden.

- Um die weitere Hashtabelle für das Ergebnis einzusparen, wird die Tabelle der untersten Join-Prozesse (die die rückgekoppelten Daten erhalten) verwendet. Nachdem ein Tupel der Probing Relation einen solchen Prozeß passiert hat, werden die Tupel aus der Building Relation gelöscht, die sich qualifiziert haben. Dieses Vorgehen ist jedoch nur dann zulässig, wenn die Joinattribute bei der Probing Relation Schlüsseleigenschaft haben.

Im vorangegangenen Text war die Rede von *aufeinanderfolgenden* Iterationsschritten. Dies heißt, daß der Rückkopplungszweig einen Puffer enthalten muß, der die Tupel eines Iterationsschrittes aufnehmen kann, denn ein an den Join-Prozeß gesendetes Tupel erscheint ja nach kurzer Zeit wieder im Strom der Ergebnistupel. Ist dieser Puffer voll, dann entsteht ein Deadlock. Kritisch ist die Puffergröße vor allem in Phasen der Berechnung, bei denen pro Eingabetupel mehrere Ergebnistupel entstehen. Dennoch ist die Verwaltung dieses Puffers kein wirkliches Problem. Es wäre außerdem wünschenswert, die Iterationsschritte nicht streng sequentiell, sondern überlappend auszuführen – während die Basisrelation gelesen wird, können bereits Tupel des Rückkopplungszweiges verarbeitet werden. Dies erfordert zusätzlichen Verwaltungsaufwand, auf den an dieser Stelle nicht eingegangen werden soll.

2. 4. Ergebnisse erster Messungen

Ein einfacher Hash Algorithmus (Standard-Hashverfahren, keine Rekursion) wurde auf einem TANDEM System unter Verwendung des TANDEM-Datenbanksystems NonStop SQL [Tand88] implementiert. Die folgende Tabelle gibt eine Übersicht über die ersten Leistungsmessungen.

Antwortzeiten (in Sekunden):

Anfrage	Phase 1	Phase 2	Phase 3	Summe
3-Wege-Join, links-tief 40 000 Tupel, 8 Part.	30	40	45	115
3-Wege-Join, rechts-tief 40 000 Tupel, 8 Part.	45	—	50	95
3-Wege-Join, rechts-tief 60 000 Tupel, 12 Part.	90	—	110	200
6-Wege-Join, rechts-tief 60 000 Tupel, 12 Part.	200	—	130	330
3-Wege-Join, Sort-Merge 80 000 Tupel, SQL[1]	—	—	—	1300
3-Wege-Join, rechts-tief 600 000 Tupel[2], 12 Part.	540	—	1960	2500

Zur Messung wurde eine Wisconsin-Datenbank [Bitt83] mit 80 000 bzw. 800 000 Tupeln in einer Relation verwendet. Als Meßumgebung diente das 16-Prozessorsystem des Tandem High Performance Research Center in Frankfurt. Die Relationen wurden partitioniert auf 16 Platten abgespeichert. Es wurden 3-Wege- und 6-Wege-Joins unter Verwendung von 8 bzw.

---

1)   Dies ist eine Vergleichsmessung mit dem Standard-Interface zu NonStop SQL

2)   Während bei den anderen Joins fünf Attribute mit insgesamt 26 Byte pro Relation verwendet wurden, wurde dieser Join mit nur jeweils einem Attribut (4 Byte) durchgeführt.

12 Partitionen durchgeführt. Die Messungen von 60 000 und 600 000 Tupeln sind leider nicht ganz mit den anderen Werten vergleichbar, da hier weniger Ausgabepuffer verwendet wurden. Es fällt hier z. B. auf, daß das Einlesen von 12 Partitionen 90 Sekunden benötigt, während 8 Partitionen in 45 Sekunden gelesen werden. Bei gleicher Zahl von Puffern sollten die Zeiten in etwa gleich sein. Dies gilt auch für die dritte Phase.

3. Zusammenfassung

Neben der physischen Clusterung von logisch zusammengehörigen Daten ist auch eine breite Verteilung aller Daten auf mehrere Prozessoren und Platten ein Ansatz zur Effizienzsteigerung in Datenbanksystemen. Insbesondere bei technischen Anwendungen, bei denen komplexe, netzwerkartige Beziehungen, Generalisierungshierarchien und rekursive Beziehungen auftreten, scheint die zweite Möglichkeit bedenkenswert. Die vorliegende Arbeit sollte zeigen, daß die Verteilung von Daten über Hashverfahren eine einfache Möglichkeit bietet, Anfragen auf komplexe Objekte zu parallelisieren. Auch rekursive Berechnungen können durch Hash Joins effizient bearbeitet werden.

4. Literatur

[Bitt83]   D. Bitton, D. J. DeWitt, C. Turbyfill
Benchmarking Database Systems - A Systematic Approach
Proc. VLDB 1983, pp. 8-19

[Blas77]   M. W. Blasgen, K. P. Eswaran
Storage and Access in Relational Data Bases
IBM Systems Journal No. 4, 1977, pp. 363-377

[DeWi84]   D. J. DeWitt, R. H. Katz, F. Olken, L. D. Shapiro, M. Stonebraker, D. Wood
Implementation Techniques for Main Memory Database Systems
Proc. ACM SIGMOD Conference, 1984, pp. 1-8

[DeWi85]   D. J. DeWitt, R. H. Gerber
Multiprocessor Hash-Based Join Algorithms
Proc. 1985 VLDB, pp. 151-164

[Dupp87]   N. Duppel, P. Peinl, G. Schiele, H. Zeller
Progress Report #2 of PROSPECT
University of Stuttgart, Department of Computer Science, Internal Report

[Enbo88]   R. J. Enbody, H. C. Du
Dynamic Hashing Schemes
ACM Computing Surveys 20, 2 (1988), pp. 85-113

[Gerb86]   Gerber, Robert Howard
Dataflow Query Processing Using Multiprocessor Hash-Partitioned Algorithms
Dissertation, University of Wisconsin-Madison, Computer Sciences Technical Report #672, Oct.86

[Haer85]   Th. Härder, A. Reuter
Architektur von Datenbanksystemen für Non-Standard-Anwendungen
Proc. GI-Fachtagung Karlsruhe, Springer Informatik-Fachberichte Nr. 94

[Reut86]   A. Reuter, N. Duppel, P. Peinl, G. Schiele, H. Zeller
An Outlook on PROSPECT
University of Stuttgart, Department of Computer Science, Internal Report

[Tand88]   S. W. Thompson (Ed.)
TANDEM Systems Review (Several Papers on NonStop SQL)
Vol. 4, No. 2, (July 1988): TANDEM Computers, 18922 Forge Drive, LOC 216-05, Cupertino, CA 95014

Wissensbasierte Werkzeuge zur Leistungsoptimierung objektorientierter Datenbanksysteme

Karol Abramowicz

Forschungszentrum Informatik
an der Universität Karlsruhe
Haid-und-Neu-Straße 10–14
D–7500 Karlsruhe 1
CS-Net: abram@ira.uka.de

Zusammenfassung

Verschiedene Anwendungsbereiche objektorientierter Datenbanksysteme zeichnen sich durch sehr unterschiedliche Anforderungsprofile aus. Bisher ist es noch nicht gelungen, allen diesen Anforderungen mit Hilfe eines statisch konfigurierten Datenbanksystems auf eine effiziente Weise genüge zu tun. Obwohl aus der Literatur sehr viele Methoden der Leistungssteuerung, welche eine Anpassung an die erwarteten Anforderungen erlauben, bekannt sind, werden diese nur selten in vollem Umfang eingesetzt. Gründe dafür liegen im großen Aufwand, der mit manueller Leistungssteuerung verbunden ist, und in unpräzisen oder inkonsistenten Informationen über die Einsatzbereiche, Nebenwirkungen und Interferenzen zwischen den einzelnen Methoden der Leistungssteuerung. Einen Vorschlag zur Verbesserung dieser Situation stellt der Einsatz wissensbasierter Werkzeuge dar.

Abstract

Object-oriented database management systems are currently proposed for many application areas. Profiles of these areas differ significantly from each other. Up to now, it has not been achieved to build a single statically-configurated DBMS which may be used in any application areas with the desired efficiency. Although many methods of performance control may be found in the literature on database systems, only few of them are used simultaneously in single DBMS implementations. The high effort of manual performance control and a missing or inconsistent knowledge about methods (side-effects, possible interactions between them) are reasons for this situation.
In this paper we propose to develop a knowledge-based toolkit for the acquisition and management of information for performance control. A generator of application programs and an expert system have been developed and implemented at FZI. We describe the architecture of our first prototypes and directions for our next steps.

1 Einleitung

In letzter Zeit wurden mehrere objektorientierte Datenbanksysteme entwickelt (*PROBE* [Daya87], *PRIMA* [Härd88], *POSTGRES* [StRo85], O_2 [Banc88], *ORION* [Kim87], *GENESIS* [Bato86], *EXODUS* [Care86], *DAMOKLES* [DiGL87]), welche für verschiedene Anwendungsbereiche (CAD/CAM–Systeme, Elektronik — Entwurf von VLSI-Chips, Softwareproduktionsumgebungen, Verwaltung von Multimediadatenbeständen oder komplexen Wissensbasen) vorgesehen sind. Die verschiedenen Anwendungen stellen allerdings ganz unterschiedliche Anforderungen an die eingesetzten Datenbanksysteme. Als wichtigste Unterschiede zwischen den Anwendungsprofilen können hier genannt werden: Größe einfacher Objekte, Komplexität strukturierter Objekte, Kardinalität von Beziehungen zwischen Objekten, Überlappung von strukturierten Objekten, Anzahl und Größe langer Felder, Größe des Datenbestandes, Zugriffsmethoden, Art der Anfragen (interaktiv/batchorientiert), Ein- oder Mehrobjektschnittstelle, Frequenz und Dauer jeweiliger Anwendungen (rund um die Uhr, einige Anfragen pro Tag).

Bei heutigem Stand der Hardwareentwicklung und der Datenbanktechnologie ist es noch nicht gelungen, ein Datenbanksystem zu implementieren, das ohne jegliche Änderung das breite Spektrum der so unterschiedlichen Anforderungen auf eine effiziente Weise befriedigen könnte. Andererseits gestatten es die hohen Kosten der Softwareentwicklung nicht, für jeden Anwendungsbereich ein spezielles, dediziertes Datenbanksystem zu realisieren. Ein Ausweg aus diesem Dilemma besteht in der Entwicklung sehr flexibler Datenbanksysteme, die sich auf möglichst einfache Weise an die aktuellen Anforderungen anpassen lassen. Da eine solche Anpassung ein nicht triviales Problem darstellt, müssen entsprechende Unterstützungswerkzeuge (z. B. zum Sammeln und Bereitstellen von Informationen über Anpassungsmöglichkeiten, zur Durchführung der Anpassung und zur Leistungsmessung) entwickelt werden. In diesem Beitrag wird vorgeschlagen, wissensbasierte Werkzeuge zu diesem Zweck einzusetzen.

2 Methoden der Leistungssteuerung

In der Datenbankliteratur wurden viele Verfahren beschrieben, die zur Leistungsteuerung eingesetzt werden können. Diese Verfahren lassen sich nach mehreren Kriterien klassifizieren. Die folgende Klassifizierung basiert auf den Einsatzpunkten der einzelnen Verfahren – von der Softwareerstellung bis zu automatischer Optimierung im laufenden Betrieb.

KONFIGURATION

Aufgrund ihrer Komplexität werden Datenbanksysteme nur selten "am Stück" implementiert, sondern zumindest konzeptuell in eine Menge unabhängiger, überschaubarer Komponenten zerlegt ([Lien87]). Auf diese Weise ist es möglich, für bestimmte Teilaufgaben mehrere Alternativlösungen zu implementieren. Die einzelnen Alternativen haben die gleichen Schnittstellen, was problemlosen Austausch ermöglicht. Die *leistungsbezogene* Konfiguration besteht in der Auswahl solcher Module, die in ihrem Zusammenwirken den erwarteten Anforderungen am besten genügen. Beispielsweise würden für eine geowissenschaftliche Anwendung spezielle mehrdimensionale physische Zugriffspfade und eine Speicherverwaltung ausgewählt, die sehr große Datenbestände unterstützen können. Existiert für ein bestimmtes Anwendungsprofil keine effiziente Implementierung eines Moduls, kann mit Hilfe einer Modulschablone[1] eine Reimplementierung eines Moduls durchgeführt werden.

Um die leistungsbezogene Softwarekonfiguration eines Datenbanksystems erfolgreich durchzuführen, braucht man einerseits eine möglichst genaue Beschreibung der Anwendung und der vorgesehenen Umgebung (Hardware, Betriebssystem, benutzte Software usw.), andererseits müssen die Einsatzbereiche der einzelnen Implementierungsalternativen und die Interferenzen zwischen Modulen bekannt sein.

TUNING

Bei vielen Problemen ist es möglich, die Systemkonstanten (z. B. Größe des Seitenpuffers, Abstand zwischen Reorganisationszeitpunkten) variabel zu halten. Durch Änderungen der Werte kann das Verhalten des Datenbanksystems beeinflußt werden. Systemvariable lassen sich in drei Klassen aufteilen:

- Variablen, deren Werte jederzeit im laufenden Betrieb geändert werden können;
- Variablen, deren Änderung eine Stillegung des Betriebs und anschließend einen Warmstart erfordert;
- Variablen, die nur einmal beim Kaltstart gesetzt werden müssen und später nicht mehr geändert werden dürfen.

DATENTRANSFORMATIONEN

Aus der Literatur sind mehrere Transformationen des primären/sekundären Datenbestandes bekannt, die eine Leistungsoptimierung des Datenbanksystems als Ziel haben. Als Beispiele solcher Transformationen können hier genannt werden:

- Clusterung aller Unterobjekte eines strukturierten Objektes;
- Änderung des physischen Zugriffspfades (z.B. Umwandlung eines B^*-Baumes in eine Hashtabelle oder umgekehrt);

---

[1] die Schablone eines Moduls besteht aus den Schnittstellen der angebotenen Prozeduren, den nach außen sichtbaren Datenstrukturen und den potentiell anwendbaren Prozeduren anderer Module.

- Reorganisation des Hintergrundspeichers.

PRE-/POSTWORKING

Pre-/Postworking sind Techniken, welche auf der Verschiebung der Durchführungszeitpunkte für bestimmte Aufgaben basieren, wobei man beim Preworking Aufträge auf Verdacht bearbeitet und beim Postworking die Aufträge speichert, die später durchgeführt werden können. Beispiele:

- Werden in einem Anwendungsprogramm nur wenige Suchausdrücke erwartet, so können sie vorher übersetzt und optimiert werden.
- Prefetching von Objekten, die in einer Beziehung zu den bereits angeforderten Objekten stehen.
- Die Änderungen innerhalb einer Transaktion werden nur in einer Logdatei vermerkt. Erst nach dem Commit werden die eigentlichen Datenbereiche aktualisiert und die Logdatei gelöscht.

UNTERSTÜTZUNG DER LAUFZEITENTSCHEIDUNGEN

Im laufenden Betrieb werden im Datenbanksystem viele Entscheidungen getroffen, z. B. Auswahl der Seite, welche aus dem Seitenpuffer ausgelagert werden muß, Strategie zur Verteilung des Datenbestandes über mehreren Knoten in einem verteilten Datenbanksystem. Diese Entscheidungen können entweder nach einer statischen Strategie oder unter Berücksichtigung des aktuellen Zustandes des Datenbanksystems und der zu erwartenden Belastungen fallen.

3 Einsatz von Maßnahmen zur Leistungsteuerung

SZENARIUM DER LEISTUNGSSTEUERUNG

Der Prozeß der Leistungssteuerung in einem Datenbanksystem kann unter Berücksichtigung der eingesetzten Maßnahmen und Einsatzzeitpunkte in vier Phasen (Abb. 1) aufgeteilt werden.

1. *Die erste Phase besteht in der Softwareentwicklung des Datenbanksystems.* Während dieser Zeit werden Entscheidungen sowohl über die Auswahl der Implementierungsalternativen als auch über die Flexibilität des gesamten Systems getroffen.

2. *Die Anpassung beim Softwarehersteller auf die spezifischen Anforderungen des Kunden (customization)* [Haas88]. In dieser Phase wird vor allem Softwarekonfiguration und Grobtuning des Systems durchgeführt.

3. *Die Installation und die Systempflege des Datenbanksystems durch den Datenbankadministrator oder durch den Anwender.* Dabei kann ein Feintuning des Systems und die Anpassung der in Anspruch genommenen Software-/Hardwarekomponenten durchgeführt werden.

4. *Die automatische Optimierung ohne Einsatz des Datenbankadministators (Anwenders).* Zu dieser Phase gehören automatische Reorganisationsverfahren, Wahl der Laufzeitentscheidungen usw.

Während jeder Phase werden die aktuellen Ergebnisse der Leistungssteuerung ausgewertet. Falls die Leistung im laufenden Betrieb das erwartete Niveau nicht erreicht hat und alle in Frage kommenden Methoden eingesetzt worden

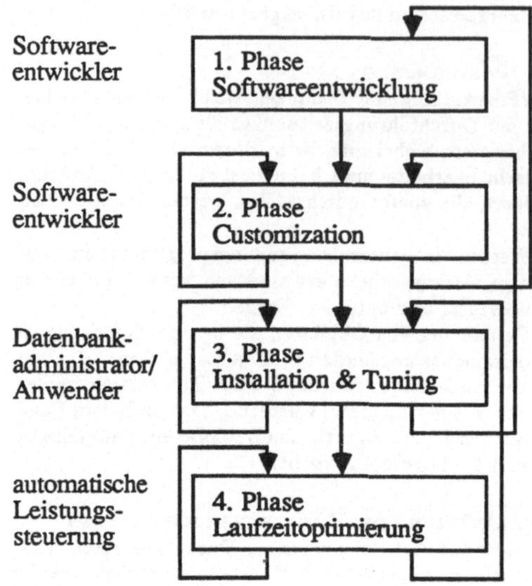

Abb. 1. Phasen der Leistungssteuerung eines Datenbanksystems

sind, ist es erforderlich die Phase (3) — die Systempflege — erneut durchzuführen. Bringen die iterativ nacheinander folgenden Phasen (3) und (4) nicht das gewünschte Ergebnis, muß die Phase (2) nochmals durchlaufen werden.

Ein wichtiger Punkt stellt das Gewährleisten der Konsistenz innerhalb aller Phasen dar. Während der Durchführung jeder Phase müssen die Ergebnisse und eingesetzten Methoden der vorherigen Phase bekannt sein. Das Problem wird dadurch erschwert, daß es für jede Phase einen unterschiedlichen Kreis (Softwareentwickler, Datenbank- /DV-Administrator, Anwender) von zuständigen Personen gibt. Deswegen ist es wichtig, den Informationsaustausch zwischen den Personengruppen maschinell zu unterstützen.

TRADE-OFF DER LEISTUNGSSTEUERUNG

Während des Prozesses der Leistungssteuerung muß darauf geachtet werden, daß alle Aufwände, die im Laufe der Optimierung anfallen (Monitoring des Datenbankverhaltens, Entscheidungsvorbereitung und Durchführung), niedriger sind als die erwarteten Leistungsgewinne. Dies ist keine Selbstverständlichkeit — für manche Speicherreorganisations- oder Clusterungsverfahren kann das Trade-off Verhältnis durchaus schlecht sein. Um solche Situationen zu vermeiden, müssen folgende Regeln beachtet werden:

- Viele Methoden der Leistungssteuerung können nur unter ganz besonderen Bedingungen eingesetzt werden. Werden diese Bedingungen nicht erfüllt, disqualifizieren sich die Methoden. Es gibt so gut wie keine Methoden, die keine Nebenwirkungen verursachen.
- Die Ergebnisse der Optimierung sind umso besser, je genauer die Anforderungen (Lasten, Laufzeitumge-

bung, Optimierungskriterien) spezifiziert sind. Wenn die Anforderungen nicht genau genug bekannt sind, sollen keine Optimierungsmaßnahmen eingesetzt werden, die als Nebeneffekte Effizienzeinbußen verursachen könnten.

- Zwischen einzelnen Optimierungsmaßnahmen können Interferenzen existieren. Die Einsatzentscheidungen müssen also aufeinander abgestimmt werden.

Aus diesen Gründen gibt es bisher nur wenige Datenbanksysteme, in denen parallel mehrere Methoden der Leistungsoptimierung eingesetzt werden.

QUALITATIVES UND QUANTITATIVES WISSEN ÜBER METHODEN DER LEISTUNGSSTEUERUNG

Das Wissen über Methoden der Leistungssterung setzt sich aus qualitativen und quantitven Teilen zusammen. Der qualitative Teil macht eine Aussage darüber, zu welchem Zweck ein Verfahren eingesetzt werden kann: (z. B. verringert die Clusterung komplexer Objekte die Zahl der Plattenzugriffe). Der quantitive Teil beschreibt dagegen, wann ein Verfahren eingesetzt werden kann (z. B. Clusterung komplexer Objekte, deren Gesamtgröße 100 KB übersteigt, beschleunigt das Bereitstellen eines Objekts durchschnittlich um 20 %).

Das qualitative Wissen über Methoden der Leistungssterung kann aus den Erfahrungen anderer Systeme gewonnen werden. Das quantitative Wissen dagegen wird fast ausschließlich durch eigene empirische Erfahrungen gesammelt. Damit das quantitative Wissen eingesetzt werden kann, ist es wichtig, daß zur Formulierung der Ursachen-Folge-Abhängigkeiten die DML-Termini benutzt werden. Beispielsweise kann keine Ersetzungsstrategie für den Seitenpuffer gewählt werden, solange die Folgen einer DB-Operation für den Puffer unbekannt sind. Das Einfügen eines Objektes verlangt mehrere Seitenoperationen. Dies ist wieder abhängig von der Realisierung und Konfigurierung der Abbildung der Objekte auf Seiten, Art der Zugriffspfade usw.

Das Sammeln des quantitativen Wissens über die Möglichkeiten der Leistungssteuerung in einem Datenbanksystem stellt einen recht komplexen Prozeß dar, der im Folgenden kurz skizziert wird.

1. Analyse der Einzelfälle (Situation X → Methode Q);
2. Synthese der Einzelfälle zu möglichst allgemeinen Faustregeln (Situation X oder Situation Y → Methode Q);
3. Aggregation der Methoden (Folgen(Q & R) = Folgen(Q) & Folgen(R)?)

Angesichts der Komplexität dieses Problems ist es nicht möglich, über das gesamte Wissen zu verfügen. Man sollte also solche Modelle der Leistungskontrolle konstruieren, die mit vagem und unvollständigem Wissen arbeiten können.

4 Werkzeuge zur Unterstützung der Leistungssteuerung

In der Datenbankgruppe des FZI werden zur Zeit Arbeiten an Werkzeugen zur Unterstützung der Leistungsoptimierung objektorientierter Datenbanksysteme geführt. Diese Aktivitäten haben als Ziel eine Unterstützung des Pro-

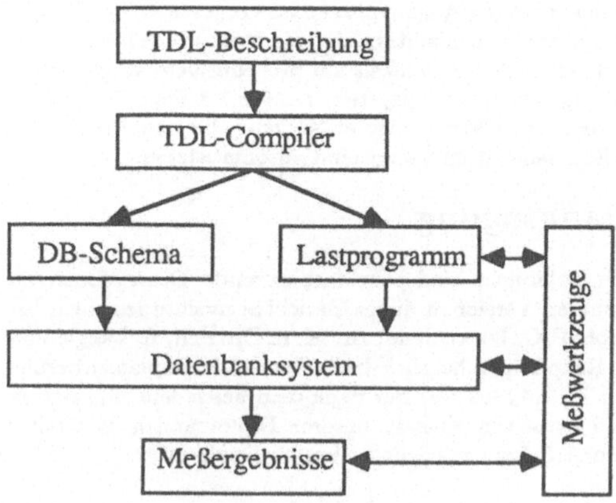

Abb. 2. Einsatzschema eines Lastgenerators

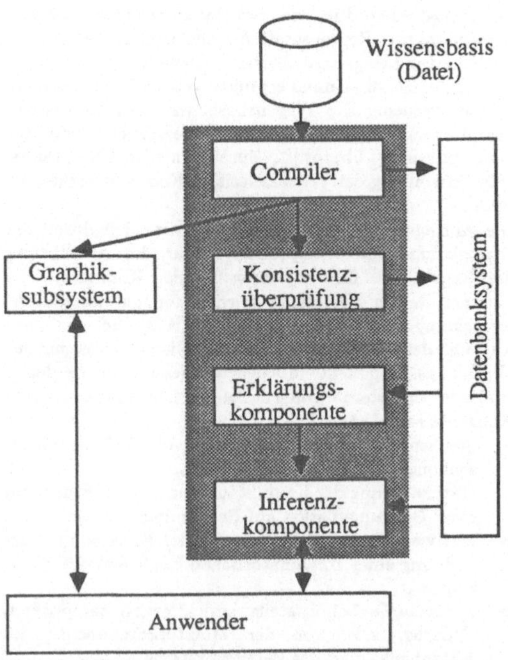

Abb. 3. Architektur des Expertensystems zur Leistungssteuerung von Datenbanksystemen.

zesses der Leistungssteuerung existierender Datenbanksysteme und gleichzeitig das Beschaffen der Grundlagen zum Konstruieren neuer Datenbanksysteme, die über eine erhöhte Flexibilität verfügen. Es ist geplant, eine integrierte, automatische, lernfähige Umgebung zu entwickeln. Bisher wurden zwei Werkzeuge, ein Lastgenerator und ein Expertensystem implementiert. Die ersten Prototypen, welche im Augenblick getestet werden, sind für unser eigenes Datenbanksystem *DAMOKLES* ([DiGl87]) vorgesehen. Eine Portierung auf andere Datenbanksysteme, obwohl wegen der Anpassung an eine neue Datenbankschnittstelle aufwendig, ist denkbar.

In Folgenden werden die Architektur, die Aufgaben und Besonderheiten dieser Werkzeuge skizziert.

LASTGENERATOR

Das Sammeln des quantitativen Wissens über Methoden der Leistungssteuerung kann entweder durch Erstellen eines Simulationsmodells beziehungsweise durch Messung des Verhaltens des Datenbanksystems erfolgen. Das Erstellen eines Simulationsmodells für ein Datenbanksystem ist sehr aufwendig. Zusätzlich muß berücksichtigt werden, daß jede Änderung im Datenbanksystem eine Modifikation des Simulationmodells zur Folge hat. Im Falle der Leistungsmessung am Datenbanksystem sind entsprechende Anwendungsprogramme notwendig. Der Vorteil des Simulationsverfahrens besteht in der Möglichkeit der Simulation von Laufzeitumgebungen, die momentan nicht vorhanden sind (z. B. ein 10-mal schnellerer Prozessor).

Der im FZI [Schm88] entwickelte Lastgenerator funktioniert nach folgendem Schema (Abb. 2): Der Anwendungsbereich, für welchen eine Leistungsoptimierung stattfinden soll, wird mit Hilfe der Sprache TDL[2] beschrieben. Die Mächtigkeit der implementierten Sprache umfaßt sowohl einfache DML-Operationen (z. B. Einfügen, Löschen eines Objektes) als auch komplexe Ausdrücke (z. B. Einfügen eines Baumes beliebiger Höhe). Die Operationen können kombiniert werden. Die Sprache ist so konstruiert, daß die Beschreibung einer Last mit möglichst geringem Aufwand erfolgen kann. Die TDL-Beschreibung wird übersetzt und

---

[2]Task Description Language

als Ergebnis ein Anwendungsprogramm (und ein Datenbankschema) erzeugt. Das generierte Programm kann dann ausgeführt werden. Während des Programmlaufs kann die Leistung des Datenbanksystems und die Effektivität der einzelnen Leistungssteuerungmaßnahmen mit Hilfe der Werkzeuge des Betriebssystems gemessen werden. Die Messungen werden unter ständigem Einsatz der unterschiedlichen Maßnahmen so oft wiederholt, bis das gewünschte Ergebnis erreicht wird. Der Lastgenerator ermöglicht das Feststellen der Abhängigkeiten zwischen den Lasten und der Leistung des Datenbanksystems.

EXPERTENSYSTEM ZUR LEISTUNGSOPTIMIERUNG

Das Wissen über die Einsatzbereiche von Maßnahmen zur Leistungsoptimierung ist zwischen mehreren Personen aufgeteilt (vgl. Kapitel 2). Bei der Implementierung eines Datenbanksystems sind mehrere Softwareentwickler engagiert. In den späteren Phasen des Lebenszyklus wird die Leistungssteuerung entweder durch einen lokalen Datenbankadministrator (falls vorhanden) oder durch den Anwender durchgeführt. Für die Qualität der Leistungsoptimierung ist also eine gute Kommunikation zwischen allen Teilnehmern des Optimierungsprozesses und das kontinuierliche Gewährleisten der Konsistenz des Wissens wichtig. Zur Erfüllung dieser Aufgabe wurde das Expertensystem *DION* realisiert [Grei88], welches seine Wissensbasis durch *DAMOKLES* verwalten läßt.

Die Komponenten des Expertensystems werden auf der Abbildung 3 veranschaulicht. Das Wissen wird in einer regelbasierten Sprache formuliert. Diese externe Wissensrepräsentation wird in eine vom Datenbanksystem akzeptierbare interne Repräsentation transformiert und in den Datenbestand eingefügt. Dieser Prozeß erfolgt inkrementell, das heißt, die einmal erzeugte Wissensbasis kann erweitert werden. Die Wissensbasis wird auf Konsistenz (Zusammengehörigkeit, Zyklen-, Widerspruchs- und Redundanzfreiheit) überprüft. Zusätzlich wird eine graphische Darstellung der Wissensbasis zu Kontrollzwecken erstellt.

Die Anfragen an das Expertensystem werden durch die Dialogkomponente interpretiert. Für die Ausführung der Regeln und für die Auflösung der Konflikte, falls mehrere Regeln ausgeführt werden können, ist die Inferenzkomponente verantwortlich. Während des Dialogs mit dem Benutzer können die Dienstleistungen der Erklärungskomponente in Anspruch genommen werden.

Im Expertensystem wurden außerdem folgende zusätzliche Konzepte realisiert:

- Strukturierung der Wissensbasis mit Hilfe des Klassenkonzepts;
- Unterstützung der Konfliktauflösung durch Einführen einer Ordnungrelation auf Regeln und Klassen;
- Aktivierung und Deaktivierung der Klassen zur Vermeidung einer kombinatorischen Explosion des Suchraumes.
- Prozedurale Schnittstelle zum Erwerb temporären Wissens, z. B. von der Monitorkomponente des Datenbank- oder des Betriebssystems.

Die enge Kopplung des Expertensystems mit dem Datenbanksystem hat sich als Erfolg erwiesen. Neben dem wesentlich kleineren Implementierungsaufwand ist es möglich, auch sehr große Wissensbasen auf eine effiziente Weise zu verwalten. Da *DAMOKLES* die Überlappung von komplexen Objekten zuläßt, kann der Speicherbedarf einer Wissensbasis erheblich reduziert werden, da die Teilprämissen, welche in mehreren Regeln teilnehmen, nur einmal gespeichert werden.

ERSTELLEN DER WISSENSBASIS

Das Erstellen der Wissensbasis erfolgt in zwei Etappen; in der ersten Etappe, während der Softwareentwicklung, werden die Informationen über eingesetzte Verfahren aus dem Bereich der DB-Technologie und über Abhängigkeiten zwischen Modulen des Datenbanksystems in Form von Regeln eingetragen. In der zweiten Etappe, nach der Fertigstellung des Datenbanksystems, wird mit Hilfe des Lastgenerators eine Menge von Anwendungsprogrammen erzeugt. Die Programme werden mehrmals ausgeführt, jeweils mit Verwendung unterschiedlicher Optimierungsmaßnahmen. Das auf diesem Wege gewonnene qualitative und quantitative Wissen wird durch das Expertensystem verwaltet.

5 Ausblick und weitere Arbeiten

Die Testphase der skizzierten Werkzeuge ist zwar noch nicht abgeschlossen, erste Versuche deuten aber auf eine gute Laufzeiteffizienz hin. Eine frühe Erzeugung der Wissensbasis ermöglicht das Erkennen von Widersprüchen und erleichtert eine Verallgemeinerung der gewonnenen Erfahrungen. Dadurch wird vermutlich eine Verkürzung der Zeit erreicht, die zur Erstellung der Wissensbasis notwendig ist.

In den weiteren Ausbauphasen ist vorgesehen, das Expertensystem so zu erweitern, daß die Module des Datenbanksystems auch zur Laufzeit auf prozeduralem Wege Anfragen an das Expertensystem richten können. Zusätzlich werden neue Werkzeuge entwickelt, die den Prozeß der Wissensaquisition weitgehend automatisieren.

Danksagung

Für zahlreiche und sehr inspirierende Disskusionen an früheren Versionen dieses Berichtes möchte ich mich bei Prof. P. C. Lockemann, Dr. K. R. Dittrich, R. Längle und T. Raupp sehr herzlich bedanken. Die Implementierung der Prototypen war nur dank dem besonders engagierten und kreativen Einsatz unserer Diplomanden M. Greiter und A. Schmutz möglich – besten Dank dafür.

Literaturverzeichnis

[Banc88] F. Bancilhon et al: *The Design and Implementation of O_2, an Object-Oriented Database System*, Proc. 2nd Int. Workshop on Object-Oriented Database Systems, 1988

[Bato86] D. S. Batory et al: *GENESIS: A Reconfigurable Database Management System*, Department of Computer Science, University of Texas at Austin, TR-86-07, 1986

[Care86] M. J. Carey et al: *The Architecture of the EXODUS Extensible DBMS*, Proc. 1st Int. Workshop on Object-Oriented Database Systems, 1986

[Daya87] U. Dayal et al: *Simplifying Complex Objects: The PROBE Approach to Modelling and Quering Them*, Proc. BTW 1987, pp. 17–37

[DiGL87] K. R. Dittrich, W. Gotthard, P. C. Lockemann: *DAMOKLES – the Database System for the UNIBASE Software Engineering Environment*, IEEE Data Engineering 10 (1987) 1, pp. 2–21

[Haas88] L. M. Haas et al: *An Extensible Processor for an Extended Relational Query Language*, IBM Research Report RJ 6182 (60892), 1988

[Härd88] T. Härder (ed.): *The PRIMA Project – Design and Implementation of a Non-Standard Database System*, Report No. 26/88, University Kaiserslautern, 1988

[Grei88] M. Greiter: *DION – Ein Expertensystem zur Unterstützung der Leistungssteuerung eines objektorientierten Datenbanksystems*, Diplomarbeit FZI, 1988

[Kim87] W. Kim: *Features of the ORION Object-Oriented Database System*, MCC Technical Report, 1987

[Schm88] A. Schmutz: *Lastgenerator für ein objektorientiertes Datenbanksystem*, Diplomarbeit FZI, 1988

[StRo85] M. Stonebraker, L. A. Rowe: *The Design of POSTGRES*, Memorandum No. UCB/ERL 85/95, University of California, Berkeley 1985

Eine Anfragesprache
für ein strukturell-objektorientiertes Datenmodell

Bernhard Schiefer   *Simone Rehm*

Forschungszentrum Informatik an der Universität Karlsruhe
Haid-und-Neu-Straße 10-14, D-7500 Karlsruhe 1

Kurzfassung

Semantisch reichhaltige Datenmodelle, wie sie beispielsweise in Entwurfsdatenbanken verwendet werden, erfordern angemessene Anfragesprachen, die deren Konzepte widerspiegeln. Im Mittelpunkt dieses Beitrags steht CERMoQL, eine Anfragesprache für ein strukturell-objektorientiertes Datenmodell, welches sich dadurch auszeichnet, daß es neben der Beschreibung von Objekten und allgemeinen n:m Beziehungen auch ein Konzept zur Modellierung strukturierter Objekte vorsieht. Diese Beschreibungsmittel finden in CERMoQL-Anfragen ihre Entsprechung. Die Struktur der abgelegten Entwurfsobjekte sowie deren Einbettung in ein Objekt-/Beziehungsgeflecht wird somit für den Benutzer sichtbar. CERMoQL ist mengenorientiert und gleicht auf den ersten Blick SQL. Unterschiede liegen in der Formulierung der FROM-Klausel. Mit Hilfe der FROM-Klausel kann ein Benutzer beliebige Wege entlang eines Objekt-/Beziehungsgeflechts beschreiben und so strukturbezogene Einschränkungen formulieren, die die Ergebnismenge betreffen sollen. Wertbezogene Einschränkungen sind in der WHERE-Klausel enthalten, während die SELECT-Klausel die Form der Ausgabe bestimmt. Die Möglichkeit, rekursive Anfragen bezogen auf die transitive Hülle einer Beziehung und deren "Geschichte" zu formulieren, verleiht der Sprache eine höhere Ausdruckskraft als die vergleichbarer ER-Sprachen. Die Leitlinien des Sprachentwurfs, insbesondere diejenigen, die sich aus dem Datenmodell ableiten, werden grob geschildert. Die Syntax von CERMoQL wird an Beispielen verdeutlicht.

Abstract

Appropriate high-level query languages are needed to reflect the semantics of advanced data models, as they are used in design data bases. This paper presents CERMoQL, a high-level query language for a structurally object-oriented data model. Queries against data structures of any complexity can be expressed by means of CERMoQL. Thus, the complex structure of the stored design objects and associations between them are visible to the user. The language is similiar to SQL. The FROM-clause represents structural conditions concerning the data to be retrieved, whereas value-based restrictions have to be specified in the WHERE-clause. The SELECT-clause determines the output of the result. The power of CERMoQL goes beyond the power of existing ER-languages by allowing a large class of recursive queries. Some general features that are useful for querying structured objects are summarized in this paper followed by an informal description of CERMoQL. Examples are given to illustrate the semantics of the basic concepts.

1. Einleitung

Der Einsatz von Datenbanktechnologie zur Unterstützung von Entwurfsanwendungen erfordert ein geeignetes Datenmodell, das eine problemgerechte Abbildung der Entwurfswelt auf die Datenbank erlaubt. Anforderungsanalysen, die u.a. im Bereich der Softwareentwicklung durchgeführt wurden ([Lock85], [Ditt87], [DAMO87]), ergaben die Notwendigkeit, geeignete Beschreibungsmittel für *komplexe Sachverhalte* zur Verfügung zu stellen. Die komplexen Sachverhalte spiegeln sich in der inneren Struktur einzelner Gegenstände (z. B.: Dokument besteht aus ...) ebenso wider, wie in den Abhängigkeiten, die diese Gegenstände untereinander eingehen (z. B.: Ein Dokument beschreibt ein Modul).

Diese Sachverhalte sollten auch im Ergebnis des konzeptuellen Entwurfs sichtbar sein. Auf der Suche nach Datenmodellen, die dieser Anforderung gerecht werden, bot sich das *Entity-Relationship (ER) Modell* an, das 1976 von Chen vorgestellt [Chen76] wurde. Es findet im Bereich semantischer Datenmodellierung weite Verbreitung. Gegenstände der Umwelt werden darin als *Objekte* und deren Zusammenhänge als *Beziehungen* beschrieben. Sowohl Objekte als auch Beziehungen können mit Attributen versehen sein. Sie repräsentieren deren Eigenschaften. Das ER-Modell eignet sich für den konzeptuellen Datenbankentwurf, da es sich in einfacher Weise auf das Relationenmodell oder andere implementierte Datenmodelle abbilden läßt.

Die oben beschriebenen komplexen Sachverhalte finden in diesem Modell jedoch keine direkte Entsprechung, denn es sind lediglich "flache" Objekte und Beziehungen zwischen diesen vorgesehen. Es gibt keine Möglichkeit, *strukturierte* Objekte zu definieren. Der Objektbegriff mußte daher entsprechend angereichert werden.

Das Datenbanksystem DAMOKLES[1], das am Forschungszentrum Informatik an der Universität Karlsruhe entwickelt wurde, weist an seiner Schnittstelle ein solches angereichertes Datenmodell auf, das strukturierte Objekte nebst allgemeinen Beziehungen kennt und das zusätzlich ein Konzept zur Modellierung von Versionen vorsieht. Es zählt zur Klasse der *strukturell-objektorientierten Datenmodelle* [Ditt86] und erlaubt die Modellierung beliebiger Objekt-/Beziehungsgeflechte ohne Einschränkungen bezüglich deren Größe oder Struktur. Das heißt, ein strukturiertes Objekt kann ein Unterobjekt desselben Typs besitzen ("rekursive Struktur") und zwei verschiedene strukturierte Objekte können ein und dasselbe Unterobjekt besitzen ("überlappende Struktur"). Die Struktur eines Objekts wird zunächst im Schema auf Typebene beschrieben. Die Definition eines *Objekttyps* kann demzufolge aus einem deskriptiven Teil und einem strukturellen Teil bestehen. Im deskriptiven Teil werden die Attribute des Objekttyps und deren Wertebereiche festgelegt, während im strukturellen Teil der Typdefinition die direkten Unterobjekttypen oder -beziehungstypen bestimmt werden. Ein Objekttyp kann außerdem als Generalisierung von speziellen Objekttypen angesehen werden und als solche wieder in Strukturen eingebracht werden. Die Beziehungen, die zwischen Objekten bestehen können, werden ebenfalls im Schema als *Beziehungstyp* definiert. Deren Ausprägungen bilden wie die einfachen und strukturierten Objekte Einheiten der Speicherung und des Wiederauffindens. Jedes Objekt des betrachteten Umweltausschnittes läßt sich also - unabhängig von seiner inneren Struktur - auf ein Datenbankobjekt abbilden. Mit dieser Eigenschaft erfüllt DAMOKLES eine der wesentlichen Anforderungen, die an ein System zur Unterstützung von Entwurfsanwendungen gerichtet werden.

DAMOKLES unterstützt die Datenhaltung von Werkzeugen, die in eine Softwareproduktionsumgebung integriert sind. Im Kontext dieser Entwurfsumgebung greift ein Entwerfer über die Werkzeuge auf die Daten zu. Ein *Anwendungsprogrammierer* formuliert diese Werkzeuge in einer höheren Programmiersprache und organisiert dabei den Zugriff auf *einzelne Objekt- oder Beziehungsexemplare* der Datenbasis über eine prozedurale Datenmanipulationssprache.

Im Entwurfsbereich finden jedoch auch Algorithmen Anwendung, die auf großen Mengen gleichartiger Daten arbeiten. Um diese Art der Anwendung zu unterstützen, ist es erforderlich, *Mengen von einfachen oder strukturierten Objekten* von der Datenbasis in das Anwendungsprogramm zu transferieren, wo sie weiterverarbeitet werden können. Hierfür ist neben einer navigierenden Ein-Exemplar-Schnittstelle eine mengenorientierte Schnittstelle notwendig. Darüberhinaus soll ein

---

1 Database Management System of Karlsruhe for Environments for Software Engineering

Endbenutzer die Möglichkeit haben, sich unabhängig von einem bestimmten Anwendungsprogramm Informationen über den Zustand der Datenbasis zu beschaffen. Dazu eignet sich ebenfalls eine mengenorientierte Datenbanksprache, mit der ein Benutzer ad-hoc Anfragen an das Datenbanksystem richten kann.

Ziel dieses Papieres ist es, den syntaktischen Entwurf einer Sprache vorzustellen, die eben dies leistet und das Aufsuchen einer Menge gleichartiger Objekte in einem beliebig komplexen Objekt-/Beziehungsgeflecht ermöglicht. Die Behandlung von Manipulationsoperatoren, mit denen eine Menge von Objekten eingefügt, verändert oder gelöscht werden kann, wird in diesem Papier ausgeklammert.

Zunächst werden im zweiten Kapitel Anforderungen an die Sprache untersucht, die sich im wesentlichen aus dem Datenmodell ableiten. Ausgehend von diesen Anforderungen wurde am FZI eine Anfragesprache entwickelt und implementiert, die sich an SQL-Sprachmitteln orientiert und die dem Benutzer erlaubt, in gebotener Einfachheit hinreichend komplexe Anfragen an das System zu stellen. Das System liefert ihm eine Menge von Objekt- bzw. Beziehungsexemplaren zurück, wobei auf Wunsch die Struktur einzelner Objektexemplare sichtbar gemacht wird. Diese Sprache - CERMoQL[1] - wird im dritten Kapitel dieses Papieres vorgestellt. Dabei werden aus Platzgründen die Sprachmittel, mit denen sich Anfragen auf Versionen formulieren lassen, nicht behandelt. Die Syntax wird an Beispielen verdeutlicht. Daran schließen sich Betrachtungen bezüglich der Mächtigkeit dieser Sprache an. Das Papier endet mit einer Zusammenfassung und einem Ausblick auf weitere Vorhaben.

2. Anforderungen

In der Literatur existieren bereits verschiedene Vorschläge für Anfragesprachen, die auf dem ER-Modell basieren. Nachdem erste Sprachentwürfe von Poonen (CLEAR) [Poon79] und Shoshani (CABLE) [Shos79] vorlagen, wurde von Atzeni und Chen [Atze81] im Zusammenhang mit der Beschreibung der Sprache ExL die Definition eines ER-Kalküls vorgestellt. Dieser kann generell als Maß für die Mächtigkeit von ER-Sprachen herangezogen werden. Die Autoren unterscheiden Sprachen, die der *einfachen* ER-Vollständigkeit genügen, von denen, die ER-vollständig sind. Die einfache ER-Vollständigkeit garantiert lediglich die Selektion einer Menge von Instanzen genau eines Typs, während in ER-vollständigen Sprachen auch Anfragen zugelassen sind, die Daten verschiedenen Typs zurückliefern. CLEAR und CABLE erfüllen nach dieser Klassifikation nicht einmal die Kriterien für die einfache ER-Vollständigkeit, während ExL der einfachen ER-Vollständigkeit genügt. Mit GORDAS haben Elmasri und Wiederhold [ElWi81] eine Sprache entworfen, deren Mächtigkeit die ER-Vollständigkeit noch übersteigt. Für die Formulierung von GORDAS-Ausdrücken ist eine graphische Sicht auf das ER-Schema wie auch auf die ER-Datenbasis von Nutzen. Einen anderen Charakter weist die Sprache ERROL [MaRa83a] auf, deren syntaktische Konstrukte sich an natürlich-sprachlichen Sätzen orientieren. Mit der Sprache ERROL wurde eine modifizierte Relationenalgebra (RRA) [MaRa83b] vorgestellt, die als Maß für deren Mächtigkeit dient. Sie liefert außerdem ein probates Mittel für die Beschreibung der Semantik von ERROL-Ausdrücken. Die Sprache LAMBDA [Velez85] ist ebenfalls RRA-vollständig. Sie bildet die Schnittstelle für ein spezielles erweitertes ER-Modell, das ein Konzept zur Modellierung strukturierter Dokumente anbietet. Das Aufsuchen dieser strukturierten Dokumente wird von LAMBDA in besonderer Weise unterstützt. LAMBDA-Anfragen ähneln auf den ersten Blick SQL-Ausdrücken. Sie bestehen ebenfalls aus einer SELECT-, einer FROM- und einer WHERE-Klausel. Die FROM-Klauseln beschreiben Wege im ER-Diagramm, einer graphische Repräsentation eines ER-Schemas ([Chen76]). Diese Idee wurde für die Formulierung von CERMoQL-Anfragen übernommen. Eine SQL-ähnliche Sprache dient auch als Schnittstelle für das Molekül-Atom-Datenmodell (MAD) [Mits88], das zur Modellierung nicht-konventioneller Anwendungen vorgeschlagen wird und daher ein Konzept zur Verwaltung von komplexen Objekten anbietet. Die Sprache MQL ist auf das MAD-Datenmodell zugeschnitten und beinhaltet insbesondere eine interessante Möglichkeit, nach der Auswertung einer Anfrage eine nachträgliche

---

1 Complex Entity Relationship Model Query Language

Strukturierung des Anfrageergebnisses vorzunehmen ("qualified projection").

Zusammenfassend sehen alle Sprachen die Möglichkeit vor, Bedingungen über Beziehungen, die zwischen bestimmten Objekten bestehen sollen, zu formulieren und ebenso Attributwerte von Objekten oder Beziehungen miteinander zu vergleichen. Es entspricht dem Vorgang einer natürlich-sprachlichen Anfrageformulierung, diese beiden Arten von Bedingungen, struktur- und wertebezogene, in beliebiger Reihenfolge aneinanderreihen zu können. Dieser Freiheitsgrad, der dem Benutzer in den meisten der oben genannten Anfragesprachen eingeräumt wird, erleichtert ihm jedoch weder die Formulierung eigener Anfragen noch das Verstehen einer Anfrage, die ein anderer Benutzer formuliert hat. Im CERMoQL-Sprachentwurf wurde deshalb bewußt die Ähnlichkeit zur natürlichen Sprache nicht in den Vordergrund gestellt. Statt dessen wurde eine klare Gliederung der Anfrageformulierung, wie sie auch in SQL anzutreffen ist, postuliert. Spezielle Konzepte, die sich aus der Anpassung an das strukturell-objektorientierte Datenmodell ergeben, beziehen sich dabei lediglich auf den strukturorientierten, nicht auf den wertorientierten Teil einer Anfrage. Eine Anpassung der Sprache an andersartige ER-basierte Datenmodelle ist daher leicht möglich.

Die wesentlichen Kriterien, die den CERMoQL-Sprachentwurf begleiteten, werden im folgenden herausgearbeitet und am Ende dieses Kapitels zusammengefaßt.

2.1 Transparenz der Konzepte

Von verschiedenen Seiten (vgl. [Lori83]) wurde der Versuch unternommen, relationale Systeme dahingehend zu erweitern, daß sie sich für die Abbildung semantischer Datenmodelle eignen. Ausgehend von der Implementierung eines strukturell-objektorientierten Datenmodells auf der Grundlage eines relationalen Systems sollen die Unzulänglichkeiten demonstriert werden, die sich durch dieses Vorgehen auf der Sprachebene ergeben.

Ein Charakteristikum von strukturell-objektorientierten Datenmodellen ist die Identität der einzelnen, darin beschriebenen Objekte, die diese - auch wenn sich ihre Eigenschaften ändern - beibehalten. Diese Eigenschaft wird durch die Einführung eines systemvergebenen Identifikators (Surrogat) realisiert, der dem Objekt bei dessen Entstehung zugewiesen wird und der vom Benutzer nicht verändert werden kann. Eine Menge gleichartiger Objekte kann in einem relationalen System durch eine Relation beschrieben werden, deren Spalten die Eigenschaften der Objekte wiedergeben. Eine Spalte bleibt dem Surrogatattribut vorbehalten. Jedes Tupel dieser Relation repräsentiert genau ein Objekt, und der Wert des Surrogatattributs ist dessen Identifikator.

Ein strukturiertes Objekt oder eine Beziehung zwischen Objekten kann schließlich durch eine Anzahl von Tupeln dargestellt werden, die verschiedenen Relationen angehören. Ein Attribut des einen Tupels verweist dabei auf den Identifikator eines anderen Tupels. Der Zusammenhang zwischen diesen Tupeln kann jedoch erst bei der Auswertung einer Anfrage über die Gleichheit von Attributwerten (Join) ermittelt werden.

Dies soll an einem Beispiel verdeutlicht werden. Im allgemeinsten Fall einer $n{:}m$ Beziehung wäre zur Modellierung dieser Beziehung eine eigene Relation erforderlich. Diese Beziehungsrelation hätte für jeden Objekttyp, der an dieser Beziehung teilnehmen kann, ein Rollenattribut. Betrachten wir dann eine Anfrage, mit der alle Objekte vom Typ A ermittelt werden sollen, die über eine Beziehung vom Typ B mit einem bestimmten Objekt vom Typ C verknüpft sind, so erfordert diese Anfrage zwei Join-Operationen. Dabei wird jeweils das Surrogatattribut eines Objekts (#) mit dem entsprechenden Rollenattribut der Beziehung verglichen. In der relationalen Anfragesprache SQL (Structured Query Language) [ANSI86] wird diese Anfrage wie folgt formuliert:

```
SELECT A.*
FROM A, B, C
WHERE C.att = "value"
  AND A.#A = B.role1
  AND B.role2 = C.#C
```

Das Relationenmodell bietet nicht die Möglichkeit, zu definieren, daß die Relationen A und C in einer Beziehung zueinander stehen. In der Anfrage kann auf diesen Zusammenhang deshalb nicht zurückgegriffen werden. Das gleiche gilt auch für strukturierte Objekte.

Eine andere Situation ergibt sich, wenn Relationen zugelassen sind, die selbst relationenwertige Attribute haben können. Entsprechende Erweiterungen der Relationenalgebra sieht das NF^2 Modell [Sche86] vor. Es ermöglicht die Modellierung hierarchischer Beziehungen, bietet jedoch keine direkten Konzepte für die Definition allgemeiner $n:m$ Beziehungen an. Das NF^2 Modell impliziert außerdem, daß zwei strukturierte Objekte disjunkt sind, d. h. keine gemeinsamen Unterobjekte besitzen können. Diese Überlappungen treten jedoch in der Realität der Entwurfswelt ebenso wie allgemeine Beziehungen häufig auf. Sie sollten sich deshalb im Datenmodell direkt beschreiben lassen.

In jedem Fall gilt der Grundsatz, daß eine Anfragesprache die Konzepte des ihr zugrunde liegenden Datenmodells widerspiegeln sollte. Die Verwendung einer relationalen Sprache - wie SQL - als Anfragesprache für ein ER-basiertes Datenmodell führt zu einer Verdeckung der semantischen Mächtigkeit des Modells. Die Sprache sollte vielmehr mit speziellen Konstrukten die direkte Bezugnahme auf Objekt- und Beziehungstypen und das Navigieren entlang beliebiger Objekt-/Beziehungsgeflechte unterstützen. Es sollte ebenso möglich sein, die Struktur der Elemente eines Anfrageergebnisses sichtbar zu machen. Die Abstraktionsmechanismen der Aggregation und Generalisierung sollten, wenn sie vom Datenmodell angeboten werden, eine Entsprechung in der Sprache finden.

2.2 Ad-hoc Join

Wie oben bereits angedeutet wurde, existieren in der Literatur verschiedene Vollständigkeitsbegriffe für ER-Sprachen. Als strittiger Punkt erweist sich die Zulassung eines wertebezogenen Joins, der den Attributwertvergleich zweier Objektexemplare auch dann erlaubt, wenn diese nicht über eine Beziehung miteinander verknüpft sind. Mehrere ER-Sprachansätze verfolgen die Leitlinie, ein Vergleich zweier Objekte sei nur dann zulässig, wenn diese Objekte im ER-Diagramm über einen Weg miteinander verbunden sind. Sie setzen voraus, daß alle interessierenden Zusammenhänge bereits im Datenbankschema modelliert werden. Diese Restriktion schränkt den Einsatzbereich der Sprache wesentlich ein. In einem System, das zum Beispiel zur Unterstützung von Entscheidungsfindungen herangezogen wird, kann es erforderlich sein, Datenansammlungen zu interpretieren, die auf eine nicht vorhergesehene Weise zusammengestellt wurden. Deshalb sollte in einem ER-basierten Datenmodell die Möglichkeit geboten werden, auf einfache Weise auch dann Objekte miteinander zu vergleichen, wenn sie nicht in Verbindung zueinander stehen (= Ad-hoc Join).

2.3 SQL-Sprachmittel

Die Sprachen LAMBDA und OSQL [Beech88] dokumentieren, daß die Verwendung von SQL-Sprachmitteln einen lohnenswerten Ausgangspunkt für den Entwurf einer ER-Sprache darstellt. Dasselbe gilt auch für eine Sprache, der ein strukturell-objektorientiertes Datenmodell zugrunde liegt. Neben der Garantie für eine leichte Erlernbarkeit und Handhabbarkeit stellt die Verwendung von SQL-Sprachmitteln die Entwicklung einer einheitlichen Schnittstelle für relationale Systeme und objektorientierte Datenbanksysteme in Aussicht. Sie erleichtert ebenso den Übergang von der Verwendung eines relationalen Systems zu der Verwendung eines objektorientierten Datenbanksystems.

2.4 Aggregationsfunktionen

Im Bereich der relationalen Anfragesprachen haben sich zwei Sprachkonzepte als wesentliche Ausdrucksmittel bewährt, die das Maß der relationalen Vollständigkeit übersteigen. Dies sind zum einen die Aggregationsfunktionen, Funktionen, die auf eine "Menge" von Werten angewendet werden (z.B.

MIN, MAX, SUM, AVG). Sie lassen sich auf eine Relation anwenden und liefern einen einfachen, meist numerischen Wert zurück. In SQL werden, begründet durch den Einsatz der Sprache im kommerziellen Bereich, arithmetische Funktionen als Aggregationsfunktionen angeboten. Das Konzept der Aggregationsfunktionen läßt sich in direkter Weise auf das ER-Modell übertragen. Eine Aggregationsfunktion wird auf eine Menge gleichartiger Objekte (oder Beziehungen) angewendet und liefert genau einen Wert zurück. Es wäre darüber hinaus wünschenswert, je nach Einsatzgebiet der Sprache einen Satz von *anwendungstypischen Aggregationsfunktionen* in die Sprache mitaufzunehmen, die zum Sprachinterpretierer hinzugebunden werden könnten. Im Bereich des Software Engineering wäre es denkbar, komplexe Funktionen wie *compile* oder *unparse* zu definieren.

2.5 Transitive Hüllen

Ein zweites Konzept, das die Ausdrucksmächtigkeit der Relationenalgebra übersteigt [AhU179], stellt die Möglichkeit dar, Anfragen zu formulieren, die sich auf die transitive Hülle einer Relation beziehen. Übertragen auf ein ER-basiertes Datenmodell gewinnt dieses Konzept eine besondere Bedeutung. Denn es ist zulässig, *rekursive Beziehungen*, also Beziehungen, die einen Objekttyp mit sich selbst verknüpfen, zu definieren. Gerade bei Entwurfsobjekten bietet sich häufig die Modellierung mit Hilfe einer rekursiven Ober-/Unterobjektbeziehung an. Als Beispiel sei die Modellierung einer Baumstruktur genannt. Jeder Baum besteht aus einer Wurzel, die mit einem oder mehreren Unterbäumen verknüpft ist (siehe Beispiel in Kap.4). Die Berechnung einer transitiven Hülle kommt hier der Bestimmung aller Wege von der Wurzel bis zu den Blättern eines Baumes gleich. Gleichwohl genügt es nicht, diese Wege zu bestimmen. Der Benutzer will in vielen Fällen in seinen Anfragen auf die "Geschichte" eines Weges Bezug nehmen. Mit der "Geschichte" eines Weges sind all die Knoten - d. h. die Objekte - gemeint, die entlang des Weges berührt werden. Will der Benutzer beispielsweise zwei Wege in einem Netz bestimmen, die nur den Anfangs- und Endpunkt gemeinsam haben, muß er die "Geschichten" beider Wege miteinander vergleichen können. Diese Möglichkeit sollte ihm im Rahmen einer ER-Sprache gegeben sein. Der Berechnungsaufwand, der erforderlich ist, um die Lösung der allgemeinsten Form einer Fixpunktgleichung zu bestimmen, ist enorm hoch. Das zu erwartende Anfrageprofil rechtfertigt diesen Aufwand nicht. Statt dessen soll es genügen, eine Teilmenge von Fixpunktfragen in der Sprache zuzulassen, die sinnvolle Fragestellungen repräsentieren, welche häufig auftreten und die zudem effizient auszuwerten sind.

2.6 Zusammenfassung

Der Entwurf von CERMoQL wurde an den oben beschriebenen Kriterien ausgerichtet. Die Syntax selbst ist dem DAMOKLES-Datenmodell angepaßt. Sie enthält bestimmte Schlüsselworte für fest vorgegebene Schritte entlang eines Weges in einem DAMOKLES-Schemagraphen. Sie erlaubt den Vergleich zweier Objekte, auch wenn die entsprechenden Objekttypen im Schemagraphen nicht miteinander verbunden sind. CERMoQL gleicht auf den ersten Blick SQL. Unterschiede liegen in der Formulierung der FROM-Klausel. Mit Hilfe der FROM-Klausel kann ein Benutzer beliebige Wege entlang eines Objekt-/Beziehungsgeflechts beschreiben und so strukturelle Einschränkungen formulieren, die die Ergebnismenge betreffen sollen. Wertbezogene Einschränkungen sind in der WHERE-Klausel enthalten, während die SELECT-Klausel die Form der Ausgabe bestimmt. In CERMoQL werden - wie in SQL - Aggregationsfunktionen angeboten. Jedoch beschränken sich diese bisher auf die aus SQL bekannten Funktionen SUM, AVG, MIN, MAX und COUNT. CERMoQL beinhaltet die Möglichkeit, Anfragen auf die transitive Hülle einer Beziehung und deren "Geschichte" zu formulieren. Damit übersteigt die Ausdruckskraft von CERMoQL die Ausdruckskraft vergleichbarer ER-Sprachen. Weitere Unterschiede, die zwischen CERMoQL und anderen ER-Sprachen, insbesondere der Sprache LAMBDA, bestehen werden in [Schi88] diskutiert.

3. Der Sprachentwurf

3.1 Begriffe

Vor der Diskussion der Anfragesprache ist zunächst noch die präzise Definition einiger Begriffe notwendig, die die Beschreibung der Sprache erleichtern.

Unter einem *Schemagraph* wird im folgenden die graphische Veranschaulichung einer Schemadefinition verstanden. Hierbei werden die Beziehungs- und Objekttypen jeweils durch Knoten dargestellt. Diese werden durch drei unterschiedliche Typen von Kanten (ER, UP_DOWN, UNION_INST) miteinander verbunden.

Beziehungs- und Objekttypen werden für jede Rolle, in der der Objekttyp an der Beziehung teilnimmt, durch je eine ungerichtete Kante vom Typ ER miteinander verbunden. Diese Kante wird mit dem Namen der Rolle beschriftet. Betrachtet man nur einfache Objekttypen, das heißt keine Generalisierungen und nur solche, die über keinen strukturellen Teil in ihrer Typdefinition verfügen, so entspricht der Schemagraph einem ER-Diagramm, wie es zum Beispiel in [Chen76] eingeführt wird.

Zwischen einem Oberobjekttyp und seinen Unterobjekt- bzw. Unterbeziehungstypen besteht je eine gerichtete Kante vom Typ UP_DOWN während zwischen einem Generalisierungstyp und seinen Spezialisierungen je eine gerichtete Kante vom Typ UNION_INST besteht.

Der zu einem Schemagraphen gehörende *Datenbasisgraph* stellt eine graphische Repräsentation einer Datenbasis dar, die zu der durch den Schemagraphen dargestellten Schemadefinition erzeugt wurde. In diesem Sinne kann man einen Datenbasisgraph auch als Instanz des zugehörigen Schemagraphen bezeichnen. Die Knoten sind hier die Objekt- und die Beziehungsexemplare. Zwischen einem Objekt und einer Beziehung existiert eine ungerichtete Kante vom Typ ER, wenn der Benutzer des Systems angegeben hat, daß das Objekt in einer gewissen Rolle an der Beziehung teilnimmt. Zwei Exemplare werden durch eine Kante vom Typ UP_DOWN verbunden, wenn die nach dem Schema mögliche Ober/Unterobjektbeziehung vom Benutzer zwischen diesen Exemplaren explizit eingerichtet wurde. Ausprägungen von UNION_INST Kanten sind im Datenbasisgraph nicht sichtbar.

Mit *Datenbasisteilgraphtyp* wird im folgenden die Spezifikation eines Teilgraphen eines Datenbasisgraphen bezeichnet. Die Spezifikation eines Datenbasisteilgraphtyps erfolgt durch die Beschreibung eines Graphen, dessen Kanten nur Knoten verbinden dürfen, die auch im Schemagraphen über eine Kante miteinander verbunden sind.

Ein Datenbasisteilgraphtyp unterscheidet sich von einem Schemagraph in drei wesentlichen Punkten:

1. Im allgemeinen wird nur eine Teilmenge der Knoten des Schemagraphen in einem Datenbasisteilgraphtyp auftreten.

2. Jeder Knoten des Schemagraphen darf beliebig oft in einem Datenbasisteilgraphtyp vertreten sein.

3. Ein Beziehungstyp muß in einem Datenbasisteilgraphtyp nicht mit all seinen im Schemagraphen spezifizierten Rollen angegeben werden. Ebenso gilt, daß zu einem Oberobjekttypen nicht alle Untertypen angegeben werden müssen und umgekehrt.

Eine Instanz eines Datenbasisteilgraphtypen wird in Analogie zu der Beziehung zwischen Typ- und Exemplarebene im folgenden *Datenbasisteilgraphexemplar* genannt.

3.2 Aufbau einer Anfrage

Eine CERMoQL-Anfrage gliedert sich wie eine SQL-Anfrage im wesentlichen in drei Teile.

Den Kopf der Anfrage bildet die SELECT-Klausel. Sie ermöglicht die Spezifikation des Formats der Daten, die das Anfrageergebniss bilden. Dabei kann es sich um ganze Objekte, einzelne Attribute, arithmetische Ausdrücke oder Aggregationsfunktionen sowie eine Kombination dieser handeln. Bei der Ausgabe von Objekten kann eine zusätzliche Einschränkung auf den deskriptiven Teil erfolgen, sonst wird das Objekt mit allen Unterobjekten und Unterbeziehungen geliefert.

Die FROM-Klausel ermöglicht die Spezifikation der Beziehungen, die zwischen den auszuwählenden Exemplaren bestehen sollen, den sogenannten strukturorientierten Bedingungen. Dies geschieht durch die Beschreibung allgemeiner Graphen.

In der WHERE-Klausel werden die Bedingungen angegeben, die sich auf Attributwerte beziehen, die sogenannten wertorientierten Bedingungen.

3.3 Strukturorientierte Bedingungen

In der FROM-Klausel werden die Datenbasisteilgraphtypen, die für die Anfrage relevant sind, spezifiziert. Das heißt, es wird die Struktur von Datenbasisteilgraphexemplaren vorgegeben. Das Ergebnis der FROM-Klausel bilden die zu einer bestimmten Datenbasis gehörenden Datenbasisteilgraphexemplare.

Die Spezifikation eines Datenbasisteilgraphtyps erfolgt durch die Angabe von *Navigationsschritten* im Schemagraph.

Dabei kann von einem Objekttyp ausgehend
☞ zu einem Unterobjekttyp (DOWN_TO sub_objecttype),
☞ zu einem Oberobjekttyp (UP_TO sup_objecttype),
☞ zu einem Generalisierungstyp (TO_UNION union_objecttype),
☞ zu einer Instanz (TO_INST inst_objecttype),
☞ zu einem Beziehungstyp, an dem der Ausgangstyp beteiligt ist (TO relationtype) oder
☞ direkt zu einem weiteren Objekttyp, der an einem Beziehungstyp teilnimmt, an dem der Ausgangstyp ebenfalls teilnimmt (TO role),
navigiert werden.

Von einem Beziehungtyp ausgehend kann
☞ zu einem Oberobjekttyp (UP_TO sup_objecttype) oder
☞ zu einem Objekttyp, der an dem Beziehungstyp in einer Rolle teilnimmt (TO role),
navigiert werden.

Die unterschiedlichen Navigationsmöglichkeiten werden anhand eines Beispiels näher erläutert. Auf die Spezifikation von Teilgraphtypen des Versionsgraphen kann hier aus Platzgründen nicht eingegangen werden. Interessenten an diesem Problembereich seien auf [Schi88] verwiesen.

3.4 Wertorientierte Bedingungen

Die Bedingungen, die in der WHERE-Klausel angegeben werden können, beziehen sich nur noch auf die in der FROM-Klausel ausgewählten Datenbasisteilgraphexemplare. Aufgrund gewisser Attributwerte der zugehörigen Objekte oder Beziehungen werden einige von ihnen ausgewählt, die dann im durch die SELECT-Klausel spezifizierten Format ausgegeben werden.

Zur Auswahl von Datenbasisteilgraphexemplaren können alle aus SQL gewohnten Arten von Bedingungen verwendet werden. Das heißt, daß sowohl der Vergleich von Attributwerten mit Konstanten als auch der Vergleich beliebiger Attributwerte (*Ad-hoc Join*) sowie der Vergleich mit dem Ergebnis einer geschachtelten Anfrage möglich ist.

Zusätzlich zu den Möglichkeiten, die SQL bietet, können in CERMoQL Anfragen auf der "Geschichte" eines transitiv berechneten Ergebnisses formuliert werden. Dies wird dadurch ermöglicht, daß auf die dieser Art berechneten Werte an jeder Stelle zugegriffen werden kann, an der das Ergebnis einer geschachtelten Anfrage stehen kann. Dadurch wird im wesentlichen die Anwendung von Aggregationsfunktionen sowie die Durchführung von Mengenoperationen wie Vereinigung, Schnitt und Abfrage von Elementzugehörigkeit ermöglicht.

4. Anfragebeispiele

Im folgenden Kapitel wird die Sprache CERMoQL anhand von Beispielen vorgestellt. Eine ausführliche Beschreibung der Grammatik findet sich in [Schi88]. In dieser Arbeit wird auch eine Abbildung der Sprache auf algebraische Ausdrücke beschrieben, mit deren Hilfe eine formale Spezifikation der Semantik erfolgen kann.

Die Demonstration der CERMoQL-Syntax erfolgt mit Hilfe eines Schemas, das die Modellierung einer Baumstruktur repräsentiert (Abb. 1). Dabei wird ein Baum als ein komplexes Objekt, bestehend aus einem Wurzelknoten und einer Menge von Teilbäumen aufgefaßt. Der Wurzelknoten steht in einer Vater_Sohn-Beziehung zu den Teilbäumen. Diese Modellierung ermöglicht es, jeden Teilbaum als eigenständiges strukturiertes Objekt aufzufassen, auf das Operationen wie z.B. Kopieren und Löschen anwendbar sind.

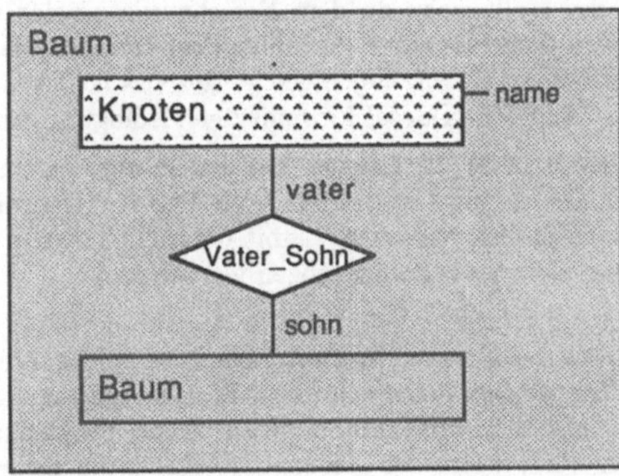

Abb. 1 Beispielschema

Abbildung 2 gibt einen Ausschnitt aus einer möglichen Datenbasis zum obigen Schema wieder. Diese Datenbasis wird zur Demonstration der Ergebnisse der folgenden CERMoQL-Anfragen verwendet.

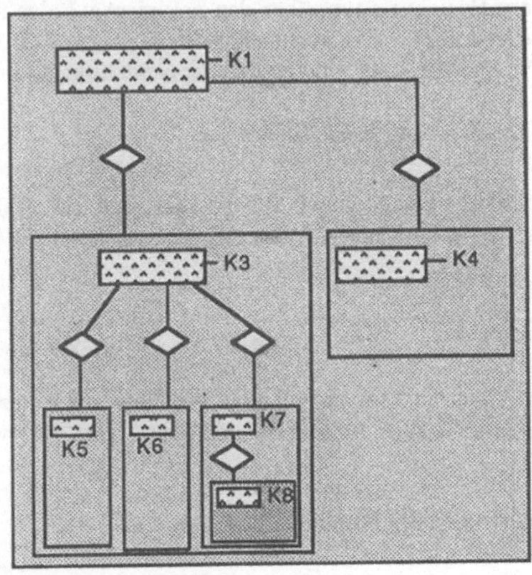

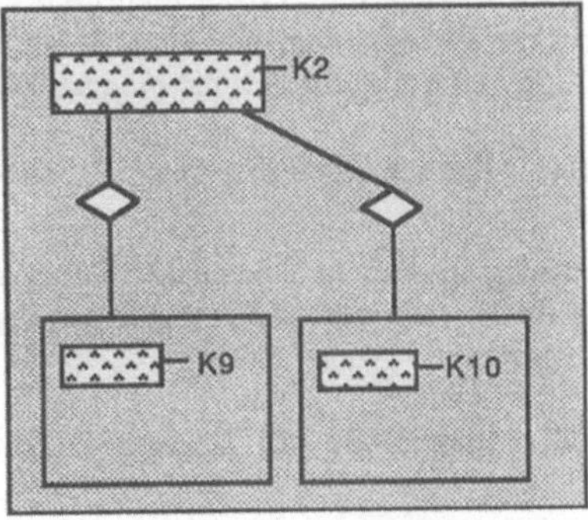

Abb. 2 Exemplarbild

Die erste Beispielanfrage demonstriert sowohl die **Navigation über Beziehungen** als auch die **Navigation in strukturierten Objekttypen**.

1. Suche die Namen aller Söhne des Knotens mit Namen "K1".

```
SELECT ks.name
FROM    Knoten kv TO sohn DOWN_TO Knoten ks
WHERE   kv.name = "K1"
```

Ergebnis: K3, K4

Der erste Teil der FROM-Klausel (**Knoten kv TO sohn**) wählt alle Tripel von Exemplaren der Typen (*Knoten*, *Vater_Sohn*, *Baum*) aus, wenn das Objekt vom Typ *Knoten* in der Rolle *vater* und das Objekt vom Typ *Baum* in der Rolle *sohn* an dem Beziehungsexemplar vom Typ *Vater_Sohn* teilnehmen. Der Objekttyp *Knoten* wird mit einer Variablen (**kv**) versehen, da die Menge der auszuwählenden Tripel in der WHERE-Klausel auf diejenigen eingeschränkt werden soll, bei denen die Exemplare dieses Typs der in der WHERE-Klausel formulierten Bedingung genügen.

Der nächste Teil der FROM-Klausel (**DOWN_TO Knoten ks**) drückt aus, daß das Exemplar vom Typ *Baum* in den zuvor ausgewählten Tripeln ein Unterobjekt vom Typ *Knoten* enthalten muß. Der Unterobjekttyp wird mit einer Variablen (**ks**) versehen, damit dessen Attribut *name* in der SELECT-Klausel zur Spezifikation des Ausgabeformats herangezogen werden kann.

Die Navigation über eine Beziehung erfordert lediglich die Angabe der Rolle, in der der zu erreichende Objekttyp an der Beziehung teilnimmt. In zwei Fällen ist jedoch zuerst die Navigation zu dem Beziehungstyp notwendig. Dies ist zum einen erforderlich, wenn Bedingungen über Attribute des Beziehungstyps formuliert werden sollen, und zum anderen, wenn die Angabe des Rollennamens mehrdeutig ist. Letzteres ist der Fall, wenn der Ausgangsobjekttyp an mehreren Beziehungstypen beteiligt ist, die über ein gleichnamiges Rollenattribut verfügen. Die FROM-Klausel müßte in diesen Fällen folgendermaßen aussehen:

```
FROM    Knoten kv TO Vater_Sohn TO sohn DOWN_TO Knoten ks
```

Wenn der Ausgangsobjekttyp in mehreren Rollen am Beziehungstyp, über den navigiert werden soll, teilnimmt, so ist außerdem die Angabe der Rolle erforderlich. Die ausführlichste, in jedem Fall eindeutige Formulierung der FROM-Klausel bei der Navigation über eine Beziehung sieht dann so aus:

```
FROM    Knoten kv VIA vater TO Vater_Sohn TO sohn DOWN_TO Knoten ks
```

Die Richtung, in der ein Datenbasisteilgraphtyp spezifiziert wird, spielt für die Semantik der Anfrage keine Rolle. Die erste FROM-Klausel im obigen Beispiel könnte völlig gleichwertig auch so formuliert werden:

```
FROM    Knoten ks UP_TO Baum TO vater kv
```

Um beliebige Graphen in der FROM-Klausel beschreiben zu können, wird ein Konzept zur **Spezifikation von Verzweigungen** benötigt. Ein einfaches Beispiel für die Spezifikation einer Verzweigung wird im folgenden Beispiel vorgeführt.

2. Bestimme alle Bäume, deren Wurzelknoten ein Bruder des Knotens mit Name "K7" ist.

```
SELECT bruder
FROM    Knoten (TO sohn DOWN_TO Knoten ks, TO sohn bruder)
WHERE   ks.name = "K7"
```

Ergebnis: Baum(K5), Baum(K6), Baum(K7)

Bem: Durch die Angabe von **bruder** in der SELECT-Klausel werden komplexe Objekte vom
Typ Baum mit allen Unterobjekten und Unterbeziehungen ausgewählt.

Durch die mehrfache Verwendung des gleichen Variablennamens für den gleichen Typ innerhalb eines Datenbasisteilgraphtyps in der FROM-Klausel können mehrere strukturorientierte Bedingungen
angegeben werden, die ein Exemplar diese Typs erfüllen muß, um sich für das Ergebnis zu qualifizieren. Verzweigte Wege können auf diese Weise in andere Äste des Graphen münden. Mit diesen einfachen Mitteln ist die Beschreibung jedes komplexen Geflechtes möglich.

Ein wesentliches Sprachmerkmal von CERMoQL ist die Möglichkeit der **Spezifikation transitiver Hüllen** sowie der Formulierung komplexer Anfragen auf diesen.

Der Begriff der transitiven Hülle einer Relation bedeutet, übertragen auf das ER-Modell, die Berechnung aller Entities, die direkt oder indirekt in der bestimmten Relation zueinander stehen. Dabei
muß *Relation* hier nicht für eine konkrete im Schema modellierte Beziehung stehen. Zwei Exemplare
eines Objekttyps können auch dann in Relation zueinander gesetzt werden, wenn sie über mehrere
Beziehungs- und Objektexemplare unterschiedlichen Typs miteinander verbunden sind.

Dies bedeutet in der oben eingeführten Terminologie:
Die Bestimmung der transitiven Hülle eines Objektes bezüglich eines geschlossenen Datenbasisteilgraphtyps entspricht der Berechnung aller Datenbasisteilgraphexemplare, deren Startknoten eben
dieses Objekt bildet, und die sich in ihrer Struktur lediglich um Vielfache von Exemplaren des spezifizierten Datenbasisteilgraphtyps (**trans_dbtg_typ**) voneinander unterscheiden.

Die Formulierung *komplexer* Anfragen auf einer transitiven Hülle bedeutet nun Formulierung von
Anfragen, in denen auf jedes Attribut eines Objekt- oder Beziehungsexemplars, das einem Knoten in
einem der durchlaufenen Teilgraphen entspricht, Bezug genommen werden kann.

CERMoQL ermöglicht den Bezug auf die Attributwerte solcher Exemplare durch die Möglichkeit
der Verwendung von Variablen innerhalb der Spezifikation eines mehrfach zu durchlaufenden Teil-
graphs. Wird auf eine solche Variable (**mtg_variable**) in der Anfrage zugegriffen, so entspricht sie
dem jeweils bei der letzten Wiederholung des Teilgraphen erreichten Exemplar.

Da CERMoQL auch Anfragen auf der "Geschichte" eines transitiv berechneten Wertes unterstützt,
erfordert das Erkennen von Zyklen bei der Berechnung einer transitiven Hülle nur einen sehr geringen Mehraufwand. Die Berechnung wird abgebrochen, wenn der Endknoten nach einem Durchlauf
eines Exemplars von **trans_dbtg_typ** mit einem der Knoten, die bei der Berechnung dieses Daten-
basisteilgraphexemplars als Startknoten eines zuvor durchlaufenen Exemplars von **trans_dbtg_typ**
auftraten, identisch ist.

Ein einfaches Beispiel für die Spezifikation einer transitven Hülle:

3. Finde die Namen aller Knoten des Baumes, dessen Wurzelknoten den Namen "K1" hat.

```
SELECT  ks.name
FROM    Knoten kv { TO sohn DOWN_TO Knoten ks } X
WHERE   kv.name = "K1"
```

Ergebnis: K3, K5, K6, K7, K8, K4

Die Tiefe, bis zu der die transitive Hülle betrachtet werden soll, kann durch die Vorgabe der maximalen Anzahl von Wiederholungen eines Teilgraphen bestimmt werden.

4. Bestimme die Namen aller Söhne und Enkel des Knotens mit Namen "K1".

```
SELECT ks.name
FROM   Knoten kv { TO sohn DOWN_TO Knoten ks } 2
WHERE  kv.name = "K1"
```

Ergebnis: K3, K5, K6, K7, K4

Mit <mtg_variable> kann auf die Liste aller bei der Berechnung einer transitiven Hülle erreichten Werte ("Geschichte") Bezug genommen werden. Eine solche Listenspezifikation darf an jeder Stelle der Anfrage auftreten, an der die SQL-Syntax das Auftreten einer Menge von Ergebniswerten gestattet. Das heißt an den Stellen, an denen eine geschachtelte Anfrage stehen darf.

Zusätzlich ist es möglich, eine solche Liste oder einen mittels einer Aggregationsfunktion auf einer solchen Liste berechneten Wert im Ergebnis, d.h. in der SELECT-Klausel, zu spezifizieren.

5. Finde die Namen aller Blätter des Baumes, dessen Wurzelknoten den Namen "K1" hat sowie die Weglänge jedes dieser Blätter.

```
SELECT ks.name, COUNT (<ks>) + 1
FROM   Knoten kv { TO sohn DOWN_TO Knoten ks } X
WHERE  kv.name = "K1"
AND    NOT EXISTS ( SELECT *
                    FROM   Knoten k TO sohn
                    WHERE  k = ks )
```

Ergebnis: (K5,3) , (K6,3) , (K8,4) , (K4,2)

Bem1: Die Weglänge des Wurzelknotens beträgt 1.

Bem2: Die Blätter eines Baumes sind die Knoten, die keine Söhne mehr haben. Dies wird in der Anfrage dadurch ausgedrückt, daß in der geschachtelten Anfrage gerade die Knoten aus dem Ergebnis ausgeschlossen werden, die in einer Vater_Sohn Beziehung stehen.

Ein abschließendes Beispiel verdeutlicht den Unterschied zwischen der üblichen Verwendung von Aggregationsfunktionen und der Verwendung einer solchen Funktion im Zusammenhang mit Werten, die auf der Berechnung einer transitiven Hülle beruhen.

6. Finde den Wurzelknoten des Baumes mit der größten Tiefe und bestimme die Anzahl seiner Äste, die diese Tiefe aufweisen.

```
SELECT kv, COUNT (ks)
FROM   Knoten kv { TO sohn DOWN_TO Knoten ks } X
WHERE  COUNT (<ks>) = ( SELECT MAX (COUNT (<ksohn>))
                        FROM   Knoten { TO sohn DOWN_TO Knoten ksohn } X )
GROUP BY kv
```

Ergebnis: (Knoten(K1), 1)

5. Betrachtungen zur Mächtigkeit

Betrachtungen zur Mächtigkeit einer Anfragesprache setzen ein formales Vergleichskriterium voraus. In der Regel dient eine Algebra (oder ein Kalkül), die das zugrunde liegende Datenmodell ausreichend beschreibt, als Maß für die Mächtigkeit. Die Relationenalgebra eignet sich nicht oder nur mit Einschränkungen für die Beschreibung eines ER-basierten Modells. Wie bereits angedeutet gibt es verschiedene formale Ansätze, das ER-Modell mathematisch zu beschreiben. In dem von Atzeni und Chen vorgestellten ER-Kalkül [Atze81] ist ein Prädikat, das die Attributwerte von verschiedenen Objekttypen miteinander vergleicht, nur dann zulässig, wenn diese in Beziehung zueinander stehen. Dieser Kalkül ist daher restriktiver als die später vorgestellte RRA-Algebra [MaRa83b], in der diese Einschränkung aufgegeben wird. Die Sprachen GORDAS, ERROL und LAMBDA sind RRA-vollständig. In [Schi88] wird gezeigt, daß CERMoQL mindestens genauso mächtig ist wie die Sprache LAMBDA, sieht man von den speziellen LAMBDA-Konzepten ab, die das Aufsuchen strukturierter Dokumente unterstützen.

Die Möglichkeit, in einer CERMoQL-Anfrage Bezug auf transitive Hüllen zu nehmen, und deren "Geschichten" wie Pfade selbst zu betrachten, trägt wesentlich zur Ausdruckskraft von CERMoQL bei. Hier bietet sich ein Vergleich zu verschiedenen Hüllenoperatoren an, die als Erweiterungen der Relationenalgebra bisher vorgestellt wurden. Mit CERMoQL lassen sich Anfragen formulieren, die sich mit Hilfe des in [Agra87] vorgestellten α-Operators nicht ausdrücken lassen. Der formale Nachweis, daß die Klasse der rekursiven Anfragen, die sich in CERMoQL ausdrücken lassen, eine Obermenge der um den α-Operator erweiterten relationalen Algebra ist, steht jedoch aus. Er wird im Zusammenhang mit einer Formalisierung des Datenmodells erfolgen.

6. Zusammenfassung und Ausblick

CERMoQL ist eine mächtige Anfragesprache, die die Auswahl einzelner Attribute oder ganzer Objekte ermöglicht, sowie die Ausgabe von Werten, die aufgrund bestimmter Attributwerte berechnet wurden.

Dadurch, daß sich CERMoQL streng an den syntaktischen Regeln von SQL ([ANSI86]) orientiert, erleichtert die Sprache den Benutzern relationaler Datenbanksysteme den Übergang zu einem objektorientierten System. Bei einer geeigneten Abbildung der Relationen auf ein dem ER-Modell oder sogar einem erweiterten ER-Modell ähnliches Datenmodell müssen die vorhandenen SQL-Anwendungsprogramme kaum, in manchen Fällen sogar überhaupt nicht geändert werden.

Eine Besonderheit der Anfragesprache CERMoQL besteht darin, daß sie die Formulierung von Anfragen ermöglicht, die auf einer transitiven Hülle basieren. Auf der "Geschichte" eines transitiv berechneten Wertes sind alle Arten von Anfragen möglich, die auch auf einer Relation, die mit diesen Werten gefüllt ist, in SQL möglich sind. Dadurch ermöglicht CERMoQL eine größere Klasse von Anfragen, als zum Beispiel die, die durch den α-Operator (siehe [Agra87]) definiert wird.

Ein in der Programmiersprache C implementierter Prototyp von CERMoQL ist zur Zeit als interaktive Schnittstelle zum DAMOKLES-Datenbanksystem realisiert.

Offen sind noch viele Fragen im Zusammenhang mit der Optimierung bei der Auswertung von CERMoQL-Anfragen. Insbesondere ist es notwendig, gemeinsame Teilausdrücke geschachtelter Anfragen zu erkennen. Eine besondere Rolle spielt dabei die Erkennung von gemeinsamen Teilgraphbeschreibungen in den FROM-Klauseln von ineinander geschachtelten Anfragen.

Ein Weg zu möglichen Optimierungen wird durch eine Abbildung der Sprachkonzepte in algebraische Ausdrücke in [Schi88] untersucht. Dadurch wird einerseits das Erkennen gleicher Teilausdrücke vereinfacht sowie andererseits ein Zugang zu den vielfältigen Möglichkeiten der Optimierung durch algebraische Äquivalenzumformungen geschaffen. Hierbei ist jedoch ein algebraisches Konzept zur Formulierung der transitiven Hülle notwendig, das die Vielfalt der möglichen Anfragen, die CERMoQL auf diesen Hüllen erlaubt, berücksichtigt.

Ein weiterer interessanter Punkt für die Weiterentwicklung von CERMoQL stellt die Modifikation der Benutzerschnittstelle dar. Der Entwurf der vorgestellten Schnittstelle erfolgte insbesondere für im Umgang mit Datenbanksystemen geübte Benutzer, wie sie bei einem Einsatz des Systems in einer Softwareproduktionsumgebung erwartet werden können. Durch die besondere Strukturierung der Anfragen erscheint die Sprache jedoch auch an die Bedürfnisse von gelegentlichen und ungeübten Benutzern leicht anpaßbar.

Hierbei liegt der Schwerpunkt auf einer Vereinfachung der FROM-Klausel, denn sie stellt für diese Benutzergruppe ein großes Problem bei der Formulierung komplexer Anfragen dar. Dies liegt darin begründet, daß in dieser Klausel die sprachliche Spezifikation eines komplexen Graphen erforderlich ist. Wesentlich natürlicher und einfacher läßt sich ein Graph jedoch mit Hilfe einer graphischen Schnittstelle angeben, bei der in dem angezeigten Schema nur bestimmte Pfade markiert werden müssen. Eine so modifizierte Schnittstelle läßt sich mit relativ einfachen Mitteln verwirklichen und läßt eine höhere Akzeptanz bei der oben angesprochenen Benutzergruppe erwarten.

Zum Schluß stellt sich nun die Frage, ob CERMoQL, das hier für ein Datenbanksystem entwickelt wurde, dessen Datenmodell auf dem ER-Modell basiert, nicht auch als Schnittstelle auf konventionellen Datenbanksystemen denkbar ist. Diese Überlegung scheint berechtigt, da das ER-Modell von Chen als einheitliches Modell zur Beschreibung von Daten in unterschiedlichen semantisch ärmeren Datenmodellen wie dem Netzwerkmodell und den Relationenmodell konzipiert wurde.

Durch die Ähnlichkeit mit SQL erscheint CERMoQL ohne Modifikationen insbesondere für ein relationales Datenbanksystem als Anfragesprache geeignet zu sein.

Eine Anwendung von CERMoQL auf einem relationalen System kann man sich etwa folgendermaßen vorstellen:

Der Anwender braucht nicht zu wissen, wie sich seine Daten auf Relationen verteilen. Er benötigt zur Formulierung seiner Anfragen lediglich das ER-Schema, das den modellierten Umweltausschnitt widerspiegelt. Dieses enthält für ihn erheblich mehr Semantik als das auf Relationen abgebildete Schema. Die Vorschriften für die Abbildung von Entities und Beziehungen auf Relationen muß nur dem Datenbanksystem bekannt sein. Damit ist es diesem möglich, aus den vom Benutzer angegebenen Pfaden durch das ER-Schema die Relationen zu bestimmen, die durch eine *Join*-Operation verknüpft werden müssen. Diese Vorgehensweise bringt eine Reihe von Vorteilen mit sich:

1. Die Formulierung von Anfragen wird für den Benutzer wesentlich erleichtert, da er keine *Join*-Operationen auf für ihn bedeutungslosen Surrogatattributen formulieren muß. Die Anfrage wird dadurch kompakter und besser verständlich.

2. Fehler durch die versehentliche Definition falscher *Join*-Operationen sind nicht mehr möglich.

3. Der Wunsch nach der Berechnung einer transitiven Hülle über einer oder mehreren Relationen läßt sich auf einfache Art und Weise formulieren.

4. Das Datenbanksystem verfügt über die Information, welche Attribute nur eingefügt wurden, um Surrogate für die Definition von *Join*-Operationen aufzunehmen, und zwischen welchen Attributen bevorzugt *Joins* durchgeführt werden müssen. Dies kann automatisch zu Optimierungszwecken, wie das Anlegen von Zugriffspfaden, verwendet werden.

Der Einsatz von CERMoQL in einem relationalen Datenbanksystem gewinnt auch durch die Ähnlichkeit der Sprache mit SQL an Attraktivität, da nahezu jeder Benutzer eines solchen Systems mit den Grundzügen dieser Sprache vertraut ist. Bei einem späteren Wechsel zu einem objektorientierten System, das auf dem ER-Modell basiert, sind keinerlei Änderungen in den Anwendungsprogrammen notwendig.

Zusammenfassend kann über CERMoQL gesagt werden, daß sich die Sprache als universelle Anfragesprache sowohl für relationale als auch für ER-basierte Datenbanksysteme empfiehlt, wobei beim Einsatz der Sprache in einem ER-basierten System die Auswertung der Anfragen effizienter durchgeführt werden kann, da die Konzepte der Sprache dann 1:1 auf Konzepte des Datenmodells abgebildet werden können.

Literaturverzeichnis

[Agra87]   R. Agrawal: *ALPHA: An Extension of Relational Algebra to Express a Class of Recursive Queries*, in [DE87]

[AhUl79]   A. V. Aho, J. D. Ullman: *Universality of Data Retrieval Language*, 6th ACM Symposium on Principles of Programming Languages, San Antonio, Texas, Jan. 1979

[ANSI86]   American National Standards Institute: *Database Language SQL*, Document ANSI X3.135-1986 auch erhältlich als: International Standards Organization Document ISO/TC97/SC21/WG3 N117

[Atze81]   P. Atzeni, P. P. Chen: *Completeness of Query Languages for the Entity-Relationship Model*, in [ER81]

[Beech88]   D. Beech: *A Foundation for Evolution from Relational to Object Databases*, in Advances in Database Technology EDBT'88, J.W. Schmidt & S. Ceri & M. Missikoff (eds.), Lecture Notes in Computer Science Bd.303, 1988

[Chen76]   P. P. Chen: *The Entity-Relationship Model — Towards a Unified View of Data*, ACM TODS, Vol. 1, No. 1, 1976

[DAMO87]   K. Abramowicz, K. R. Dittrich, W. Gotthard, R. Längle, P. C. Lockemann, T. Raupp, S. Rehm, T. Wenner: *Datenbankunterstützung für Software-Produktionsumgebungen*, in Proc. GI Fachtagung Datenbanksysteme in Büro, Technik und Wissenschaft, Informatik-Fachberichte 136, 1987

[DE87]   *Proceedings of 1987 Data Engineering Conference*, Los Angeles, California, Feb. 1987

[Ditt86]   K. R. Dittrich: *Object-oriented Database Systems: The Notions and the Issues*, in Proc. ACM/IEEE Int. Workshop on Object-oriented Database Systems, 1986

[Ditt87]   K. R. Dittrich: *Complex Entities for Engineering Applications*, Entity-Relationship Approach, S. Spaccapietra (ed.), 1987

[ElWi81]   R. Elmasri, G. Wiederhold: *GORDAS: A Formal High-Level Query Language for the Entity-Relationship Model*, in [ER81]

[ER81]   P. P. Chen (ed.): *Proceedings of the 2nd International Conference on Entity-Relationship Approach to Information Modeling and Analysis*, Washington, D.C., 1981

[ER83]   C. Davis, S. Jajodia, P. Ng, R. Yeh (eds.): *Proceedings of the 3nd International Conference on Entity-Relationship Approach to Software Engineering*, Anaheim, California, Oct. 1983

[Lock85]   P. C. Lockemann et al.: *Anforderungen Technischer Anwendungen an Datenbanksysteme*, in Proc. GI Fachtagung Datenbanksysteme in Büro, Technik und Wissenschaft, Informatik-Fachberichte 94, 1985

[Lori83]   R. A. Lorie: *Complex Objects and Their Use in Design Transactions*, in Proc. 1983 ACM Engineering Design Applications, San Jose, CA, May 1983

[MaRa83a]   V. M. Markowitz, Y. Raz: *ERROL: An Entity-Relationship, Role Oriented Query Language*, in [ER83]

[MaRa83b]   V. M. Markowitz, Y. Raz: *A Modified Relational Algebra and Its Use in an Entity-Relationship Environment*, in [ER83]

[Mits88]   B. Mitschang: *Towards a Unified View of Design Data and Knowledge Representation*, 2nd Int. Conf. on Expert Database Systems, Virginia 1988

[Poon79]   G. Poonen: *CLEAR: A Conceptual Language for Entities and Relationships*, Centralized and Distributed Systems, IEEE Computer Society, Silver Springs, Maryland 1980

[Sche86]   H. - J. Schek, M. H. Scholl: *The Relational Model with Relation-Valueed Attributes*, Information Systems, 1986

[Schi88]   B. Schiefer: *Entwurf einer Mengenorientierten Deskriptiven Anfragesprache für ein Erweitertes Entity-Relationship Modell*, Diplomarbeit an der Universität Karlsruhe, Fakultät für Informatik, April 1988

[Shos79]   A. Shoshani: *CABLE - A Chain-Based Language for the Entity-Relationship Model*, Proc. 1st Int. Conf. on the Entity-Relationship Approach to Systems Analysis and Design, LA, California, Dec. 1979

[Velez85]   Fernando Velez: *LAMBDA: An Entity-Relationship Based Query Language for the Retrieval of Structured Documents*, in Proc. of the 4th Int. Conference on Entity-Relationship Approach, Chicago, Illinois, Oct. 1985

Rekursion im MAD-Modell:
Rekursivmoleküle als Objekte des Datenmodells

Harald Schöning
Universität Kaiserslautern

Überblick

Das Molekül-Atom-Datenmodell unterstützt die Datenbank-Verwaltung komplexer Objekte. Es bietet Operationen zum Zugriff, Ändern, Löschen und Einfügen an, die auf Mengen von dynamisch definierten Objekten arbeiten. Diese Objektdefinitionen können direkte und indirekte Rekursion enthalten, so daß die Berechnung der transitiven Hülle möglich ist. Im Gegensatz zu vielen anderen Vorschlägen für die Integration von Rekursion in Datenbanksysteme ist diese Hülle mit ihrer Struktur ein Objekt des Datenmodells, kann also mit dessen Operationen weiterverarbeitet werden. Eine Auswahl von Aggregations- und Verkettungsoperatoren ermöglicht die Lösung von Pfadproblemen durch Berechnung der generalisierten transitiven Hülle.

Abstract

The molecule atom data-model (MAD model) supports the management of complex objects in a database. There are operations to retrieve, update, delete, and insert sets of dynamically defined objects. The object definitions may contain direct and indirect recursion. Thus, transitive closure computations are possible. In contrast to many proposals for the integration of recursion in a database system published earlier, the transitive closure together with its structure can be represented within the data model. Path problems can be solved by a choice of various aggregation and concatenation operators, which may be applied to the generalized transitive closure.

1. Einleitung

Schon seit einigen Jahren wird der Einsatz von Datenbanksystemen nicht nur für die bekannten "klassischen" Anwendungsgebiete, sondern auch für die Datenverwaltung in Expertensystemen /vgl. Re87/, CAD-Systemen und ähnlichen "Non-Standard-Anwendungen" erwogen /BTW85, BTW87/. Für diese Anwendungsgebiete sind jedoch die herkömmlichen Datenbanksysteme ungeeignet /HR85/. Daher werden weltweit sogenannte Non-Standard-Datenbanksysteme entwickelt, von denen man sich eine bessere Unterstützung neuer

Anwendungen verspricht. Neben neuen Verarbeitungskonzepten basieren diese auf Datenmodellen, die sich durch Eigenschaften wie

- Integration von Zeit und Unterstützung von Versionen und Alternativen,
- Fähigkeit zur Behandlung von Rekursion und
- Abbildung von "mehr" Semantik im Datenmodell, z.B. durch die Fähigkeit zur Darstellung komplexer (strukturierter) Objekte und zur Definition komplexerer Integritätsbedingungen

auszeichnen. Diese Datenmodelle sind entweder Erweiterungen bekannter Datenmodelle (meist des Relationenmodells) oder Neuentwicklungen. Im folgenden soll die Behandlung von Rekursion näher betrachtet werden. Dabei geht es nicht um Auswertungsaspekte, sondern um die Einbettung der Rekursion in Datenmodell und Anfragesprache. Als Motivation werden zunächst einige Beispiele für Rekursion gezeigt, die in den obengenannten Non-Standard-Anwendungen vorkommen.

2. Anwendungsbeispiele

Deduktive Datenbanken

Deduktive Datenbanksysteme sollen die Datenhaltung z.B. in Expertensystemen verbessern, die im allgemeinen weder die Nutzung von Sekundärspeicher noch Mehrbenutzerbetrieb unterstützt. Solche Datenbanksysteme besitzen die Fähigkeit zur Herleitung einer sogenannten intentionalen Datenbank. Aus einer "extensionalen" Datenbank (also aus explizit gespeicherten Daten) wird die intentionale Datenbank bei Bedarf durch einen Inferenzmechanismus rekursiv gewonnen. Eine einfache extensionale Datenbank könnte z.B. aus der Relation PERSON (Name, Elternteil) bestehen. Die intentionale Datenbank beinhaltet dann z.B. die Relation AHNEN (Name, Vorfahr), deren Daten aber nicht explizit abgespeichert sind, sondern bei Bedarf abgeleitet werden.

VLSI-Entwurf

Die Verwendung von Rekursion bietet sich natürlicherweise überall dort an, wo eine stufenweise Zerlegung oder Verfeinerung auftritt, besonders, wenn die Anzahl der Zerlegungsstufen nicht von vorneherein festliegt. Ein Beispiel hierfür ist der VLSI-Entwurf, bei dem ein bestimmter Chip aus Zellen bestimmter Funktionalität besteht, die wiederum aus anderen (ggf. Standard-) Zellen zusammengesetzt werden können, usw.

Beim VLSI-Entwurf bestimmt ein sogenannter Floorplan die geometrische Lage von Zellen. Dieser Floorplan kann durch einen sogenannten Slicing-Baum dargestellt werden (vgl. /Hä85/), der eine rekursive Flächenaufteilung beschreibt, und somit ein weiteres Anwendungsgebiet von Rekursion darstellt.

Versions- und Zeitverwaltung

Eine wichtige Forderung von Entwurfsanwendungen (CAD, VLSI-Entwurf) an Datenbanksysteme ist die Unterstützung der Darstellung eines Objektes in verschiedenen Beschreibungen. Dabei kann zwischen Versionen, Alternativen, Repräsentationen /Mi85/ unterschieden werden. Verschiedene Darstellungen stehen miteinander in Beziehung (z.B. "ist hervorgegangen aus" bei Versionen) und bilden zusammen ein Entwurfsobjekt. Da hierarchische Beziehungen zwischen den Darstellungen in nicht vorhersagbarer Tiefe vorliegen können, ist auch hier eine rekursive Vorgehensweise erforderlich.

3. Rekursion in Datenbanksystemen

Es gibt einige Vorschläge für die Integration einer stark eingeschränkten Rekursion in Datenbanksysteme, z.B. kennt QBE nach /DS86/ Rekursion nur bei binären Relationen, die einen Baum bilden. POSTGRES /SR86/ bietet die Möglichkeit, die transitive Hülle zu berechnen.

Eine Vielzahl von Aufsätzen (einige neuere sind: /HN84/, /Io86/, /De87/, /LMR87/) behandelt die effiziente Berechnung rekursiver Anfragen, ohne jedoch Aussagen über die Einbettung der Rekursion in das Datenmodell zu machen. /RS86/ und /Ul85/ fordern die Erweiterung von Datenbanksprachen um Horn-Klauseln, womit Rekursion formulierbar würde. Eine solche Vermischung herkömmlicher Datenbanksprachen mit völlig anders gearteten Konstrukten scheint aber zu inhomogenen Sprachansätzen zu führen, die die natürliche Integration der Rekursion im Sinne einer "einheitlichen", homogenen Sicht der Datenbank nicht unterstützen.

Wie in /DS86/ festgestellt wird, ist es nicht sinnvoll, Rekursion in ihrer vollen Allgemeinheit in Datenmodelle einzubetten, da die Anfragesprache dann nicht mehr entscheidbar wäre. Als eine Rekursionsklasse mit "gutem Verhalten" wird dort die Klasse der Pfadprobleme weiter betrachtet. Das einfachste Pfadproblem ist die Berechnung der transitiven Hülle (also aller erreichbaren Knoten in einem Graphen). Zur Lösung komplexerer Pfadprobleme wird die Berechnung des sogenannten verallgemeinerten Hüllenoperators ("generalisierte transitive Hülle") benutzt. Das bedeutet, daß neben der Ermittlung aller erreichbaren Knoten eines Graphen auch Informationen entlang der dabei verfolgten Wege (Pfade) berechnet werden. Dabei werden zwei Operatoren benötigt:

- der *Verkettungsoperator* berechnet aus den Informationen über einzelne Kanten Werte innerhalb eines Pfades.

- Durch den *Aggregationsoperator* werden diese zwischen den Pfaden zusammengefaßt.

Tabelle 1 zeigt die Wahl beider Operatoren für typische Pfadprobleme.

Problemtyp	Gesuchte Eigenschaft	Aggregations-operator	Verkettungs-operator
Kürzester Pfad	Länge oder Dauer	Minimum	+
Kritischer Pfad	Länge oder Dauer	Maximum	+
Breitester Pfad	Kapazität	Maximum	Minimum
Zuverlässigster Pfad	Verfügbarkeit	Maximum	*
Stückliste	Häufigkeiten	+	*
Alle Wege	Teilstrecken	∪	Aneinanderfügen
Irgendein Weg	Teilstrecken	irgendeiner	Aneinanderfügen
Logische Deduktion	Prädikate	irgendeiner	Aneinanderfügen

Tabelle 1: Varianten des verallgemeinerten Hüllenoperators /Re87/, /DS86/

In /DS86/ wird die Berechnung des verallgemeinerten Hüllenoperators als vorläufiges Ziel der Integration von Rekursion in Datenbanksysteme gesehen. Drei Arten der Formulierung von Anfragen werden untersucht:

- **prozedural**: Solch eine auswertungsorientierte Rekursionsspezifikation durch den Benutzer führt u.a. zu schlechter Optimierbarkeit.

- **logik-orientiert**: Eine Formulierung mittels Horn-Klauseln führt - in geringerem Maße - zu demselben Problem.

- **schablonenartig-deskriptiv**: Da die Rekursionsspezifikation nur über Aggregations- und Verkettungsoperator erfolgt, steht dem System ein großes Optimierungspotential offen.

Datenmodelle, die keine strukturierten Objekte kennen (wie etwa das Relationenmodell), können eine transitive Hülle nur über ihre Knoten, nicht aber in ihrem Zusammenhang darstellen, so daß die Information über die Struktur der transitiven Hülle nicht repräsentiert wird ("flache" Darstellung). NF^2 /Da86, SS86/ kennt statisch strukturierte Objekte (nicht-normalisierte Relationen mit fester Struktur). Da die Tiefe einer transitiven Hülle zum Anfragezeitpunkt nicht feststeht, kann sie nicht als strukturiertes Objekt des Datenmodells dargestellt werden /Li87/. Das in /KCB87/ vorgestellte Datenmodell erlaubt direkte Rekursion in sogenannten Konfigurationen, die aus einer Hierarchie von komplexen Objekten bestehen, so daß eine einfache transitive Hüllenberechnung möglich ist. Inwieweit die berechnete transitive Hülle im Datenmodell dargestellt und weiterverarbeitet werden kann, bleibt allerdings unklar.

Das Molekül-Atom-Datenmodell unterstützt dynamische strukturierte Objekte. Es erlaubt eine "strukturierte" Darstellung mit unbestimmter Tiefe, also auch die Darstellung der transitiven Hülle als Objekt des Datenmodells. Zusammen mit den angebotenen Operationen zur Berechnung der transitiven Hülle und der generalisierten transitiven Hülle stellt es ein mächtiges Werkzeug zur Behandlung von Rekursion dar.

Im folgenden werden zunächst einige grundlegende Eigenschaften dieses Modells vorgestellt. Anschließend werden die Ausdrucksmöglichkeiten für Rekursion präsentiert und an Beispielen verdeutlicht.

4. Einige Grundzüge des Molekül-Atom-Datenmodells

Das Molekül-Atom-Datenmodell (kurz MAD-Modell, /Mi88/) ist ein auf dem Relationenmodell aufbauendes Datenmodell zur Handhabung von komplexen Objekten, den sogenannten Molekülen. Diese werden zum Bearbeitungszeitpunkt dynamisch aus Basisobjekten, den sogenannten Atomen, aufgebaut. Atome entsprechen in etwa den Tupeln des Relationenmodells. Ein Atom gehört immer zu einem bestimmten Atomtyp (der einer Relation vergleichbar ist), und setzt sich aus Attributen verschiedener Datentypen zusammen.

Neben den aus vielen herkömmlichen Datenmodellen bekannten Datentypen (wie INTEGER, REAL, etc.) sind für Attribute auch komplexere Datentypen wie TIME, LIST und ARRAY zugelassen. Jedes Atom besitzt genau ein Attribut vom Typ IDENTIFIER, das die eindeutige Identifikation des Atoms durch Verwendung eines Surrogatkonzeptes garantiert. 1:1, 1:n und n:m-Beziehungen zwischen Atomtypen lassen sich mittels Attributen des Typs REFERENCE darstellen: In jedem der beiden zu einer solchen Beziehung gehörenden Atomtypen gibt es ein REFERENCE-Attribut, das explizit an seinen Partner im anderen Atomtyp gebunden ist. Auf diese Weise entstehen sogenannte Atomtypnetze. Beispiel 1 zeigt ein Atomtypnetz für das angegebene Entity-Relationship-Diagramm: für jeden Entity-Typ wird ein Atomtyp definiert; die 1:n-Beziehung Staat-Stadt und die n:m-Beziehung Stadt — Flugverbindung werden jeweils durch ein Paar von REFERENCE-Attributen modelliert. In dem Atomtypgraphen wird diese Tatsache durch die ungerichtete Verbindung der Atomtypen dargestellt.

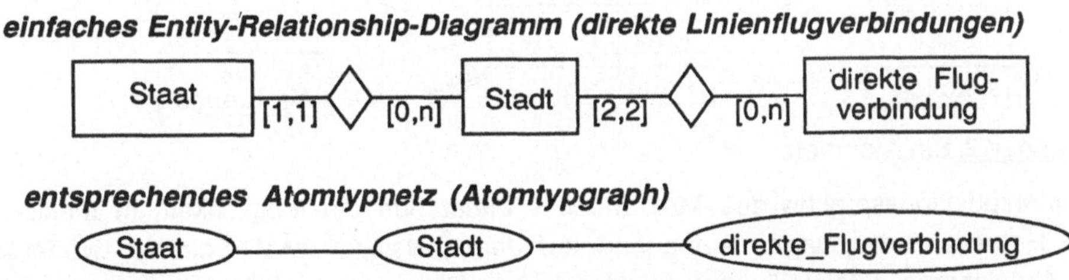

Beispiel 1: Umsetzung eines Entity-Relationship-Diagramms in ein Atomtypnetz

Der Wert eines REFERENCE-Attributes des einen Atomtyps ist eine Menge von IDENTIFIER-Werten der an der Beziehung beteiligten Atome des anderen Atomtyps, und umgekehrt. Dabei kann für die Kardinalität der Menge eine Ober- und eine Untergrenze angegeben werden. Somit könnte obiges Atomtypnetz durch folgende Atomtypdefinitionen beschrieben werden:

```
CREATE_ATOM_TYPE Stadt:
    (Stadt_Id : IDENTIFIER;
    Name : String;
    Nation : REFERENCE TO Staat.Städte (1,1)
    Flüge : REFERENCE TO direkte_Flugverbindung.zwischen (0,VAR);
    ...)
```

```
CREATE_ATOM_TYPE Staat:
    Staat_Id : IDENTIFIER;
    Name : String;
    Städte : REFERENCE TO Stadt.Nation (0, VAR);
    ...)

CREATE_ATOM_TYPE direkte_Flugverbindung:
    Flug_Id : IDENTIFIER;
    Flug_Nr : INTEGER;
    Linie : String;
    zwischen: REFERENCE TO Stadt.Flüge (2,2);
    ...)
```

Die Werte der REFERENCE-Attribute spezifizieren eine Netzstruktur auf Atomen, die bidirektional ist, da es zu jeder Referenz eine sogenannte Gegenreferenz gibt (Aus dem oben Gesagten folgt nämlich: Wenn es ein REFERENCE-Attribut des Atoms a1 den Wert {b1,b2} hat, dann gibt es in b1 und in b2 jeweils ein REFERENCE-Attribut, das den Wert a1 enthält). Beispiel 2 zeigt ein Atomnetz zu dem Atomtypnetz aus Beispiel 1. IDENTIFIER-Attribute sind nicht dargestellt. Die Werte von REFERENCE-Attributen sind durch die Verbindungslinien zwischen den Atomen symbolisiert. Jede ungerichtete Verbindung entspricht einem Referenz-/Gegenreferenz-Paar.

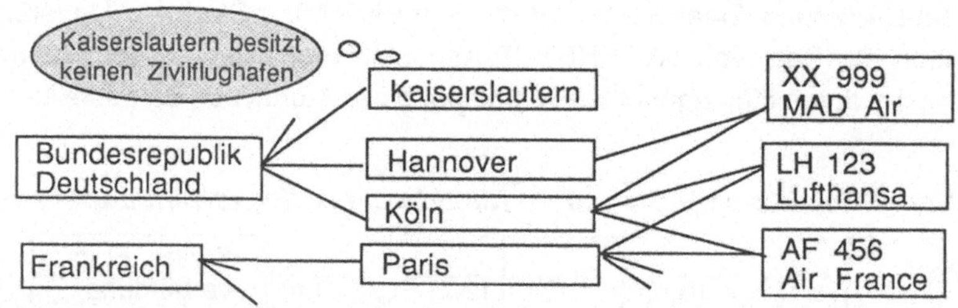

Beispiel 2: Ein Atomnetz

Die Datenmanipulationssprache des MAD-Modells bietet nun die Möglichkeit, in Manipulations- und Retrieval-Anweisungen aufbauend auf dem jeweiligen MAD-Schema dynamisch komplexe Objekttypen (Molekültypen) zu definieren. Dazu werden Knoten des Atomtypnetzes ausgewählt und Kanten zwischen diesen mit einer Richtung versehen, so daß ein zusammenhängender gerichteter Graph (Molekültypgraph) entsteht. Von genau einem Atomtyp dieses Graphen, dem sogenannten Wurzelatomtyp, müssen allen anderen erreichbar sein. Da die über REFERENCE-Attribute ausgedrückten bidirektionalen Beziehungen symmetrisch verwendbar sind, wird die Richtung der Beziehungen zwischen Atomtypen erst zu diesem Zeitpunkt festgelegt. Die Notation zur Definition eines Molekültyps soll in etwa die Graphstruktur widerspiegeln. Ausgehend vom Wurzelatomtyp werden die zu verwendenden REFERENCE-Attribute und die abhängigen Atomtypen angegeben. Eine (gerichtete) Beziehung wird durch "-" symbolisiert. So entspricht z.B. **Staat.Städte - Stadt** dem Molekültypgraphen:

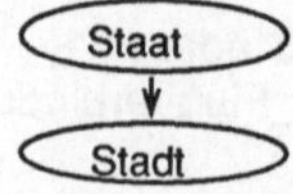

Der Attributname des zu verwendenden REFERENCE-Attributes kann entfallen, wenn die Beziehung eindeutig ist, wenn es also zwischen den beiden Atomtypen nur eine Beziehung gibt. Im obigen Fall wäre daher **Staat - Stadt** auch erlaubt. Verzweigungen im Molekülgraphen werden durch entsprechende Klammerung ausgedrückt. **Stadt - (.Nation - Staat, .Flüge - direkte_Flugverbindung)** beschreibt folgenden Molekültypgraphen:

Auch hier ist die Kurzfassung zulässig: **Stadt - (Staat, direkte_Flugverbindung)**

Da der Wurzelatomtyp erst durch die Definition des Molekültyps festgelegt wird, ist natürlich auch die Molekültypdefinition **direkte_Flugverbindung - Stadt -Staat** erlaubt. Die mehrfache Aufnahme eines Atomtyps in einen Molekültyp ist möglich. Jedes Auftreten desselben Atomtyps muß dann zur Identifikation einen sogenannten Rollennamen erhalten. Sollen z.B. Start- und Zielflughafen in einem Molekültyp differenziert werden, obwohl es im Atomtyp direkte_Flugverbindung eine solche Unterscheidung nicht gibt, kann dies durch Vergabe von Rollennamen geschehen: **Start (Stadt) - direkte_Flugverbindung - Ziel (Stadt).**

Die Moleküle, die zu einem Molekültyp gehören, lassen sich folgendermaßen beschreiben:

• Für jedes Atom des Wurzelatomtyps existiert genau ein solches Molekül.

• Zu einem Molekül gehören alle Atome, die über eine in der Molekültypdefinition angegebene Beziehung direkt oder transitiv mit dem Wurzelatom verbunden sind.

• Ein Molekül entspricht somit einem gerichteten zusammenhängenden Graphen über dem Atomnetz.

Moleküle bestehen aus Atomen mit deren Attributen und sogenannter Strukturinformation, die die Molekülstruktur beschreibt und aus den REFERENCE-Attributen der Atome abgeleitet wird. Bei der graphischen Darstellung von Molekülen wird die Strukturinfomation mit Hilfe von Pfeilen ausgedrückt.

Die Definition **Start (Stadt) - (Staat, direkte_Flugverbindung - Ziel(Stadt))** bildet aus dem Atomnetz von Beispiel 2 folgende vier Moleküle:

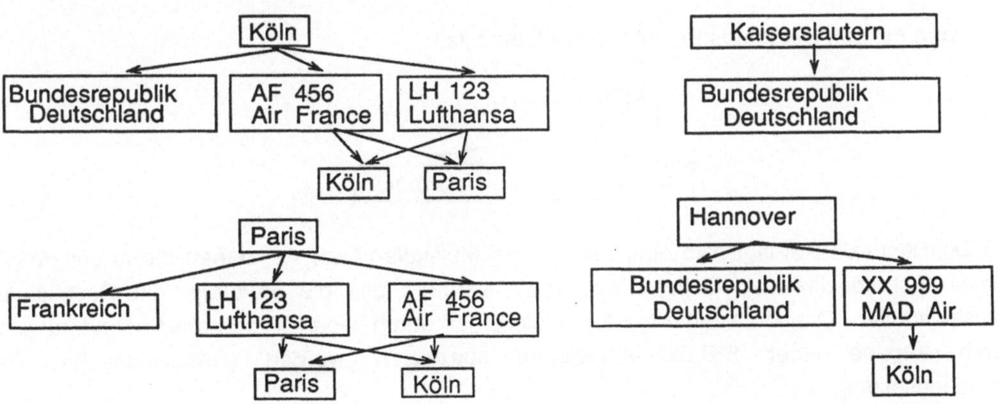

In der Rolle **Ziel** sind aufgrund der Molekültypdefinition beide Endpunkte jeder Flugverbindung enthalten. Daher kommt es, daß Köln bzw. Paris zweimal in demselben Molekül enthalten sind.

Als Beispiel für die Anwendung von Molekültypdefinitionen soll im folgenden die Retrieval-Anweisung SELECT näher beschrieben werden. Um die Lesbarkeit zu gewährleisten, werden die Molekültypgraphen zu den einzelnen Beispielen nicht im Text, sondern im Anhang angegeben. Eine SELECT-Anweisung besteht aus einer Projektionsklausel, einer Definitionsklausel und einer Restriktionsklausel und beschreibt eine (dynamisch zu erzeugende) Menge von Molekülen:

        SELECT <Projektionsklausel>
        FROM   <Definitionsklausel>
        WHERE <Restriktionsklausel>

Die **Definitionsklausel** spezifiziert den Molekültyp, auf den sich die Anfrage bezieht. Es können auch mehrere Molekültypen spezifiziert sein, wodurch ein kartesisches Produkt der Molekültypen gebildet wird. Nur solche Moleküle gehören zum Ergebnis, die den in der **Restriktionsklausel** angegebenen Ausdruck erfüllen. Jeder nicht-quantifizierte Term dieses Ausdrucks wird als existentiell quantifiziert angesehen. Die **Projektionsklausel** spezifiziert die Teile der ermittelten Moleküle (also Attribute oder Atome), die zum Ergebnis gehören sollen. Das Schlüsselwort ALL steht für alle vorkommenden Atome und Attribute. Mit ALL_BUT können gezielt Atome oder Attribute ausgeschlossen werden. Dabei muß allerdings immer ein zusammenhängendes Atomnetz bestehen bleiben, das das Wurzelatom enthält. In der Projektionsklausel können auch sogenannte virtuelle Attribute enthalten sein, deren Wert mittels einer Berechnungsvorschrift zu ermitteln ist.

Die Frage: *Von welchen französischen Städten aus und mit welchen Fluglinien kann man direkt nach Köln fliegen?* wird folgendermaßen formuliert:

        SELECT Start (Name), direkte_Flugverbindung (Linie)
        FROM   Start(Stadt)-(Staat, direkte_Flugverbindung-Ziel(Stadt))   
        WHERE Staat.Name = 'Frankreich' AND Ziel.Name = 'Köln'

und liefert mit den Daten aus Beispiel 2 das Ergebnis:

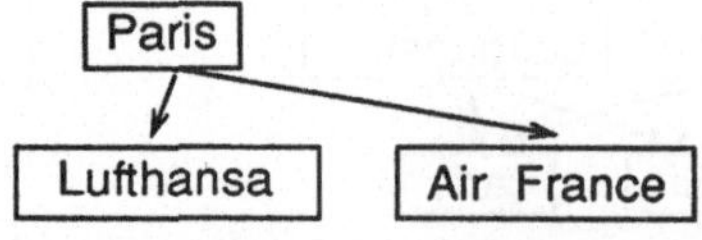

Die Definitionsklausel legt also eine Menge von Molekülen fest, von denen die in der Projektionsklausel spezifizierten Teile ausgegeben werden, falls die Moleküle die Restriktionsklausel erfüllen. Die Molekülmenge kann nicht nur durch einen Typgraphen, sondern auch durch Angabe einer SELECT-Anweisung spezifiziert werden (Geschlossenheit des Sprachansatzes).

Die Konvertierungsfunktion **VALUE** erzeugt aus Molekülmengen, deren Moleküle aus genau einem Atom mit genau einem Attribut (vom Datentyp t) bestehen, eine Liste des Typs t. Soll aus Atomen *innerhalb eines Moleküls* eine Liste erzeugt werden, so steht hierfür die Funktion **MOLAGG** zur Verfügung.

Beispiel: *Welche Stadt hat überdurchschnittlich viele Flugverbindungen?*

```
SELECT  ALL
FROM    Stadt
WHERE   COUNT (Flüge) > AVG (VALUE ( SELECT Anzahl:=COUNT (Flüge)
                                     FROM   Stadt))
```

Die Verwendung von SELECT-Anweisungen ist auch in der Projektionsklausel möglich. Dadurch können Teilmoleküle wertabhängig aus dem Ergebnismolekül ausgeblendet werden (qualifizierte Projektion). Das Schlüsselwort **RESULT** in der Definitionsklausel verdeutlicht, daß es sich dabei um eine Operation auf dem durch Definitions- und Restriktionsklausel der umgebenden Anfrage bestimmten Ergebnis handelt.

Beispiel: *Welche <u>anderen</u> Städte erreicht man von Köln direkt mit welchen Linien?*

```
SELECT  Start(Name), direkte_Flugverbindung(Linie),
              Ziele :=( SELECT Ziel (Name)
                        FROM    RESULT
                        WHERE   Ziel.Name <> 'Köln')
FROM    Start(Stadt)-direkte_Flugverbindung-Ziel(Stadt);
WHERE   Start.Name='Köln'
```

Da Köln, wie bereits gesehen, auch als Ziel-Stadt im Ergebnismolekül vorhanden ist, muß es explizit ausgeblendet werden. Die qualifizierte Projektion darf die Zusammenhangseigenschaft des Ergebnismoleküls nicht zerstören.

5. Rekursion im MAD-Modell

Nachdem nun einige Grundzüge des MAD-Modells vorgestellt wurden, soll die Handhabung von Rekursion näher betrachtet werden. In diesem Kapitel werden die wichtigsten Aspekte der Berechnung der transitiven Hülle vorgestellt, während das anschließende Kapitel dann die generalisierte transitive Hülle behandelt.

Die Integration von Rekursion in das MAD-Modell erlaubt es, einen Atomtyp nicht nur in einer festen Anzahl in verschiedenen Rollen in ein Molekül aufzunehmen, sondern "beliebig oft" entlang einer bestimmten Beziehung. So ist es in unserem Beispiel nicht nur interessant, welche Städte von einem bestimmten Startpunkt aus direkt erreicht werden können, sondern auch, welche Städte überhaupt (mit beliebig vielen Zwischenstops) zu erreichen sind. Es ist also nach der transitiven Hülle von direkte_Flugverbindung-Stadt gefragt. Ein entsprechender Molekültypgraph muß eine Schleife enthalten. Moleküle mit einem solchen

Molekültypgraphen heißen Rekursivmoleküle. Rekursionsbildung ist im MAD-Modell dort möglich, wo Beziehungen zwischen Atomtypen definiert sind. Dies entspricht den in der Literatur (z.B. /DS86/, /Re87/) zur Rekursionsbildung herangezogenen Primärschlüssel-Fremdschlüssel-Beziehungen.

Ein Rekursivmolekül setzt sich aus einer unbestimmten Anzahl von typmäßig gleichen Komponentenmolekülen zusammen, die über eine ausgezeichnete Beziehung (die sogenannte rekursionsbildende Beziehung) miteinander verbunden sind. Der Typgraph eines Rekursivmolekültyps enthält also eine Schleife. Zu einem Rekursivmolekül gehört genau ein Komponentenmolekül in der Rekursionsstufe 0 (in Analogie zum Wurzelatom eines Moleküls). Zur Rekursionsstufe n+1 gehören alle Moleküle des Komponentenmolekültyps, auf deren Wurzelatom ein Wert der rekursionsbildenden REFERENCE-Attribute von Komponentenmolekülen in Stufe n verweist. Allerdings gehört ein Komponentenmolekül nur in der kleinstmöglichen Rekursionsstufe zum Rekursivmolekül, ist also nur einmal in jedem Rekursivmolekül enthalten. Durch diese Definition wird ein maximaler, gerichteter azyklischer Ausschnitt des Atomnetzes betrachtet (analog zu /Li87/ werden Schleifen vermieden). Da die Datenbank endlich ist, existiert ein endlicher Fixpunkt der Rekursion, so daß nur endliche Rekursivmoleküle entstehen können.

Beispiel: Berechnung der transitive Hülle **Stadt-direkte_Flugverbindung** für jede Stadt.

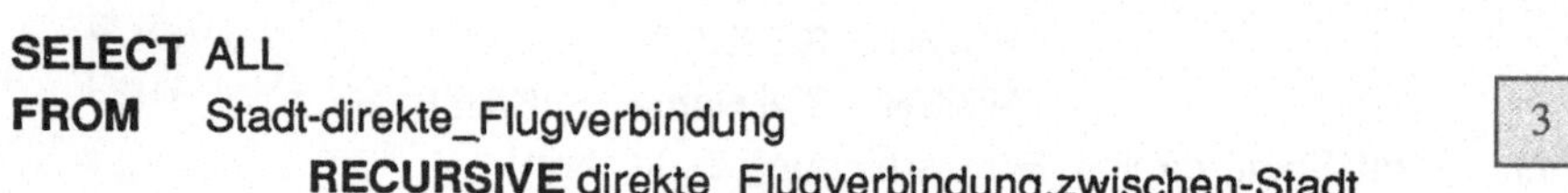

```
SELECT ALL
FROM    Stadt-direkte_Flugverbindung
              RECURSIVE direkte_Flugverbindung.zwischen-Stadt
```

3

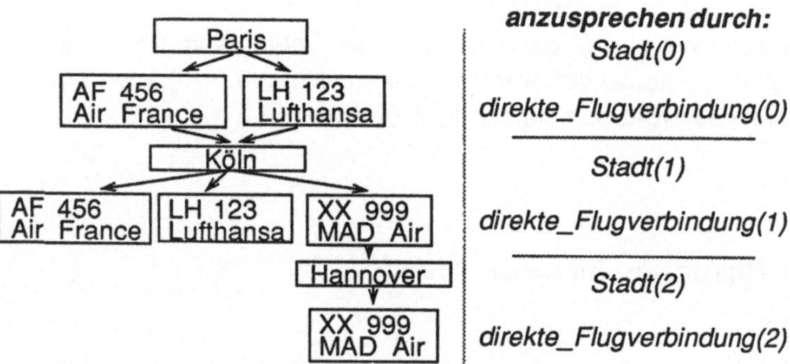

Teile von Rekursivmolekülen können folgendermaßen angesprochen werden:

- ALL_REC bezeichnet die Zusammenfassung aller Rekursionsstufen.

- [n] bezeichnet die Rekursionsstufe n. Das oberste Komponentenmolekül hat die Rekursionsstufe 0.

- [n..m] bezeichnet die Rekursionsstufen n bis m

- eine spezielle Aggregationsfunktion MAX_RECDEPTH gibt die Länge des längsten Pfades in dem Rekursivmolekül (also die größte Rekursionsstufe) an.

- LAST bezeichnet Blätter des Rekursivmolekülgraphen.

So könnte aus der oben berechneten transitiven Hülle die letzte Flugverbindung folgendermaßen entfernt werden:

    SELECT ALL_BUT direkte_Flugverbindung(LAST)
    FROM   Stadt-direkte_Flugverbindung
                      RECURSIVE Flugverbindung.zwischen-Stadt

Die Molekülstruktur stellt die transitive Hülle "strukturiert" dar. Soll lediglich eine "flache"
Sicht der erreichbaren Städte erzeugt werden, kann folgende Anfrage formuliert werden, die
die Definition des virtuellen Attributes *erreicht* als Liste von Städtenamen enthält:

    SELECT Stadt (0)(erreicht:=MOLAGG (Stadt (ALL_REC).Name))
    FROM   Stadt-direkte_Flugverbindung
                      RECURSIVE Flugverbindung.zwischen-Stadt

Die Rekursion muß nicht an der Wurzel des gesamten Moleküls beginnen; vielmehr kann ein
beliebiger nicht-rekursiver Molekültyp als Wurzel des Ergebnisses spezifiziert werden, wie
Start im folgenden Beispiel:

    SELECT ALL
    FROM   Start(Stadt) - direkte_Flugverbindung - Stadt
                      RECURSIVE Stadt.Flüge-direkte_Flugverbindung

Oft soll nicht die gesamte transitive Hülle berechnet werden, sondern nur ein bestimmter
Ausschnitt. Dabei sind mehrere Auswahlkriterien für diesen Ausschnitt denkbar:

- Die Rekursionstiefe soll ein bestimmtes Maximum nicht überschreiten.

- Sobald ein Rekursionspfad eine bestimmte Bedingung erfüllt, soll dessen Aufbau beendet
  werden. Diese Bedingung könnte zum Beispiel sein: "Die Stadt *Köln* ist im Pfad enthalten".

- Nur solche Teile der transitiven Hülle sollen betrachtet werden, bei denen die rekursionsbildende Beziehung bestimmte Bedingungen erfüllt (z.B. Weiterflug nur mit einer Maschine
  derselben Linie).

Solche Auswahlkriterien können im MAD-Modell in der **UNTIL**-Klausel formuliert werden,
die beliebig komplexe Bedingungen enthalten darf. Sie bezieht sich auf den jeweils gerade
betrachteten Rekursionspfad und hat folgende Semantik: Wenn durch die Hinzunahme eines
weiteren Komponentenmoleküls zum aktuellen Pfad die Bedingung erfüllt würde, wird die
Berechnung des Pfades abgebrochen. In der UNTIL-Klausel kann auf MAX_RECDEPTH
Bezug genommen werden, so daß die Rekursionstiefe jedes Pfades beschränkt werden
kann.

Beispiel: *Welche Städte sind von Paris aus mit höchstens einem Zwischenstop erreichbar?*

    SELECT ALL
    FROM   Start (Stadt) - direkte_Flugverbindung-Stadt
                     RECURSIVE Stadt.Flüge-direkte_Flugverbindung
                     UNTIL MAX_RECDEPTH > 1
    WHERE Start.Name='Paris'

Ferner sind die Schlüsselwörter CURRENT und PREVIOUS erlaubt, um das aktuell untersuchte Komponentenmolekül bzw. seinen direkten Vorgänger anzusprechen.

Beispiel: *Welche Städte sind von Paris aus ohne Linienwechsel erreichbar?*

> **SELECT** ALL
> **FROM**   Start (Stadt) - direkte_Flugverbindung-Stadt
>   **RECURSIVE** Stadt.Flüge-direkte_Flugverbindung
>   UNTIL direkte_Flugverbindung (CURRENT).Linie <>
>   direkte_Flugverbindung (PREVIOUS).Linie
> **WHERE** Start.Name='Paris'

Bisher wurden nur "lineare" Rekursivmoleküle vorgestellt, also solche, bei denen jedes Atom
der Komponentenmoleküle in dem Pfad vom Wurzelatom zum "untersten" Atom des Rekursivmoleküls enthalten war. Daß auch andere Rekursivmoleküle definierbar sind, zeigt folgendes
Beispiel: *Welche innerfranzösischen Flugverbindungen gibt es? (Wie kann man durch Frankre-
ich reisen, ohne eine Flugverbindung mehrmals zu benutzen?)*

> **SELECT** ALL
> **FROM**   Start (Stadt) - (direkte_Flugverbindung-Stadt-Staat
>   **RECURSIVE** Stadt.Flüge-direkte_Flugverbindung
>   UNTIL Staat (CURRENT).Name <> 'Frankreich');
> **WHERE** Start.Name='Paris'

Die Hinzunahme der jeweils ersten Stadt außerhalb Frankreichs zum Rekursivmolekül würde
zur Erfüllung der UNTIL-Klausel führen. Daher werden außerfranzösische Städte nicht in das
Rekursivmolekül aufgenommen.

6. Die Berechnung der generalisierten transitiven Hülle

Die bisher eingeführten Rekursivmoleküle erlauben die Berechnung der transitiven Hülle. Zu
jedem Atom der transitiven Hülle sind alle (bzgl. der Anzahl der zu traversierenden Beziehungen) minimalen Wege in Form von Strukturinformation im Ergebnis enthalten. Zur Berechnung der generalisierten transitiven Hülle, also zur Auswahl bestimmter Pfade über die
Pfadeigenschaften, eignet sich das Ergebnis der Anfrage in dieser Form jedoch nicht.

Daher wird neben der RECURSIVE-Klausel eine weitere Klausel **REC_PATH** angeboten. Tritt
diese in einer Anfrage auf, so werden statt der transitiven Hülle alle entsprechenden maximalen schleifenfreien linearen Pfade als Moleküle geliefert. Das heißt, daß nicht alle Werte
des rekursionsbildenden REFERENCE-Attributes zum Aufbau des Rekursivmoleküles
benutzt werden, sondern jeweils nur einer. Wo RECURSIVE also ein Molekül liefert, das die
transitive Hülle (oder einen Ausschnitt daraus) enthält, liefert REC_PATH für jeden Pfad, der
über die rekursivmolekülbildende Beziehung spezifiziert wird, ein eigenes Molekül. Die Komponentenmoleküle werden dabei einer speziellen qualifizierten Projektion unterworfen: alle
Atome des Komponentenmoleküls gehören nur dann zum Rekursivmolekül, wenn ihr Atomtyp

nicht zur Rekursionsbildung beiträgt (wie etwa Staat im vorhergehenden Beispiel), oder wenn die Atome direkt zu dem Rekursivpfad gehören, den das Rekursivmolekül darstellt.

Beispiel: *Welche Stadt- und Linienkombinationen gibt es für den Flug ab Paris (wenn keine Stadt mehrmals erreicht werden soll)?*

```
SELECT ALL
FROM    Stadt-direkte_Flugverbindung
            REC_PATH Flugverbindung.zwischen-Stadt
WHERE Stadt(0).Name = 'Paris'
```

Der Ausschluß von direkte_Flugverbindung (LAST) ist aufgrund der Semantik der Rekursiv-molekülbildung hier nicht nötig. Als Ergebnis entstehen folgende zwei Moleküle:

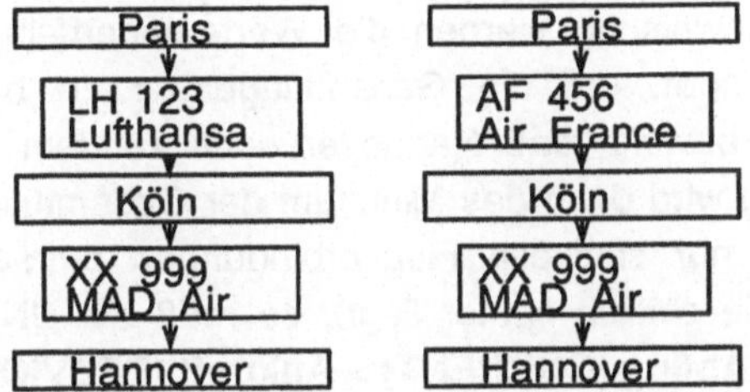

Mit dieser REC_PATH-Klausel kann nun die sogenannte generalisierte transitive Hülle berechnet werden. Tabelle 2 zeigt die im MAD-Modell zur Berechnung der einzelnen Problemtypen (vgl. Tabelle 1) zu verwendenden Operatoren. *MOLAGG* und *VALUE* liefern - wie in Kapitel 4 bereits erläutert - jeweils Listen von Werten, auf die dann die Operationen MIN, SUM, etc. angewendet werden können. Der Operator *MULT* bildet das Produkt aller Listenelemente.

Problemtyp	Gesuchte Eigenschaft	Aggregations-operator	Verkettungs-operator
Kürzester Pfad	Länge oder Dauer	MIN (VALUE...)	SUM (MOLAGG...)
Kritischer Pfad	Länge oder Dauer	MAX (VALUE...)	SUM (MOLAGG...)
Breitester Pfad	Kapazität	MAX (VALUE...)	MIN (MOLAGG...)
Zuverlässigster Pfad	Verfügbarkeit	MAX (VALUE...)	MULT (MOLAGG...)
Stückliste	Häufigkeiten	SUM (VALUE...)	MULT (MOLAGG...)
Alle Wege	Teilstrecken		MOLAGG
Irgendein Weg	Teilstrecken		MOLAGG
Logische Deduktion	Prädikate		MOLAGG

Tabelle 2: Operatoren des MAD-Modells für die Berechnung von Pfadproblemen

Für "irgendein Weg" ist kein spezieller Aggregationsoperator notwendig, da jedes Molekül einen solchen Weg darstellt. Analog kann für die logische Deduktion argumentiert werden. Die Ergebnismenge besteht aus allen Wegen. Daher kann ein Aggregator für "alle Wege" entfallen.

Ein Beispiel für den Problemtyp "kürzester Pfad" ist die folgende Anfrage: Wie lange sind die Passagiere, die in Paris mit Ziel Hannover starten, mindestens in der Luft? (Dazu muß es natürlich ein Attribut Dauer bei dem Atomtyp direkte_Flugverbindung geben.)

```
                                                    Aggregation
                                     ⎛⎯⎯⎯⎯⎯⎯⎯⎯⎯⎯⎯⎯⎯⎯⎯⎯⎯⎯⎯⎯⎯⎯⎯⎯⎯⎯⎯⎯⎯⎯⎯
SELECT  Start (In_der_Luft :=MIN (VALUE (SELECT Flugdauer FROM RESULT)))
FROM    (SELECT Start (Name),
                (SELECT  Flugdauer := SUM (MOLAGG
                                (direkte_Flugverbindung (ALL_REC) .Dauer)))      Ver-
                FROM     RESULT                                                   kettung
                WHERE    Stadt (LAST).Name = 'Hannover')
         FROM     Start (Stadt) - direkte_Flugverbindung-Stadt
                           REC_PATH Stadt.Flüge-direkte_Flugverbindung
                           UNTIL Stadt (PREVIOUS) = 'Hannover'
         WHERE    Start.Name = 'Paris')
```

In einer inneren SELECT-Anweisung werden die Werte innerhalb eines Pfades verkettet, falls dieser in Hannover endet, um die Gesamtflugdauer zu berechnen. **UNTIL Stadt (PREVIOUS) = 'Hannover'** bewirkt, daß Hannover noch zu dem Pfad dazugehört. In der äußeren SELECT-Anweisung wird dann das Minimum der Gesamtflugdauer aller Pfade Paris-Hannover bestimmt. Sollen nur sinnvolle Flugverbindungen betrachtet werden (Weiterflug nur mit einer Verbindung, die zeitlich später liegt), so muß die UNTIL-Klausel ergänzt werden, etwa um den Ausdruck: **Abflug (CURRENT) > Ankunft (PREVIOUS)**.

An diesem Beispiel wird die Nützlichkeit parametrisierter Anfragen, wie MAD sie unterstützt, deutlich: Statt Hannover bzw. Paris könnte in dieser Anfrage auch ein symbolischer Parameter $ZIEL oder $START stehen. Für diese Parameter können dann bei der Ausführung der vorübersetzten Anfrage aktuelle Werte angegeben werden. Aus Platzgründen kann dieser Aspekt hier leider nicht vertieft werden.

7. Beispiele für komplexere Rekursionsbeziehungen

Mehrfachrekursion

Für die folgenden Betrachtung führen wir eine Erweiterung des Beispielschemas ein:

```
CREATE_ATOM_TYPE Stadt :
   (Stadt_id : IDENTIFIER;
   Name : String;
   Nation : REFERENCE TO Staat.Städte (1,1)
   Flüge : REFERENCE TO direkte_Flugverbindung.zwischen (0,VAR);
   Züge : REFERENCE TO Zug.zwischen (0,VAR);
   ...)
```

```
CREATE_ATOM_TYPE Zug:
   Zug_Id : IDENTIFIER;
   Zug_Nr : INTEGER;
   zwischen: REFERENCE TO Stadt.Züge (2,2)
   ...)
```

Die Frage: *Wie gelangt man von Kaiserslautern mit dem Zug zu einem Flughafen und per Flugzeug nach Paris?* bedingt eine Verbindung der Rekursivmoleküle für Flugverbindung und Zugverbindung. Dies kann durch Verbindung (Join) zweier Rekursivmoleküle erreicht werden, der die Zugverbindung von einer Stadt X nach Kaiserslautern mit der Flugverbindung von X nach Paris verbindet (Voraussetzung: Zug- und Flugverbindung sind symmetrisch):

```
SELECT ALL
FROM     Bahn (Stadt-Zug REC_PATH Zug.zwischen-Stadt
                        UNTIL Stadt (PREVIOUS).Name='Kaiserslautern'
         Flug (Stadt - direkte_Flugverbindung
                        REC_PATH direkte_Flugverbindung.zwischen-Stadt         6
                        UNTIL Stadt (PREVIOUS).Name='Paris')
WHERE Bahn.Stadt(0).Name=Flug.Stadt (0).Name
      AND Flug.Stadt (LAST).Name = 'Paris'
      AND Bahn.Stadt (LAST).Name='Kaiserslautern'
```

Ein weitere Variante "verschachtelt" die Rekursivmoleküle ineinander. Für jede per Zug erreichbare Stadt wird untersucht, ob sie eine Flugverbindung nach Paris hat. Die unterstrichene UNTIL-Klausel bewirkt, daß die Bahnverbindung von dieser Stadt aus nicht weiter verfolgt wird, wenn eine entsprechende Flugverbindung exisitert.

```
SELECT ALL
FROM     Start(Stadt) - Zug - Stadt -
                        Flug := (SELECTALL
                                 FROM   Flug(direkte_Flugverbindung - Ziel(Stadt)
                                        REC_PATH Ziel.Flüge - direkte_Flugverbindung
                                        UNTIL Ziel (PREVIOUS).Name='Paris')
                                 WHEREZiel(LAST).Name = 'Paris')                7
                        REC_PATH Stadt.Züge - Zug
                        UNTIL EXISTS Flug (PREVIOUS)
WHERE Start.Name = 'Kaiserslautern'
```

Rekursion über mehrere REFERENCE-Attribute

Ein vielverwendetes Beispiel zur Demonstration von Rekursion, insbesondere im Bereich deduktiver Datenbanken, ist das Vorfahren-Problem: Zu einer gegebenen Person sind alle Vorfahren gesucht.

Wird das MAD-Modell-Schema folgendermaßen gewählt:

```
CREATE ATOM_TYPE Person:
   (Id : IDENTIFIER;
   Name : String;
   Mutter : REFERENCE TO Person.ist_Mutter_von (0,1);
   Vater : REFERENCE TO Person.ist_Vater_von (0,1);
   ist_Mutter_von: REFERENCE TO Person.Mutter (0,VAR);
   ist_Vater_von: REFERENCE TO Person.Vater (0,VAR);
   ...)
```

so müssen zur Bestimmung aller Vorfahren die Referenzen auf Mutter und Vater vereinigt werden (& ist der Konkatenationsoperator für REFERENCE- und LIST-Attribute.):

```
SELECT ALL
FROM    P:=( SELECT Name, Vorfahren:=Mutter&Vater
             FROM Person)
          RECURSIVE P.Vorfahren-P
WHERE  P(0).Name = 'Hugo'
```

8. Zusammenfassung und Ausblick

Die Integration von Rekursion in ein Datenmodell ist ein wichtiger Schritt auf dem Weg zu Datenbanksystemen für Non-Standard-Anwendungen. Erwünscht ist dabei nicht nur die Fähigkeit zur Berechnung der transitiven Hülle, sondern auch einer generalisierten transitiven Hülle, um die wichtige Rekursionsklasse der Pfadprobleme behandeln zu können. Im Molekül-Atom-Datenmodell können die transitive Hülle und die generalisierte transitive Hülle berechnet werden, so daß Pfadprobleme auf azyklischen Graphen gelöst werden können. Mechanismen anderer Datenmodelle zur Integration einer solchen Fähigkeit sehen meist nur eine flache Sicht der transitiven Hülle vor, also nur die Erfassung aller Objekte innerhalb dieser Hülle. Das MAD-Modell bietet darüberhinaus die Möglichkeit, diese transitive Hülle - ebenso wie einzelne Pfade - in ihrer Struktur darzustellen, und zwar als Objekt innerhalb des Datenmodells. Damit ist es auch möglich, Pfade darzustellen, deren einzelne Knoten wiederum strukturiert sind. Rekursion läßt sich im MAD-Modell deskriptiv spezifizieren, so daß der Anwender von der Erstellung eines effizienten Abarbeitungsplanes befreit wird.

Die Implementierung des MAD-Modells im Projekt PRIMA (Prototyp-Implementierung des MAD-Modells, /HMMS87, Hä88/) enthält die Realisierung der RECURSIVE-Klausel. Eine in Vorbereitung befindliche zweite Version von PRIMA wird den vollen Umfang des hier vorgestellten Sprachvorschlags realisieren.

Literatur

BTW85 Proceedings Datenbank-Systeme für Büro, Technik und Wissenschaft, GI-Fachtagung, Karlsruhe, März 1985, Springer IFB 94.

BTW87 Proceedings Datenbank-Systeme für Büro, Technik und Wissenschaft, GI-Fachtagung, Darmstadt, April 1987, Springer IFB 136.

Da86 Dadam, P. et al.: A DBMS Prototype to Support Extended NF^2-Relations: An Integrated View on Flat Tables and Hierarchies, in: Proc. ACM SIGMOD, Washington, DC, 1986, pp. 356-367.

De87 Demo, B.: Recursive versus Iterative Schemes for Least Fix Point Computation in Logic Databases, in: Proc. Third Int. Conf. on Data Engineering, Los Angeles, California, Feb. 3-5, 1987, pp. 130-137.

DS86 Dayal, U., Smith, J.M.: PROBE: A Knowledge-Oriented Database Management System, in : Brodie, M.L., Mylopoulos, J. (eds.): On Knowledge Base Management Systems, Springer, 1986, pp 227-257.

Hä85 Härder, T., et al.: Datenstrukturen und Datenmodelle für den VLSI-Entwurf, Forschungsbericht 26/85 des SFB 124, Universität Kaiserslautern, 1985.

Hä88 Härder, T. (ed.): The PRIMA Project - Design and Implementation of a Non- Standard Database System, Forschungsbericht 26/88 des SFB 124, Universität Kaiserslautern, 1988.

HMMS87 Härder, T., Meyer-Wegener, K., Mitschang, B., Sikeler, A.: PRIMA - A DBMS Prototype Supporting Engineering Applications, in: Proc. 13. Int. Conf on VLDB, Brighton, 1987, pp. 433-442.

HN84 Henschen, L.J., Naqvi, S.A.: On Compiling Queries in Recursive First-Order Databases, in: Journal of the ACM, Vol. 31, No. 1, January 1984, pp. 47-85.

HR85 Härder, T., Reuter, A.: Architektur von Datenbanksystemen für Non-Standard-Anwendungen, in /BTW85/, S. 253-286.

Io86 Ioannidis, Y.E.: On the Computation of the Transitive Closure of Relational Operators, in: Proc. 12. Int. Conf on VLDB, Kyoto, August 1986, pp. 403-411.

KCB87 Kim, W., Chou, H-T., Banerjee, J.: Operations and Implementation of Complex Objects, in: Proc. Third Int. Conf. on Data Engineering, Los Angeles, California, Feb. 3-5, 1987, pp. 626-633.

Li87 Linnemann, V.: Non First Normal Form Relations and Recursive Queries: An SQL Based Approach, in: Proc. 3rd IEEE Int. Conf. on Data Engineering, Los Angeles, Feb. 1987, pp. 591-598.

LMR87 Lu, H., Mikkilineni, K., Richardson, J.P.: Design and Evaluation of Algorithms to Compute the Transitive Closure of a Database Relation, in: Proc. Third Int. Conf. on Data Engineering, Los Angeles, California, Feb. 3-5, 1987, pp. 112-119.

Mi85 Mitschang, B.: Charakteristiken des Komplex-Objekt-Begriffs und Ansätze zu dessen Realisierung, in: /BTW85/, S. 382-400.

Mi88 Mitschang, B.: Ein Molekül-Atom-Datenmodell für Non-Standard-Anwendungen -Anwendungsanalyse, Datenmodellentwurf und Implementierungskonzepte, Dissertation, Universität Kaiserslautern, 1988.

Re87 Reuter, A.: Kopplung von Datenbank- und Expertensystemen, in: Informationstechnik it, 29. Jg., Heft 3/87, S. 164-175.

RS86 Raschid, L., Su, S.Y.W.: A Parallel Processing Strategy for Evaluating Recursive Queries, in: Proc. 12. Int. Conf on VLDB, Kyoto, August 1986, pp. 412-419.

SR86 Stonebraker, M., Rowe, L.A.: The Design of POSTGRES, in: Proc. ACM SIGMOD, Washington, DC, 1986, pp. 340-355.

SS86 Scheck, H.J., Scholl, M.H.: The Relational Model with Relation-Valued Attributes, in: Information Systems, Vol. 11, No. 2, 1986, pp. 137-147.

Ul85 Ullman: Implementation of Logical Query Languages for Databases, in: ACM TODS, Vol. 10, No. 3, pp. 289-321.

Anhang

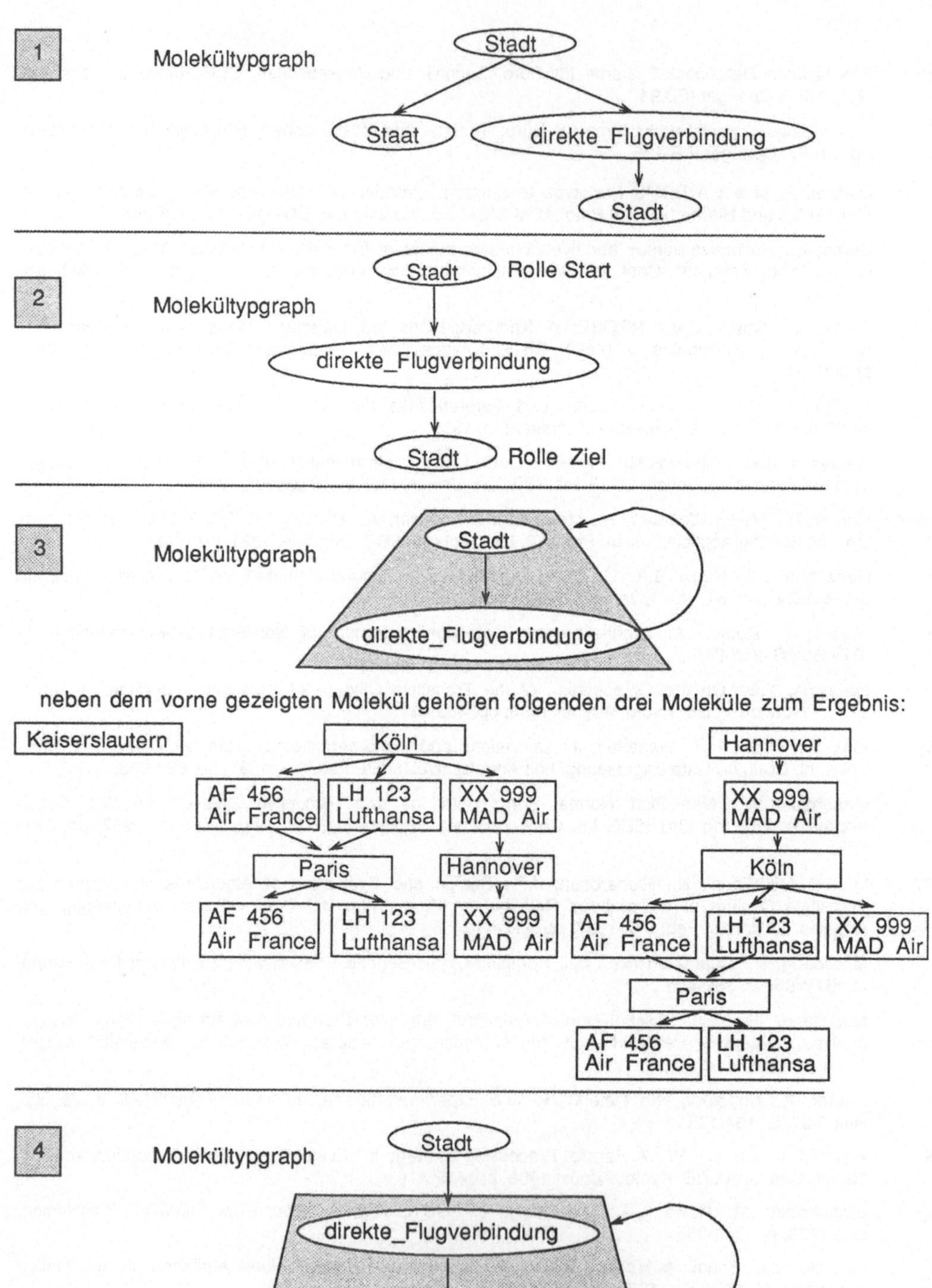

1
Molekültypgraph
Stadt
Staat
direkte_Flugverbindung
Stadt

2
Molekültypgraph
Stadt   Rolle Start
direkte_Flugverbindung
Stadt   Rolle Ziel

3
Molekültypgraph
Stadt
direkte_Flugverbindung

neben dem vorne gezeigten Molekül gehören folgenden drei Moleküle zum Ergebnis:
Kaiserslautern
Köln
AF 456 Air France
LH 123 Lufthansa
XX 999 MAD Air
Paris
Hannover
AF 456 Air France
LH 123 Lufthansa
XX 999 MAD Air
Hannover
XX 999 MAD Air
Köln
AF 456 Air France
LH 123 Lufthansa
XX 999 MAD Air
Paris
AF 456 Air France
LH 123 Lufthansa

4
Molekültypgraph
Stadt
direkte_Flugverbindung
Stadt

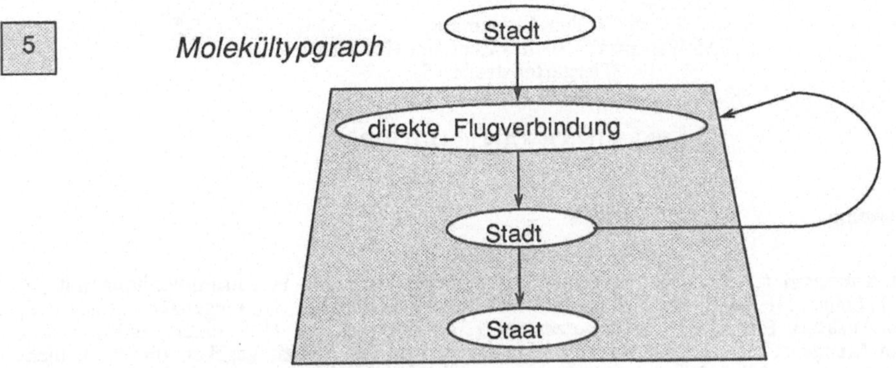
5
Molekültypgraph
Stadt
direkte_Flugverbindung
Stadt
Staat

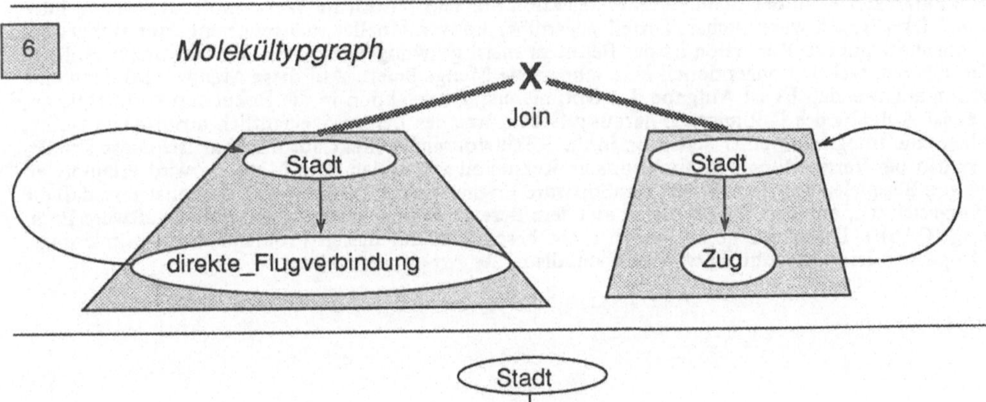
6
Molekültypgraph
X
Join
Stadt
direkte_Flugverbindung
Stadt
Zug

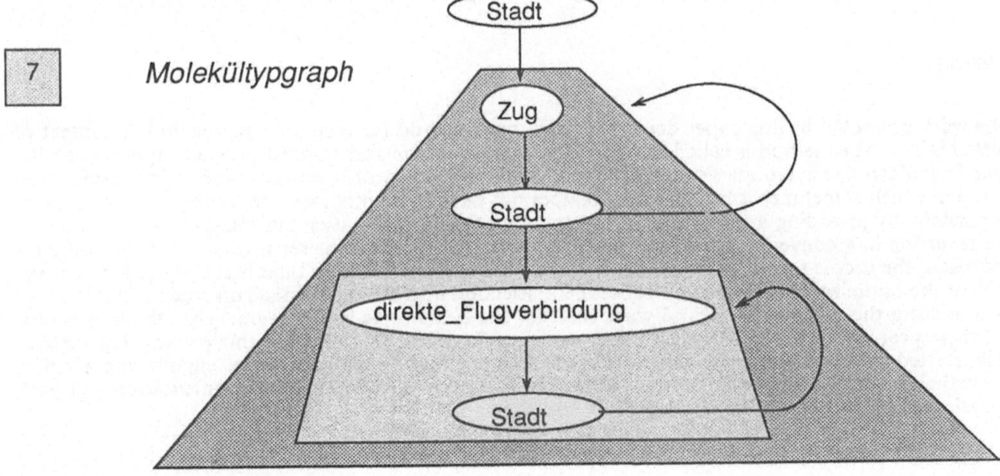
7
Molekültypgraph
Stadt
Zug
Stadt
direkte_Flugverbindung
Stadt

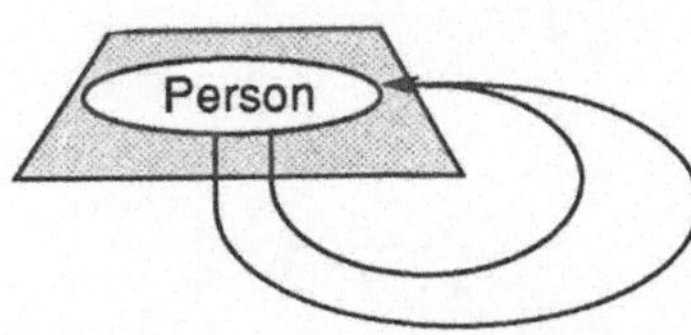
8
Molekültypgraph
Person

Funktional rekursive Anfragen
auf der Basis von geschachtelten Tabellen

Volker Linnemann
IBM Wissenschaftliches Zentrum Heidelberg
Tiergartenstraße 15
D-6900 Heidelberg

EARN: LINNEMAN at DHDIBM1

Zusammenfassung

Diese Arbeit demonstriert eine neue Methode für rekursive Anfragen in Zusammenhang mit geschachtelten Tabellen. Die Methode wird funktionale Rekursion genannt. Im Gegensatz zu den meisten früheren Ansätzen formuliert der Benutzer rekursive Anfragen mit Hilfe einer Funktion statt
einer üblichen Mengenrekursion. Das Terminierungskriterium ist implizit gegeben und muß nicht
wie bei einer konventionellen Programmiersprache explizit programmiert werden. Durch entsprechende Parameter kann der Benutzer eine Selektion auf sehr natürliche Weise in die Rekursion integrieren. Dies ist ein wesentlicher Vorteil gegenüber konventioneller mengenorientierter Rekursion.
Bei mengenorientierter Rekursion ist der Benutzer meist gezwungen, zunächst eine rekursive Anfrage
zu formulieren, welche konzeptionell eine sehr große Menge liefert. Auf diese Menge wird dann eine
Selektion angewendet. Es ist Aufgabe des Optimierers, die Selektion in die Rekursion zu integrieren,
d.h. es ist Aufgabe des Optimierers, herauszufinden, was der Benutzer eigentlich ausdrücken wollte,
weil hier eine Integration einer Selektion in die Rekursion nicht direkt ausdrückbar ist. Diese Probleme werden bei Verwendung von funktionaler Rekursion vermieden. Die Methode wird erläutert an
Hand von Beispielen aus dem Gebiet des Software Engineering. Hierdurch wird demonstriert, daß die
Methode sich u.a. anbietet für Probleme aus dem Bereich des computerunterstützten Software Engineering (CASE). Die Methode ist jedoch nicht beschränkt auf diesen Problemkreis. Optimierungs-
und Implementierungstechniken werden ebenfalls in der Arbeit angegeben.

Abstract

The work presented in this paper demonstrates a new method for recursive queries in the context of
nested tables. The method is called functional recursion. In contrast to most previous approaches, the
user formulates recursive queries by writing a function instead of a set recursion. The termination
criterion which sometimes is rather complex does not have to be programmed by the user but is given
implicitely. By providing appropriate parameters to a function, the user can integrate a selection into
the recursion in a convenient and natural way. This is not the case for set recursion. When using set
recursion, the user is forced to formulate a query which computes more than is really needed. It is the
task of the optimizer then to push a subsequent selection into the recursion. This means that the user
cannot write the query in a natural way. Instead, the system has to figure out what the user wants.
All these problems are avoided when using recursive functions as defined in this paper. The method
is illustrated by several examples taken from the area of computer aided software engineering (CASE).
Nevertheless, the method is not restricted to CASE problems. Moreover, implementation and optimization techniques are given in the paper.

1. Einleitung

Diese Arbeit demonstriert eine neue Methode für rekursive Anfragen in Zusammenhang mit geschachtelten Tabellen. Die Methode wird funktionale Rekursion genannt. Im Gegensatz zu den meisten früheren Ansätzen formuliert der Benutzer rekursive Anfragen mit Hilfe einer Funktion statt einer üblichen Mengenrekursion. Das Terminierungskriterium ist implizit gegeben und muß nicht wie bei einer konventionellen Programmiersprache explizit programmiert werden. Durch entsprechende Parameter kann der Benutzer eine Selektion auf sehr natürliche Weise in die Rekursion integrieren. Dies ist ein wesentlicher Vorteil gegenüber konventioneller mengenorientierter Rekursion. Bei mengenorientierter Rekursion ist der Benutzer meist gezwungen, zunächst eine rekursive Anfrage zu formulieren, welche konzeptionell eine sehr große Menge liefert. Auf diese Menge wird dann eine Selektion angewendet. Es ist Aufgabe des Optimierers, die Selektion in die Rekursion zu integrieren, d.h. es ist Aufgabe des Optimierers, herauszufinden, was der Benutzer eigentlich ausdrücken wollte, weil hier eine Integration einer Selektion in die Rekursion nicht direkt ausdrückbar ist. Diese Probleme werden bei Verwendung von funktionaler Rekursion vermieden. Die Methode wird erläutert an Hand von Beispielen aus dem Gebiet des Software Engineering. Hierdurch wird demonstriert, daß die Methode sich u.a. anbietet für Probleme aus dem Bereich des computerunterstützten Software Engineering (CASE). Die Methode ist jedoch nicht beschränkt auf diesen Problemkreis. Optimierungs- und Implementierungstechniken werden ebenfalls in der Arbeit angegeben. Als Basissprache für die Methode wird eine SQL-ähnliche Datenbanksprache für komplexe Objekte verwendet.

Die Arbeit ist wie folgt aufgebaut: Abschnitt 2 enthält einen kurzen Überblick über existierende Ansätze für komplexe Objekte und rekursive Anfragen. Abschnitt 3 gibt einen Überblick über die zugrundeliegende SQL-ähnliche Anfragesprache und skizziert einen früheren Ansatz zur Unterstützung rekursiver Anfragen. Abschnitt 4 ist der zentrale Teil der Arbeit. Er führt funktional rekursive Anfragen ein, sowohl formal als auch durch Beispiele. Die Beispiele sind in erster Linie Beispiele aus dem Software Engineering. Darüberhinaus wird eine wichtige Unterklasse von generell rekursiven Funktionen angegeben, welche einerseits eine effiziente Implementierung ermöglicht und andererseits allgemein genug für praktische Anwendungen erscheint. Abschnitt 5 stellt einige Optimierungstechniken für funktionale Rekursion vor. Abschnitt 6 schließlich beendet das Papier mit einer Zusammenfassung und einem Ausblick auf zukünftige Arbeiten.

2. Rekursive Anfragen und komplexe Objekte

In den letzten Jahren wurde an vielen Stellen erkannt, daß konventionelle relationale Systeme mit relational vollständigen Anfragesprachen /Co72/ die Anforderungen von fortschrittlichen Anwendungen wie wissensbasierten Systemen oder Ingenieuranwendungen nicht erfüllen /Ke84/, /ISW84/, /GMN84/, /JaLiSc85/, /Li86/, /RHDM86/, /St86/, /Ag87/, /CMW87/, /SP82/, /DaKü86/, /PA86/, /SS86/, /St86/, /La84/, /LaMSc84/, /HL82/, /AB84/, /RKB85/, /JaClVa84/, /Ap85/ etc. Dies hat im wesentlichen 2 Gründe:

- Konventionelle relationale Systeme mit flachen Tupeln haben keine adäquaten Strukturierungsmöglichkeiten welche es erlauben würden, die Daten, welche zu einem Objekt gehören, zu gruppieren

- Vergleichsweise einfache Anwendungen wie die Berechnung der transitiven Hülle einer Relation können nicht ausgedrückt werden mit Hilfe einer relational vollständigen Anfragesprache /AhUl79/.

Die Forschung in diesem Gebiet läßt sich grob in 3 Gruppen aufteilen:

1. Die erste Gruppe von Arbeiten benutzt Hornklausel-Logik als Datenbanksprache /Ko81/, /GMN84/. Die meisten Ansätze gehen von der Programmiersprache PROLOG /ClMe81/ aus welche in engem Zusammenhang mit Hornklausel-Logik steht und koppeln sie in der einen oder anderen Weise mit einer relationalen Datenbank /JaClVa84/, /Ap85/ etc.

2. Die zweite Gruppe von Arbeiten geht von einem relationalen Datenbanksystem aus und erweitert es durch rekursive Anfragen /Ke84/, /ISW84/, /JaLiSc85/, /Li86/, /St86/, /Ag87/.

3. In der dritten Gruppe von Arbeiten wird ein nichtkonventionelles Datenmodell benutzt /DaKü86/, /PA86/, /SP82/, /SS86/, /St86/, /La84/, /LaMSc84/, /HL82/, /AB84/, /RKB85/ welches bessere Strukturierungsmöglichkeiten erlaubt. Einige behandeln das Problem der rekursiven Anfragen im Model /RHDM86/, /CMW87/, /AG87/, /TZ86/.

Stellvertretend für die Fülle der Arbeiten auf dem Gebiet der rekursiven Anfragen sollen hier DATALOG , LDL, COL, MAD und PROBE erwähnt werden. Aus Platzgründen können wir uns nur auf die wesentlichen Eigenschaften beschränken und müssen auf Details verzichten.

Der Begriff 'DATALOG' wurde eingeführt von einer Gruppe von Wissenschaftlern der Stanford University und der Microelectronics and Computer Technology Corporation (MCC) in Austin/Texas. DATALOG ist eine eingeschränkt Fassung von PROLOG. Die Einschränkungen sind im wesentlichen, daß keine Funktionen zugelassen sind und daß zweifelhafte Sprachkonstrukte wie CUT und FAIL weggelassen sind. Darüberhinaus gibt es keine Negation. Durch diese Einschränkungen läßt sich die Semantik von DATALOG durch eine mengenorientierte Fixpunktsemantik beschreiben, welche eine effiziente Datenbankunterstützung erlaubt im Gegensatz zu PROLOG. Insbesondere ist, im Gegensatz zu PROLOG, die Reihenfolge der Angabe von Regeln in DATALOG irrelevant. Weil keine Funktionen zugelassen sind, unterstützt DATALOG nur flache Tabellen. Es gibt inzwischen eine Fülle von Arbeiten, welche sich mit der Optimierung von DATALOG Anfragen beschäftigen, siehe z.B. /Ul85/, /BMSU86/, /BaRa86/, /Ga87/.

LDL ('A Logic-Based Data Language') /TZ86/ kann als Verallgemeinerung von DATALOG aufgefaßt werden. Die wesentlichen Verallgemeinerungen betreffen mengenwertige Komponenten und eine besondere Art der Negation. Hierdurch eignet sich LDL u.a. zur Unterstützung von komplexen Objekten. Auf der anderen Seite ist LDL eine generelle Programmiersprache, d.h. LDL Programme müssen nicht unbedingt terminieren. Dies erscheint für eine Anfragesprache nicht akzeptabel.

Auch COL /AG87/ ist eine Verallgemeinerung von DATALOG in Richtung auf komplexe Objekte. Neben Basistabellen und abgeleiteten Tabellen gibt es Basisdatenfunktionen und abgeleitete Datenfunktionen. COL ist jedoch nicht als Endbenutzersprache anzusehen, sondern mehr als Metasprache zur Definition von Endbenutzersprachen.

MAD /Mi87/ ist ein Datenmodell für den Kern eines Non-Standard-Datenbanksystems. Es unterstützt rekursive Anfragen, allerdings wird in der Regel die Angabe eines expliziten Terminierungskriteriums verlangt.

Rekursive Anfragen in PROBE /RHDM86/ kommen der in dieser Arbeit diskutierten funktionalen Rekursion am nächsten. Die Rekursion in PROBE, auch 'traversal recursion' genannt, behandelt die Rekursion in Zusammenhang mit Graphalgorithmen, d.h. die traversal recursion ist eine Rekursion über Graphen. Darüberhinaus basiert PROBE auf dem funktionalen Datenmodell DAPLEX /Sh81/ während der in dieser Arbeit vorgeschlagene Ansatz geschachtelte Tabellen zur Grundlage hat.

3. Modellierung von Software Engineering-Problemen mit HDBL

3.1 Datenmodell und Sprache

Das Datenmodell, das im folgenden kurz skizziert werden soll, ist eine objekt-orientierte Verallgemeinerung von Non-First-Normal-Form (NF^2) bzw. geschachtelten Relationen. Die Heidelberg Data Base Language (HDBL), eine SQL-artige Sprache, wurde entwickelt, um dieses Datenmodel zu unterstützen /PT86/, /PA86/, /Pi87/, /ALPS88/.

Die **Objekttypen**, die von HDBL unterstützt werden, sind:

- mengenwertig
- listenwertig
- tupelwertig
- atomar

Atomare Datentypen sind: DATE, TIME, REAL, INTEGER, BOOLEAN, CHARACTER, und
SURROGATE. Die Elemente oder Attributwerte eines beliebigen Objekttypen (Ausnahme: atomare
Werte) können Werte von einem der oben aufgelisteten Typen sein. Zum Beispiel können die Attribute eines tupelwertigen Objekts atomar, mengenwertig, listenwertig oder wieder tupelwertig sein.
Abbildung 1.a zeigt eine graphische Repräsentierung dieses Datenmodells. Man kann dieser Abbildung entnehmen, daß sowohl das 1NF Datenmodell als auch das pure NF^2 Datenmodell Spezialfälle
dieses Datenmodells sind. Das Datenmodell wird auch *Extended NF^2 Data Model* genannt, weil es in
evolutionärer Weise aus dem NF^2 Datenmodell entstanden ist. Implementierungsdetails, z.B. Clustering von Subobjekten, werden in /DaKü86/ diskutiert.

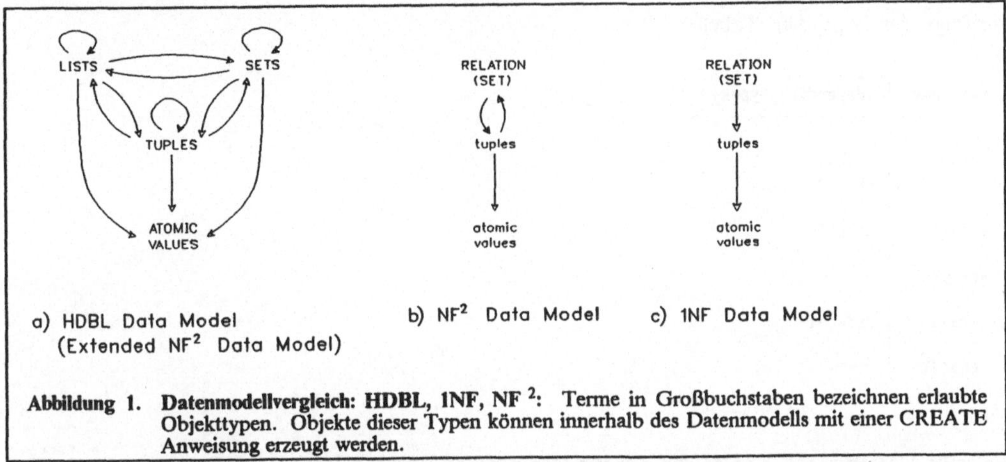

Abbildung 1. Datenmodellvergleich: HDBL, 1NF, NF²: Terme in Großbuchstaben bezeichnen erlaubte
Objekttypen. Objekte dieser Typen können innerhalb des Datenmodells mit einer CREATE
Anweisung erzeugt werden.

Da HDBL-Anweisungen später zur Einführung von funktionaler Rekursion verwendet werden, soll
jetzt eine kurze Einführung in diese Sprache gegeben werden. Eine ausführliche Darstellung findet sich
in /PT86/, /PA86/, /Pi87/.

Die folgenden Beispiele zeigen die CREATE Anweisung von HDBL und einige einfache Anfragen.
Um übersichtlich zu bleiben, wurde eine relativ einfache Struktur gewählt.

Als Beispiel benutzen wir einen Teil eines Software Engineering Systems welches es erlaubt, Informationen über Softwaresysteme zu speichern. Das erste Beispiel generiert eine Tabelle zur Abspeicherung von Typabhängigkeiten in einem Softwaresystem.

Beispiel 1:

```
CREATE type_defs
  { [ typename: string,
      depending_types: { string }
  ] }
END
```

Mengen werden durch geschweifte Klammern angedeutet ({...}), Tupel durch eckige Klammern ([...]),
Listen (geordnete Mengen) durch spitze Klammern (<...>); alternativ können die Konstruktoren
set(...), tuple(...), und list(...) benutzt werden /ALPS88/. Dies bedeutet, daß 'type_defs' eine Menge
von Tupeln ist. Das Attribut 'depending_types' ist eine Menge von Zeichenketten. 'typename' repräsentiert einen Typnamen, und 'depending_types' repräsentiert alle Typen die direkt von diesem
Typ abhängen. Dies Beispiel zeigt einen Unterschied zu normalen geschachtelten Relationen. Geschachtelte Relationen in reiner Form erlauben nur Mengen von Tupeln. Das Beispiel benutzt eine
Menge von Zeichenketten für das 'depending_types' Attribut. Hierdurch wird die Einführung eines
künstlichen einattributigen Tupels überflüssig. Zum Beispiel führen die PASCAL Typdeklarationen

```
TYPE range  = 1 .. 1000;
     array1 = ARRAY [ range  ] OF REAL;
     array2 = ARRAY [ range  ] OF INTEGER;
     array3 = ARRAY [ 1..50  ] OF array1;
     record1 = RECORD
                    a1: REAL;
                    a2: array3
                END;
```

zur folgenden 'type_defs' Tabelle:

typename	{depending_types}
range	array1 array2
array1	array3
array2	——
array3	record1
record1	——

Es sollte klar sein, daß eine solche Tabelle sehr nützlich ist wenn in einem Softwaresystem ein Typ verändert werden soll, da die Tabelle die Information enthält, welche Typen von einem Typ abhängig sind, d.h. eventuell von der Änderung betroffen sein könnten. Es folgen nun einige Beispielanfragen, welche sich auf diese Tabelle beziehen. Mit HDBL kann die Anfrage 'Welche Typen hängen direkt vom Typ "range" ab ?' wie folgt ausgedrückt werden:

Beispiel 2:

```
SELECT d
FROM t IN type_defs, d IN t.depending_types
WHERE t.typename = "range"
```

Das Ergebnis der Anfrage ist die Menge {"array1", "array2"}. Natürlich reicht es in praktischen Anwendungen in der Regel nicht, wenn man nur die direkt abhängigen Typen kennt. Man benötigt normalerweise auch die indirekt abhängigen Datentypen. Im Beispiel wäre das die Menge {"array1", "array2", "array3", "record1"}. Diese Anfrage kann nicht in reinem HDBL ausgedrückt werden, da sie im wesentlichen die Berechnung der transitiven Hülle erfordert. Abschnitt 4 zeigt, wie dieses Problem mit funktionaler Rekursion gelöst werden kann.

Das nächste Beispiel ergänzt Beispiel 1 um Informationen über Prozedurabhängigkeiten.

Beispiel 3:

```
CREATE types_and_procedures
   [ types:
         { [ typename: string,
             depending_types: { string },
             depending_procs: { string }
           ] },
       procedures:
         { [ procname: string,
             depending_procs: { string }
           ] }
     ]
END
```

Um das Beispiel übersichtlich zu halten, nehmen wir an, daß Typen nicht von Prozeduren abhängen können, d.h. es gibt keine Prozeduren als Komponenten von Records. 'depending_types' und 'depending_procs' enthalten immer direkt abhängige Größen. Zu bemerken ist noch, daß in diesem Beispiel das Objekt auf oberster Ebene ein Tupel mit den Komponenten 'types' und 'procedures' ist, d.h. es ist keine Menge von Tupeln wie im 1NF- oder NF^2- Fall. Falls wir die Typdeklarationen wie vorher und die Prozedurdeklarationen

```
PROCEDURE proc1(p1:array1);
BEGIN ... proc3(...) ... proc4(...) ... END;

PROCEDURE proc2(p2:record1);
BEGIN ... proc1(...) ... proc4(...) ... END;

PROCEDURE proc3(p3:INTEGER);
BEGIN  ... proc2(...) ... END;

PROCEDURE proc4(p4:REAL);
BEGIN  ... proc4(...) ... END;
```

annehmen, sieht das entsprechende 'types_and_procedures' Tupel wie folgt aus:

types			procedures	
typename	{depending_types}	{depending_procs}	procname	{depending_procs}
range	array1 array2	—	proc1	proc2
array1	array3	proc1	proc2	proc3
array2	—	—	proc3	proc1
array3	record1	—	proc4	proc1 proc2 proc4
record1	—	proc2		

Wir können alle Prozeduren, die direkt von "proc2" abhängen, wie folgt erhalten:

Beispiel 4:

```
SELECT dp
FROM p IN types_and_procedures.procedures, dp IN p.depending_procs
WHERE p.procname = "proc2"
```

Wie bei den Typen ist es in reinem HDBL nicht möglich, alle indirekten Abhängigkeiten zu finden. In diesem Beispiel haben wir nicht nur einfache Abhängigkeiten, sondern auch Abhängigkeiten zwischen verschiedenen Attributen. Abschnitt 4 wird zeigen, wie alle indirekten Abhängigkeiten in sehr natürlicher Weise mit Hilfe von funktionaler Rekursion gefunden werden können.

Natürlich gibt es in HDBL auch Update- Operationen wie DELETE, INSERT und ASSIGN. Da diese Operationen in dieser Arbeit nicht benötigt werden, werden diese Operationen hier aus Platzgründen weggelassen. Einzelheiten und weitere Beispiele finden sich in /DaKü86/, /PT85/, /PA86/, /Pi87/, /ALPS88/.

3.2 Mengenorientierte Rekursion

Wie Aho und Ullman schon 1979 bewiesen haben /AhUl79/, kann die transitive Hülle einer Relation nicht berechnet werden mit Hilfe einer lediglich relational vollständigen Anfragesprache /Co72/. Um dies zu tun, ist entweder Iteration oder Rekursion notwendig. Es gibt mittlerweile viele Vorschläge für die Integration von Rekursion in eine relationale Anfragesprache, siehe zum Beispiel /Ko81/, /Ke84/, /ISW84/, /GMN84/, /JaLiSc85/, /Li86/, /RHDM86/, /St86/, /Ag87/, /CMW87/ etc. Während die meisten Ansätze sich nur mit Rekursion über flachen Tabellen befassen, wurde in /Li87/, /Li88a/ ein SQL-basierter Vorschlag für mengenorientierte rekursive Anfragen über geschachtelten Tabellen gemacht. Die wesentliche Idee von diesem Mechanismus ist es, Attribute rekursiv zu definieren. Diese rekursiv definierten Attribute können auf einer beliebigen Hierarchiestufe einer geschachtelten Tabelle auftreten. Beispielsweise können alle indirekten Typabhängigkeiten mit dieser mengenorientierten Rekursion wie folgt erhalten werden:

```
SELECT
  [ typename: t.typename ,
    all_depending_types:
        t.depending_types UNION
          ( SELECT dp
            FROM t2 IN type_defs,
                 dp IN t2.depending_types
            WHERE
                EXISTS d IN all_depending_types:
                  d = t2.typename )
  ]
FROM t IN type_defs
```

Die Semantik dieser Rekursion ist definiert durch konventionelle Fixpunktberechnung welche bekanntlich immer terminiert falls die Mengensequenz monoton ist. Diese Art der Rekursion ist mengenorientiert, da Mengen von Tupeln, im Beispiel 'all_depending_types' rekursiv definiert werden. Obwohl dieser Ansatz sich in einfachen Fällen als brauchbar herausgestellt hat, hat die Erfahrung im Umgang mit dieser Spracherweiterung gezeigt (die Spracherweiterung wurde prototypisch im Rahmen einer Diplomarbeit implementiert /Wo88/), daß die Anfragen für den Benutzer sehr komplex werden und schwer zu durchschauen sind. Dies liegt in erster Linie daran, daß mengenorientierte Rekursion zuviel gleichzeitig tut. Der Benutzer ist immer gezwungen in einer Rekursion über Mengen zu denken obwohl das übliche mentale Model bzgl. Rekursion eigentlich eine rekursive Funktion ist. In /Li88a/ wird ein Beispiel gegeben in welchem mehrere Subattribute rekursiv definiert werden mit nur einem rekursiven Namen auf höchster Ebene. Das Beispiel ist sehr kompliziert und es zeigt, daß für viele Problemkreise eine mengenoriertierte Rekursion sehr unnatürlich und nicht adäquat ist. Dieses Beispiel soll hier nicht wiederholt werden, weil funktionale Rekursion so wie sie im nächsten Abschnitt eingeführt wird, eine wesentlich elegantere und übersichtlichere Lösung darstellt.

4. Funktionale Rekursion

Im Gegensatz zur mengenorientierten Rekursion, wo Mengen rekursiv definiert werden, werden bei der nun einzuführenden funktionalen Rekursion Funktionen rekursiv definiert. Dies erlaubt, wie die Beispiele zeigen werden, eine wesentlich natürlichere und übersichtlichere Darstellung. Dies liegt vor allem daran, daß bei der funktionalen Rekursion die Selektion ein integraler Bestandteil der Rekursion ist. In unserem Beispiel der Typen und Prozeduren ist der Benutzer in der Regel nicht interessiert an allen Abhängigkeiten zwischen Typen, sondern nur an den Typen, die von einem bestimmten Typ abhängen. Die folgende Notation erscheint sinnvoll:

```
all_depending_types( Names: {string} ) =
    directly_depending_types(Names) ∪
        all_depending_types(directly_depending_types(Names))
```

wobei directly_depending_types(Names: {string}) definiert ist durch die folgende HDBL Anweisung:

```
SELECT dt
FROM t IN types_and_procedures.types,
     dt IN t.depending_types
WHERE
    EXISTS t2 IN Names: t2 = t.typename
```

'types_and_procedures' wurde definiert in Beispiel 3. Falls der Benutzer beispielsweise alle Typen wünscht, die indirekt von "range" abhängen, so kann er einfach sagen

```
depending_types({"range"})
```

Man sieht also, daß die Beschränkung auf die von "range" abhängigen Typen sehr leicht durch ein entsprechendes Funktionsargument ausgedrückt werden kann, d.h. die Selektion ist in die Rekursion integriert.

Natürlich stellt sich die Frage, wo diese Rekursion zum Ende kommt. Wie im Falle der Mengenrekursion erscheint es nicht sinnvoll, vom Benutzer zu verlangen, das Ende der Rekursion explizit zu programmieren, da das Terminierungskriterium ziemlich komplex sein kann. Würde man dies tun, hätte man letztlich keinen Unterschied mehr zu einer rekursiven Funktion in einer Programmiersprache. Eine Anfragesprache muß den Benutzer von dieser Last befreien und nur terminierende Anfragen zulassen, d.h. endlose Rekursionen sollten nicht möglich sein. Wir müssen daher Ausdrücken der obigen Art eine sinnvolle Semantik zuordnen. Dies wird im folgenden geschehen.

4.1 Syntaktische Definition der funktionalen Rekursion

Die allgemeinste Form für eine Menge von n wechselseitig rekursiven Funktionen ist die folgende:

$$g_1(rel{:}greltype_1) = f_{1,1,1}(...(f_{1,1,p_{1,1}}(rel))...) \cup ... \cup f_{1,m_1,1}(...(f_{1,m_1,p_{1,m_1}}(rel))...)$$

$$...$$

$$g_n(rel{:}greltype_n) = f_{n,1,1}(...(f_{n,1,p_{n,1}}(rel))...) \cup ... \cup f_{n,m_n,1}(...(f_{n,m_n,p_{n,m_n}}(rel))...)$$

$$h_1(rel{:}hreltype_1) = HDBL_1(rel)$$

$$...$$

$$h_k(rel{:}hreltype_k) = HDBL_k(rel)$$

wobei die Funktionen $HDBL_1(rel)$, ..., $HDBL_k(rel)$ legale HDBL SELECT Ausdrücke bezeichnen, die vom Parameter 'rel' abhängen. Die Indizes in einem Funktionsaufruf $f_{i,j,u}$ haben die folgende Bedeutung:

```
i: bezeichnet die zu definierende Funktion (1 ≤ i ≤ n)
j: bezeichnet die Nummer eines geschachtelten Aufrufs (1 ≤ j ≤ m_i)
u: bezeichnet die Position in der Schachtelung (1 ≤ u ≤ p_i,j)
m_i ≥ 1
p_i,j ≥ 0
```

Darüberhinaus haben wir

$$f_{i,j,u} = g_{r_{i,j,u}} \quad (1 \le r_{i,j,u} \le n)$$

$$\text{oder}$$

$$f_{i,j,u} = h_{r_{i,j,u}} \quad (1 \le r_{i,j,u} \le k)$$

Wir nennen die Gleichungen $g_1, ..., g_n, h_1, ..., h_k$ **Funktionsgleichungssystem.**

Beispiel 5:

Ein einfaches Beispiel war schon zu Beginn dieses Abschnitts angegeben worden:

```
all_depending_types(Names: {string}) =
    directly_depending_types(Names) ∪
        all_depending_types(directly_depending_types(Names))

directly_depending_types(Names: {string}) =
    SELECT dt
    FROM t IN types_and_procedures.types,
        dt IN t.depending_types
    WHERE
        EXISTS t2 IN Names: t2 = t.typename
```

In diesem Beispiel haben wir

$n = 1$, $k = 1$, $m_1 = 2$, $p_{1,1} = 1$, $p_{1,2} = 2$, $g_1 = $ all_depending_types, $h_1 = $ directly_depending_types,
$f_{1,1,1} = $ directly_depending_types, $f_{1,2,1} = $ all_depending_types, $f_{1,2,2} = $ directly_depending_types.

4.2 Semantische Definition der funktionalen Rekursion

Intuitiv wird die funktionale Rekursion definiert durch rekursiven Aufruf bis sich nichts mehr ändert. Wenn wir von endlichen Domänen ausgehen, muß dies irgendwann eintreten. In Abschnitt 4.3 werden sinnvolle Einschränkungen angegeben, welche eine effizientere Implementierung erlauben. Der Leser, welcher nicht an den Semantikdetails interessiert ist, kann den Rest von Abschnitt 4.2 an dieser Stelle überschlagen.

Wir definieren die Semantik der funktionalen Rekursion wie folgt. Zunächst definieren wir zu dem Gleichungssystem eine kontextfreie Grammatik. Die nonterminalen Zeichen der Grammatik sind die Funktionssymbole $g_1, ..., g_n$. Die terminalen Zeichen sind die Funktionssymbole $h_1, ..., h_k$. Die Regeln der Grammatik werden wie folgt definiert:

$$g_1 ::= f_{1,1,1}...f_{1,1,p_{1,1}} \mid ... \mid f_{1,m_1,1}...f_{1,m_1,p_{1,m_1}} \quad ... \quad g_n ::= f_{n,1,1}...f_{n,1,p_{n,1}} \mid ... \mid f_{n,m_n,1}...f_{n,m_n,p_{n,m_n}}$$

Es soll jetzt die Bedeutung von $g_i(\text{rel})$ definiert werden. Um dies zu tun, benutzen wir die Sprache, die vom Nonterminal g_i der kontextfreien Grammatik erzeugt wird. Diese im allgemeinen unendliche Sprache wird bezeichnet durch $L(g_i)$. Die Elemente von $L(g_i)$ werden bezeichnet durch $z_1, ..., z_j, ...$ Für $z_j = h_{j,1} ... h_{j,r_j}$ können wir dann die Semantik für $g_i(\text{rel})$ durch die folgende Gleichung definieren:

$$g_i(\text{rel}) = \bigcup_{j=1}^{\infty} h_{j,1}(...(h_{j,r_j}(\text{rel}))...)$$

Wenn nur endliche Domänen betrachtet werden, so gibt es nur endlich viele semantisch unterschiedliche Funktionen. Daher kann g_i (rel) in endlich vielen Schritten berechnet werden. Effiziente Auswertungsstrategien werden in Abschnitt 5 gegeben. Die Semantik entspricht also sehr intuitiv rekursiven Aufrufen der g-Funktionen. Die Rekursion wird modelliert durch die Ableitung der Sprache $L(g_i)$. Jedes Wort der Sprache entspricht den HDBL Funktionen die letztlich in der Rekursion aufgerufen werden.

Beispiel 6:

Die Grammatik für Beispiel 5 ist:

```
all_depending_types ::= directly_depending_types |
                        all_depending_types directly_depending_types
```

wobei all_depending_types das einzige Nonterminal ist. Das einzige Terminal ist directly_depending_types. Wir haben offenbar:

```
L(all_depending_types) = { directly_depending_types ¹ | i>0 }
```

4.3 Restriktionen für eine effiziente Implementierung

Obwohl funktionale Rekursion prinzipiell implementiert werden kann wie beschrieben, benötigt eine effiziente Implementierung einige Einschränkungen. Die Beispiele werden zeigen, daß die Einschränkungen im allgemeinen theoretischer Natur sind. Sie haben wenig Auswirkungen auf praktische Anwendungen. Auch an anderer Stelle wurde erkannt, daß allgemeine Rekursion wenig interessant ist, da es schwierig ist, Anwendungsbeispiele zu finden für Rekursionen, die nicht mindestens linear sind /NeSt88/. Die erste Einschränkung läßt nur monotone HDBL Ausdrücke zu:

$$rel_1 \subseteq rel_2 \rightarrow h_i(rel_1) \subseteq h_i(rel_2)$$

Diese Einschränkung ist erfüllt, falls kein FORALL und kein NOT vorkommt.

Die zweite Einschränkung fordert, daß die HDBL Funktionen linear sind:

$$h_i(rel_1 \cup rel_2) = h_i(rel_1) \cup h_i(rel_2)$$

Diese Einschränkung ist erfüllt, falls der Parameter nur einfach auftritt im HDBL Ausdruck.

Die dritte Einschränkung fordert, daß eine geordnete Partition der Funktionen existiert, so daß für die Definition einer Funktion nur Funktionen aus derselben oder einer vorhergehenden Partition verwendet werden. Höchstens eine Funktion darf derselben Partition angehören wie die zu definierende Funktion. Dies kann ähnlich der Stratification in COL /AG87/ formal wie folgt festgelegt werden.

Es muß eine Partition der Menge $T = \{g_1, ..., g_n\}$ wie folgt existieren (+ bezeichnet disjunkte Vereinigung):

$$T = T_1 + ... + T_s, \quad s \geq 1$$

mit einer Ordnung

$$T_1 < ... < T_s$$

und einer Funktion 'partition' definiert durch

$$partition(g_i) = T_a \Leftrightarrow g_i \in T_a$$

so daß die folgenden 2 Bedingungen erfüllt sind:

1.

$$f_{i,j,u} = g_{r_{i,j,u}} \rightarrow partition(g_{r_{i,j,u}}) \leq partition(g_i)$$

2.

$$f_{i,j,u} = g_{r_{i,j,u}} \quad \text{und} \quad \text{partition}(g_{r_{i,j,u}}) = \text{partition}(g_i) \quad \text{und} \quad v \neq u \rightarrow$$

$$f_{i,j,v} = h_{r_{i,j,v}} \quad \text{oder} \quad (f_{i,j,v} = g_{r_{i,j,v}} \quad \text{und} \quad \text{partition}(g_{r_{i,j,v}}) < \text{partition}(g_i))$$

Dies kann wie folgt intuitiv erläutert werden: Falls die Partition nur aus einer Menge besteht, d.h. $s = 1$ und $T = T_1$, so sagt die Restriktion aus, daß in jedem geschachtelten Funktionsaufruf höchstens eine Funktion eine rekursiv definierte Funktion sein darf. Falls die Partition mehrere Elemente enthält, so müssen alle bis auf eine Funktion in einem geschachtelten Aufruf einer vorhergehenden Partition angehören. Dies bedeutet, daß diese Funktionen vorher ausgewertet werden können. Beispiel 9 ist ein Beispiel wo die Partition mehrere Elemente enthält. In allen anderen Beispielen ist keine echte Partition notwendig.

Man kann leicht sehen, daß jede Funktion eines Funktionsgleichungssystems jetzt linear ist.

Beispiel 5 erfüllt offenbar die Einschränkungen. Alle anderen Beispiele in dieser Arbeit werden diese Einschränkungen erfüllen.

4.4 Beispiele

In diesem Abschnitt werden einige Beispiele gegeben, welche die Nützlichkeit der funktionalen Rekursion zeigen. Wir setzen die Tabellen aus Abschnitt 3 voraus.

Beispiel 7:

Dies Beispiel basiert auf Beispiel 5. Der Funktionsaufruf

```
all_depending_types({"range"})
```

resultiert in den folgenden Auswertungsschritten:

```
directly_depending_types({"range"}) ∪
    all_depending_types(directly_depending_types({"range"}))
```

ergibt

```
array1  array2
```

und den Aufruf

```
all_depending_types({"array1","array2"})
```

Dieser Aufruf resultiert in

```
directly_depending_types({"array1","array2"}) ∪
    all_depending_types(directly_depending_types({"array1","array2"}))
```

welcher als Ergebnis liefert:

```
array3
```

und den Aufruf

```
all_depending_types({"array3"})
```

Dieser Aufruf wiederum liefert

```
directly_depending_types({"array3"}) ∪
    all_depending_types(directly_depending_types({"array3"}))
```

mit dem Ergebnis

```
record1
```

und dem Aufruf

```
all_depending_types({"record1"})
```

Dieser Aufruf wiederum resultiert in

```
directly_depending_types({"record1"}) ∪
    all_depending_types(directly_depending_types({"record1"}))
```

mit der leeren Menge als Ergebnis und dem Aufruf directly_depending_types({}) welcher {} liefert.
Daher bricht die Rekursion ab. Das Ergebnis ist:

```
array1   array2   array3   record1
```

Wir können die all_depending_types Funktion in einer SELECT Anweisung wie folgt verwenden:

```
SELECT
   [typename: t.typename,
    alltypes: all_depending_types({t.typename}) ]
FROM t IN types_and_procedures.types
```

Diese Anfrage resultiert in der folgenden Tabelle:

typename	{indirecttypes}
range	array1 array2 array3 record1
array1	array3 record1
array2	—
array3	record1
record1	—

Beispiel 8:

Dieses Beispiel behandelt Prozedurabhängigkeiten:

```
all_depending_procs(Names: {string}) =
    directly_depending_procs(Names) ∪
        all_depending_procs(directly_depending_procs(Names))

directly_depending_procs(Names: {string}) =
    SELECT dp
    FROM p IN types_and_procedures.procedures,
        dp IN p.depending_procs
    WHERE
        EXISTS p2 IN Names: p2 = p.typename
```

Der Aufruf

```
all_depending_procs({"proc1"})
```

resultiert in den folgenden Auswertungsschritten:

```
directly_depending_procs({"proc1"}) ∪
    all_depending_procs(directly_depending_procs({"proc1"}))
```

ergibt

```
proc2
```

und den Aufruf

```
all_depending_procs({"proc2"})
```

Dieser Aufruf resultiert in:

```
directly_depending_procs({"proc2"}) ∪
    all_depending_procs(directly_depending_procs({"proc2"}))
```

ergibt

```
proc3
```

und den Aufruf

```
all_depending_procs({"proc3"})
```

Dieser Aufruf resultiert in:

```
directly_depending_procs({"proc3"}) ∪
    all_depending_procs(directly_depending_procs({"proc3"}))
```

ergibt

```
proc1
```

Der Aufruf

```
all_depending_procs({"proc1"})
```

ist redundant weil {"proc1"} enthalten ist in der Vereinigung der vorherigen Parameter und weil directly_depending_procs linear ist. Die Rekursion bricht also ab. Das Ergebnis ist:

```
proc2   proc3   proc1
```

Beispiel 9:

Die Basis für dieses Beispiel ist wieder das types_and_procedures Tupel aus Beispiel 3. Wir wollen alle Prozeduren berechnen, die von einem gegebenen Typ abhängen. Wir definieren die folgenden HDBL Funktionen:

```
types_directly_depending_on_types(TNames: {string}) =
   SELECT dt
   FROM t IN types_and_procedures.types,
        dt IN t.depending_types
   WHERE
      EXISTS t2 IN TNames: t2=t.typename

procs_directly_depending_on_types(TNames: {string}) =
   SELECT dp
   FROM t IN types_and_procedures.types,
        dp IN t.depending_procs
   WHERE
      EXISTS t2 IN TNames: t2=t.typename

procs_directly_depending_on_procs(PNames: {string}) =
   SELECT dp
   FROM p IN types_and_procedures.procedures,
        dp IN p.depending_procs
   WHERE
      EXISTS t2 IN PNames: t2=t.typename
```

Jetzt können wir die folgenden rekursiven Funktionen definieren:

```
types_depending_on_types(TNames: {string}) =
   TNames ∪
      types_depending_on_types(types_directly_depending_on_types(TNames))

procs_depending_on_procs(PNames: {string}) =
   PNames ∪
      procs_depending_on_procs(procs_directly_depending_on_procs(PNames))

procs_depending_on_types(TNames: {string}) =
      procs_depending_on_procs(
         procs_directly_depending_on_types(
                     types_depending_on_types(TNames)))
```

Die Partition entsprechend unseren Einschränkungen ist die folgende:

```
T₁ = { types_depending_on_types, procs_depending_on_procs }
T₂ = { procs_depending_on_types }
T₁ < T₂
```

Diese Partition reflektiert die Tatsache, daß die Funktionen types_depending_on_types und procs_depending_on_procs ausgewertet werden können vor der Auswertung von procs_depending_on_types. Die Angabe der einzelnen Auswertungsschritte wird dem Leser überlassen.

In /Li88a/ wird dieses Problem mit Hilfe von mengenorientierter Rekursion gelöst. Man sieht, daß funktionale Rekursion dem Problem wesentlich besser angepaßt ist.

Beispiel 10:

Dieses Beispiel behandelt das bekannte 'same generation cousins' Problem. Wir benutzen die folgende Basistabelle:

```
CREATE families
  { [ parent: string,
      child:  string
    ] }
END
```

Der Stammbaum

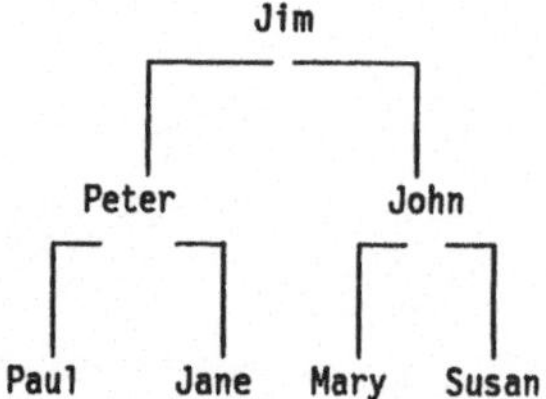

kann beispielsweise modelliert werden durch die Tabelle

parent	child
Jim	Peter
Peter	Paul
Peter	Jane
Jim	John
John	Mary
John	Susan

Wir definieren die folgenden HDBL Funktionen:

```
parents( persons: {string} ) =
  SELECT f.parent
  FROM f IN families
  WHERE EXISTS p IN persons: p=f.child

children( persons: {string} ) =
  SELECT f.child
  FROM f IN families
  WHERE EXISTS p IN persons: p=f.parent
```

Die same_generation_cousins Funktion kann jetzt wie folgt definiert werden:

```
same_generation_cousins(persons: {string}) =
        persons ∪
                children(same_generation_cousins(parents(persons)))
```

Die Angabe der einzelnen Auswertungsschritte wird wieder dem Leser überlassen.

5. Implementierungstechniken

Entsprechend unseren Einschränkungen aus Abschnitt 4.3, können wir für die Implementierung einer Funktion aus T_c induktiv annehmen, daß wir schon die Auswertung der Funktionen aus T_1, ..., T_{c-1} kennen. Wir können offenbar annehmen, daß alle Funktionen in T_i das folgende Aussehen haben:

$$g_a(rel) = hh_{a,1}(rel) \cup hh_{a,2}(g_{j_{a,2}}(hhh_{a,2}(rel))) \cup ... \cup hh_{a,m_a}(g_{j_{a,m_a}}(hhh_{a,m_a}(rel)))$$

$$\vdots$$

$$g_b(rel) = hh_{b,1}(rel) \cup hh_{b,2}(g_{j_{b,2}}(hhh_{b,2}(rel))) \cup ... \cup hh_{b,m_b}(g_{j_{b,m_b}}(hhh_{b,m_b}(rel)))$$

wobei die hh- und hhh- Funktionen entweder die Identität bezeichnen oder eine Funktionsschachtelung deren Auswertung bereits bekannt ist.

Alle Funktionen sind linear, wie in Abschnitt 4.3 vorausgesetzt. Die generelle Auswertungsstrategie akkumuliert die Parameter für alle rekursiven Funktionsaufrufe und führt einen Funktionsaufruf dann nicht aus, wenn die Parametermenge schon in der entsprechenden akkumulierten Menge enthalten ist. Da es nur endlich viele verschiedene Parametermengen gibt, muß dieses irgendwann eintreten. Daher bricht die Rekursion stets ab. Wir können den generellen Algorithmus, der gewisse Ähnlichkeiten mit dem Query-Subquery Ansatz von Vieille /Vi85/ aufweist,wie folgt skizzieren:

Zum Akkumulieren der Parameter definieren wir die globalen Variablen

$$params_{a,2}, ..., params_{a,m_a}$$

$$...$$

$$params_{b,2}, ..., params_{b,m_b}.$$

Darüberhinaus benötigen wir das boolesche Feld

$$first_{a,2}, ..., first_{a,m_a}$$

$$...$$

$$first_{b,2}, ..., first_{b,m_b}.$$

Dann definieren wir die folgenden rekursiven Funktionen:

```
FUNCTION g_p (rel: ...): ...;
VAR result: ...;
BEGIN
    result := hh_{p,1}(rel);
    result := result ∪ subfunct_{p,2}(rel);

             .
             .
             .

    result := result ∪ subfunct_{p,m_p}(rel);
    g_p := result
END;

FUNCTION subfunct_{p,q} (rel: ...): ...;
VAR result: ...; intermediate: ...;
BEGIN
    intermediate := hhh_{p,q} (rel) \ params_{p,q} ;
    IF NOT first_{p,q} AND intermediate = {}
    THEN result := {}
    ELSE BEGIN
            params_{p,q} := params_{p,q} ∪ intermediate;
            first_{p,q} := FALSE;
            result := hh_{p,q}(g_{j_{p,q}} (intermediate));
        END;
    subfunct_{p,q} := result;
END;
```

Ein Funktionsaufruf des Benutzers der Art

$$g_p \ (rel)$$

resultiert in den folgenden Anweisungen:

```
params_{a,2} := {}; first_{a,2} := TRUE;
             .
             .
             .
params_{b,m_b} := {}; first_{b,m_b} := TRUE;

g_p (rel)
```

Das boolesche Feld 'first' wird benötigt für den Fall eines Funktionsaufrufs mit der leeren Menge als Parameter. In diesem Fall ist der Funktionsaufruf in der Regel nicht redundant.

Beispiel 11:

Die Evaluierung von Beispiel 5 kann wie folgt skizziert werden:

```
FUNCTION all_depending_types(Names: ...): ...;
VAR result: ...;
BEGIN
    result := directly_depending_types(Names);
    result := result ∪ subfunct_{1,2} (Names)
    all_depending_types := result;
END;
```

```
FUNCTION subfunct₁,₂ (rel: ...):...;
VAR result, intermediate: ...;
BEGIN
    intermediate := directly_depending_types (rel) \ params₁,₂ ;
    IF NOT first₁,₂ AND (intermediate = {})
    THEN result := {}
    ELSE BEGIN
            params₁,₂ := params₁,₂ ∪ intermediate;
            first₁,₂ := FALSE;
            result := all_depending_types(intermediate);
        END;
    subfunct₁,₂ := result;
END;


params₁,₂ := {}; first₁,₂ := TRUE; all_depending_types({"range"})
```

In diesem Beispiel werden die Indizes nicht benötigt. Wir können außerdem ′params′ mit {″range″}
initialisieren statt mit {}. Darüberhinaus wird hier $first_{1,2}$ nicht benötigt da alle Funktionen die leere
Menge liefern, wenn sie mit der leeren Menge als Parameter aufgerufen werden.

6. Zusammenfassung und Ausblick

In dieser Arbeit wurde eine neuartige Art von rekursiven Anfragen vorgestellt, nämlich die funktionale Rekursion. Mit Hilfe von mehreren Beispielen aus dem Gebiet des Software Engineering wurde
demonstriert, daß diese Art der Rekursion übersichtlicher und natürlicher ist als mengenorientierte
Rekursion. Dies zeigt sich besonders dann, wenn die zugrundeliegenden Datenbankobjekte strukturiert sind, also keine normalisierten Relationen im Sinne des Relationenmodells sind. Dies ist sehr
häufig der Fall bei Anwendungen aus dem Ingenieurbereich und im Bereich des Software Engineering.
Die Methode ist also unter anderem sehr geeignet für CASE (Computer Aided Software Engineering)
Anwendungen. Die funktionale Rekursion wurde einerseits formal definiert, andererseits wurden
Implementierungs- und Optimierungstechniken angegeben, welche eine effiziente Implementierung
ermöglichen.

In einer weitergehenden Arbeit wird auf den Aspekt von Listen und von arithmetischen Operationen
in Zusammenhang mit der funktionalen Rekursion eingegangen. Hierdurch lassen sich unter anderem
kürzeste Wege und Stücklistenprobleme behandeln /Li88b/.

In der Zukunft wird es wichtig sein, noch genauer über Queryoptimierung in Zusammenhang mit
funktionaler Rekursion nachzudenken und entsprechende Architekturüberlegungen im Hinblick auf
ein Gesamtsystem anzustellen. Darüberhinaus erscheint es interessant, herauszufinden, ob einige der
in der Arbeit angegebenen Restriktionen abgeschwächt werden können. Es wird noch mehr praktische Erfahrung notwendig sein, um herauszufinden, welche der Einschränkungen in der Praxis eine
reale Bedeutung haben.

Danksagung

Der Autor ist den Kollegen aus dem AIM-Projekt, insbesondere P. Dadam, P. Pistor, G. Saake und
N.Südkamp zu Dank verpflichtet für wertvolle Anregungen und Diskussionen zu dieser Arbeit

Literatur

AB84   S.Abiteboul, N.Bidoit: Non First Normal Form Relations: An Algebra Allowing Data Restructuring. Rapports de Recherche No 347, Institut de Recherche en Informatique et en Automatique, Rocquencourt, France, Nov. 1984.

AG87   S.Abiteboul, S.Grumbach: COL: A Logic-Based Language For Complex Objects, INRIA Rapports de Recherche No. 714, September 1987

Ag87   R.Agrawal: An Extension of Relational Algebra To Express a Class of Recursive Queries, Proc. Third IEEE Conference on Data Engineering, Los Angeles, 1987, 580-590

AhUl79   A.V. Aho, J.D. Ullman: Universality of Data Retrieval Languages, 6th ACM Symp. on Principles of Programming Languages, San Antonio, Texas, January 1979, 110-117

ALPS88   F.Andersen, V.Linnemann, P.Pistor, N.Südkamp: Advanced Information Management Prototype: User Manual for the Online Interface of the Heidelberg Data Base Language (HDBL) Prototype Implementation, Release 2.0, 21 January 1988, IBM Scientific Center Heidelberg TN 86.01

Ap85   Appelrath,H.J.: Von Datenbanken zu Expertensystemen, Informatik-Fachberichte 102, Springer-Verlag 1985

BMSU86   F.Bancilhon, D.Maier, Y.Sagiv, J.D.Ullman: Magic Sets and other strange ways to implement logic programs, Proc. ACM SIGMOD-SIGACT Symp. on Pronciples of Database Systems, Cambridge, Mass., March 1986

BaRa86   F. Bancilhon, R.Ramakrishnan: An Amateur's Introduction to Recursive Query Processing Strategies, Proc. ACM SIGMOD Conf., Washington,D.C., 1986, 16-52

ClMe81   W.F. Clocksin, C.S. Mellish: Programming in PROLOG, Springer Verlag 1981

CMW87   I.F. Cruz, A.O. Mendelzon, P.T. Wood: A Graphical Query Language Supporting Recursion, Proc. ACM SIGMOD Conf., San Francisco, 1987, 323-330

Co72   E.F.Codd: Relational Completeness of Database Sublanguages. In Database Systems, ed. R. Rustin, Courant Comp. Sc. Symposia Ser. Vol. 6, Englewood Cliffs, N.Y. Prentice Hall, 1972.

DaKü86   P.Dadam, K.Küspert, F.Andersen, H.Blanken, R.Erbe, J.Günauer, V.Lum, P.Pistor, G.Walch: A DBMS Prototype to Support Extended NF^2 Relations: An Integrated View on Flat Tables and Hierarchies, Proc. ACM SIGMOD Conf., Washington,D.C., 1986, 356-367

Ga87   G. Gardarin: Magic Functions: A Technique to Optimize Extended Datalog Recursive Programs, Proceedings of the 13th Conference on Very Large Data Bases, Brighton, 1987, 21-30

GMN84   H. Gallaire, J. Minker, J.M. Nicolas: Logic and Databases: A Deductive Approach, Comp. Surveys, Vol.16, No.2, June 1984, 153-185

HL82   R.L.Haskin, R.A.Lorie: On Extending the Functions of a Relational Database System. Proc. SIGMOD 82, Orlando, June 1982, 207-212.

JaClVa84   M.Jarke, J.Clifford, Y.Vassiliou: An Optimizing PROLOG Front-End to a Relational Query System, Proc. ACM SIGMOD Conference, Boston 1984, 296-306

ISW84   Y. Ioannides, L.L. Shinkle, E. Wong: Enhancing INGRES with Deductive Power, in /Ke84/, 847-850

JaLiSc85   M.Jarke, V.Linnemann, J.W.Schmidt: Data Constructors: On the Integration of Rules and Relations, Proc. 11th Intern. Conf. on Very Large Data Bases, Stockholm, August 1985, 227-240

Ke84   L. Kerschberg (ed.): Proc. of the First International Workshop on Expert Database Systems, Kiawah Island, South Carolina, October 1984

Ko81   R.Kowalski: Logic as a Database Language, Department of Computing, Imperial College, London, 1981

La84   W.Lamersdorf: Recursive Data Models for Non-Conventional Database Applications, Proc. First Intern. IEEE Conference on Data Engineering, Los Angeles, 1984

LaMSc84   W.Lamersdorf, G.Müller, J.W.Schmidt: Language Support for Office Modelling. VLDB Proc., Singapore, 1984, 280-288.

Li86   V.Linnemann: Constructorset's Database Support for Knowledge Based Systems, Proc. Second IEEE Conference on Data Engineering, Los Angeles, 1986, 244-251

Li87   V.Linnemann: Non First Normal Form Relations and Recursive Queries: An SQL-Based Approach, Proc. Third IEEE Conference on Data Engineering, Los Angeles, 1987, 591-598

Li88a   V.Linnemann: On the Relationship Between Recursive Queries and Complex Objects, IBM Scientific Center Heidelberg Technical Report TR88.02.003, February 1988

Li88b   V.Linnemann: Functional Recursion and Complex Objects, IBM Scientific Center Heidelberg Technical Report TR88.12.017, December 1988 (in preparation)

Mi87   B.Mitschang: MAD - ein Datenmodell für den Kern eines Non-Standard-Datenbanksystems, Proc. GI Fachtagung 'Datenbanksyteme in Büro, Technik und Wissenschaft', Darmstadt 1987, Informatik Fachberichte 136, pp. 180-195

NeSt88   E.Neuhold, M.Stonebraker (ed.): Future Directions in DBMS Research, International Computer Science Institute Technical Report TR-88-001, May 1988

PA86   P.Pistor, F.Andersen: Principles for Designing a Generalized NF^2 Data Model with an SQL-type Language Interface, 12th Intern. Conf. on Very Large Data Bases, Kyoto, Japan, Aug. 1986, 278-285

Pi87   P. Pistor: The Advanced Information Management Prototype: Architecture and Language Interface Overview, 3. Journee Base Donnees Avancees, Port Camargue, France, May 1987

PT85   P.Pistor, R.Traunmüller: A Database Language for Sets, Lists, and Tables, IBM Scientific Center Heidelberg Techncal Report TR 85.10.004, Oct. 1985.

PT86   P.Pistor, R.Traunmüller: A Database Language for Sets, Lists, and Tables, Information Systems Vol. 11, No. 4, pp. 323-336

RHDM86   A.Rosenthal, S.Heiler, U.Dayal, F.Manola: Traversal Recursion: A Practical Approach to Supporting Recursive Applications, Proc. ACM SIGMOD Conf., Washington,D.C., 1986, 166-176

RKB85   M.A. Roth, H.F.Korth, D.S.Batory: SQL/NF: A Query Language for $\neg$1NF Relational Databases, Deptm. Comp. Scienc. Univ. of Texas, Austin, TR-85-19, Sept. 1985.

SP82   H.-J.Schek, P.Pistor: Data Structures for an Integrated Data Base Management and Information Retrieval System, Proc. VLDB Conf. Mexico, Sept. 1982, 197-207

SS86   H.-J.Schek, M.Scholl: The Relational Model with Relation-Valued Attributes, Information Systems 1986, Vol.11, No.2, pp. 137-147

Sh81   D.Shipman: The Functional Data Model and the Data Language DAPLEX, ACM Transactions on Database Systems, Vol.6, No.1, March 1981, pp. 140-173

St86   M.Stonebraker, L.A.Rowe: The Design of Postgres, Proc. ACM SIGMOD Conf., Washington,D.C., 1986, 340-355

Ul85   J.D. Ullman: Implementation of Logical Query Languages for Databases, ACM TODS 10(3), Sept. 1985, 289-321

Vi85   L.Vieille: Recursive Axioms in Deductive Databases: The Query-Subquery Approach, European Computer-Industry Research Centre GmbH (ECRC) Internal Report KB-10, Sept. 1985

Wo88   M.Woschko: Implementierung Rekursiver Anfragen in einem Datenbanksystem, Diplomarbeit Fachhochschule für Technik Mannheim 1988

TZ86   S.Tsur, C.Zaniolo: LDL: A Logic-Based Data Language, Proc. 12th Intern Conf. on Very Large Data Bases, Kyoto, Japan, August 1986, 33-41

Informatik — Fachberichte

Band 112: Wissensbasierte Systeme. GI-Kongreß 1985. Herausgegeben von W. Brauer und B. Radig. XVI, 402 Seiten, 1985.

Band 113: Datenschutz und Datensicherung im Wandel der Informationstechnologien. 1. GI-Fachtagung, München, Oktober 1985. Proceedings, 1985. Herausgegeben von P. P. Spies. VIII, 257 Seiten. 1985.

Band 114: Sprachverarbeitung in Information und Dokumentation. Proceedings, 1985. Herausgegeben von B. Endres-Niggemeyer und J. Krause. VIII, 234 Seiten. 1985.

Band 115: A. Kobsa, Benutzermodellierung in Dialogsystemen. XV, 204 Seiten. 1985.

Band 116: Recent Trends in Data Type Specification. Edited by H.-J. Kreowski. VII, 253 pages. 1985.

Band 117: J. Röhrich, Parallele Systeme. XI, 152 Seiten. 1986.

Band 118: GWAI-85. 9th German Workshop on Artificial Intelligence. Dassel/Solling, September 1985. Edited by H. Stoyan. X, 471 pages. 1986.

Band 119: Graphik in Dokumenten. GI-Fachgespräch, Bremen, März 1986. Herausgegeben von F. Nake. X, 154 Seiten. 1986.

Band 120: Kognitive Aspekte der Mensch-Computer-Interaktion. Herausgegeben von G. Dirlich, C. Freksa, U. Schwatlo und K. Wimmer. VIII, 190 Seiten. 1986.

Band 121: K. Echtle, Fehlermaskierung durch verteilte Systeme. X, 232 Seiten. 1986.

Band 122: Ch. Habel, Prinzipien der Referentialität. Untersuchungen zur propositionalen Repräsentation von Wissen. X, 308 Seiten. 1986.

Band 123: Arbeit und Informationstechnik. GI-Fachtagung. Proceedings, 1986. Herausgegeben von K. T. Schröder. IX, 435 Seiten. 1986.

Band 124: GWAI-86 und 2. Österreichische Artificial-Intelligence-Tagung. Ottenstein/Niederösterreich, September 1986. Herausgegeben von C.-R. Rollinger und W. Horn. X, 360 Seiten. 1986.

Band 125: Mustererkennung 1986. 8. DAGM-Symposium, Paderborn, September/Oktober 1986. Herausgegeben von G. Hartmann. XII, 294 Seiten, 1986.

Band 126: GI-16. Jahrestagung. Informatik-Anwendungen – Trends und Perspektiven. Berlin, Oktober 1986. Herausgegeben von G. Hommel und S. Schindler. XVII, 703 Seiten. 1986.

Band 127: GI-17. Jahrestagung. Informatik-Anwendungen – Trends und Perspektiven. Berlin, Oktober 1986. Herausgegeben von G. Hommel und S. Schindler. XVII, 685 Seiten. 1986.

Band 128: W. Benn, Dynamische nicht-normalisierte Relationen und symbolische Bildbeschreibung. XIV, 153 Seiten. 1986.

Band 129: Informatik-Grundbildung in Schule und Beruf. GI-Fachtagung, Kaiserslautern, September/Oktober 1986. Herausgegeben von E. v. Puttkamer. XII, 486 Seiten. 1986.

Band 130: Kommunikation in Verteilten Systemen. GI/NTG-Fachtagung, Aachen, Februar 1987. Herausgegeben von N. Gerner und O. Spaniol. XII, 812 Seiten. 1987.

Band 131: W. Scherl, Bildanalyse allgemeiner Dokumente. XI, 205 Seiten. 1987.

Band 132: R. Studer, Konzepte für eine verteilte wissensbasierte Softwareproduktionsumgebung. XI, 272 Seiten. 1987.

Band 133: B. Freisleben, Mechanismen zur Synchronisation paralleler Prozesse. VIII, 357 Seiten. 1987.

Band 134: Organisation und Betrieb der verteilten Datenverarbeitung. 7. GI-Fachgespräch, München, März 1987. Herausgegeben von F. Peischl. VIII, 219 Seiten. 1987.

Band 135: A. Meier, Erweiterung relationaler Datenbanksysteme für technische Anwendungen. IV, 141 Seiten. 1987.

Band 136: Datenbanksysteme in Büro, Technik und Wissenschaft. GI-Fachtagung, Darmstadt, April 1987. Proceedings. Herausgegeben von H.-J. Schek und G. Schlageter. XII, 491 Seiten. 1987.

Band 137: D. Lienert, Die Konfigurierung modular aufgebauter Datenbanksysteme. IX, 214 Seiten. 1987.

Band 138: R. Männer, Entwurf und Realisierung eines Multiprozessors. Das System „Heidelberger POLYP". XI, 217 Seiten. 1987.

Band 139: M. Marhöfer, Fehlerdiagnose für Schaltnetze aus Modulen mit partiell injektiven Pfadfunktionen. XIII, 172 Seiten. 1987.

Band 140: H.-J. Wunderlich, Probabilistische Verfahren für den Test hochintegrierter Schaltungen. XII, 133 Seiten. 1987.

Band 141: E. G. Schukat-Talamazzini, Generierung von Worthypothesen in kontinuierlicher Sprache. XI, 142 Seiten. 1987.

Band 142: H.-J. Novak, Textgenerierung aus visuellen Daten: Beschreibungen von Straßenszenen. XII, 143 Seiten. 1987.

Band 143: R. R. Wagner, R. Traunmüller, H. C. Mayr (Hrsg.), Informationsbedarfsermittlung und -analyse für den Entwurf von Informationssystemen. Fachtagung EMISA, Linz, Juli 1987. VIII, 257 Seiten. 1987.

Band 144: H. Oberquelle, Sprachkonzepte für benutzergerechte Systeme. XI, 315 Seiten. 1987.

Band 145: K. Rothermel, Kommunikationskonzepte für verteilte transaktionsorientierte Systeme. XI, 224 Seiten. 1987.

Band 146: W. Damm, Entwurf und Verifikation mikroprogrammierter Rechnerarchitekturen. VIII, 327 Seiten. 1987.

Band 147: F. Belli, W. Görke (Hrsg.), Fehlertolerierende Rechensysteme / Fault-Tolerant Computing Systems. 3. Internationale GI/ITG/GMA-Fachtagung, Bremerhaven, September 1987. Proceedings. XI, 389 Seiten. 1987.

Band 148: F. Puppe, Diagnostisches Problemlösen mit Expertensystemen. IX, 257 Seiten. 1987.

Band 149: E. Paulus (Hrsg.), Mustererkennung 1987. 9. DAGM-Symposium, Braunschweig, Sept./Okt. 1987. Proceedings. XVII, 324 Seiten. 1987.

Band 150: J. Halin (Hrsg.), Simulationstechnik. 4. Symposium, Zürich, September 1987. Proceedings. XIV, 690 Seiten. 1987.

Band 151: E. Buchberger, J. Retti (Hrsg.), 3. Österreichische Artificial-Intelligence-Tagung. Wien, September 1987. Proceedings. VIII, 181 Seiten. 1987.

Band 152: K. Morik (Ed.), GWAI-87. 11th German Workshop on Artificial Intelligence. Geseke, Sept./Okt. 1987. Proceedings. XI, 405 Seiten. 1987.

Band 153: D. Meyer-Ebrecht (Hrsg.), ASST'87. 6. Aachener Symposium für Signaltheorie. Aachen, September 1987. Proceedings. XII, 390 Seiten. 1987.

Band 154: U. Herzog, M. Paterok (Hrsg.), Messung, Modellierung und Bewertung von Rechensystemen. 4. GI/ITG-Fachtagung, Erlangen, Sept./Okt. 1987. Proceedings. XI, 388 Seiten. 1987.

Band 155: W. Brauer, W. Wahlster (Hrsg.), Wissensbasierte Systeme. 2. Internationaler GI-Kongreß, München, Oktober 1987. XIV, 432 Seiten. 1987.

Band 156: M. Paul (Hrsg.), GI – 17. Jahrestagung. Computerintegrierter Arbeitsplatz im Büro. München, Oktober 1987. Proceedings. XIII, 934 Seiten. 1987.

Band 157: U. Mahn, Attributierte Grammatiken und Attributierungsalgorithmen. IX, 272 Seiten. 1988.